McGRAW-HILL SERIES IN MARKETING

RETAIL MANAGEMENT

Ron Hasty
University of North Texas

James Reardon
University of Tennessee

The McGraw-Hill Companies, Inc.
New York • St. Louis • San Francisco • Auckland
Bogotá • Caracas • Lisbon • London • Madrid
Mexico City • Milan • Montreal • New Delhi • San Juan
Singapore • Sydney • Tokyo • Toronto

McGraw-Hill

*A Division of The **McGraw·Hill** Companies*

Retail Management

Copyright © 1997 by The McGraw-Hill Companies, Inc. All rights reserved. Printed in the United States of America. Except as permitted under the United States Copyright Act of 1976, no part of this publication may be reproduced or distributed in any form or by any means, or stored in a data base or retrieval system, without the prior written permission of the publisher.

This book is printed on acid-free paper.

Photo credits appear on page PC1 and on this page by reference.

1 2 3 4 5 6 7 8 9 0   VNH   VNH   9 0 9 8 7 6

ISBN 0-07-027031-7

The editors were Karen Westover, Dan Alpert, and Richard Mason.
The production supervisors were Tanya Nigh and Richard DeVitto.
Project supervision was done by The Total Book.
The interior and cover design was by Vargas/Williams Design.
The photo researcher was Elyse Rieder.
This book was set in Stone Serif by GTS Graphics.
This book was printed and bound by Von Hoffmann Press, Inc.

Library of Congress Cataloging-in-Publication Data

Hasty, Ronald W.
  Retail management / Ron Hasty, James Reardon.
    p.   cm. —(The McGraw-Hill series in marketing)
  Includes bibliographical references.
  ISBN 0-07-027031-7 (hardcover)
  1. Retail trade—Management. 2. Retail trade—Management—Case studies. I. Reardon, James, (date). II. Title. III. Series.
HF5429.H329   1997
658.8'7—dc20   96-15987

International Edition
Copyright © 1997. Exclusive rights by The McGraw-Hill Companies, Inc. for manufacture and export. This book cannot be re-exported from the country to which it is consigned by McGraw-Hill. The International Edition is not available in North America.
When ordering this title, use ISBN 0-07-114315-7.

ABOUT THE AUTHORS

Ron Hasty is Department Chair and Professor of Marketing at the University of North Texas. He received his Ph.D. from the University of Colorado. He has prior administrative and teaching experience at the University of Texas at El Paso and Colorado State University. He has been on the Faculty of Administrative Sciences at Middle East Technical University in Ankara, Turkey and has taught in the University of Pittsburgh's Semester at Sea Program. He has served on the board of the American Marketing Association Retail Management Special Interest Group.

Dr. Hasty is the author/coauthor of textbooks in retailing and marketing. His research has appeared in such journals as the *Journal of Marketing, Journal of Retailing, Journal of Microcomputer Management, Journal of Marketing Theory and Practice, Journal of Personal Selling and Sales Management, International Journal of Retailing and Distribution Management, Journal of Retailing and Consumer Science*, and the *Journal of the Academy of Marketing Science*. He has taught numerous executive development seminars and workshops including Retail Store Management Series, Market Analysis and Buyer Behavior, Advertising for the Small Business, New Product Development, and Business Ethics.

James Reardon is Assistant Professor of Retailing and Consumer Science at the University of Tennessee, Knoxville. He received his Ph.D. from the University of North Texas. His publications have appeared in such journals as the *Journal of Retailing, Journal of Marketing Theory and Practice, Journal of International Advertising, Journal of Applied Business Research, Journal of Business and Economic Perspectives, International Journal of Retailing and Distribution Management, Journal of Retailing and Consumer Science,* and *International Journal of Management.* He has received research grants from the American Collegiate Retail Association and the University of Tennessee. His research interests include the productivity of marketing functions, retail competitive structure, store image development, and retail strategy.

This book is dedicated to our wives for their support, encouragement, and constant love.

Thank you Sharlott and Tricia.

Contents in Brief

Contents

PART 2: THE RETAIL CUSTOMER   116

CHAPTER 4: UNDERSTANDING AND IDENTIFYING THE CUSTOMER   118

CHAPTER 7: STORE DESIGN AND LAYOUT   252

CHAPTER 8: HUMAN RESOURCE MANAGEMENT AND STORE ORGANIZATION   290

CHAPTER 9: FINANCIAL ANALYSIS AND MANAGEMENT   332

PART 4: RETAIL MERCHANDISING AND PRICING   368

CHAPTER 10: PLANNING MERCHANDISE NEEDS AND MERCHANDISE BUDGETS   370

PART 5: COMMUNICATING WITH THE RETAIL CUSTOMER   490

CHAPTER 13: RETAIL ADVERTISING   492

CHAPTER 14: RETAIL SELLING, SALES PROMOTION, AND PUBLICITY 530

PART 6: RETAILING CHALLENGES AND CHANGES 566

CHAPTER 15: THE VIRTUAL STORE AND RETAIL DATABASE MARKETING 568

CHAPTER 16: GLOBALIZATION AND CHANGING RETAIL FORMATS   606

PREFACE

This book is for students in Principles of Retailing, Retail Management, and Fashion Merchandising classes in two- and four-year colleges, universities, and technical institutes. We believe you are enrolled in a class that has the potential to be one of the most interesting and stimulating in your educational career. Retailing is a world of change featuring goods, services, and entertainment that make our lives more comfortable and enjoyable. You may be interested in a career in the exciting and dynamic world of retailing with its tremendous opportunities for well-paid positions. Business majors may be interested in understanding how consumer markets and retailing are the driving forces in business development and expansion. Nonbusiness majors can become better consumers by understanding the retail environment and the role of retailing in the economy. Whatever your objective, we believe this textbook is an important resource to refer to as a student and throughout your career.

We wrote the book because the world of retailing has changed so much in recent years that a fresh new approach was needed. The changes have been driven by several forces in the retailing environment. The first of these is the explosion in information technology, which has changed the way retailing is practiced. Your text integrates coverage of information technologies such as electronic data interchange, quick response, electronic mail, geographic information systems, computer-aided design, and the use of the Internet. In addition a unique technology-based chapter on the *virtual store and database retailing* opens a whole new world of nonstore merchandising. Technology has also been responsible for the globalization of retailing, the second major force of change.

This is not an international retailing book, but it recognizes that the *globalization of retailing* is as much a reality as the globalization of manufacturing or finance. Virtually every retailer is affected by *global sourcing*. Buyers search the world for quality goods at the lowest possible price, assisted by efficient global logistics and distribution providers who keep the cost of getting the goods to the store or distribution centers low. Many retailers face competition from foreign retailers who have entered North American markets in search of new opportunities. Dozens of the largest European and Asian retailers own operations in the United States. America is a nation of immigrants. In many urban markets there are growing ethnic neighborhoods where the *customers* have many of the attitudes, languages, and cultures similar to those found in their home countries. Retailing in these markets requires the firm to have the same sensitivity to cultural differences as it would in entering a foreign market.

Your text recognizes that retailers are actively exploring *global opportunities* as domestic markets become more saturated. To compete in a global economy, retailers must build on skills, expertise, and knowledge of diverse attitudes, languages, and cultures, and form synergistic business partnerships with vendors and logistics providers around the world. Therefore, the text features an integrated coverage of the impact of globalization on retailing practice. Also, a comprehensive treatment of global concepts is included in Chapter 16, which also considers other significant factors including retailing as entertainment, retail theater, and the changing retail formats.

The third major force of change is the dramatic reduction in the number of retailers as a result of competition, technology, and globalization. In the United States, where we have seen a reduction of nearly 500,000 stores in just over a decade, not only are there fewer stores, but they are larger as well. This change requires more and better trained professional managers. The number of firms recruiting professionally educated young people to enter retailing is rapidly growing.

There are many other new concepts that are important to understanding today's retail environment. We have provided up-to-date coverage on strategic alliances, just-in-time delivery, supply chain management, total quality management, continuous quality improvement, relationship marketing, and partnering.

Many of you are working in stores while completing your education. We hope the book helps you do your job better by providing a more complete understanding of contemporary retailing practice. At the end of the class you will have mastered fundamental principles and be able to apply the more complex technical aspects of retailing, including market analysis and market research, merchandise budgeting, assortment planning, markups, markdowns, inventory control and evaluation, and analysis of financial statements. You will be able to implement the latest concepts in areas such as advertising, selling, buying, store design and layout, and display. And you will understand how changes in the legal environment—like the Americans with Disabilities Act and the Family Leave Act—impact retailing practice.

ORGANIZATION OF THE BOOK

The sixteen chapters of the book are based on a logical flow of concepts and skills as suggested and defined by a survey of numerous professors. It is designed to take you through the course much the way you would think of retailing if you were starting a store. The first part of the book provides an overview. Chapter 1 describes the world of retailing. Chapter 2 provides a comprehensive strategic and operational framework for the rest of the book as it examines how retailers seek to create a competitive advantage. Chapter

3 offers the framework for understanding the external competitive, social, economic, and legal environment. An examination of the ethical dilemmas retailers face completes the chapter. The second part of the book discusses the tools and concepts that help retailers understand markets. Chapter 4 offers approaches to understanding and identifying the customer, and Chapter 5 looks at how research can help us gain a better understanding of the customer and markets. Part 3 takes an in-depth look at the store itself. Chapter 6 is a comprehensive treatment of the critical area of store location and site evaluation. Chapter 7 covers store layout and design. Human resource management and store organization are the subject of Chapter 8. Chapter 9 examines in detail the important area of planning and managing financial resources. Chapters 10 and 11 in Part 4 discuss merchandise planning and the buying function. Chapter 12 covers pricing the merchandise and managing the pricing process. In Part 5 we explore the role of retail communications through advertising (Chapter 13) as well as sales promotion, personal selling, and publicity (Chapter 14). Part 6 begins with the exciting new areas of the virtual store and retail database marketing (Chapter 15). The book concludes with a more comprehensive treatment of retailing in a global environment, the changes associated with retailing as entertainment, and possible changes in retail formats (Chapter 16).

Learning features

Learning objectives, chapter summaries, and key terms. Each chapter begins with six to eight learning objectives that frame the content of the chapter in terms of outcomes. These will help guide your study of the chapter as will the chapter summaries and lists of key terms with page number references.

The presentation of the material. The design of the book was created to capture the colors and textures of contemporary retailing environments. Our students and colleagues who have read our manuscript praised the writing style, calling it "clear," "engaging," and "user-friendly." We believe that this style will reinforce your learning and help you absorb and retain important chapter concepts. The book contains numerous relevant examples, which follow the presentation and explanation of principles and concepts. Students and faculty have noted that "the examples are up to date and valuable."

Cases, situations, questions, and problems. Each chapter has a "wrap case" consisting of an opening and closing section. The opening section is based on an actual retail firm's experience and current practice, bringing to life important concepts that are later addressed in the body of the chapter. Many of these stores—such as Gap, L. L. Bean, Nordstrom, and Wal-Mart—will be familiar to you. The closing section "revisits" the same retailer and examines issues that the firm will face in the future. Each chapter concludes with questions, situations, and additional cases that will help you apply the material you've studied.

Photo essays. One of the unique features of your book is the photo essay program. The authors selected key concepts in every chapter, chose photo examples to match the concepts, and then wrote detailed photo captions that teach the concepts. The photos help make the concepts come alive and help you remember them.

Boxed material and figures. Throughout your text boxed material is used to highlight and expand on key concepts, including at least one retailing ethical dilemma per chapter. About 100 attractive full-color figures illustrate key chapter coverage.

An understandable approach to the quantitative elements of retailing. It has long been our experience that students occasionally have difficulty understanding quantitative concepts in retailing such as the retail method of inventory, merchandise budgets, inventory control and evaluation, ratio analysis, location models, and markup. To facilitate student comprehension, each quantitative concept is carefully explained, worked, and illustrated with an example.

A World Wide Web page for career information and updates. You can access our Web site at http://www-LAN.UNT.EDU/HASTY for current career information, ideas for resume preparation, and interviewing techniques. When you have news about your job search, interesting experiences at work, or just want to talk about retailing, E-mail us at Hasty@Cobaf.unt.edu or Reardon@utkuki.utk.edu.

INSTRUCTOR TEACHING FEATURES

A complete set of instructors' materials is available to adopters. The *Instructor's Manual* (IM) has discussion guidelines and suggested solutions for all the cases, situations, and problems. Chapter outlines are keyed to the boxed material, figures, and end-of-chapter material. There is also a "Projects and Activities" section for each chapter in the *Instructor's Manual* along with additional cases. A semester project, "Starting a Retail Store," is included in the IM. The project is keyed to the text so that the students are working on each section of the project as they go through the course. The project includes spreadsheet problems that can be worked with a calculator or with a spreadsheet program. This project and the spreadsheets are available to adopters on disk. Nearly 1,600 multiple-choice and true-false exam questions are available to instructors in a printed test bank and on computer disk.

A set of videotapes provides additional current examples to enhance the teaching and learning process. Also, a set of full-color transparencies is available to adopters of *Retail Management.*

ACKNOWLEDGMENTS

A VERY SPECIAL RECOGNITION

In February 1994 the Professional Services and Certified Public Accounting Firm of Coopers & Lybrand and Lebhar-Friedman, Inc., sponsored a CEO-level symposium entitled "The 21st Century: Thriving in a Global Market." At the symposium, Coopers & Lybrand unveiled an exhaustive groundbreaking study, *Retailing in the 21st Century: A Global Perspective.* The study set forth the many and complex dimensions of the strategic imperative of retail globalization. The study was directed by Michael J. Gade, who at the time was partner and chair of International Retail Group. Mr. Gade graciously granted the authors permission to use portions of the study throughout the text, which are integrated with global materials and examples from many sources and the international experience of the authors. Tom Dodderidge, then vice president of AT&T Global Information Solutions, D. Michael Grimes, president of Retail Technology Group, and James Traxler, vice president of Telxon Corporation, played significant roles in shaping the study. Citicorp—through Arnold Ziegel, managing director of Citicorp Securities Inc.—was the corporate sponsor for the project.

A special issue (Volume 69, No. 12/Special Issue) of *Chain Store Age Executive* published under contract from Coopers & Lybrand by Lebhar-Friedman, Inc., was devoted exclusively to an executive summary of *Retailing in the 21st Century: A Global Perspective.* It was prepared and written by Michael Gade and the professionals at Coopers & Lybrand. *Chain Store Age Executive* regularly publishes such special studies and reports that provide insight into how rapidly the practice of retailing is taking on a global dimension.

The authors are also indebted to Murray Forseter, editor of *Chain Store Age Executive,* at Lebhar-Friedman for his role in organizing the symposium. The presentations by the speakers were exceptional. The keynote speech by Alfred F. Lynch, president of J. C. Penney International, Inc., and the luncheon address by Clark A. Johnson, chairman and CEO of Pier One Imports Inc., were particularly helpful in crystallizing the way the global dimensions of your text would be presented. The findings, analysis, and insight provided under Michael Gade's direction will give each of you as business and retail leaders of tomorrow a valuable start as you prepare to enter the business world of the twenty-first century.

Numerous retail firms allowed us to use their materials and photos. We are indebted to them for their support. Robert Kahn, former retail executive and now editor and publisher of *Retailing Today,* allowed the use of material from his publication for the preparation of ethical dilemmas that are current and relevant. This book also carries the imprint of Ted Will, coauthor and mentor of the senior author, who is now a retail executive in Colorado. His guidance is deeply appreciated.

The professional staff at McGraw-Hill College Division are responsible for making the ideas and words of the authors come alive in this book. The support and encouragement of Karen Westover, the editor, are deeply appreciated. Dan Alpert's constant concern for innovation that would make the book interesting and useful for students, and his attention to detail, made an indelible mark on the work. We are grateful for his long-term commitment to the success of the project. Kate Scheinman did a masterful job in her role as project supervisor. She constantly held the authors to high standards of quality and excellence, and did so with humor and grace. Your senior author has worked with a number of copy editors on book projects, none were as capable as Leslie Weber. She handled the technical aspects of her job with accuracy and insight. The book reflects her constant concern that students clearly understand every concept. Elyse Rieder did the photo research for the book. She conducted a worldwide search for photos that would capture the concepts in the photo essays. Richard Mason served as senior editing supervisor. The designer, Juan Vargas, created a colorful and exciting design to enhance student learning.

The authors are indebted to Betty Tuggle and Richard Brown, professional staff in the marketing department at the University of North Texas, for their assistance and encouragement. Richard is always ready to help the faculty create the best possible learning materials for students. Betty's constant attention to detail and delightful approach to work and life are responsible for creating an administrative environment that lets the faculty concentrate on students, research, and service.

Students are never bashful about telling a professor what can make his or her teaching better. Hundreds of our students have contributed immeasurably to this project as they have used cases, projects, and problems, and have read the manuscript. Kim Miller, now a customer service manager at Sprint, was particularly helpful. She read the manuscript numerous times. Former graduate students at the University of North Texas—Phil Wilson, Charlotte Allen, and Victor Massad—contributed to the manuscript.

This book reflects the feedback from numerous professors as they read various drafts of the manuscript. Our hope is that we have faithfully incorporated the excellent suggestions made by the following individuals: Vicki Blakney, University of Dayton; David J. Burns, Youngstown State University; Louis M. Capella, Mississippi State University; Joseph C. Hecht, Montclair State College; Charlane Bomrad Held, Onondaga Community College; Tony Henthorne, University of Southern Mississippi; John Lloyd, Monroe Community College; Irving Mason, Herkimer County Community College; Roger A. Pae, Siena Heights College; Duane Schechter, Muskegon Community College; Ray Tewell, California State University, Sacramento; Joan Weiss, Bucks County Community College; and David Wiley, Anne Arundel Community College.

Ron Hasty
James Reardon

PART 1

THE RETAILING ENVIRONMENT

1

Chapter Goals

After reading this chapter, you should be able to:

- Define retailing.
- Identify and understand the differences between the various types of retail transactions.
- Describe how retailing benefits customers, manufacturers, and wholesalers.
- Explain the nature of retailing in terms of its economic characteristics.
- Understand the different types of store classifications.
- Describe the important factors that will contribute to success in retailing in the future.

An Overview of Retailing

GAP INC.[1] COMPETING WITH PRIVATE-LABEL FASHION

True relaxed attitude! Donald G. Fisher did not intend to create a retailing superstar. He simply wanted to exchange a pair of Levi blue jeans. When he discovered that what should have been a simple transaction was impossibly frustrating at the local department store, he decided that America needed a new kind of specialty shop. His original concept was to cater to the tastes of the midteen market with three kinds of goods: records, cassette tapes, and Levi's. Levi's were the real draw, and the tapes and records were quickly dropped from stock. Opened in 1969, Gap Inc. has become one of the most successful chains in retailing history. Although the early target market was primarily young people, the convenience of a neatly organized Levi Strauss jeans store appealed to customers of all ages. By 1972, there were twenty-five stores in six states. Mr. Fisher dreamed of a chain of specialty stores with the Gap label. His vision "to be unique; to create, produce and sell" began to be realized as the company soon added private-label clothing to the merchandise mix.

In 1976, federal laws that allowed manufacturers to control retail prices in some states were changed and stores began discounting Levi's. Mr. Fisher had always disliked price-driven businesses, and he became even more convinced that Gap's competitive advantage could not depend on low prices.

In the early 1980s Gap implemented a new product development program. Every garment offered by the company would be sourced, manufactured, inspected, shipped, distributed, displayed, advertised, and sold by or under the control of Gap employees. Gap's trademark pocket tees and fleece active wear were introduced. Gap went upscale, with more pure cotton goods, "image" advertising, and a more mature target market: Ages twenty to forty-five were sought. As the company continued to increase its market share with new products, Levi's fell to 21 percent of total Gap sales.

The phenomenally successful 1988 "Individuals of Style" advertising campaign established Gap—with its extensive merchandise assortment of men's and women's goods, accessories, active wear, and denims—as a worldwide creative and fashion force. The campaign brought an upscale clientele to the stores. Down-to-earth Gap basics became status symbols, and the classic pocket tee, chambray shirt, and denims held their own with some of the biggest names in the world of fashion.

In 1991, Gap announced that Levi's products would no longer be sold in Gap stores; all merchandise would be under the company's own label. Today, Gap Inc. purchases its own label merchandise from over 1,000 suppliers located domestically and overseas.

While Gap was growing, the company was actively starting and acquiring new formats. The 1980s were a period of dynamic growth in new formats for Gap Inc. First, Banana Republic, famous for military-surplus-style clothing and supplies for fashion individualists, was acquired in 1983. The company rapidly began to add new stores and expand the selection of merchandise, adding unique private-label fashions inspired by function. In two years there were thirty-five Banana Republic stores.

The company also recognized an unmet need for well-designed, good-quality garments for children. The solution was GapKids, which opened in 1986. It was conceived as a store with comfortable, fashionable children's wear, much like the grown-up Gap. The borrowed-from-Gap basics were enhanced by styles designed by the GapKids product development team.

In 1990, babyGap made its first appearance as a department in twenty-five GapKids stores. The babyGap apparel line was a miniversion of the GapKids lines with bright colors and similar styling and quality. It provided an exciting alternative to traditional pastel baby clothes. Record sales laid the groundwork for a major jump in the size of GapKids stores. By the mid-1990s, Gap operated nearly 900 Gap, 360 GapKids, and 200 Banana Republic stores and was opening nearly 200 new stores each year. In 1995 the president said, "My goals are to grow earnings, boost employee satisfaction and performance, and exceed the expectations of our customers."[2]

1. **What factors have contributed to the success of Gap Inc.?**
2. **Where do you think management might look for further expansion opportunities?**

INTRODUCTION

We are living in an exciting time to be studying retailing. The opportunities for each of us to benefit from changes in retailing have never been better. Just think, while returning home on a flight from Montreal to Phoenix, you may remember that you needed to shop for a birthday gift for a friend or family member. You know on-demand retailing is available to you at 35,000 feet. Using an in-flight catalog and an airline telephone, you can place an order and have your merchandise waiting when you arrive at the airport. If you prefer, your order can be shipped to any address in the world with next-day delivery. While on a camping trip you can watch one of several television shopping networks on a personal-sized television, place an order by cellular phone, and have the items delivered to your home or campsite. Or sitting at home with your laptop PC, you can visit a virtual store for ideas before you actually go shopping.

You are about to embark on a learning process that will be very important in your life and in your career—the study of retailing. You will soon increase your understanding of the wide variety of activities that retailers perform and the many services that they provide. Because a significant part of each retail dollar you spend pays for these retailing activities, we also want you to become a more astute shopper. We will show you how retailing fits into the broader scope of marketing and plays an important role in the total business system. You will see the positive effect that retailing has on the American economic system by fueling almost 70 percent of the gross domestic product, providing jobs for about 18 percent of the U.S. workforce, and delivering one of the highest standards of living in the world.[3]

No matter how you look at retailing, it is dynamic. It is the world of merchandising. It is a world of things and ideas that contribute to excitement and beauty. Look at what you see all around you—attractive, well-lighted, and air-conditioned stores where you may shop at your leisure. Look at the way stores are locating in areas near you and staying open at times most convenient to you.

Look, too, at the way stores have adjusted their merchandise offerings to provide for one-stop shopping. Retailers continue to change retailing in whatever ways are necessary to satisfy their customers.

Retailing is a global activity, occurring from a street vendor in Bombay to Macy's in Manhattan. In one way or another, retailers must compete in a global environment. Throughout this text we will return to global issues—the paramount element of change for today's retailer.

Retailing as Customer Satisfaction

It is the task of marketing to create as well as deliver a standard of living. Specifically, marketers must be sensitive to equating new and improved goods and services with the needs, desires, and fancies of consumers. Retailing is the institution most closely in touch with consumers and, in many ways, the best able to interpret these needs. To the extent that retailers are skillful in interpreting consumer needs, and to the extent that they develop good assortments of merchandise (e.g., styles, materials, colors, prices, sizes) and present them in an effective manner so that consumers find it easy and attractive to buy, retailing truly serves society.

BOX 1.1 THE PENNEY IDEA

- To serve the public, as nearly as we can, to its complete satisfaction

- To expect for the service we render a fair remuneration and not all the profit the traffic will bear

- To do all in our power to pack the customer's dollar full of value, quality, and satisfaction

- To continue to train ourselves and our associates so that the service we give will be more and more intelligently performed

- To improve constantly the human factor in our business

- To reward men and women in our organization through participation in what our business produces

- To test our every policy, method, and act in this wise: "Does it square with what is right and just?"

6543217

In 1940, a young man by the name of Sam Walton accepted a position with the J. C. Penney company and reported to the Des Moines, Iowa, store.[4] As a part of his training program, he committed to memory the seven principles of "The Penney Idea" adopted in 1913 by James Cash Penney (see Box 1.1).

Sam Walton borrowed Penney's ideas about how to succeed in retailing by putting *customer satisfaction* ahead of profit. In 1945, after serving in World War II, Walton bought a franchise for a Ben Franklin five-and-dime store in Newport, Arkansas. He went on to become founder of Wal-Mart, the world's largest retailer.

The idea of "customer satisfaction first" was not new to Penney or Walton. In fact, over a century ago in the mid-1890s, the Sears, Roebuck, and Company catalog was a retailing success story. Richard Sears called his catalog "the farmer's friend." It was almost like a personal letter from Richard to his customers. With a friendly folksiness, Sears would write copy for the catalog and reassure rural families that it was safe to order merchandise from the "big city" that they had not seen in the store. Because Sears realized that orders could go astray or customers could misinterpret his product descriptions, he understood that a guarantee was important. The original pledge, "We Guarantee Satisfaction and Safe Delivery on Everything You Order," evolved into today's familiar slogan of "Satisfaction Guaranteed or Your Money Back."[5]

Unfortunately, as the years went by, Sears managers let success distract them from their focus on customer satisfaction, leading to a number of major changes. Sears managers closed their catalog stores and reduced their workforce by some 50,000 employees as a result of their decision to discontinue the general merchandise "Big Book" catalog for which they had been famous for over a century. Box 1.2 raises an ethical dilemma faced by having to lay off employees. Sears struggled in the early nineties to regain its former glory as it adjusted product and service assortments in its more than 1,000 retail

BOX

1.2 AN ETHICAL DILEMMA: HOW WOULD YOU LAY OFF 900 PEOPLE?

The day that Kmart Corporation headquarters laid off 900 management people, Robert Kahn received a phone call from a reporter for the Fox-affiliated television station in Detroit asking if this condition were evidence of something seriously wrong with the retail industry. He explained that Kmart faces problems not typical of the industry, informing the reporter that as early as July 1994 Kmart had announced its plan to release 2,300 or 10 percent of its management people. At that time, Kmart also employed 260,000 hourly workers. Shortly after, in September, it announced that only 1,650 in management would be released and that 100 to 110 unprofitable stores would be closed, resulting in 6,000 layoffs among hourly employees. By November, the planned management layoff had been reduced to 650.

Kahn pointed out that Kmart had suffered seven consecutive quarters of declining earnings. It had announced a plan to dramatically reduce expenses: The original goal was $1 billion in two years, but present references are between $600 million and $800 million. A new senior officer was brought in to head the program.

To fund Kmart through this difficult time, it raised about $2 billion by selling Thrifty Drug NW, its 21 percent interest in Coles Myer Ltd. (the largest retailer in Australia), and a minority interest in Sports Authority.

Adequate notice of the layoffs was given but not to individual employees. Apparently, none of the employees believed they would be among the 4 percent finally cut. The reporter said that 900 terminated management employees were notified at the start of work on December 12, when each was presented with a box for personal belongings and told to leave the building immediately. Outside security people were brought in to see that they did exactly that! Kmart may have been concerned about sabotage by some of its terminated employees, especially against its computer records. A computer consultant said this was not an uncommon procedure when terminating information systems personnel.

Questions

Do you think there is an ethical issue in laying off employees two weeks before Christmas? The method used by Kmart is one way. But is it a fair way? No notice—not even the customary two weeks—when the employees have broken no rules?

Source: Used by permission from Robert Kahn, "How Would You Lay Off 900 People?" *Retailing Today,* February 1995, p. 1.

6543217

outlets. A focused merchandising strategy, which you will read more about, turned the company around.

Despite how a firm chooses to compete, whether it is a general merchandise discounter like Wal-Mart focusing on the "always low price" or a specialty apparel retailer like Nordstrom providing "premium services," customer satisfaction will be the cornerstone to successful retailing into the twenty-first century.

W. Edwards Deming, a man who lived most of the twentieth century, was the foremost advocate of change in American business to meet the world's competitive challenges. His philosophy was basic and built on three principles: (1) customer satisfaction, (2) continuous quality improvement, and (3) taking care of your employees with training and giving them the tools for success.[6]

In the broadest sense, everything that retailers do revolves around providing service. As our earlier examples have shown, a customer satisfaction focus is not new. Unfortunately, it is a focus that many American business managers have lost. Let's look for a moment at how retailing fits in the larger picture of marketing and its need for a customer satisfaction focus.

Retailing Is Marketing

The global economy is very complex. Within our U.S. economic system, literally tens of thousands of different goods and services are produced and distributed each day. It is **marketing** that delivers these goods and services to provide the standard of living we enjoy today. Formally the American Marketing Association has defined marketing as "the process of planning and executing the conception, pricing, promotion and distribution of ideas, goods, and services to create exchanges that satisfy individual and organizational objectives." Retailing is marketing, too. **Retailing** is defined as "the activities involved in the sale of goods and services to consumers for their personal, family, or household use." An expanded definition of retailing is "marketing activities designed to provide satisfaction to final consumers and profitably maintain these customers through a program of continuous quality improvement." Retailing provides customer satisfaction through continuous quality improvement across all areas, not just by selling goods and services. For example, the benefits delivered by retailing may satisfy emotional, economic, or social motivations of customers.

To execute this marketing process and facilitate customer satisfaction, a retailer develops a **retail marketing strategy.** This retail marketing strategy involves selecting a **retail target market** and implementing a **retail marketing mix.** See Figure 1.1. The retail target market is the carefully identified group of final consumers that a retailer seeks to satisfy. The retail marketing mix consists of the product, price, promotion, and distribution strategies that will satisfy the members of the retail target market. The **product** element of the marketing mix encompasses all facets of providing goods and

FIGURE 1.1

The retail
marketing mix.

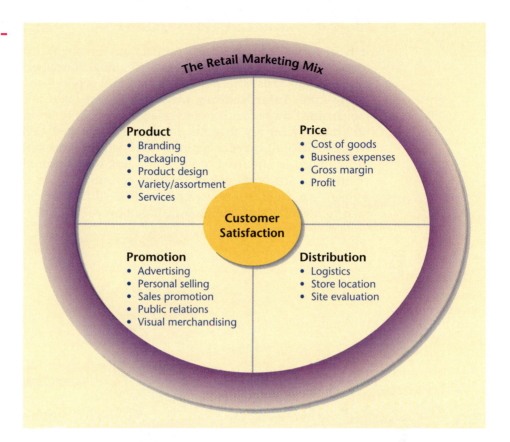

The Retail Marketing Mix

Product
- Branding
- Packaging
- Product design
- Variety/assortment
- Services

Price
- Cost of goods
- Business expenses
- Gross margin
- Profit

**Customer
Satisfaction**

Promotion
- Advertising
- Personal selling
- Sales promotion
- Public relations
- Visual merchandising

Distribution
- Logistics
- Store location
- Site evaluation

services, including branding, packaging, and product design. **Price** is designed to recover the expenses of doing business, as well as the cost of the goods, and to make a profit for the owners or shareholders of the firm. The difference between the selling price and the cost of a good is the gross margin.

Promotion involves a wide range of advertising, personal selling, sales promotion, and public relations activities. **Distribution** involves the location, logistics, change of ownership, transportation, and storage of goods activities. As we will see throughout this book, the members of the retail distribution system perform all of the marketing activities needed to satisfy the final consumer.

Retailing is the link in our marketing distribution system that makes goods and services available to consumers. The key difference between marketing and retailing is that *retailing* applies only to those activities related to marketing goods and services to final consumers for personal, family, or household use. Let's examine this in a little more detail.

Identifying Retail Transactions

It is important to distinguish transactions involving industrial buyers and intermediary buyers from those involving final consumers. **Industrial buyers** are individuals who purchase goods and services on behalf of manufacturing firms. **Intermediary buyers** are wholesalers and retailers who buy merchandise for resale. For convenience, we will group industrial buyers and intermediary buyers together in a category called organizational buyers. **Organizational buyers** are individuals within firms whose purchase behavior is guided by the need to perform a task or sell a product effectively, efficiently, and at a profit. We define final consumers to be individuals who buy for personal, family, or household use. This distinction permits us to separate sales to organizations and intermediary buyers from sales to final consumers.

FIGURE 1.2

Retail and wholesale transactions.

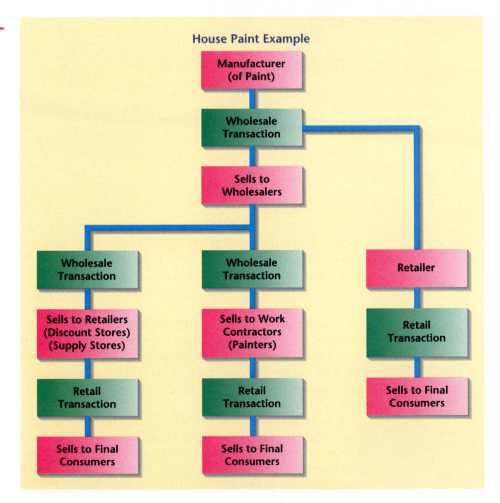

Providing goods and services to final consumers is a retail transaction. Retailers include street vendors, local supermarkets, Motel Six, Macy's department store, and a Schwinn bike shop. Anything that involves a purchase by an individual for personal, family, or household use is retailing.

Sales to organizational buyers are called **wholesale transactions,** and sales to final consumers are called **retail transactions.** We can illustrate the distinction between wholesale and retail buying situations by describing the sale of a gallon of house paint.

There are many sellers of house paint. Discount stores like Wal-Mart, Kmart, and Venture sell paint as do building supply stores like Lowe's, Payless Cashways, and Home Depot, as well as hardware stores like Ace, Westlake, and True Value. When a paint manufacturer sells directly to a retail store, the sale is considered a wholesale transaction (see Figure 1.2) because the store is not the final consumer. The store represents an organization that is in business to sell paint to final consumers. When one organization (a paint manufacturer) sells to another organization (Wal-Mart, Payless Cashways, Ace Hardware), this is a wholesale transaction.

On the other hand, if a store sells a gallon of paint to Barbara Jones to paint the living room of her condominium, this is considered a retail transaction. A final consumer like Barbara Jones does not buy paint for manufacture or resale. Rather, she purchases the paint to enjoy the benefits of a freshly painted living room.

Does a store like Payless Cashways always engage in retail transactions? The answer is no. Not everyone who shops at Payless Cashways or Home Depot is a final consumer. Some of these individuals are painting contractors who make their living painting homes and buildings. Painting contractors function as organizations, because they buy paint on behalf of the individuals for whom they are doing the painting.

Many types of stores, other than paint dealers, engage in both retail and wholesale transactions. For example, business supply stores like OfficeMax, General Office Supply, and Office Depot make both retail and wholesale sales. For example, if you buy a box of paper clips or a roll of tape for your home, we would consider that a retail transaction. On the other hand, if you bought the same box of paper clips or roll of tape for a business, that purchase would constitute a wholesale transaction.

Some types of sellers, such as apparel stores and restaurants, complete virtually no wholesale transactions. Almost all the customers who frequent an apparel store will be retail customers purchasing for themselves, friends, or family, unless uniforms are purchased for employees. Similarly, people frequenting a restaurant will not be buying prepared food for resale to others.

Despite the exceptions, many stores see one-half or more of their annual revenues generated from wholesale sales, although they may appear from the outside to be "retail stores."

Another situation that we often encounter is a store advertising that they "sell wholesale to the public." Carpet and furniture stores often use this type of advertising. Although the "public" may or may not be paying the same price as wholesale customers, sales to final users are retail transactions. The use of the word *wholesale* in advertising or even in the store name is simply to get attention or to suggest low prices. The distinction between wholesale and retail is not the store, its name, or the advertisement, but the transaction. The legal implications of this are discussed in Chapter 13.

The difference between wholesale and retail transactions centers on five characteristics: buying motives, trade discounts, stocking requirements, application of sales taxes, and price differentials.

Buying motives. Generally speaking, an individual buying at wholesale is making an organizational buying decision based on the profit motive, or maybe a service motive for a nonprofit organization like the Red Cross. Unlike organizational buyers, final consumers are neither manufacturers nor resellers and do not focus on long-term profitability as their principal buying motive. Rather, an individual buying at retail makes a purchase simply for the satisfaction derived from using the product or service. A wholesale buyer, such as a painting contractor, must select a paint with color characteristics and durability that will enhance any guarantee the contractor may offer customers. Price per gallon is important to the contractor so that a certain profit level can be obtained on a painting job.

Trade discounts. Another major difference between retail and wholesale exchanges is that wholesale buyers are typically offered a trade discount. A **trade discount** is a price reduction for performing services. It may be as much as 70 percent off the retail price. The principal reason that a trade discount is offered to organizational buyers is because they will typically perform selling and storage functions. In the case of a painting contractor, the contractor performs the selling function to the home owner. Chapter 11 discusses how a trade discount is a price reduction from a suggested list retail price for performing services. In a retail sale, store personnel would perform the selling function. Consequently, the contractor earned the trade discount by selling the painting job. The trade discount actually becomes an important part of the painting contractor's overall profit margin. Because final consumers rely on the selling efforts of the store, they do not earn a trade discount.

Stocking requirements. Painting contractors maintain a broad array of tools to apply paint that will last from job to job. When they buy paint, they will not need to buy scrapers, brushes, rollers, and pans every time they start a job. When the contractor does buy supplies, they will typically be very durable and quite expensive. This is not likely to be the case when final consumers buy paint and painting supplies. Most final consumers will buy paint and supplies for a single painting task. They will want economy and may prefer "disposable" supplies. Because of this, sellers who deal with final consumers will typically carry a much different variety of merchandise than sellers catering principally to organizational buyers.

Sales taxes.   Most states and cities levy sales taxes. Typically, these sales taxes apply only to retail sales. On the sale to the painting contractor, a sales tax would not be collected by the store, but would have been collected by the contractor. In our example of a consumer buying paint to refinish a living room, the retail store would have collected the appropriate sales tax. This taxing method keeps intermediate transactions relatively simple and ensures that the tax will be applied at the highest price point. In many countries a value-added tax (VAT) is added at every transaction. It's like a cumulative sales tax.

Price differentials.   A firm that is selling at wholesale is limited in the price differentials it can charge to competitive firms. As we will see in Chapter 12, a wholesaler that sells to two organizational buyers cannot charge them different prices for the same quantity and quality of goods if the two retailers are competitors. Retail transactions, however, are not restricted in the types of discounts or differences in prices given to final consumers.

You have seen that there may be a significant price differential between a wholesale and a retail transaction, but there is a real blurring of price differentials in some industries. With the rise of the category killer stores such as OfficeMax (business supplies), and Home Depot (building materials), price differentials are disappearing in many transactions. A home builder can purchase lighting fixtures at Home Depot at a price equal to or less than the price at a traditional wholesale outlet. The consumer replacing a light fixture in the dining room will pay the same price as the home builder.

THE BENEFITS OF RETAILING

Retailing benefits customers in many ways. It also benefits manufacturers and wholesalers. See Figure 1.3.

How Retailing Benefits Customers

Retailers make it easier for us to buy. If it were not for retailers, we would be forced to go from manufacturer to manufacturer to purchase goods that we need daily. Clearly, retailers provide critically needed services by acting as our

FIGURE 1.3

Retailing benefits
customers,
manufacturers,
and wholesalers
and creates
economic utility.

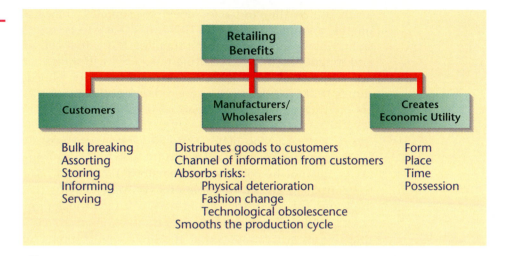

buying agent. To complete this task for us, retailers perform the basic functions of bulk breaking, assorting, storing, informing, and serving. The retailer who can provide these functions efficiently and pleasantly at a price that is proportionate to their value will be successful.

Efficiency in buying and distribution is derived from the bulk-breaking function. **Bulk breaking** means that retailers buy goods in large quantities (e.g., ton, gross, dozen, carload) so that they can earn significant quantity discounts. By so doing, not only do they usually earn quantity discounts on their purchase price, but freight rates are generally much lower for large shipments of goods. They then take these bulk shipments and break them into smaller sizes for their customers (e.g., pound, unit, quart). The smaller sizes are more convenient for the customers and allow them to spend less at any given time. Warehouse stores like Costco and Sam's, however, have identified a segment of customers willing and able to buy in bulk and provide their own in-home storage in return for lower prices.

Retailers perform the **assorting** function by evaluating all the different products that are available and offering us the optimum array of products from which to choose. The products the retailer selects must be those that are best suited to meet the needs and demands of the particular community in which the retailer hopes to sell them. As a result, consumers benefit by having a more efficient buying process and are able to take advantage of increased levels of "one-stop shopping."

So that customers do not have to anticipate their desires too far in advance of their needs, retailers keep goods in inventory until customers are ready to buy and use them. **Storing** means the retailer acquires and keeps safe a vast inventory of products so that they will be there when the customers need them. This is a very important function. For example, many of us have become accustomed to "picking up dinner on the way home from work" or "getting a few snacks before the game" at grocery or convenience stores. Such instantaneous shopping trips would be impossible if retailers did not maintain adequate assortments and store them in inventory. The storing function is also one of the most risky for the retailer.

When the retailer carries goods in inventory, there are the risks of physical deterioration, fire, theft, flood, fashion change, and even technological obsolescence. Many retailers, for example, lost a great deal of money on their large stocks during the early 1990s when the cost of personal computers fell by as much as 50 percent over a three-year period. You probably know of retailers who often stock merchandise toward the end of a fashion trend only to see the merchandise drastically marked down in an effort to sell it. In each of these examples, it was the retailer who had to absorb the loss of devalued inventory. Inventories also have a cost because they occupy space on which the retailer has to pay taxes and insurance premiums. An additional consideration is the opportunity cost of inventory if those dollars could have been invested in another asset that would earn a greater return.

Consumers expect a great deal of information from the retailing system. **Informing** means that the retailer provides the advertising and the in-store sales personnel necessary to complete a transaction. By so doing, we can "shop" by going through the newspaper, instead of having to visit numerous different stores and have a salesperson present to explain the characteristics and features of the goods.

Retailers provide many services for customers. Serving the customer may mean providing convenient hours, delivery, credit, alterations, exchange privileges, parking, education in the use of products, and help from courteous and knowledgeable sales associates. The retailer must decide what level of service is needed or appropriate, given the price that the customer wants to pay. We see value-oriented stores like Target working to improve the level of customer service they provide, such as by installing scanners on the sales floor so that shoppers can verify price prior to checkout.

After a retailer buys goods, they are marked up to the retail selling price. This **markup** is expressed as a percentage of the selling price of the item and may range from 18 percent for canned vegetables in the supermarket, an average of 30 percent on appliances and 40 percent on clothing, to something like 50 percent on jewelry and home furnishings. Part of the markup we pay the retailer is because the retailing system performs the task of buying in large quantities and selling to us in the small quantities we want. Furthermore, the costs and risks associated with storing inventory are a major component in the markup percentage. The variety of services that a specific retailer offers will also affect the markup percentage.

How Retailing Benefits Manufacturers and Wholesalers

The retailing system that brings goods to consumers is viewed by producers as the means of getting their goods to market. Only by making sales to retailers can manufacturers and wholesalers return revenues to their firms to pay their employees, buy more materials, and renew the cycle. Just as we said that the retailer can be viewed as the buying agent for the consumer, the retailer is the selling agent for the producer. Producers need and expect a retailing system that gives them the opportunity to present their goods to consumers.

Manufacturers and wholesalers expect retailers to be part of an established channel through which information can flow back from consumer to manufacturer. This feedback is vital to manufacturers, who must anticipate current and future consumer needs. The retailer provides this vital link between the manufacturer and their customers.

As retailers attempt to match a wide selection of many manufacturers' goods with the anticipated needs of consumers, they take some of the risks of being in business that the manufacturer would otherwise have to assume. For example, when the retailer purchases the goods, a financial burden is shifted from manufacturer to retailer. The manufacturer has been paid even though the ultimate consumer has not made a purchase. The retailer also assumes three kinds of obsolescence risk: physical, technological, and fashion. If goods sit on the floor or shelf and get shopworn, it is the retailer who bears the burden of reduced value (e.g., greeting cards). If a technological breakthrough increases product performance while lowering price, it is the retailer whose inventory becomes obsolete or devalued (e.g., personal computers). If style or fashion changes during or before a season, it is up to the retailer to decide what to do with merchandise customers no longer want (e.g., new styles, colors, or fabrics).

In addition to the risk burden that the retailer assumes, manufacturers benefit by pushing inventory from their storage warehouses to retailers' storage facilities. Why and when does this occur?

You will notice in Figure 1.4 that the production level of these toys is in excess of demand from March to October and falls far short of demand for November and December. Retailers offer toy manufacturers the ability to

FIGURE 1.4

Retailers help manufacturers smooth out differences between production and sales.

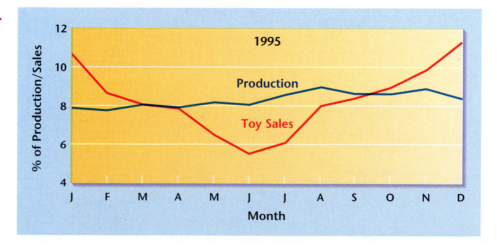

smooth their production cycles by placing orders for Christmas toys in February or March and receiving shipments of toys throughout the year. By working in a partnership, toy prices to retailers can be minimized and toy manufacturers can confidently make toys year-round.

Retailing and Economic Utility

Another way to think about retailing is from an economic point of view. Economists often describe elements of the economy in terms of their ability to provide the four basic economic utilities from which satisfaction is derived. The term **utility** simply means the ability to satisfy needs. The importance of marketing and retailing stems from the fact that it is necessary for an economy to provide four basic utilities: form, time, place, and possession. **Form utility** is created by manufacturing and other means of production and when goods are sorted into smaller units. Form utility is embodied in physical goods and intangible services. Goods and service production, however, is insufficient. The retailer adds value to goods and services by providing time, place, and possession utilities.

   Time utility is created when the retailer stores goods and makes them available when the customer wants to make a purchase. **Place utility** is created by the transfer of goods from the place of production to the place where they can be easily accessed by consumers. **Possession utility** occurs when the retailer assists the customer in acquiring a good or service through purchase, lease, or trade. It is by providing such utilities that the retailer is able to satisfy the needs of each and every customer who comes into the store.

   In an attempt to provide utility to consumers, many different retail structures have emerged ranging from the small boutique to the huge discount warehouse.

THE NATURE OF THE RETAILING INDUSTRY

The nature of retailing may be categorized in terms of diversity in store types, competitiveness, and the fact that buyers seek sellers. See Figure 1.5.

Diversity in Store Types

There are more than 1.5 million retail stores in the United States. Some of them are very small, with monthly sales of a few thousand dollars like your local used paperback bookstore; others are very large like Target Greatland, with monthly sales exceeding $5 million. Retail stores are different in many other ways as well. In the next section we will explore differences based on type and breadth of merchandise handled, type of ownership, and methods of operation. However, there are some common elements in the diversity. One

FIGURE 1.5

The nature of the retailing industry.

of the most obvious is that retailing is highly competitive. Because there are so many new types of retailing and so many types of retailers, there is always someone thinking of a way to do a better job, and to do it more efficiently. These retailers seek to provide a new way or a better way to give the consumer goods and services with the best possible value. With so many stores competing, retailing also is dynamic. There are constant changes in operations and in the goods and services offered.

Practitioners and students of retailing have searched for a theory or theories to help explain the changes that have taken place in stores as retailing has evolved to meet the challenges of economic, competitive, social, technological, and political pressures. Even though none fully explain change, they all lend credence to our position that change is going to occur and there will be ever greater diversity. Several of these changes will be discussed in Chapter 3.

Buyers Seek Sellers

One of the unique characteristics of in-store retailing is that the buyer seeks out the seller. Manufacturers and wholesalers typically employ salespeople who call on their customers. The retailer waits for the customer to come to the store. When those customers do come, they generally expect instant satisfaction. They expect to have the goods available to them to take home at the time they purchase them. And when customers come to the seller, they expect service, a convenient location, and a choice of product at a price they are willing to pay. Retailers soon learn that they live or die by merging the desires of the customer with the variety and quality of the goods they carry, along with the atmosphere, service, and location of the store.

Because buyers must seek out the sellers of the goods in retailing, retailers spend a great deal of time and money on information programs. They rely on advertising and selling efforts as well as location to guide the consumer to their store. Since so many retail transactions consist of unplanned purchases, the elements within stores—such as displays, layout, and merchandise presentation—mean a great deal.

Competitiveness

Competition in retailing is fierce. Every day entrepreneurs with a new idea, a new twist on an old idea, or a proven successful idea open hundreds of new stores. At the same time, major chains are opening thousands of additional stores annually. As a result, tens of thousands of stores disappear. The intensely competitive nature of the retail industry is discussed in more detail in Chapter 3.

RETAIL COMPETITION: TYPES OF STORES

If anything characterizes retailing in the United States today, it is variety in types of stores! Retail operations range from the little lemonade stand you or your friends may have opened for a day one summer to the giant that is Wal-Mart, where more than 50 million customers each week go to shop. We have looked at retailers by size and ownership. We now look at stores by types of merchandise and type of operations. See Figure 1.6.

Like the sizes of retail operations, the products sold through retailing vary widely. They range from the most intangible services like those of home

FIGURE 1.6

Retailers may be classified by ownership, by size, and by assortment and variety of merchandise.

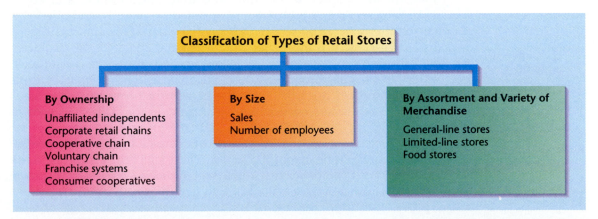

Classification of Types of Retail Stores

By Ownership	By Size	By Assortment and Variety of Merchandise
Unaffiliated independents	Sales	General-line stores
Corporate retail chains	Number of employees	Limited-line stores
Cooperative chain		Food stores
Voluntary chain		
Franchise systems		
Consumer cooperatives		

cleaning or secretarial services to very tangible goods like women's apparel and used sporting equipment at Play It Again Sports.

Along with variations in size of operation and products sold, there is also variety in type of retail institution. Types vary from old established organizations like Montgomery Ward to Nature Virtual Store. All are competing, in one way or another, for the consumer's dollar. With all this variety, it is helpful to categorize and describe retail operations by form of ownership, by size, and by general-line versus limited-line retailing, service retailing, and nonstore retailing.

Any categorization scheme has to recognize that consumers throughout the world have a ferocious appetite for choice. Retailers will be challenged by competitors that are local, regional, national, and even global in scope. Knowledge transfer will be instantaneous and will be the new mechanism for competitive advantage. Yet there will be opportunity for the innovative concept or for the successful rejuvenation of an existing business.

Classification by Type of Ownership

Retail operations may be classified into at least four basic categories according to form of ownership. The first category consists of independents who are not affiliated with other retail operations (i.e., sole proprietorships and partnerships). Corporate retail chains consisting of two or more stores make up the second category. This includes relatively small retail chains as well as large ones. The third category includes cooperative and voluntary chains of independently owned operations organized by retailers or their wholesalers. The largest portion of this category exists through franchise agreements. The fourth category consists of consumer cooperatives, which are retail establishments owned and managed by consumers.

Unaffiliated independents are establishments owned and operated as single-unit operations. For example, the Cauldron is a limited-line store selling a wide selection of prints, paintings, pottery, handcrafted jewelry, and ready-made picture frames. In addition, the store offers custom and do-it-yourself framing services. It is owned and operated by a family, and offers the personalized atmosphere and service that so often characterize independently owned stores. Because it is independently owned and operated, the Cauldron can reflect the tastes and preferences of its owners and customers; it can therefore be very flexible and responsive to change. On the other hand, a store like the Cauldron does not experience the benefits of being part of a large-scale operation, and its success depends exclusively on the skills of its owner-managers.

The ability of unaffiliated independents to compete in today's aggressive discount marketplace is being put to the test. These small merchants are finding that attempts to compete against the discounters on price usually prove fatal. They typically don't have the sales volume to get the most favorable cost of goods terms from vendors, and their overhead as a percentage of sales is higher than the discounters'. In fact, as Archie Nivins in Charlotte, North Carolina, said so succinctly, "You can't keep food in your employees' mouths [on a 10 percent markup]" as an independent retailer competing in a world of discounters.[7] As pointed out by other small retailers, independents must concentrate on a personal touch, friendly and helpful service, offering product lines that the chains do not, and showing an honest concern for customer needs.

Corporate retail chains.   In contrast to the single retail store that is independently owned and operated, a **corporate retail chain** is made up of multiple retail units under common ownership and management. This type of retail chain is defined as two or more stores selling similar lines of merchandise, having similar architectural motifs, and featuring centralized buying. Corporate chains may vary in size from just two stores to organizations with hundreds of outlets. The Art Adventure, for example, is part of a chain consisting of only two stores located in college communities about forty miles apart. Both sell the same lines of art and drafting supplies. At the other extreme, stores such as Home Depot, BabySuperstore, Sears, and J. C. Penney have hundreds of retail outlets in the United States and are expanding around the world.

In addition to varying in size, corporate chains are not found with equal frequency in all types of retail businesses. For example, corporate chains account for more than 50 percent of sales for stores selling women's apparel, and in department store retailing, corporate chains account for nearly all sales.

The success of corporate chains can be attributed to a number of factors. Generally speaking, corporate chains have the advantages of centralized management, computerization, bargaining power, and economies of scale.

Of course, chains also have disadvantages including inflexibility, local management without the commitment of a local owner, and high return on investment requirements.

Associations of Independent Retailers

Many **independent retailers** voluntarily associate with wholesalers, manufacturers, service firms, or other retailers to gain some of the advantages of a corporate chain while still maintaining their status as individual owners. These groups offer independent retailers volume buying power, advertising efficiencies, site selection, store layout, technology systems, and image campaigns.[8]

Cooperative chain.   One type of voluntary association is the **cooperative chain.** For example, a hardware store in your city may be a member of the cooperative chain called True Value Hardware Stores. This store would be one of the more than 5,000 hardware stores that together own Cotter & Company, the wholesale distribution and merchandising organization developed and managed to serve True Value Hardware Stores. Cotter & Company provides its member stores with large-scale buying and warehousing operations. Ten regional distribution centers, with a combined warehousing capacity of 3.6 million square feet, are strategically located across the nation. In addition to warehousing and assistance in buying, Cotter & Company provides member stores with other services. For example, Cotter sponsors national advertising in magazines like *Better Homes & Gardens* to the benefit of member stores who could not individually afford expensive national advertising of this type. Other services include assistance in accounting, selecting store sites, planning store layouts, inventory control, merchandising, sales training, and financing.

Voluntary chain. The **voluntary chain** is also an association of independent retailers, but it is sponsored by a wholesaler rather than by the retailers themselves. Like cooperative chains, voluntary chains are also found in the food industry as well as in other industries. The Colony Market, for example, belongs to a voluntary chain called Western Grocers. As a member of such a chain, the Colony Market buys a considerable amount of merchandise from the Western Grocers' wholesale operation, but it still can maintain its identity as an independent grocer.

The voluntary chain is sponsored by a wholesaler; the cooperative chain is sponsored by cooperating retailers. But the basic purpose of both groups is the same—to enable independent retailers to compete more effectively with corporate chain stores. Ace Hardware stores are independent, often family-owned firms that voluntarily join the Ace Hardware buying group. The association buys for the 5,000 independent stores and provides them with merchandising and promotion support.

Franchise Systems

Another association of independent retailers is created by franchise agreements. Many independent retailers are members of **franchise systems sponsored by manufacturers, distributors, and service firms.** Gas stations, for example, are usually owned by independent retailers who operate according to franchise agreements with their distributors or manufacturers. Comparable franchise arrangements are commonly sponsored by manufacturers of cars, trucks, motorcycles, appliances, and lawn and garden equipment. A service firm may also sponsor a chain of franchised operations. In this case we would have a franchise system sponsored by a service firm, usually a large retail organization. The growth of franchise systems in the fast-food industry is illustrated best by the success of McDonald's. Since the first restaurant was opened in 1955, the chain has expanded to more than 13,000 stores with sales over $22 billion; about 70 percent of them are franchised. In other service-oriented types of retailing, franchise systems are common for motels, hotels, auto rentals, and recreation services.

Franchise organization.[9] Today more than 500,000 U.S. business establishments are franchised, and franchised organizations—including both franchised units and company stores—account for nearly a third of all retail sales.

Owning a franchise amounts to paying for the right to distribute products, use trademarks, and use a business format for a set period of time. Among the oldest and largest of franchises are auto and truck dealerships. General Motors occasionally has some for sale, but they cost anywhere from less than a million dollars in a small rural community to several million dollars in a large urban area. The more recently developed franchises, like McDonald's and Midas Muffler, do more than authorize the distribution of their products; they provide a complete format for doing business as well. Many companies find the best location, put up the building, and instruct the franchisee on how to keep the books.

Companies are willing to provide these services for one primary reason. As they locate franchisees who invest their own money in the franchise, they are able to expand the company's sales and market penetration without having to raise their own capital. Typically, franchise buyers (franchisees) pay an initial franchise fee, remodel and lease a store, buy their own equipment and inventory, and then pay a continuing royalty based on sales, usually between 5 and 12 percent. Most franchisers require buyers to have 25 to 50 percent of the initial costs in cash.

The franchises most people are familiar with are concentrated in a handful of industries: fast foods, motels, car rental, office services, and consumer services such as income tax preparation and child care. But it is possible to choose a franchise in almost any sector of the economy. The fastest-growing franchising areas include car repair centers, home remodeling, equipment rental, and specialized stores for everything from maternity clothes to sporting goods.

Advantages and disadvantages of a franchise. As with any business, there are good and bad points to franchising. When you go into business with a franchise, you often get a proven product or service to sell, one backed by an established profit record. A company representative will be on hand to spot problems and tell you how to solve them. Franchising is a way for an inexperienced businessperson to take advantage of the managerial knowledge of others. And with a multi-million-dollar ad campaign behind you, it is usually less necessary to drum up business.

However, owners of labor-intensive franchises can find themselves unprepared to deal with personnel problems. Others run into trouble because they start out deep in debt and short of working capital. While using franchising to become their own boss, some new retailers don't realize that they give up a lot of their rights as independent businesspeople when they sign the contract. While an independent business can be sold to others or passed on to heirs, a franchise usually can't be transferred without the company's

BOX 1.3 — FOUR KEY QUESTIONS TO ASK WHEN EVALUATING A FRANCHISE

1. Does the franchise have a strong chance of competing in your community? A well-known fast-food franchise might have little trouble luring enough customers away from a local deli, but a dry-cleaning franchise without a famous name might find it hard to draw customers away from an established favorite.

2. Does the franchise have potential for future growth, or does its success depend on a fad, such as disco roller skating? Other franchises deserving extra scrutiny include worm farms, envelope-stuffing businesses, and vending-machine routes. Though some companies in these areas may be honest, such businesses have been the staples of con artists in recent years.

3. Will franchise ownership be an advantage in the business you are considering, or could you do as well on your own? If the franchise offers a well-known trademark or a unique service, there is little question of its value. But if it only provides you with equipment you could buy on your own, then you can probably make more money without it.

4. What is the company's attitude toward developing new products? A fast-food franchise that was not continually introducing new menu items and developing promotions would be chewed up by the competition.

6543217

approval—approval that franchisers are sometimes reluctant to give. Before purchasing a franchise it is important to obtain answers to a number of questions. Four important questions are outlined in Box 1.3.

Consumer Cooperatives

In contrast to the large number of stores that are part of chains and franchise systems, relatively few retail operations are owned and managed by consumers. Such operations are appropriately called **consumer cooperatives,** because member consumers usually cooperate in buying, transporting, and pricing the goods sold for the store. Consumer cooperatives saw their peak during the inflation-ridden 1970s as individuals sought to get control of prices. In addition, some consumers seek to save money by substituting their own labor; consumer cooperatives also may allow customers access to products such as "health foods" that may not be available from traditional stores. Although consumer cooperatives are most prevalent in the food business, they account for less than one-tenth of 1 percent of supermarket sales. Because members share at least some of the work required to buy and distribute the goods, prices may be lower than at other food stores, particularly for working members.

Classification by Size

We noted that there are about 1.5 million retail stores in the United States. Most are small in terms of their annual sales. Small retail stores dominate our retailing system in terms of the number of establishments, but the large-scale retailers are more powerful in terms of sales. In 1995, the four largest firms—Wal-Mart, Kmart, Sears, and Kroger Stores—accounted for more than $200 billion in net retail sales. With total gross retail sales in the United States exceeding $2,300 billion, the four largest retailers accounted for a disproportionate share of this sales volume, illustrating the concentration of power that characterizes American retailing.

Two basic types of retailing have evolved in the United States. In their purest forms, these two types may be called *general-line retailing* and *limited-line retailing*. As the name suggests, general-line retailing refers to operations that carry a wide variety of product lines with at least some depth of the assortment in each line. In contrast, limited-line retailing refers to operations that carry a considerable assortment of goods within only one or a few related product lines. In spite of the fact that there is not always a clear distinction, we can use these categories in describing many of the retail institutions.

We will begin with department stores and discount stores, which are two types that clearly represent general-line retailing. Next, we will look at the types of stores that exemplify limited-line retailing. Then we will focus on food retailers, including supermarkets, convenience stores, superstores, and hypermarkets, since they are in many ways distinctly different from other retail institutions. The section will conclude with a look at nonstore forms of retailing and service retailing.

General-Line Retailing

Department stores.   Department stores like J. C. Penney, Sears, Macy's, Burdines, Foley's, Rich's, Dillard's, and Montgomery Ward are familiar names in retailing. See Table 1.1, and notice how few pure department stores are among the top retailers in the world. Dillard's is a typical department store. It is a large-scale, general-line retail operation that carries many product lines. Like most department stores, the varied product lines of Dillard's include a wide selection of women's wear attractively displayed and available in several price ranges. In addition, a department store like Dillard's tends to carry many other lines of merchandise, including men's wear, children's wear, dry goods, household linens, housewares, furniture, and home furnishings.

The organization of department stores varies considerably, but as their name suggests, all are departmentalized for the purposes of buying, accounting, and general management. Although most have continually tried to

TABLE 1.1

The World's Largest Retailers, by Sales

Top Retailers	Main Type of Trade	Home Country	Sales $ Billions (1993)	Number of stores (1993)
Wal-Mart	Discount	United States	68.0	2,540
Metro Int	Diversified	Germany	48.4	2,750
Kmart	Discount	United States	34.6	4,274
Sears, Roebuck	Department	United States	29.6	1,817
Tengelman	Supermarket	Germany	29.5	6,796
Rewe Zertrale	Supermarket	Germany	27.2	8,497
Ito-Yokado	Diversified	Japan	26.0	13,482
Daiei	Diversified	Japan	22.6	5,920
Kroger	Supermarket	United States	22.4	2,208
Carrefour	Hypermarket	France	21.7	647
Leclerc, Centres	Hypermarket	France	21.1	524
Aldi	Supermarket	Germany	20.9	3,435
Intermarche	Supermarket	France	20.7	2,890
J. C. Penney	Department	United States	19.6	1,766
Dayton Hudson	Discount	United States	19.2	893
American Stores	Supermarket	United States	18.8	1,697
Edeka Zentrale	Supermarket	Germany	17.9	11,670
Promodes	Hypermarket	France	16.0	4,675
J. Sainsbury	Supermarket	Britain	15.9	514
Jusco	Diversified	Japan	15.8	2,452
Price/Costco	Warehouse club	United States	15.5	200
Safeway	Supermarket	United States	15.2	1,078
Koninklijke Ahold	Supermarket	Holland	14.6	2,152
Otto Versand	Mail order	Germany	14.4	na
Tesco	Supermarket	Britain	12.9	430

Source: "A Survey of Retailing: Change at the Check-out," *The Economist,* March 4, 1995, p. 4.

modernize their operations and offer current fashions and furnishings, the department store is a relatively old form of retailing in this country. The concept of the department store developed in the 1860s, and the number of stores grew rapidly from 1860 to about 1920. From the 1920s on, the impact of department stores has increased primarily through the establishment of branch stores located in suburban shopping centers. Being no exception, May Department Stores has opened a number of branches in suburban areas of major cities as well as smaller (75,000 population and up) communities in

Department stores must have a wide variety and deep assortments in many merchandise categories. Four restaurants and a deli in Marks and Spencer in London add to the total shopping experience. Restaurants, produce, and grocery sections are common in department stores outside the United States.

the trade area. Although branch stores tend to be smaller and less impressive than the original downtown stores, they dominate department store retailing in terms of sales.

Recent trends show that department stores are benefiting the most from changes in the 1990s. A recent Arthur Andersen & Co. survey indicated that 80 percent of all U.S. shoppers who had gone shopping anywhere shopped at a department store, an increase from 60 percent the year before.[10] In its effort to capture this increased traffic, May Department Stores is planning to spend $4.6 billion from 1994 to 1998 to open 100 new stores and remodel another 100. Federated Department Store managers anticipate spending $1.2 billion over the 1994–1997 period to build 40 new stores and upgrade 217.

General merchandise discount stores. Discount department stores are departmentalized retail stores with limited customer service and low markup, carrying diversified product lines, including soft lines like apparel and linens and hard lines like computers, furniture, and consumer electronics. These stores typically consist of a sales area of at least 20,000 square feet and are usually housed in a one-level structure.[11] General-line discount stores like Kmart, Wal-Mart, and Target may have 100,000 square feet. They try to

The concept of offering goods in almost every category including a full grocery store originated in Europe. Such stores struggled in the United States. They were just too big for
American customers, who wanted convenience and one-stop shopping but were unwilling to
search for goods in a huge store. Wal-Mart was one of the firms that tried this concept. Its
USA hypermarche store contained more than 250,000 square feet. Wal-Mart scaled back to
less than 200,000 square feet and created the Wal-Mart supercenters.

keep operating costs as low as possible by hiring a minimum of personnel,
relying on self-service merchandising, and locating in less expensive buildings with less expensive equipment and fixtures. Service is kept at a minimum, and price is the most frequently used promotion appeal. These discount stores vary in size, merchandise assortment, operations, and
management. The phenomenal growth experienced by full-line discount
houses is illustrated by the success of Kmart. In the early 1960s S. S. Kresge
moved from the faltering variety store business into discounting and called
the new discount department stores Kmart. The Kmart general merchandise
stores' sales exceed $30 billion.

At one time there were a large number of regional discount department
store chains. In fact, there was a time when regional chains such as Bradlees
and Caldors in the Northeast were blamed for taking the life out of downtown shopping districts. Now they have filed for bankruptcy protection as
they have succumbed to the national discounters: Dayton Hudson's Target,
Kmart, and Wal-Mart. Discount specialty retailers—ranging from Price/Costco
membership warehouses and Home Depot home improvement stores to Baby-
Superstores—have contributed to the regional discounters' demise. Against
such competition they lack the capitalization and computer systems for man-

aging inventory and orders, and they have not found a profitable niche to make themselves stand out.[12]

Membership warehouse stores. Membership warehouse stores, or wholesale clubs as they are sometimes called, have been around since 1976. They have familiar names like Sam's and Price/Costco. This retail phenomenon commands over 600 stores nationwide and boasts a total sales volume of $33 billion.[13] The success of this format lies in volume selling, averaging about $60 million per unit, operating at about half the expense rate of its primary competitors, and surviving on about half their gross margin.[14] These performance figures are driven by the fact that industry experts believe approximately 60 percent of all U.S. households will belong to at least one club by 1997. Clearly, in exchange for lower prices, many customers appear quite ready to give up many amenities, and services, to purchase in bulk.

Variety stores. Variety stores, although dead in many U.S. cities, are also a form of general-line retailing. The F. W. Woolworth Company, the largest variety and general merchandise store operation, closed 970 general merchandise and specialty stores in the United States and Canada in 1993 and 1994, eliminating 13,000 jobs.[15] For many of the more senior Americans, Woolworth was one of the first places they spent their money as children. Variety stores like Woolworth were appealing because they sold a wide selection of merchandise in the low and popular price ranges.

Typically, variety stores carry stationery, gift items, women's accessories, toilet articles, light hardware, toys, housewares, and confectioneries, all at prices that nearly every consumer can afford. Although you still see variety stores like Woolworth, Dollar General, and Ben Franklin stores in small towns or in downtown urban areas, their numbers are decreasing across the country because of the competition from discount stores. As retailing evolved to meet the needs of consumers, the variety store, with its wide collection of merchandise and low price range, was superseded by the more complex discount store meeting a wider variety of customer needs, often at lower prices. Presently, variety store formats are being revised to include 99 cent merchandise and craft stores.[16]

Limited-Line Retailing

In contrast to general-line retailing, limited-line retail encompasses all operations that carry only one or a few related lines of merchandise. Limited-line stores sell a single but broad category of merchandise. One example of a limited-line store would be a shoe store that carries a variety of styles of footwear for men, women, and children. A typical men's apparel store, such as the Men's Warehouse, is another example of what we call a limited-line store. It might be limited to apparel for men, but it carries a deep assortment of suits, shoes, shirts, sweaters, slacks, coats, underwear, neckties, scarves, and other fashion accessories.

Specialty stores.   A specialty store is a limited-line store that sells one or a few lines of merchandise within a broader category such as food, furniture, or hardware. Specialty stores also compete on uniqueness of offerings, rather than price. The Shoe Boat is a specialty store that carries only children's shoes, whereas a limited-line store like Gallenkamp's handles footwear for adults as well as children. Lane Bryant is another example of a specialty store. It carries women's apparel but specializes in the sale of fashions for tall and large women. Like department stores, large limited-line stores and specialty stores may be departmentalized for the purposes of promotion, buying, accounting, and control. However, they are clearly different from department stores, since both are limited to the sale of merchandise within some broad category. The specialty store concept can be built around narrow and deep selections versus wide and shallow selections. Good Guys, a clothing retailer in southern California, is an example of the former; and Home Club home improvement stores are an example of the latter.

Boutiques.   Another type of limited-line store is the boutique. The rise in the number of boutiques is an example of the changing attitudes of today's customers. They expect and want more from their purchases, including not only practicality but also individuality. Such stores are much like specialty stores, but they are smaller and appeal to more limited target markets. They are usually found in downtown areas, fashionable shopping districts, and

F.A.O. Schwarz is a specialty toy retailer. A category dominant limited-line store like Toys 'R' Us sells toys but carries far more lines within the category. The specialty store typically competes with a deep assortment but less variety, knowledgeable salespeople, and services like layaway, credit, delivery, and gift wrapping.

large upscale shopping centers. Boutiques are also found in self-contained areas within department stores. A typical boutique, for example, might carry an assortment of women's apparel selected for a particular and rather limited target market, such as furs. Such stores are small operations with distinct personalities, and they provide a unique product assortment that usually consists of special types of goods like expensive clothes, high-quality sporting goods, or shoes in special sizes.

Category dominant limited-line stores. The late 1980s saw the emergence of a new segment of limited-line discount retailers who focused on the public's appetite for one-stop shopping and the desire for value. Large discount-oriented stores specializing in one or a few product lines like Toys 'R' Us, CompUSA, OfficeMax, BabySuperstores, and Circuit City grew rapidly. The appeal of these *category dominant stores or category killers* is based not only on low price but also on extensive assortment and variety within a narrow product line. Sales for these stores can be extensive. Toys 'R' Us, for example, has sales of over $8.7 billion, and Circuit City posted 1995 sales exceeding $5.5 billion.[17] What is probably more intriguing from an analytical perspective is the market share that a store of this type can garner. Toys 'R' Us sales, for example, constitute 25 percent of the total U.S. toy market.[18]

Factory Outlet Stores

Recent years have seen a tremendous growth in factory outlet limited-line stores. These stores are typically in a strip center located at least fifty to seventy-five miles from a major metropolitan area. Originally these stores were viewed by manufacturers as a place to dispose of production overruns, seconds, and returns. In many cases they still are. Some manufacturers produce products and brands especially for their outlet stores. Van Heusen will have different brands and slightly different styles in their outlet stores than in the department stores in the nearby towns.

Major developers like HGI and Exposition Mills built outlet stores across the country. Freeport, Maine, is a city known for its factory outlets. It is a convenient drive from Boston and the New York City area, and customers come from as far as the West Coast, Europe, and Latin America looking for bargains. The factory outlet trend reflects the customer's desire for low prices on branded goods. It also indicates that manufacturers are looking for ways to be less at the mercy of department store and specialty store chain buyers.

Food Retailing

Food sales in supermarkets, convenience stores, membership warehouse stores, and other types of stores exceed $400 billion.[19] Of this total, supermarkets represent the most significant segment in food retailing, having garnered 75 percent of total grocery sales while constituting only 22 percent of all grocery stores.[20] Independent supermarkets have seen their market share decrease from 42 percent of supermarket sales in 1972 to less than 29 percent now.

Supermarkets. The term *supermarket* is generally used to describe a complete, full-line, self-service, departmentalized food store with a sales volume of over $2 million per year and an average size of 25,000 square feet. The first supermarkets were opened in the 1930s, and to this retail institution is attributed the introduction of true self-service shopping. The original supermarkets were successful for several reasons. The economic conditions of the 1930s made consumers more price-conscious, and supermarket retailing was based on a low-price appeal. Supermarkets could offer lower prices than other food stores because they saved money by locating in low-rent areas. They sold nationally advertised, presold brands, so they did not need large advertising budgets. This form of retailing allowed the supermarket to cut costs as well as increase volume.

When they were first introduced, supermarkets were stocked with dry groceries, and shoppers boxed and carried out their own purchases. The supermarket of today often carries over 10,000 items displayed for convenient self-service shopping. Along with the aisles of food products are special departments like the store's own bakery or its delicatessen. Some supermarkets are adding restaurant-type additions such as Chinese Kitchens and Pizza Parlors inside the store where you can sit down and eat or take the food home.

Combination superstores. Supermarkets will probably continue to dominate the food industry in the foreseeable future, but several new store types are carving up the market. The superstore is a new form of competitor in the food retailing area. A superstore is like a supermarket in that it is a low-cost, high-volume, limited-service operation with a high proportion of its sales in food products. However, the superstore is much larger, combining the grocery store with general merchandise. Combining unrelated merchandise across categories is called **scrambled merchandising.** The superstores have from 160,000 to 200,000 square feet, which gives them the space of a supermarket and a traditional general merchandise discount store. One of the key advantages of carrying food items in the superstore format is frequency of customer visits. To compete with superstores, more and more nonfood products are found in today's supermarket; the items range from auto accessories to magazines at the checkout counter. Items like candy and tabloid newspapers may be located to encourage pure impulse buying, but an increasing number of nonfood items are stocked throughout the store to encourage consumers to buy more and more of their convenience goods at their local supermarket. Predicted trends for the future of supermarkets include continued scrambling and an increase in customer services ranging from check cashing to film processing.

A *hypermarche* is the name given to a huge superstore. The concept is the same but with as much as 300,000 square feet devoted to the store. The hypermarche originated in Europe. One of the earliest in the United States was attempted when a drugstore, supermarket, and discount store combined in a vacated mall.

Membership warehouse store. Another relatively new entry that is taking a piece of the food business is the membership warehouse store. As noted above, these stores carry many food items as well as a wide range of auto tires, batteries and accessories, home furnishings, office supplies, consumer electronics, and clothing.

Convenience stores. Convenience stores, also called C-stores, have made a significant impact on the food retailing business. Such stores do not carry many items in comparison to a supermarket, but they tend to be more conveniently located and they are open longer hours. The largest single operator of convenience stores is 7-Eleven Stores (owned by Southland Corporation, which was taken over by the Japanese firm Ito-Yokado) with sales of $7.475 billion from 6,395 stores.[21] These stores carry a small but balanced inventory of convenience items, including milk and other dairy products, bread, snack foods, meats, tobacco, paper products, soft drinks, beer, and personal care items. Food sales through convenience stores are about $30 billion or 7 percent of total food sales.

The convenience store's natural market advantage is its usefulness for immediately needed merchandise when a shopper does not want to wait in long lines or when the local supermarket is closed. In 1957 there were only 500 convenience stores in the United States. More than 68,000 C-stores today have a total sales volume greater than $63 billion.[22]

Generally speaking, convenience stores are very profitable. And a good share of their success can probably be attributed to the fact that most are located in the neighborhoods where their customers live. However, it should be noted that the concept of having a small neighborhood food store is not at all new! Before the era of supermarkets, food retailing was characterized by small neighborhood stores.

SERVICE RETAILING

The service sector of the U.S. economy has dominated economic growth over the past two decades, and as much as 80 percent of the growth in employment over the next decade will be in services. Retailing is itself a service-oriented activity. The selling of services, instead of goods, will be referred to as *service retailing*. As the growth in the service sector continues, service retailing also grows.

To truly appreciate the breadth of retailing, consider the Egyptian merchant selling camel rides out on the desert in the shadow of the pyramids. He is one small component of leisure and entertainment service retailing that includes your hairstylist, Disney World, and the Mirage in Las Vegas. This merchant is an example of the millions of individuals who make a living with small-scale retailing.

Services with Merchandise

Service retailing is associated directly or indirectly with merchandise that consists mainly of three types: rental goods, owned goods, and nongoods services. *Rental-goods services* consist of customers renting some type of good, usually a consumer durable. This may include anything from small household appliances to large farm vehicles. *Owned-goods services* include those services that are performed on goods owned by the consumer. Perhaps the best example of this is repair services. The last category is *nongoods services* and includes services provided by the retailer to customers who make goods purchases at their store. While providing these services is not the major function of the store, it is nonetheless necessary to offer them. Examples include delivery, wrapping, providing credit, and check cashing.

Services without Merchandise

Some retailers are involved in selling pure services such as telephone answering, hair care, dry cleaning, and financial services. These retailers face special challenges as dictated by their unique offering. The principles of good retailing that will be covered in this book will also apply to the retailing of pure services. A bank must focus on customer satisfaction as much as any other retailer, deciding on which services to offer, what prices to charge, and how to communicate with the customer through location, store design, advertising, personal selling, and publicity. Certainly today banks look for opportunities in the global environment and face competition at home from foreign banks.

NONSTORE RETAILING

More than half of all U.S. adults make purchases by mail order or over the phone, and more than half of these individuals spend over $75 each year.[23] Clearly, more and more consumers are taking advantage of nonstore retailing. With the advent of new technologies and deregulation, direct access to the customer has increased dramatically. Some of the more popular forms of nonstore retailing that have developed recently include telephone sales through the use of 800 and 900 numbers, broadcast infomercials, in-home videotape infomercials, on-line CD-ROM systems, on-line computer networks (e.g., CompuServe, America Online, and Prodigy, as well as Microsoft's MSM and InternetMCI), interactive direct response TV systems, and buying clubs. These forms supplement the traditional nonstore retailing base of catalog, direct mail, telephone, vending, and door-to-door selling. The importance of nonstore retailing is growing dramatically as new types of retailers enter the marketplace and traditional retailers look for ways to increase their business. For example, in-store vending represents a great opportunity for toy vendors to broaden their reach. Restaurants already use toys to complement food service with everything from kid's meals to team logo glasses. Now, Pizza Hut units are vending stickers and sports trading cards to lure more families. Burger King also has installed machines to vend trading cards.[24]

While many organizations have become heavy users of new technologies to gain access to consumers at home and at work, others rely on more traditional means to accomplish the same objective. Some of the more popular methods include in-home selling, mail order, catalogs, and vending machines. Organizations such as Avon and Amway rely almost exclusively on in-home selling and mail order or catalogs to sell their products.

Nonstore retailing attempts to provide the organization with a competitive advantage through greater access and service to the customer. However, as more and more organizations develop these specialized skills, the advantage of existing firms is diluted. Chapter 15 is devoted to nonstore retailing, particularly the virtual store on the World Wide Web and database retail marketing.

From craft shows at the county fairs in New England to the night market in Taipei, merchants sell goods outside of what retailers call the "box." Today, getting out of the box includes everything from QVC and direct mail catalogs to 800 and 900 phone numbers and the virtual store on the Internet.

WINNING IN THE TWENTY-FIRST CENTURY

Let's conclude this introductory chapter with a brief look into the future of retailing. In this book we will return again and again to the idea that retailers in the future will have to compete in an increasingly competitive environment. That environment will include lower costs and lower margins, the use of new technology, smaller stores with less inventory in stock, a focus on long-term customer value, and a global marketplace.

In the twenty-first century, retailers' survival will depend on being leaner and more efficient in all aspects of their operations, including being superior to the global competition in the utilization of technology to reduce costs and dramatically improve customer service levels. For example, restaurants are using computer technology to track customers, take orders, and plan menus. Computer programs track sales of each item every hour and determine cooking schedules to meet anticipated sales. To direct new-product decisions and promotions, Brinker International Inc. uses its frequent-diner program at Chili's to determine eating habits of the company's best customer.

More companies will be continually driving costs down so that savings can be passed on to consumers. This, in turn, increases sales, providing greater profits to reinvest in achieving further cost efficiencies.

Retailers thus must learn how to thrive in an environment in which living with thinner margins and continually searching for productivity improvements will be a continuous process and a normal part of doing business. (See Box 1.4.)

BOX 1.4 ATTRIBUTES OF A WINNING RETAILER

- Low-cost provider in an industry segment in which it operates
- Superiority in the use of technology
- Excellence in global product sourcing
- Clear missions communicated throughout the organization

- Providing a "value-added" shopping experience, not just meeting but exceeding customer expectations

6543217

Lower Cost/Lower Margins

More and more retailers in the United States and those headquartered in other countries have undertaken restructuring of their organizations. No longer will they be able to count on the traditionally high gross margins that have characterized their business structures. Instead, they will find themselves under intense margin competition from the rapid global growth in discount and category dominant formats. These retailers will also face greater competition from electronic shopping channels and other such services, which will grab significant market shares in many developed nations.

When consumers choose to actually go into a store, they will be expecting more "value added." They will be demanding even more variety in merchandise offerings, more assurances of quality, and better service levels. At the same time, the competitive nature of the industry will dictate that retailers around the globe keep their prices as low as possible—no matter what products they are selling.

New Technology

Application of technology to achieve greater efficiencies and generate higher productivity will continue to be critical to retail success. New and emerging technologies will play a critical role in strengthening each of the areas in Box 1.5. Technology will be the tool used to help retailers fulfill a continuing

BOX 1.5 RETAILERS WILL BENEFIT FROM TECHNOLOGY IN SIX KEY AREAS

- **Logistics,** the ability of retailers and their suppliers to move merchandise through the entire supply chain faster and at lower cost than the competition

- **Improving service levels** at point-of-sale and throughout the store

- **Direct communication** with retail customers and with newer technology applied to facilitate creative, effective relationship marketing and individualized micromarketing

- **Enhancing within company communication and control** and among its stores, providing retailers with the ability to build and maintain strong, fluid global organizations

- **Eliminating repetitive tasks** and excessive layers of corporate management so that retailers can more efficiently and more rapidly respond as market conditions change and opportunities emerge

- **Handling the scores of financial issues** that arise when business is being done in multiple countries

6543217

imperative of increased sales per square foot. Achieving this is an essential goal for any retailer that wants to be financially strong enough to compete on a global level.

To accomplish increased sales per square foot, technology can be used to add entertainment, excitement, and fun to the in-store shopping experience—another mandate for retail success. This can include the use of video walls, the creation of in-store video networks, the strategic use of kiosks, and experimentation with interactive applications. Not only will these provide more excitement within the stores, but they can also be used to provide more complete and in-depth product information to tomorrow's well-educated, increasingly selective consumers.

Smaller Stores

Stores are likely to be smaller. Again, technology will play an important role, especially when it comes to those applications linked directly to improved customer service. Technology will aid in better forecasting and speedier movement of merchandise from initial order to delivery. Technology will make it possible for stores to have far less inventory on the selling floor, but still effectively service their customers.

Retailers will benefit from making it possible for consumers to purchase product choices not physically present in their stores. Consumers will be able to use technologies ranging from CD-ROM to interactive media to virtual reality in order to select and buy products.

Purchases can then be sent directly to the customer via the manufacturer. Emerging technologies will also facilitate just-in-time manufacturing of certain products within the actual store. This is already taking place in the music and greeting card industries, for example.

Focus on Long-Term Customer Value

Chapter 4 examines the concepts that are involved in customer satisfaction. In the highly charged and competitive environment of the rest of the nineties and into the twenty-first century, understanding the lifetime value of a customer will be extremely important. *Lifetime value* is the dollar value of all the sales your store will receive from a given customer over the lifetime of that customer. As Chapter 4 will explain, it makes far more sense to keep a loyal customer than to try to find, convert, and keep a new one. It would be possible for a car dealer to sell a family fifteen cars over a 30-plus-year period. At an average cost of $25,000, that's $375,000! Throughout your text, the strategies and concepts you will explore are designed to aid in keeping the customer coming back.

A Global Marketplace

Taking a more strategic approach to other aspects of merchandising will be required for retailers to win on the global playing field. For example, taking a global approach to product sourcing becomes critical because, when done effectively, it can help retailers to further lower total product costs and increase product quality.

Particularly for specialty niche players, seeking out new products throughout the far reaches of the world will become more and more essential to their ability to offer an unusual and distinctive product selection to their customers.

Similarly, many retailers will continue to succeed by making themselves the destination stores for certain branded lines and categories of merchandise, such as Toys 'R' Us in toys or Staples in office supplies. Alternatively, stores may leverage their strengths in private label development, such as Gap, Benetton, and IKEA, the Swedish-based retailer of modest-priced home furnishings. These and other retailers will need to continually build on and refine their core competencies. For instance, one of IKEA's core strengths is its consistency in product design and quality.

There must be communication throughout the organization so that people are both inspired and empowered to serve the customer. Motivated, well-trained, service-oriented employees will remain an absolutely essential ingredient to retail success.

In essence, those retailers who meet and exceed customers' expectations, who consistently differentiate themselves from the competition, and who execute all aspects of their business with superior skills will be the winners on the twenty-first century's global playing field.

GAP INC.—REVISITED:[25] TAKING A RISK IN THE GLOBAL ENVIRONMENT?

The success of Gap increased imitation by other retailers. Such imitation has made and will continue to make its retail environment more competitive. Gap's continued success depends on its ability to increase sales at existing store locations and to expand domestically and internationally.

In 1993, Gap tested a new line of value-priced merchandise at converted Gap locations under the name of Gap Warehouse. This format was renamed Old Navy Clothing Co. The concept is simple. "Shoppers who can't afford the Gap or other such retailers deserve better than the bland, poorly made and often carelessly displayed offerings of many stores with low prices."[26]

Old Navy follows the formula of the "category dominant" retailers like Toys 'R' Us, Home Depot, and OfficeMax: low prices, large selection, and recognized brand names. The storefront originally identified the Old Navy Clothing Co. as a Gap store, but the merchandise always carried only the Old Navy label.

Old Navy "resembles other no-frills, high volume, large inventory stores with its vast expanse of concrete floor and a ceiling padded with exposed insulation and laced with ducts. Customers wheel around shopping carts and pay for purchases at supermarket-style checkout counters. The prices mimic a discounter's: about 80 percent of the merchandise sells for $22 or less."[27]

Because they were aware that customers would make comparisons between Gap and Old Navy, management differentiated the stores with a new emphasis on fashion in Gap. Gap has added products like hand-crocheted sweaters, floral-print dresses, chiffon skirts, and suede loafers. In addition to offering more trendy clothes, the stores now carry shoes and workout gear like leotards and bicycle pants under the Gap Athletic label. The fashion lines mean that Gap will have less stock of its traditional basics such as T-shirts, jeans, denim shirts, and other commodity-type apparel.[28]

In keeping with the strategic emphasis on worldwide markets, the international division has expanded its Gap and GapKids store base in Canada, Great Britain, and France to over 100 stores, and new ones have opened in Japan and Germany. Gap International Sourcing has the responsibility for all offshore sourcing. For each country, the division narrows and focuses merchandise assortments in order to better meet the needs and wants of overseas customers. Plans call for further European and Asian expansion. Expansion of Banana Republic stores overseas is planned for the mid- and late 1990s.

1. **What are the advantages and disadvantages of Gap's moving away from their emphasis on denim and traditional khakis and branching out into other newer fashion directions?**
2. **How do you think the customers of Gap and Old Navy differ?**
3. **In what ways might customers in non-U.S. markets have different needs and wants from their American counterparts?**

SUMMARY

Retailing is dynamic. It is an ever changing activity that is full of opportunities and risk. It is made up of many distinct types of businesses, customers, products, and environments. Retailing succeeds or fails on how accurately it markets its goods, services, and ideas to the customers and how well it satisfies those customers.

Anytime products or services are sold to the final customers, a retail transaction occurs. Wholesale transactions take place when organizations sell to other organizations. Retail and wholesale transactions have several different characteristics that set them apart.

Retailing benefits customers, manufacturers, and wholesalers in numerous ways. Retailing makes it easier for the consumer to purchase goods, and it aids producers in getting those goods to the consumers. Retailing also provides the economic utilities of form, time, place, and possession that drive customer satisfaction.

There are many methods to help classify retail establishments. Some of the more popular are classifications by ownership, by size, and by the assortment and amount of goods carried.

In the future, retailers will need to have a clear mission that is communicated and implemented throughout the organization. Along with the mission, the retailer will have to constantly lower costs and margins as competition increases in their industry segment. New technology will aid retailers by improving logistics operations, raising levels of customer service, increasing the efficiency of store space, and enhancing communications with customers and within the company. Retailers will need to understand the value of a lifetime customer and how to win the game on a global playing field. There is not one single factor that will cause a retailer to be successful in the future, but rather a multitude of choices and factors that will combine to guide retailers into the twenty-first century.

KEY TERMS AND CONCEPTS

Assorting, 16

Bulk breaking, 16

Buying motives, 14

Consumer cooperatives, 26

Cooperative chain, 23

Corporate retail chains, 23

Distribution, 11

Form utility, 19

Franchise systems sponsored by manufacturers, distributors, and service firms, 24

Independent retailers 23

Industrial buyers, 12

Informing, 17

Intermediary buyers, 12

Marketing, 10

Markup, 17

Organizational buyers, 12

Place utility, 19

Possession utility, 19

Price, 11

Price differentials, 15

Product, 10

Promotion, 11

Retail marketing mix, 10

Retail marketing strategy, 10

Retail target market, 10

Retail transactions, 13

Retailing, 10

Sales taxes, 15

Scrambled merchandising, 34

Stocking requirements, 14

Storing, 16

Time utility, 19

Trade discounts, 14

Unaffiliated independents, 22

Utility, 19

Voluntary chain, 24

Wholesale transactions, 13

Questions

1. Define retailing.

2. Define marketing. Is retailing a subset of marketing?

3. In your estimation, does our retailing system really work?

4. Would our retailing system benefit if firms were larger or smaller than they are now?

5. How might the retailing mix be different for a motorcycle shop and a teen specialty clothing shop?

6. Explain the trends in retailing as you see them.

7. What role does retailing play in our economic system?

8. Explain the difference between retail and wholesale transactions.

9. What evidences of the globalization of retailing do you see around you?

10. How do the functions of retailing relate to the concepts of economic utility?

Situations

1. You own a small (about 1,000 square feet) woman's clothing boutique in a town of 60,000 people. A Wal-Mart is moving to your area in the next few months. What are the characteristics that your store, as a boutique, has that will allow you to stay in business? What threats does the opening of a Wal-Mart in your area have? What buying motives could you appeal to in order to overcome these threats? What retail functions will you be able to perform better than Wal-Mart? Which will Wal-Mart be able to perform better than you?

2. You are a manager of a local hardware store. You need to charge sales taxes on all retail transactions, but not on wholesale transactions. A customer claiming to be a contractor enters your store and purchases several items. He does not have his tax exemption number with him, but promises to bring it next time. Do you charge the sales tax?

3. You are manager of a large retailer located at the edge of a small community. The local city council is proposing to spend tax dollars for a "shop downtown" campaign. What is your response to the city council?

Cases

CASE 1A
Around Your Neck Co.

Bob Baumann built his business like most people build their wardrobe—one piece at a time. Baumann's Around Your Neck Co. started more than three years ago selling ties to businessmen in

their offices. As the company grew, Baumann's wares grew to include shirts, suits, and shoes.

Around Your Neck's growth has been fueled by a simple premise: Men don't like to shop. And Baumann's portrait of shopping isn't a pretty one: "Men hate loading the kids in the car, shutting the garage door, fighting traffic to get to the mall, hunting for a place to park, walking half a mile after you park, and fighting the crowds in the store only to find they don't have what you want."

So Baumann brings the store to the customer. Clients include employees at American Airlines Inc., NationsBank of Texas, Frito-Lay Inc., and KPMG Peat Marwick.

Looking sharp in the office has helped Around Your Neck win repeat business. Baumann said many executives have told him that they like the way their employees look after one of Baumann's visits.

The idea for Around Your Neck started with a $75 tie Baumann bought in 1989. At the time, he was working for Westcott Communications Inc. and drawing a six-figure salary. One day, instead of going to lunch, he went walking through the Galleria, a very large fashion-oriented mall in North Dallas. "Wham!" he said. "There it was. The tie." Baumann saw a tie he had to have, but the price tag said $75. "The most I'd ever spent was $40," he said. But he couldn't help himself.

On the way back to the office, Baumann began wondering how a piece of silk could cost $75. So he spent the next four hours tracking down the San Francisco–area manufacturer and the information he wanted: The wholesale price of the $75 tie was $18.

Baumann asked people in his office if they liked the tie. They did. He asked whether anyone would buy it for $20. "Within 10 minutes I sold 60 ties," he said. Then he began calculating how much money he could make in Dallas selling 50 ties a day at just $2 profit.

In 1991, Baumann made his first presentation with 300 ties. About ten months later, he added shirts. In January 1993, he started selling suits, and the next year he added shoes. His 1994 revenue exceeded $1.5 million.

1. *What changing market factors have contributed to Bob Baumann's initial success with his different kind of retail operation?*

CASE 1B
Around Your Neck Co. Again

"In 1989, times were tough," Bob Baumann, owner of Around Your Neck, said. You could buy a new tie and have a whole new wardrobe. However, as the economy improved, there was a growing demand for additional products. The addition of shirts, suits, and shoes contributed much to the growth of Around Your Neck Co. But the additional inventory made Baumann's operations more complicated. New issues of product display, inventory control, coordination, and pricing emerged. Selling suits takes more time and care, he said. "It's a lot different from buying a tie. Because if you don't like the tie, you can just pick out a new one." He spent a year fine-tuning the suit-selling operation.

As Baumann added garments, he also added distributors. His one-man operation grew to sixteen distributorships in Dallas, Houston, Milwaukee, St. Louis, Detroit, Denver, and Buffalo, New York. He and his distributors make appointments with the companies to display their wares to employees.

Baumann has also teamed with firms like Merrill Lynch & Co. Inc. and Sewell Lexus to provide clothing as part of company sales incentive programs. "So many companies give away things like trips that never come back to benefit the company," Baumann said. "But companies want everyone to look sharp. So they give them the opportunity to win three ties or a whole new wardrobe."

After several years of tinkering with the process and improving his basic retail strategy, Baumann said it's time to focus on growing the business. He said he would like to open offices in Atlanta, Boston, New York, Los Angeles, San Francisco, San Diego, and Washington, D.C.[29]

1. *Are there other possible markets that he could seek out where he could use the current retail format?*

2. *How else could he grow his business?*

CHAPTER 2

Chapter Goals

After reading this chapter, you should be able to:

- Understand the basic dimensions of retail strategies.
- Know the various tactics available to retailers to achieve strategic positioning.
- Explain how quality is the result of a successful strategy.
- Identify the steps in retail planning and understand why planning is essential to the retailer.
- Define competitive advantage and realize how competitive advantage aligns with a global retailing strategy.

Retail Strategy: Creating the Competitive Advantage

TIFFANY AND CO.[1]
COMPETING WITH QUALITY

Tiffany & Co., the famous New York–based jewelry and other luxury item retailer, has extended its reach far beyond the Fifth Avenue flagship store with the "Atlas" clock over the entrance. It currently operates more than ninety-six locations worldwide with net sales of over a half billion dollars. Tiffany's operates with a high-margin, low-turnover strategy. Its turnover hovers near two with inventory averaging 150 to 200 days in stock and gross margins that average nearly 50 percent.

Tiffany's reaches out to existing and potential customers in a very personal way. The company features exclusive merchandise, but its attitude and approach are congenial and inviting. Get-acquainted receptions are held for potential customers. Tiffany's introduces its stores to prospective customers as one would expect to be introduced into a new family. It commonly hosts a "Breakfast at Tiffany's" event whenever it opens a new store, extends a product line, or introduces new merchandise. These events have become more and more elaborate.

Tiffany's also attempts to educate potential customers by publishing a free booklet entitled "How to Buy a Diamond." This booklet includes a toll-free 800 number that customers can use to ask questions. More than 40,000 people call the number each year. High-profile cultural and charitable events are held annually in the communities where the company has stores.

The Tiffany sales staff is highly trained in selling and service skills. The salespeople work hard at establishing a helpful dialogue with patrons, considering their past preferences and future needs. The salespeople make appropriate suggestions of new items particularly suited to the individual tastes of customers. Part of the service through sales approach involves reaching out to active customers through the Tiffany Register program of special communications that let customers know about new products and services and target special events and days in the customer's life.

Tiffany's does not believe value is synonymous with bargain pricing; rather it is a wealth of quality product designs in exclusive styles, shapes, and textures at a fair price. For Tiffany customers quality does not mean the best at any price, but rather the best within each customer's chosen price range, which leads the company to offer a broad range of selections and pricing with each product category.

Tiffany's not only uses high levels of customer service to enhance its image but also locates in the most prestigious of properties. Tiffany's rarely has to seek out new properties. Instead, it is often asked to locate where developers wish to establish an exclusive image. For instance, when developer Douglas Stitzel built Two Rodeo Drive in Beverly Hills,

he made several concessions to encourage Tiffany's to locate in his minimall. These included building a facade that resembles Tiffany's Fifth Avenue location and lump-sum concessions totaling $200 per foot. The $200 million complex was designed to be a one-stop shop for the "Rolls-Royce set" in stores like Tiffany's, Cartier, and Christian Dior. The cost for the project was more than $1,500 per square foot, compared to less than $400 a foot for the fanciest shopping centers.[2] The concept must be working. Mr. Stitzel was able to sell a 90 percent interest in the minimall for "well in excess" of the $200 million cost.

1. **What services do customers purchasing high-price high-quality goods expect?**
2. **How has Tiffany & Co. met these expectations?**

INTRODUCTION

Every day, many retailers permanently close their doors, often the victim of a competitor who has done a better job of meeting customer needs. In fact, from 1975 to 1987 the United States saw some 400,000 retailers going out of business for one reason or another. Retailers from Stanley Marcus, former CEO of Neiman Marcus, to David Glass, CEO of Wal-Mart, forecast that the decline in the number of retailers would continue and that by the year 2001 the United States would have fewer than 1.4 million stores. The most critical factor is that there has been a growth in the square feet of selling space with a decline in the retail sales per square foot in constant dollars. See Figure 2.1.

Retailers, together with all U.S. firms, are realizing that they are in an economic war in which only the strong will survive. Instead of entering the war, some firms give up and go out of business. Others hang on hoping that state

FIGURE 2.1

Too much selling space is chasing fewer sales. (*Source:* Reprinted from November 27, 1995 issue of *Business Week* by special permission, copyright © 1995 by The McGraw-Hill Companies.)

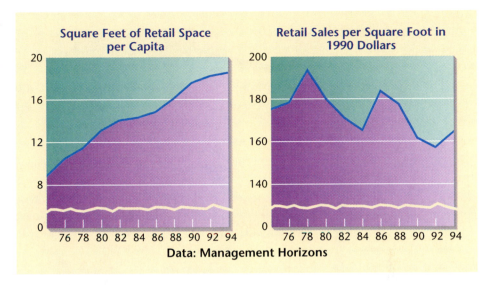

Square Feet of Retail Space per Capita

Retail Sales per Square Foot in 1990 Dollars

Data: Management Horizons

or local governments will bail them out with some type of protection or subsidy. Sometimes governments have done this by creating barriers to the entry of firms like Wal-Mart and other large retailers with the use of restrictive zoning and other regulations in an effort to protect smaller local merchants. Still others pursue a strategy designed to stay in business, but not simply to maintain the status quo—a strategy to prosper, grow, and become more profitable. These retailers are marshaling all of their resources and directing the use of those resources to the task of constantly changing to be the most competitive firm possible.

STRATEGIES FOR A COMPETITIVE ADVANTAGE

Development of a strategy defines for the store its business relative to its competitors. As shown in Figure 2.2,[3] there are five major dimensions of a retail strategy: (1) location, (2) merchandise, (3) price, (4) service, and (5) communications. These dimensions are supported by (1) store operations, (2) logistics, (3) purchasing, (4) market research, (5) finance, and (6) technology. The retailer attempts to achieve the end result of quality as it relates to the customer.

Each retailer should determine which dimensions will best serve its advantage by examining its own position relative to its competition. Let's look briefly at each of the five strategies.

FIGURE 2.2

Retail strategy for positioning the store.

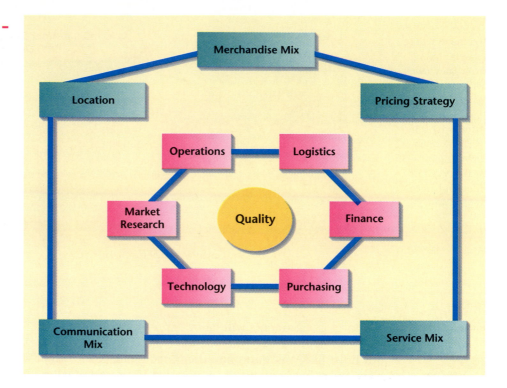

Location

Competition, to most Americans, is a good thing. It leads to better products and services at lower prices. It can inspire a retail manager to do a better job. However, numerous and/or aggressive competitors in a limited geographical area are costly to the retailer. Too many similar stores serving too few customers cause the sales volume of each store to suffer.

For some types of stores, however, the best strategy can be to locate as close as possible to the competition. Competing stores located in the same area may increase customer traffic. Some cities, for example, have an area with many antique shops. Customers are drawn to the area because of this convenience, and each store's traffic helps the other stores. Retailers should not be afraid of competition, but their mission statement should guide the finding of a market where there is an unfilled demand for the type of store they are planning. Also, complementary stores create shopping areas where customers can find everything they need in a single area. Likewise a smaller store, such as a candy shop, can depend on traffic from larger stores in the vicinity, like Home Depot.

The location strategy can be examined by mapping retailers according to the amount of traffic at the location (pedestrian and/or vehicular) and the

FIGURE 2.3

Drawing power of
the store versus
pedestrian
vehicular traffic.

High Drawing Power

Wal-Mart

Target   Toys 'R' Us   J. C. Penney
                                         Sears
Kmart

Stand Alone   Strip Mall   Anchor Stores
High Drawing Power Anchors

**Low   High
Traffic   Traffic**

Candy Store

Unsuccessful   McDonald's
Stores   Burger King

Suffer from Lack   Stores Dependent
of Traffic   on High Traffic

Low Drawing Power

Some goods may not be
purchased often, but may be
needed on short notice.
Prescriptions are one example.
The strategy for Walgreen Drug
Stores is to be dominant in
medium-size markets and to be
convenient to customers in
those markets. Walgreen wants
to have multiple stores in these
markets and be on the corner
of "main and main" for as
many customers as possible. Its
stores are linked by satellite so
that a customer can refill a
prescription in thousands of
towns across America.

retailer's **drawing power,** as shown in Figure 2.3. This graph allows retailers to examine their retail strategy in comparison to competitors. The pedestrian or vehicular traffic is usually fixed at the location unless the retailer has
the ability to draw customers to the area just because that is where the store
is located. Drawing power represents the natural ability of a store to encourage customers to travel farther to shop there. For example, 7-Eleven and other
convenience stores have very little drawing power, while high-end specialty
stores, such as The Sharper Image, have very high drawing power.

BOX

2.1 WHEN MERCHANDISE IS THE CENTRAL PREMISE[4]

Merchandise is the single most important variable in shaping the character of a retail business and a consumer's decision where to shop. Especially in a climate where low price has been effectively neutralized as a purchase motivator, retailers will have to focus on their merchandise as the variable most capable of moving them to the next stage of development. It's crucial to establish a governing concept for the business that will determine the character of merchandise offered to targeted shoppers. Conventional retailers, particularly department stores, have relied too much on suppliers' labels to mold the identity of their business.

Specialty chains offer the best examples of **concept-grounded merchandising.**

The Nature Company sprang from the concept of selling products associated with a major societal trend—understanding and caring for the environment. This concept determined the character of both the merchandise and the store design, which are perfectly in tune with each other and unique as a total "package." Warner Brothers is another retailer that has formulated a unique concept and translated it successfully into a one-of-a-kind store/merchandise combination. Both cases demonstrate that where merchandise and the selling environment are unique and compelling, there is no need to rely on low price or price promotions to motivate purchases.

6543217

Merchandise

Planning the merchandise mix is one of the most important aspects of store operations. The merchandise mix represents the full range of products the retailer offers to potential customers. The merchandise a retailer carries defines the store for the customer. This will be discussed in some depth in Chapters 10 and 11. Box 2.1 offers an excellent commentary on using merchandise as the central strategy element.

Marketing the **store as a brand** is another effective means of competitive differentiation based on merchandise rather than price appeal. This approach is heavily employed in the United Kingdom and to a growing extent in the United States. Not only has Victoria's Secret understood the sensual side of intimate apparel, but its powerful assortments have built the company into an industry trendsetter and a major brand that has been successfully extended to toiletries. Gap is another example of the power of own-label merchandise to establish the store as a brand, which is then extended to other product categories—GapKids, babyGap, exercise wear, and shoes.

One manner in which retailers can examine their merchandising strategy is by using an assortment/variety graph, as shown in Figure 2.4.

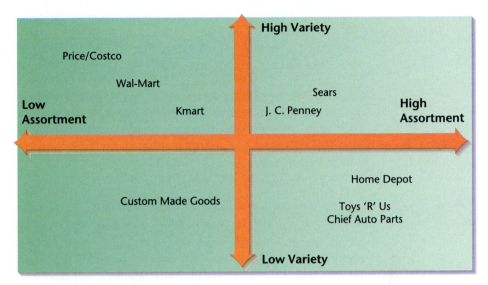

FIGURE 2.4

Positioning variety versus assortment.

The Container Store seeks to be category dominant in the $1.2 billion "organize it" sector. The store uses a merchandise strategy to appeal to customers who are "neat-niks." Shopping at the Container Store also gives hope to the disorganized "non-neat-niks" who visit the store and see employees sitting on the floor assembling merchandise.

Variety refers to the number of different types or classes of products that a retailer carries. Retailers such as Target carry a large variety of merchandise, but a relatively small assortment. The **assortment** refers to the depth of a product line, or how many different styles and brands a retailer carries in each product line. Specialty shops, such as M. J. Designs, carry few product lines, but a great assortment in each. Stores often have to make the choice to carry either a large assortment or a large variety. Attempting to carry both would increase inventory costs to the point of being uncompetitive.

Price

One way to examine the relative strategic positioning of a store is to plot your own retailer against competitors on a margin/turnover graph, as shown in Figure 2.5. To a large extent, these two variables will define not only the success or failure of the retailer but also how that retailer is perceived by the public. As shown on the graph, it is difficult, if not impossible, to maintain both high margins and high turnover. As retailers increase their prices in an attempt to improve margins, customers start seeking out competitors from which to purchase goods. In this instance, competition will quickly drive such a retailer out of business. Likewise, it is also impossible to maintain low margins and low turnover. In this instance, the retailers will not make enough money to survive.

This leaves the retailer a choice of either a low margin–high turnover or a high margin–low turnover strategy. Discount stores, such as Target, and category killers, such as Toys 'R' Us and Circuit City, depend partly on lower prices (and thus lower margins) to achieve the high rates of turnover that they need to be profitable. Whereas specialty stores, such as Hallmark, and high-end stores, such as Nordstroms, depend on higher prices to make up for lower turnover.

While turnover and margins are a good way to examine a relative pricing strategy, this classification is insufficient by itself. Retailers, such as Macy's, found that high margins were insufficient to make up for low turnover. Others have run into the opposite problem—that of having a high turnover during sales at less than needed margins. During the mid-1980s, Sears found it was having problems selling merchandise at full price. Most merchandise was being sold at reduced margins as customers learned to expect periodic sales.

FIGURE 2.5

Positioning turnover versus gross margin.

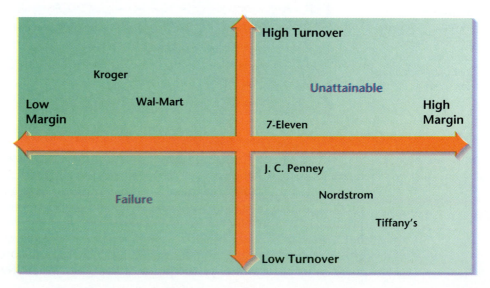

2.2 WHEN PRICE IS THE CENTRAL PREMISE[5]

If it is determined that low or lowest price is the central selling proposition, as it is for many commodity-centered businesses, a retailer's strategy must embrace four key elements. First, the company must make sure that it is a low-cost operation and, if not, squeeze or reengineer excess costs out of the business. Only in this way can a company consistently have a lower price than competitors. Second, the company must establish sufficient critical mass in its primary product areas to be the destination store. This is increasingly important for retailers dealing in commodity merchandise like electronics, linens, and home improvement products. Third, company stores must provide a level of service that meets and, where possible, exceeds shoppers' expectations. Because most retailers cannot afford to provide superior service and/or do not have a culture to support it, the real issue is to meet shoppers' service expectations. Finally, the **price-driven company** must have a communications and marketing program that projects dominance. A good example is "Nobody Beats The Wiz"; the slogan clearly and succinctly declares that this New York–based electronics retailer will not be undersold.

Instead of paying full price, customers waited for the sale and bought merchandise at discount. This led to a customer image that was inconsistent with Sear's strategy. Pricing issues are discussed in detail in Chapter 12. Another perspective on the low-price strategy is provided in Box 2.2.

Service

Each store owner-manager must determine the level of service that is appropriate for the store. This includes both the quality of services provided by the salespeople and the quantity of associated services provided by the store, such as gift wrapping and mailing.

It should be recognized that high levels of service increase costs, and unless increases in sales follow, it may be necessary to raise prices. The trade-off in service versus price is illustrated in Figure 2.6. Walter Levy has noted that a retailer must examine the character of the business to identify the feature(s) that can be best exploited to create a compelling point of differential from competition. In every type of retail business there are features and variables that, while shared by competitors, can be manipulated in a manner to establish a special character for a retailer over the competition. For example, all retailers provide *service* of some sort, but service can take many forms. If service is to be employed as a positive differentiator, the key is to understand

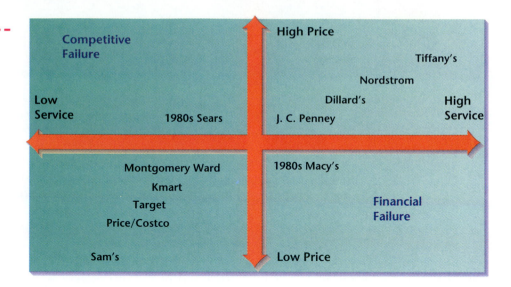

FIGURE 2.6

Positioning with price versus service.

Competitive Failure

High Price

Tiffany's

Nordstrom

Low Service

Dillard's

High Service

1980s Sears

J. C. Penney

Montgomery Ward

1980s Macy's

Kmart

Target

Financial Failure

Price/Costco

Sam's

Low Price

Customers today are busy and tired. Saving them time and energy should be a part of providing customers a full bundle of benefits. This can include everything from knowledgeable, caring sales associates to providing a full customer shopping service. Goods are delivered on approval to the customer's home.

what particular aspect of service is most appropriate for the type of merchandise being sold and is most important to the shoppers being targeted.[6] While basic services are necessary for a retailer, many firms, such as Wal-Mart and other discounters, have tried to minimize their cost. Other retailers, such as Nordstroms, have built a strategic advantage around the idea of providing better quality service than their competitors. The legendary retailer, Stanley Marcus, recalls that he learned his most valuable lessons during the hard times of the Depression. "I took to heart the instructions my father drilled into my head," he recalls. "Respect the customer. Pay attention to her. Take her package to her car. You broke your neck to get what she wanted because you never knew when the next customer would come along."[7] As the ethical dilemma in Box 2.3 suggests, a quality service reputation can be easily damaged.

Choosing services. In contrast to an overall focus on customer service, the store must choose the services that support the sale of merchandise and those that might be a profit center. The latter are often important to overall image and strategy. Examples include home decorating advice at a Home

2.3   AN ETHICAL DILEMMA: FOOLS' NAMES AND FOOLS' FACES

In the August 1995 issue of *Consumer Reports* the heading of an article was "Wooly Puffery at the Department Store." The department store was Lord & Taylor, which has fifty stores, does $2.3 billion in sales a year, and is owned by The May Department Stores, Inc.

Consumer Reports reported on some $99 "wool and cashmere blend" women's jackets that looked "a bit stiff and wrinkled" and not what one would expect of a cashmere garment. The tag on the sleeve stated "wool and cashmere," but the tag inside the jacket stated "75% wool, 20% nylon, and 5% recycled cashmere." The labeling laws require that any fiber content more than 10% must be disclosed.

Consumer Reports then found $99 sweaters bearing labels that described the material as "two-ply cashmere" but, with the correct label stitched into a side seam, stated "90% cashmere, 10% wool." There is an organization called the Cashmere and Camelhair Manufacturer's Institute that investigates such matters. In this instance, the institute contacted Lord & Taylor and insisted it correct the sweater labels. However, when *Consumer Reports* called Lord & Taylor for a comment, the call was not returned.

Questions

Do you see an ethical issue in this situation? How do you feel about a fine store like Lord & Taylor using two labels, a potentially misleading one on the sleeve and the required label less prominently displayed? More than 3 million middle- to higher-income families subscribe to *Consumer Reports*. Many are or may be potential Lord & Taylor customers. If you are a Lord & Taylor customer, what is your reaction? And what do you now think of Lord & Taylor's parent company, May Department Stores?

Source: Adapted with permission from Robert Kahn, "Fools' Names and Fools' Faces," *Retailing Today,* September 1995, p. 4.

6543217

Depot, grooming and veterinarian service at PetsMart, and the Starbucks Cafe at Barnes & Noble Bookstores. A list of the nongoods services retail stores offer would be very long indeed. It would be of small benefit to a manager, however, to attempt to develop such a list. Most retailers cannot, and *should not,* attempt to provide for all possible customer needs. One of the first decisions retailers must make is to select which services they will offer.

Although it is expensive to provide services, retailers must offer those services customers expect to find in stores. In certain businesses, servicing the merchandise sold is sometimes at best a break-even operation, but so important to customers that if it is not offered, it will actually decrease sales.

The problem for the retailer is, of course, to determine what services customers expect. In making this decision, the retailer may classify services into a hierarchy based on customer needs. Services may be classified in one of three categories.

Services that provide convenience.

These services are basic to the operation of any retail store. They make shopping convenient and are used by all the store's shoppers. Such services include convenient shopping hours, attractive displays, adequate parking, effective personal selling, pleasing and effective store layout and appearance, convenient store location, and so on. Other examples that have been developed with new technologies include computer-aided centers to help locate products and shopping carts that inform customers of sale items as they pass by.

Services that facilitate sales.

These services are used by some shoppers and are tied directly to the kind and the amount of merchandise purchased. Such services include credit, installation, engraving, and delivery. Frequently, sales cannot be made if these services are not offered. This is especially true for specialty or high-priced luxury items. Decisions about credit have a significant impact on how strategy is implemented. Today customers rely on charge accounts, installment buying, and bank and store credit cards. "Buy now—pay later" is an accepted form of consumer behavior. The offering of store credit poses problems for retailers, however. They must decide (1) whether to offer credit, (2) who may receive credit, (3) what credit limit to give each customer, and (4) how to follow up on bad debts.

Whether or not a firm decides to offer credit will depend on customer expectations, credit privileges offered by the competition, and the cost of credit services measured against expected returns. These considerations should be examined in light of the obvious advantages of offering credit: increased sales volume, increased sales of expensive merchandise, and the advantage of leveling the daily sales volume throughout the month.

Credit cards are popular with consumers who maintain a credit account with a bank affiliated with the VISA or MasterCard program. Customers are permitted to charge merchandise at the establishment of any participating merchant, and purchases are subsequently billed through the local bank. With the card scanners, it is often only a matter of minutes before the payment is charged to the cardholder's account and paid to the retailer. Retailers do not have to maintain their own credit departments, which may cost them as much as 6 percent of sales. Retailers also like bank cards because they are not responsible for collecting unpaid bills. The bank credit card programs cost grocery retailers 2 percent, whereas specialty stores pay as much as 5 percent.

Auxiliary services.

These services are usually promotional in nature and are auxiliary to the successful operation of the store. The include gift certificates, layaway plans, gift wrapping, check cashing, special orders, mail orders, telephone orders, baby-sitting, and fashion consulting. Many of these services have been aided by technological advances. Until the advent of scanners and communication devices, many retailers were reluctant to accept checks because of the large number returned for insufficient funds. Today, a retailer can simply run a personal check through the scanner, which communicates with a central computer, to identify bad checks.

The areas in which retailers can decide whether or not to offer services are in the second and third categories: services that facilitate sales and auxiliary services. Some level of convenience services must be offered; only in the nature of the offering is there room for decision making. In general, a firm decides whether it will offer services that facilitate sales and auxiliary services on the basis of five factors: customer need, type of merchandise sold, store image, competitive climate, and cost.

Selecting which services to offer. The first step in deciding what specific services to offer is to carefully examine the needs of your customers. What do they expect? Are there basic services that you can provide everyone, and are there others for which you can charge a small fee, such as home delivery of grocery orders?

General guidance can often be found by examining store, industry, or research databases. Impact Resources, for example, profiles the "service shopper."[8] These customers generally:

- Own their own home
- Have an above-average household income
- Are married
- Eat at full-service restaurants
- Do not listen to telephone solicitations
- Use the Yellow Pages more often than the general population
- Read newspaper circulars
- Have higher-than-average education levels

Most notably, some 61 percent of these individuals list shopping as one of their leisure activities. However, this tells only part of the story.

Service expectation by product category completes the picture. For each of the listed product categories, the service shoppers rank the need for service in the following order: clothes, shoes, children's clothing, televisions, VCRs, stereo equipment, toys, health and beauty aids, home and improvement items.

Communications

Each retailer should have an overall strategy to reach potential consumers. One manner in which this strategy can be examined is in the context of the objectives of the promotional mix. There are four strategic dimensions that can be examined in the communication policy: reach, frequency, content, and personalization. **Reach** represents the number of people who will see a promotion or advertisement at least once, whereas **frequency** is the average number of times that a customer sees the advertisement. As discussed in Chapter 13, most retailers use newspapers to communicate with potential consumers. However, with the advant of inexpensive cable television, more retailers are depending on higher levels of frequency with less reach, to target a specific consumer group. The Lands' End winter sale catalog illustrates low frequency and high reach to its customer base.

The content of an advertisement can be described as either image- or information-oriented. Many larger retailers use national television ads to promote the image of their stores. A good example of this is the highly successful advertisement by Sears that promotes "the softer side of Sears." However, most retail ads tend to be oriented toward providing the consumer with store, product, and price information. Each newspaper carries a great deal of this type of advertisement. These ads tend to inform the consumer of the products being carried by the store and the price of the products.

Achieving Strategic Positioning

Retailers depend on operations management, purchasing/logistics, market research, financing, and technology to achieve their **strategic positioning.** These variables act as the tactics to achieve a given strategy. Their functions must be performed on a daily basis, often without the consumer's direct involvement, to ensure success.

Operations

The manager must pay attention to the day-to-day requirements of running a retail outlet. Included in operations are staffing, maintenance, and general management of the store. While each store should have a grand plan or strategy to compete, the daily operations will determine the success or ability to achieve a given strategy. The managers must ensure that the staff provides services consistent with the retail strategy and that the store appearance is maintained to provide an appealing atmosphere.

Purchasing/Logistics

Retailers are using purchasing and logistics as a competitive advantage. Integrated into the distribution system is the retail buyer. This person is responsible not only to maintain stock levels in the store but also to ensure that the goods are those that the consumer wants. Stores are defined by the products that they choose to stock. The importance of the buying decision is discussed more in Chapters 4 and 11.

Logistics planning is also becoming more of a competitive weapon. For example, firms such as Wal-Mart use cross-docking, and The Limited has reduced turnaround times because of its efficient distribution system. These and other firms have learned to substantially reduce costs or increase service to the customer by better controlling the distribution channels of their goods. While these options have traditionally been reserved for only the largest retailers, new technologies in distribution are allowing even the smallest of retailers to take advantage of more efficient distribution. Those retailers who maintain more traditional distribution channels may find themselves left behind.

Market Research

In order to satisfy a customer and have a quality store, as discussed later in the chapter, the retailer must be in touch with consumer expectations, desires, needs, wants, and behaviors. This is often accomplished through a formal market research program as discussed in Chapter 5. Store managers should always keep in mind that their tastes and preferences do not represent those of the consumers. Too much inventory has been bought with the attitude of "I like it" instead of "the consumer wants this." Market research is also necessary to continually adjust to changing consumer trends.

Financing

The financial performance of a retailer is often viewed as an end result, instead of a planning function. However, store managers need to realize that financial planning is an imperative for success. This is often a weak area for store managers. For example, many small retailers are financed with short-term debt that causes problems as it comes due. Often, little attention is paid to the return on debt and equity. By planning for the future, retailers ensure that they have the capital to be successful. Chapter 9 explores important financing issues.

Technology

The use of technology has become so pervasive in retailing that it is often considered a strategic decision. In most smaller stores technology is used as a support function for the other functional areas of business. In retail chains and franchises, technology is often the centerpiece of the system. It allows corporate and store managers to interact on an efficient basis. Technology not only provides store managers with information but also reduces inventory losses and reduces costs. You will see continuing references to the role of technology in retailing as you go through your text.

RETAIL PLANNING

Retailing is a challenging and dynamic field. To function successfully, the retailer draws on knowledge from such areas as marketing, psychology, finance, accounting, and management. The study of management principles tells us that planning is one of the most important functions of the retail manager. It is a function often neglected under the pressure of day-to-day business activity, but it is so important that it must be given top priority.

Why planning? Retail managers must decide how to make the best use of limited resources, such as people, funds, and inventories. In order to use these resources in the most productive way, the manager plans for the future. The most important planning occurs before a retail store even opens for business. Careful planning at this time greatly enhances a store's chance of success. By gathering and synthesizing the relevant information into a retail business plan, the retail manager can make better decisions. Here are some of the advantages of planning:

1. Planning helps the manager deal with the future more effectively.
2. Planning helps managers focus effort on the main objectives of the business.
3. Planning helps to unify and coordinate the activities of everyone involved.
4. Planning minimizes costs and helps a manager solve problems creatively.
5. Planning enables a manager to evaluate and measure progress and performance.

Without planning, there is no predetermined course of action, and without some predetermined course of action, managers do not know what to do, where to do it, or why it should be done. They waste their own energies and the resources of the store. Planning involves selecting objectives and developing specific programs, policies, and procedures for achieving them. The basic retail planning process consists of four major steps.

Step 1: Identifying Market Opportunities

Both new and existing retailers must continually identify market opportunities. Retailing operates in a much more dynamic industry than many other businesses. Opportunities arise and disappear with amazing speed. Because of the changing environment, there is a limited period of time when the market offers opportunities that "fit" the abilities of a firm. A firm must continually scan the environment to identify these opportunities.

A full bundle of benefits can include category dominance. Incredible Universe offers "electronics and appliances as far as the eye can see. If it's not in the Universe, it doesn't exist." As for service, "Come by the main stage and enjoy FREE popcorn while our cast members demonstrate to you our huge selection of educational software and kids' computer accessories. Register your kids for Kidz Computer Camp, our computer training course for kids."

Gap analysis. **Gap analysis** is commonly used to identify marketing opportunities. A retailer can use it to identify where there is a gap between customer desires and other retailers' offerings. Early on, Kmart identified a desire for low-priced goods that the consumer could trust. Other stores have taken a different approach, such as Nordstrom, which identified a desire of high customer service and quality goods.

Gap analysis for the retailer differs from that of a manufacturer in that a manufacturer identifies a customer desire and creates a product to fulfill this desire. On the other hand, a retailer does not typically create new products. Instead, it is a retailer's job to bring products and people together. Therefore a retail must continually scan the environment and find the assortment of products that will best fulfill the customer's needs at a given price level and offer them in a setting that is appropriate.

SWOT analysis. Another way of finding opportunities is by using a **SWOT** (strengths, weaknesses, opportunities, and threats) **analysis.** A retailer must ask, what are the strengths and weaknesses of a business? By assessing these factors, a manager can maximize the use of all available assets and can limit or eliminate the obstacles imposed by the inherent weaknesses of these resources.

At least as important as knowing the strengths of the retailer is analyzing its weaknesses. Awareness of weak areas is the first step in overcoming them. Some weaknesses can be overcome by hiring an outside expert in areas in which the manager's knowledge and experience are limited. Additional training and outside reading are other answers to many weak areas.

A manager with general retailing experience but little knowledge of, say, the shoe business could benefit greatly by hiring experienced shoe salespeople before planning to open a shoe store. A manager who is weak in the areas of financial planning and control needs to work closely with a good accountant.

However, as suggested by SWOT, knowing your strengths and weaknesses is insufficient. A retailer must also be able to identify opportunities and the threats that go along with these opportunities. A retail organization is a part of many larger systems that include the local business community, the community itself, the state, the nation, and the world. Thus, there are environmental constraints, customs, and responsibilities that can be considered as specific objectives are set and operation decisions are made. A discussion of the external environment including the legal and ethical aspects is the topic of Chapter 3.

Step 2: Determining a Market Position

After identifying the opportunities and matching the retailer's ability with these, it is important that a retailer develop a market position to take advantage of these opportunities.

In their book *In Search of Excellence,* Peters and Waterman describe their study of successful companies and the factors that lead to enhanced competitiveness.[8a] They found several attributes that served to make this distinction:

- A belief in innovation
- A belief in being aggressive
- A belief in producing quality products and services
- A belief in looking to people to solve problems

Five years later, Peters concluded, in *Thriving in Chaos,* that for a company to be successful, it must continuously adapt to the changes taking place in today's competitive environment.[8b]

The search for a differential advantage. Traditionally, many firms have spared no expense as they have searched for a **differential advantage** that would let them compete. New technology was adopted, financial techniques that resulted in lower cost of funds were relentlessly pursued, new organizational designs were implemented, new store designs developed, new distribution systems implemented, and new products offered—all in the interest of beating the competition to the punch in today's fast-track global world of business. The problem with these and many other competitive strategies is that no sooner has an advantage been found than the competition copies what the original firm worked so hard to develop. A sustainable competitive advantage is difficult to achieve and maintain.

Formats for success. The implementation of a retail store's market position determination begins with the store format, which focuses the store on a target market. As introduced in Chapter 1, store formats take on a variety of forms. The objective of a store format is to differentiate a retailer from competitors while appealing to a target market. For example, Price/Costco's format resembles a warehouse in order to create the image of low prices. Yet it lacks the order of a Wal-Mart or Kmart, thus differentiating it in the minds of the consumer.

The format is important to the retailer because it positions the retailer with respect to competition over a long period of time. Often, the store's format is even more enduring than locations. Witness Kmart. While the company has been dramatically removing and rebuilding stores, the basic format has remained. The persisting qualities of a store format require that every aspect be carefully and fully planned out in advance. Decisions at the initial stages of format development will continue to haunt or benefit the store throughout its lifetime. "Store design is a part of the format that can be used for effective differentiation. For example, store design can create an environment that is visually exciting or otherwise distinctively attractive; make the shopping process especially user-friendly via layout, lighting, and signage; or employ materials and design features that capture the essence of a retailer's positioning and attributes."[9]

Step 3: Developing a Formal Marketing Plan

A workable retail business plan should be detailed, specific, and in writing. Indeed, a major advantage of planning is that it forces the retail manager to put ideas on paper. Box 2.4 contains the keys to a good plan.

Setting objectives. Planning requires the establishment of overall objectives. These can include survival, growth, market share increases, high returns on investment, and development of a good store image. Objectives will also be established for the specific operational areas. Some objectives are more important than others. Profit, of course, is a fundamental objective of retail organizations. Social concerns, however, must often be given consideration too if the store is to be a "good citizen" of its business community.

Objectives are difficult to apply to real situations and decisions if they are stated in vague terms. An objective should establish a measurable goal—a

BOX 2.4 THE KEY ELEMENTS OF A GOOD PLAN

1. A good plan should first specify specific objectives that will be achieved by implementing the plan.

2. The focus of a good plan is attainment of the objectives set by management.

3. Use of *all* resources should be planned. Often, use of funds is overplanned and use of people is underplanned.

4. A good plan should contain specific written strategies and tactics that will help management achieve its objectives.

5. A good plan takes alternatives into account.

6. A good plan is simple, flexible, and economical.

7. A good plan includes periodic evaluation and updating.

6543217

yardstick to compare results with efforts. Objectives such as "to increase sales by 18 percent this year" or "to break even in his first year of operation" or "to reach 30 percent of our target market with the winter sale catalog" are examples of clearly defined and measurable goals. They must be supported with concrete plans that specify the steps for reaching these goals.

In forming the retail business plan, be as specific as possible. Remember to be customer-oriented in setting objectives; it is one of the keys to successful retailing. Do not lose sight of these objectives once they are formulated. Schedule quarterly or, if appropriate, monthly reviews of progress.

In the following section of this chapter we will look at planning as associated with defining a mission statement and setting objectives in the context of the material presented in each chapter in the text.

The mission statement. The **mission statement** is a general statement that answers basic questions about the store's business: In what business are we? What is the scope of the business? What is our vision? What is our growth direction?

Objectives must match the intent and overall goals of the retailer. These are defined largely by the mission statement. When a mission statement is developed, the managers can begin to set overall objectives. The objectives then guide the firm's analysis and decision making. Ben and Jerry's is well known as a manufacturer and franchise retailer of high-quality ice cream and other products. Its mission statement clearly sets forth the basis by which the company will approach doing business. Compare the mission statement of Ben & Jerry's with that of PetsMart, a fast-growing pet food, supplies, and services firm. See Boxes 2.5 and 2.6. What differences and similarities do you see?

2.5 BEN & JERRY'S STATEMENT OF MISSION

Ben & Jerry's is dedicated to the creation and demonstration of a new corporate concept of linked prosperity. Our mission consists of three interrelated parts: product, economic, and social. Underlying the mission of Ben & Jerry's is the determination to seek new and creative ways of addressing all three parts, while holding a deep respect for individuals inside and outside the company and for the communities of which they are a part.

Product—To make, distribute, and sell the finest quality all natural ice cream and related products in a wide variety of innovative flavors made from Vermont dairy products.

Economic—To operate the company on a sound financial basis of profitable growth, increasing value for our shareholders and creating career opportunities and financial rewards for employees.

Social—To operate the company in a way that actively recognizes the central role that business plays in the structure of society by initiating innovative ways to improve the quality of life of a broad community: local, national, and international.

Source: *Ben & Jerry's 1993 Annual Report.*

2.6 PETSMART MISSION STATEMENT[10]

It is the mission of our company to be the dominant retailer of pet food, supplies, and services in each of the markets that we serve.

- For the caring and value-oriented pet owners . . .
  To be the most complete and exciting store for all pet food, supplies, and services.

- For the many valuable associates of our company . . .
  To be an enjoyable, challenging, and rewarding place to work.

- For the manufacturers and vendors of the product that we sell . . .
  To be a true partner in meeting the needs of the pet owner.

- For the communities in which we operate . . .
  To be a good corporate citizen and to add overall value to the community.

- For the investors in our company . . .
  To provide pride of ownership and to be a financially rewarding investment.

In our dealing with the communities of interest which make up our stakeholders, we will always conduct ourselves at a level of *integrity* beyond approach.

Budgeting. Every marketing plan should have a budget. Without a budget, plans tend to be "dream sheets" that have little practical relevance. A budget ensures that a retailer faces the realities of planning. Many plans fail because of poor budgeting on the part of the planner, usually because the budget was not large enough to accomplish the plan. While it is a common practice to overbudget, every attempt should be made to make sure this is not done. Allocating unnecessary resources to a plan either ties up valuable resources or encourages waste through overspending.

Step 4: Implementing the Plan

The success of a retail business plan depends on how well it is implemented. There is no plan in the world that can survive poor execution. How many times have we seen advertisements and in-store promotions making claims that the store did not live up to? If a store claims that it has the highest customer service and the consumer does not find it, the store will quickly receive a poor reputation.

Poor execution of a plan is often the result of either limited resources allocated to achieving the plan, an overambitious plan that cannot be achieved, or the lack of interest and involvement of store-level personnel in the planning process. It is important that a plan be executable. When it is not, the retailer often makes promises to consumers that it cannot live up to. An important part of executing a plan is that it not only produces quality but also provides for continually improving quality. Let's explore what a commitment to quality might mean.

QUALITY: THE RESULT OF SUCCESSFUL STRATEGIC PLANNING[11]

The retailer's planning success is frequently determined by a commitment to improve quality. Therefore, it is important for us to understand what we mean by quality. This understanding is critical because our definition will guide our actions. It will determine the programs, people, products, and services that are selected to reach the goal of quality. Unfortunately, *quality* is a word that has many different meanings, although it generally conveys an implication of a high level of excellence. In reality, quality is a dimension that has a continuum of levels. As firms have studied the concept of quality and its implications, the definition has gradually changed. We define **quality** as all of the features and characteristics of store, product, service, and people that combine to contribute to the ability to satisfy stated or implied needs and wants of the customer. Simply stated, quality means meeting and exceeding the consumer's shopping expectations.[12] We should notice that the essential word is *customer* and the word *excellence* does not appear. Because excellence is in the eye of the beholder, that is, our customer, we as retail managers cannot define it independent of our customer.

It does not matter what the product looks like, how long it will last, how much it costs, or how much status it conveys to others. If the product does not satisfy the customer's needs and wants, then quality is low or inadequate. It often requires changing the way we think to see quality as associated with low price, but when we view quality as whatever satisfies customers, every store can be built around quality. Sam Walton recalls in his autobiography:

> I realize that so much of what we did in the beginning was really poorly done. But we managed to sell our merchandise as low as we possibly could, and that kept us right-side-up for the first ten years. . . . The idea was simple: when people thought of Wal-Mart, they should think of low prices and satisfaction guaranteed. They could be pretty sure they wouldn't find it cheaper anywhere else, and if they didn't like it they could bring it back.[13]

At the other end of the spectrum, Stanley Marcus recalls in *Minding the Store* the statement made by his father, Herbert Marcus: "There is never a good sale for Neiman Marcus unless it's a good buy for the customer." The idea of what made a good buy was articulated in a full-page advertisement that appeared in the *Dallas Morning News* on September 8, 1907, announcing "the opening of the New and Exclusive Shopping Place for Fashionable Women . . ." The ad copy proclaimed:

> We have spent months in planning the interior, which is without equal in the south. . . . We have secured exclusive lines which have never been shown in Texas before, garments that stand in a class alone as to character and fit. . . . Every article of apparel shown will bear evidence, in its touches of exclusiveness, in its chic and grace and splendid finish, to the most skillful and thorough workmanship.[13a]

This product policy, combined with a passion for providing personal attention to each customer, defines quality for the store.

Sounds simple, doesn't it? Why doesn't every firm simply satisfy its customers? First, many firms really do not know who their customers are and what they really want. It is so easy for buyers to purchase what they want, for associates on the floor to sell the features and benefits they think are important, and for the advertising to reflect the image management has decided the store should have. Understanding the customer takes continual listening, testing, and researching. Many firms are using "competitive benchmarking" to see how other firms are understanding and responding to the customer and formulating successful strategies. There is nothing wrong with the imitation of success.

Second, most managers often do not know what quality is and, worse, how to achieve it; they simply give it lip service. When asked about quality, they always agree that it's important, but when you look at what they do, it's clear there are other performance measures that are more important. To identify what is really important to managers, look at what they spend their time on, what kinds of data they track and analyze, what they talk about first and most often, and what criteria influence their decisions. All too often, you find a focus on sales, profits, growth, new products, and market share. All of these are important, of course, but when the retail manager focuses primarily on these other kinds of performance, quality becomes secondary and there is a high probability that quality is a problem.

Total Quality Management: Continuous Quality Improvement

The search for ways to accomplish change and enhance the competitiveness of American business led many scholars and practitioners to rethink the role of quality as a determinant of competitiveness.[14] What has emerged is **total quality management** (TQM). Feigenbaum was the first to use the term in his book *Total Quality Control,* and Shores applied the term to management practices in his book *Survival of the Fittest.*[14a] A very concise definition of TQM states it to be a participative management style that focuses on satisfying customer expectations by continuously improving the way business is conducted.

Successful retailing today is based on an attitude that is centered on customer satisfaction as the outcome and is operationalized by a commitment to **continuous quality improvement** (CQI). Knowing that the measure of all planning is the reality and perception of quality in everything the people in a store accomplish, more and more firms monitor quality through a philosophy and program of CQI. Our model of successful retailing suggests that there are five elements that make up a CQI program. See Figure 2.7.

- Leadership with a vision for quality
- A broad view of customer focus
- Teamwork
- Training
- Measuring for quality

Leadership with a vision for quality. There must be a framework that supports the activities necessary to develop and implement a quality program. The proper environment is created by top management, but it must be maintained throughout the firm. If any part of the organization is omitted, the program will fail. It begins by developing a vision of where the store is going. The vision must include a genuine acceptance of the fact that the environment of customer needs and wants and competition are going to change. The vision requires a commitment to change and a commitment to quality

FIGURE 2.7

Total quality management requires a continuous quality improvement program.

in every aspect of the business. This vision must then be communicated to everyone within the organization and to everyone who does business with the firm, from vendors to consumers. This requires a considerable amount of leadership. Leadership is different from management: Leaders guide whereas managers direct. This point is significant; a program that is forced on people by managerial mandate is doomed to fail. A program will succeed when people have a stake in its success and believe in it. Remember the Nordstrom's example of giving decision-making power to the sales associates on the floor? Leadership means giving everyone the means to do the job right—the resources, the materials, the knowledge, the training, and the responsibility for doing the job right the first time.

A broad view of a customer focus.

If customer satisfaction is the desired outcome, then the input must be a customer focus. A hospital is a retailer of health care services. Consumers and politicians agree that health care change in the United States is no longer an option. Joe Dawson, administrator of Blount Memorial Hospital in Tennessee, is one who believes that the customer (patient) can no longer be treated according to the needs of the hospital.[15]

We have noted that a focus on the customer being supreme is not a new concept for many firms. The CQI philosophy requires the firm to view the people within the store as customers or suppliers for the final consumers. The buyer must look at sales associates as customers in a process that includes the final consumer. The buyer is a customer who depends on accurate and timely support from the information systems in order to be efficient and effective.

Store maintenance people are suppliers of services for the store display personnel, and so on. The dynamics of internal customer requirements means everyone needs to have a continual awareness of the consumers' needs if they are to be met. Everyone in the organization needs to know who the customer is and needs to have an attitude of continuously looking for ways to improve those customer relationships and requirements. Those requirements might include availability, delivery, reliability, accuracy, maintainability, cost, and so forth.

The key to providing quality to internal and final consumers is understanding needs and wants. All too often people within a firm have one version of what those needs and wants are and have not developed the art of continually modifying their views. Developing this art requires regular emphasis and training.

Teamwork. To continuously improve quality requires teamwork among the individuals who are involved in each process within the store. A **process** is any of the series of activities necessary to carry out one of the business functions within the firm: buying, selling, promotion, store operations, maintenance, accounting, and so forth. A team approach involves everyone in describing the process, establishing boundaries of responsibility, identifying standards that address customer requirements, and developing measures with respect to standards. When people are simply given instructions on what to do and have no freedom to change a process, they typically develop an attitude of "who cares." In order to improve the process and quality of the services produced by that process, people need to be empowered to make changes, and they must be given incentives to make changes—typically a reward and recognition system.

Teamwork to produce quality improvement requires breaking down boss/employee divisions. There must be recognition that the people doing the work are often the ones most likely to have ideas about how change can enhance the level of customer satisfaction.

Training. A training and education system is critical for the proper environment to flourish. Education is never ending for everyone in the firm if a quality program is going to succeed. The education must be directed toward acquiring specific knowledge and skills that will continuously improve every process. Remember, the idea that customer satisfaction is the driving force in the firm must always be reinforced. Continuous education not only keeps people thinking about improvements in the process in which they are involved but also helps them improve themselves—perhaps to qualify for advancement or an increase in salary. People who see themselves growing will always be an asset to the store.

Measuring for quality. We have discussed the more intangible elements of a program for continuous quality management. We said that understanding a process required the development of standards for customer requirements. We also noted that the customer may be the final consumer or an internal customer who uses our services. In addition, we must develop measurements with respect to those standards. Measures are important because they force the establishment of current levels of performance in a precise manner. "We're doing fine" is imprecise and therefore unacceptable. Measurements are also necessary to determine the effect of decisions—to see if improvement has occurred. There are many people who do not understand the need to measure and, in fact, are reluctant to gather or use quantitative data. There is room in a store for making descriptive decisions based on subjective, intuitive evaluation of alternatives. In the management of quality, however, this is not true. Quality decisions must be based on measurements because you can't tell if improvement has occurred unless you measure before and after.

Let's look at an example. Consider a possible process involving the exchange of a garment in a boutique. A typical process might involve the sales associate greeting the customer, asking how she can help the customer, taking the garment to a sales supervisor who verifies the previous purchase, and issuing a form authorizing a return or exchange. The quality team—consisting of the store manager, sales supervisor, and sales associates—may have set a standard of having the exchange approval process completed in five minutes. Timing this process for a period of several days may show that the average time is five minutes and forty seconds. If we believe that five minutes and forty seconds is unsatisfactory, then the team can look for ways to improve the quality of service by reducing the time a customer has to wait for exchange approval.

Placing more authority closer to the customer may result in significant retail service quality improvement. Illustrating this point, the Target Stores division of Dayton-Hudson has embraced employee empowerment to the extent that store personnel can give customers the "sale price" even if the sale has ended, accept the customer's word for a shelf price up to $20 if the item fails to scan at checkout, and offer comparable merchandise at sale prices if the sale item is out of stock.[16] Other retailers, much smaller than Target, have also had success with TQM-type programs.[17] For example, M & D Supply, an Ace Hardware affiliate in Beaumont, Texas, has introduced six quality teams of ten employees each. The teams have focused each employee on the fact that what they do affects others. The result is increased job satisfaction, reduced turnover, and increased productivity.

We have described what we believe to be the key to survival throughout the remainder of the 1990s and into the twenty-first century. A successful store will adapt to environmental change by having a program of continuous quality improvement. That same store must be vigilant so that it does not fall prey to the insignificant outcomes that appear to befall two-thirds to four-fifths of the firms that have attempted to adopt CQI.[18] Such factors as an inward focus rather than a customer focus, a focus on statistical standards rather than customer needs, the tendency to become bureaucratic, and a failure to forge entirely new relationships with outside partners must be actively avoided. A recent report by Ernst and Young suggests that firms begin implementing TQM through CQI simply by using a "bottom-up" approach and empower front-line employees to handle simple customer complaints without constant supervisory approval.[19] The next step in the process is to implement teamwork and a quality focus for nonmanagement employees.

ACHIEVING A COMPETITIVE ADVANTAGE IN A GLOBAL ENVIRONMENT

*G*lobalization is the single most important issue confronting retail industry executives now and in the future. A global strategy will be imperative if they are to increase their revenue base and defend their competitive position against both indigenous as well as foreign-owned retail players.

That's because in developed countries such as the United States, retailing has already become a zero sum game, with growth in market share only possible through stealing it away from other players.

The Global Frontier

Therefore, not only does globalization of retailing become inevitable, but pursuing a global strategy is critical. Leading retail companies must fulfill their revenue objectives by developing new channels of distribution and entering new geographic markets. If they do so successfully, they will strengthen their leadership position by leveraging their infrastructure, achieving greater economies of scale, and thereby lowering their overall cost structures. This allows retailers to boost productivity and pass savings on to their customers around the globe.

In the past, however, the primary driver for the expansion of these retailers beyond their national boundaries was the search for greater market potential than was available in the home markets. One result is that most retailers tended to take an opportunistic approach to becoming multinational players, usually going first to where the easiest and most obvious opportunities for entry presented themselves. In the future, however, retailers will need to take a much more strategic approach to global expansion. Box 2.7 explains some other motivators for retail globalization.

For purposes of definition, international players include both cross-border and cross-seas retailers. Cross-border retailers tend to venture only into markets close to home, that is, French retailers expanding into Spain, German retailers moving into Austria, Japanese retailers expanding to Singapore and Malaysia, and United States retailers venturing into Mexico and Canada. Cross-seas retailers tend to be somewhat more daring in their international

2.7 OTHER DRIVERS OF RETAIL GLOBALIZATION

- Rapid communication of information and trends, contributing to the homogenization of consumer tastes; as a result, consumer groups with similar aspirations and needs are becoming identifiable throughout the world.

- Increasing political and economic stability of many nations, coupled with changes in governmental policies that encourage, not discourage, foreign investment.

- Emergence of free trade blocks occurring not only in North America and in Europe but also in Asia (including ASEAN in southeast Asia) and South America. In South America alone there are discussions about MERCOSUR (Argentina, Paraguay, and Brazil), ANCOM (Peru, Bolivia, Ecuador, Colombia, and Venezuela), and CARICOM (Caribbean nations), all representing efforts to create a Pan-Latin American market.

- The economic viability of emerging and developing technologies that facilitate all aspects of retail globalization, including communication and control.

6543217

In today's global environment, electronic data interchange (EDI) allows manufacturers to track the sale of their goods in stores. The manufacturer can ship just what is needed so that it will be in the store to avoid both stockout and excess inventory. Third party logistics suppliers such as Federal Express have distribution centers designed with cross-docking capabilities. Goods arrive at the center and are prepared for smaller shipments to individual stores without having to actually go into storage.

BOX

2.8 J. C. PENNEY GOES GLOBAL

The J. C. Penney global strategy includes:

- Exporting the J. C. Penney store format to Mexico as well as to other Latin American countries

- Exploring a joint-venture arrangement to open J. C. Penney stores in China

- Developing licensed stores, named the J. C. Penney Collection, that will sell private-label goods (plans call for ten of these stores to be open in the Middle East by the year 1998)

- Selling its private-label merchandise in Portugal through a new department store chain, Plaeto, created by a Portuguese hypermarket developer

- Selling licensed products through department stores in other countries, including agreements with El Corte Ingles, a department store chain in Spain, and Japan's Aoyama's men's wear chain

- Marketing the company's catalog merchandise (excluding electronics) to Russians through a special licensing agreement

"We are unwilling to compromise over quality standards anywhere in the world," emphasizes Alfred F. Lynch, president and chief executive officer, J. C. Penney International, Inc.

6543217

ventures, although often first targeting countries where language and/or habits are very similar. Thus consider the moves of United Kingdom retailers into the United States and Australia, or Carrefour leveraging its experiences in Spain to move into Spanish-speaking Latin American countries.

Truly Global Retailers

Global retailers who have created significant market presence in a number of countries and on more than one continent are still relatively few in number. Examples include fast-food chains such as McDonald's; specialty retailers including Benetton, Bally, The Body Shop, and IKEA; diversified retailers such as C&A Brenninkmeyer, Pinault-Printemps, and Rallye; and food and hypermarket operators like Promodes. J. C. Penney is an example of the more typical situation as companies take small steps toward being truly global retailers. Box 2.8 describes how J. C. Penney is going global.

In the future, global retailers will be those who take a strategic approach to expansion into both developed and undeveloped countries.

Other examples of United States–based companies already beginning to pursue this strategic approach include Toys 'R' Us, Saks Fifth Avenue, Gap, Staples, T.J.X. Cos., and Blockbuster Entertainment.

Kmart Corporation likewise has made several aggressive international moves. The most widely publicized of these is Kmart's acquisition of Maj, which operates twelve department stores located in the Czech and Slovak Republics. While certainly considered a risky move by some, this gives Kmart an important foothold in the Eastern European countries just opening up to retail development.

Several years ago Spain represented a major expansion opportunity because of the rapid economic growth taking place coupled with the fragmented state of its retail marketplace. However, French-, and to some extent, British-, and German-based retailers with nearer vantage points were able to recognize the potential early and entered quickly, taking dominant positions in certain Spanish retail sectors.

This means that even as the twenty-first century begins, every major developed country, and many of the developing ones as well, will have international retailers competing among themselves and with domestic stores. Areas where the competitive threshold will rise include the creative use of technology, new approaches to supply chain management, the rethinking of the organization, and new approaches to financial issues.

TIFFANY'S—REVISITED: GLOBAL EXPANSION

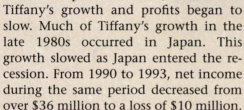

Tiffany and Co. operates stores throughout North America, Europe, the Middle East, and the Asia Pacific region. The worldwide recession of the early 1990s had a strong impact on Tiffany's. As consumers throughout the world became more price-conscious, Tiffany's growth and profits began to slow. Much of Tiffany's growth in the late 1980s occurred in Japan. This growth slowed as Japan entered the recession. From 1990 to 1993, net income during the same period decreased from over $36 million to a loss of $10 million.

By the mid-1990s income had recovered to exceed $30 million.

To curb recessionary effects, Tiffany's adopted several strategies. First, it is attempting to appeal to a wider market by offering a broader range of products and creating awareness that solitaire diamond rings start at $850. Tiffany's has started to promote its diamonds as affordable. For example, its catalog now shows Tiffany diamonds at less than $1,000. This is a significant change from the previous catalog that had no rings priced less than $4,500. The campaign is part of an ongoing effort to build awareness of the affordability of Tiffany diamonds. The company indicates that it has brought in customers who never thought they could afford a Tiffany diamond ring. Interestingly enough, even with its uptown image, the average purchase at Tiffany's is only about $200.[20]

Second, the company decided to increase its control over operations in Japan. It had previously sold its products wholesale to Mitsukoshi Ltd., which sold the products at retail in Japan. Tiffany and Co. assumed direct management of twenty-nine retailers that were previously operated by Mitsukoshi. This buyout was in response to Mitsukoshi's sales dropping nearly 35 percent. Tiffany's management believes it can expand into the Japanese market for jewelry, which is about the same size as the market in the United States at nearly $20 billion a year.

Third, Tiffany's has extended its reach by cultivating sales affiliations with fine jewelers, specialty retailers, and better department stores in the United States, Europe, Canada, the Middle East, and the Asia Pacific region. This provides an effective and cost-efficient method of bringing a selection of Tiffany & Co. jewelry, watches, gift items, and fragrance products to the attention of shoppers outside of the company's major retailing areas.

Tiffany's expansion into the global market continues at a relatively fast pace. Stores have been opened in Singapore, Japan, Australia, and the Philippines. International sales account for more than 40 percent of total sales. The company continues to sell wholesale to independent retailers and distributors in Asia Pacific, Europe, Canada, and the Middle East.

For customers who prefer the convenience of shopping at home, Tiffany's mails 15 million copies of its Selections catalog worldwide. The distribution by catalog has increased rapidly in recent years and now includes new single-category editions, such as the Jewelry Collections catalog and a brochure featuring Elsa Peretti's distinctive jewelry. The company sees the worldwide catalog operation as not only generating direct mail and telephone sales but also attracting potential retail customers for the stores.

1. Can Tiffany's appeal to a broader market and still maintain the image and reputation necessary to sell to the really affluent customer?
2. What will happen to the perception of the service level if Tiffany's starts appealing to a larger market segment?
3. Will this change in perception occur even if the services don't change?
4. Is there a group of customers in most countries who would patronize a store with Tiffany's goods and services?
5. How would you find and identify these customers?

SUMMARY

Strategy defines the retailer and its competition. The basic dimensions of retail strategy are location, merchandise, price, service, and communication. These dimensions work together as an integrated package that indicates to the consumer who the retailer is and what the retailer has to offer of value to the consumer. Tactics, or functions that must be performed on a daily basis, support these strategies. These tactics include operations management, purchasing, logistics, market research, financing, and technology.

A retailer should be concerned about how the consumers perceive the quality of services and products offered to the public. The goal of a successful strategy should be first and foremost to continuously improve all areas of the business in order to meet and exceed consumer expectations.

Retailers have limited resources available to buy products, to hire the right employees, and to perform the many other functions required to run a retail business. This is why planning is so important. It provides a blueprint for making those decisions. Retail planning consists of identifying market opportunities, determining market population, developing a formal marketing plan, and implementing the plan.

Because of the increased competitiveness in the U.S. market, many retailers are exploring global strategies for future success. All retailers are looking for ways to position their business as better than the competition or, in other words, to develop a competitive advantage. Retailers who sustain a competitive advantage over time will prosper in the increasingly competitive global environment.

So is there any way to create a durable competitive differential advantage—an advantage that cannot easily or quickly be copied even when others know and understand what you are doing? Yes, says Gerald D. Sentell, the chairman of the board and CEO of Tennessee Associates International Inc.:

> Successful management of change requires huge investments of time, commitment and belief. Competitors will need more than a fat checkbook to copy that. Any company with the willpower and patience necessary to put in place continuous improvement and innovation ahead of its competition will establish a virtually unassailable lead.[21]

The key is to keep focused on customer satisfaction.

Deming, in his classic book, *Out of Crisis*, argues that:

> There is a multiplying effect on sales that comes from a happy customer and opposite effect from an unhappy customer. The happy customer that comes back is worth more than 10 prospects. If he comes without advertising or persuasion, he may even bring in a friend. Profit in retailing comes from repeat customers, customers that boast about your products and services, and that bring their friends with them. Fully allocated costs may well show that profit in a transaction with a customer that comes back voluntarily may be 10 times the profit realized from a customer that responds to advertising and other persuasion.[22]

KEY TERMS AND CONCEPTS

Assortment, 53

Auxiliary services, 58

Concept-grounded merchandising, 52

Continuous quality improvement, 70

Differential advantage, 64

Drawing power, 51

Frequency, 60

Gap analysis, 63

Mission statement, 66

Price-driven company, 55

Process, 72

Quality, 68

Reach, 60

Services that facilitate sales, 58

Services that provide convenience, 58

Store as a brand, 52

Strategic positioning, 60

SWOT analysis, 63

Total quality management, 70

Variety, 53

QUESTIONS

1. What elements make up the basic strategies for retailers? If you were to open a retail store, show where you would want your store to be on each of the following dimensions:
   a. Traffic drawing power (Figure 2.3)
   b. Assortment/variety (Figure 2.4)
   c. Margin/turnover (Figure 2.5)
   d. Service/price (Figure 2.6)
   e. Communications: reach/frequency
   f. Communications: image-oriented/information-oriented

   Are all the positions that you indicated practical?

2. How does a retailer go about achieving a strategic position? Is there a single manner in which this can be accomplished for every retailer? Why or why not?

3. There are five advantages of planning:
   - Planning helps the manager deal with the future more effectively.
   - Planning helps a manager focus efforts on the main objectives of the business.
   - Planning helps to unify and coordinate the activities of everyone involved.
   - Planning minimizes costs and helps a manager solve problems creatively.
   - Planning enables a manager to evaluate and measure progress and performance.

   Discuss these advantages and give examples of each.

4. What are the similarities and differences between a gap analysis and a SWOT analysis? In your opinion, which would work better for defining a market position? Why?

5. What characteristics should objectives have? Why did you choose these?

6. Can a manager implement a strategic plan straight from the plan itself? Is it ever necessary to make adjustments? What degree of latitude should the operation manager have for making adjustments in a retail plan?

7. Discuss the key elements of a good plan. Which element(s) should be given higher priorities than the others? Why?

8. Discuss the elements that make up a continuous quality improvement program. How can CQI enhance competitiveness?

9. Do global retailers have an advantage over purely domestic retailers?

SITUATIONS

1. Sheldon Bromberg is the "new" manager of El Cambio Market, a neighborhood grocery store, in Albuquerque, New Mexico. Sheldon and his brother once owned El Cambio before they sold it to the Sanchez family of Corrales, New Mexico. The Sanchez brothers did not manage the store themselves, but hired a Safeway manager to run it. Business soon faltered in what once was a very successful store. Customers were leaving for higher-priced and more distant competitors. The Sanchez brothers believed the fault lay in how the customers were being treated under the new manager. Their decision was to terminate the manager and hire Sheldon Bromberg to resurrect their store. What steps do you suggest that Sheldon take to demonstrate to the customers that they are the focus of El Cambio's operations?

2. Betty Velarde has managed a sporting goods store targeted to women for the last seven years. She has become concerned recently that her store does not project an image of quality. Betty has hired you to measure the "quality" of her store. How do you propose to do that?

3. You are the owner-manager of a greeting card (limited-line) store selling primarily greeting cards, candles, and calendars. Several of your customers have suggested adding an assortment of T-shirts and baseball caps. What changes would this move bring about in your store and your ability to serve customers? How would this affect your business as a whole?

4. You are the owner-manager of a small specialty dress shop in a middle-class suburb of a major city. You opened the store five years ago. After four years of success, you decided to open an identical store near the central business district of the city. What factors should be taken into consideration in the addition?

5. You are the junior fashions department assistant manager in a medium-sized department store located in the community in which you are now attending school. The store manager has asked you to explore the possibility of opening a subteen fashion boutique in the store. What factors will you include in your analysis? Where will you obtain the information you need?

6. You are the store manager of a gift shop located in a large suburban strip shopping center. The center manager has proposed that it be a matter of policy for all stores in the center to stay open until 9 p.m. Monday through Saturday. How will you respond? What factors might have prompted the center manager to make this suggestion?

CASES

CASE 2A
Star's Center

In 1993 the Minnesota North Stars, a National Hockey League team, relocated from their home in Minneapolis to their new home in Dallas, Texas. Although this was not Dallas's first exposure to professional hockey, it finally came to Dallas to stay. The Dallas Stars located their practice facility in an ice skating rink in nearby Valley Ranch, a subdivision of Irving, Texas. The Stars recognized that their practice facility was not up to NHL standards and built a new practice facility adjacent to their current one. This rink, Star Center, primarily serves the Stars but also provides a facility for amateur hockey leagues and figure skaters. The new facility includes a 3,000-square-foot pro shop, workout facilities, restaurant, and rooms for dance classes. The pro shop sells a full line of hockey equipment. The workout facilities are for fitness club members and skaters. Dance facilities are for figure skaters.

1. *The Stars believe that by promoting hockey at the amateur level, fan interest in the sport will be heightened. Imagine that you have been assigned the position of general manager of the new Star's Center. It is your responsibility to suggest a mission statement. Develop one.*

CASE 2B
Customer Service: A New Competitive Advantage in Singapore[23]

The competitive advantages of excellent customer service are well documented by retailers in the United States. Its dividends are less apparent in the practices of local shoppers in Singapore who have come to expect less than excellent customer service from retailers. However, many competitive changes are occurring that have caused retailers to improve existing customer service. Sales per square meter (approximately 10.76 square feet) have been on the decline since 1991. With sales decreases, more retail space being built, increased competition, and a drop in average spending per tourist, retailers are looking for ways to attract and keep customers. Also, local shoppers have less real income to spend on shopping and are spending more of their real income overseas (11 percent versus the average of 7 percent through the late 1980s). A retail shakeout is predicted for Singapore with the survivors being those with "deep pockets" and those with a competitive niche in the market.

A considerable number of local Singapore residents do not frequent the large downtown department stores but shop in local HDB (Housing Development Board) neighborhood stores. Customer service is one of the main reasons that the neighborhood stores are favored over downtown department stores. Neighborhood stores are closer to home for most residents, and they like the ability to "bargain" with a salesperson, one aspect that will not be found in large department stores with fixed prices. Overall, neighborhood stores were rated as having more of a personal touch than department stores. Residents may shop in local neighborhood stores every day; therefore, shop owners and salespeople are likely to know their names and shopping preferences. Likewise, residents normally shop in department stores only on occasion and find them to be quite crowded and lacking in quantity and quality of salespeople.

Some retail stores in Singapore are turning to good customer service in an attempt to attract and retain customers. Top management support, staff training, and strategic plans are key aspects in providing good customer service. Some retailers are offering higher than market wages in order to retain trained salespeople and cut turnover costs. These retailers have extensive training programs for full-time, part-time, and temporary workers. They follow up on the training by rewarding good workers and counseling workers who have received customer complaints.

An interesting aspect of Singapore retailing is the two-tiered price structure for locals and tourists. Local residents normally receive less attention by salespeople when shopping, but pay a lower price. On the other hand, tourists pay a higher price than locals, but receive more attention while shopping.

1. *Can customer service provide a competitive advantage for Singapore retailers who choose this strategy?*

2. *How else could retailers in Singapore change to handle the dilemma of declining sales?*

3. *Are there any lessons to be learned from Singapore that are applicable to the U.S. market?*

4. *Do you feel that there are any ethical issues that need to be addressed over the two-tiered price structure? What are those issues? How would you feel if you were a local resident of Singapore? How would you feel as a tourist?*

3

Chapter Goals

After reading this chapter, you should be able to:

- Discuss how external environments affect retailing.
- Describe what constitutes a personal ethical framework.
- Explain the social responsibility of retailers and give examples of their responses to this challenge.
- Understand the basic laws that affect retailing.
- Describe how the economic environment has affected retailing.
- Discuss the competitive market structure and how retailing has changed in response to competition.
- Explain how technological and global environments will transform retailing.

THE ENVIRONMENT OF RETAILING AND DECISION-MAKING ISSUES

FOOD LION INC.:
A SUPERMARKET UNDER SIEGE

In the highly competitive supermarket business Food Lion Inc. was once among the supermarket industry's fastest growing firms, with sales climbing from $2.4 billion in 1986 to $6.4 billion in 1991. Earnings more than tripled in the same period, reaching $205 billion. Since the 1960s, Food Lion has been an innovator of everyday low pricing (EDLP) with claims that prices are 8 percent below its competitors. However, increasingly cost-conscious customers, low inflation, and rough competition began to take their toll in 1992 as sales increased to $7.2 billion while profits fell to $178 million.

Food Lion's president noted that the company has always been committed to efficiencies that improve quality, customer service, and cost control. Today's computer technology is helping Food Lion continue the quest for efficiency using electronic data interchange and vendor maintained replenishment systems as well as cross-docking and freight consolidation to benefit distribution system operations. Computerized warehouse systems help Food Lion maintain proper product levels while at the same time reducing distribution center inventory and paperwork. These innovations assure customers that they will find the products they are looking for and help keep sales and administrative expenses down to about 13 percent of sales, compared with the industry average of 19 percent. The company boasted net profit margins of 3 percent, which is far above the industry average of 1 percent of sales, until a TV report hit the company.

Food Lion was rocked by an ABC Prime Time Live program that aired an exposé of alleged food-handling abuses. Allegations included rewrapping outdated meat products and covering tainted food with sauces and repackaging. Food Lion filed a lawsuit against ABC and obtained unedited videotape that vindicates the chain on at least one charge the show made against it.[1] Food Lion also accused the United Food and Commercial Workers Union of concocting allegations contained in the ABC report. Food Lion, with its non-unionized employees in more than 1,000 stores, is a major target for the union, which had clashed with the company in the past.[2] The company's problems were further compounded when the U.S. Department of Labor announced that Food Lion had agreed to pay $16.2 million in back pay for overtime and child labor violations.[3] Following the allegations, Food Lion profits fell to less than $4 million the next year, down from the high of more than $200 million.

1. **With legal, ethical, union, and public relations problems creating a cloud over Food Lion, how should management proceed?**

INTRODUCTION

The decades since World War II have been a period of unprecedented prosperity in the United States. But there have also been consumer boycotts, protests, periods of high unemployment, recession, and inflation. Whether the issue is the problems of the ghetto, consumerism, ecology, or the price of goods, retailing is the business segment with which people have the most intimate contact, and it is retailing that must often take the brunt of arguments made against business. If for no other reason than simple survival, retailing has a great deal at stake in society's welfare.

To help you understand the complex external environment in which retailers function, this chapter explores several different dimensions of the environment. First, we examine some historical attitudes and thoughts about how people view the world of business. The chapter then turns to the issue of personal decision making as it is influenced by ethics and social responsibility, codes of professional behavior, and economic utilitarianism. The chapter then discusses the legal, competitive, and technological environments and concludes with a discussion of global market influences and opportunities.

THE SOCIAL RESPONSIBILITY ENVIRONMENT

The traditional role of American business has been an economic one—that of providing goods and services to the ultimate consumer. It was expected to perform this role in a way that made profits for the firm so that the business could survive and continue to provide the goods and services that society wanted. In performing this task, business traditionally relied on its own devices and its own conscience. Some businesspeople, including some retailers, seemed to believe it acceptable to operate on the basis of ***caveat emptor***—"let the buyer beware." Just because goods were scarce and the nation needed capital accumulation to further economic growth, did such an attitude have its place? The argument was made that government, religious institutions, schools, and other social organizations, as instruments of the people, should have responsibility for the noneconomic aspects of people's lives.

A Change in Attitudes

In the early 1990s, society's expectations of business changed. New attitudes were formed. At that time it became no longer sufficient for business simply to provide goods and services. Business was expected to do so in an ethical manner. Furthermore, business became responsible for fulfilling social as well as economic needs.

At the turn of the twentieth century, society began to evaluate business and to take action to ensure that it would act in society's best interests. Specifically, society employed the law to curb bad business practices. Legislation curtailed business's freedom to some degree, and the government assumed an active role in making sure the economic needs of society were being met (Figure 3.1).

In the early 1950s, people aggressively began to object to business practices. Some claimed that business was not meeting its obligation to society. Two indictments were associated with this statement. First, business was not performing well enough at those activities it was engaged in. People com-

FIGURE 3.1

Changing role of business in meeting government, economic, and social needs.

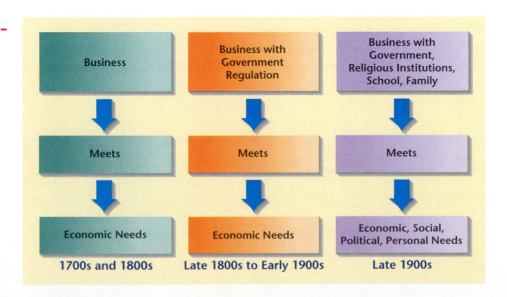

plained of shoddy merchandise, misleading advertising, the emphasis on materialistic values, and the general inefficiency and ineffectiveness of business institutions. Second, business felt its responsibility was much more limited in scope than society thought it should be. Society believed business had a responsibility to help alleviate social ills. Business was given still less freedom in performing its economic role, but it now shared the responsibility for fulfilling some of society's noneconomic needs.

Nonbusiness Influences on Decision Making

Retailers are forced to make decisions that do not necessarily call for simple business answers in this new environment. There are several nonbusiness influences on every decision that retailers make, as shown in Figure 3.2. The three major nonbusiness influences on the decision-making process include the law, professional codes of behavior, and personal ethics. The figure also shows **economic utilitarianism** as the business influence on the decision-making process. Utilitarianism is an attitude that business should act in its economic best interest. The Nobel prize winning economist Milton Friedman epitomized this form of thought when he stated that "there is one and only one social responsibility of business . . . to increase its profits so long as it . . . engages in open and free competition without deception or fraud."[3a] Economic theory indicates that under certain conditions, society as a whole will maximize utility if each member (including business) maximizes its own utility. This philosophy is often justified by the relationship between stockholders and business. Since business represents the owners, it should act only in the best interests of the stockholders since they own the firm. For example,

FIGURE 3.2

Influences on individual decision making.

it can be justified that business should not engage in philanthropy but instead should transfer money to stockholders, who can then contribute to the well-being of society. While this line of thought has some logic, several problems arise. The major problem concerns the firm's relationship with its customers. Without customers, the retailer has no purpose. The relationship between business and its customers is dictated by the image of the business. This image is directly affected by the attitude and actions that business takes in relation to society. We believe business should return something to society for the privilege it has in operating for profit in our free enterprise system.

Criticism of Business

The indictment by society for acting unethical was not new to business in the nineteenth and twentieth centuries. Among the earliest to criticize business practices were the Greek philosophers Plato and Aristotle. Plato characterized merchants as "unfriendly and unfaithful." Aristotle argued that tradesmen were to be carefully excluded from what now would be called the corridors of power. It was not until this century that society began to demand social responsibility from business. Virtues such as integrity and honesty are expected of businesspeople. The goal of personal gain could tend to overshadow other values.

In a mature society, there is the implication that business has an obligation to any or all of the following: the poor, the young, the elderly, minority groups, consumers, the environment, schools, cities, rural areas, and the unemployed.

In a single management decision a company must take into consideration the simultaneous demands of several stakeholder groups—customers, employees, stockholders, and the community. When a decision is ultimately made, there may be no "right answer." Businesspeople evaluate the economic gain inherent in a particular situation, but social responsibility requires that they respond to many demands.

From a pragmatic standpoint, business has a stake in initiating changes and working for progress, which benefits business and the total society. Business could not enjoy the progress society might achieve without contributing to that progress. Therefore, business must administer its affairs so that it acknowledges not only its economic role but also its social role.

Retailing and Social Needs

It is difficult to conceive how a business today could be immune to the pressures for social involvement. Retailers have often been at the forefront in responding to community needs. The Ronald McDonald House is a good example of how a company can take an active part in community needs and concerns. Other examples are numerous. For instance, Wal-Mart creates jobs with its "Buy America" program. Anita Roddick, CEO of the England-based worldwide retailer The Body Shop, has made commitment to women's and environmental issues a cornerstone of her company. Many firms have successful minority hiring and training programs, open new stores in inner-city neighborhoods, and sponsor Little League teams. The issue is no longer whether business should be socially involved, but rather in what ways it can make contributions to society. Retailers have contributed toward the solutions of social problems in many areas. Let us take a closer look at some major issues.

Consumerism

Consumerism is a term encompassing the activities of government, business, independent organizations, and concerned shoppers designed to protect the rights of consumers.[4] These activities have run the gamut from consumer protection laws to consumer boycotts and reflect society's rejection of the doctrine of *caveat emptor.*

People have become frustrated as consumers because they feel they have little control over the buying situation. At a time when they possess great sophistication, they often feel abused and even insulted. Consumers are offended, especially when they cannot rely on business to provide needed services for a product, safe products, and truthful information. To them, the free-wheeling nature of the marketplace is sometimes a source of confusion, irritation, and resentment.

Several factors have enhanced the expression of consumerism. Increased leisure time, income, and education have tended to magnify and intensify the forces of consumerism as the buyer seeks products that fulfill the quest for individuality. Demands for product improvement have led to increased product complexity, which causes increased service difficulties and introduces performance reliability problems.[5]

As technology solved many of the problems of production, and as lifestyles of consumers changed to meet a society characterized by abundance, successful retailers have adjusted by turning to a consumer orientation that embodied the idea that the proper way to run a business is to find out the customer's wants and needs, both felt and unfelt, and then to offer a product that fills those needs and wants better than anything else on the market.

Yet another view of the causes of consumerism has been expressed by the National Goals Research Staff. This organization feels that the abundant flow of new consumer goods has been viewed as a clear indication that the economy, with its strong technological base, brings vast direct benefits to the American people. Yet in the past few decades this virtue has been questioned.

Consumerism contends that the rapid introduction of new products produces confusion; that the technical complexity of new products makes it impossible to evaluate their benefits or dangers and makes them difficult to repair; and that pressure on business firms to introduce new products and services breeds marketing practices of a dubious nature, particularly as promotion has centered on nonprice competition instead of price competition. An argument can be made that the consumer just does not have the information needed to make an informed choice.[6]

Retail competition is fierce. Service Merchandise Inc. carries a wide variety of general merchandise goods. It is the nation's largest jewelry retailer. To keep costs low, the firm displays sample merchandise. Sold goods are delivered to a pickup area from the warehouse, with the exception of jewelry, which is stocked in the jewelry department and given directly to customers. The low-price guarantee is similar to dozens of others. How many retailers can guarantee lowest price before the claim loses a competitive advantage? Do you believe Best Buy, Circuit City, Montgomery Wards, Zellers, Wal-Mart, or . . . the list goes on and on.

Basic Consumer Rights

The foundation for a consumer bill of rights was laid when President John F. Kennedy, in his first consumer message to Congress in 1962, set forth the four **basic consumer rights:** the right to safety, the right to be informed, the right to choose, and the right to be heard. See Box 3.1.

In theory, a competitive market system and the laws of contracts are designed to ensure that consumers get real value for their money.[7] Unfortunately, because of poor quality merchandise, or because of misleading advertising and high-pressure sales tactics, consumers may still not get their money's worth. Retailers must continue to express their concern with warranties and guarantees, the handling of consumer complaints, and product performance testing, and must continue to rectify fraudulent and deceptive advertising, packaging, pricing, and credit practices.

Consumer interests have moved beyond the traditional concerns of fair quality and quantity of the product into areas such as package size, unit pricing, and credit disclosure. Consumers are now also concerned with major social and economic issues such as pollution, welfare systems, health care, poverty, taxes, and the government. They are involved in all areas of the political, economic, and social spectrums, and retailers must learn how to expand their vision.

What Can Retailers Do?

If retailers make a commitment to excellence where they are best equipped to excel—by insisting on products that are fairly priced, that perform as they

BOX 3.1 THE FOUR BASIC CONSUMER RIGHTS

1. **The right to safety**—to be protected against the marketing of goods that are hazardous to health or life. The belief in the right to safety has been the basis of many laws that protect the consumer when he cannot be expected to have sufficient knowledge to protect himself. Laws that regulate the quality of the food we eat, the clothing we wear, the cosmetics we buy—all are designed to prevent danger to health and safety, and many require clear warnings to be issued if the possibility to danger can occur because of misuse.

2. **The right to be informed**—to be protected against deceitful, fraudulent, and misleading information whether in advertising and labeling or in other such practices and to be given the facts needed to make an informed choice. This right is fundamental to the economic interests of the consumer. We hope no one questions the fact that the consumer should not be deceived. Not only does the consumer have a right not to be deceived, but the buyer has a right to sufficient information to make intelligent purchases.

3. **The right to choose**—to be assured whenever possible of access to a variety of products and services at competitive prices and, in those industries in which government regulations are substituted for competition, to be assured of satisfactory quality and services at fair prices. Much of the antitrust legislation has focused on protecting and encouraging competition. Fundamental to our economic system is the belief that significant numbers of competitors competing in a fair and open market are the critical factor in providing the consumer the right to choose.

4. **The right to be heard**—to be assured that consumer interests will receive full consideration in the formulation of government policies. The Office of Special Assistant to the President for Consumer Affairs is the central focus to ensure that consumer interests are given fair consideration in the formulation of government policy and during regulatory proceedings in administrative deliberations.

6543217

are supposed to, and that meet the claims made for them; on warranties that protect the buyer as much as the seller; and on services that truly serve—then they have little to fear from government or the consumer.

Better goods and services. Consumers have expressed dissatisfaction with retailers primarily for two reasons. First, consumers have been especially irritated with service (or lack of service) offered by retailers. They complain of ill-informed and indifferent salespeople, of poor postsale services, and of the general lack of attention given to their needs. In many ways, these are the strongest indictments consumers have against retail operations.

Second, consumers complain that retailers operate on the premise that they are justified in offering any merchandise as long as it will sell. Consumers argue that retailers are not as concerned with product safety, durability, and warranty as they should be. More than any other institution in the marketplace, retailing has the opportunity to select goods that promote consumer welfare. If it did this job well, many consumer criticisms would be eliminated.

Aid in urban affairs. One area in which retailing can play and has to some extent been playing a significant role is urban affairs. It is in this area that retailing contributes to the solution of problems arising from the social fabric. Retailers have both the personal skill and the commitment required for meaningful involvement in community activities. The activities retailers can and do engage in are illustrated in Box 3.2.

Employment opportunities and needs. Because retailers employ such a large segment of the labor force, they have a unique opportunity to make a contribution to society's needs through improvement in employment opportunities and job enrichment to make work meaningful. Through enlightened training programs, many retailers have responded to employee needs for greater job variety and increasing of skills that lead to higher wages and greater productivity.

BOX 3.2 HOW CAN RETAILERS AID IN URBAN AFFAIRS?

1. Assist in training programs for the unemployed and minorities.

2. Aid in police-community relations.

3. Engage in self-policing of sales and credit practices.

4. Conduct traffic surveys for better city planning.

5. Encourage consumer education programs within the community.

6. Contribute money for 4-H scholarships, Little League, city symphony, and so on.

7. Work with community leaders and planners before locating a particular store.

8. Invest in and improve low-income property.

9. Encourage entrepreneurship among minority groups.

10. Work with city leaders to find ways to alleviate pollution in the community.

11. Be concerned for the occupational health and safety of their own employees.

6543217

Many companies take a long-run perspective on their responsibility to provide employment opportunities by helping to ensure that theirs is a pool of qualified applicants. Kmart again is a good example. The company supports education all the way from the elementary to the college level. The company participates in Invent America!—a national program developed by the U.S. Patent Model Foundation that encourages children to develop problem-solving skills while competing for prizes. The company is a strong financial supporter of higher education and the United Negro College Fund. Kmart also matches employees' gifts to colleges and universities dollar for dollar from a minimum of $25 to a maximum of $1,000 annually.[8]

We have been examining the topic of how retailers handle the area of social responsibility. However, social responsibility comes down to an ethical framework that individual managers and associates of the firm bring to each decision.

PERSONAL ETHICAL DECISION MAKING

Each individual either explicitly or implicitly has an ethical framework that guides his or her beliefs and behaviors. *Ethics* is simply the word we use to describe our standard of "right beliefs" and "right behavior." This is an area where there are many differing views and many ways of expressing similar concepts. For the purpose of simplicity we are going to suggest that there are three basic frameworks: a legalistic framework, a professional code of ethics, and a personal ethic. Within the personal ethic we explain a range of ideas from the self-oriented ethic to an others-oriented ethic.

Every day a retail manager faces the possibility of making an ethical decision. As you have already noticed in Chapters 1 and 2, the boxes throughout your text present ethical dilemmas that retailers face. The issues range from placing stores in the inner city to selling cigarettes and from marketing shoddy goods to labeling merchandise in a questionable manner and falsely advertising "sale prices." How you or any retailer deals with these issues stems from the ethical framework you bring to the decision-making table. Let's begin with a look at what we call the legalistic ethic.

A Legalistic Ethic

Many people use the law, or absence thereof, as a justification for their actions. However, the law provides only maximum allowable limits on the actions that may be taken by a retailer and provides little assistance in making decisions on a day-to-day basis. Senator Tom Harbin introduced a bill in Congress that would prohibit firms from bringing into the United States goods made by children under fourteen years of age. Current law simply requires that the secretary of labor list countries and industries that use child labor in the manufacture of goods. The International Labor Organization esti-

Federal laws may restrict the global business activities of retailers. These laws include those dealing with bribery, currency flows, fabric content and labeling, food safety, and the importing of goods made with child labor. Many of the laws are difficult to enforce. Strong personal ethical standards are often better guides to "right" behavior than legislation. A company code of ethical conduct can also help.

mates that there are between 100 million and 200 million children under the age of fifteen employed. In Brazil thousands of children work in the shoe industry. More than half earn less than the country's minimum wage and receive no basic benefits such as vacation or sick leave.[9] Even if buyers were concerned about the situation, the most they may be able to do is look for alternative sources of supply.

The law is reactive in nature. It rarely indicates a specified course but rather a limitation of choices. For example, the Sherman Act of 1890, discussed below, specifies that monopolies may not be formed; however, there is no indication on what type, size, or framework a business should take.

Using the law as a justification for actions has led to a **legalistic ethic** that some people try to use to guide their decisions. This ethic indicated that any action that was not specifically illegal was all right. However, using the law as the sole source of information in the decision-making process has led to many decisions that fall short of society's expectations. Continued behavior that is legal but fails to satisfy society often leads to more legislation. Continued use of the legalistic ethic could lead to more restrictions placed on how a business can operate. Business groups have sometimes taken a proactive role to avoid legislation through self-regulation. This has often included professional codes of behavior.

Professional Codes of Ethical Behavior

Many retailers and manufacturers have taken a proactive role in delineating proper and improper behavior for their employees by establishing a professional code of ethics. Many of these codes were developed in response to society's demands that a business act in a more ethical manner. Professional codes often explicitly state types of behavior that are forbidden, such as accepting or offering bribes.

Many professional codes directly affect vendor-retailer relations and retailer-customer relations. The main purpose of these codes is twofold. First, they attempt to avoid conflicts with the law, often by stating and interpreting it. Second, they serve to maintain relationships, usually between vendors and retailer or between retailers and customers. Box 3.3 illustrates the guidelines used by The Body Shop in looking for vendors, which it refers to as trading partners.

BOX

3.3   THE BODY SHOP'S FAIR TRADE GUIDELINES

We look for potential trading partners using the following guidelines:

- **Community.** Our aim is to respect people's right to control their resources, land, and lives.

- **Communities in need.** Our aim is to pay special attention to minority groups, women, and people who are socially and economically marginalized.

- **Environmental sustainability.** Our aim is to respect all environments and trade in renewable natural materials.

- **Direct benefits.** Our aim is to benefit the primary producer and treat trading partners with commercial viability.

- **Commercial viability.** Our aim is to create successful and sustainable trade links and encourage small-scale community economies that can be easily duplicated.

Source: From the Internet home page, The Body Shop International Plc. http:\\the body shop.com. Copyright 1996.

6543217

While professional codes of behavior may be used to guide decision making, they usually fall short of indicating a specific course of action. Much like the law, they often define forbidden behaviors. However, most codes also offer some general guidelines that assist in making decisions.

A Personal Ethical Framework

Decisions in any business are made by people. The decisions to put forth, defend, support, and initiate a course of action are made at all levels of retailing by individuals. As shown above, the law indicates only forbidden behaviors, and professional codes offer slightly more guidance. We will now take a look at ethics from an individual viewpoint.

Individual or personal ethics can be organized into four categories to help guide our thinking. Decisions can be made in relation to one's self, the situation, societal norms, or the impact on others affected by the decision. Again, there are many ways to view the development of a personal ethical framework. The four-level framework suggested here is illustrated in Figure 3.3. The "self ethic" is the most primitive. The "situation ethic" adds another consideration to the decision issue. A higher level is the "social ethic," while the "others ethic" requires the highest level of thinking regarding ethical issues.

Self ethic. Decisions made using a **self ethic** are based on the welfare of the individual decision maker. Ernest Hemingway best epitomized this type of decision when he said, "What's good is what I feel good after, and what's bad is what I feel bad after."[9a] Thus, the deciding factor is self-satisfaction.

In its extreme form, egoism can be defined as the practice of **hedonism:** Essentially this is pleasure as both a means and an end. The only justification for an action is the amount of pleasure derived for the decision maker. Thus the actions taken depend entirely on the ways in which the decision maker derives pleasure. An employee who steals from the store may not think of the consequences, only that he or she will feel better because of what can be obtained with the stolen item or money. The same situation applies when management decides to sell shoddy goods.

Situation ethic. Decisions based on a **situation ethic** are unique to each situation. A decision or act itself is not deemed right or wrong unless the situation in which the act takes place is specified. For example, a person may consider a million-dollar bribe unethical, and yet buying lunch for a potential client may be considered normal business practice. Using a situation ethic as a basis for decision making can lead to people taking the path of least resistance and using the situation as a justification for their action or inaction.

The extreme form of the situation ethic is **Machiavellianism,** which is the term applied when a decision is made on the basis that the end justifies the means. In such a case the actions taken are justified using the outcome of the situation. Some argue that economic utilitarianism is based in part on the idea that the means justify the means. The only real issue is "profitable

A framework of increasing commitment to ethical decision making.

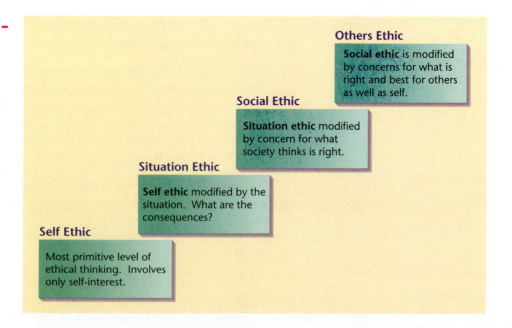

Others Ethic

Social ethic is modified by concerns for what is right and best for others as well as self.

Social Ethic

Situation ethic modified by concern for what society thinks is right.

Situation Ethic

Self ethic modified by the situation. What are the consequences?

Self Ethic

Most primitive level of ethical thinking. Involves only self-interest.

or not." Much like any other ethic the situation ethic can lead to inaction or inappropriate action depending on how a person views a particular dilemma.

Societal ethic.   Many years ago Alfred Whitehead defined the **societal ethic** when he said, "What is morality in any given time or place? It is what the majority then and there happen to like and immorality is what they dislike."[9b] In other words, what is considered right is what everyone else considers right. Most adolescents have used this ethic when justifying an action to their parents by saying that "everyone else does it." The obvious problem of using this type of ethic is shown by the parent's response: "If everyone else jumped off a bridge, would you?"

Others ethic.   Ethics that are based on the effect a decision has on *others* are referred to as **consequential ethics.**

We have said that ethics is the word we use to describe our concern for right (or good) behavior. At the highest level of thinking the concern must consider not only our own well-being but also that of others and all of society. This "others" ethic requires that the individual manager or associate consider the impact of a business decision on the firm, employees, customers, and suppliers as well as how it will contribute to the stability and strength of the society. It is important that an "others" ethic orientation to decisions based on the greatest good principle not ignore the rights and desires of economic and ethnic minority groups. An example from a company whose employees take an "others ethic" seriously is that of Kmart. Kmart Corporation annually donates more than $10 million to charities and community service projects. But, just as important, each year Kmart associates contribute more than 48,000 food baskets with the fixings for a holiday feast to needy families. Because of this hands-on approach to community service, Kmart was a national retail winner in the Good Citizenship Award for Community Service.[10]

An others-based personal ethic is often seen as having a theological basis because it is found in many religious teachings. Such an ethic does not necessarily have to be held by an individual because of a religious conviction. A prominent single-rule idea behind an others ethic is the Golden Rule: "Do to others what you would have them do to you." Major religions such as Confucianism, Hinduism, Buddhism, Judaism, and Christianity all have some form of the Golden Rule as cornerstones of their structure. A less common, but often used, rule is the Silver Rule: "Don't do to others what you would not have them do to you." Where the Golden Rule is proactive, indicating a course of action, the Silver Rule is reactive, indicating only courses of action to avoid. A theological-based ethic is concerned primarily about the "rightness" of the action as it impacts others as well as the individual decision maker.

Each individual retailer should come to some conclusion about his or her own ethical framework and how it impacts decision making. How might the ethical framework influence the ethical dilemma in Box 3.4?

3.4 AN ETHICAL DILEMMA: CAMELS, COFFEE, AND CAULIFLOWER

Dr. D. Kirk Davidson is a professor in the department of business and economics at Mount Saint Mary's College in Emmitsburg, Maryland. He conducted a survey of thirteen chains that account for the sale of approximately two-thirds of all cigarettes sold in the United States including A&P, Kroger, and Safeway supermarkets; Circle K and 7-Eleven stores; plus Wal-Mart discount stores. His research produced several interesting findings.

The percentages of cigarettes sold by various types of stores were as follows: (1) convenience stores, 35 percent; (2) supermarkets, 25 percent; (3) grocery stores, 8 percent; (4) drugstores, 6 percent; (5) mass merchandisers, 6 percent; and (6) other outlets, 20 percent. Cigarettes, which are the major cause of lung cancer, represent 26 percent of convenience store sales, exclusive of gasoline, and about 4 percent of supermarket sales. Cigarettes are a high-margin item on which there may be price competition between types of stores (warehouse clubs, supermarkets, and convenience stores) but little competition between stores of the same type. With all of the hundreds of pages of advertising that a food chain runs during the course of a year, it is seldom that you would see prices cut on major brand cigarettes.

Dr. Davidson also asked retailers what they had done in the situation where apples allegedly had traces of the pesticide Alar on them and whether or not they "edited" the pornographic magazines and periodicals sold. He was interested in learning what they carried and whether or not they were subject to any organized pressure groups. The sale of cigarettes, apples sprayed with Alar, and allegedly pornographic magazines is legal. He found that there were local pressure groups against pornographic literature and apples sprayed with Alar but none against carrying cigarettes. Dr. Davidson found that supermarkets and convenience stores were concerned that if they did not carry cigarettes they would lose the purchases of smokers, who would then go to a competitive store that *did* carry cigarettes. However, there was no such concern connected with the sale of pornographic magazines!

Between one-third and one-half of the firms offer smoking-cessation programs as a benefit to their *employees*. In addition, many have smoke-free stores. Although helping employees to stop smoking is of benefit to the employees, it also represents a savings to the employer in the cost of medical coverage.

Questions

Is selling cigarettes an ethical issue? How might the economic realities influence your response? Is carrying cigarettes considered an acceptable act because it is legal? Is something wrong? Theory says that free enterprise will always work to the benefit of society. Has theory failed in the case of cigarettes?

Source: Adapted with permission from Robert Kahn, "Camels, Coffee, and Cauliflower," *Retailing Today,* July 1995, p. 3.

6543217

We have looked at the concepts of social responsibility and a personal ethic framework. Let's turn to an introduction of how the legal environment influences retail decision making.

THE LEGAL ENVIRONMENT

In retailing, almost every aspect of day-to-day operations is affected by government regulations. The American economic system is characterized by consumer and producer sovereignty: suppliers of capital and land can use these resources as they wish; workers can work where they please; and consumers are free to spend their income where, when, and how they desire.

The Constitution of the United States gives the federal government the power "to regulate interstate commerce . . . among the several states" and "to promote the general welfare." As monopoly power increased in the late nineteenth century, the United States government began to regulate the economic system for the protection of consumers. Much of the government's protective regulation is expressed in laws designed to encourage and maintain competition and to prevent deceptive, fraudulent, and harmful practices. State and local governments also became active in the regulation of business.

Because business activities are governed and restricted by laws, and are parts of the social process, retailers must have some legal knowledge as they respond to social needs. In each chapter where appropriate we discuss the specific laws that constrain and govern behavior.

Laws and Regulation and Their Effect on Retailing

The basic ideas of competition and free markets were expressed by Adam Smith in 1776 when *The Wealth of Nations* was published. He proposed that the "invisible hand of competition" would control economic systems so that they would respond to the needs of society. His notion of *laissez-faire* in economic regulation was the cornerstone of early American domestic policy toward business. **Laissez-faire** is a doctrine opposing governmental interference in business affairs and advocating little interference with individual freedom of choice and action beyond the minimum necessary to maintain peace and property rights. However, as the American economic system evolved and grew, the invisible hand doctrine proved inefficient in controlling business and ensuring competition in the short run. In order to encourage the competition expounded by Adam Smith, the United States began in 1890 to pass laws designed to restrict the misuse of market power by large business and to make sure competition was allowed to flourish.

Regulation of competition. By regulating competition, government tries to ensure that no one group gains too much economic power and that consumers have a wide variety of choice. The regulations used by government fall into three categories: (1) antitrust laws, (2) price competition laws, and (3) unfair trade practice laws.

Antitrust Laws

In the late nineteenth centuries Americans found that where there was absolute freedom of action in the marketplace, the economy failed to function properly. Unrestrained economic activity led to monopolies, which restricted competition and fixed prices. Firms in some industries were so large and economically powerful that they formed combinations and monopolies to reduce competition and otherwise restrain trade. So-called robber barons emerged who controlled large segments of the oil, railroad, steel, banking, and sugar business in the United States.

The Sherman Antitrust Act. The first important legislation designed to combat monopolies was the **Sherman Antitrust Act,** passed in 1890. The act's key provisions are *Section 1* (every contract, combination, or conspiracy in restraint of trade is illegal) and *Section 2* (monopoly and attempts to monopolize are illegal).

By 1911, the U.S. Supreme Court found that firms such as Standard Oil Company, American Tobacco, Northern Securities, and Addison Pipe and Steel had unlawful monopoly power. Many other attempts to ensure competition were unsuccessful.

The Clayton Act. Because the provisions of the Sherman Antitrust Act were generally too vague to be effective, Congress passed the Clayton Act in 1914. The **Clayton Act** made illegal four types of practices that might substantially lessen competition or tend to create a monopoly. Its key provisions are found in Sections 2, 3, 7, and 8.

Section 2 says that it is unlawful to discriminate in price among different purchasers when the effect may be to substantially lessen competition or to tend to create a monopoly. (Section 2 was amended in 1936 by the Robinson-Patman Act.) *Section 3* states that tying agreements and exclusive dealings are unlawful when the effect is to substantially reduce competition or to tend to create a monopoly. *Section 7,* as amended by the Celler-Kefauver Act in 1950, prohibits the acquisition of the stocks or assets of other corporations (mergers) in any line of commerce in any section of the country if the effect is to substantially reduce competition or to tend to create a monopoly. Finally, *Section 8* says that a person is prohibited from being a member of the board of directors of two or more corporations when the effect would be to substantially lessen competition or to tend to create a monopoly.

The antitrust laws and associated court rulings have established the following legal guidelines for retailers:

1. Retailers cannot put pressure on manufacturers to prevent them from selling products to competitive retailers.

2. Retailers cannot acquire other retail firms if the intent is to substantially lessen competition or to tend to create a monopoly.

3. Retailers cannot conspire to fix the prices of goods they sell. In other words, retailers cannot agree to eliminate price competition among themselves.

4. Retailers cannot undersell other retailers to gain control of a market. This prevents a large chain, for example, from lowering prices to drive smaller competitors in one area out of business while the chain maintains standard prices in other areas.

The actions of the retailer, manufacturer, supplier, and customer are intertwined in a complex maze of law and legal precedent. Retailers must understand what rights they have in pricing merchandise, what provisions they should make for customer relations, what rights and responsibilities they possess when making a sale, what rights their employees have, and what liabilities they may face in selling products to customers.

THE ECONOMIC ENVIRONMENT

The type of economic system that exists in a country has a direct bearing on retailing's ability to be innovative and to adjust to meet the changing needs of the society. In our private enterprise system, individuals make decisions concerning business activity. Firms and individuals provide products and services demanded by consumers and seek to make a profit by balancing income against costs. In other words, suppliers of capital and land may use resources as they wish; workers may work where they please; and consumers are free to spend their income where, when, and how they desire. The foundations of capitalism are a free marketplace and the ownership of private property. The private enterprise system permits, and in fact requires, retailing to respond to consumers' needs. If the demand for a product exists, manufacturers and retailers are free to try to meet the demand, with competition ensuring fair value to the customer.

In the United States, the private enterprise system has yielded a dynamic, growing economy powered by vast productive and natural resources and by talented, knowledgeable individuals. This system of private enterprise has made possible the highest standard of living in the world for U.S. residents. Today, countries around the world have thrown off the shackles of communism and socialism for a more free enterprise economic system. The free enterprise system is capable of adapting to provide for future needs for goods, services, and jobs.

The retailer cannot ignore the factors in the overall or *macroeconomic environment,* both domestic and global, that influence the local market. One measure of the health of the overall economy is the long-run rate of real growth in gross domestic product (GDP). When the term *real* is used, it refers to infla-

Stores in countries within the former Soviet Union are struggling to learn how to compete in a free market economy. In the Gum Department store in Moscow, a customer would stand in line to pick out a pair of shoes. Often the only choice might be size. The customer would then stand in another line to pay for the goods and then in a third line to pick them up. As consumers have more choices, they quickly defect to other merchants.

tion-adjusted numbers. The GDP growth is expressed as the sum of the individual growth rates of four components: (1) the number of available workers in the economy (the labor force), (2) the rate at which these workers are employed (the employment rate), (3) the number of hours worked per year (which is proportional to the average workweek), and (4) the quantity of goods and services produced by an hour of labor (labor productivity). The average annual rate of growth of GDP is about 2.3 percent per year. However, averages can be deceiving. In the 1980s GDP grew at a rate exceeding 2.5 percent per year. Retailers generally did very well. In the first half of the 1990s growth declined to about 2.1 percent per year, and many retailers struggled.

Growth and Inflation

Unfortunately, growth and inflation tend to go hand in hand. However, there are periods when one outpaces the other. The times when growth increases faster than inflation, thus allowing for real GNP growth, are commonly referred to as "boom periods," such as in the mid-1980s. When inflation increases faster than growth, causing negative real growth rates, it is referred to as an inflationary period, such as the mid- to late 1970s.

Effect of real growth on retailing. Real growth has a positive effect on most sectors of the economy, and retailing is no exception. Because people have more income, they tend to spend more. This leads to higher sales and more profits for the retailer. One of the most important benchmarks for retailers is to "beat yesterday." Investors and management regularly compare the real growth in same-store sales to comparable previous quarter or annual data. However, growth also tends to lead to greater competition over the long run. As the economy expands, people and firms tend also to expand in response to higher demand levels. This leads to more firms in the market trying to fulfill the consumers' needs.

Inflationary effects on retailing. The consumer price index (CPI) is the government's measure of the cost of living to consumers. CPI is derived from a group of retail goods and measures the amount of price increase or decrease over periods of time. When the CPI increases, consumers can purchase less with their paycheck. (See Figure 3.4.) This leads to less goods being bought at higher prices. Inflation has an immediate impact on retailers. As retailers' cost of goods increases, they attempt to pass on this increase to the consumer. However, it is often not possible to pass on the entire amount. This cuts the retailers' profits.

Recession and depression. The common definition of an economic recession is when your neighbor is out of work. An economic depression is when you are out of work. The U.S. economy tends to move in cycles from boom times to recessionary periods. In relatively rare cases the economy will have high levels of sustained growth or detraction. Retailers must plan for

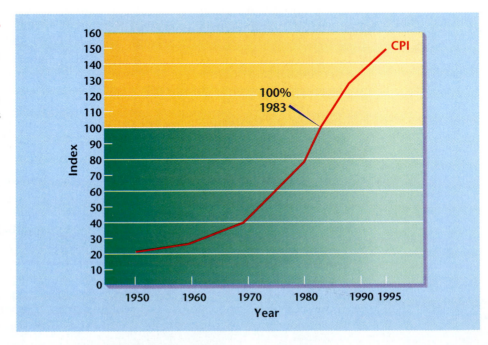

FIGURE 3.4

The consumer price index reflects the changing cost of goods for consumers because of inflation. It does not do a good job of reflecting changes in the quality of goods reflected in the changing prices.

changes in the business cycle. Usually upward shifts are not a problem. However, sudden recessionary times are difficult for retailers. Often they get caught with excess inventory and payroll. Inventory can be reduced through attrition or sales. However, payrolls are often fairly stable. Most businesses are reluctant to drop wages or employees during downward shifts. This leaves the retailer with the same level of fixed costs and fewer sales to pay for them.

THE COMPETITIVE ENVIRONMENT

Part of the reason retailing is so competitive is that it is easy to enter and exit from the industry. It takes a relatively small amount of capital and relatively unskilled labor to enter the retailing business. For example, there might be a vacant building in a secondary part of the downtown business area that could be rented for just a few dollars per square foot per year on a month-to-month basis. It is also possible to find suppliers willing to place goods in the store on a consignment basis so that inventory would require little capital. With homemade fixtures, an advertisement in the local paper, and a cash drawer, you have another retail store. It may not be tremendously successful, but because expenses are low and the individual who opened the store may be willing to live on a very low salary, this store could be competitive with others nearby.

Effects of a Competitive Environment

Retail stores are different in many ways. In Chapters 1 and 2 we explored differences based on size and number of employees, type and breadth of merchandise handled, type of ownership, and differences due to methods of operation. However, there are some common elements in the diversity. One of the most obvious is that retailing is highly competitive. Because there are so many new types of retailing and so many types of retailers, there is always someone thinking of a way to do a better job, and to do it more efficiently. These retailers seek to provide a new way or a better way to give the consumer goods and services with the best possible price and value. With so many stores competing, retailing also is dynamic. There are constant changes in operations and in the goods and services offered.

Practitioners and students of retailing have searched for a theory or theories to help explain the changes that have taken place in stores as retailing has evolved to meet the challenges of economic, competitive, social, technological, legal, and political environmental changes. We will briefly examine several of the more popular theories of retail change that are useful in helping to understand the dynamic nature of retailing. The wheel of retailing, the accordion theory, the dialectic theory, and natural selection are alternative explanations of how retailers and retailing change over time.

Changes in Retailing in Response to Competition

An attempt to understand the changes in retailing that have occurred in response to the changing environment and increasing competition has led to several popular theories.

Wheel of retailing. Harvard University professor Malcolm McNair offered the best-known explanation for changes in the competitive structure: the **wheel of retailing.** Figure 3.5 depicts this as a framework with three phases of change. In the *entry phase* an innovative retailer penetrates the market primarily on the basis of low price and minimal services. The assumption is that those price-sensitive customers will give up service, selection, and maybe location convenience in exchange for lower prices. This theory also assumes that those price-sensitive customers are not loyal to one store. After the innovative retailers have been in business for a while, they move into a *trading-up phase* in an attempt to increase sales, improve the store image, and reach additional markets. As store types enter the *maturity phase,* they become more like a traditional retailer as facilities, selection, services, and locations are improved.

The wheel of retailing suggests that with success comes maturity, management top-heaviness, and conservatism, which makes the store vulnerable to another innovative retailer. This theory helps explain changes in some types of retailing, particularly general-line retailers such as food and general merchandise stores, but it is not very helpful in thinking about specialty

FIGURE 3.5

The wheel of retailing.

Higher prices
Excellent facilities
Excellent service
Falling profit
Conservative management

Maturity Phase

Low price
Limited service
Modest facilities
Limited product line, variety, and assortment
Innovative management

Entry Phase

Trading Up

Moderate prices, good facilities
Higher service levels, highest profit
Increasing product variety and assortments

stores. For example, not so many years ago the mom and pop grocery store was a mature retailer. Services ranged from personal credit to special ordering and in-store butchering services. These stores were conveniently located for the consumer. Enter the supermarket with low prices, fewer convenient locations, no credit, and no carryout offerings. The supermarkets soon added services ranging from accepting credit cards to carryout prepared foods, and they also added larger and larger selections. With maturity, the supermarket has become not only a full-line food store but also an extensive nonfood store. This has been accomplished by providing an in-store bakery, fish market, pharmacy, video shop, and, in some parts of the Southwest, a tortilla factory.

Several innovative nonfood retailers are also pursuing the food business. Warehouse clubs, such as Sam's, now offer to individual and business members low prices and minimal service, while requiring bulk purchasing. Sack 'N' Save stores offer minimal service with a breadth of product lines but not much depth. So the wheel goes full circle from the entering grocers to the full-service supermarkets and hypermarkets and back to the no frills discounters.

Retail accordion theory.   A second explanation for changes in the structure of retail stores is known as the **retail accordion theory.** This theory suggests that stores evolve in a general-specific-general pattern resembling the bellows of an accordion. The small-town general store carried a wide assortment (i.e., many product lines) but not much variety (e.g., number of brands, colors, styles). As urbanization occurred, merchants opened drugstores, hardware stores, apparel stores, and so on. With suburbanization and ease of transportation, customers became interested in one-stop shopping and merchants saw opportunities for "scrambled merchandising," the adding of goods and services unrelated to the stores' original business. With the growth of store size and the somewhat limited breadth, merchants again saw opportunities for single-line and specialty stores that offer a limited assortment but a greater degree of variety. Witness the accordion effect of generalization and specialization.

Natural selection.   We know environmental changes occur on a continuing basis. The theory of **natural selection** suggests that change in retail store structure is a natural reaction to the environmental change as merchants seek to adapt. Those that do adapt survive; those that do not, disappear or face great stress. This theory is an adaptation of basic Darwin theory. The variety store as a category has been pushed to the brink of extinction by discount stores. Some firms stayed at the forefront of change: Witness how S. S. Kresge evolved into Kmart.

Dialectic process.   Several other theories of retail change also exist. Among these is the **dialectic process,** which suggests that change occurs through thesis, antithesis, and synthesis. In other words, the process of change is one in which a concept is preserved and fulfilled by its opposite.

What does that mean? Supermarkets (the thesis) sell food and a wide variety of nonfood items in a full-price, full-service, convenient location. Discount stores (the antithesis) sell nonfood items and some food items in a low-price, low-service, less convenient location. The synthesis may be seen in a Wal-Mart superstore—a combination discount store and economy supermarket. In a similar way the department store (thesis) has as its antithesis the budget discount store. The synthesis is the promotional discount store such as Dayton-Hudson's Target.

THE TECHNOLOGICAL ENVIRONMENT

Perhaps the most dynamic changes in retailing have come as a result of changing technology. Bar code scanners, computers, software, point-of-sale terminals, and management information systems (MIS) have provided retailers with more, better, and more timely information about their operations. However, technology is not limited to increasing information; it is also used to prevent theft, promote the store's goods, and create a better shopping atmosphere.

Technology will be the tool used to help retailers fulfill a continuing imperative of increased sales per square foot and sales per employee. Achieving this is an essential goal for any retailer that wants to be financially strong enough to compete on a global level.

To accomplish this, technology can be used to add entertainment and excitement to the in-store shopping experience—another mandate for retail success. This can include the use of video walls, the creation of in-store video networks, the strategic use of kiosks, experimentation with interactive applications, and creative utilization of a host of other applications just now being developed. Not only will these provide more kinetic energy within the stores, but they can also be used to provide more complete and in-depth product information to tomorrow's well-educated, increasingly selective consumers.

Stores themselves are likely to be smaller. Again, technology will play an important role, especially when it comes to those applications linked directly to improved consumer demand forecasting and speedier movement of merchandise from initial order to delivery. Technology will make it possible for stores to have far less inventory on the selling floor, but still effectively service their customers.

Retailers will benefit from making it possible for consumers to purchase product choices not physically present in their stores. Consumers will be able to use technologies ranging from CD-ROM to interactive media to virtual reality to select and buy products. Purchases can then be sent directly to the customer via the manufacturer. Emerging technologies will also facilitate just-in-time manufacturing of certain products within the actual store. This is already taking place in the music and greeting card industries, for example.

THE GLOBAL ENVIRONMENT

Economic theory as well as business practice has shown that countries benefit from trade. However, many countries have been slow to adopt free trade. It is only in the past few decades that free trade has started to become a reality. Countries throughout the world have lowered tariffs. The General Agreement on Tariffs and Trade (GATT) has been instrumental in creating free trade by lowering tariffs and other barriers such as quotas. The result of expanded free trade is increased product selection, reduced prices, and an expanded world economy. Retailers can now obtain a greater selection of goods at lower prices on the world market. This allows them to offer customers greater selection at lower prices.

Regional economic agreements such as the North American Free Trade Agreement (NAFTA) can reduce economic barriers that restrict retailers' entry into new markets. NAFTA makes it easier and less expensive for Wal-Mart to ship goods to the stores in Mexico, and lower duties mean lower prices. Increased economic activity can mean a rising standard of living resulting in new customers in the overseas market.

GATT's importance can also be seen in the global imports available to today's retailers. J. C. Penney imports apparel and other goods from over 100 countries. Even a more specialized retailer like Pier One imports goods made in 40 countries.

Countries are also opening their borders through bilateral and multilateral free trade agreements. The United States, Canada, and Mexico have created the North American Free Trade Agreement, NAFTA, which creates greater opportunities for retail expansion in these countries. For example, Wal-Mart recently expanded into Mexico with great success and has chosen to expand into Canada through the purchase of Woolco stores. It is expected that NAFTA will soon include other Latin American countries. Several, such as Chile, have expressed an interest in joining.

Other free trade areas and agreements exist throughout the world. One of the largest is the European Economic Community, also called the Common Market, which is now known as the Economic Union (EU). This group consists of Belgium, Denmark, France, Germany, Greece, Ireland, Italy, Luxembourg, Netherlands, Portugal, Spain, and the United Kingdom. Norway, Sweden, Iceland, Finland, and Austria are also tied to this group through the European Free Trade Association. These countries make up the largest and most established economic group. Retailers, and most other business sectors, have been aggressive in expanding internationally within the Economic Union nations.

The Asia-Pacific Economic Cooperation (APEC) group has seventeen Pacific Rim members including the United States. Business development among the members is their primary focus.

An interesting aspect of the economic groups is that they create additional opportunities for retailers from within the group. At the same time the preferences granted to members may create a competitive disadvantage for nonmembers.

There are countries such as Japan that have some of the lowest tariffs in the world and yet continue to restrict foreign goods through nontariff barriers. Nontariff barriers, such as ownership restrictions, have the greatest effect on the international expansion of retailing. Many countries restrict the ownership of land and also limit investments in their countries. For example, two of the largest trade partners of the United States, Canada and Japan, both restrict direct foreign investment in their countries. Other areas that offer the best prospect for growth, such as India, do not allow any foreign ownership of land. While these restrictions only marginally affect industrial traders, retailing is much more limited because it often requires high direct investment in the country.

Global Expansion of Retailing

No challenge is greater than that faced by retailers as they adapt their operations to handle the globalization of retail competition. Many retailers are meeting global competition by expanding into other markets.

Continued slow growth of the U.S. domestic economy also encourages retailers looking for international opportunities. In addition to the dim prospects for real economic growth, other significant factors force consideration of global opportunities. The quantity and quality of retail supply are a serious concern. The retail square foot per capita is excessive, nonstore retail is growing, and many retail facilities are in need of major updating and remodeling.[11] In Chapter 16 we discuss how different world economies offer different levels of opportunity and risk for the retailer.

FOOD LION—REVISITED:
LEGAL PROBLEMS CONTINUE

In 1993, the president of Food Lion noted in the Annual Report that the company had incurred an increase in advertising, legal, and public relations costs associated with addressing "continuing tactics from the United Food and Commercial Workers Union International's corporate cam-paign to discredit or damage Food Lion's credibility." As a side note, *Progressive Grocer* indicated that some in the supermarket industry dismissed the ABC Prime Time Live exposé as media hype. Yet most were motivated to examine and reinforce food-handling and sanitation procedures and policies. Many believe the ABC report caused supermarket shoppers to look closely at stock rotation, sell-by dates, and overall look of freshly prepared foods.[12] Also, regulators are endorsing the hazardous analysis control point (HACCP) system—an on-site, process-specific method of ensuring safety of high-risk products by predicting potential risks and taking steps to prevent them.

After the Prime Time Live report, it took a while, but profits at Food Lion began to recover and were up 42 percent; sales reached $7.9 billion by 1994. Food Lion's consumer research and sales results affirmed that customers have learned to shop for value. Food Lion continues its aggressive cost controls and has responded to the desires of its customers by offering them an increased variety of regional brand products and by expanding its private-label merchandise to include approximately 1,000 such products, up from 500 two years ago. These private-label products now account for about 10 percent of sales. In addition, Food Lion implemented a new marketing strategy that included additional advertising to focus on quality products, customer service, and "extra low prices." The company's Gold Lion Guarantee initiative now communicates the commitment to quality, freshness, cleanliness, and service.[13]

The legal shoe dropped again when thirteen current and former employees of Food Lion filed suit alleging that the company engaged in racial discrimination. The suit claimed that black employees were discharged for minor work rule violations and were passed over for promotion. The complaint seeks restitution and unspecified compensatory and punitive damages. A company spokesperson said that the company "recruits, hires and develops its employees without regard to race."[14]

In the summer of 1995 consumer advocates stormed local Food Lion stores, returning hundreds of dollars worth of allegedly outdated food. The mass return of merchandise along with press releases alerting the media was part of a national campaign against the company by the "Consumers United with Employees." According to Food Lion, this is a union front organization of the United Food and Commercial Workers Union. The president of the union has been quoted as saying, "A very real threat to the market share of organized stores are the nonunion chains—the Food Lions . . . we must either reduce these chains' market share or put them out of business."[15]

1. Now that you have been introduced to the legal environment of retailing, what do you think about the amount and kind of government regulation?
2. Has all of the regulation been effective?
3. Because of its continuing problems, do you think Food Lion has become an obvious target for legal pressure?
4. What ethical issues can you identify in the Food Lion situation?

SUMMARY

Retailers are affected by the environment in which they operate; it influences how and why they conduct business. Many businesses use the law as a guideline for business decisions; however, law is reactive and rarely gives guidelines for ethical actions. In response, many retailers have joined together to develop professional codes of ethics to guide decision making.

Nevertheless, businesses do not make decisions; people make decisions. Each individual person must decide the ethics that he or she will live and make decisions by. A personal ethical framework is composed of a self ethic, a situation ethic, a societal ethic, and an others ethic (or consequential ethic).

Businesses are also affected by the social environment. Retailers today are constantly involved in making contributions to society in the forms of better goods and services and aiding in urban affairs. Governmental decisions and laws also affect businesses and retailing. Laws, such as the Sherman Antitrust Act and the Clayton Act, are geared toward the regulation of competition.

The economic system that a country operates under also influences how business operates. While individual retailers normally have little control over macroeconomic issues like growth, inflation, and recession, business decisions must take these issues into account.

One of the reasons that makes retailing so competitive is the relative ease to enter and exit from the industry. This is one of the factors that causes retailing to be an extremely dynamic industry. Many theories of retailing have been offered to address this dynamic nature.

In the last few years, the face of retailing has been irrevocably altered as a result of new and emerging technologies. Along with the technological environment, the global environment has also permanently altered the nature of retailing. The global expansion of retailers, aided by free trade agreements and the increasing number of business opportunities overseas, has exploded in the last decade. In order to be successful, retailers in the future must take into consideration the many environments in which their business operates.

KEY TERMS AND CONCEPTS

Basic consumer rights, 91
Caveat emptor, 87
Clayton Act, 101
Consequential ethic, 98
Consumerism, 90
Dialectic process, 107
Economic utilitarianism, 88

Hedonism, 97
Laissez-faire, 100
Legalistic ethics, 95
Machiavellianism, 97
Natural selection, 107
Retail accordion theory, 107
Self ethic, 96

Sherman Antitrust Act, 101
Situation ethic, 97
Societal ethic, 98
The Wealth of Nations, 100
Wheel of retailing, 106

QUESTIONS

1. How do antitrust laws affect retailers?

2. What effect did the Clayton Act have on trends in retailing?

3. Do the poor pay more? Explain.

4. There is a limit to which a retailer can be socially conscious. Do you agree? Explain.

5. Discuss what might be done to increase customer confidence in retailing.

6. Can retailers truly exercise the function of being buying agents for customers and therefore operate in the best interests of consumers? Explain.

7. Evaluate this statement: Society, it seems, is insisting that there must be a consumer bill of rights. Do you agree? Explain.

8. What are the effects of growth and inflation on retailing? What effects do they have on the consumer?

9. Which retail theory best explains the changing retail environment (wheel of retailing, retail accordion, natural selection, or dialectic process)? What faults do these theories suffer from?

10. How has the expansion on retailing into the global environment affected consumers?

SITUATIONS

1. You are the buyer of private-label kitchen appliances for a large chain discount firm. Your plans call for purchasing 217,000 electric can openers for the coming year. You believe that several manufacturers will give you a substantial price concession if the order is placed now and if one manufacturer receives the entire order. Current economic and market conditions support this belief. However, you are somewhat hesitant to press too hard even though you are in a favorable bargaining position. Why? What legal constraints do you face?

2. You are the owner-manager of a store located in the downtown area. Your store is well known to the other merchants in the area because of your ability to attract customers from a great distance. Recently, you heard a report that a major regional shopping mall is coming into town, and you are giving serious consideration to relocating your store in this center. The decision will not be easy to make, because if you leave the downtown area, other stores might follow your lead and leave the remaining merchants in an unfavorable competitive position. In addition, customers who reside near the downtown area will be adversely affected, as will salespeople who live near this area. You, however, do not see how you can maintain your present sales volume when the new center comes to town. What will you do?

3. You are the owner-manager of a pet shop in a community of 50,000. Recently, a group of interested citizens gathered to develop what they considered to be an appropriate sign code for the city. As a result of their meetings, they have called for legislation that would prohibit the use of any signs not attached to the building and that would limit

the size of signs to no larger than three feet by five feet. In addition, they are proposing that revolving signs and signs with blinking lights be forbidden. Your store is located in a block with many other retail stores. You have recently paid $3,000 for a new sign, which in your estimation makes it easier for people to see your store and know what services you offer. This new sign would be in violation of the proposed code. There will be a grandfather clause that existing signs in violation will not have to be taken down for five years. What position will you take?

4. You are the manager of an apparel store and have decided to give a bonus to the salesper-

son with the highest volume. At the end of the month you find that the salesperson with the highest volume has acted in an excessively competitive manner. This person has achieved volume by ignoring all duties other than selling and has had a tendency to "steal" customers from other employees. You do not wish to encourage this type of behavior, but you did announce the bonus. Furthermore, the store has no written rules on ethical behavior. Do you give the salesperson a bonus? What can you do to prevent this type of behavior in the future?

CASES

CASE 3A
Retailers Imposing Conduct on Manufacturers

Retailers have started to impose codes of conduct on international manufacturers from which they purchase. For example, whenever J. C. Penney Co. awards contracts to apparel makers in Guatemala City, it makes them sign a code of conduct forbidding any violation of local labor law, including the use of underage workers. Jose Asians, director of Penney's buying office in Guatemala City, states, "Our suppliers know how strict we are regarding these conditions." However, the company has come under fire for not checking for compliance among its vendors. Recent visits to factories supplying J. C. Penney revealed workers under the legal age of fourteen and workers paid less than the $2.80 per day minimum wage. Furthermore, some workers were forced to put in unpaid overtime for workdays as long as fifteen hours.

The lax enforcement of rules defined by Penney's and other retailers is drawing fire. Observers say that codes represent little more than public relations gambits, designed to coax Americans into believing they can shop with a clear conscience. Retailers say they can't realistically be expected to enforce the codes. Mr. Davine, director of imports for Target stores, states, "We don't have a fleet of people to inspect plants—we have to rely on our contractors" to police themselves. Other retailers, such as Wal-Mart, conduct inspections, but largely depend on suppliers to honor the codes.

While visits to vendors in Guatemala City uncovered violations of the codes, they also uncovered an important fact: The codes do make some difference. None of the seven- and eight-year-old workers common in some other industries were found in the plants with codes. Also, many of the workers were earning relatively more than their industry counterparts.

While retailers tend to be lax in inspection, enforcement for the vendors caught breaking their code can be severe. When Wal-Mart found underage workers at Sam Lucas SA, it immediately canceled its orders from the plant. Not only did Sam Lucas lose the contract, but it also lost its relationship with America's largest retailer. For many producers, this is a matter of survival.

1. *Does a U.S. retailer have the right to tell an international vendor how to run its business? Should retailers put more effort into inspecting and enforcing their codes of conduct?*

2. *Are codes of conduct a "public relations gambit" or an honest attempt to improve the quality of life in other countries?*

Source: Adapted and quoted with permission from Bob Ortega, "Conduct Codes Garner Goodwill for Retailers, but Violators Go On," *The Wall Street Journal*, July 3, 1995, p. 1. Copyright © Dow Jones & Company, Inc. All rights reserved worldwide.

CASE 3B
The Global Economic Environment—Discounting in Japan[16]

Traditionally, Japan's retail industry was as stable as it was protected. Retailing was dominated by two kinds of stores: giant department stores and small neighborhood stores. Both were kept alive by a complex distribution system characterized by layers of middlemen and by manufacturers who expected their suggested high retail prices to be the actual retail prices. Now, many economic and political factors are changing this scene. Competition has entered the Japanese retailing industry; old department stores are being threatened by efficient new retailers that are cutting out layers of middlemen. The rise of large specialty retailers that are both efficient and profitable has forced many Japanese retailers to reinvent how they do business.

Foreign companies, who had never seriously considered entering the Japanese market, have made inroads into a market that had been considered too complex and closed for non-Japanese companies. Toys 'R' Us has opened discount stores, forcing department stores in Osaka and Tokyo to begin discounting toy prices for the first time in their history.

Ameyayokocho, or "American Store Street," is a discount area in Tokyo for newly price-conscious shoppers. Sale signs have appeared in most Tokyo department stores advertising 30, 50, and even 70 percent off list prices. After years of price setting, Japanese shoppers are discovering price disparities in their favorite products. For example, a can of Coors costs 240 yen in a neighborhood liquor store, 178 yen in a supermarket, and 139 yen in a discount store. The department stores know that transformations are needed, but most are unsure of how they want or need to change to meet the increased competition. Small neighborhood stores, who cannot offer the low prices of the discounters, are going out of business and being replaced by discount drugstores, optical stores, factory outlets, and sidewalk bazaars.

One of the problems Japanese retailers face is that the careful customers are not big-spending customers. Japanese families have very high savings rates. Consumer spending accounts for 56 percent of the Japanese economy compared to 68 percent in the U.S. economy.

1. *Why has it taken foreign-based retailers entering the market to force Japanese retailers to change the way they do business?*

2. *What social issues are raised when large discount firms eliminate small retailers and wholesalers?*

PART 2

THE RETAIL CUSTOMER

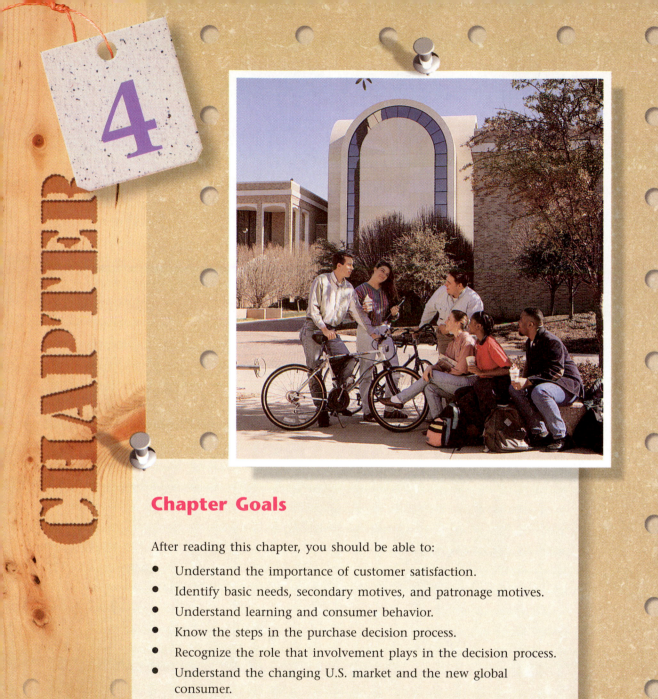

CHAPTER 4

Chapter Goals

After reading this chapter, you should be able to:

- Understand the importance of customer satisfaction.
- Identify basic needs, secondary motives, and patronage motives.
- Understand learning and consumer behavior.
- Know the steps in the purchase decision process.
- Recognize the role that involvement plays in the decision process.
- Understand the changing U.S. market and the new global consumer.

UNDERSTANDING AND IDENTIFYING THE CUSTOMER

TCBY ENTERPRISES INC.: ADAPTING TO THE CHANGING CUSTOMER MARKET

"The Country's Best Yogurt." TCBY is the nation's largest chain of soft-serve yogurt stores. Consumers have found that with about 120 calories and 4 grams of fat, yogurt is a great way to have a dessert. The $1.2 billion market grew nearly 50 percent from 1986 to 1990, and Americans' appetites for frozen yogurt continue to grow at 12 percent annually.[1] However, there has been continued growth in the number of frozen yogurt shop competitors and an increase in the number of sources for the product ranging from grocery stores to self-serve gasoline stations.

Some stores have added baked goods and even salads to their menus in an attempt to satisfy customers. Ice cream companies and ice cream retail shops have also added frozen yogurt to their product line.[2] Even McDonald's has yogurt on the menu.

There are approximately 2,700 TCBY outlets. Over 1,200 are in nontraditional locations including airports, roadside travel plazas, college student unions, superstores, factories, schools, and hospitals. For example, the company has over 270 airport locations. It is now one of the foremost branded concepts in airports and travel plazas throughout the country.

After years of successful growth, a period of revenue and earnings decline marked the early 1990s. By the mid-1990s the profit-eroding decline in same-store sales that caused a number of TCBY stores to close stabilized. However, earnings growth did not respond to a dramatic increase in TCBY's nontraditional locations.

One major strategy being used now to increase earnings growth is to develop retail sales for new products such as TCBY brand hard-packed frozen yogurt, TCBY brand refrigerated yogurt, pies and cakes, a nonfat with no-sugar-added variety, and an indulgent gourmet line. TCBY and other frozen yogurt companies are introducing variations of the traditional product with everything from fat-free fruit flavors to nut, brownie, and candy versions that vary greatly in calorie count and fat content. TCBY has also launched a supermarket line with such flavors as honey almond vanilla and brazil and cashew nut crunch.[3] In the face of intense competition, the company is continuing its efforts to reverse declines in same-store sales through menu extensions, national and local media advertising, store decor upgrades, and relocations. TCBY's nontraditional locations and menu variety indicate the company is trying hard to satisfy customer needs and wants.

The major growth potential for frozen yogurt may come from new customers among the 70 percent of consumers who have not tried the product. TCBY continually looks for ways to reach these customers. Considerations include kiosks, carts, "express" franchises, and additional satellite units. Expanded telemarketing programs allow customers to fax, mail, or telephone orders for pickup and delivery.

The Nutrition Labeling and Education Act of 1990 that took effect in May 1994 may stimulate sales of healthful products and particularly benefit the nonfat segment of the frozen yogurt market. Did you know that just half a cup of premium ice cream can have 190 calories, 15 grams of fat, and 45 milligrams of cholesterol? In contrast, a nofat, no-sugar-added yogurt would have 80 calories, 0 grams of fat, and 0 milligrams of cholesterol.

1. **Is there a typical profile of the customer purchasing frozen yogurt?**
2. **Is that profile different for customers purchasing TCBY yogurt if the purchase is made in a traditional franchised soft-serve frozen yogurt store, in a nontraditional location, or in a supermarket?**
3. **Is the customer's motivation for purchasing frozen yogurt compatible with adding the new product lines?**

INTRODUCTION

The primary responsibility of every retail sales associate, manager, and owner is to provide long-term customer satisfaction by selling goods and services at a profit. To do this, we must first remember that people who enter your store do so because they have one or more specific needs and they believe that you can help satisfy them. Even if someone has never visited your store before, you must quickly try to understand their needs and treat them as a valued customer. They may become one of your best customers. You may satisfy some new customers by simply offering them a way to pass time while waiting for a friend at a mall. By browsing through your store and asking questions of your sales staff, customers may get the information they will need later. Other needs may be satisfied by selling them a product, offering a special service, or correcting a problem.

A Focus on Customer Satisfaction

Customer satisfaction is created by correctly matching the needs of customers with the information, goods, and services that you offer. If there is one guiding retail principle to follow, it is to "know your customers and their needs." By focusing on customer satisfaction you will enhance the lifetime value of every customer as he or she continues to patronize your store for years to come and refers friends or family members.

Do not underestimate the value of your ability to uncover customer satisfaction problems. This may sound like an easy proposition except for one factor: Half of the customers who have a problem will not talk to anyone in your company and only between 9 and 37 percent of them will ever return.[4] The implications of these numbers are clear. Not only must we strive to create an environment within the store that will foster customer satisfaction, but we must also seek to train employees to be alert to customer problems.

In the mid-1800s, Marshall Field of Chicago and John Wanamaker of Philadelphia were pioneers in the movement to emphasize what the customer wanted and needed, rather than what the merchant wanted to sell. These merchants initiated the slogan "The customer is always right." While not always true, the statement is a much better way to conduct retail business than the *caveat emptor,* or "let the buyer beware," policy of the early 1800s. More and more, we see the "customer is right" philosophy being supported. Many specialty, department, and discount stores offer liberal policies that permit customers to exchange items or get refunds without a receipt. Grocery stores frequently offer merchandise free if the automatic scanner prices an item in error at checkout.

We see that successful retailers offer goods, services, and customer service policies that match the expectations of their customers. At the same time merchants must take measures to protect themselves from consumer fraud. For example, stores now have no-return policies on dresses and gowns. Wal-Mart now requires a receipt to return goods. By tracking customer returns the company learned that a few people were regularly returning stolen goods for cash. Don Sodequist, a senior company executive, tells the story of sitting in a café in Wisconsin and hearing a lady tell a friend she had gathered up a bunch of old jewelry and taken it to the local Wal-Mart. The store gave her money back when she said she bought the jewelry there and was dissatisfied. She then told her friend, "Why don't you do that?"

Lifetime Value

We all have had the experience of visiting a store or making a purchase and not being satisfied with some part of the transaction. You have undoubtedly shopped at a store or visited a restaurant where advertising messages and slogans heralded customer satisfaction yet you left dissatisfied. Somehow, you were undervalued as a customer and were not satisfied with the treatment that you received. This type of outcome must be avoided. The value of a customer can be quantified. Let's look at a grocery store example.

If a family of four spends 80 percent of their grocery budget at a single store, they will have an approximate annual value of $5,000 to that store. Clearly, there are financial rewards to be earned by the store for keeping even a single customer satisfied. The **lifetime value** (LTV) of a customer is the dollar value of all the sales your store receives from a given customer over the lifetime of that customer. In our example, if we can expect the family to continue shopping at our store for five years, then the LTV for that household is $25,000. By simple multiplication we can expand this calculation to value a market segment or target market. For example, if there are 1,000 families in a particular target market who patronize this store and each family has an LTV of $25,000, then the LTV of that target market of 1,000 families is $25 million.

Retailers are making conscious efforts to examine strategies in the context of LTV. Brookstone is a store and catalog retailer of what might be categorized as gadgets. Like most catalog retailers they are continuously looking at how they can obtain new customers and turn current customers into repeat buyers. Alternatives include frequent-shopper rewards, discounts and price promotions, and discounts on shipping charges. Shipping charges are a major cost center as well as a significant irritation for customers. The vice president of mail order for Brookstone is experimenting with flat fee shipping charges as well as free shipping, which really means shipping is included in the price. He doesn't like price discounts because the new customers a firm gets from price promotions have a lower lifetime value. "They are in search of a deal every time."[5]

LTV helps focus attention on the importance of satisfying each and every customer for the long term. A failure to satisfy one customer often means that we are failing to satisfy others with similar needs. For example, incidents like those described in Box 4.1 may drive many customers away who never return. Because every satisfied customer has a lifetime of spending and because losing a customer means more than losing a single sale, we need to see how best to attract and retain customers.

Market Segmentation

You know a market is a group of people with the ability, desire, and willingness to buy. No retailer can serve everyone's needs because the needs and desires of people are too varied and the resources available to retailers too limited. Rather than trying to serve everyone, successful retailers try to serve a **market segment,** a group of customers who have some common characteristics. In other words, if we look at all customers, we have a heterogeneous group. The goal of **market segmentation** is to find homogeneous

4.1   AN ETHICAL DILEMMA: SECOND QUALITY GOODS

Carol Lynn Lee owns and manages a moderately successful Lynn's Younger Fashions store in a North St. Louis suburb. She carries several lines of juniors' and children's apparel for girls. Carol's store is located in a strip center next to a video rental store and a Drug Emporium. A supermarket anchors the center.

Carol purchases most of her goods through two West Coast importers. Several months ago she bought a large quantity of spring dresses that were "seconds." She had the imperfections repaired by a tailor and then priced and sold the garments in her store as if they were first-quality goods.

Yesterday, Carol inspected her latest shipment of children's sleepwear from a new vendor located in southeast Asia. She had ordered the goods directly from the vendor when she went to the spring market at the Dallas Apparel Mart.

During her inspection she determined that the material did not meet federal laws requiring such garments to be made from flame-retardant material. She can't imagine how the goods got through customs.

Carol knows there is little chance of recovering her investment from the vendor or the importer. She does know a store owner in a Latin American country that does not have similar government restrictions. She decided to sell the garments to that owner, who accepted the goods she offered at a significant discount from what she paid.

Questions

Are there similar ethical issues in the two situations presented? If neither action is illegal, does that make a difference? What would you do in each situation? What are the consequences if Carol's customers discover what she is doing? How might the concept of long-term customer value be relevant here?

6543217

groups that the store can profitably serve. The idea of niche retailing is to find a relatively small and carefully defined group of customers with common characteristics and then appeal to them with a unique and carefully tailored offering.

Many variables may be used in an analysis of markets. In this chapter we begin with a look at some of the psychological concepts involved in customer behavior including motivation, learning, attitudes, and opinions. The next section of the chapter examines population, income and expenditure, and cultural and social characteristics. The third section looks at a customer purchasing decision model. The chapter concludes with a discussion of some global customer groups.

IDENTIFYING CUSTOMER NEEDS AND WANTS

Think about retail stores in your own community or hometown. Can you identify retailers who satisfy their customers by offering the lowest prices? Are there others who believe that service is more important than price? How about those retailers who go out of their way to satisfy their customers by offering unique or distinctive products? Do some retailers offer easy credit terms? Because each of these retailers seeks to satisfy customer needs in different ways, they are responding to basic needs that differ from person to person.

We all have some similar needs. For example, food, personal safety, and transportation are needed by everyone. How individuals choose to satisfy these needs is a matter of personal preferences or resources. We define **needs** to be those basic underlying motivations that move people to action. People engage in shopping behavior to satisfy needs. The specific goods or services that individuals buy to satisfy those needs, however, may be entirely different from one person to another. While people shop based on their needs, they buy based on their wants. We define **wants** to be the specific ways that people choose to satisfy their needs. For example, you may need a new suit for work. While there are many varieties of suits from which to choose, a customer may want a two-piece wool blend Hickey-Freeman in medium gray. A friend may also need a suit for work. That individual, however, may want the same color suit but a Stratford brand marketed by J. C. Penney in a herringbone weave. In either case, the person will shop at a retail store to satisfy his overall clothing need. He will buy, however, according to his specific wants.

Maslow's Hierarchy of Needs

You may have already learned Abraham Maslow's postulation that at any given time a person may be faced with a number of needs, but probably cannot act on all of them at the same time.[6] Therefore, each person is said to have a hierarchy of motives. The most urgent motive is acted on first. Motives representing needs and wants lower in the hierarchy remain unsatisfied, at least temporarily. **Maslow's hierarchy of needs** is illustrated in Figure 4.1.

Motives arising from physiological needs—such as water, air, food, exercise, sleep, and freedom from pain and discomfort—are basic to existence. Motives involving safety needs result from the individual need to feel loved and secure. The word *safety* sometimes suggests a striving for the financial security obtained through insurance, good wages, and savings. However, financial security is not as important to humans as emotional security. Emotional security makes us feel that we are needed by others and that we are confident of our own abilities and capacities for success and happiness. Emotional security has to do with belonging and love needs.

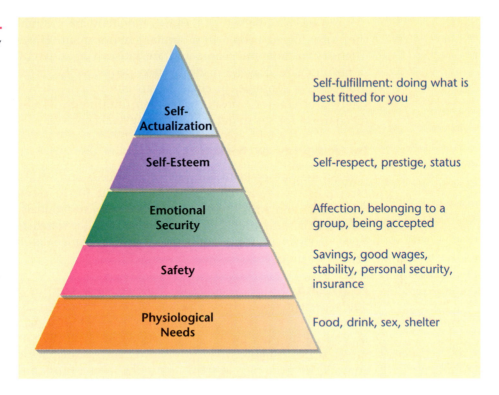

FIGURE 4.1

Maslow's hierarchy of needs.

The need for emotional security leads directly to motives involving recognition, status, and prestige. Maslow identified these as esteem needs. We all need to be treated as unique individuals who are wanted and are important.

Closely associated with the need for recognition is the need for acceptance: We all need to be part of and to identify with groups. So strong is this motive that our primary means of punishment is to remove people from social contact. Ample evidence exists to suggest that much of our purchasing behavior is influenced by the motive to be a part of a group—to do that which is acceptable to friends and associates.

Self-actualization needs involve the individual's desire to be independent—to do things on one's own and to obtain a sense of accomplishment—that is, the desire to reach one's potential. We all seek that inner feeling of enjoyment and accomplishment we experience when we have done a job well or when we achieve one of our goals. Egoism is closely linked to the need for recognition. Although egoistic motives may be satisfied even if no one else is aware of our accomplishment, most of us like others to know what we have done. Therefore, we may try to find a way of showing them. For this reason, egoistic motives are especially evident in purchasing behavior. We frequently look for products that help us let others know we have accomplished our objectives and achieved our goals.

The needs classified by Maslow's hierarchy are presumed to be essentially the same for all people in a similar environment. However, they differ in intensity in different people and are satisfied in different ways. In fact, the same purchase may be made by two people acting from entirely different motives. For example, in choosing an automobile, people are motivated by safety and comfort, prestige, and self-fulfillment. The product serves as a mechanism for satisfying any one or several motives.

Inventories of Motives

A different way of identifying customer needs and wants was developed by Melvin Hattwick. Hattwick[7] identified eight **basic needs** that are desired most often and with the greatest intensity by individuals. These basic needs are referred to as primary motives. They are illustrated in Figure 4.2. These basic needs fit perfectly our requirement for understanding what motivates people to shop.

Food and drink.   Food and drink are necessary for physical sustenance and represent needs. How a person chooses to act on these needs will vary depending on the person and situation. For example, one person, when *needing* food, may *want* prime rib. Someone else, with the same basic need, may prefer seafood. Quite frequently, needs are satisfied within situational constraints. For example, an individual may be in a hurry and just have enough

FIGURE 4.2

The basic needs.

Food and drink

Comfort

Freedom from fear and danger

To be superior

To attract the opposite sex

Welfare of loved ones

Social approval

To live longer

time for a quick hamburger and fries. The person may choose to use the drive-thru window at a fast-food establishment or telephone a restaurant for in-office delivery. This type of situation has encouraged many restauranteurs to expand the number of quickly prepared menu items; to provide take-out meals, featuring fifteen-minutes-or-it's-free offers; and to set up drive-thru windows.

Personal comfort. Personal comfort encompasses a broad range of retail products and services. Climate-controlled living areas, convenience products, well-fitting clothing, and smooth-riding automobiles are but a few of these items. As people spend an increasing amount of their day working or in the pursuit of leisure activities, many individuals and families are seeking to make their lifestyle more comfortable. In addition, the stresses arising from commuting to and from work, urban crowding, or the pressures of the workplace have also motivated people to make their car or home as comfortable as possible. Personal comfort can be a motivating factor in the selection of an automobile or casual shoes.

Freedom from fear and danger. Increasingly we see products designed, manufactured, and retailed that appeal to our need to be free from fear and danger. Smoke detectors, dual air bags, tamper-proof packaging, and deadbolt locks are among the products that can satisfy this need. In fact, cellular telephones, automobile tires, and credit card protection agreements have also been marketed in such a way as to satisfy this basic need.

To be superior. The competitive spirit of the individual compels this need. Whether it is to be the fastest, smartest, strongest, or highest test scorer, a multitude of products have been developed and retailed to satisfy this basic need to be superior. We can see numerous retail examples where a particular brand of running shoe will help you run faster, the right kind of suit will help you be more successful, or the right kind of study aid will help you be smarter than your peers. Reebok and Nike have developed very successful marketing strategies for athletic shoes based on the need to be superior.

Personal attractiveness. Archaeological finds from the pyramids and other places show us that ancient Egyptians valued personal attractiveness. People from cultures of all types and times have adorned themselves with beads, worn colorful makeup, or placed a variety of items in their hair. Many of today's cosmetics, lines of wearing apparel, fashion accessories, and health products are directed at satisfying this basic need of personal attractiveness. Interestingly, this need is shared by young and old alike. GapKids uses personal attractiveness to promote its products to the target market: mothers.

Welfare of loved ones. Insurance, passenger-side air bags, college education funds, flame-retardant infant clothing, and home safety devices are among the products and services that appeal to this need. Closely tied to our

Dual-income married couples with children and single parents are both very busy and concerned with quality child care. Star Markets of Boston meets these needs with in-store child care provided by Bright Horizons Child Care Centers, one of the nation's leading providers of quality child care. Trained day care personnel care for children for up to two hours. The cost to parents is $4 an hour or $2 an hour with a purchase of $100 or more.

personal need to be free from fear and danger, the "welfare of loved ones" need addresses the well-being of family members or people emotionally important to you. Whether your loved ones are at home, in the car, in college, or in a patient-care facility, you want only the best for them. Many consumer product managers have utilized the welfare of loved ones need in developing their marketing strategies. Michelin uses this appeal in its tire ad. The babies in the Michelin TV and print advertisements attract attention and help make a connection to the welfare of loved ones motivation.

Social approval.   People everywhere have a need to be accepted by others and to be part of a group. Many children have learned to "eat all their vegetables" for the singular purpose of winning the approval, or at least avoiding the disapproval, of a parent. Countless shoppers closely follow fashion trends because they want to be wearing the "right" clothes. Personal hygiene products of all kinds, from toothpaste to deodorant to antidandruff shampoo, support our need for social approval. Retailers promote personal grooming products with this need in mind.

To live longer.   Long before Ponce de Leon sought the Fountain of Youth in what we now call Florida, people have sought to live longer. More recently, however, health care services, hot mineral springs in Arkansas, multivitamins, and health/fitness programs have all been developed to respond to this basic need. A fitness club, which is a service retailer, builds its strategy around this motivation.

Secondary Motives

In addition to to these primary motives consumers may have needs associated with secondary motives. For example, they want to be efficient, to have conveniences, to be healthy, and so forth, but these motives are more remote from the primary ones just listed. The secondary wants are learned or socially acquired. They are those we learn to value and satisfy in ways that are unique to us as individuals. Many of our wants develop as we grow older and more experienced and become conscious of our role in society. A listing of such **secondary motives** would include the following:

1. Bargains   **6.** Convenience

2. Information   **7.** Dependability and quality

3. Knowledge   **8.** Economy

4. Cleanliness   **9.** Curiosity

5. Efficiency

While these motives help us understand the behaviors of individual shoppers in their daily interaction with others, they may not offer the retail manager a clear picture of the process of store choice. The secondary motives listed above are culture-sensitive and therefore not constant across nations. Patronage motives, on the other hand, give us better insight into the critical area of understanding the retail customer.

Patronage Motives

Whether the retailer considers motivation from the Maslow point of view or by studying Hattwick's inventory of motives, the objective of the retail manager is to develop a profile of store characteristics that can be associated with a consumer's motivation to shop at a specific store. The basic and secondary

According to *American Demographics,* customers have a morbid fear of being caught behind a slow person in the express lane in the supermarket. "Checkout phobia" is spurred by visions of other customers counting twenty-seven cans of cat food as one item, haggling with the cashier over the receipt, writing a check . . . one . . . letter . . . at . . . a . . . time, or digging for exact change coupons. The desire for fast service has staffing and store design implications (Baker, Ross K., "Play a Simple Malady," *American Demographics,* August 1995, pp. 16–18.)

motives that influence product selection must be identified with factors the store can use to influence consumer store choice. **Patronage motives** are the underlying forces that influence the choice of a store. Most patronage motives can be classified into one of the following categories: price/value; location; convenience; parking; accessibility; friendly and helpful salespeople; merchandise, assortments, varieties, and brands; atmosphere; store image; and services offered.

LEARNING AND CONSUMER BEHAVIOR

Each individual forms attitudes and opinions about stores from a systematic learning process. It is often helpful to organize the retailing mix in such a way that customers can *learn* about a store and how it can provide them with the best shopping alternative for one or more given product or service categories. Learning theory can be applied effectively to help understand the importance of the store choice dilemma and retail patronage.

Learning

Learning refers to changes in behavior that result from experience. These changes in behavior may be expressed in thoughts, words, or overt actions. Learning theory relies on the concepts of need, cue, response, and reinforcement to help explain behavior. Again, a need is the basic underlying motivation that moves people to action. Another way to think about a need is that it is the internal force that initiates action. The consumer will typically have many possible retail alternatives that will satisfy any given need. **Cues** exist as a prompt in the environment and/or in the individual and frequently trigger need recognition. The fragrance counter of a department store, the aroma of a barbecue restaurant, and a grocery display are cues that can trigger need awareness. If purchase behavior in **response** to the need and cues produces satisfaction, positive **reinforcement** occurs. Learning occurs when a specific want or need has been satisfied by a specific retail response. Accordingly, an association is formed between a retail stimulus (cue) and the response (retail behavior). This association may be formed because of reinforcement (reward or punishment mentally tied to the stimulus) or simply because stimulus and response occurred at the same time.

Learning theory suggests several roles for the retailer. Providing a product at the right price, in the right place, in the right quantity, and at the right time to satisfy drives is the retailer's role. Purchasing is the desired response. Sales associates, advertising messages, or the store environment may be among the stimuli (cues) by suggesting problem solutions, heightening the relevance of the motive, or reinforcing the response. Attitudes and opinions are typically formed during the learning process.

Attitudes and Opinions

The difference between an attitude and an opinion is subtle. Psychologists and sociologists define an **attitude** as a predisposition or tendency to act in a particular way, and an **opinion** as the verbalization of an attitude. Thus, a woman who says she prefers Gap to The Limited is offering an opinion that expresses one aspect of her attitudes toward stores and fashion. Our cumulative experience in our total environment—in our family, peer groups, society, and culture—causes us to develop preferences for and evaluate beliefs about the objects and ideas in our world.

Attitudes perform several functions for consumers. As a person develops positive or negative attitudes about products, services, or stores because of experience or other information, the decision process is expedited. Attitudes also serve to protect the self-image or ego of the consumer. Many attitudes may be held simply to enhance the ego. In other words, they are used to reduce tensions created by unpleasant stimuli. Further attitudes are formed to give expression to basic values. Finally, and perhaps most important, attitudes give meaning and organization to the world around us.

Attention and Perception

Every waking moment our five senses receive a great number of stimuli. We hear the radio announcer, see a sign, or taste a new product at a supermarket demonstration. Thousands of times a day our brain is stimulated by inputs received by our senses. **Attention** and **perception** are elements of the complex process by which we sense, select, organize, and interpret sensory stimulation so that we can receive a meaningful picture of the world.

In a single day, a customer may be exposed to more than a thousand commercial messages. As a person drives to work, there are hundreds of billboards and signs. The daily newspaper, television shows, and radio broadcasts are filled with commercials for stores, products, and services. Our friends and coworkers talk about their experiences with stores and products. Obviously, an individual cannot efficiently receive and process all this information. Therefore, **selective attention** occurs. The person unconsciously controls the reception of information by either paying attention or ignoring it.

Conditions influence the buyer's willingness to receive information. For example, our needs and wants make us sensitive to information that will help us satisfy them. Attitudes also influence our attention and perception processes. In general, consumers tend to select information that reinforces attitudes they hold and reject information that conflicts with existing attitudes. Consumers are also likely to be receptive to information concerning areas about which they are uncertain or lack knowledge. Products, packages, displays, store location, prices, advertising, signs, and so on, are all information messages that may or may not be received by potential customers. If messages are to be received, they must first be made compatible with customers' needs, desires, and attitudes. In addition, the messages should be designed to reduce uncertainty and to supply meaningful information.

When buyers receive information, they organize and interpret it during the perception process. In other words, once information is perceived, buyers distort it to make it consistent with their frame of reference from previously received information. How the information is organized and interpreted is a function of thought processes that call on past experiences, on ideas of the product's desirability, and on an evaluation of the information received.

CONSUMER LIFESTYLES

An individual's manner of living is called his or her **lifestyle.** Because of differences in values and resources, each family has unique qualities that will distinguish it from other families. What a family purchases, the way it purchases, and the manner in which purchases are consumed reflect the family's lifestyle. Closely associated with lifestyle are values and goals.

One of the most popular lifestyle indicators is the Values and Lifestyles profile, VALS™2, developed by SRI International in 1989.[8] The VALS™2 framework is designed to segment consumers into one of eight basic classifications: Actualizers, Fulfilleds, Believers, Achievers, Strivers, Experiencers, Makers, and Strugglers. Lifestyle characteristics of target consumers may be valuable in development of store image, merchandise assortments, and advertising messages. Figure 4.3 is a visual description of the segmentation system. Box 4.2 is a description of the VALS™2 groups. Figure 4.3 and Box 4.2 were downloaded from the World Wide Web at the SRI International home page. You will also find there an interesting questionnaire that you can complete. The results allow you to see what segment you fit into and how the information could be used to understand consumer characteristics.

Consumers pursue and acquire products, service, and experiences that provide satisfaction and give shape, substance, and character to their identities. They are motivated by one of three powerful self-orientations: principle, status, and action. Principle-oriented consumers are guided in their choices by abstract, idealized criteria, rather than by feelings, events, or desire for approval and opinions of others. Status-oriented consumers look for products and services that demonstrate the consumers' success to their peers. Action-oriented consumers are guided by a desire for social or physical activity, variety, and risk taking.

Resources, a dimension in the VALS™2 system, refers to the full range of psychological, physical, demographic, and material means and capacities consumers have to draw upon. They encompass education, income, self-confidence, health, eagerness to buy, intelligence, and energy level. They are a continuum from minimal to abundant. Resources generally increase from adolescence through middle age but decrease with extreme age, depression, financial reverses, and physical or psychological impairment.

The VALS™2 segmentation system sorts respondents to the VALS™2 question-naire system into eight groups. The main dimensions of the system are *self-orientation* (the left-to-right dimension in the figure above) and *resources* (the top-to-bottom dimension in the figure above). © SRI International. All rights reserved. Unauthorized reproduction prohibited.

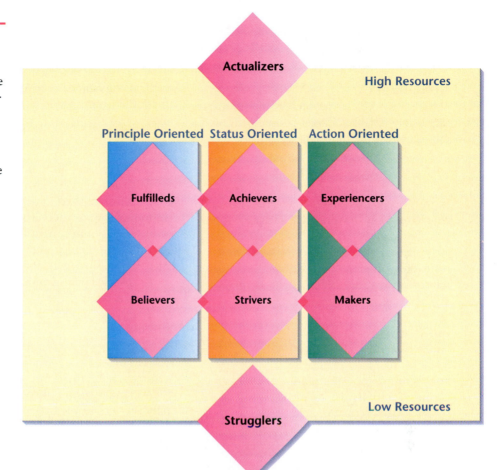

Teens are a potent $110 billion plus market for everything from clothing and snack foods to music. Average spending is $50 a week for young teens and more than $100 for eighteen- to nineteen-year-olds. They are very brand-conscious and watch closely what their TV, movie, music, and sports idols are wearing, using, or eating. Teens are fickle consumers, which puts a premium on inventory control. The merchant must stock, but cannot afford to be caught off guard with unsalable inventory.

BOX 4.2 VALS™ 2 ONLINE DESCRIPTIONS OF GROUPS

Actualizers

Actualizers tend to be successful, sophisticated, active, "take charge" people with high self-esteem and abundant resources. They seek to develop, explore, and express themselves in a variety of ways.

Image is important to Actualizers as an expression of their taste, independence, and character. They have a wide range of interests, are concerned with social issues, and are open to change. Their possessions and recreation often reflect cultivated tastes for relatively upscale, niche-oriented products and services.

Fulfilleds

Fulfilleds tend to be mature, satisfied, comfortable, reflective people who value order, knowledge, and responsibility. Most are well educated and in (or recently retired from) professional occupations. Relatively content with their career, families, and station in life, their leisure activities tend to center around the home.

Fulfilleds generally have a moderate respect for the status quo institutions of authority and social decorum, but they are open-minded to new ideas and social change. While their incomes allow them many choices, Fulfilleds are conservative, practical consumers; they look for durability, functionality, and value in the products they buy.

Believers

Believers are predominantly conservative, conventional people with concrete beliefs based on established codes: family, church, community, and the nation. They follow established routines, organized in large part around home, family, and social or religious organizations to which they belong.

Believers favor familiar products and established brands. Their income, education, and energy are modest but sufficient to meet their needs.

Achievers

Achievers tend to be successful career and work-oriented people who like to, and generally do, feel in control of their lives. They value consensus, predictability, and stability over risk, intimacy, and self-discovery. They are deeply committed to work and family. Work provides them with a sense of duty, material rewards, and prestige. Their social lives tend to be structured around family, career, and church.

Achievers live mostly conventional lives, tend toward political conservatism,

Source: SRI International. VALS™2 is a trademark of SRI International.

The eight segments of consumers defined by the dimensions of self-orientation and resources have different attitudes and exhibit distinctive behavior. The segments are balanced in size so that each truly represents a viable target market.

The way people act on their needs and wants, given their lifestyle, differs greatly. Some families wait for sales and shop for bargains: Other families may and respect authority. They favor established, prestige products and services that demonstrate success to their peers.

Strivers

Strivers tend to seek motivation, self-definition, and approval from the world around them. Strivers are concerned about the opinions and approval of others. In effect, they are striving to find a secure place in life.

Strivers have an unusually strong drive for material rewards, but they often feel constrained in their ability to realize their ambitions. Consequently, Strivers have a relatively strong antipathy toward "the system." As consumers, they tend to be impulsive, style conscious, and quick to emulate those of greater material wealth.

Experiencers

Experiencers tend to be young, vital, enthusiastic, impulsive, and rebellious. They seek variety and excitement, savoring the new, the offbeat, and the risky. They quickly become enthusiastic about new possibilities but are equally quick to cool.

Experiencers combine an abstract disdain for conformity with an outsider's desire of others' wealth, prestige, and power. Their energy finds an outlet in exercise, sports, outdoor recreation, and social activities. Experiencers are avid consumers, spending a comparatively high proportion of their income on clothing, fast food, music, movies, and videos.

Makers

Makers are practical people who have constructive skills and value self-sufficiency. They live within a traditional context of family, practical work, and physical recreation and often have little interest in what lies outside that context. Makers experience the world by working on it—building a house, raising children, fixing a car, or canning vegetables—and, in general, have enough skill, income, and energy to carry out their projects successfully.

Makers are unimpressed by material possessions other than those with a practical or functional purpose (such as tools, utility vehicles, and fishing equipment).

Strugglers

Strugglers' lives are constricted. With limited material and educational assets, without strong bonds, and often elderly and concerned about their health, strugglers are often resigned and passive. Their chief concerns are for security and safety.

Strugglers are cautious consumers. They represent a very modest market for most products and services, but are loyal to favorite brands.

spend their whole paycheck when they receive it and may also be credit users. The expenditures of two families with the same income may differ greatly. For example, one family may buy a boat or camper, whereas another may save for retirement. Yet another group of customers may have a lifestyle that includes purchasing environmentally friendly merchandise. Woodward & Lothrop's Planet Earth shops have signage pointing out the reasons for environmentally themed merchandise made from recycled materials or designed to conserve energy. Some of the profits from these sales go to support environmental causes.[9]

The purchasing behavior of a family, then, is directly influenced by the goals and values of its members. Goals depend on the family's economic structure, its group of friends, the number and age of family members, and the needs of the family as a group. Goals can reflect the need for basic necessities or desires of the family and its members. For example, decisions must be made about whether the family most wants a larger apartment, a new home, a cabin in the mountains, or a new car.

Customers Buy Benefits

Regardless of the need being satisfied, we must always remember that the customer is buying **benefits.** It is much like the old example of the one-quarter-inch electric drill. Although the customer may have compared brands, features, and prices, he didn't buy it because he wanted a drill: He bought it because he wanted a one-quarter-inch hole. Other examples are easily envisioned. Customers will not buy The Club because they want an attractive red iron bar in their car: They want the *benefit* of theft protection the manufacturer promises them. It is important to remember that we satisfy needs and wants by focusing on the benefits that our products or services offer our customers. To do this effectively, we must understand our customers. If we do not understand why our customers come into our store, we cannot assemble the best assortment of goods and services to satisfy them. The same can be said of advertising, displays, in-store service, or sales consultation. If we do not understand how customers gather information and make choices, we cannot satisfy them effectively.

As we have discussed, the need structure of the customer is the basic motivator for the decision-making process. The way that our customers make decisions and build their expectations for product or service performance will, in large part, characterize the extent to which they will be satisfied or dissatisfied with a purchase. It is incumbent upon retailers to anticipate the needs and wants of their target consumers. We now turn to a discussion of the population, income and expenditure, and cultural and social characteristics of markets.

THE CHANGING U.S. MARKETPLACE

For a retail manager, tomorrow's marketplace will be very different from the retail landscape you see today. Our total population is growing more slowly than at almost any time in the past; geographic dispersion is continually changing, immigration is presenting multicultural challenges, the population is aging, and there are an increasing number of single and single-parent households. Despite the depth of these changes, our real disposable incomes are plateauing and people are becoming increasingly value-conscious. Our needs for goods and services have altered markedly in response to these changes. We begin our view of the changing marketplace with a population perspective.

Population

While individual retailers are most interested in the population of their own retail trade area, they must also understand national events and trends. Because the changes that occur in the aggregate consumer market affect all retailers, they must be prepared to react to alterations in the composition of the U.S. population. Changes in population growth, immigration, migration, age composition, and the socioeconomic status of households dramatically affect retailers. Let's examine each of these factors to see how they can provide opportunities.

Growth. By 1970, the U.S. population was more than double the 1915 figure of 100 million, and by 1996 the population had reached 262 million. Although the rate of population growth has slowed since the mid-1960s, the growth in numbers of people has remained fairly constant since then. For example, the population increased approximately 23 million during the 1970s and 22 million during the 1980s. Table 4.1 illustrates these U.S. population changes for the period 1970 to 1990. What significant trends do you see?

Historically, many retailers have relied on a continually expanding population for their sales growth. However, during periods of slower growth, successful retailing will depend to a greater degree on increased customer purchasing power and the ability of individual retailers to gain market share at the expense of other retailers. A growing number of larger retailers with little growth in population or incomes mean increasing competition.

TABLE 4.1

Changing Age Distribution of the American People (in 1,000s)

	1970	1980	1990
19 and under	77,020	72,458	71,735
20–29	29,868	40,840	40,460
30–39	22,550	31,526	41,679
40–49	24,112	22,759	31,333
50–59	21,090	23,325	25,057
60–69	21,066	25,669	28,670
70+	7,530	9,969	13,033

Migration.   Soon after the Eastern seaboard was settled, the United States experienced a steady population shift westward. This trend has continued. The Pacific, Mountain, and Southwest regions continue to grow more rapidly than the Northeast, Midwest, and South. Many retailers have been successful because they moved with or in anticipation of the population shifts. Stores like Macy's followed the population as it grew on the West Coast and in the Southeast and Southwest. Macy's expansion, however, didn't save it from bankruptcy!

Despite the significance of regional population shifts, it has been the population changes among urban, suburban, and rural areas that have had the most dramatic effect on retailing over the last half-century. Largely as the result of migration from rural areas, the percentage of the population living in central cities continued to grow until the 1950s. Beginning in the 1930s, the country also began to experience substantial growth in the suburbs partly as a result of widespread automobile ownership, inexpensive automotive fuel, and the growth of multilane highway systems. These combined factors made it efficient to commute from the suburbs to urban workplaces. Even today, the greatest growth continues to occur in suburban areas and the population in rural areas continues to decline.

The population redistribution during the past half-century has created challenges throughout the business world. Many downtown retailers have moved to suburban areas or have opened branch outlets there. Some retailers were forced to close unprofitable downtown stores, and those who remained have experienced a dwindling market share. Retailers have generally followed population shifts by moving to locations accessible by the automobile. Strip shopping areas, large centralized suburban shopping centers, and the development of sprawling regional shopping malls reflect how retail strategies have adapted to dynamic population shifts.

The United States and Canada have always been nations of immigrants. During the 1980s the pace of immigration accelerated dramatically. U.S. immigrants (who identify strongly with their cultures) are now primarily from Asia and Latin America. Canada has been a destination for many Hong Kong Chinese and Indians. Successfully meeting their needs requires retailers to communicate in the immigrant's native language.

FIGURE 4.4

Changing patterns of immigration to the United States. (*Source:* U.S. Immigration and Naturalization Services, *Statistical Yearbook,* annual; and releases.)

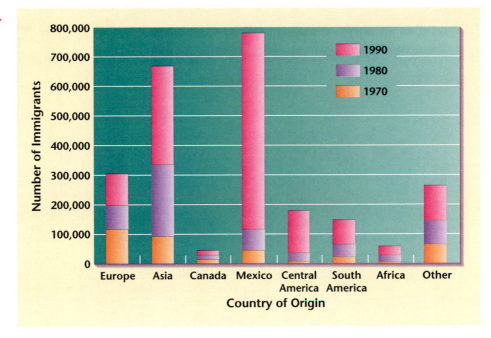

The central cities experienced a decrease in their rate of population decline during the 1980s. Many people have chosen to return to the central cities to reduce commuting time, renovate older housing, and take advantage of cultural and entertainment activities concentrated there. This return to the central cities again offers retailing opportunities and challenges.

Immigration.   Much of the recent U.S. population growth has been a result of immigration from other countries. During the 1960s, 14 percent of the total U.S. population growth was a result of immigration. This figure increased to 20 percent of the total growth during the 1970s and 33 percent during the 1980s.

Immigration is creating dramatic changes in the retail marketplace. Immigrant groups bring with them their culture. They often want to maintain their language, religion, food preferences, and marriage rituals. For example, English will become a second language for populations in many Southwestern retail trade areas before the next century. Retailers will be serving customers with different cultural backgrounds from those they have traditionally dealt with. Retailers must be aware of subculture differences. It is easy to simply identify the migrants from Mexico, Central, and South America as Hispanic or Latino. In reality, Cubans, Puerto Ricans, Mexicans, and other groups have unique subculture characteristics. Figure 4.4 illustrates the changes in immigration patterns and the number of legal immigrants in the years 1970, 1980, and 1990.

FIGURE 4.5

Changing
percentage distrib-
ution of the U.S.
population by
race/ethnicity.
(*Source:* U.S.
Bureau of the
Census, Current
Population
Reports,
P 25–1104.)

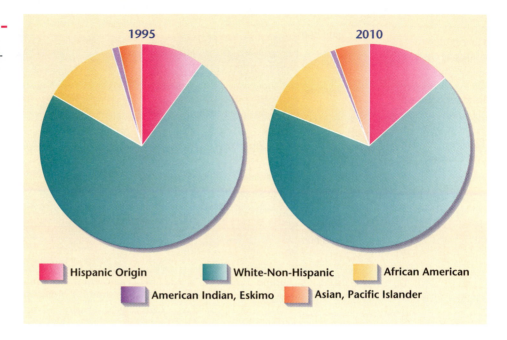

Race and Ethnicity

Cultural and racial diversity is increasing in importance in our country and
is dramatically affecting retailing strategies. In 1970, for example, 11.1 percent of the U.S. population was African American and 1.4 percent was classified as "other" races. By 1990, the black population increased to 12.1 percent and "other" races constituted 7.6 percent. In 1970, the Hispanic
population represented 4.5 percent of the U.S. population. This number had
doubled to 10 percent by 1995. See Figure 4.5. Retailers have only recently
begun to recognize the opportunities in targeting ethnic populations. For
example, the African-American market has been estimated to have an approximate annual "value" of $280 billion to marketers.[10] Successful retailers in the
future will actively target these markets and seek to provide goods and services related to their cultural needs and wants.[11] For example, supermarket
retailers have responded to the growing Hispanic population with Viva stores
in Los Angeles, Danal's Food Stores in Dallas, and Fiesta Marts in Houston.
In various parts of the United States, ethnic shopping centers are being targeted at African Americans, Asian Americans, and Hispanic Americans.[12]

Age

A change in the age distribution of the population is also very important to
retailers. With the onset of the industrial revolution family size decreased as
families migrated from the farm to the city. The number of births again
dropped during the Great Depression of the 1930s. With the return of the

GIs and renewed economic prosperity following World War II, the number of births increased as dramatically as it had dropped only two decades before. This sharp increase in births became known as the "baby boom" and would significantly change the nature of retailing for years to come. Increases in sales of single-family homes, home furnishings, baby clothing, and affordable automobiles led to an upward swing in the retail business.

The importance of age can be seen in the 46 million people in the United States aged eighteen to twenty-nine who have been labeled as members of generation X. This is a group that is said to feel uncertain about its future and to believe that it has been ignored, since marketers have been focusing on baby boomers and the elderly. But for restaurant owners, generation X has become the most popular targeted group. Xers spend over $30 billion, about 25 percent of their discretionary income, on dining out.[13] Generation X is the group that shops for music and software most frequently. They like music superstores. With significant disposable income and brand consciousness, this group also likes shopping in full-price apparel stores.

Exercise is a part of the senior consumer lifestyle. Many work out at health clubs and attend aerobics classes. As they get older, exercise tends to become more home-centered, with an interest in equipment that is designed for them. In addition, major expenditure categories include health care, food, clothing, and pharmacy. Price is important for this group, which spends $500 billion annually. Ease of shopping in the store, feelings of safety, and knowledgeable employees are also important. ("Americas' Aging Consumers," *Discount Merchandiser,* September 1993, pp. 16–18.)

Baby boomers are moving into their peak earning years during the 1990s with major family commitments and social and community obligations triggering major shifts in retailing. Their busy lifestyles will be the driving force in the shift of market share toward nonstore retailing. Electronic retailing, catalog retailing, and television shopping continued to expand their market share through the mid-1990s, and baby boomers have led the shift. Baby boomers, born from 1946 to 1964, are in control of the nation's economy. They will be the most significant consumer group in terms of size and purchasing power for the next twenty to thirty years. There are twice as many boomers shopping for music and computer software as Xers. They prefer buying hardware and software together at superstores like Best Buy. They tend to stay away from full-price apparel outlets.[14]

The fifty-five and over group has the highest per capita income and represents a major market segment for health and related items, travel, and financial services. They are generally more conservative shoppers who tend to be careful, value-conscious advertisement readers and coupon clippers.[15] (See Figure 4.6.)

FIGURE 4.6

The growing population of individuals more than 60 years old (000,000). (*Source:* U.S. Bureau of the Census, *Current Population Reports.*)

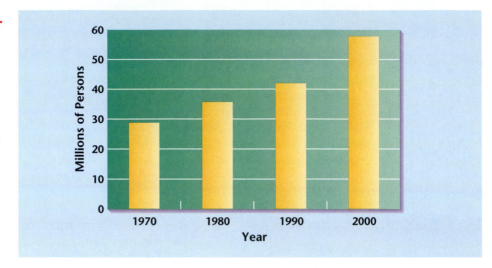

Household Composition

The size and composition of households largely determine the manner in which people spend their money. Marriages, divorces, and births influence family composition and household size. Family life in the United States has changed dramatically during the last half of the century. Today, people are delaying marriage and choosing to have fewer children. In 1990, 63 percent of the women and 79 percent of the men under age twenty-five had never been married. Companies like BabySuperstore are positioning themselves for the mini baby boom that is beginning for couples who have delayed having children.

The birthrate in terms of per thousand women of childbearing age declined over the past thirty years, even though many "baby boomers" were in their childbearing years during that time. This decline was due in part to women delaying marriage and starting a family after they had established their career. The median age of a woman at first marriage is now about twenty-four years, compared to almost twenty-one years in 1970.

During the 1980s, the proportion of women who had given birth before age thirty reached a near record low. However, the fertility rate for women in their thirties rose dramatically. A mini baby boom is beginning.

Several factors have contributed to this increase. Because of the baby boom from 1946 to 1964, more women were in their thirties. Many of them are having the children they delayed in their twenties. Additionally, large increases in immigration during the 1980s boosted the fertility rate. The Juvenile Product Manufacturing Association says that industry sales of infant and children's merchandise are growing rapidly.[16] The baby boomlet creates demand for toys and bikes, basketball backboards and backyard playground equipment, and car seats. Scholastic sells 150 million premium-quality books a year aimed at kindergarten through sixth grade children.[17]

Families with only one or two children have become predominant. More married mothers are in the labor force. Other general trends present today suggest significant changes in the family. For example, fewer young adults marry, a third of the births are to unmarried mothers, and children are more likely to live with only one parent. These changes make identifying market opportunities more complex, but they enlarge the opportunities available to retailers to meet needs and wants.

Education

Since World War II, Americans in record numbers have pursued higher levels of formal education. More people than ever before want higher education and advanced training. Increasingly, large numbers of students are pursuing higher education not only in colleges and universities but also in vocational and trade schools. Students forego immediate jobs in anticipation of higher future earning capacity so that they can join the already large numbers of affluent individuals and families who demand goods and services to satisfy a high standard of living. In 1950, the median number of years of school completed by persons twenty-five years and over was 9.3. This increased to 12.7 years in 1990. Even more impressive, however, is the fact that in 1990, 21.3 percent of the population aged twenty-five and over had received a college degree. Figure 4.7 shows the educational attainment of persons in the United States since 1960.

FIGURE 4.7

The percentage of Americans completing high school and attending college is growing significantly. (*Source:* U.S. Bureau of the Census, *Current Population Reports.*)

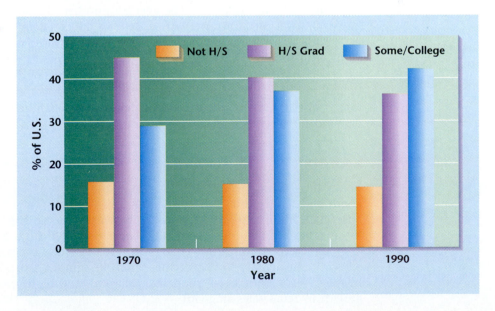

Higher levels of formal education are associated with higher income levels. A Department of Commerce survey showed that high school graduates with no college had half the monthly earnings of those persons with a bachelor's degree. In addition, higher levels of formal education tend to change the tastes and buying patterns of customers and increase the purchase of fashion-oriented items. Many adults pursue higher education solely for cultural enrichment or other reasons that have nothing to do with increased earning power. A highly educated population offers many benefits and opportunities to today's retailers. To illustrate, stores such as The Sharper Image did not exist two decades ago. Today, such retailers prosper by satisfying the needs of highly educated and affluent segments of our population.

Occupation

In an increasingly global and technological economy, today's occupational shifts are generally toward jobs that require a higher level of education. Such shifts have been both the cause and the result of the rising education level of people in the labor force. Occupational shifts have also occurred because of changes in the demand for goods and services and from changes in the level of technology.

A changing workplace means changing work styles. Fewer people will spend their entire lives in one type of work or at the same job. The changing requirements of the working environment will necessitate frequent retraining and additional education. Occupational shifts will also cause people to relocate more frequently. As people improve their skills and move from job to job, many retail opportunities become available as their needs change.

Another important change in the occupational environment is the declining length of the workweek. The average number of hours worked per week has declined from 37.1 in 1970 to 34.5 in 1990. Large numbers of people with additional discretionary time are free to pursue leisure activities. This, alone, will present vast opportunities for many types of retailers.

There have also been significant increases in the number of women participating in the labor force. In 1990, 58 percent of women were in the labor force. Working wives bring additional income to families and increase the demand for services and laborsaving products.

Income

The ability of individuals to buy is measured not only by the availability of goods and services but also by the amount of money they have to spend. To appreciate the important relationship between income level and retail activity, it is helpful to understand different types of income as defined in Box 4.3. Numerous factors affect changes in each of these types of income. Overall economic activity, cost of living, inflation, and tax issues each play a part. In the 1990s tax increases, moderate inflation, and high unemployment kept growth in retail sales stagnant.

4.3 DEFINITIONS OF DIFFERENT TYPES OF INCOME

- **Personal gross income** includes salaries, wages, interest income, rental income, and other forms of income before taxes have been deducted.

- **Disposable income** is personal income after taxes and reflects the amount of money that is available for personal consumption and savings.

- **Discretionary income** is the amount of disposable income that is available after spending for basic household operation and fixed commitments (e.g., auto loans, medical insurance).

- **Real income** reflects actual purchasing power of today's income relative to the purchasing power of the same dollar-value income in a previous period.

- **Psychic income** represents the personal reward or satisfaction that a person enjoys from his or her work, rather than money income.

6543217

Income distribution. The personal income of Americans grew dramatically between the late 1940s and the early 1970s. However, despite the rising educational levels and the increasing number of women in the labor force, real family income is about the same now as it was in 1977. Although income growth has presently plateaued, the total number of individuals and families with high levels of discretionary income continues to increase. These changes should affect retailing profoundly by increasing the demand for both new and existing goods and services. At the same time single-parent households have less income.

The retailer must also be aware of income distribution differences across the country. Over the last two decades, for example, personal income has been increasing most rapidly in the Far West, the Southwest, and the Southeast. Clearly, since retailers exchange products and services for money, these income distribution considerations are important in making decisions concerning merchandise mix, store location, store image, and merchandise offerings.

Credit and savings. The total purchasing power of an individual consumer consists of disposable income, savings, and credit. Americans use credit extensively for all types of retail purchases. Installment credit, noninstallment credit such as single-payment loans, and credit card debt total almost $1,500 billion. This indicates how an expanding population translates needs and desires into demand for goods and services through the use of credit.

Saving creates a reserve of funds available to customers for major purchases. In 1970, personal savings accounted for 8.0 percent of personal income. It is now less than 5 percent.

BOX 4.4 ENGEL'S LAWS

Four generalizations, known as Engel's laws, have become benchmarks for the study of consumer expenditures. Simply, they state that as income increases:

- A smaller percentage will be spent for food.
- The percentage spent for clothing will remain approximately the same.

- The percentage spent for housing and household operations will remain about the same.
- The percentage spent for miscellaneous items (e.g., recreation, religion, education) and savings will increase.

Expenditure patterns. The analysis of customer expenditure patterns aids retailers when attempting to estimate:

- The dollar size of markets
- Market growth rates
- The proportion of the customer's dollar spent for various products and services
- Changes in expenditures associated with changes in income

Aggregate customer expenditure data and changes in disposable personal income represent only part of the total retail consumption picture. Significant variations in purchase behavior can be associated with such factors as place of residence, family income, and age of household head. A study of customer spending patterns has led to some useful generalizations about the relationship between income and expenditure patterns. See Box 4.4.

These relationships describing purchase behavior given changes in personal income have generally been confirmed by studies of personal consumption expenditures. For example, the percentage of consumption expenditures for food purchased in grocery stores was 16 percent in 1970, compared to less than 10 percent in 1995. However, the amount spent for purchased meals and beverages increased. Thus, as income increases, the proportion spent for food prepared at home tends to decrease, but individuals and families tend to spend more for dining out. Similarly, the proportion of consumption expenditures spent for housing has stayed relatively the same since 1970. The proportion of consumption expenditures spent for recreation has not only kept pace with increased income but represents a slightly greater share. This increased amount spent for recreation items presents great opportunities for retailers selling sports-related items, televisions, CD players, Sony Walkmen, and VCRs.

SOCIOCULTURAL CHARACTERISTICS

Retail market behavior is strongly influenced by the interaction of individuals within groups and the values imposed by those groups. These individual interactions and group values are largely shaped by the culture of the group to which an individual belongs. **Culture** is defined as the "complex of values, ideas, attitudes, and other meaningful symbols created by man, and the artifacts of that behavior, as they are transmitted from one generation to the next."[18]

Within each culture, there typically exist two or more subcultures. For example, the United States has more subcultures with identifiable values than many other countries. Retailers typically look at important religious, ethnic, or geographical subcultures instead of focusing on broad cultural values. Because culture so strongly influences the patterns of motivation, the attitudes, and the perceptions of customers, it has direct bearing on purchasing behavior. What people want or will accept largely reflects cultural values, particularly as those values are filtered and transmitted to individuals through the family, reference groups, and social classes.

Reference Groups

A **reference group** consists of people with whom a person identifies. Reference groups may be groups to which individuals belong or desire to belong. Social psychologists believe that reference groups are a major source of values, norms, and perspectives. Reference groups influence purchasing behavior in at least two major ways. First, they influence aspiration and achievement levels. This is to say that the reference group can provide a frame of reference against which someone can base his or her satisfaction or frustration. For example, if your friends wear a certain brand of clothing, you may be influenced to obtain clothing of a similar brand. Second, reference groups set standards of behavior by establishing acceptable and approved purchasing patterns and by inducing conformity to the group. The desire for conformity is one explanation for the existence of fads.

Social Classes

Societies are frequently stratified into groups called *social classes*. Sociologists have suggested a six-level social class system based on occupation, income source, education, type of housing, and location of residence. Belonging to one of these social classes reflects one's attitude toward such factors as future orientation, lifestyle, or leisure time. Although social class itself is difficult to apply as a segmenting variable, a people's perception of their membership in some particular social class influences their retail motives and attitudes. Because members of the same social class tend to share similar values and standards of behavior, we know that their retail patronage behavior will be closely aligned as well.

Family Life Cycle

The family represents a basic unit in the American social structure and exerts a major influence on the purchasing behavior of individuals within that unit. Three aspects of family life are especially important in affecting expenditures: (1) the family life cycle, (2) the family lifestyle, and (3) the family goals. Family life has changed greatly over the last three decades. The number of nonfamily households and changes in living arrangements have affected the allocation of income and personal consumption expenditures. Postponement of marriage and childbearing, increases in divorce and separation, and increases in life expectancy have also changed the allocation of income among various groups.

There are several identifiable stages in the family life cycle that are predominantly characterized by the age of the family members. The needs and desires of individuals within that family change as a family moves through these stages. Some inferences that may be drawn for purchasing behavior from the various stages are described below.

Singles. Singles (persons living alone or with nonrelatives) constitute 35 percent of all households. Aggregate income for this group as a percentage of the aggregate income of all households is about 25 percent. Although many young singles have yet to realize their potential earning capacity, they often have a relatively large discretionary income because they have no family responsibilities. Members of this group tend to be consumers of fashionable clothing, automobiles, sports-related merchandise, and other products that are associated with recreation and leisure. This has given rise to the expansion of stores like Eddie Bauer and Lands' End.

Young married couples with no children. With marriage, expenditure patterns begin to change. Young couples establish their household in apartments or homes and purchase furniture and household appliances. At this stage, many wives work and discretionary income may be quite high. Besides household items, these couples also tend to be interested in products associated with sports and recreation.

Young married couples with young children. With the birth of children, some wives may leave the workforce, although an increasing number are choosing to return to work. Even with two incomes, these families may still be at the lower end of their potential income scale, and the needs of young children are added to the needs of their parents. These families are purchasers of household items, furniture, and children's clothing and tend to be highly price-conscious.

The emerging children's superstore chains like Lil' Things and BabySuperstores are growing in response to the increasing birthrate among late baby boomers and immigrants. Parents are motivated to help their children learn in a fun and educational way with computer software. CD ROM multimedia computers are the basis for software departments. The two major growth areas in home computing are kids' titles and "infotainment" programs in subjects like gardening, cooking, health care, and parenting.

Single parents with young children. The demographics of the family have changed greatly as the number of single parents continues to increase. The income of the single-parent family tends to be considerably below that of married couples with children. Many of these single parents and their children live with relatives. Single parents spend most of their income on child care and maintaining a household. They tend to be highly price-conscious.

Married couples with older children living at home. As children grow, families' needs and income levels change. Family heads approach their peak earning capacity, and wives who may have left the workforce return to work. Although the essential needs of the family have been met, many purchases represent the replacement of products obtained during the family formation phase such as furniture and major household appliances. Often, because of higher levels of disposable income in this phase of the family life cycle, the replacement items will be of better quality than the originals.

Older singles with older children living at home. The demands on the single parent with older children will be different from those faced by single parents with smaller children. The influence of athletic events, social activities, and school projects will place considerable demands on the nonworking hours of the single parent. Consequently, the single parent will be attracted by convenience items and time-saving devices, although they will still tend to be price-conscious because of a lower income level.

Older married couples with no children living at home. When children leave home, several major changes take place. Family income may still be high, so discretionary income may increase dramatically. Couples travel and engage in other leisure activities. They may become involved in community activities to fill the gap in their lives left by the children's absence. A move to a smaller house may create the need for new household furnishings.

Sole survivors. As the life span of our citizens continues to increase and medical science develops new procedures to help us live longer, the likelihood of becoming the sole survivor of a marriage increases. Products that make life more convenient, health care aids for in-home medical assistance, memberships in social organizations, and patronage of senior citizen transportation systems are among the products and services that this growing population segment will need in the coming years.

Older married couples with family heads retired. When heads of households retire, a reduction in income may cause changes in consumption patterns. Needs change to match income level, and purchases will reflect basic necessities. However, this segment has experienced a considerable rise in household income in recent years, as more working wives leave the workforce with retirement income. This group will continue to have increased buying power in the future.

Older singles/couples with at least one parent living in the home. As we see the life span of individuals continue to increase, the incidence of older parents living with their children instead of living in a planned community setting or nursing home increases as well. This change in household structure holds extensive implications for household building modifications, home health care equipment, and professional services.

THE PURCHASE DECISION PROCESS

A group of friends may discuss for several minutes the pros and cons of several alternative restaurants before selecting one that will most closely match each of their needs. All in all, individuals have devised interesting ways to search out information about products or services, compare the alternatives available to them, and make a final purchase decision. The successful retailer seeks to understand customer shopping behavior and the steps involved in the purchase decision process. As you enhance your understanding of these important issues, you will be able to satisfy better each of your customer's needs.

The search for a better understanding of customer shopping behavior has led to the development of numerous models explaining the **purchase decision** process.[19] In each case, the researcher has sought to diagram or flowchart the way that individuals seek to satisfy their needs. These models are important to retail managers because of their desire to create customer satisfaction. One such model, shown in Figure 4.8, proposes buyer behavior as a problem-solving activity. In your studies you may take a course in consumer behavior that will examine many models in detail.

In this model, there are six stages a buyer will go through in the buying process: unsatisfied need (problem) recognition, alternative identification and information search, alternative evaluation, the purchase decision, postpurchase evaluation and action, and decision feedback.

As a customer moves through the decision process, a number of different kinds of decisions must be made. **What to buy** questions involve choosing among the various products, brands, and prices. The customer might be trying to decide **where to buy.** In this case, the choice may be among types

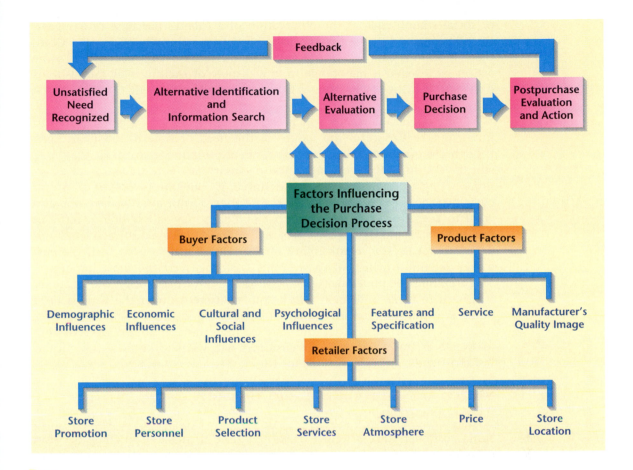

FIGURE 4.8

The purchase decision process.

of stores and the services they offer or whether to shop downtown, in a suburban mall, or in a neighborhood store. **How to buy** questions require the customer to decide if the purchase will be made in a store, from a vending machine, from a catalog, by telephone order, or maybe from a door-to-door salesperson. The customer must also make decisions about paying cash or using credit. **When to buy** decisions involve the choice of time of day, day of week, and time of year. Each customer decision requires an effort to solve a problem and make a decision by searching for and evaluating information.

Unsatisfied Need Recognition

The purchase decision process starts when the customer recognizes an **unsatisfied need.** An unsatisfied need creates tension, which is a problem for the person. The need may be triggered by any number of stimuli. A physical drive may be aroused by our internal senses; that is, hunger, thirst, sex, or pain avoidance drives may give rise to tension. The tension may also arise because of social stimuli such as the observation of a friend's purchase or a suggestion by someone that we would look good in a new style of sweater. Commercial stimuli can also create this tension. This occurs because of some action by a seller. It may range from a display of exciting new fall fashions or a sign in front of the store to a newspaper advertisement or elaborate TV commercial.

Quite often, a customer will walk into your store with a general need in mind, but be unsure of the nature of the need or how to satisfy it. Even though customers may know what wants are important to them, they may still have a difficult time making the necessary attribute trade-offs to determine a single product choice. For example, if someone is looking at winter coats, we should not assume it is because they do not already have one and want to keep from being cold. A coat purchase may satisfy one or more of the eight basic needs, such as personal comfort, personal attractiveness, or social approval. The responsibility of the sales associate is to help the customer determine which of these needs is strongest or the most important. This step must be undertaken first because the information that the customer will need to make a decision will be quite different under the various need options. If **personal comfort** is the need being satisfied, then fit, warmth, waterproofing, or ease of closure may be important. If **social approval** is identified as the need, then the customer will want to know about current fashion trends and expectations for the next season's lines.

Search for Information and Identification of Alternatives

Some customers take a longer or shorter time to make a purchase decision depending on their previous experience with the product, the complexity of the product, the price, or the buying situation. These individuals desire to reduce their level of uncertainty to a manageable level. The source, kind, and degree of this uncertainty are evaluated and weighed against the strength of the stimuli that aroused the need. The source of uncertainty may arise from choices of products and/or brands, places of purchase, or methods of purchase. The degree of uncertainty is determined by the likelihood of making a wrong purchasing decision. The buyer knows that making a wrong decision may be worse than making no purchase at all. To resolve these uncertainties, the buyer searches for information before making the decision.

Once a person recognizes that a specific need exists and believes that purchasing a product or service will satisfy that need, then he or she must discover and evaluate the alternatives. At the most fundamental level, customers will **search** their memory **for information** they already know about the product, services, brands, or store alternatives. This memory search may reveal that the item they bought previously was satisfactory, and the person may make a routine purchase this time. This type of decision-making process is frequently used with most convenience goods or other regularly purchased items.

In other situations, however, a person will be uncertain of the alternatives available or the best course of action to take. He or she will need much additional information. At this point, it is the responsibility of the retailer to provide the appropriate information to the customer. In fact, if one retailer does not supply the needed information, the customer is likely to go to another. Customers will search for information until they believe they can comfortably make a decision. Only with adequate information will the customer be able to reduce uncertainty about the product, brand, or store to an acceptable level and move closer to a purchase decision.

The buyer has many information sources. Friends, product labels, advertising, and in-store sales personnel are but a few of the sources that a buyer may use. Even if the buyer already knows a great deal about the product category, he or she may seek additional information about brands, features, prices, service, and seller. Information on location, hours of operation, return policies, and services may be gathered for one or more stores. Additional information about the buyer's current financial situation may also be needed. For example, in the case of major purchases like automobiles or appliances, the buyer may ask, "How much money do I have or can I borrow?" If two different needs with two different purchase outcomes are present, but there is only enough money for one or the other, the buyer must ask, "Which need would I rather satisfy?" As the buyer collects information on all of these issues, the amount of uncertainty surrounding the decision will begin to decrease. Typically, the buyer will continue to collect information until he or she is satisfied that the risk of purchase is within their personal range of acceptance.

Alternative Evaluation

When the customer has collected enough information to feel comfortable, he or she will examine the **alternative** retail solutions to the problem. The buyer must compare factors such as product, brand, price, store, service contract, guarantee, credit, and delivery. As they arrive at their final choice, customers will form some ranking of preference among each alternative. At this point, the buyer can select from among the alternatives, seek additional information, or delay the purchase until more alternatives are discovered. Usually, however, the customer will form a purchase intention for the preferred choice and move toward making a purchasing decision. It is frequently the role of the sales associate to help the customer arrive at a satisfactory decision.

Purchase Decision

If nothing interferes with the purchase intention established in the previous step, the person must engage in an action that leads to the exchange of money for the good or service. Often, the purchase intention includes only a decision about the choice of good or service. The purchasing decision process may have to be repeated to determine the choice of a store, price to be paid, and terms of purchase.

Postpurchase Behavior

Almost every decision carries with it the possibility of some dissatisfaction or doubt. This negative feeling is called **cognitive dissonance,** and it describes the tension that results from holding two conflicting ideas or beliefs at the same time. More specifically, cognitive dissonance refers to the negative feelings that can occur after a commitment to purchase has been made. Cognitive dissonance, per se, is not unusual. Many of us have brief doubts about purchases. If this doubt is strong and persistent, purchase dissatisfaction will occur. For example, if the decision was important or the choices were unclear, the chance of cognitive dissonance is high.

After the purchase is made and the customer begins to use the product, he or she will start to develop attitudes about it. The buyer may, at this point, begin a critical reevaluation of the decision. In fact, the buyer may even look for ways to obtain postdecision reinforcement by seeking additional information to confirm the wisdom of the purchase decision. Retailers must be prepared to follow up with their customers after the sale when items are expensive, are difficult to use, or may affect the social status of the purchaser. Thank you cards are frequently used by retailers as a follow-up to high-ticket purchases. The key point to be made here is that you should expect your customers to have "second thoughts." If they call you to ask questions or even to make a minor complaint, it is likely that they just want some additional reinforcement. You should not avoid these people, and their calls should be returned by the salesperson promptly!

Retailers need to plan strategies to reduce the chance of negative outcomes. A "satisfaction guaranteed" policy may reduce dissonance because customers who know they can reverse a decision within, say, thirty days after a purchase will not worry about it as much. This assurance will give you and your customer the time needed to learn how to use the product and to realize its full benefits.

Decision Feedback

Decision feedback is the phenomenon by which information arising from making a previous purchase or using the product or service becomes input for subsequent purchase behavior. Throughout the decision-making process, the buyer records and stores information that may change motives, attitudes, and perceptions about the product or the retailer. This decision feedback process will influence the decision-making process the next time a similar need arises. In fact, the feedback received from a single purchase may be such that the overall satisfaction with the store will motivate the customer to return there the next time a similar need arises.

Involvement in the Decision Process

Earlier, we mentioned that customers sought information about products, services, and store options until they reduced their uncertainty to a manageable level. We use the term **involvement** to capture the extent to which customers engage in decision-making activities prior to purchase. The extent of buyer involvement at each stage of the purchase decision process may be at any of three different levels: routine-involvement responses, limited-involvement problem solving, and extensive-involvement problem solving.

Routine-Involvement Responses

In many situations, customers buy primarily from habit. Essentially, they move instantaneously through the decision stages. This occurs when customers have few uncertainties because of experience. The items are usually low-cost and regularly purchased. The customer has experience with the product and brand, has a known and acceptable price range, and is familiar with the choices for place of purchase. An example of a **routine-involvement response** would be purchasing a candy bar.

Because of the many purchasing decisions we have to make as customers, we often seek to avoid giving a lot of thought, time, and effort to the selection of many products we use regularly. This is a favorable form of behavior for your customers if you or your brands or your services are being patronized. On the other hand, if you are a competitor of the store being patronized or brand being routinely purchased, you must make a special effort in terms of price, promotion, or display to get customers engaged in more complex decision processes and possibly switch stores or brands.

Limited-Involvement Problem Solving

When customers have somewhat limited experiences, or the product is more expensive or purchased less frequently, buyers move toward **limited-involvement problem solving.** In this case, they still go through each stage of the decision process but with more effort. They do not need to spend a great deal of time in each stage because they are generally familiar with the product class and the major alternatives. Customers may seek or utilize information about new brands they have heard about. They may be aware that a new line is available or that the market has become more competitive, and they are not sure which store has the best price and so are willing to spend some time shopping.

This is the level of involvement for customers when they break their shopping routine and stop engaging in routine-involvement responses. At this point, they will collect more information about stores they have not patronized. If you are the store that the customers are thinking of leaving, you need a strategy to retain them at this stage. When customers are at this level of problem solving, you want to make sure that your store, your brands, or your services are considered. An example of a purchase requiring limited-involvement problem solving would be buying a television set or car tires.

Extensive-Involvement Problem Solving

Customers engage in **extensive-involvement problem solving** when they are considering new or very infrequently purchased products, when they are not familiar with sources for a product, or when the product is very expensive. Time will be spent searching for information and evaluating it. Uncertainties about brand alternatives, price, service, performance, and choice of store cause customers to be very careful and take time to make a deliberate decision. Major purchases and specialty goods often fall into this category. Personal selling at the store level is often found to be quite important when customers are spending extensive amounts of effort to make comparisons prior to a decision. While repurchase rates of a single customer may be slower with goods purchased in this way, do not underestimate the value of referrals. The lifetime value of these customers must include the value of their referrals and complementary purchases. An example of a decision that often requires extensive-involvement problem solving is buying a car.

THE GLOBAL CONSUMER

Global consumers are extremely important to understand as they have diverse needs and wants, and marketing plans and products need to be differentiated to meet these needs.

Enormous differences exist among consumers throughout the world. These differences are related to language, age, income, as well as the physical and political environment and culture.

Media and communications are changing the nature of consumer demand. Around the world, people are being exposed to the same messages, concepts, and ideas, whether in movies, television, advertising, video games, news, or music.

Programs first shown on American television receive high ratings around the world, as does network programming such as MTV, CNN, and BBC. Consumers throughout the world are being exposed to many of the same fashions and product choices, raising their awareness and desire. This is an important factor in the continuing development of global retail formats and brands. Computer networks—like InternetMCI, Prodigy, and America Online—create instant global communication.

As media becomes global, the influence of foreign brands and images is readily apparent. Brands like Pizza Hut, McDonald's, Burger King, and Giorgio Armani are catching on. For example, in the Czech Republic, satellite television arrived in the early part of 1993, bringing with it an advertising jingle for Fruit of the Loom. Walking down the streets of Prague, one can hear young people singing the tune.

All of these factors are combining to help create homogeneous worldwide consumer groups. Let's look at just four possible global consumer groups and how retailers are now reaching them, and could reach them in the future.

The "Carriage Trade"

The so-called carriage trade consumer segment refers to very financially well-to-do consumers. Many retailers (like Saks Fifth Avenue in Mexico and Barney's New York in Japan) have recognized that affluent customers travel frequently, are willing to seek out and pay for quality, and have a tremendous appetite for new products, services, and retail formats. They constitute one of the most homogeneous lifestyle segments.

The Only Child

In some countries many parents have opted to have only one child. Families spend a disproportionate amount of money on these children. They are responding to the child's demand for toys, consumer electronics, compact discs, video games, and trendy clothing, with the same styles popular throughout the world.

Toys 'R' Us has already capitalized on this in numerous international markets with broad but locally tailored assortments and value pricing.

"Emerging Middle Class"

In countries like Argentina, the Republic of Korea, Mexico, Turkey, and India, a sizable middle class is beginning to develop. These middle-class consumers are demanding many of the same basic goods and services that Americans and Western Europeans take for granted, such as apparel, household items, health and beauty aids, appliances, and consumer electronics. These consumers are willing to pay a premium for what they perceive to be high-quality, high-status products.

However, when it comes to basics, these consumers are extremely value-conscious. This characteristic will provide opportunities for the further development of traditional and limited-line discount retailers as well as category dominant formats. Department stores that combine many categories of "necessities" under one roof and offer brands at "value" prices will also do well.

Two-Income Families

In developed countries the labor force participation of women is relatively high: over 40 percent. Labor force participation of women is also high in some developing countries, such as the Republic of Korea, and is growing rapidly in Brazil and Argentina.

Two-income families represent an important segment for convenience-oriented, time-saving products, such as convenience foods, easy-to-use home appliances, and services such as child care and home care, regardless of the country where they live. This segment will demand more convenient store formats and longer operating hours.

Implications for Global Retailers

Despite the existence of groups such as those just described, no truly global consumer exists. Striking differences remain between consumers even in neighboring countries, where ethnicity is often an issue.

However, there are striking similarities around the globe. Consumers worldwide are under significant financial pressure—in developing markets like China and Brazil, as well as in developed markets like the United States, Japan, and Germany. "Value" is taking on new meaning. Discount formats, unheard of in Japan a decade ago, are developing rapidly, while in Europe limited-line discount formats are becoming commonplace.

Value-oriented formats like Toys 'R' Us and Staples (office products) benefit directly from this trend, but all retailers must take it into consideration. Twenty-first century global retailers must carefully design each element of their strategy—image, positioning, assortment, service, ambience, the channel of distribution, and price.

TCBY—REVISITED: EXPANDING THE CUSTOMER BASE

Companies in the frozen yogurt business see expansion of the market as a more logical strategy than trying to take market share from each other. There is a proliferation of brands and flavors that vary widely in calorie and fat content. The hope is that a continued emphasis on the healthful aspects of frozen yogurt will appeal to customers who count grams of fat and calories, while flavors such as caramel pecan and french silk chocolate will bring new customers into the market, particularly ice cream addicts, who are seeking a slightly lower fat content.[20]

TCBY is also seeking to expand the total market by looking outside the United States. The company has international licenses for stores in more than thirty countries including China, Korea, and Egypt. The company's licensees plan to open an additional fifty-two outlets in the Middle East alone by 1998. Countries include Bahrain, Kuwait, Qatar, Saudi Arabia, and the United Arab Emirates, in addition to Egypt. Hartsell Wingfield, president of TCBY's international division, said that "initial sales of frozen yogurt in the region have exceeded all expectations."[21] NAFTA, the North American Free Trade Agreement, has allowed significant expansion of TCBY franchisees in Mexico.

The company had about twenty stores when NAFTA was passed. The agreement ends a 20 percent import duty on yogurt that the company ships to Mexico from its Dallas facility. The hope is that in addition to lower tariffs, and therefore lower prices, NAFTA will also mean a Mexican middle class that likes American products and will have more income to buy them.[22] Devaluation of the peso and a difficult economy have slowed Mexico's expansion.

1. In analyzing international markets, what problems do you think might be associated with gaining information necessary to understand customers and focus on their satisfaction?
2. What changes do you think a local TCBY franchisee might need to make to be successful in Middle East or Mexican markets?
3. How would you seek to appeal to customers who really prefer the rich taste and texture of ice cream and have not tried yogurt?

Summary

The ability of a retailer to accurately match the needs of consumers with the information, goods, and services that it offers is dependent on how well the retailer knows the customers and their needs. The future financial well-being of the retailer relies on its capacity to satisfy customer needs over the long term.

Needs are the basic underlying motivations that move people to action. Maslow's hierarchy of needs is essentially the same for everyone in a similar environment; however, needs are satisfied in different ways by different people, and some needs will be more important to some people. Primary motives are basic needs that are desired most often and with the greatest intensity by individuals. Secondary motives also influence consumer behavior. Each of these needs influences what retail products the consumer is interested in and how that consumer will shop for that product. Patronage motives, such as price/value or location, direct the consumer's choice of retail store.

Consumer learning occurs when a specific want or need is satisfied by a retail response. Attitudes and opinions are normally formed during the learning process.

Consumers go through various stages before finally deciding on whether to buy a product. The normal stages a buyer will go through are problem recognition, alternative recognition and information search, alternative evaluation, the purchase decision, postpurchase evaluation and decision feedback. It is important for the retailer to understand which stage in the process the consumer is at and what actions are required by the retailer to move the customer farther along in the process.

The amount of involvement of the consumer in the decision process depends on the product and the information requirements of the consumer. Involvement can range from routine to limited to extensive.

Furthermore, changes in the U.S. market have driven many retailers to alter what products they offer and how those products are offered. Population growth, geographic distribution, multicultural diversity, and changes in family structure alter our need for goods and services now and in the future.

With many retailers expanding globally, the similarities and differences that exist in the global market must be addressed in terms of products and services offered. The emergence of an international media has helped to create global consumer markets that are similar in nature. The major underlying principle for both national and international retailers is to know your customers and their needs.

KEY TERMS AND CONCEPTS

Alternative evaluation, 153

Attention, 131

Attitudes, 131

Basic needs, 126

Benefits, 136

Cognitive dissonance, 154

Cues, 130

Culture, 147

Customer satisfaction, 121

Decision feedback, 154

Discretionary income, 145

Disposable income, 145

Extensive-involvement problem solving, 156

How to buy, 151

Involvement, 155

Learning, 130

Lifestyle, 132

Lifetime value, 122

Limited-involvement problem solving, 155

Market segment, 122

Market segmentation, 122

Maslow's hierarchy of needs, 124

Needs, 124

Opinions, 131

Patronage motives, 130

Perception, 131

Personal comfort, 152

Personal gross income, 145

Postpurchase behavior, 154

Psychic income, 145

Purchase decision, 150

Real income, 145

Reference group, 147

Reinforcement, 130

Response, 130

Routine-involvement responses, 155

Search for information and/or alternatives, 152

Secondary motives, 129

Selective attention, 131

Social approval, 152

Unsatisfied need recognition, 151

Wants, 124

What to buy, 150

When to buy, 151

Where to buy, 150

QUESTIONS

1. What different motives might influence your choice of a restaurant?

2. What information sources might be used to reduce each of the following uncertainties?
   a. Fear of product failure
   b. Peer group approval
   c. Product quality
   d. Store reputation

3. Why do you think some people develop strong brand loyalties and others do not?

4. How would a computer retailing superstore such as CompUSA determine the lifetime value of a customer?

5. What are the eight basic needs as presented by Hattwick?

6. What are the decisions a customer makes in the purchase process?

7. What are some causes of postpurchase cognitive dissonance?

8. Explain why two families of the same size and with the same income might spend substantially different amounts of money on recreation and choose different types of recreation. Would stages in the family life cycle be important? If so, in what way? Would social class be important? Why or why not?

9. Has rising educational attainment influenced buying habits? Why or why not?

SITUATIONS

1. You are the head chef of a restaurant chain. How would your clientele's basic needs affect your selection of menu items? Describe three age groups and develop a menu for each.

2. Kimberly has just started her new job as assistant sales manager at Friendly Computers. Her first task is to design a program for her sales representatives that will help them overcome customers' postpurchase anxiety. What recommendations would you make to Kimberly?

3. Amanda Christine has just transferred from Billings, Montana, where she was the assistant manager of a sporting goods store that specialized in sports equipment and sports attire for women and girls. She is now the manager of a new store in Dallas, Texas. How should Amanda go about identifying the needs and wants of her targeted customers: sports-minded women and girls in Dallas and its suburbs?

4. Kenneth Henry is a recent marketing graduate from a state university. He is taking over the family business, a wallpaper store. How can he get potential wallpaper customers to engage in more complex decision processes and consider his store as a potential source that would satisfy their wallpaper needs?

CASES

CASE 4A
Highland Shores Fitness Center[23]

Kelly Mitchell has been charged with developing the marketing program for Highland Shores Athletic Club, a fitness center in an Atlanta suburb.

Most of the residents of Highland Shores are young to middle-aged professionals. The population of Highland Shores includes physicians, attorneys, dentists, airline pilots, and so forth. The price of homes in Highland Shores begins at approximately $250,000 and can cost over $1 million. The majority of households in Highland Shores are single-income households where one of the spouses remains at home to care for children.

Kelly believes he should identify the needs of his target market and prioritize those needs. If you were to assist him, how do you perceive the needs of the Highland Shores residents?

1. *How should Kelly position his fitness center in light of the demographic characteristics of the residents of Highland Shores?*

CASE 4B
"Eldermall"[24]

Recent research sponsored by the International Council of Shopping Centers Educational Foundation studied the shopping habits and preferences of consumers over the age of fifty-five. There were a number of important findings.

Most customers said that they want to feel comfortable in the mall and wanted a map or directory at major entrances. Color coding of levels was considered helpful along with comfortable and numerous benches or rest areas. Lack of security in mall areas was listed as a concern. A considerable number of those surveyed would like the mall to look like yesterday's downtown.

Most felt that downtown shopping had an element of class to it that mall shopping today does not possess.

Many of the respondents felt that today's mall was geared toward younger shoppers. However, those surveyed wanted a mall that represented all ages, not just the older or younger population. Older shoppers in general wanted more specialty retailers and dress shops, but not expensive boutiques.

Most of the older consumers remembered the close relationships they had with salesclerks in the downtown stores, where the staff knew their names, sizes, and what styles they liked. Most older shoppers did not like stores that were too crowded with merchandise or people. In general, they want good quality and service and are willing to pay for it.

Older customers spend a considerable amount of time at the mall shopping. About 40 percent of those surveyed spent over two hours at the mall, and 53 percent spent one to two hours shopping at the mall per visit. Women spent significantly more time at the mall than men. In general, the shoppers went to the mall once a week and spent an average of $80 per visit.

1. *What does the above information tell you about the shopping habits and motivation of older customers?*

2. *You are the manager of a local neighborhood mall. The demographics show that over 40 percent of your market will be over the age of fifty-five within a few years. On the basis of the above information, what changes would you recommend for the mall? What types of stores or services would you recommend? Be specific.*

CASE 4C
Tourists in the West Edmonton Mall

If you attend an International Council of Shopping Centers (ICSC) annual meeting, you can be sure that the developers will be talking about creating a total entertainment experience when they build or remodel a shopping mall. For years most developers and retailers have thought of malls as places where people shop for goods and services. In Edmonton, Canada, the people who developed the West Edmonton Mall had a different view. They saw it as a place where people could stop, be entertained, be amused, and be educated and where they could have every basic necessity of life taken care of in a climate-perfect environment. That vision has resulted in the biggest complex of its type in the world with 5.2 million square feet—the size of 115 football fields.

West Edmonton Mall includes over 800 retail stores with 11 major department stores, over 150 restaurants and kiosks, an amusement park with 25 rides, a 7-acre waterpark, an NHL-size ice arena, 4 seaworthy submarines, an exact replica of the Santa Maria ship, a dolphin show, world-class aquarium facilities, an aviary, a 360-room hotel, a miniature golf course, 19 movie theaters, a casino, original art and sculptures, 58 entrances, and parking for 20,000 vehicles.

A woman traveling with her boyfriend stood in amazement pointing at the Mindbender Roller Coaster and stammered, "This is not at all what I expected." Like many people who come to West Edmonton Mall for the first time, she had imag-ined it to be a big shopping mall with a lot of stores. "I had to keep my eyes closed all the time," she said, adding "I can handle most roller coasters, but I don't know if I can do this one again!"

By night, at a country bar on Bourbon Street, patrons line up at a barrel to fill their baskets with peanuts in the shell; the shells are discarded on the floor. Steak and kidney pie, West Coast salmon, and blackened Cajun snapper will be washed down with British ale and fine wines along Bourbon Street on just about any night. Others will choose a trusty and familiar hamburger, hot dog, or slice of pizza in one of the two food courts.

One merchant said that the traffic in the mall, 2 million people a month during the summer, justified the rents that he estimated at more than $60 per square foot for a smaller retailer. Rents for restaurants and coffee shops near the ice palace exceed the $100 level.

1. *How might the idea of shopping as part of an entertainment experience be explained by what you know about consumer behavior?*

2. *The "Mall of America" built in 1992 in Minneapolis, Minnesota, rivals the West Edmonton Mall in size (4.3 million square feet) and entertainment options. If you were one of the owners or managers of the West Edmonton Mall, how might you attempt to differentiate your mall and continue to attract large numbers of Americans and other international visitors?*

Chapter Goals

After reading the chapter, you should be able to:

- Realize why retailers engage in research.
- Understand the steps in the research process.
- Describe how to select a research design.
- Explain how to locate and use secondary information.
- Know the different methodologies available to collect primary data.
- Guide a retailing problem through the research process.

CUSTOMER INFORMATION FROM RESEARCH

THE BODY SHOP INTERNATIONAL PLC: COMPETING WITH VALUE AND INFORMATION

In 1976, Anita Roddick opened a small shop in Brighton on England's south coast, selling twenty-five naturally based skin and hair care preparations. Today, The Body Shop is a manufacturer and retailer of a wide range of innovative, high-quality hair, skin, and color cosmetic products, trading in over 1,300 branches in 45 countries throughout the Americas, Europe, and Asia.

But The Body Shop is not just a retailer or manufacturer in the traditional sense. Its management focuses on a strategy of improving society and the environment: It actively attempts to minimize the company's impact on the environment, promotes fair trading relationships with communities in need, is against animal testing in the cosmetics industry, champions human rights initiatives by embracing issues that are close to its heart, and encourages education, awareness, and involvement among staff and customers. According to Bombay Company's Robert Nourse, The Body Shop goes further than any other retailer in returning something to its source communities and in making that the foundation of its marketing strategy.[1]

The Body Shop sells through company-operated and franchise retail stores that are small, but elegant, and full of bright colors anchored by the company's signature shade of green. As a merchandiser, The Body Shop displays its products in much the same manner as upscale department stores. However, the company also provides a great deal of additional information, both printed and through salespeople.

The sales staff are trained on various aspects of each product, including the ingredients. They acquaint customers with the environmental aspects of the products, as well as the company's minimal use of disposable packaging and its "against animal testing" policy. The Body Shop does not test its products or ingredients on animals, nor does it commission others to do so. The company actively supports an end to such tests worldwide and is at the forefront of the campaign to achieve that goal. Its employees run in-store campaigns and lobby governments and official bodies.

In two short decades, The Body Shop has grown from a sharply focused niche market of customers in Britain concerned with environmental and animal rights issues to a more mainstream global market. This expansion is due to its concentration on a market trend that has continually expanded as consumers have begun to believe in the need to protect the environment while also demanding consumer friendly products.

The Body Shop has served its market by providing consistently high-quality goods that promote environmental and social concerns. It has been extremely successful in communicating its values to both the public and its employees. This competitive strategy has paid off as customers have become more educated about the norms for manufacturing and testing in the cosmetics industry and how The Body Shop differs in principles

and practice. Expansion and earnings are expected to increase for many years to come.[2]

The Body Shop competes in an industry that is dominated by strategies of discounting, price promotions, and other margin giveaways. Instead of mindlessly following the industry trend, The Body Shop has concentrated on a value and information strategy. The prices of The Body Shop's goods are relatively high, but the company maintains that few manufacturers can match its quality at that price. Management has been concentrating on developing more efficient operations. It has restructured product lines to improve turnover, increase transaction size, and encourage repeat buying. It has also expanded the market for specific products by encouraging customers to sample and experiment with new items in the store.

1. **How does a relatively high-priced retailer, such as The Body Shop, survive and prosper in the globally competitive cosmetics industry?**
2. **What research questions would help The Body Shop as it further expands its business?**

INTRODUCTION

Managers must increasingly rely on research information for help in making intelligent decisions. Regularly needed information is provided through the store's electronic data processing system. However, good management decisions also benefit from information that must be sought out to answer specific questions. Much of this information is obtained through marketing research. We will examine retailing problems requiring marketing research and explore how to approach the research process.

The large chain organizations can afford full-time, trained employees to conduct research projects. However, the small and medium-sized retailer should not neglect the opportunity to improve operations through decisions based on research. Information in this chapter on how to design and implement these projects can produce significant benefits in customer satisfaction and service and overall better management for all retailers.

PROBLEMS THAT REQUIRE RESEARCH

The problems that require information inputs from marketing research are numerous and varied. (See Box 5.1.) One of the most common uses of research is to conduct a market analysis. For the store, a market analysis would include profiles of customer characteristics discussed in Chapter 4. Because

BOX 5.1 RETAILERS USE OF RESEARCH INFORMATION

1. Research on markets
   a. Analyzing market potentials for products
   b. Sales forecasting
   c. Characteristics of product markets
   d. Analyzing sales potentials
   e. Studying trends in markets
   f. Research on customer characteristics, attitudes, and desires

2. Research on products
   a. Customer acceptance of proposed new products
   b. Comparative studies of competitive products
   c. Studying customer dissatisfaction with products
   d. Product-line research

3. Research on promotion
   a. Evaluating advertising effectiveness
   b. Analyzing advertising and selling practices
   c. Selecting advertising media
   d. Motivational studies
   e. Evaluating present and proposed sales methods
   f. Analyzing salesperson effectiveness
   g. Establishing sales quotas

4. Research on distribution
   a. Location and design of stores
   b. Handling and packing merchandise
   c. Cost analysis of transportation methods
   d. Supply and storage requirements

5. Research on pricing
   a. Studying competitive pricing
   b. Demand elasticities
   c. Perceived prices
   d. Cost analysis
   e. Margin analysis

6543217

retailers more and more are trying to understand consumer behavior, market analyses increasingly emphasize customer buying habits and motives.

Research is also needed to provide information for merchandise planning, development, and evaluation. Understanding the needs of the market provides the input necessary for new product ideas, such as adding or deleting a line. Every store should know how a suggested product contributes to the total offering of the store in terms of both image and profitability. Information from customers may be needed to develop warranty plans, package designs, and service offerings. Advertising and pricing policies may depend on the results of product or service image studies. *Discount Store News* reported on research conducted by Lisa Frank Inc. that studied children as consumers. The value of the study can be seen in the suggestions it made for retailers.

> Merchandise should be colorful, exciting and well-coordinated. Child-safe fixtures and height-appropriate presentation should be considered. Special classes or demonstrations that inform kids about product benefits and how to get the most for one's money would be especially appreciated. A special kids' section should include food, music, and age-specific merchandise and hands-on demonstrations. Events should be planned around times when kids receive additional spending money.[2a]

Communications analyses are almost as frequent as market analyses. A market analysis that yields profiles of customers may serve as the basis for determining the theme and content of advertising and sales messages. Media-audience studies ensure that the medium being considered delivers an audience that matches the profile of the target market. Content analyses of broad-

Customer research has revealed that families want shopping to be fun. PetsMart is one firm that has positioned itself around this concept. Owners are encouraged to bring their pets to the store. The trip provides a special social experience for the animals as well as the children or adult owners. The store has grooming facilities where owners can watch their pet get a bath, cut, and curl.

cast programming and printed media help a store choose a medium that projects the desired image. Measuring the results of advertising, sales promotion, and personal selling programs is another vital area of communications analysis.

In talking about research we will frequently use the terms *primary research* and *secondary research*. Primary research is that which involves collecting original data to answer a specific problem. For example, a bank trying to develop new products and services that would appeal to its upscale customers might use a detailed questionnaire to test retail customer preferences and decision factors relating to the customers' banking relationships.[3] Secondary research involves using data and information that are already collected for a purpose other than solving the particular problem at hand. For instance, a bank may purchase the "connect lists" of names from the utility company. Since a bank change is often associated with an address change, the bank tailors its new product offering to those customers.

Types of Investigations

Two types of investigations are carried out by retailers—applied research and fact gathering. **Applied research** refers to the application of basic principles and other existing knowledge to the solution of problems. Common examples are finding causes of declining sales or poor morale of salespeople, evaluating various promotion alternatives, or making site selections. In applied research, the investigator generally has a tentative problem condition identified, and the job is to gather data that will provide insight into the solution of this problem. **Fact gathering** differs from applied research in that the researcher's task is merely one of gathering data. For instance, in order to decide whether or not to send a technician to school, the manager of Acme Television may want to know how many households in Omaha have satellite signal receiving systems. Knowing the number of such systems and the manufacturer's estimates of repair frequency would answer the question. The task here is merely one of collecting this information.

Thus, the type of research assigned determines which activities must be performed by the researcher. In fact-gathering studies, the direction and nature of the study have already been chosen. In applied or problem-solving research, general direction for the study has been designated for the researcher.

THE RESEARCH PROCESS

The **research process** includes a number of steps: (1) situation analysis, (2) preliminary investigation, (3) defining specific objectives, (4) developing the research design, (5) searching for secondary data, (6) selecting a methodology to collect primary data, (7) analyzing and interpreting the data, and finally (8) presenting the findings. Ignoring any of these steps commonly leads to research that is incomplete or does not fit the problem that is being examined. Figure 5.1 diagrams the steps involved in the research process.

Situation Analysis

The situation analysis identifies the activities undertaken to narrow a broad subject area down to one that lends itself to research. It is necessary when the researcher feels uncomfortable with the breadth of the assignment or feels that the identified problem may not be the central issue. Then it is necessary

Steps in the
research process.

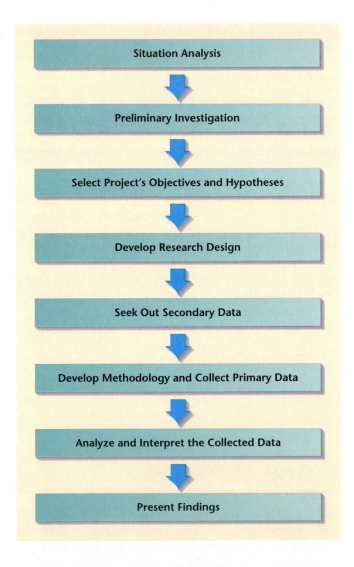

to analyze the total situation before choosing the specific direction of the research.

A situation analysis may involve examination of the general economic condition, new competitors, and competitors' retailing activities, as well as each element of the store's own activities. For example, the store manager at Ronda's Bike-O-Rama may say to the researcher: "Bicycle sales have fallen drastically because our price lines are too high. We need data that will shed light on what is a more effective price." Actually, the decline in sales may have been caused by any number of factors—poor product quality, competitors' actions, poor personal selling, and so on. Research dealing solely with price would not provide the data needed to overcome the real problem.

Preliminary Investigation

Out of the initial situation analysis, a tentative problem will emerge. The researcher identifies the general subject matter of the research. Conducting a preliminary investigation may take the form of a review of the general topic through unstructured interviews with customers or employees; a review of literature in trade journals, popular press, and academic journals; and gathering secondary data. The intent of this investigation is to obtain a generalized knowledge base from which to start. For example, if the problem was an incomplete understanding of the buying patterns of potential customers, an appropriate objective would be to conduct a behavioral market analysis.

Project Objectives and Hypotheses

After the preliminary investigation has been completed, the researcher is ready to select the specific objectives of the study. An effective tool for guiding a research project is the establishment of *hypotheses,* tentative statements describing relationships among concepts or possible cause-and-effect relationships. These statements reflect a belief about real-world relationships, but they must be supported or rejected based on evidence gathered from the research effort. For example, one hypothesis might be that "more than 60 percent of the potential shoppers at Ronda's Bike-O-Rama, as determined by the expression of a favorable store image, are less than forty years of age." Notice the direction this hypothesis gives the researcher. Information must be obtained from potential buyers (not present buyers) about the image of the store, and age data must be collected.

Developing the Research Design

The heart of research is the **research design,** the overall plan that determines information needed and that specifies how the investigation to obtain it will be conducted. A complete research design would include five elements: (1) a statement of the evidence necessary to solve a problem and the basic methods whereby the solutions will become revealed or validated, (2) specification of the evidence—where and how it will be obtained, (3) anticipation of how the data will be analyzed to produce answers to the problem, (4) guidelines for the calculation and approval of the feasibility and cost of the project, and (5) a plan to guide the implementation of the project.[4]

A major purpose of the research design is to provide the researcher with a blueprint of the research process, which will provide better insight into the potential costs and time commitments associated with the project. The next step in the research process is to collect the necessary data. This process may involve secondary or primary data collection methods, which are discussed later in the chapter.

Analysis and Interpretation

Once the data have been gathered, the task of analysis and interpretation begins. Analysis and interpretation involve putting the data into a form that is applicable to the study's objectives and is also useful to those who apply the research findings. Box 5.2 presents the findings of a study that requires management action.

BOX 5.2 **AN ETHICAL DILEMMA: CUSTOMER PERCEPTIONS OF ETHICAL BEHAVIOR**

A supermarket chain in the Southwest commissioned a research firm to conduct a general study of customers' beliefs and ethical perceptions regarding various retailing practices.

Several of the findings surprised the management:

1. Minority customers, particularly Hispanics, believed the supermarket charged higher prices in low-income areas. They believed this to be highly unethical, much more so than whites.

2. Many customers believed that the supermarket hired part-time employees primarily to avoid paying fringe benefits. Most said this was unethical behavior.

3. Some of the customer segments seemed to believe they have been treated unethically by retailers in general. The study suggested that perceived or actual injustices in retail shopping experiences may cause consumers to view the adoption of unethical behavior on their part as acceptable.

4. The higher the income of the customer, the less likely they were to view a given retail practice as unethical.

Questions

How would you, as a manager for the supermarket chain, use the findings of this study? How much should a firm rely on research such as this? Do you see an ethical issue in charging higher prices in low-income areas, particularly if your cost of doing business is higher? How about hiring part-time workers if it reduces costs?

The data must be processed before a meaningful analysis can be carried out. This processing includes editing, coding, and tabulation. Editing involves preparing the data for tabulation and inspecting the data-gathering forms for accuracy, completeness, and consistency.

Raw data from a research study generally must be organized to give them meaning. During editing, but before coding and tabulating the data, categories must be established to subdivide the information, summarizing the results and providing the basis for statistical manipulation. For example, in a customer survey respondents may be grouped by characteristics such as age, income, occupation, number of children, geographical location, and so on.

Coding involves preparing individual answers for data entry. Data may be scanned if responses have been recorded on forms such as those used for multiple choice exams. Skilled data entry people can input data very quickly with today's computer software.

When data entry has been completed, the difficult task of analysis and interpretation begins. Analysis and interpretation involve the assembly of the data in a form that can be used to test the hypothesis. The methods by which data are to be analyzed should be specified as part of the research design.

Appropriate statistical methods help the researcher determine how well sample results reflect the characteristics of the entire population, whether significant differences exist among categories, and whether there are relationships between categories that will help explain differences. If the data are drawn from a sample, it is necessary to determine how close the sample results are likely to be to the actual characteristics of the population.

One of the most important phases of data analysis is the attempt to determine relationships that help explain differences. For example, if there are differences in the frequency of customer store visits, it may be important to know if these differences are associated with demographic or socioeconomic characteristics. Facts must be interpreted; they must be placed in the context of the research study, used to test the hypothesis, and compared to other known facts. What if a retailer discovered that 20 percent of the households with children less than six years of age shop at her store at least four times a year? This fact does not have much meaning until the question is asked: Is 20 percent more or less than she expected (hypothesized), and how does this compare with past results or competitors' performance?

Presentation of Findings

It is essential that research findings be reported in an organized manner appropriate for potential users. The report should include a brief summary of the key findings and a full explanation of the procedures, findings, and conclusions for that part of the audience interested in more detail.

We have looked briefly at the steps involved in the research process. We now return to a more specific look at the nature of secondary and primary data.

SECONDARY DATA

Secondary data provide information collected for some purpose other than to solve a current problem. It is information that already exists and can be obtained. There are many secondary sources available to retailers, inside and outside the firm. Government, trade and professional associations, and many private firms are valuable sources for secondary information.

Retail Uses of Secondary Data

Secondary data in retailing are used for (1) market identification, (2) customer purchasing patterns, (3) targeting advertising, (4) customer and vendor credit, (5) merchandise planning, (6) inventory control, (7) employee management, and (8) assisting other managerial decisions. The first four typically involve collecting data external to the store. The last four involve using information gathered within the store.

Most information-gathering efforts should begin with a search of secondary sources. The information used to solve a problem can often be found in secondary sources more quickly and inexpensively than from primary sources. Even when the secondary information does not solve the problem, the research results may refine the problem definition, suggest alternative solutions, and help plan the collection of primary data.

Although secondary information can be obtained quickly and at relatively low cost, it must be evaluated before use by the researcher. Because the data were gathered for some other purpose, they may provide valuable background information but not lead to a solution. The data must satisfy four criteria to be useful: They must be accessible, pertinent, accurate, and sufficient.

Accessibility.   Data have been gathered for many purposes in both private and public organizations. While almost all governmental data are readily accessible to the public, private data are often harder to obtain. Unfortunately, many of the data collected by private organizations are considered proprietary and therefore not released for public consumption.

Pertinence.   The data must be directly applicable to the identified problem. With the exception of standardized format data that the government collects, most data are collected for a specific purpose. While similarities to the original purpose may exist, the data may not include necessary variables to solve the problem at hand.

Accuracy.   Several distortions in the accuracy of secondary data are quite common. Among the most common of these are precision and bias distortions. The original collectors make the decision on what level to aggregate the data. For instance, if the data were broken down into customers less than sixty-two and those sixty-two or older, they may not be of much use to the retailer. You must also evaluate the integrity and bias of the data source. Whenever possible, the data should be obtained from the original source.

Sufficiency. It is not unusual to find much of the information that is needed to study a particular problem but still be unable to find a few of the necessary variables to solve the problem. For example, it is relatively easy to obtain aggregate data on the demographics of customers in a given area. However, if the research requires both demographic and behavioral variables, this information is insufficient to fulfill the researcher's needs. The information found can be accessible, pertinent, and accurate without being sufficient to answer the question of the researcher.

Where to Find Secondary Information

Many sources of information for retailing decisions are readily available in university and public libraries. A search for information in a published source should begin with the use of an indexing service. All of the indexes are available in electronic format for easy computer access. Many are available on the Internet through Prodigy, CompuServe, America Online, and MSN. Of the many such services, these four are among the most widely used by business students: *ABI/INFORM,* which contains abstracts and titles of journals on compact disk; *The Business Periodicals Index,* which covers the contents of general business magazines; *The Wall Street Journal* annual index, which lists articles that have appeared in the publication during the year; and *The Readers' Guide to Periodical Magazines,* which indexes general-interest magazines.

Trade publications. Much important information will be found in periodical trade publications covering almost every aspect of retailing. Examples of retailing publications are *Stores, The New York Retailer, Display World, Chain Store Age, Discount Merchandiser, Progressive Grocer, National Jeweler, Merchandising Weekly, Women's Wear Daily, Journal of Retailing, Supermarket News, Journal of Franchising, International Journal of Retail Distribution,* and *International Journal of Retailing and Consumer Services.*

Many of the trade periodicals devote one or more issues a year to statistical information. These issues provide up-to-date facts on industry sales, operating results, financial results, growth rates, and trends. Most trade associations gather and publish information on sales, costs, returns and allowances, expenses, profits, stock turnover rates, accounts receivable, bad debt losses, and the like. Check listings in the *Directory of National Trade and Professional Associations of the United States* and in the *Encyclopedia of Associations.*

Other secondary publications. The U.S. Government Printing Office is the world's largest publisher. Through the various government agencies, an unbelievable amount of information is available covering almost every conceivable topic. The three agencies that publish the most information directly

BOX

5.3 SUMMARY OF SELECTED SECONDARY INFORMATION PUBLICATIONS

1. *The Statistical Abstract of the United States* publishes annually a summary of statistics from all the census publications, as well as other important facts.

2. The *Census of Population* is published every ten years: Volume I contains general population, social, and economic characteristics; Volume II details cross-relationships on families, marital status, education, employment, occupation, income, and the like.

3. *Census Tract Reports* contain detailed information on population and housing, and the *County and City Data Book* summarizes statistics for small geographical areas.

4. The *Census of Housing* is published every ten years. Volume I includes detailed occupancy, structural, and financial characteristics of housing. Volume II contains cross-classifications of housing and household characteristics. Volume III details block statistics on plumbing, size, rent, value, and occupancy. Volume IV documents physical changes since the previous census for the metropolitan housing characteristics (Volume II).

5. The *Census of Retail Trade* has six volumes. Volumes I, III, and V summarize statistics for retail, wholesale, and selected service trades by geographic area. Volumes II, IV, and VI contain statistics organized by business for counties, cities, and standard metropolitan statistical areas. The service trade census provides data on receipts, employment, number of units, and organization.

6. The *Census of Business—Selected Services* contains special reports on selected businesses, including motion picture theaters, gasoline service stations, eating and drinking places, laundry and cleaning establishments, and travel agencies.

7. *County Business Patterns* has statistics on number of business units, employment, and payroll figures.

8. *The Survey of Current Business* regularly brings up to date over 2,500 statistical series.

9. The *Monthly Labor Review* reports current labor statistics, including employment, wages, labor turnover, and price indexes.

10. *The Federal Reserve Bulletin* is a monthly source of statistics on banking, government, business, real estate, and consumer finance. In addition, it provides data in such areas as savings, national product and income, department store sales, prices, and production.

6543217

related to the retailer are the Department of Commerce, the Bureau of the Census, and the Small Business Administration. The major guide to government documents is the *Monthly Catalog of United States Government Publications,* which provides a comprehensive list. Box 5.3 provides additional detail for selected secondary information publications.

The reports can provide valuable insight for retailers. One report notes that in about 6 percent of America's counties, nonwhite consumers are the majority of the population, and the minority population in this country is growing faster than the population as a whole.[5] The African-American population (30 million) constitutes 12 percent of the U.S. population and earns $262 billion a year. The Hispanic population (22.4 million) has a collective buying power of $180 billion. The report notes that these markets are fast-growing and are loyal customers for retailers who use a niche strategy to meet their unique needs.

SRDS publishes some seventeen source books which provide comprehensive media and marketing information needed by retailers to prepare and place advertising in the media, including coverage, costs, and timing. Four of the source books are of particular interest: *SRDS Interactive Advertising Source; SRDS TV & Cable Source; SRDS Radio Advertising Source;* and *SRDS Newspaper Advertising Source.* A sample page from *SRDS Newspaper Advertising Source* with information for the *Journal* in Ithaca, New York is illustrated in Figure 5.2.

FIGURE 5.2

Page from *SRDS Newspaper Advertising Source* with information for the Ithaca, New York *Journal*.

Sales and Marketing Management Survey of Buying Power contains population, income, and retail sales data for states, counties, metropolitan areas, and cities. A user's guide has examples of applications with research on buying trends which indicate that consumers with the same profiles buy similar quantity and quality products.

There are several potential sources of secondary data other than publications. The easiest to access are store data that have been collected at the point of purchase or for other research. Since this information has been gathered from a specific store or firm, it is often the most pertinent.

In-store data have both advantages and disadvantages. The major advantages are accessibility, cost, ease of collection, and pertinence. However, one of their finest assets, pertinence, is also a limitation. For instance, if questions arise concerning attracting new customers to the store or new stores, current data sets are limited because most of the information concerns current customers.

Information from other noncompetitors.

The second unpublished source of information involves other organizations, usually not direct competitors. Most firms routinely gather information on customers and trends. Several large and small firms are willing to sell these data to retailers, as long as they are not competitors. For instance, many credit card companies and magazines sell lists of their customers to retailers. These lists often include some basic demographic information such as age, income level, and marital status. However, more extensive information is often available. This can include credit or purchase information, which would be especially valuable to a specialized retailer.

Marketing research firms.

Finally, some companies survive solely by collecting and selling marketing information on everything from specific products to extensive customer lists. Companies such as A. C. Nielsen and Infotrac collect and sell data captured from point-of-purchase scanners. These companies can be invaluable sources of information for both manufacturers and retailers. Although sometimes expensive, these firms will often provide very specific data in a ready-to-use format. We now turn to a discussion of collecting primary data.

Marketing research firms can be used to carry out projects for both large and small retailers. Firms such as M/A/R/C hire college students to work in the evening making calls on behalf of their clients. Telephone surveys are an effective and relatively inexpensive way to gather data. The students must learn to handle the rejection that comes when people use verbal abuse and hang up in anger because they have been disturbed.

SELECTING A METHODOLOGY TO COLLECT PRIMARY DATA

Primary data can take two forms: those gathered through *survey/interviews* and those obtained through *observation*. Major changes have taken place in survey data collection in the past few years. Personal interviewing has declined because of the significant cost and difficulty of getting consumers to cooperate. Centralized facilities for large-scale telephone interviewing have become common and utilize computer-assisted telephone interviewing systems (CATI). Mall intercept interviewing has increased. Asking people to take a few minutes from their shopping time to answer questions, when they are probably closer psychologically to the behavior and attitudes associated with the questions, is more effective than interrupting them at meal or family time. Focus group interviewing has also been expanded. Bringing a small number of individuals together to be interviewed at the same time has the advantage of lower cost, and the individuals can react to ideas raised by other members of the group.[6]

Survey/Interview

Questioning respondents properly helps provide information about past, current, or intended behavior as well as data that may be associated with attitudes and opinions, or demographic and socioeconomic characteristics. Questioning or interviewing of respondents may be structured or unstructured, direct or indirect. If the questioning is to be structured, a formal questionnaire is prepared, with specific questions to be asked in a specific order. Structured questioning has the advantage of asking for the desired information in a systematic manner. Careful wording of questions helps avoid the possibility of ambiguities and misunderstandings. However, it is difficult for the retailer to get at motivational factors through structured questioning. If unstructured questioning is used, the wording of the questioning and the question order are adapted to each interview, the only guideline being the type of information desired. Unstructured questioning is more flexible and

Qualitative research utilizing focus groups depends on the researcher encouraging targeted discussion among group participants. Opinions Unlimited in Houston, Texas, employs the latest communication technology to enhance the research process. This discussion is being videoconferenced live to a client in another city. A note taker is using software designed to analyze the transcripts of a focus group by key words, respondent data, and discussion topics.

allows the interviewer to pursue the motive or cause behind an answer. With an unstructured format it may be difficult to cover all desired information areas, and more open-ended responses are sometimes difficult to interpret and tabulate.

In indirect questioning, the purpose for asking the questions is disguised and the questioning is often conducted with what are called *projective techniques.* Indirect interviews are most useful when the researcher wants to obtain information about deep-seated motivations or values. There are several commonly used projective techniques. A familiar one involves word association and sentence completion tests. Here a respondent is asked to give a spontaneous reaction to a word or sentence, which in turn tells the investigator something about how the respondent is thinking. One of the projective techniques that is used to accomplish this is the Cartoon Test. Cartoons depicting people and a problem such as illustrated in Figure 5.3 are used to gain information that may suggest additional research. The respondent is asked to assume the role of one of the persons in the situation and to describe what the person is doing or saying. In the Third Person technique, the respondent is asked for the opinions or views of a third person. This presumably allows the respondent to project his or her own opinions without feeling pressured to give an acceptable answer.

Another way to find out what the customer wants is through use of a consumer panel. Retailers of all sizes can organize a small group of customers who will be questioned on new products, styles, store policies, and other issues. For example, stores selling primarily to teenagers have successfully used panels of young people to keep management aware of their wishes. Unfortunately, consumers are not always able to provide objective evaluations of products, services, or stores. They may be in too much of a hurry to think over their answers, or they may want to be nice and say what they think the

FIGURE 5.3

The Cartoon Test is one of the many projective techniques that can be used by researchers to gain insight into consumers' attitudes and opinions.

This man has just told his wife that he has opened a charge account at the new sports megastore in town. What is she thinking?

_____

_____

_____

_____

Questioning customers is important if retailers are going to understand their changing needs and wants. The Age Wave Inc. research firm told *Discount Store News* (July 1995, p. 11) that "men tend to want clear, no nonsense, hassle-free shopping. Time savings is of the essence and items and signs need to be color-coded and well-organized. Mature women tend to enjoy the shopping experience, appreciate liberal merchandise exchange policies and money-back guarantees."

interviewer wants to hear. To guard against these problems, retailers should not rely solely on shopper interviews or questionnaires.

Mail surveys are particularly useful for structured direct questioning. Mail survey questionnaires are economical and make large samples possible. People are often more willing to report personal information, such as income, anonymously by mail rather than by telephone or in person. But mail surveys also have their limitations. One of their weaknesses is lack of personal communication, which can help explain misunderstandings and misinterpreted questions. In addition, the mail surveys are dependent on the individual's willingness to fill out and return the forms. Mail questionnaires generally need to be short and the questions must be very clear.

Telephone interviewing has the advantages of being quick and relatively inexpensive. Interviewers must be well trained to handle situations when respondents do not understand the questions. The list of questions must be short and the questions carefully worded.

Personal interviews may be used for any form of questioning. The more unstructured and/or indirect the questions, the more likely personal interviewing will be needed and the better trained the interviewers must be. Personal interviewing is slow and expensive, but it is often the only way to obtain complete, detailed information. Personal interviews can be conducted in several settings. One is to distribute a questionnaire to people as they shop in the store. An example of a questionnaire is illustrated in Figure 5.4. This questionnaire was handed to customers as they were intercepted in a mall. Do you see advantages in doing this? Disadvantages?

Observation

Observing the behavior of respondents is sometimes an excellent source of information. Furthermore, although it is often difficult for respondents to verbalize the reasons for their behavior, observation may demonstrate those reasons. Observational studies may also be undertaken simply to validate information obtained by questioning. If, for example, the research was concerned with a store layout, some of the most valuable information might be obtained by observing the movement of people in stores. Other counts (observations) might be used to determine peak selling days and peak time of day for sales and/or customer traffic.

FIGURE 5.4

A personal interview questionnaire to measure attitudes and behavior.

Fashion Mall

This is a customer profile study for the Fashion Mall. Through this study we hope to better know you, our customer, so that all the merchants in the mall can better serve your needs.

Thank you very much for your cooperation.

1. Male ____   Female ____

2. Stage in the family life cycle:
    _____ Single, not living at home.
    _____ Single, head of household.
    _____ Married, no children.
    _____ Married couple, with youngest child under six.
    _____ Married couple, with dependent children over six.
    _____ Married couple, with children living away from home. Household head in labor force.
    _____ Married couple, children living away from home. Household head retired.

3. My occupation: _____
    Spouse's occupation: _____

4. Family income bracket:
    _____ $10,000–$19,999
    _____ $20,000–$29,999
    _____ $30,000–$39,999
    _____ $40,000–$49,999
    _____ $50,000–or over

5. Do you rent ____ , or own your own home ____ ?

6. Where is your place of residence?
    _____ Altus
    _____ Duncan
    _____ Jacksonville
    _____ St. Albana
    _____ Rutland
    _____ Other: _____

7. Do you have a favorite day to shop?
    Yes ____   No ____
    If yes, what day is it?
    _____ Monday
    _____ Tuesday
    _____ Wednesday
    _____ Thursday
    _____ Friday
    _____ Saturday
    _____ Sunday

8. Are the hours that the Fashion Mall is open: 10:00 a.m.–9:00 p.m. Monday through Saturday, and 12:00–6:00 p.m. Sunday, satisfactory to you?   Yes ____   No ____
    If no, what hours would be better? _____

9. How often do you shop at the Fashion Mall?
    _____ More than once a week
    _____ Once a week
    _____ Twice a month
    _____ Once a month
    _____ Other

The Children's Research Council of the Advertising Research Foundation conducted an in-store observational study.[7] On seeing a shopper, observers estimated the child's age, recorded basic information about the shoppers, and took notes about what was said and done. Box 5.4 (on page 184) shows an example of the data that were collected by observation.

Observational studies may be made to count foot traffic or to measure the number of potential shoppers, the proportion of window shoppers, or the percentage of passersby entering the store. Vehicular traffic counts are important in location and site selection decisions.

A fashion count might be used periodically in an attempt to recognize trends in clothing. Observations of potential customers might simply involve

9-a. Are you shopping in the mall today for an advertised sale? Yes____ , No____ .

10. How did you hear about the sale at the Mall?

_____ Mail received at your home?

_____ Radio: What station?_____

_____ Newspaper: Which?_____

_____ TV: What station?_____

11. Which of the following newspapers do you read regularly? (You may check more than one.)

_____ Altus Post

_____ Duncan Banner

_____ Second Thursday

_____ Guthrie News

_____ Burlington Review

_____ The Collegian

_____ Other: _____

Questions 12–19 refer to your feelings toward the Mall itself in relation to the various items mentioned. Please place a check mark in the spot that best expresses your opinion.

	Very good	Accept-able	Below standard
12. Availability of fashion or quality merchandise . . .	_____	_____	_____
13. Selection and variety of merchandise . . .	_____	_____	_____
14. Price appeal (lower prices good bargains, and good values)	_____	_____	_____
15. Salesclerk service	_____	_____	_____
16. Access routes to the Mall	_____	_____	_____
17. Parking availability on arrival	_____	_____	_____
18. Satisfaction with returns and adjustments	_____	_____	_____
19. Mall events	_____	_____	_____

20. What percentage of your purchases for clothes are made at the Fashion Mall?

_____ 0–25% _____ 25–50% _____ 50–75%

_____ 75–100%

21. Do you have any comments on anything in particular that you like or dislike about the Mall? _____

_____

22. What have been your favorite Mall special events? _____

_____

_____

recording the number (percentage) of customers wearing a particular style or color. Research firms may use audits and recording devices to observe behavior. A pantry audit of consumer households—to record brands, quantities, and sizes of products—is useful for determining past behavior.

Censuses and Samples

From whom, when, and where to collect the data are primarily data-gathering issues. If a data source to be studied is small, or if there are no limitations of time or money, a census may be conducted. In a **census,** every member or item in the group is approached to provide data; that is, the

BOX **5.4** **EXAMPLE OF DATA RECORD COLLECTED BY OBSERVATION**[8]

Case #171 (young child). Observer: Julie Seyfert. Store: supermarket: Waldbaum's, Mt. Kisco, N.Y. Aisle: breakfast cereals. Shopping party: mother, girl age seven, boy age one. Both children in cart. No shopping list visible; no coupons visible.

Field observations. Party enters section, girl in bottom of cart, boy in top. Girl immediately points to Count Chocula box and exclaims something to the effect of "Look at those eyes!" Boy then joins in, "Oh yes, let's get that one, can we get that one?" Mom says something in Spanish as she picks up the box of Count Chocula. Group talks in Spanish; a few things are said—neutral in tone. Mom puts Count Chocula in cart and wheels away.

Field thoughts. Mom seems willing to please; didn't look at side panels or anything. Children were obviously drawn to the box and seemed to make decisions based solely on eyes on box. Girl in bottom of cart less vocal than boy. Count Chocula picture on the box had plastic piece over the face that made the eyes appear to move as the viewer walked by.

6543217

entire population of the universe is included in the study. A **population or universe** refers to all items or elements under consideration. However, even without the limits of money, time, and/or physical constraints, it is often impossible to locate or obtain the cooperation of everyone in the population or universe. The results obtained from a carefully selected portion of the universe may well present a better picture of that universe than a census.

The process of selecting a limited group to represent a larger group is known as **sampling.** The purpose of sampling is to obtain statistical measures that approximate the characteristics of the entire universe faster, as accurately, and at a lower cost than would be the case with a census. To be able to fulfill its purpose, the sample should be collected by using the principles of random sampling, to ensure that every item in the universe has an equal chance of being included. The basic assumption of random sampling is that the results derived from a sample, when subjected to strict statistical analysis, will allow conclusions that are valid for the entire universe.

A major cause of inaccuracy arises from bias. Assuming that the researcher is not intentionally trying to influence the results of the study, bias is caused primarily by inadequate planning and improper data collecting, recording, or analysis. These kinds of errors are not inherent in the sampling process and are called *nonsampling errors. Sampling errors* are inherent to the process, because sample results may differ from the true characteristics of the universe as a result of chance alone. The effects of sampling error can be estimated by statistical methods.

It is important that a time and place be appropriate to capture a random sample of the population of interest. For instance, a retailer may wish to know about women who purchase specific brands. If this researcher limits the research to a specific store, he or she is also limiting the population to people who shop there. Because each store is unique in some characteristic, the people who shop at a given store may also be unique in some way.

RETAIL INFORMATION SOURCES

You have learned a great deal about the more formal aspects of obtaining information from marketing research that can assist in making retailing decisions. There are many additional sources of information. Just a few are discussed in the next section.

WANT SLIP
Report every WANT.
Report every OUT.

Customers make "best sellers" – let's find them early. Give complete information about colors, sizes, and styles needed.

_____
_____
_____
_____

SKU: _____
Associate no. _____

Want Slips

Want slips can help retailers make buying decisions. Many retailers, both large and small, have employees fill out a form for each item of merchandise that is requested but is either currently out of stock or not carried. Such forms are called want slips. When buyers plan their purchases for the upcoming season, they review the want slips. Most of them include (1) the name of the article requested and a description of it by style, price, and color; (2) the quantity requested; (3) information on whether the sale was lost or whether the customer accepted a substitute; and (4) comments or suggestions made by the customer or the salesperson. See Figure 5.5.

Information from Store Records

FIGURE 5.5

Want slips help anticipate customer wants and needs.

A store's records can aid managers and buyers in their purchasing decisions. An investigation of sales records will reveal such information as which price lines sold best, which sizes were the most popular, which periods were the peak selling seasons, which vendors had the fastest moving merchandise, and which styles or colors were the most popular. Many firms go to extra lengths to collect information that enhances the use of in-store data. Radio Shack asks customers for their names and addresses so that they can build a database of exactly who their customers are and what they purchase. They are careful to protect the privacy of customers and not press them for the information.

Comparison Shopping

Information on product offerings, pricing, and sales promotions of competitors is important to retailers. They obtain this information by shopping in competitive stores. Comparison shopping information should, however, be used in conjunction with other data. There is no reason to stock an item merely because the competitor has it.

Information from Vendors

Vendors, wholesale suppliers, manufacturers, and importers can provide valuable input regarding what consumers are seeking. In deciding what to purchase, retailers should consider their suppliers to be important sources of information. Suppliers have worked hard to find the best available merchandise. As they have visited buyers in other retail stores, they have seen what is being purchased and, in many cases, have obtained information on customer responses to individual items. Although a supplier's total line may not be appropriate for a store, the manager should listen to the supplier and welcome advice and suggestions.

Similarly, a resident buying office can provide information to assist with decision making. The resident buying office is an organization that services noncompeting stores with merchandise and general market information. It reports to clients concerning items that seem to be good buys. There are also special buying reports, such as the *TOBY Fashion Reports*. In fact, there is often so much material that buyers cannot absorb it all.

Information from Sales Personnel

Retailers should never make a buy without first soliciting ideas from salespeople. First of all, they are in a position to know what merchandise the customer is talking about and buying. Second, merchandise is sold by salespeople; if it is unacceptable to them, it may go unsold. Soliciting their ideas about merchandise before it is purchased can aid in selling it on the floor.

In addition to sales personnel, buyers may seek advice from fashion coordinators, display personnel, their own superiors, and other buyers. Display personnel, for example, may realize that a good display window could not be built around an item under consideration. This type of knowledge is extremely valuable to the buyer when selecting merchandise and critical to the design of the retail marketing strategy.

A RETAILING RESEARCH EXAMPLE

In the section above we discussed how to conduct a research project involving primary research. Now we will apply this knowledge in a step-by-step example. The scenario for the research is as follows: You are the marketing

TABLE 5.I
Sales Report: Year-to-Year Comparison for Selected Weeks in Produce Section of Supermarket

		1996	1997
May	week 1	$5,250	$5,002
	week 3	5,689	5,300
June	week 1	6,230	5,671
	week 3	4,760	4,517
July	week 1	4,987	4,601
	week 3	5,790	5,212

manager for a grocery store. The divisional manager has received your sales figures by department for the last several months. While visiting your store, he asks why the produce department has suffered from a continual drop in sales over the past several months, especially in the face of increasing expenditures for inventory and display. See Table 5.1. You respond that you have been trying to expand the produce section to include a wider assortment and variety and that the customers have not responded well. The divisional manager has given you one month to find an explanation and cure for the problem.

Situational Analysis

You decide that there are several possible reasons that the produce expansion could be failing. These include customers not wanting the new produce, competitors offering better value, customers unwilling to pay higher prices for a larger selection of produce, or some overall mismanagement of the produce section. Discussions with the store manager and produce manager indicate that other problems may exist as well. These include inefficient display of the produce, lack of customer knowledge about the exotic fruits that have been added, and failure of the employees to remove damaged or dated produce.

Preliminary Investigation

In order to help you define the problem, you write down what you have learned so far.

Problem symptom

1. Sales continually have dropped in the produce section.

Sales in the produce section have fallen for several months in a row. The produce manager must design a research project that attempts to identify possible reasons.

Potential causes

1. Customers who shop here do not want the expansion.
2. Competitors are offering the customers greater selection.
3. The prices of the new items are too high.
4. The produce section is mismanaged.
5. Displays are poor.
6. Customer knowledge is lacking.

Considerations

1. The problem started shortly after the expansion.
2. Other stores that underwent an identical expansion are doing well.
3. Your customers are not unique compared to those of other stores that underwent this expansion. You decide that the causes need to be narrowed down to a more manageable level. In order to do this, you ask the customers shopping in your store a few preliminary questions.

After spending a full day introducing yourself and questioning store patrons, you are even more baffled by the problem. All of the customers indicate that they like the new expansion and they also seem familiar with many of the new types of produce. You noticed while doing the interviews that the produce section is clean and well-ordered and that the employees are pleasant. At the end of the day you check sales and compare them with those of previous days. You find that they are still below last year's sales.

Looking through your list of potential problems, you decide to eliminate them one at a time. At the end of the process there is only a single one left—

competition. You decide it's time to do some comparison shopping. You find that the two nearest stores had dramatically expanded their produce section and seem to be selling their new additions at about the prices in your store. You believe you have found the problem—increased competition.

Choosing Specific Objectives

The realization that action by the competition was the probable source of the sales drop was not enough. You now need to find out the specific reasons why customers are switching stores and devise a strategy to correct the situation. First, the specific differences between the competition and your store need to be examined. In order to do this the objective for further research should be specifically stated. You therefore define the objective as follows: Find the specific differences that are causing customers to switch to the competition. To do this you set up specific hypotheses:

H1. Customers perceive that the neighboring stores have lower prices on produce.

H2. Actual price differences are causing customers to believe the prices are lower in neighboring stores.

H3. Customers perceive that the neighboring stores have a greater selection of produce than our store.

H4. Actual assortment differences are causing customers to believe that neighboring stores have a larger assortment.

H5. Customers will shop for produce wherever it is less expensive.

H6. Customers will shop for produce where the selection is best.

The hypotheses are stated in a way that:

1. They are testable.
2. They specify the relationship between two variables.

Developing a Research Design

After defining specific hypotheses, you need to develop a plan for testing them. This is done through the five steps outlined above.

A statement of evidence.   The first thing that needs to be done is to determine what data need to be collected in order to test the hypotheses. The hypotheses as stated above require a comparison of prices, a comparison of selection, customers' reactions to price, and customers' reactions to selection. Thus, you decide to collect the following information:

1. Customers' opinions of the difference in produce prices between your store and the neighboring stores
2. Customers' opinions of the difference in produce selection between your store and the neighboring stores

3. Actual differences in produce prices between stores
4. Actual differences in produce selection between stores
5. Customers' opinions of the importance of price in determining where they shop for their produce
6. Customers' opinions of the importance of selection in determining where they shop for their produce

Specification of evidence.   How the evidence will be obtained is an important part of the research design. This part of the research process leads to further considerations in the methodology section. Therefore, the more comprehensive this section is, the less work you will have to do later.

There are two distinct types of data that are needed in this research: (1) customer opinions of price, of selection, and of their relative importance must be obtained, as well as (2) the actual prices and selection of different stores. These two types of data require different collection techniques. The first type will take the form of a survey, and the second will be derived from observation.

Analyzing data.   Looking up analytical techniques from a basic research book reveals that the proper test for the difference between two means is a t-test. This is a versatile test that is often used in basic research. Although more sophisticated tests are available for these types of data, they are more appropriate for a statistics or research book.

Planning.   There are two major things that must be taken into consideration at this stage: time and money. The district manager has only given you a month to develop and conduct the research. Therefore, the calendar can be developed with this constraint in mind. It is always wise to include some extra time for each stage of the research. It is usually the case that something goes wrong and requires extra time to fix. This is also true to some extent with the monetary budget.

Selecting a Methodology

You have decided that both objective and opinion data need to be collected for your research. Opinion data will require that customers be surveyed. Objective data need to be collected through observation and recording. Thus a methodology needs to be outlined that includes both collection procedures.

There are various survey instruments that can be used to collect opinion data. Given your time constraints, you decide to use either a telephone or a personal interview format. Also, to aid in the collection and coding and because you have specific hypotheses, you decide to use a structured format for the survey questions. Since the questions will be structured and therefore are simple enough to be answered over the phone, you decide to use a telephone survey to avoid the additional expense of personal interviews.

The objective data with regard to prices and assortment can be gathered using secondary or primary data. You decide that your competitors are unlikely to give you any existing price information (secondary data), and therefore you will send a researcher to collect it (primary data). You decide to hire someone not affiliated with your store to collect and record the price and assortment information from the other stores.

Collecting Data

The first thing that needs to be done is the development of a survey instrument. Since you have decided on a structured interview format, the questionnaire needs to ask questions regarding the hypotheses while providing several answers from which the respondent can choose.

After the questionnaire was developed, you determined that you needed to define a population from which to sample. The population that concerns this problem is grocery shoppers or, more specifically, produce shoppers. However, you soon realize that you cannot take a census and therefore must use a sample. Because you have decided to use a statistical technique called the t-test in the analysis of the data, you must take a random sample. You determine that a sample of 300 shoppers will be enough to satisfactorily use the t-test. These can be obtained by taking a random sample of 300 names with the zip codes that your store serves from the local phone book.

Analysis and Interpretation

The results of your study lead you to conclude the following:

1. Customers believe that the competition has lower produce prices.
2. In fact, there is little or no actual price difference between you and your competition.
3. Customers perceive no difference in the assortment level between you and your competition.
4. In fact, there are no significant differences in the assortment between stores.
5. Customers perceive the price of produce to be very important in determining where they shop.
6. Customers perceive the level of an assortment as important in determining where they shop.

You decide that your assortment level is appropriate. However, you notice that the customers hold the opinion that your price levels are too high. This is in spite of the fact that there is no actual price difference between you and your competitors. A key finding is revealed: Your store is not communicating its price level to the customers.

Presentation of Findings

Usually, presentations of research are written in a research report that explains the steps taken, the results, and a recommended course of action. You complete a report recommending that the store use comparative advertising. Thus the customers can see that your store's prices are at the same level as those of your competitors. As a secondary recommendation, you consider lowering your price level and then using comparative advertising showing that your prices are lower than your competitors'. Through analysis of the data, you know at what level your prices need to be in order to make the claim of lower prices.

THE BODY SHOP
INTERNATIONAL PLC—REVISITED

There has been a dramatic shifting in cosmetic sales from traditional department stores to mass merchandisers. Consumers throughout the world have become more price-conscious, and competition has become fierce. During this period The Body Shop has continued to prosper by promoting value as well as social and environmental concerns.

More than forty companies in the United States have tried to copy The Body Shop's format, yet The Body Shop has continually outperformed them. Less than 25 percent of these copycat stores have developed into recognizable chains. Similarly, The Body Shop has also been successful in outperforming its United Kingdom competition. The continuing competitive success is partially attributed to the constant innovation in The Body Shop's product line. In one year more than 160 new products were introduced, including an endangered species range of soaps and the Colourings® line of color cosmetics. More than 60 percent of these are manufactured by The Body Shop.

The Body Shop's store branding strategy has been called "passion branding" by David Adler of Cone Communications. The Body Shop not only fulfills the traditional needs of customers, but it also attempts to solve tangible social problems, and this commitment has been successfully communicated to potential customers. For example, The Body Shop provides detailed information about its products, including development, ethical sourcing, manufacture, ingredients, and testing. It has also been a leader in using minimal packaging and unique design elements to communicate its strategic position to the consumer.

The Body Shop represents a truly international brand. It has proved its potential to expand into both developed and rapidly growing markets. Currently,

The Body Shop is experimenting with new retail formats. In the United Kingdom, for example, the company has begun testing direct distribution in the home through a party format, much like that of Tupperware. It has introduced a mail-order catalog that provides detailed information on each product. More concentration is also being paid to holiday promotions.

1. **What research would help identify buying motives of customers of The Body Shop?**
2. **The management of The Body Shop prefers to use brand differentiation and its social and environmental agenda, rather than price discounts, to attract customers. Is this a realistic strategy in today's global environment? Why or why not?**
3. **What secondary research would help The Body Shop identify locations in the United States that would have a high probability of success?**

SUMMARY

Retailers conduct research for one main reason: to gather information that they do not already have access to. Retailers possess a great deal of information from computerized management systems; however, the system may not have the information needed for market analysis, communication analysis, or merchandise planning.

The research process consists of the following steps: situational analysis, preliminary investigation, defining specific objectives, developing the research design, searching for secondary data, selecting a methodology to collect primary data, analyzing and interpreting the data, and presenting the findings.

The research design determines what information is needed and how that information will be obtained. The research design is the outline of the general research process. Without this step, the research may not be gathering the information that is needed or may not be addressing the problem correctly.

Secondary sources contribute information that was collected for another purpose than to answer the current research problem. Secondary sources are available from trade and professional organizations; from the state, local, and federal government; and from private companies specializing in secondary information. As with any form of data, there are advantages and potential problems arising from the use of secondary information.

Primary research involves collecting original data to answer the research problem. The two most popular methodologies to use when collecting primary date are survey/interview and observation. The selection of methodology depends on the information requirements to answer the problem.

There are many additional sources of information available to the retailer from store records, vendors, sales personnel, and so on. A step-by-step example provides the reader with a detailed voyage through the research process.

KEY TERMS AND CONCEPTS

Accessibility, 174

Accuracy, 174

Applied research, 169

Census, 183

Fact gathering, 169

Mail surveys, 181

Personal interviews, 181

Pertinence, 174

Population or universe, 184

Primary data, 179

Research design, 171

Sampling, 184

Secondary data, 174

Sufficiency, 175

Telephone interviewing, 181

The research process, 169

QUESTIONS

1. What types of retail problems require research?

2. Describe the research process. Is there a shortcut to this process?

3. What are the advantages of using secondary data? What are the disadvantages?

4. How much assistance will the Internet be to retailers? Give an example of how retailers could use this resource to help run their stores.

5. What are the advantages and disadvantages of collecting primary data? Should it always be used to solve a retailer's problem?

6. If retailers want to measure customer satisfaction, what methodology would they use?

7. Is it ever possible to use a census instead of a sample? If so, give an example. If not, explain why not.

8. How can a retailer identify the difference between a symptom and a problem? Does the question above require research for a retailer?

9. Why would a retailer want to do a preliminary investigation?

10. Should the retailer conduct research projects alone?

Situations

1. You are the assistant manager in a medium-sized junior department store located in the community in which you are now attending school. The store manager has asked you to explore the possibility of opening a subteen fashion boutique in the store. What factors will you include in your analysis? Where will you obtain the information you need?

2. You are the store manager of a gift shop located in a large suburban shopping center. The center manager has proposed that it be a matter of policy for stores in the center to stay open until 9 p.m, Monday through Saturday. How will you respond? What factors might have prompted the center manager to make this suggestion?

3. Sports for Her is a sporting goods store that specializes in sports equipment and sports attire for women and girls. Design a questionnaire for the manager of the store to determine the customers' expectations.

4. Find a store that is having a drawing for a free gift or prize. Enter yourself in the drawing, but use "Z" for your middle initial or add Jr. to your name. Track your mail for the next two months to see where the information from the entry form appears.

Cases

CASE 5A
Bass Pro Shops[9]

Outdoor World, the Bass Pro Shops' extraordinary shopping experience that is bundled into 158,000 square feet, prides itself on carrying anything and everything that a sports person would ever need or want. Outdoor World was Missouri's number-one tourist attraction last year, welcoming 3.5 million visitors. Outdoor World could be compared to a Disney World for sportsmen and sportswomen complete with designated photo opportunities and loanable cameras. Natural surroundings abound with a four-story waterfall, a trout stream that runs through the departments, a collection of big-game mounts, aquariums galore, and a two-story log cabin. To help navigate through the many attractions and departments, maps are available for visitors.

Outdoor World departments include fishing tackle, shooting and hunting equipment, rod and reel repair, sportswear, outdoor books, gifts, boats and marine accessories, along with departments geared toward specific sports, such as golf or baseball. Many services are also provided for visitors; you can have your knife sharpened while you wait to have the wildlife print framed that you bought in the art gallery or while you test-fire hunting rifles or bows on the practice ranges. And if you are hungry, you can eat either at the McDonald's located on the fourth floor or at Hemingway's Blue Water Café, a fine restaurant located near McDonald's.

John Morris, the president of Bass Pro Shops, is steering the organization into becoming "the finest sporting goods company and the finest vacation resort in the United States." Big Cedar

Lodge, south of Branson, Missouri, is a sixty-two-acre resort with a three-star *Mobil Travel Guide* rating. Luxury lodges include natural touches such as cedar siding, mounted game animals, massive stone fireplaces, and handcrafted chandeliers. Also available are various styles of wilderness cabins. Big Cedar Lodge offers guest activities like guided trail rides on horseback, hayrides, lighted tennis courts, nature trails, a miniature golf course, and fishing trips and guides for excursions on Table Rock Lake.

For those not able to visit Outdoor World, purchases can be made all day and night from a 22,000-item master catalog and numerous specialty catalogs.

1. *You are the vice president in charge of looking into the possible expansion of Bass Pro Shops in the Dallas, Texas; Orlando, Florida; and southern California areas. What information will you need to discover about each area in order to decide whether expansion would be a viable possibility?*

2. *What secondary sources could you use to find this information?*

3. *What primary research methodology(ies) would you use to find the information you want?*

4. *On the order form in the middle of the catalogs is the 800 phone number and the following statement: "Fill out our order form with the appropriate information. Have your order card, VIP number, and key code from the back of your catalog handy when you call. We recommend you order by phone so we can provide product availability information." From a research information perspective, why would you want to talk to the customer? What information could be obtained for the catalog database?*

CASE 5B
Research Information for Merchandising and Promotion[10]

The regional manager of an auto parts chain was reading the results of a study reported in *Stores* magazine, copyrighted by the National Retail Federation.

The study confirms that consumers buy motor oil frequently, use it regularly, and have definite opinions about brands and packaging. The research drew on telephone interviews from 450 nationwide households. It indicates that more than 60 percent of Americans who own a car will add oil to it when the dipstick shows that they are a quart low or more. About 50 percent of those surveyed say that they change their own oil at least occasionally, while 38 percent report that they change their oil "most of the time."

About 76 percent are able to state a preference in motor oil brands.

A definite majority (83 percent) prefer the lightweight, quick-opening, easy-to-pour plastic bottles. About 13 percent say they prefer the cans, which require a spout for pouring. Approximately 45 percent of those surveyed favor regular motor oil, while 47 percent favor premium motor oil.

Nearly half of the respondents shop for motor oil first at a discount store. More than one-third of those surveyed would shop at either a supply store, a service station, or a specialty chain.

Seven quarts of motor oil are purchased each year by the average consumer. The amount is slightly higher among those who change their own oil (eight quarts) and slightly lower among service station customers (six quarts).

A majority of those surveyed (59 percent) bought motor oil at regular price, while 37 percent bought motor oil on sale or with a promotion. Consumers who bought motor oil on sale purchased a higher number of quarts on average (nine quarts) than consumers who bought motor oil at regular prices (six quarts).

About 60 percent of those surveyed purchased motor oil because it was needed; however, 40 percent bought it on impulse (they did not set out specifically to buy motor oil). Consumers who purchased motor oil at a discount store were more likely to have bought it on impulse than consumers who purchased it in an auto parts store.

1. *As regional manager for the specialty auto store chain, what information from this study would be of most use to you? Why?*

2. *What other kinds of primary and secondary information would be of use to the company if it had a goal of increasing the sale of motor oil?*

PART **3**

THE RETAIL STORE

6

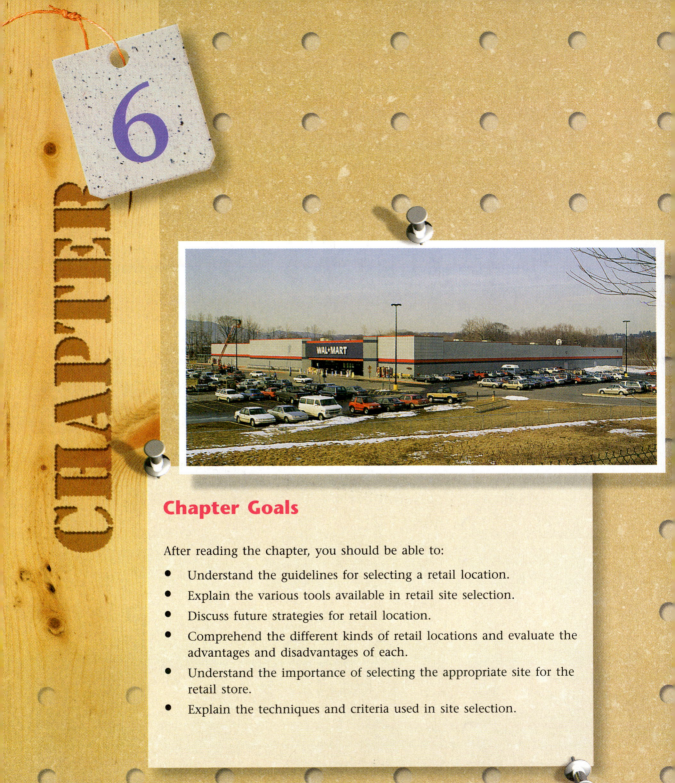

Chapter Goals

After reading the chapter, you should be able to:

- Understand the guidelines for selecting a retail location.
- Explain the various tools available in retail site selection.
- Discuss future strategies for retail location.
- Comprehend the different kinds of retail locations and evaluate the advantages and disadvantages of each.
- Understand the importance of selecting the appropriate site for the retail store.
- Explain the techniques and criteria used in site selection.

Store Location and Site Evaluation

WAL-MART:[1] COMPETING WITH LOCATION STRATEGY

Wal-Mart became the world's largest retailer in 1990. Sam Walton took Wal-Mart from its founding to more than $44 billion in the company's first thirty years. Even in the tough retail environment of the 1990s Wal-Mart continued its record sales and earnings. By 1996 Wal-Mart had sales of $100 billion, operating more than 2,200 Wal-Mart stores and 450 Sam's stores in all 50 states. Sales are projected to reach $200 billion in 2001. Wal-Mart's success has been attributed to many things, including the format of the store, high-tech merchandising and distribution strategies, customer service, the strategy of everyday low prices, and location strategies. Regardless of the reason for today's success, one thing is certain: Sam Walton developed his initial base through selection of promising small markets.

In its early years, markets chosen by Wal-Mart were in smaller communities that had not previously received large investments in the retailing sector. Many of the retail stores in these markets were smaller family-owned businesses that had existed for decades. These communities were often overlooked by large retailers because of perceived lack of market potential. However, these markets presented a good opportunity for Wal-Mart because of the lack of serious competition and the fact that many of these communities were growing and served as the center of a significant trading area.

Most smaller communities responded to the opening of a Wal-Mart in their area with enthusiasm, but some reacted with an all-out fight. The consumers in these small towns benefit from higher selection and lower prices. However, the increased efficiency often drives smaller retailers out of business. For this reason, Wal-Mart has become the scapegoat for a variety of politicians, preservationists, and small retailers. Wal-Mart has been accused of causing many societal ills, including business failures, job losses, the deterioration of the downtown area, and even "the decline of neighborliness." These criticisms arise, in part, from

Wal-Mart's location strategy where the entry of a large store on the edge of town diverted traffic away from the downtown area. The existing retailers in these communities were in districts with limited parking, were often located in deteriorating stores, had limited store hours, and sometimes engaged in poor merchandising. Wal-Mart entered the market with stores that offered a larger variety of merchandise, lower prices, and free parking.

Some communities have attempted to stop Wal-Mart from entering their area through restrictive zoning and other legal maneuvers. Most of the anti-Wal-Mart activists are characterized by growth proponents as local protectionists, attempting to restrict competitive entry into their market. See Box 6.1. Most communities realized that if Wal-Mart did not enter their market, then another efficient retailer would soon do so. Also, these communities realized that Wal-Mart not only benefits the consumers but also tends to create a net increase in employment. In one year, Wal-Mart created 77,000 jobs, more than any other U.S. company.

Wal-Mart's location strategy relies on developing a very strong market presence. The chain often simultaneously opens several stores of more than 90,000 square feet, eventually putting them so close together that they compete with each other.

Wal-Mart's strength has been in small markets, but as it built critical mass in distribution in an area, urban markets were no longer ignored. In fact, if you look at the top urban markets and the top three discounters in each, Wal-Mart is either first or second in market share in twenty-four of them.[2]

The company is rapidly expanding its supercenter concept. The Wal-Mart supercenters have approximately 196,000 square feet, with 45,000 square feet devoted to groceries and a McDonald's, optical shop, garden shop, photo center, and so on.

Kmart is expanding its Super K concept into many of the same areas as Wal-Mart. For example, in Sherman, Texas, a town of slightly more than 30,000 people, a Super K and Wal-Mart superstore are located directly across the highway from each other. Both stores operate twenty-four hours a day. Most analysts contend that consumers simply do not need more than one big combination store in a market.

1. **What market factors led to Wal-Mart's success with its market dominance location strategy?**
2. **Are there any strategies a small store such as a downtown hardware store might use to survive?**
3. **Are there ethical questions in Wal-Mart's market dominance strategy?**

INTRODUCTION

Have you driven around a town and thought, "Why would anyone ever have put that store there? I would have put it out on the loop." Indeed, you may be right, given what you know today. Unfortunately, the decision to place that store where it is was made many years ago. The site that was chosen may have been the best one available at that time. The one rule of thumb that applies to location and site selection is that today's best location decision is probably not tomorrow's. Because neighborhoods change, cities grow, competitors arrive, competitors move, and roadways change, retailers must recognize that they must make the best decision that they can with today's best information. We have organized this chapter to help you assess your objectives, examine your alternatives, and make the retail location decision.

BOX

6.1   **POEM IN RESPONSE TO CRITICISM OF WAL-MART'S IMPACT ON SMALL COMMUNITIES**

On the 26th of May,
"Pepper . . . and Salt" chose to play
Howard Upton's poem called "Civic Shock."
The meter was catching,
The words were fetching,
But the content? What a crock!
In eight lines of rhyme,
He blamed the decline
Of Main Street on Sam Walton's store.
But we create jobs
And taxes in gobs.
Is someone else offering more?
The facts, sir, are these:
Main Street's maladies
Had started before our arrival.
Folks drove to the city
And there spent their kitty.
And threatened small towns' survival.
When Wal-Mart sets up,
Local spending picks up;
The values are just down the block.
Hundreds are hired
And many retire
With plenty of Wal-Mart Stores stock.
We can't be beholding
When some firms are folding.
The fact is that many do better
By heeding Sam's verse,
"The Customer First,"
And marking down that green-and-blue sweater.

Source: Reprinted with permission of the author, Don E. Shinkle, vice president, Corporate Affairs, Wal-Mart Stores Inc., Bentonville, Arkansas.

6543217

IMPORTANCE OF LOCATION DECISION

Even though nonstore retailing is growing, most of the nearly 1.5 million retailers in the United States are selling from retail store space. Some of these retailers are very small single-store operators, and some are huge superstore discounters. Each location selected resulted from an effort to satisfy the needs of the particular market each was designed to serve.

Whether it was the consumer's need for convenience, their desire to do comparison shopping, the extent of the purchasing power in a market area, or the transportation facilities available, many factors together led to the development of different kinds of retail locations. There is an old saying that the value of real estate is determined by three things: location, location, and location. Nowhere is that more the case than with stores. A *Wall Street Journal* study looked at the largest store as measured by gross sales of the twenty largest brands.[3] Not surprisingly, in nearly every case, a unique location was a major factor. The study provides some interesting examples. A Baskin-Robbins store is in a Waikiki mall where it is the only food store. Crowds of tourists, year-round summer weather, and a known brand lead to sales exceeding $1 million a year. An on-base Domino Pizza store on a military installation with 11,000 Marines and their families sells as many as 4,000 pizzas a week. In New York, across from Macy's, which generates enormous traffic, where Sixth Avenue and Broadway converge, a Florsheim men's shoe store serves some 30,000 customers a year.

Retail stores should be located where market opportunities are best. After a country, region, city or trade area, and neighborhood have been identified as satisfactory, a specific site must be chosen that will best serve the desired target market. Site selection can be the difference between success and failure. A thorough study of customers and their shopping behavior should be made before a location is chosen. The finest store in the world will not live up to its potential if it is located where customers cannot or will not travel to shop.

Generally, retail location evaluation focuses on the idea expressed in the preceding paragraph—that the primary role of the retail store or center is to attract the shopper to the location. Alternatively, retailers must take the store to where the people are, either at home or in crowds. Examples of taking the store to where the crowds are include airport locations, theme parks, and vending machines. A study by the National Restaurant Association found that the highest number of restaurants per number of residents was in major tourists destinations such as Martha's Vineyard, Massachusetts; Williamsburg, Virginia; and Yosemite National Park, California.[4] Taking the store to the customer is the topic of Chapter 15, which looks at subjects ranging from the virtual store to home shopping networks and database retailing.

Chapter 2 discussed how every retail store strives for its competitive advantage. For some stores, it is price. For others, it is promotional expertise

More and more retailers are seeking ways to take the store to the customer. One unique example is a train store. In mid-November, the Neiman Marcus Holiday Express Train, using eleven renovated railcars made between 1948 and 1958, rolls out on a tour of ten cities that do not have a Neiman Marcus store. The train is filled with holiday gifts ranging from a $7.50 chocolate toy soldier to a $4,500 jeweled evening bag. Customers call an 800 number to confirm a boarding time to shop. (Castabeda, Laura, "NM Train to Go on Holiday Tour," *Dallas Morning News,* November 18, 1995, pp. F1, F3.)

or the special services that are offered. Despite any differences among the various stores that may be competing for the shopper's dollar, location offers a unique asset for all stores because once a site is selected, it cannot be occupied by another store. This advantage, however, points to the importance of location analysis and site selection. Once a facility is built, purchased, or leased, the ability to relocate may be restricted for a number of years. In short, location and site selection is one of the most important decisions made by a retail owner. We need to look for ways to optimize this process.

Retailing Strategy and Location

Before deciding where your retail location should be, you first need to decide what business you are actually in. In Chapter 2, we discussed retailing strategy and objectives. A retailer should first begin with a mission statement. This helps the retailer, its employees, and its customers understand the purpose of the business. The core concepts and culture that come from a mission statement flow from the choice of the strategies selected in an attempt to achieve a competitive advantage. Location may be the primary strategy selected, or it may be merchandise, pride, service, or communication. Whatever strategy is emphasized, location is a critical variable.

Owners or managers who wish to emphasize merchandise quality will require an entirely different location than managers of a low-margin discount house.

Just as the strategy and objectives of a retailer are integral to the location decision process, so is the importance of market research, as discussed in Chapter 5. The use of marketing research criteria in deciding on a location depends on what type of information or answer is needed from the research, time and cost factors, and the importance of the decision in the overall strategy.[5]

Characteristics Used in Location Analysis

There are several characteristics used in location analysis. The key ones include demographics, economic, cultural, demand, competition, and infrastructure. Some of the characteristics will be more helpful in the discussion of the "macro" areas (country and region) as opposed to the "micro" areas (trade area and site evaluation), and vice versa. We introduce each characteristic in the discussion of country and region analysis and then return to each as appropriate in the micro areas. See Figure 6.1.

FIGURE 6.1

Location analysis begins with a study to select a country such as the United States. Next, the examination would be narrowed to a region of the country such as the South Atlantic States. A market area like Tampa–St. Petersburg, Florida, could then be explored, followed by analysis of a site in the Eastlake Mall near the intersection of I-75 and I-4.

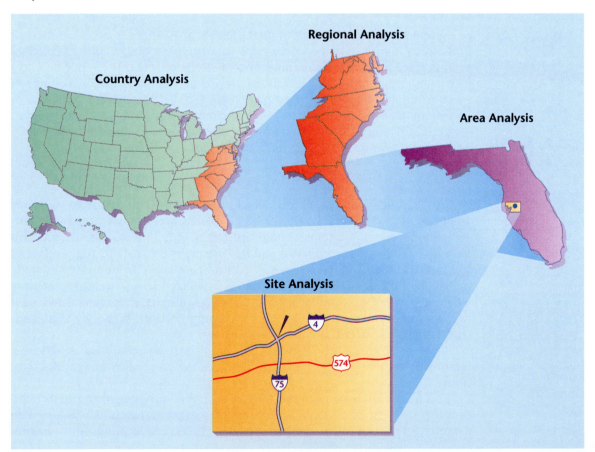

COUNTRY AND REGIONAL ANALYSIS

Many retailers have found success establishing locations in other countries. Because of the high market saturation in the United States, many U.S. retailers ranging from Toys 'R' Us and McDonald's to J. C. Penney have expanded overseas in an effort to improve their bottom line. On the other hand, there are many important market characteristics in the United States that have attracted overseas retailers like Laura Ashley, Benneton, and The Body Shop.

There is a need to recognize that country analysis will be an increasingly important aspect of the location strategy as merchants look for growth opportunities. Table 1.1 listed the largest global retailers. If you look at a listing of the 100 largest, you will see that while U.S. firms dominate the list with 30 chains, their share of total international sales is falling as European and Asian companies are expanding rapidly.[6]

After the decision is made as to what country or countries are to be considered, a regional analysis will need to be done. Most countries are not completely homogeneous and need to be broken down into regions in order for a retailer to better understand the market characteristics. For example, the United States is normally divided into the following regions: Pacific, Mountain, West North Central, East North Central, West South Central, East South Central, South Atlantic, Middle Atlantic, and New England. Regions may differ in many characteristics such as population demographics and density, climate, cultures, and distribution infrastructure.

The importance of examining countries and regions by their macro characteristics can be illustrated by the importance of today's distribution infrastructure to the concept of **flow-through replenishment.** This concept is based on having information on consumer demand that allows the flow of goods to be regulated by actual needs in the retail stores. Consumer demand is acquired at the point-of-sale terminal when the UPC bar code is scanned for each product sold. Computers maintain continuous records of product flow. Daily or weekly reorders go directly to manufacturers so that exact quantity replacement can be shipped to each individual store or routed to the retailer's central distribution center.[7] If this is a part of the firm's competitive advantage, the country or region must have the transportation, computer, and warehousing infrastructure necessary to support the strategy. A regional map of the United States published by the Census Bureau is shown in Figure 6.2.

Demographics

Demography is the study of population characteristics that are used to describe consumers. Retailers can obtain information about the consumer's age, gender, income, education, family characteristics, occupation, and many other items. These **demographic variables** may be used to select market segments, which become the target markets for the retailer.

FIGURE 6.2

Regions of the
United States.
(*Source:* U.S.
Department of
Commerce, Bureau
of the Census,
1990.)

Demographics aid retailers in identifying and targeting potential customers in certain geographic locations. Retailers are able to track many consumer trends by analyzing changes in demographics. Demographics provide retailers with information to help locate and describe customers. Linking demographics to behavioral and lifestyle characteristics helps retailers find out exactly who their consumers are. The Vancouver airport in Canada conducted a study of travelers who passed through the facility and categorized them into the eight VALS™2 Values and Lifestyles groups discussed in Chapter 4. The study found that the largest share of respondents were Actualizers (upscale independent intellectuals) followed by Experiencers (younger action-oriented consumers). Therefore, the airport decided to attract retailers like The Sharper Image or Nature Company whose customers would fit into those groups.[8] Retailers who target certain specific demographics characteristics should make sure that those characteristics exist in enough abundance to justify locations in new countries or regions.

Economic

Businesses operate in an economic environment and base many decisions on economic analysis. Economic factors such as a country's gross domestic product, current interest rates, employment rates, and general economic conditions affect how retailers in general perform financially. (**Gross domestic product** is a measure of the goods and services produced in the country.) For example, employment rates can affect the quantity and quality of the labor pool available for retailers as well as influence the ability of customers to buy. Figure 6.3 shows the gross domestic product for selected countries and the United States.

Normally, growth in a country's gross domestic product indicates growth in retail sales and disposable income. Retailers want to locate in countries or regions that have steadily growing gross national products. As interest rates rise, the cost of carrying inventory on credit rises for retailers and the cost of purchasing durable goods rises for consumers. Countries that have projected significant increases in interest rates should be evaluated very carefully by retailers. Retailers will also be affected by a rise in employment rates; this lowers the supply of available workers to staff and support retail locations.

Let's consider the example of China. The country has a billion people, a low but growing per capita income, and major urban areas even though the country is largely rural. Consumers are used to purchasing food products on an almost daily basis. They pay close attention to prices and often prefer to haggle. Japan's supermarket chain, Yaohan, sees increasing economic well-being as a signal for opportunities in China. A *Wall Street Journal* article tells how the Japanese firm is attacking the market: "Yaohan's joint-venture supermarket, a 7,000-square-foot store wedged into the ground floor of an apartment complex in a working class district, sells mostly locally produced fresh and packaged goods at prices that match or beat those at local stores."[9] The company plans to open 1,000 stores by the year 2010.

Cultural

Cultural characteristics impact how consumers shop and what goods they purchase. The values, standards, and language that a person is exposed to while growing up are indicators of future consumption behavior. Consumers

FIGURE 6.3

Gross domestic product (GDP) is the total output of goods and services produced by labor and property valued at market prices (current U.S. $ 1993). (*Source:* U.S. Department of State Background Notes.)

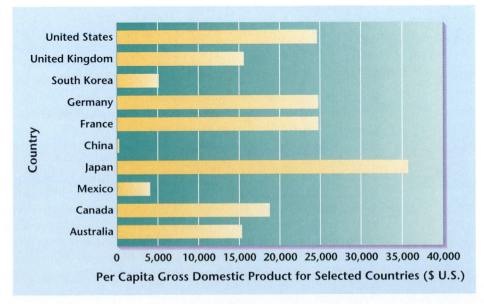

Per Capita Gross Domestic Product for Selected Countries ($ U.S.)

want to feel comfortable in the environment in which they shop. To accomplish this, retailers must understand the culture and language of their customers. In a bilingual area, a retailer may need to hire employees who are capable of speaking both of the languages spoken by the customers.

Some retailers have found it useful to market to the cultural heritage of their consumers, while other retailers seek to market cross-culturally. Normally larger cultures are made of many distinct subcultures. Retailers need to be aware of the different aspects of culture that will affect the location decision. For example, greeting cards sold in the United States normally have verses on the inside, while greeting cards sold in Europe normally do not. Figure 6.4 is one author's idea of how U.S. regions can be defined based largely on cultural and economic differences.

Demand

The demand for a retailer's goods and services will influence where the retailer will locate its stores. Not only must consumers want to purchase the goods, but they must have the ability or money to do so as well. Demand characteristics are a function of the population and the buying power of the population that the retailer is targeting.

Population and income statistics are available for most countries and regions with developed economies. In developing countries the income data may be little more than an informed guess. These statistics allow for comparisons of populations and a basic determination of who will be able to purchase the goods carried in the store. This is of utmost importance for retailers, whether they carry higher-priced goods—such as durables, furniture, jewelry, and electronics—or lower-priced goods—such as basic apparel or toys.

Competition

Levels of competition vary by nation and region. In some areas, retailers will face much stiffer competition than in other areas. Normally, the more industrialized a nation is, the higher the level of competition that exists between its borders. Again, one of the reasons U.S. retailers are looking beyond their borders is the level of sophistication of the competition. As an example, the lower level of competition in Mexico compared to the United States caused many U.S. retailers to expand there.

One of the environmental influences on the success or failure of a retail establishment is how the retailer is able to handle the competitive advantages of its competition. A retailer must be knowledgeable concerning both direct and indirect competitors in the marketplace, what goods and services they provide, and their image in the mind of the consumer population.

Sometimes a retailer may decide to go head to head with a competitor when the reasons are not entirely clear. *Discount Store News* notes that Baby-Superstore is opening a 40,000-square-foot store almost in the shadow of the 47,000-square-foot flagship location of LiL' Things in Arlington, Texas. The

The nine nations of North America. (*Source: The Nine Nations of North America* Copyright © 1981 Joel Garreau. Reprinted by permission of Houghton Mifflin Company. All rights reserved.)

stores offer a full line of furniture, bedding, apparel and accessories, hard goods, child development items, toys, and gifts. Both stores have an every-day low price policy, gift wrapping, a gift registry for expectant mothers, prominent display of upscale brands, a strong private-label program, broad price-point offerings, and preference for power-center locations.[10]

Infrastructure

Infrastructure characteristics deal with the basic framework that allows business to operate. Retailers require some form of channel to deliver the goods and services to their door. Depending on what type of transportation is involved, distribution relies heavily on the existing infrastructure of highways, roads, bridges, river ways, and railways. Legal infrastructures—such as laws, regulations, and court rulings—and technical infrastructures—such as level of computerization, communication systems, and electrical power availability—also influence store location decisions.

Distribution plays a key role in the location decision especially for countries and regions. There is a significant variance in quantity and quality of infrastructures across countries. A retailer whose operation depends on reliable computerization and communications would not need to even consider a country or a region that did not meet those criteria. The need for refrigerated trucks to distribute frozen juice might limit a retailer like Orange Julius in its ability to expand to India. The multilevel small wholesaler infrastructure in Japan has been a major hurdle for retailers attempting to enter that market.

The legal environment is a part of the overall infrastructure a firm must consider. For example, many countries require nonnative businesses to have a native partner before establishing retail locations. The legal requirements a retailer operates under in one country will not be the same for another country or region and may be different from state to state within the United States.

Another part of the location analysis at the country or regional level may be the simple fact of whether or not locations are available and can be had at rents that fit the business strategy. Retail space is hard to find in Hong Kong, and rents are double those in Tokyo and New York. A corner juice stand of thirty square feet pays rent in Hong Kong of $38,000 (US$4,918) each month. Bossing Marketing Ltd., a clothing retailer, pays HK$1,000,000.[11]

In conclusion, the demographic, demand, competition, cultural, infrastructure, and economic characteristics are important in analyzing a country or region. Our topic next turns to market and trade area analysis.

TRADE AREA ANALYSIS

It is important to define the market area of any potential location. You know that a retail market is any group of individuals who possess the ability, desire, and willingness to buy retail goods or services. The residents of any neighborhood, city, region, country, or group of countries may constitute a **retail market.**

The **retail trade area** is defined as the geographic area within which the retail customers for a particular kind of store live or work. For example, Jaxon's restaurant serves the residents and office workers in the downtown and Westside areas of El Paso as well as visitors from across the border in Mexico. Harrod's in London serves customers not only from the London area but from Europe, the United States, and many other countries as well. The customer profile of a segment of the people within the geographic area that the store decides to serve is the target market. For example, some retailers are finding a strong customer base in downtown urban areas. Filene's Basement Corporation has long been a major player in downtown Boston. It has now opened stores in downtown Washington, D.C., New York, and Philadelphia.[12]

Trade Area Considerations

Demographic. We have said that perhaps no variables are more important to the retail manager than the demographic dimensions of a market. Whether the retail trade area is the central city, a growing suburb, or a quiet rural area, you must understand the people who live and work there.

To illustrate the application of segmentation, Just Add Water managers have identified their target market to be females aged sixteen to thirty-five who enjoy water sports and desire a wide selection of swimwear. Managers of the discount grocery chain Sack 'N' Save identify their target market to be budget-minded adults with children who are willing to bag their own groceries to save money. Despite the great number of possible retail product or food store categories, Just Add Water and Sack 'N' Save managers have carefully identified their respective target markets. By doing so, the ability of each store to meet the needs of its respective target customers is greatly enhanced. Once the basic characteristics are identified and a judgment is made as to how far one of the customers would travel for the goods, the total market has been determined.

Factors such as the current population, potential population, population density, age, income, gender, occupation, race, proportion of home ownership, average home value, and proportion of single versus multifamily dwellings are important considerations.

Where consumers live, their commuting patterns, and whether their numbers are increasing or decreasing are but a few of the dynamic characteristics of the trade area population that the retailer must consider. It may be quite helpful to construct maps that display where certain types of customers reside. A retailer could start with census tract maps such as that illustrated in Figure 6.5. The U.S. Bureau of the Census provides extremely detailed information for each census tract. For example, a retailer looking at a location in census tract 21 at the corner of Skyline Drive and Wedgewood Drive in Knoxville, Tennessee, could determine that 11,514 people live in tracts 20, 32, 33, and 21. Within Figure 6.5 is a selected list of characteristics that could

Census tract data can be used to define customer characteristics in the retailer's trade area.

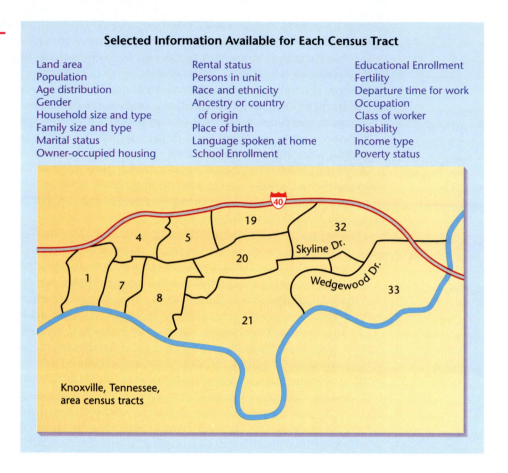

Selected Information Available for Each Census Tract

Land area	Rental status	Educational Enrollment
Population	Persons in unit	Fertility
Age distribution	Race and ethnicity	Departure time for work
Gender	Ancestry or country	Occupation
Household size and type	of origin	Class of worker
Family size and type	Place of birth	Disability
Marital status	Language spoken at home	Income type
Owner-occupied housing	School Enrollment	Poverty status

Knoxville, Tennessee, area census tracts

be used to profile the market in the tracts. While each of these characteristics affects location choice, it should not be forgotten that any retail store serves only a small part of the total population. For this reason it is important to segment the market into potential customers.

As you learned, **market segmentation** is the process of grouping individuals according to characteristics that help define their needs. Each of these groups of similar individuals is called a **market segment.** No matter how many different segments you may find within any given retail market, you may choose to satisfy only one or just a few of them. Each segment that a retailer attempts to satisfy is a **target market.** Toys 'R' Us has a target market that could be defined as parents and grandparents with infants through teens who desire a large selection of toys and related children's merchandise and are willing to sacrifice individual service for everyday low prices.

Economic. Economic characteristics have a significant impact on country and region selection. The impact on trade area is even greater. The local unemployment rate will affect the local labor pool and the amount of money that consumers have to purchase products. Throughout the 1980s and early 1990s, factory shutdowns and employee layoffs dramatically affected cities and states in the upper Midwest. In the 1990s, California, Arizona, and Texas were impacted by the devaluation of the peso. The migration of workers also had an effect on local employment and purchasing power in the Sunbelt.

The most important economic characteristics for the retailer are per capita income and employment rates. The U.S. Bureau of Labor collects massive amounts of information about these factors. Figure 6.6 shows how per capita income varies around the country.

Subculture.   Subcultures have more of an impact on market and trade area selection than on country or region selection. One must normally be at the market or trade level in order to accurately gauge the location and characteristics of a subculture. An ethnic subculture creates market segments for goods ranging from food and cosmetics to clothing and entertainment. At the same time religion, language, and family structure create both opportunities and problems.

Demand.   The economy of an area under consideration for location should provide a general indicator of the long-range retail opportunities present within an area. The number, type, trends, and stability of industries that might affect business in the market area need to be considered. Employment rates, total retail sales, segment retail sales, household income, and household expenditures all provide information from which the economic stability of the area can be ascertained.

FIGURE 6.6

Per capita income by regions in the United States ($ 1990). (*Source:* U.S. Bureau of the Census, Current Population Reports.)

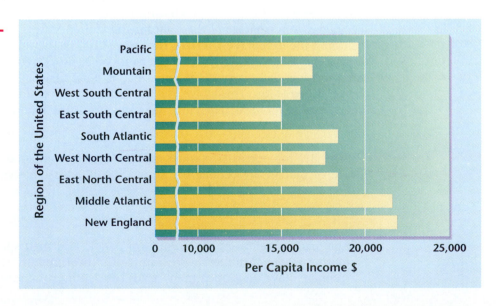

TABLE 6.1

The *Sales Management Survey of Buying Power Index* for the Top Ten Markets

Rank	Area	Buying Power Index
1	Los Angeles–Long Beach	3.328
2	Chicago	3.2821
3	New York	3.2802
4	Washington	2.1005
5	Philadelphia	2.0676
6	Detroit	1.7938
7	Boston	1.6443
8	Houston	1.4994
9	Atlanta	1.4004
10	Nassau-Suffolk	1.2810
Total top ten markets		27.67
Total top fifty markets		50.8491

Source: Reprinted from the *1995 Survey of Buying Power* published by *Sales and Marketing Management* and produced by Market Statistics, both companies of Bill Communications.

The **buying power index (BPI)** indicates the relative ability of consumers to make purchases. The BPI for most metropolitan statistical areas (MSAs) is published yearly by *Sales and Marketing Management* in their *Survey of Buying Power.* The BPI combines effective buying income (weighted 50 percent), retail sales (weighted 30 percent), and population (weighted 20 percent) in a single measure of the purchasing power of consumers. Each variable is specified as a percentage of the total for the United States. For instance, when including the **effective buying income (EBI)** in the formula (the amount of personal income after such things as income, property, and social security taxes and mandatory payments on debt), it must first be divided by the EBI of the United States. This allows the BPI to be directly compared with BPI estimates from other areas. Therefore, we can express the buying power index as:

BPI = 0.5 (% of U.S. EBI) + 0.3 (% of U.S. retail sales) +0.2 (% of U.S. population)

The BPI for potential markets can be directly compared to help make a choice of market area. Table 6.1 shows the BPI for ten major cities in the United States.

Defining the Trade Area

Since a market comprises the number of people and their spendable income, estimating where customers will shop is of critical importance to retailers.

Scholars have developed many tools for defining the size of a trade area.

We will examine Reilly's law and Huff's model, which are called gravity models because they attempt to look at the retail customers and where they will be pulled by the gravity of retail centers. We also introduce the idea of concentric circles and the use of geodemographics. Reilly's law and Huff's model depend on assumptions and data that do not fit the real world very well. At the same time they both demonstrate some of the characteristics that are important in understanding and defining a trade area and show how a model can be constructed and used.

Reilly's Law

Among the most simple of the models is Reilly's law. **Reilly's law** states that a customer will travel a distance to shop based on the population of the shopping area and the distance between areas. In essence, it specifies a break point between two population centers. People on one side of the break point will travel to the city on the same side.

Reilly's law is most useful for calculating the trade area boundaries between two cities. However, it can also be used to calculate the break point between metro areas and surrounding communities, although it is less precise. Reilly's law is based on a simple rule that population centers attract retail shoppers. A trade area can be defined by using Reilly's law to calculate the break points between a city of interest and every surrounding city. The major disadvantage of Reilly's model is that it assumes all retail characteristics are proportional to the size of the population in an area. It does not explicitly consider such things as differences in retailer types or the number of stores in an area. Let's look at an example of using Reilly's law to calculate the break point between a city and the surrounding population centers. The population data and mileage in Table 6.2, and the steps in Box 6.2, were used to calculate the break point distances that define the trade area of Flint, Michigan. The map in Figure 6.7 (on page 219) illustrates the trade area for Flint, which was determined using the break points.

TABLE 6.2

The Trade Area Break Points for Flint, Michigan, Using Reilly's Law

City	Population	Miles from Flint	Break Point Distance	
Flint	138,987	N/A		
Detroit	970,156	54	A	6.77 miles
Ann Arbor	109,252	50	B	22.01 miles
Lansing	126,509	50	C	23.83 miles
Saginaw	69,056	31	D	10.29 miles
Port Huron	35,000	62	E	12.47 miles

6.2 STEPS TO USE IN CALCULATING REILLY'S LAW

1. Draw a line from a city center to a city center between the city of interest and all surrounding cities.

2. Measure these lines with a ruler, and convert from inches to miles using the map legend (e.g., if 15.5 miles = 1 inch, then multiply the number of inches by 15.5 to get miles).

3. Find the population of each city that is connected by a line.

4. Use Reilly's formula to calculate the break point distances.

5. Complete Table 6.2.

6. Change the break point miles into inches (e.g., if 15.5 miles = 1 inch, then divide the number of miles by 15.5 to get inches).

7. In Reilly's law, all break points are always measured starting from the city with the *smaller* population. Using a ruler, measure from the smaller population city the number of inches from step 6 for each line. Mark and label these points.

8. Connect the points from step 7 to define the trade area.

$$\frac{\text{Break point}}{\text{distance}} = \frac{\text{distance between cities}}{1 + \text{square root of} \atop \text{(population of the large city/} \atop \text{population of the small city)}}$$

6543217

Huff's Model

A slightly more complex alternative to Reilly's law was developed by David Huff. **Huff's model** considers the size of the shopping center, how long it would take a customer to travel to each shopping center, and the type of product the customer is looking for. Huff's model gives retailers an approximate probability of how likely it will be for a customer to travel to a specific shopping center. The formula used to calculate Huff's model is shown in Box 6.3. It looks complicated, but it really isn't. Let's put it into English and go through an example.

First, the square footage of a shopping center is divided by the amount of travel time to reach that shopping center. Next, the same calculation is done for the rest of the shopping centers; those numbers along with the calculation for shopping center A are totaled. The proportion for the single shopping center is then divided by the proportion for all of the centers. Both of the travel time figures are modified by gamma (γ), an adjustment for the type of product to be purchased. We will explain more about the gamma in a moment.

The calculations in Box 6.3 indicate that a customer living in the Forestridge neighborhood would travel to shopping center 1 about 38 percent of

FIGURE 6.7

Reilly's law can be used to estimate the break point that defines the point from which customers will drive to a given location. This map illustrates the break point from Flint, Michigan, and surrounding cities and the resulting trade area. (*Source:* Map used with permission. *Rand McNally Road Atlas: United States Canada Mexico 1996 Deluxe Edition,* p. 47. Copyright © Rand McNally, 8255 N. Central Park Avenue, Skokie, Illinois.)

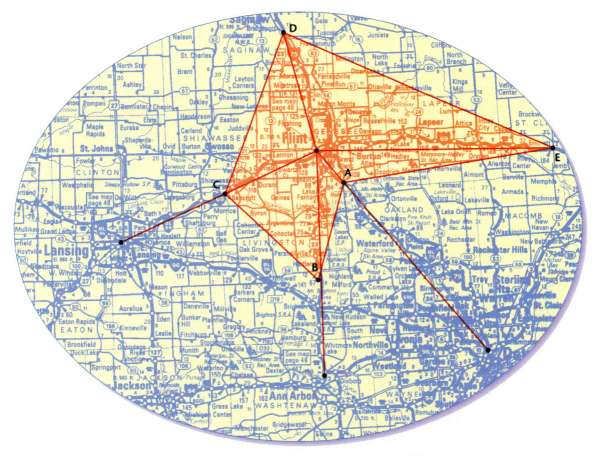

the time. Another way to interpret the result is to say that 38 percent of the residents would travel to shopping center 1 to purchase the type of goods represented by a gamma of 2. Comparing the percentage estimate for shopping center 1 with the other three shopping centers, we see that consumers are about three times more likely to travel to either shopping center 1 or 2 as opposed to shopping center 3 or 4. The percentages for all the shopping centers should total 100 percent.

As stated earlier, gamma (γ) is an adjustment for the type of good that the consumer is looking for at the shopping center. Previous research has calculated gammas of 2.723 for furniture and 3.191 for clothing.[13] The larger

BOX 6.3 CALCULATIONS FOR CUSTOMER TRAVEL TIME TO A GIVEN SHOPPING CENTER USING HUFF'S MODEL

	Shopping Center 1	Shopping Center 2	Shopping Center 3	Shopping Center 4
Travel time (minutes)	5 min	7 min	12 min	15 min
Amount of space in square feet (000)	150 sq ft	300 sq ft	250 sq ft	400 sq ft

Use a gamma of 2.0 and the formula in column 2 to calculate an estimate of how often a consumer would shop at each of the shopping centers.

Shopping center 1 = $(150/5^2) / (150/5^2 + 300/7^2 + 250/12^2 + 400/15^2) = 38.37\%$

Shopping center 2 = $(300/7^2) / (150/5^2 + 300/7^2 + 250/12^2 + 400/15^2) = 39.15\%$

Shopping center 3 = $(250/12^2) / (150/5^2 + 300/7^2 + 250/12^2 + 400/15^2) = 11.10\%$

Shopping center 4 = $(400/15^2) / (150/5^2 + 300/7^2 + 250/12^2 + 400/15^2) = 11.37\%$

$$prob = \frac{sqft_i}{travtime_i^Y} \sum_{j=1} \frac{sqft_j}{travtime_j^Y}$$

where prob = the probability of a shopper traveling to a center

$sqft_i$ = the square footage of the shopping center

$travtime_i$ = the travel time to the shopping center

$sqft_j$ = the square footage of competing shopping centers

$travtime_j$ = the travel time to competing shopping centers

Y (gamma) = an estimated effect of travel time based on the type of good and the kind of purchase

The denominator term is the sum of calculations for each of the shopping centers including the one under consideration.

shopping center 3 (250,000 sq ft)
travel time 12 min
shop here 11.10% of the time

shopping center 1 (150,000 sq ft)
travel time 5 min
shop here 38.37% of the time

Forestridge neighborhood

shopping center 4 (400,000 sq ft)
travel time 15 min
shop here 11.37% of the time

shopping center 2 (300,000 sq ft)
travel time 7 min
shop here 39.15% of the time

6543217

the estimated value of gamma, the smaller the time expenditure will be. Also, as gamma grows larger, the scope of the trading area will become smaller. Obviously, the more important the item is to the customer, the less important travel time becomes. Consumers who are shopping for a specialty good will spend more time traveling than consumers who are shopping for a convenience good. The estimate of the travel time can also vary greatly depending on the form of transportation used by the consumer.

Concentric Zones

One way to analyze a market area is to use maps and census tracts to construct concentric zone maps. Survey data from existing stores can determine how far customers will travel to shop. Obviously this depends on the type of goods and the pulling impact of the location. Customers will travel much farther to shop for home entertainment equipment in a regional mall than to pick up medicine at a pharmacy.

Assume our data show that 60 percent of our customers come from less than four miles (primary zone), 25 percent come from four to eight miles (secondary zone), and 15 percent (tertiary zone) are occasional customers who come more than eight miles. The firm can now take census tract data and determine how many potential customers (owner-occupied household with income over $35,000) live in each zone. Figure 6.8 shows a map of Cincinnati with concentric circles drawn at four, eight, and twelve miles, which

FIGURE 6.8

For one firm located at the intersection of Highway 284 and State Street Avenue in Cincinnati, the concentric zones at 4, 8, and 12 miles define the primary, secondary, and tertiary trade areas. (*Source:* Map used with permission. *Rand McNally Road Atlas: United States Canada Mexico 1996 Deluxe Edition*, p. 71. Copyright © Rand McNally, 8255 N. Central Park Avenue, Skokie, Illinois.)

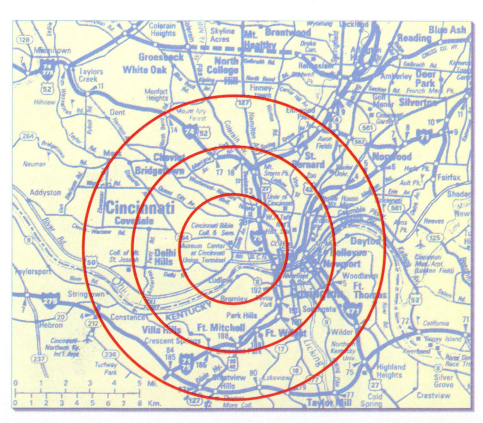

describe the primary, secondary, and tertiary zones around the intersection of Highway 284, State Street Avenue, and 6th Street. The concentric zones help describe a trade area, but as you will see, the actual market may be limited by accessibility factors. Look again at the map of Cincinnati. Notice how the interstate highways could limit accessibility. The actual sales potential of the store is also going to be limited by the number and location of competitors.

Geodemographics

The term **geodemographics** is derived from the demographics of populations coupled with the geographic dimensions of populations. Retail location decisions commit large amounts of capital, and once made, the decision is fixed for a significant period of time. New techniques such as the use of geodemographic information have the potential to be very important.[14]

Geodemographic data are used with a group of software programs known as geographic information systems (GIS). GIS is a computerized system that utilizes information databases to construct digital maps of specified geographic locations. Most GIS systems have computerized mapping, database mapping, and interactive graphic features that provide easy-to-understand visual representation of the data (see Figure 6.9). GIS is becoming more widespread as a result of decreasing cost and increasing power of computer systems. Retailers of all sizes are utilizing GIS to help determine niche markets and understand customer location characteristics.[15] A major advantage of GIS

FIGURE 6.9

Retail location map on GIS.

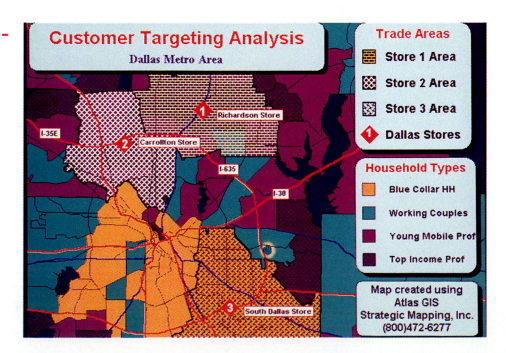

is its ability to upload current market information easily into the system. A typical database would include the demographic data down to census blocks and complete city street maps. Real estate databases can be accessed, which adds the dimension of size and type of locations as well as traffic counts. The latest generation of systems includes a number of features that will make them more user-friendly and easier to integrate into the firms' other information systems.[16]

Although we may describe a retail market in terms of geography, everyone within that geographic area is not a potential customer. To be an effective retailer, you must group together those individuals in your trade area who possess similar needs. Within the trade area, with target market defined, a retailer can stock merchandise and provide specific services to meet the needs of those potential customers.

Estimating Market Potential

Once the retail trade area has been identified and the relative segmenting variables applied, certain quantitative factors must be considered to decide if the area is suitable. These factors include the retail market potential of a retail trade area and the retail sales potential. **Retail market potential** is the total dollar sale that can be obtained by all stores selling a particular retail product, product line, or group of services within a given retail trade area. **Retail sales potential** is the total dollar volume that a particular retailer might expect to obtain within the retail trade area if everything was maximized. Therefore, retail sales potential is a part of retail market potential. A **retail sales forecast** is the specific estimate of sales volume that a retailer expects. Because the retailer is new in the area or because of the entry of a new competitor, the sales forecast may be less than the estimate of retail sales potential.

There are two major determinants of the market potential for a trade area: the number of potential customers within the area and the amount of money consumers spend for the product or product line in question. For example, a retailer can estimate the market potential by multiplying the number of potential consumers in the trade area by the average amount they spend for the product. Generally, market potential figures are based on yearly estimates. Suppose, for example, that 50,000 potential customers reside in the trade area. If it is known that each potential customer spends approximately $79 per year on gifts, the retail market potential for gift sales in that retail trade area would be $3,900,000.

Population statistics are commonly used in arriving at market potential and are expressed on a per capita, a per household, or a per family basis. The other factor is per capita expenditure.

Let's stop for a moment and look at census information as an aid in arriving at population information. Census data provide, in addition to nationwide statistics, information for every city, town, and village in the United States. For metropolitan statistical areas (MSAs), material has been tabulated for census tracts and blocks. MSA is a geographic designation that contains a central city of at least 50,000 inhabitants plus bordering counties that are socially and economically integrated with the central city. Census tracts are small areas within an MSA with about 4,000 or 5,000 population. Blocks are subdivisions of census tracts and generally include populations of around 300 people.

Summary information is available for an entire metropolitan area, for each census tract, as well as for blocks within a city. MSA and census tract data provide fairly comprehensive information, whereas block statistics give general characteristics of the population because of the smaller geographical unit.

In the census reports, tracts and blocks are portrayed on maps like that in Figure 6.5. If the trade area is defined to include blocks, it is the population characteristics within these blocks (or fractions of blocks) that are of most interest to a retailer. For the specific information within a block, the retailer can turn to another page of the census data and locate the relevant population statistics.

In using census data, merchants must be aware that the information is usually based on city and county subdivisions. A retail trade area may have little relationship to these political boundaries. The merchant may be able to get a more detailed breakdown of population by checking with:

- The local chamber of commerce for any detailed studies it may have made
- The local newspaper for circulation statistics
- The local post office for the number of box holders on delivery routes
- The local public utilities office for information on the number of residential electric or gas meters
- The city planning office, fire department, and police department for information on the number of residents within a specific retail trade area

Regardless of the sources used, however, the merchant will probably find it necessary to adjust population information for a retail trade area by using the data collected in combination with individual judgment about the area.

In addition to population information, the retailer must collect data on the number of dollars being spent by consumers for the product or product line in question. Probably the best sources of such information are established trade associations for the kind of business being started. *Gale's Encyclopedia of Associations* lists different business industries and their publications by type of business. Trade associations usually provide information on how much is being spent per capita for the products their members sell. Other sources of information include *Sales and Marketing Management's Survey of Buying Power* and the U.S. government's *Census of Retail Trade*. The latter source contains retail sales for seventy-two kinds of businesses.

For example, a merchant interested in arriving at a per capita consumption expenditure figure could use the census data by taking the total retail sales for a particular kind of business and dividing it by the population of the state or area. For example, in the state of Delaware, the last *Census of Retailing* reported that all stores selling footwear did a total sales volume (excluding toddlers and infants) of $100,863,000. If you divide this figure by the number of people living in Delaware (693,100), you would estimate the per capita footwear expenditure to be $145.52. If inflation has been 3 percent compounded each year for five years, the number would be $168.69.

Estimating Sales Potential

You learned that the retail sales potential for a firm is the estimated dollar sales that a retailer expects to obtain in a particular retail trade area over a given period. An accurate appraisal of sales is important, because it will dictate the amount of inventory that will be purchased, the number of employees that will be needed, the dollars that can be spent for expenses, and the amount of debt capital the business can comfortably afford. To arrive at such a figure, one must consider:

- The competitive strengths in the market
- The amount of business that can be drawn from substitute products
- Management's own expertise

To assess the competitive strengths in the market, the retailer can start with an assessment of the total market potential. If the retailer assumes that the business will obtain at least the average amount of sales being realized by the competitive businesses in the trade area, an estimate of the sales potential can be made. If there are five businesses (the new retail establishment makes six), each business might be expected to have one-sixth of the business available in the trade area.

Although this approach may not seem as sound as that used in measuring market potential, it does provide an analysis of competitive strength, and the figure derived is usually conservative. This approach can be useful in particular situations. Suppose, for example, that a new firm was considering entering a five-store trading area in which the market potential was $2,800,000. A sixth store would mean that the sales potential for the new store would be $466,666 ($2,800,000 divided by 6). If the new firm had to do $600,000-worth of business merely to break even, it would face a situation where profitability would be difficult.

It is possible to use other methods to gauge competitive strength. One is to obtain an approximation of the square footage, the number of employees, the linear counter footage, or the number of checkout stands in competitive establishments. Then, by using trade publications or firsthand information of typical productivity ratios—such as sales per square foot, sales per employee, sales per linear foot of counter space, and sales per checkout counter—one can estimate the amount of business being done by competitors. For example, a fabric shop does, on the average, around $155 per square foot of selling area. If two existing fabric shops had a combined selling area of 6,000 square feet, the total volume of business from these shops might be estimated at $930,000.

Going back to our shoe example, you can see how the $168.69 per person expenditure data can be helpful to estimate shoe sales. If your trade area contains 50,000 people and you believe that you can get 1 out of 10 of them to buy shoes from you, then your estimated shoe sales would be $843,450. This is, of course, an "average" estimate, and you will need to make adjustments depending on the types of shoes you carry, the income level of your customers, and numerous other factors. Regardless of these cautions, this methods gives us a good beginning estimate for our sales volume. The formal name of the calculations we have been using in formulating sales potential is the *index of retail saturation*.

Index of Retail Saturation

Competition exists when more than one store compete for the same market segment or target market. In some situations, a firm might like to be the only one of its type in a given market area. This is particularly the case for specialty or convenience goods. On other occasions, however, good strong competition will enhance the overall business potential of a given area because it will draw shoppers from a greater distance to compare prices or stores. This is particularly the case with goods for which people often make shopping comparisons. Maps may be developed to show retail locations of competitors by relative size and merchandise mix.

One measure of the competitive structure of the market is the **index of retail saturation (IRS),** which examines the level of competition and the retail sales in a given geographical area. There are several ways to formulate this measure. The typical IRS is calculated as area sales divided by a measure of competitive saturation (usually total square feet). Sales in an area can be total retail sales or sales for a standard industry classification (SIC). All retail stores are classified by different SIC codes. The first 2 of 7 digits define the very broad retail group. For example, 53 is the code for automobiles. Competition can be measured by number of stores or square footage of stores over a given time period (usually years, quarters, months, or weeks). If data were available on retail square footage, you would calculate IRS as follows:

$$\text{IRS} = \frac{\text{total market potential in the market area for the SIC code}}{\text{total square feet of stores selling goods for the SIC code}}$$

Assume that ten shoe stores with a total of 30,000 square feet were in the market area. Using our previous $168.69 per capita expenditure for shoes for 50,000 people, total sales would be $8,434,500. Then, you would divide by 30,000 square feet to arrive at $281.15 in sales per square foot. If a store of 3,000 square feet was planned, the sales potential would be $843,450.

Although sales per square foot may give a more accurate account of retail saturation, this information is often difficult to obtain. The retail census data provide sales for SIC code by county. A modified version of the IRS allows for easy access to needed data. The modified formulation is:

$$\text{IRS} = \frac{\text{retail sales by SIC code}}{\text{divided by number of stores in SIC code in that area}}$$

For example, if gasoline service stations in New York and Los Angeles were considered, the following calculations would be made:

$$\frac{\text{Gas station sales (L.A., Calif.)}}{\text{Number of gas stations in L.A., Calif.}} \quad \frac{\$2,943,151,000}{3,032 \text{ stores}} = \$970,696/\text{store}$$

$$\frac{\text{Gas station sales (N.Y., N.Y.)}}{\text{Number of gas stations in N.Y., N.Y.}} \quad \frac{\$106,442,000}{103 \text{ stores}} = \$1,033,417/\text{store}$$

The IRS may be used to compare different markets as above. For example, the IRS for furniture stores in Kansas City, Missouri, is $637,123 compared to $447,162 in Shreveport, Louisiana.[17] The IRS may also be used to compare internal data reflecting the anticipated sales level needed. Obviously, if a firm can find a differential advantage, it can achieve sales above the level suggested by the per store sales revealed in the IRS calculation.

Outshopping. A critical element of any estimate of sales potential is outshopping. **Outshopping** occurs when individuals within your retail trade area go outside your area to shop for similar goods or services. This is a serious problem for smaller shopping areas or communities located near metropolitan areas. Box 6.4 presents an interesting ethical dilemma based on an outshopping issue.

You must be careful that your market potential and sales potential estimates do not overstate the true marketplace for your community. Outshopping can also occur for specific merchandise. In fact, the presence of outshopping may be an indicator that there is a need for specific good or service assortments within your retail trade area.

It is difficult to combat the outshopping phenomenon. The most frequently cited reason for outshopping is the belief that a better assortment of goods and services exists outside the immediate area. The next concern is price. Quite often, smaller communities do not have the level of competitive intensity or the aggregate volume to get prices as low as they are often found in larger metropolitan areas. For example, your author bought an alternator from Auto Zone in a town of 30,000 people less than a one-hour drive from his home and paid $84. The price in the metropolitan city was $64. How would you have felt? The best advice for areas affected by outshopping is to emphasize your merchandise assortment, promote services such as return privileges close to home, and minimize the importance of price. The smaller store cannot compete head-to-head on price, so do not try. Offer *value;* it will be the only long-term win-win solution.

6.4 **AN ETHICAL DILEMMA: "LOCATING ON THE WRONG? SIDE OF TOWN"**

For years residents of Oak Cliff, Fair Park, and South Dallas have been very concerned about inadequate shopping opportunities and lack of large new supermarkets in their neighborhoods.* These areas of the city contain large numbers of ethnic minorities and low-income households. One community leader has said that chain stores and businesses shy away from minority communities because they have misconceptions about the amount of money they can make and the crime rate. The concerns have at times burst into vocal demands by minority groups at city council meetings and resulted in economic development programs sponsored by governments.

The Association of Community Organizations for Reform Now (ACORN) is working to address the concerns of both consumers and businesses in low- and moderate-income neighborhoods. The western regional director of ACORN said, "Everyone should have an opportunity to shop at quality places that serve quality goods. . . . There are still no major department stores or movie theaters in the community."† Merchants say that one of the problems is that residents shop in other areas of town, and things won't improve until they start spending more of their money in their neighborhoods.

A year ago it appeared that things would improve. Fiesta Mart Inc. of Houston announced plans to open six inner-city stores and won tax abatements from the city. The chain opened one location but then canceled or delayed the rest of its plans saying that prospects were marginal.

In the summer of 1994, Minyard's, a regional supermarket chain, began to take a special interest in the South Dallas area. When four public swimming pools there were targeted for closing by the city because of tough budget times, Minyard's executives delivered a $65,000 check to elected officials to pay to keep them open.‡

In 1995, Minyard's opened the first modern full-service supermarket in South Dallas with a deli, bakery, and pharmacy. The store created about 175 jobs.§

Questions

Do you see an ethical issue here? Do chains have a moral responsibility to serve the whole community? What if they cannot achieve "acceptable" profit levels?

Source: *Marcia Halkias, "Minyard's Plans Three Stores in Fair Park, Oak Cliff," *Dallas Morning News,* January 5, 1994, p. 1D.
†Shawn M. Terry, "Southern Dallasites' Support Sought," *Dallas Morning News,* December 27, 1994, p. 1Y.
‡Sylvia Martinez, "Grocery Chain Dives in to Keep Your City Pools Open," *Dallas Morning News,* May 12, 1994, p. 21A.
§Jason Sickles, "Minyard's to Open in S. Dallas," *Dallas Morning News,* August 23, 1994, p. 24.

6543217

Infrastructure

We have talked about how the infrastructure—including roads and highways, distribution warehouses, communications facilities, and labor pool—must be adequate for a country or region. The same is even more true for trade area analysis. The legal infrastructure can also impact the trade area selected for your store. State and local laws vary concerning advertising, zoning, and sign restrictions for retailers. In Vermont, Act 250 allows environmental reviews of projects. It was the last state to have a Wal-Mart. Local governments who want to control commercial development can write planning and zoning codes to accomplish their purposes. The town of Greenfield, Massachusetts, rewrote its zoning codes to accommodate Wal-Mart. The firm made several concessions, but the citizens still voted against the changes that would have allowed them to build a store.[18]

SITE EVALUATION AND SELECTION

Once a retailer has determined that a particular trade area is a good possibility for a store, the analysis turns to site evaluation. There are numerous types of locations. Let's look at these before we turn to an examination of site evaluation criteria.

Types of Locations

There are three major types of location that we will discuss in this section: (1) the shopping center, (2) the business district, and (3) the freestanding location. Where a retail store is located can dramatically impact the amount of traffic and the business the store generates.

Planned Shopping Centers

The expansion of suburbia brought with it planned residential developments. These new subdivisions were connected by many new city streets and thoroughfares along which retail businesses could be established. The notion of the **planned shopping center** was born. Developers could plan multistore facilities that would serve the needs of these new neighborhoods with grocery, drug, and apparel goods. With the availability of large tracts of relatively cheap undeveloped land located many miles from the inner city, but close to these new living areas, large centers could be designed that would offer one-stop shopping to entire clusters of residential areas. The last thirty years witnessed the widespread development of multiunit retail strip centers and the construction of multiacre shopping malls/theme parks.

Several important issues surround the choice of locating a retail business in a planned shopping center. One important consideration is the nature of the businesses sharing leased space within the center. Recent research has shown that the image of your retail business will be either positively or negatively influenced by the types of business that surround you, a process that is called *image transference*.[19] Perhaps there is no better example of how the image of a given store can be influenced by the design of a mall and by the environment created by other stores than the case of *The Forum Shops at Caesar's* in Las Vegas. The Forum Shops is designed to be the "Shopping Wonder of the World" with stores and restaurants located in palatial splendor. The Forum Shops is a visual as well as a retail attraction. Storefront facades and common areas resemble an ancient Roman streetscape, with immense columns and arches, central piazzas, ornate fountains, and classic statuary. Overhead, on a barrel-vaulted ceiling, a painting emulates the beauty of the Mediterranean sky.

Among the prestigious tenants are Gucci, Plaza Escada, Ann Taylor, Christian Dior, and Guess, as well as the Palm Restaurant, and Planet Hollywood. These retailers are benefited by the upscale environment as they appeal to customers seeking unique and high-quality merchandise.

The term *shopping center* has been evolving since the early 1950s. Given the maturity of the industry, numerous types of centers currently exist that go beyond the standard definitions. Industry nomenclature originally offered four basic terms: neighborhood, community, regional, and superregional. However, as the industry has grown and changed, more types of centers have evolved, and these four classifications are no longer adequate.

The International Council of Shopping Centers (ICSC) has defined eight principal types. Table 6.3 at the end of this section provides guidelines for understanding major differences between the basic types of shopping centers. Several of the categories shown in the table—such as size, number of anchors, and trade area—should be interpreted as "typical" for each center type. As a general rule, the main determinants in classifying a center are its merchandise orientation (types of goods and services sold) and its size.

It is not always possible to precisely classify every center. A hybrid center may combine elements from two or more basic classifications, or a center's concept may be sufficiently unusual as to preclude it from fitting into one of the eight generalized definitions presented here.

There are other types of shopping centers that are not separately defined here but nonetheless are a part of the industry. One example is the convenience center, one of the smallest of centers where tenants provide a narrow mix of goods and personal services to a very limited trade area. A typical anchor would be a convenience store like 7-Eleven or other minimart. At the other end of the size spectrum are super **off-price centers** that consist of a large variety of value-oriented retailers, including factory outlet stores, department store closeout outlets, and category killers in an enclosed megamall (up to 2 million square feet) complex. Other smaller subsegments of the

TABLE 6.3

ICSC Shopping Center Definitions

Type	Concept	Sq. Ft. Including Anchors	Acreage	Number	Type	Anchor Ratio*	Primary Trade Area†
Neighborhood center	Convenience	30,000–150,000	3–15	1 or more	Supermarket	30–50%	3 miles
Community center	General merchandise, convenience	100,000–350,000	10–40	2 or more	Discount dept. store, supermarket, drug, home improvement, large specialty/discount apparel	40–60%	3–6 miles
Regional center	General merchandise, fashion (mall, typically enclosed)	400,000–800,000	40–100	2 or more	Full-line dept. store, jr. dept. store, mass merchant, disc. dept. store, fashion apparel	50–70%	5–15 miles
Superregional center	Similar to regional center, but has more variety and assortment	800,000+	60–120	3 or more	Full-line dept. store, jr. dept. store, mass merchant fashion apparel	50–70%	5–25 miles
Fashion/specialty center	Higher-end, fashion assortment	80,000–250,000	5–25	N/A	Fashion	N/A	5–15 miles
Power center	Category dominant anchors, few small tenants	250,000–600,000	25–80	3 or more	Category killers, home improvement, discount dept. store, warehouse club, off-price	75–90%	5–10 miles
Theme/festival center	Leisure, tourist-oriented, retail and service	80,000–250,000	5–20	N/A	Restaurants, entertainment	N/A	N/A
Outlet center	Manufacturers' outlet stores	50,000–400,000	10–50	N/A	Manufacturers' outlet store	N/A	25–75 miles

* The share of a center's total square footage that is attributable to its anchor.
† The area from which 60 to 80 percent of the center's sales originate.

The enclosed mall became popular in the United States as people moved to the suburbs beginning in the 1950s. However, the concept is not new. For hundreds of years customers have gone to the Grand Bazaar in Istanbul to do their shopping. You can buy everything from fresh fish to fine gold jewelry and antique clocks from the Ottoman Empire. All of the prices are negotiated in spirited bargaining.

shopping center industry include vertical, downtown, off-price, home improvement, and car care centers.

Simply stated, a shopping center is a group of retail and other commercial establishments that are planned, developed, owned, and managed as a single property. On-site parking is provided. The center's size and orientation are generally determined by the market characteristics of the trade area served by the center.

Basic Configurations of Shopping Centers

There are two basic shopping center configurations: malls and strip centers. Malls typically are enclosed, with climate-controlled walkways between two facing rows of stores. The term represents the most common design mode for regional and supermarket centers and has become an informal term for them.

A **strip shopping center** is an attached row of stores or service outlets managed as a coherent retail entity, with on-site parking usually located in front of these stores. Open canopies may connect storefronts, but a strip center generally does not have enclosed walkways linking the stores. A strip center may be configured in a straight line or have an "L" or "U" shape.

Shopping center types.   Within the basic configurations, there are eight major types: neighborhood center, community center, regional center, superregional center, fashion/specialty center, power center, theme/festival center, and outlet center.

Neighborhood shopping center. This type is designed to provide convenience shopping for the day-to-day needs of consumers in the immediate neighborhood. Roughly half of these centers are anchored by a supermarket, while about a third have a drugstore anchor. These anchors are supported by smaller stores offering drugs, sundries, snacks, and personal services. A neighborhood center is usually configured as a straight-line strip with no enclosed walkway or mall area, although a canopy may connect the storefronts.

The relatively small size of the strip center means that it offers a rather narrow array of convenience or specialty stores. It is best designed to serve individuals living in the immediate vicinity or frequent passersby who would see the stores in the center as being "convenient." The neighborhood strip center can be placed almost anywhere that land permits. Intersections and main thoroughfares are the most popular sites.

Notably, recent changes in shopping patterns have seen a move away from urban and regional malls to these neighborhood formats.[20] A trade area of around three miles normally supports such a center. A supermarket is characteristic in these centers, and one with a significant market share is a critical factor. More than 10,000 households with an average income of $40,000 within a one-mile radius and a traffic count of more than 50,000 cars with high visibility of signs from the primary street contribute to success.[21]

The **gross leasable area (GLA)** of these types of centers ranges from 30,000 to 150,000 square feet on a site of 3 to 15 acres, with the typical size being about 50,000 square feet. Because neighborhood centers are rather similar and the trade area boundary for a neighborhood center generally extends to a point about halfway between other neighborhood centers, the market from which a given center draws is relatively easy to identify. If the target market for a retail store matches the profile of the neighborhood center, and it can survive with the number of residents within the trade area served by the center, then this may be a suitable location for the business.

Community shopping center. A community center typically offers a wider range of apparel and other soft goods than the neighborhood center. Among the more common anchors are supermarkets, super drugstores, and discount department stores. Community center tenants sometimes include off-price retailers selling such items as apparel, home improvement/furnishings, toys, electronics, or sporting goods. The center is usually configured as a strip, in a straight line, an "L," or a "U" shape. Of the eight center types, community centers encompass the widest range of formats. For example, certain centers that are anchored by a large discount department store refer to themselves as discount centers. Others with a high percentage of square footage allocated to off-price retailers can be termed off-price centers.

The community center usually has 100,000 to 350,000 or more square feet of gross leasable area. Some 90 percent of the newer centers measure less than 150,000 square feet of GLA. Developers are attracting stores like Gap,

Ann Taylor, and the Banana Republic to what amounts to specialty store malls. These facilities can be large versions of the open neighborhood centers or smaller enclosed malls. The site is typically situated on 10 to 40 acres, and a trade area of 100,000 or so people is usually required to support a center of this type.

Many of today's community centers are yesterday's regional centers. Cities have grown to surround these types of centers or larger malls have been developed, and this causes the former retail center powerhouse to lose their "regional" status. These smaller malls currently constitute approximately 87 percent of all shopping mall GLA.[22]

Having lost some of their major tenants to the newer regional malls, community centers often have a new mix of entertainment and restaurants with established merchandise outlets. The trade area for the community center crosses many neighborhood center boundaries.

A retailer's decision to locate within a community center will be based on the ability to benefit from traffic drawn from across the entire community. Because the rental rates in the community center will be much higher than those for a neighborhood or strip center, the revenue benefits must be worth the additional costs.

Regional shopping center.   This type provides general merchandise, a large percentage of which is apparel, and services in full depth and variety. Its main attractions are its anchors: traditional, mass merchant, or discount department stores or fashion specialty stores. A typical regional center is usually enclosed, with an inward orientation of stores connected by a common walkway. Parking surrounds the outside perimeter.

A regional shopping center provides full depth and variety in apparel, furniture, home furnishings, and general merchandise. Regional centers typically contain at least three large full-line department stores supplemented by numerous apparel stores, shoe stores, household appliance stores, furniture stores, drugstores, and supermarkets. More recently, off-price and discount anchors have appeared as mall operators respond to the need of retaining value-conscious shoppers. Gross leasable area for this type of mall ranges between 300,000 and 1,000,000 square feet. The typical size of a regional center is about 400,000 square feet on a 40- to 100-acre site. A trade area of 200,000 or more people is normally required.

A key point of differentiation between the community and the regional center is the extent to which people are willing to drive from one city to another to patronize a regional center. In other words, the shopping alternatives that are available in a regional center must not be present in surrounding communities. This case is often encountered in large urbanized areas that contain multiple large-scale malls, each of which contains similar anchors. A retailer's decision to locate within a regional mall is, again, dependent on the level of demand that is available given rental and utility costs. Another important mall location consideration is signage. As a nonanchor tenant, the lifeblood is not traffic drawn from the street by a sign or storefront but the interanchor traffic generated within the mall. This captured traffic, however, permits the survival of narrow-niche marketers like specialty restaurants.

Superregional shopping center. This is similar to a regional center, but because of its larger size, a superregional center has more anchors, contains a deeper selection of merchandise, and draws from a larger population base. As with regional centers, the typical configuration is an enclosed mall, frequently with multiple levels.

The superregional shopping center is the largest of the planned centers. It encompasses the largest, most complete assortments of goods and services backed by four or more department stores in the 100,000-square-foot and larger class. The gross leasable area of the superregional center ranges from 800,000 square feet to well over 1,000,000. The Mall of America in Bloomington, Minnesota, is a superregional that boasts 4.2 million total square feet, 2.6 million square feet of retail selling space, 4 anchor department stores, 7 junior department stores, 350 specialty shops, an 18-hole miniature golf course, and a Knott's Camp Snoopy amusement center with a log flume ride and roller coaster.[23] In its first year of operation, over 35 million people visited; over 40 percent were tourists from more than 150 miles away.[24] The largest superregional, the West Edmonton Mall, is located in Edmonton, Alberta, Canada, and boasts 5.2 million square feet of floor space and 3.8 million feet of GLA. More than 20 million people visited its 823 stores, 110 restaurants, and indoor amusement park in a single year.[25]

Fashion/specialty center. This type is composed mainly of upscale apparel shops, boutiques, and craft shops carrying selected fashion or unique merchandise of high quality and price. These centers need not be anchored, although sometimes restaurants or entertainment can provide the draw of anchors. The physical design of the center is very sophisticated, emphasizing a rich decor and high-quality landscaping. These centers usually are found in trade areas having high income levels.

Power center. Dominated by several large anchors, a power center includes discount department stores, off-price stores, warehouse clubs, or "category killers," that is, stores that offer tremendous selection in a particular merchandise category at low prices. Some of these anchors can be freestanding (unconnected). The center has only a minimum amount of small specialty tenants.

Power centers are usually constructed as large strip centers with at least 75 percent of the gross leasable area devoted to three or more high-traffic high-volume discount-oriented anchor-type tenants. For example, a Service Merchandise, PetsMart, Best Buy, Office Depot, and Toys 'R' Us could share a common parking area in much the same fashion as a traditional shopping center. Not all power centers are newly constructed. In fact, many viable "power centers" are traditional community shopping malls or older open centers that have been revived as discount shopping centers. In between the anchor stores are smaller leasable areas for independent or chain discount retailers. A major consideration will be price and assortment. The smaller tenant in the power center will need to be a niche discounter. While traffic counts will be very high for the power center, the anchor stores will generally cover a broad spectrum of product lines. To successfully compete in the backyard of these discount giants, a retailer will need to have carefully selected merchandise and services offered to be consistent with the needs of the power center shopper, but fall outside the competitive mix of the anchors.

Theme/festival center.   This center typically employs a unifying theme that is carried out by the individual shops in their architectural design and, to an extent, in their merchandise. The biggest appeal of this center is for tourists; it can be anchored by restaurants and entertainment facilities. The center is generally located in an urban area, tends to be adapted from an older (sometimes historic) building, and can be part of a mixed-use project. A theme/festival center normally contains from 80,000 to 250,000 square feet and covers 5 to 20 acres. Theme centers have common architectural motifs that unite a wide range of retailers. These tenants tend to offer unusual merchandise and have restaurants and entertainment centers that serve as anchors, rather than supermarkets or department stores.

Factory outlet center.   Usually located in a rural or occasionally in a tourist area, an outlet center consists mostly of manufacturers' stores selling their own brands at a discount. An outlet center typically is not anchored. A strip configuration is most common, although some are enclosed malls and others can be arranged in a "village" cluster. Factory outlet malls draw a combination of middle- and lower-class socioeconomic customers. Some contemporary factory outlet centers also include some off-price stores, particularly in newer multilevel mall-style formats. In addition, given the larger-scale formats of outlet centers, factory outlets seem ideally suited for tourist destinations.[26]

Factory outlet stores provide manufacturers with a way to sell the products that were overproduced without going through the traditional retail distribution channel. Sensitivity to location is a key issue here since many brands can be sold in both a factory outlet store and the traditional retail store. Factory outlet stores seem to be most popular among specialty clothing, sporting goods, leather goods, luggage, shoes, and housewares manufacturers. A factory outlet mall is typically located at least thirty miles from national retail chains in order to draw traffic.[27]

Central Business Districts

The **central business district (CBD)** is a shopping area located in either the central downtown area or another area in the city with a concentration of businesses. Until the mid-1970s, the CBD was the core for shopping in most cities. When cities were relatively compact and much smaller, the largest share of retail shopping was done in this downtown area. The CBD contained the largest concentration of department stores, clothing stores, jewelry stores, variety stores, and specialty stores. When the CBD was thriving, it made possible large-scale comparative shopping for all types of merchandise. Ironically, the CBD was an early "mall" concept in that stores were relatively close and comparisons could be made easily. The downtown area also met the needs of out-of-town shoppers, who would frequently be visiting on business or staying in a downtown hotel.

The 1950s and 1960s saw a mass exodus of families and individuals from the cities to the suburbs. These moves were prompted by the widespread availability and use of automobile transportation, improved intercity roadways, advanced telecommunications, and changes in family composition. The result of this population shift was a change in retail structure that permitted retail shopping to be conducted close to the customer's place of residence.

Many downtown areas have deteriorated. They grew old without being renovated. Traffic congestion became intense, and the lack of adequate parking facilities has made downtown shopping difficult. These factors, coupled with rising rental costs and urban crime problems, have made downtown retail locations increasingly hard to justify.[28]

Some downtown areas are making significant strides in combating the trend of retailers moving away. A number of cities converted to a "pedestrian mall" concept. A pedestrian mall does not allow automobile traffic into the mall area, but provides ample parking space on the periphery streets. Storefronts are often required to be remodeled to conform to a desired image. In short, the new downtown retail district adopts the layout of an open-air shopping center. Although deemed quite successful in cities such as Denver and Fort Worth, in other areas the results have been disappointing. In other cases, city planners are encouraging the construction of integrated office buildings, condominiums, restaurants, and tourist attractions. This renewal is often accompanied by aggressive expansion of meeting facilities and new hotel rooms.[29] Designing stores to fit into downtown areas often requires modifying the typical one-level suburban prototype store. A Target store in downtown Pasadena has three levels with four oversized elevators and escalators that have steps deep enough to accommodate a shopping cart. Logistics can also be a challenge. The Toys 'R' Us store in downtown Chicago

A progressive downtown renewal is a prerequisite before most retailers should consider locating in a central business district. Such renewal is neither easy nor inexpensive to successfully complete. A combination of access, parking, restaurants, apartments, and entertainment is essential to bring customers and retailers into the district. One of the most essential requirements is that potential customers feel assured of their physical safety.

Small retailers who find a niche market, have key locations, and provide personal service and expertise can prosper in the face of huge price-driven retailers. The 17th Street Surf Shop is a niche nine-store chain that targets males ages 8 through 28 with surf gear: 10 percent hard goods and 90 percent soft goods. Customers get attention from sales associates who provide special help because of their expertise. (Cockerham, Paul W., "The Little Fish Survive," *Stores*, November 1994, pp. 64–65.)

keeps the stockroom open all night because traffic restrictions limit deliveries to nighttime hours.[30]

Many cities are passing statutes that require downtown buildings to have street-level retail sites. Reuse and modernization of commercial buildings also promise to help the return of street-level retail activity to downtown areas. A retailer must decide whether renovation of downtown building space is commercially feasible. The following attributes should be considered: (1) easy access from street, (2) abundance of foot and vehicular traffic, (3) space and lighting for appropriate signage, (4) physical dimensions required to support business use, (5) a contiguous population that can correlate with the quality of shops and their brand name merchandise and the expected cost of goods, and (6) the design enticements to help make the location a unique shopping experience.[31]

Freestanding Locations

This type of retail store stands alone, physically separate from other retail stores. It does not enjoy the same benefits that shopping centers offer from the standpoint that customers of a freestanding store must have made a special trip to get there. Shoppers are not "just next door" and decide to walk in as they could in a mall or strip center. Freestanding locations constitute about 22 percent[32] of all retail space, and a recent survey of retailers shows that this category leads all others for future importance.[33]

Wal-Mart and Kmart, for example, have long traditions of building freestanding locations for their stores. Because of their overall size requirements, the need for a very large parking lot, the large volume of semitrailers arriving at their loading docks every week, and a desire for high-traffic locations, a freestanding site has traditionally been their best choice. The neighborhood convenience store can be considered freestanding because it does not require a trip tie-in with other stores. Some retailers are reevaluating their mall location. In fact, recent moves by Chick-Fil-A have been from in-mall locations to freestanding sites so that they can increase their seating capacity, add drive-through sales, and capture a portion of the booming breakfast business.[34] A freestanding Chick-Fil-A can garner sales increases of 70 percent over a typical in-mall location. The retailer who chooses a freestanding location must offer customers unique benefits to make it worth a special trip to visit the store. Frequently, the freestanding retailer will select a convenient site along the major traffic corridors. Discount stores have a price advantage that makes a trip worthwhile. Because its managers believe that freestanding locations offer greater visibility from the road, easier parking, and greater proximity to target market neighborhoods, Walgreens Drugs has recently pursued a strategy of seeking freestanding locations to supplement its current mall locations and strip centers.[35]

Drive-in locations are special cases of freestanding sites that are selected for the purpose of satisfying the needs of customers who shop in their automobile. In some situations, the drive-in aspect of the retail business is only to supplement existing in-store sales, but the same requirements of all drive-in locations apply. These sites are usually positioned along or beside heavy traffic arteries in neighborhoods, city streets, or innercity thoroughfares because, as the experience of McDonald's shows, up to 55 percent of total store sales are often attributable to drive-through business.[36] Stores that rely totally on drive-in and walk-up business, such as Fox Photo, are designed to offer extremely quick service and require a significantly smaller amount of space than more traditional park-and-shop stores. In fact, drive-in-only retailers often find that they can price competitively because of reduced overhead from smaller building and land size.

The total volume of passing traffic and the ease with which the traffic can enter and leave the store are critically important to the sales potential of the entire establishment. The greater the density of traffic, the greater the potential amount of business that is likely to be derived. An automobile traffic count is absolutely necessary to identify suitable locations for drive-ins. Furthermore, it is important that this traffic count be separated into direction, or flow.

A traffic flow analysis may be described in terms of why a customer is making the trip: whether it is to or from work, for shopping, or for pleasure or recreation. For example, drive-in services for a bank would more likely be utilized during work-to-home trips than the reverse. If the objective of a drive-in window of a fast-food chain was to increase breakfast food sales, then a home-to-work direction would be favorable. A work-trip customer may drop off cleaning on the way to work and stop for gas on the way home.

Customers on a shopping trip are more easily stopped if a location is positioned along the right side of a thoroughfare. Not all shopping is done between home and work. This is particularly true if a drive-in is located

The Cracker Barrel is a chain of restaurants featuring "country cooking." Customers enter through a retail area that contains a wide range of country-oriented merchandise. Rocking chairs are displayed next to dolls, figurines, gifts and books. The merchandise complements the food service and adds a unique competitive advantage to the total operation. The company has chosen to build its own freestanding facilities to be able to implement its strategy.

between the customer's place of residence and a major shopping area. If there are a number of stores located in the general vicinity, the drive-in should be on the same side of the street as those stores. To attract recreation or pleasure trip shoppers, locations along a heavily traveled artery are best. The location should be convenient to enter and leave, adjacent to the incoming traffic.

Assessing Site Evaluation Criteria

The description of locations you have just read provides most of the ideas about the evaluative criteria for selection of a site. Putting all of the different ideas together and coming to a decision is the trick. There is no such thing as a "perfect site." Retailers must decide which attributes are the most important to their business. As we will see in a moment, a *multiattribute weighted checklist* is one of the most common methods for doing this. Without going into detail, there are several other methods that can be used in the evaluation process. For example, the analog financial method provides a view of the store's financial performance at a set point in time by focusing on the degree of market penetration. In other words, the site is evaluated on its sales potential and cost of doing business at that site. The regression method is a statistical approach that relates sales (the dependent variable) to other independent variables or factors that are related to sales. Gravity methods, such as Reilly's law and Huff's model, can be applied to specific retail locations. The network model selects sites in accordance with the goal of maximizing profit or sales of the company's whole retail network.[37]

Let's summarize the key criteria critical to the site selection decision.

Sales potential for the site. The demographic, economic, and competition factors and the strategies by which management hopes to create a competitive advantage determine the estimate of sales for a site. *Growth potential* should be a basic consideration in the evaluation of the sales potential.

Accessibility to the site. Automobile and public transportation access to the site and adequate parking may well be defining criteria. There may be a number of barriers to the target market seeing the site as accessible. The barriers may be geographical, such as mountains or rivers. They may be psychological, such as the perceived quality of the neighborhoods that customers must travel through. Barriers are often man-made, such as one-way frontage roads, bridges, cloverleafs, and long-term public works construction projects.

Pedestrian accessibility at the site. The site must provide reasonable actual and perceived access to the store. Traffic patterns within malls or on city streets can help or hinder pedestrian access. The storefronts can intimidate or encourage entry. Neighboring stores can bring potential customers near or drive them away. Have you ever watched customers turn away when they have to try to get to a store through a group of teens waiting in line to get tickets to the movie in the mall?

Synergies from nearby stores. We discussed image transference as either a help or a hindrance to drawing traffic to the store. There is cumulative attraction when businesses can draw more customers together than they could individually. That is why auto dealers will tend to locate where shoppers can visit each of them in a single trip. In a shopping center a group of complementary stores such as apparel and accessories benefit from being near one another. There is more likely to be a **cross-shopping** benefit when the stores have similar retailing strategies on dimensions of merchandise quality and price lines, service quality, and store atmosphere.

Technology is providing new ways to fine-tune the site evaluation process in terms of the architectural fit with neighboring stores. How the store and its exterior design mesh with the neighboring stores is a concern. Advanced computer imaging allows the retailer to see how the storefront will look in the area before construction or moving begins.[38]

Site economics: leasing and occupancy terms. The terms of the lease or purchase contracts have critical implications for the retailers. In a recent survey of retail managers,[39] leasing options and terms were expressed as among their top concerns. Occupancy rates in the immediate or surrounding vicinity also have important implications to retail managers. For example, lower occupancy rates may improve your ability to negotiate a more favorable lease because the developer is anxious to fill vacant space; but low occupancy may signal poor access, poor market variables, or poor management relations with the center owner/developer. Furthermore, even if the vacant space is not a signal of poor economic viability in the market, too much vacancy can be an open door to a competitor. In fact, if the vacant space is sufficient, it can quickly be occupied by a competitor that you did not anticipate.

The full range of the costs of occupancy must be considered. Local taxes, maintenance and upkeep costs, renovation costs, utilities, as well as the cost to rent or own, are all critical factors.

Legal and political environment. Increasingly, the legal and political environment is an important consideration in site location decisions. Changes in zoning laws, taxing districts, and road maintenance projects can threaten the long-run viability of a specific site.

Physical features. The physical features of the site and neighboring area must not be overlooked. Whether it is raw land or an existing building, the physical dimensions of the site must fit your needs. Gap, for example, has adopted a standard layout for all of its stores to simplify shelving, checkout, stock room, and merchandise display needs.[40] Consequently, if a site will not accommodate this predetermined configuration, it is abandoned.

The size and shape of a site, visibility of a site for signs, age of surrounding buildings, traffic flows by time of day, traffic turning patterns, and number of traffic lanes have critical implications to factors such as access, number of cars that can be parked, or room for future expansion. Condition of building or rental space, visibility from the street, disabled and delivery access, parking lot condition and size, and interior decor must also be considered.

A site that is functional today may not be functional tomorrow as your business expands. As an area grows, you need to be able to assess whether or

Attribute	Management Importance	Existence				Score = importance × existence			
		Mall	Downtown	Stand alone	Strip Mall	Mall	Downtown	Stand alone	Strip Mall
Low rent and maintenance									
Low leasehold improvement costs									
High vehicle traffic									
High foot traffic									
Parking available									
Expansion possible									
High area population									
High income area									
Appropriate store size									
Near target market									
Low-cost promotion									
Occupancy/ terms/legal									
Tenant fit									
Visibility									
Totals									

Management importance scale

Least important ———————————— Most important

1	2	3	4	5	6	7

Existence scale

Does not describe location ———————— Best describes location

1	2	3	4	5	6	7

FIGURE 6.10

A multiattribute weighted checklist.

not the existing streets, highways, and intersections will accommodate the expanded vehicular traffic. The close proximity of older buildings may suggest that future development is unlikely or that the area is suffering from economic decline. Close attention to zoning must be paid when evaluating the physical features of a proposed site.

Multiattribute Weighted Checklist

We said that management judgment is the method used by many firms to integrate all the site evaluation factors. At the basic level, a checklist of important factors is made and the site is evaluated as to the degree to which the desired characteristics are present for the site being evaluated. Figure 6.10 is an example of a multiattribute weighted checklist that can be used to quantify the judgments when two or more sites are being evaluated. Notice that down the left-hand side of the checklist is a list of factors or attributes that management might consider important. Across the top are several possible sites. A weight from 1 to 7 for each of the factors is assigned based on that factor's relative importance. Then, for each factor for each site, a number is assigned to the degree to which that factor exists. If you multiply the management importance by the existence score, you get a total score for each factor. Adding up the total scores for each site allows you to have quantitative comparison.

To obtain information needed to make a good site evaluation, retailers who are planning new locations need to investigate secondary sources and question people who know the community, in addition to doing their own analysis. Visiting the local chamber of commerce; asking for advice from local industrial development groups; talking to bankers, real estate brokers, newspaper editors, various businesspeople, area highway departments, and city/county zoning commissions; and visiting local area shopping center developers are all ways of gaining this needed information.

WAL-MART—REVISITED: NAFTA OPENS GLOBAL MARKETS

One of the more promising areas for expansion by Wal-Mart is in the international arena. With the advent of NAFTA (the North American Free Trade Agreement), Wal-Mart has moved into two new potentially lucrative markets: Canada and Mexico.

Wal-Mart became familiar with the Latin American consumer through its store in Laredo, Texas. It is estimated that 70 percent of that store's sales are derived from Latin Americans crossing the Mexican border. With over 151,000 square feet of selling space (the size of three football fields) the store has 350 "associates" in 36 departments. In a bid to expand directly into the Mexican market, Wal-Mart formed a joint venture with CIFRA SA, Mexico's largest retailer. They opened their first two superstores in Monterrey and Mexico City. Wal-Mart had to close the doors for two hours during its grand opening in Monterrey, Mexico, because of an overflow of shoppers. That was a first for Wal-Mart! Wal-Mart's expansion plans for Mexico were put on hold in 1995 when the Mexican economy went into a tailspin. Wal-Mart expanded into Argentina and Brazil in 1995, the first U.S. retailer to operate in either country. The company is also considering locating in Chile, a country that may possibly join NAFTA.

In 1994 Wal-Mart announced its entry into Canada with the purchase of 122 Woolco discount stores throughout the country. The purchase gave Wal-Mart more than 14 million square feet of space in what they believe to be an important new market. In addition to transforming the Woolco stores, the company will rapidly add new stores, opening nearly 100 in the first two years after entering the market.

Wal-Mart is likely to concentrate on continued international expansion. The 1995 company stockholder report states, "While we will proceed cautiously in light of obvious cultural differences, we are confident that the Wal-Mart concept is 'exportable' in part because of our emphasis on providing the customer with quality, value, and service." With current operations in Brazil, Argentina, China, and Hong Kong, the company obviously plans to be an international player.

1. **Is it wise for Wal-Mart to expand into the international arena? If so, did it choose the right countries for expansion?**
2. **What are likely to be the difficulties associated with expanding into Mexico and Canada?**
3. **Wal-Mart had traditionally targeted smaller communities. However, in Mexico it entered two of the largest cities. Why do you think the company changed its usual strategy?**

 Summary

Retailers want to locate their stores in the best place possible. The best place possible will vary from retailer to retailer depending on the industry, type of product, competition, and other market factors. Basically, a retail store should be located where the market opportunities are at optimal levels.

There are basic guidelines that most retailers examine before choosing a new location. First, the retailer must select a country or region and then define the boundaries of the trade area and evaluate its population characteristics against the retailer's target market. The buying power of the area must be considered along with its market and sales potential. The size, location, and type of competition must also be taken into account. The local legal and political environment must be examined along with the leasing costs and occupancy rates. The actual physical features of the location—such as available space, traffic and access to the site, and surrounding buildings—play a role in the selection process.

Retailers possess many tools to help in the site selection decision. Reilly's law and Huff's model can aid in defining the trade area. Market segmentation and demographic segmentation provides clues to population characteristics. The buying power index and effective buying income suggest strength of the economic base, while the index of retail saturation offers a benchmark for market comparison.

Changes in consumer lifestyles will require new strategies for selecting retail locations, such as the increasing use of conve-

nience-oriented sites, the integration of food and nonfood retailing, and the placement of retail merchandising in amusement parks.

There are numerous kinds of retail locations to choose from as well. Most potential sites fall into one of these categories: business districts, shopping centers, and freestanding locations. There are eight basic types of shopping centers: neighborhood, community, regional, superregional, fashion/specialty, power, factory outlet, and theme/festival. There are specific advantages and disadvantages for each type of location. The bottom line in retail site selection should be to choose a location that will fit both today's and tomorrow's needs.

KEY TERMS AND CONCEPTS

Buying power index (BPI), 216

Central business district, 238

Community shopping center, 233

Cross-shopping, 241

Demographic variables, 207

Drive-in locations, 239

Effective buying income (EBI), 216

Factory outlet center, 236

Fashion/specialty center, 235

Flow-through replenishment, 207

Freestanding location, 238

Geodemographics, 222

Gross domestic product, 208

Gross leasable area (GLA), 233

Huff's model, 218

Index of retail saturation (IRS), 226

Market segment, 214

Market segmentation, 214

Neighborhood shopping center, 233

Off-price center, 230

Outshopping, 227

Planned shopping center, 229

Power centers, 235

Regional shopping center, 234

Reilly's law, 217

Retail market, 212

Retail market potential, 223

Retail sales forecast, 223

Retail sales potential, 223

Retail trade area, 213

Strip shopping center, 232

Superregional shopping center, 235

Target market, 214

Theme/festival center, 236

QUESTIONS

1. Describe what you believe to be the significant trends in selecting retail locations.

2. Explain what effect the following would have on retail location:

a. Population shifts

b. Changing competitive conditions

c. Customer spending patterns and habits

d. Altering transportation influences

3. Explain how the deterioration of the downtown area of cities has affected consumer buying habits.

4. Does vehicle accessibility affect the success of most new businesses? When might it not be a factor?

5. How will the flow of traffic affect the success or failure of a drive-in retail store?

6. Can competition increase your business?

7. How can traffic flow be used to forecast sales volume? Is this an accurate measure?

8. Discuss the trend of retail stores moving away from downtown locations. How might the trend be reversed?

9. What role do census data play in determining market potential? Are they important? Why or why not?

10. If you were asked to suggest ways of revitalizing your downtown shopping district, what would you propose?

SITUATIONS

1. You are given the opportunity to buy a small confectionery store. This store makes its own candy and also sells candy purchased through national manufacturers. The business is located in the downtown area of a town with a population of 80,000. Currently, downtown retail sales are equal to those of a strip shopping center located at the edge of town. Within the next two years a major shopping center—a regional mall—will come into the community. It is expected that this mall will have a substantial impact on the retail sales of the downtown area and on the sales of the other strip shopping center. The confectionery store has enjoyed profitable trade for twenty-five years in its present location. The owners will sell the business for $40,000. Last year it netted $27,000, exclusive of the owners' salaries. Would you buy this business? Explain.

2. You are considering opening a bridal shop. You hope to offer your customers merchandise including gowns for the bride and bridesmaids, bridal accessories, tuxedo rentals, and wedding invitations. In addi-

tion, you will offer a free consulting service. You have two sites from which to choose. One is in a regional shopping center located in the popular end of town. It would rent for $25 a square foot for 800 square feet. The other is located at the other end of town in a convenience shopping center, in a less populated area, renting for $10 per square foot for 800 square feet. With only this information available from which to make a decision, which site would you choose?

3. You are the owner of a small shop in a college town of about 25,000 people. There are 7,000 students attending the college. Your shop sells only submarine sandwiches. Business has been fairly good, but you feel that because you offer only take-out service, you are missing an opportunity to do more business. Therefore, you are considering expanding your business by taking over the vacated store next to yours. Then you can provide your customers with tables and chairs. What should you take into consideration as you make your decision? What alternative actions might increase business?

CASES

CASE 6A
Lloyd's Ltd. Fine Men's Wear (A)

In 1978 Lloyd Tanner opened a men's apparel store in Colorado Springs, Colorado. His store was successful, and in 1985 he opened three stores in Denver and then one in Boulder in 1988. In the spring of 1996, Tanner was considering opening a store in Fort Collins, Colorado. As in the other stores, he would carry a full line of upper-end quality men's apparel and furnishings.

To help make the decision, Tanner collected data from a number of sources, including the *1995 Survey of Buying Power*. See Box 6.6.

The following information is from Tanner's notes:

1. Enrollment at Colorado State University is 18,000.

2. Estimates of men's and boy's clothing in all stores: $36,757,000.
   Estimates of men's and boy's clothing in apparel stores: $18,747,000.

3. One source shows eighty-six stores selling all kinds of apparel. The Fort Collins phone book lists nineteen stores under men's clothing that are not department stores.

4. The U.S. government estimate is that 1.7 percent of disposable income is spent in the men's apparel category. The best estimate is that disposable income in Fort Collins is $1.4 billion.

5. Unless a men's store has very low overhead and/or high turnover, it cannot survive on less than $300 sales per square foot. A moderately successful, full-service store would average about $350 per square foot, and a very successful one $400 per square foot.

6. The typical men's store in Fort Collins has 2,000 to 3,000 square feet. One larger specialty chain store in the regional mall has 7,500 square feet, and some downtown ones are as small as 1,500 square feet.

7. Typical operating factors as a percentage of net sales:

Cost of goods	58.7
Repairs	0.4
Bad debts	0.2
Rent	5.8
Taxes (excluding federal tax)	2.2
Interest	1.4
Depreciation	1.4
Advertising	2.4
Other expenses, including payroll and employee benefits	21.6
Net income before tax	2.3

8. Additional Information—Tanner's stores:

Average sales	$695,000
Expenses	$260,000
Inventory turnover	4.5
Build out cost per sq. ft.	$20
Fixtures and equipment	$90,000
Cash on hand for expenses is needed for one inventory turn.	

1. *Based on the data Mr. Tanner collected, what are the pros and cons of locating a new store in Fort Collins?*

CASE 6B
Lloyd's Ltd. Fine Men's Wear (B)

After Mr. Turner made an initial market opportunity assessment, he turned his attention to location and site analysis. There were a number of alternatives, but he selected two as worthy of detailed consideration.

Location I

Downtown on the west side of College Avenue between Oak and Mountain. (See Figure 6.11.)

BOX 6.5 RETAIL DATA FOR FORT COLLINS, COLORADO

Population

Metro Area County City	Total Population (Thousands)	% Of U.S.	Median Age of Pop.	% of Population by Age Group				Households (Thousand)
				18–24 Years	25–34 Years	35–49 Years	50 & Over	
Larimer County	216.0	.0824	32.0	12.9	16.4	24.7	20.3	82.0
*Fort Collins	101.7	.0388	28.5	20.6	18.3	22.2	16.0	39.3

Retail Sales by Store Group

Metro Area County City	Total Retail Sales ($000)	Food ($000)	Eating & Drinking Places ($000)	General Mdse. ($000)	Furniture/ Furnish. Appliance ($000)	Auto-motive ($000)	Drug ($000)
Larimer County	2,145,070	348,377	256,790	358,100	149,181	419,451	32,610
*Fort Collins	1,395,698	222,454	169,518	225,410	114,678	274,502	19,996

Effective Buying Income

% of Hslds. by EBI Group:

(A) $10,000–$19,999
(B) $20,000–$34,999
(C) $35,000–$49,999
(D) $50,000 & Over

Metro Area County City	Total EBI ($000)	Median Hsld. EBI	A	B	C	D	Buying Power Index
Larimer County	3,467,143	35,288	16.0	23.3	18.6	31.7	.0843
*Fort Collins	1,576,827	32,505	17.8	21.8	17.0	29.7	.0442

Source: Reprinted from the *1995 Survey of Buying Power* published by *Sales and Marketing Management* and produced by Market Statistics, both companies of Bill Communications.

6543217

1. Rent $16 per square foot for 3,200 square feet.

2. Three-year lease.

3. Lessee pays all utilities (estimated $4 per square foot).

4. Estimated cost for remodeling, carpet, fixtures, and lighting: $150,000.

Location II

In the Foothills Fashion Mall located off Foothills Parkway on the east side of South College Av-

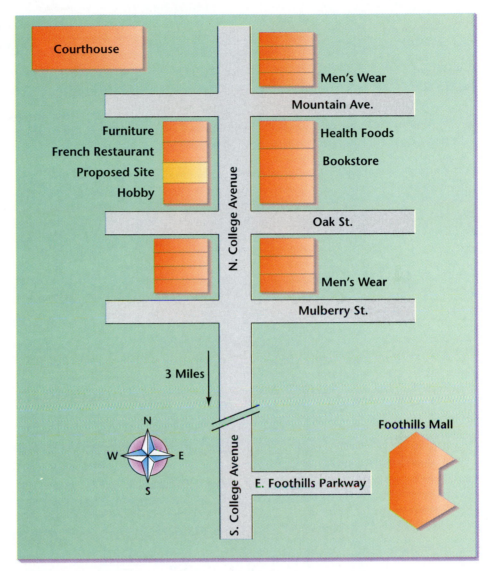

FIGURE 6.11

Potential location I, downtown.

enue, number 12. (See Figure 6.12.) (Men's stores are located at sites 8, 37, and 59.)

1. Rent $35 per square foot for 2,400 square feet and 3 percent of sales after $800,000.

2. Five-year lease.

3. Lessee pays $1 per square foot for the merchants' association and $2 per square foot

for heat; pays own electric, estimated to be $2 per square foot.

4. Estimated cost for build out: $105,000.

1. *What competitive and market factors should influence Tanner's decision?*

2. *What does an analysis of the rental costs suggest?*

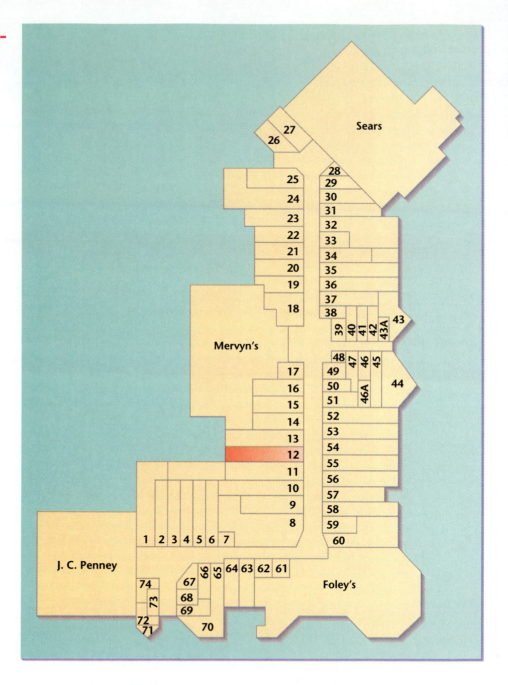

FIGURE 6.12

Potential location II, in Foothills Fashion Mall, number 12.

CASE 6C
To Move or Not to Move

A small South American import shop that has been in business for nine months in a popular ski town is considering moving to a slightly larger location. The business is operating above the break-even point, with sales approaching $250 per square foot, but a move at this time would put some strain on financial resources. The present location has good access and parking, but it is in a neighborhood center three blocks away from the main shopping area at the ski mountain.

The merchandise carried in the shop is imported directly from South America, is mostly handmade, and is of high quality. The product line consists of such items as handwoven tapestries in the $200 to $1,200 price range and gift and apparel items from $17 to $300. The primary target market is upper-middle-class tourists. Some local residents do gift shopping in the store as well.

The new location under consideration is toward the end of a string of street developments at the base of the ski mountain. This development contains about thirty shops and is considered the main shopping district at the ski area. Although the available location is at the far end of the development from the ski lifts, it is close to the main hotel and very near the bus stop. Parking is limited, and most shoppers are on foot.

Both spaces currently have the same rent of $25 per square foot, but the available location under consideration calls for rent of 7 percent of gross sales if this amount exceeds the base rent expected. This location does offer a 300-square-foot loft, suitable for a storage and office area, rent-free.

The lease on the present location is up for renewal in three months at the option of the tenant. The alternative location would require a three-year lease.

1. *What factors should the owner consider in changing locations?*

CHAPTER

7

Chapter Goals

After reading this chapter, you should be able to:

- Understand how to design a comprehensive store plan.

- Demonstrate your knowledge of the basics of external store design practices.

- Explain how interior store design is affected by existing space, stock storage, customer traffic flow, and types of goods.

- Know the basic interior design elements of a store.

- Demonstrate the basic guidelines for effective store display.

- Understand the process of developing a planogram and know how to use it.

STORE DESIGN AND LAYOUT

KMART:[1] COMPETING WITH STORE DESIGN

During the late eighties, Kmart Corporation suffered from declining sales and profits. The company had been concentrating on expansion through acquisitions and new store formats. In the 1980s Kmart operated several retail outlets in addition to the Kmart discount general merchandise stores including Builders Square, OfficeMax, The Sports Authority, PACE membership warehouse, Waldenbooks, Borders Books, Payless Drug, BizMart, Pay'n Save, and Office Warehouse. At the beginning of the 1990s Kmart was the second largest retailer in the United States with sales of more than $30 billion. However, the company was not achieving an acceptable profit level.

In 1989, in order to halt a downward spiral, the chief executive officer, Joseph Antonini, had recommended a complete restructuring plan for Kmart stores.

The restructuring called for the closure of stores that were not performing and the relocation and rebuilding of most older stores. The plan was a five-year, $3.5 billion program aimed at remodeling or removing existing discount stores. By 1993, Kmart had closed or relocated 323 stores and refurbished 874 more, but the company still lost $550 million on sales of $34 billion.

Modernization of existing stores radically changed the format of Kmart. Not only were the existing stores enlarged and given a facelift, but they were also redesigned. The remodeling included widened aisles, improved lighting, and installation of better signs and displays. An improved inventory control system was implemented to increase efficiency. On the merchandising side, Kmart started aggressive television advertising in an attempt to get rid of its image as the "Polyester Palace" and create the look of a popular-price fashion store.

A new prototype for store design is located in Auburn Hills, Michigan. The store has 116,000 square feet of selling space. There is a general refinement of the ambience with updated fixtures. The traditionally empty space near the ceiling is filled with signage, coloration, and graphics. Baffles are marked with logos of brand names to assist the customers in finding what they need. The cash registers are equipped with phones connected to all departments. The registers are angled so that the checkout associates are facing customers. Color-coded borders help shoppers locate departments. The new auto service center has a glass-enclosed lounge for customers waiting for their vehicles to be serviced. In another significant change, a cosmetics boutique has department store–style showcases containing fragrances such as Liz Claiborne, Aziza, and Giorgio. These allow customers to get service and information.[2] Finally there is a sixty-seat Little Caesars restaurant for carryout as well as eating in.

The display counters have been raised to eighty-four inches to accommodate more products and reduce back-room space. Rather than a central entrance that divides hard lines from apparel, the store opens with a corner entrance in the fashion area.

Kmart continues to explore design and merchandising strategies that will increase sales of high-margin merchandise, create greater flexibility to meet changing customer desires, and strengthen Kmart's image as a low price leader.[3]

Some of the new stores also include the ShopperTrak system. This consists of a maze of ceiling sensors to track where customers congregate and how they move through the store. It allows Kmart to reposition its products, especially impulse purchase items, to higher traffic areas. It also indicates how the stores can improve customer flow.

1. Why do you think Kmart's massive store layout and remodeling effort has had such a limited impact on increasing profits?

INTRODUCTION

Rapid changes in consumer buying behavior and demographics require that today's retailer be extremely flexible and creative when thinking about the store design, layout, and presentation plans. Store design and layout are derived from the retail format, and yet they are a part of that format. Remember in Chapter 2 we defined *retail format* as the total mix of merchandise, services, advertising and promotion, pricing policies and practices, location, store design, layout, and visual merchandising used to implement the sustainable competitive advantage. See Figure 7.1. It is the format that positions and distinguishes the firm from other competing retail companies.

The value of design and layout cannot be underestimated. A new store look, for example, could increase sales anywhere from 10 to 300 percent, according to Ann Erickson of Retail Planning Associates.[4]

The retail format positions and distinguishes the firm from the competition.

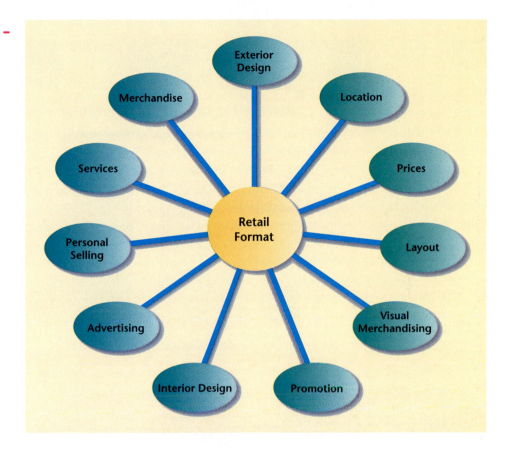

This chapter examines the factors that should be considered in planning a new store or remodeling an old one, and provides ideas for using store design and layout as a merchandising tool. See Figure 7.2. Exterior design is the complete architectural aspects of what the customer sees before entering the store including color and materials, signage, window, security, and the store entrance. The issues relating to interior design begin with layout management and determining the value of space, customer traffic flow, and the type of goods and complementary merchandise placements. The interior layout design elements include fixtures, displays, floors, color, lighting, ceiling treatments, and security.

COMPREHENSIVE STORE PLANNING

In this section we will discuss some overall planning concepts. We will then turn to more details regarding exterior design, interior design, layout management, and interior design elements.

FIGURE 7.2

The nature of store design.

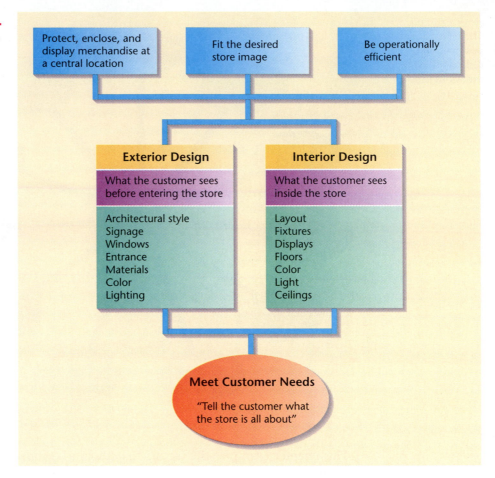

Store design is the architectural character or decorative style of a store that conveys to the customer "what the store is all about." Stores vary so much in kind, size, and geographical location that it is difficult to generalize about design. The architecture of the store's exterior creates an initial impression. For example, if a retailer chooses to remodel an older Victorian home, the customer will get a different impression from that of a store in the mall.

The remainder of the 1990s will likely see design continue to be less concerned with aesthetics and more concerned with establishing an identity and marketing a store image.[5] Key issues like the 1990 Americans with Disabilities Act and state/local ordinances will continue to affect retail design as our population ages and becomes more diverse.[6]

Because of continued pressure on costs, newer designs reflect a closer attention to all details including store size. The drive to reduce inventory levels has forced a move to smaller stores, because a large store with less merchandise looks as though it is going out of business. The stores showing an

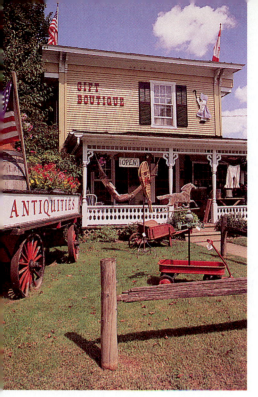

The exterior architectural design of a building can help create identity for the store. Notice how this antique store in Montgomery, Vermont, uses the older home to help capture the image of the merchandise. The "antiquities" sign on an old wagon provides further reinforcement, and the flag says "Americana." The interesting architectural features of the porch provide display opportunities.

increase in store size are those attempting to diversify and broaden merchandise lines. Higher rents, higher building costs, and the move to more localized stores because of the customer's desire for convenience hurt larger, stand-alone, and regional mall stores. Let's look at the planning process.

General Requirements

The first step of store design is the development of a comprehensive plan for the overall requirements of the store. On the basis of market potential (the sales estimate and dollars received per square foot of selling area), plans can be made to meet the need for storage and selling space. The plan must specify the ways to achieve the best traffic circulation possible throughout the store and the types and sizes of fixtures necessary to display the merchandise in an appealing manner. A careful study of these factors helps make stores attractive, conducive to shopping, and as operationally efficient as possible.

In developing a comprehensive layout plan, there are agencies to which the retailer can go to get assistance. For most retailers, getting specialized assistance makes a great deal of sense. An individual retailer may lack expertise and familiarity with the latest developments in store design and layout. Furthermore, retailers rarely have the time to check building codes, work with contractors, and shop for equipment.

Some of the agencies that help in store planning include merchandise suppliers, local architects, engineers specializing in store planning, store equipment firms, and consulting firms. Contact can be made with the consulting firm nearest the store through the Institute of Store Planners. In general, the cost of using professional store planners is about 7 percent of construction costs. Some of this can be offset by discounts made available to store planners by suppliers that may not be available to retailers acting on their own.

Comprehensive planning requires developing a customer-based holistic focus for the design and layout of the store and for the desired store image. Only after this customer focus is defined should a comprehensive plan be developed for both the exterior and the interior of the store that matches the desired store image.

Customer Focus

The focus of a store design should always be the customer. If the store design and layout are appealing, the customer will form an image that is also appealing. It is easy to get into the technical aspects of store design and forget that the retailer's reason for existence is the customer. The design should be focused on forming and maintaining an image, while at the same time making the layout as accessible as possible for shoppers. As discussed in Chapters 4 and 5, research should determine the needs, habits, and buying potential of the shoppers in the area and the need for store service and overall general customer comfort. Management must then determine the overall image that would best differentiate the store and attract the target market.

Store Image

A comprehensive plan would include a process for continuously obtaining customer feedback regarding improvements and for continuously updating the design to reflect changing customer needs and wants. Walter Loeb, a consultant and publisher of the *Loeb Retail Letter,* makes the case for a focused customer-based approach to store images in Box 7.1.

A store design serves two, often opposing, functions. First, and foremost, the design serves the functional purposes of protecting, enclosing, and dis-

---

BOX 7.1 BE FOCUSED—STORE IMAGE[7]

"Each specialty store should focus on a specific classification of merchandise and a specific customer profile. Nice merchandise is not enough. Stores that do not know the customer they want to serve will perish. Retailers must ask themselves over and over again whether certain products are relevant to the image of their stores. If not, they should be edited from the assortment.

"Store images must be focused. Some stores are *brand specific,* since all merchandise is identified with the store name. Ralph Lauren and Authentic Fitness for Speedo both typify this concept. Customers like these stores because they are shopping for a specific designer's taste or brand theme. Other stores are *category specific,* like Athlete's Foot or Home Depot, where customers know exactly what they will find. Finally, there are *signature stores* where customers expect to find trendy fashion such as Bloomingdale's or Saks Fifth Avenue. Here, however, the customer looks for the store signature as a guarantee since it backs up designer and other brand name manufacturers with the assurance of quality and integrity.

"Stores needn't carry designer labels to be brand specific. Some stores like Crate & Barrel, Victoria's Secret, Gap, and The Limited feature the store name as a brand. The absence of any competing brands enables these stores to concentrate instead on complementary, full assortments. In this way, they assure the customer that they will stand behind their products with the implied guarantee of quality and value. More importantly, they coordinate their merchandise to create focus and a specific image for the customer."

The design elements of the store interior can define the nature of the store for the customer. The high open ceilings, concrete floors, and high shelving with backup stock create the image of low price, variety, and assortment. Bold hanging banners for defining departments guide the customer through the store.

playing merchandise, while at the same time serving as a central location where customers can find the merchandise that they seek during convenient times. The second purpose relates to the symbolic needs of the customer. This includes the social aspects of shopping or owning a particular good from a particular store. The symbolic aspects of the store are anything that contributes to the overall store image. This may include environmental aspects, such as store atmosphere, or physical aspects, such as brand-name products.

When customers enter a store, they want the displays and departments to tell them what the store is all about. The image the store is attempting to project should be immediately obvious to potential customers. If the store wants price as the predominant image, departments emphasizing this aspect should be placed near the entrance. Managers should give the best space to the departments that say to the customer, "This is what I am."

Holistic Approach

A store's design should match the store's character. This means that consideration should be given to the type of store image the merchant hopes to project. It includes exterior design and interior arrangements for selling and nonselling activities. In addition, the design should match with that of other stores around it; it should also enhance the salability of the merchandise within the store and be in good taste. The store design should have a single theme or image throughout. Attempts to create several images often confuse the customer. Also, building multiple images tends to create greater competition. This is because the retailer is no longer competing against stores within a single image category, but instead with stores in several categories.

It was only a few years ago that shopping malls and theme parks were separate worlds. In the previous chapter the point was made that shopping centers today are often seen as a destination for entertainment as well as shopping. In fact, the shopping experience itself is entertainment for many people. With the Mall of America in Minneapolis offering a Snoopy playland complete with a roller coaster; the West Edmonton Mall in central Alberta, Canada, featuring a water park with a tropical beach; and the Japanese incorporating ski jumps and golf courses in their malls, it was only a matter of time before a store retailer would promote them as "the theme park of retail." And that is how Incredible Universe, Tandy Corporation's consumer electronics supercenter, is positioning itself. In a highly competitive segment of the retail business Tandy is focusing on "show biz" as its key to survival.[8] With sales of about $70 million annually, the Incredible Universe stores rank very high in consumer surveys for selection, price, and entertainment value. Rich Hollander, vice president of Incredible Universe, was quoted by David Dillon in the *Dallas Morning News* as saying, "People expect an entertainment experience. And so we decided that if they have a good time, they'll be more in the mood to buy things." Managers are trained by Disney to call customers "guests," employees "cast members," and themselves "producers" and "directors."[9] Products are "props," departments are "scenes," and the store is a "show." Design elements are critical in carrying out the planned store image. Dillon notes that the stores have no windows and no clocks so that customers can focus on consumption. The floor plan is a maze of paths that take shoppers through the 85,000 items in the store. Stereos play rock music from the 1960s and 1970s with a strong beat. Between scenes there may be clowns, trapeze artists, laser shows, or a potato peeling contest and cooking demonstration.

Technology and Planning

Store designs are becoming more complex as new formats evolve. For this and efficiency reasons, it is becoming more common to rely on technology to assist in developing a store layout and design. Computer-aided design (CAD) helps plan stores that are more space-efficient. Planning can be done quickly, and changes are easy to make. New construction design for a 200,000-square-foot store has been reduced from months to weeks with new computer-aided design software and hardware.[10]

CAD programs such as those by Autodesk Inc. allow the designer to see how fixtures and the interior design will work together to create the desired effect. See Figure 7.3.

In the store itself, new combinations of interactive and multimedia technologies will change the way retailers design for direct customer contact and information assistance. For example, a self-service concept store may be developed where kiosks replace sales associates, providing product information and updates on availability of merchandise. A customer may use a kiosk to receive information about a camera. The terminal can display the camera specifications, testimonials, and a product video. Furthermore, it may suggest accessories, tell the customer whether or not the products are in stock, and place the order.

FIGURE 7.3

Computer-aided design provides fast and efficient views of potential interior and exterior design alternatives. (*Source:* This material has been reprinted with permission from and under the copyright of Autodesk Inc.)

Technology will also contribute to the further blurring of in-store and home channels of distribution. For example, Crayola had The Walker Group design a store incorporating catalog ordering on the selling floor. Further integration of stores and catalogs is inevitable as retailers try to increase store productivity by providing consumers with access to more merchandise in less space.

Retailers will likewise be exploring creative linkages between participation in electronic home shopping channels and in-store selling. Through the use of interactive technologies, consumers will be able to view merchandise choices at home, make product selections, and conclude the purchase transaction. They will be able to choose whether to wait and receive their purchases through transportation carriers or to proceed directly to the retailer's store or depot where the merchandise will be ready for pickup.

EXTERIOR DESIGN

The exterior design must protect the interior from the elements. Just as important, it also serves to convey information to potential customers. The exterior is the first part of the store that potential customers see. They will determine from the outside whether or not they wish to enter and shop. It is critical that the outside of the store gain the attention of customers and entice them to enter. If the outside does not reflect an image appropriate to customers, they will not enter. The interior design of a Home Depot provides a specific image for the shopper. The same image is conveyed from the exterior design elements. Strong graphics, plain high walls, and long street face tell the customer: low-price warehouse and large selection.

The exterior design of the Galleria Emeruel in Milan, Italy, meshes with the cultural motifs, local customs, and habits of the market. Many of Italy's consumers are very style conscious with a taste for quality luxury items. Italy is a traditional male-dominated society. About one-third of the women work, mostly part-time. A strong sense of family is a major force in Italian life. (Gaspare Insaudo, "The Land of One Million Shops Has Room for New Concepts," *Going Global,* November 1993, p. 34. Special report by Ernst & Young, New York, NY.)

New Building versus Existing Facility

The decision to build a new facility or seek existing space is a critical element in exterior design planning. Each option has its advantages. Building allows the retailer to design all aspects of the exterior and interior. However, this option may be limited by location availability, time, or cost. Buying, renting, or leasing existing space has the advantage of being much quicker, may offer the advantage of a superior location, and may be less expensive. However, a retailer is often limited in what can be done with regard to design issues. It is often the case where major renovations of existing space are as expensive as building from the ground up.

Restrictions

Recognizing the importance of the exterior, retailers have become very competitive in their designs. Unfortunately, this has often led to many areas looking like a war zone of competing colors, signs, shapes, and sounds. Both property owners and governments alike have taken steps to ensure that consumers are not assaulted by an overwhelming amount of stimuli.

Lease requirements.   Many property owners require retailers that lease their space to adhere to certain rules regarding store design. These rules serve two purposes. First, they assure the owner that the property will be maintained in good condition; and second, they ensure that the surrounding property does not lose value. For example, most malls require that signs be certain sizes and often limit the use of intense light.

Building codes. Most cities have building codes for businesses; often many are directed at retailers. These serve several purposes. First, they protect the public. Fire codes and safety regulations are examples. Some codes include sign ordinances that try to create some kind of visual harmony. Second, they ensure equal access to shopping for those with disabilities; and third, they reflect the community's attitude with regard to appearance. For example, many towns recognize the need of retailers to promote their business through the use of signs. However, for aesthetic purposes, they have limited or abolished signs in particular areas.

Theme areas. Theme areas are those in which buildings must meet structural requirements that fit a certain theme. Many downtown areas are implementing very strict building codes that allow businesses to stay only if they fit with the atmosphere the area is trying to create. For example, the building codes in downtown Santa Fe require the exterior of the buildings to be adobe, among many other structural requirements. This adds to the enjoyment of shopping and increases tourism.

Color and Materials

The exterior color and texture of a store give a lasting first impression to the customer. Often, this will be the first and sometimes the only thing a customer sees of a store. It is important that the exterior look and "feel" right to the shopper. The colors and material should express the image of the store.

Today's retailers are increasingly using textured building materials (brick, rough-sawn wood, and so on) at the store entrance to give a pleasant feeling to the facade. Steel buildings tend to create an impression of strength, whereas glass tends to create an altogether different impression, usually of a more modern store. Concrete or block can contribute to the overall image of low cost or value. Brick may create a more upscale feeling.

Signs

Effective use of signs identifies the nature of the business, builds a corporate identity, communicates an image, ties the company to its advertising through the use of a logo, and attracts attention to the store.

The city of Burlington, Vermont, has strict codes and regulations governing the exterior of buildings, signage, and billboards. Combined with extensive landscaping of street medians and sites by business owners, the city has an environmentally friendly image.

The most common signage is in plastic-based materials despite the relatively high cost. Companies find that effective signs have individual letters that are coated in tough plastics and illuminated from within by neon tubes. This type of sign has advantages because it uses 15 to 20 percent less energy than other lighted signs and has an extremely long life. Stores desiring a very contemporary look may use exposed tubes; small strip shopping centers may use handcrafted wooden signs to maintain a low profile. Backlight signs offer a slightly more expensive possibility. Instead of the light splashing out of the front of the letter, it washes the wall with a silhouette. Mall tenants may be limited in the type and size of their sign by management rules. Signs from materials such as wood or metal that have direct lighting can be used to create different images from luxury to country. However, plastic technology today allows the creation of nearly any look.

Exterior walls and signs. Many retailers use the exterior wall space to promote their store. Painting the name and logo of a business on the exterior is often less expensive than having a custom-made sign. Examples of this vary from a simple, elegant script indicating the name of the store to more exotic art that includes not only the name but also pictures. If artwork is used on the exterior of the building, it must conform to the principles of design, appeal to the customer base, and be integrated with the rest of the architecture.

Windows

The main purpose of windows is to attract attention and create an image to potential customers standing outside. "A window should be a total environment, a complete statement on its own," states Steven Kornajcik, corporate senior vice president for R. H. Macy & Co.[11] Whether it's Macy's animated character windows during the holiday season, or Hermes Cie on 57th Street in New York introducing its summer accessories line with two dancers in its store windows,[12] or a simple display of camping equipment, each makes a statement.

Humor, theatrical flair, color, motion, or sound playing outside the windows work well to increase the effectiveness of the display. Bloomingdale's flagship store in New York has fifty-two windows, and the fact that they change every ten days[13] reflects the belief that windows as a part of the exterior can be a major component in retail design.

One of the biggest advantages of display windows is the ability to dramatically affect the exterior of the store. Most of the exterior requires major renovations to change. A retailer can take advantage of its window space to reflect changes in the store's offerings on a seasonal or monthly basis.

The window displays project the image of the store. While one store may be trying to say "quality" in its windows by showing specific brands or fashions, other stores may use window displays to project a low-price or value image. Regardless of whether it is a children's store, a sporting goods store,

Windows can make an interesting exterior design element, convey an image for the store, and demonstrate use of merchandise. Rondpoint men's clothing store in Paris, France, uses an open back window to allow a view of the elegant store interior and merchandise. Notice the photo in the window, which helps convey the image achieved with the goods.

or a home furnishings store, the window display is often one of the first efforts to communicate with customers and invite them.

Window design is a function of the physical design of the store, and not something specifically requested by the retail manager or merchandising designer. The open back, as opposed to the closed back, is a window through which the interior of the store itself becomes the display case. When open-back windows are used, the store does not have valuable selling space tied up in windows, management need not concern itself with planning window displays, and the problems of keeping windows clean and timely are usually avoided. However, the open-back window can cause unexpected display problems and exaggerate old ones. For example, the most significant concerns are reflection, sun glare, sun control, artificial lighting for both day and night, and the necessity for a general organization of merchandise within a completely exposed store.

Awnings.   The use of awnings is a subset of the window and exterior design issue and often poses a particular problem for retailers. Stores located on the shady side of the street are fortunate; they do not have to worry about faded merchandise or the daily raising and lowering of awnings. Most awnings are made of fabric and are of the old scissors or outrigger style. In recent years, fabric awnings that can be fastened into a recessed box at the end of the building have been developed. Other types of awnings are a structural part of the building.

Awnings come in many assorted sizes, colors, and styles. Merchants can take advantage of an awning to attract attention by using it as promotional space. Many companies now sell custom awnings that are designed to fit with the store's image. However, it should be noted that competing awnings can be almost as distracting, obtrusive, and unattractive as competing neon signs. When selecting an awning, merchants should find one that is interesting and also compatible with the building and the nature of the business.

The Store Entrance

One of the first and most striking impressions customers get of a store is the one they receive as they go through the front door. An entrance should be more than a device to keep people out of the store, to encourage them to come in, or to protect against the elements. An entrance should have character, and it should say to a prospective customer, "Please come through the door where you will be treated with courtesy and friendliness and served to the best of our ability." The entrance might be graceful and elegant or dull and functional; in any case, it should be compatible with the store design and provide an easy way to enter.

Store Name

Although not strictly related to external design, the choice of a store name does have an effect on the overall store image. The favorable or unfavorable image generated by the use of a name can enhance or negate the style set by store design.

At first glance, choosing a name for the business may seem to be a rather easy task. Unfortunately, this is not the case. The retailer who thought of the name Equ-ulus for a small gift shop certainly made a mistake. This name is not pronounceable, and it has little meaning for the majority of the customers to whom the store is appealing. Often it is desirable that the name sound not only attractive but prestigious. Certainly it must fit the type of store. For example, Budget Weddings was chosen as the name of a store that provided package services for brides. It failed because brides-to-be did not like the mental picture of a truck with that store name pulling up to the church and the reception hall. They liked the low price but were embarrassed by the name. See Box 7.2 for some guidelines in this area.

Theft Prevention

Another area of concern with exterior design is employee and customer theft. The design must consider the flow of people in and out of the store and how they may be observed or pass through technology-based theft prevention. Exterior doors and docks for receiving goods or trash disposal should also be

7.2   GUIDELINES FOR SELECTING A STORE NAME

- The name should be immediately understandable to the shopper. Don't choose a name that is too difficult or complicated for customers to remember or pronounce. Cute names have their place only if they can be remembered easily.

- Don't use a name that is offensive, is negative, or has a disagreeable sound.

- Consider using your name. Although some people may accuse you of egotism, using your own name enables you to identify with your business. As people begin to know you, they begin to know your name.

- Use a name that will not become dated. As your business expands or as it changes to meet changing conditions, a name that is always timely has distinct benefits over one that is not.

designed and arranged to minimize opportunities for unauthorized entrance and exit.

Multilevel Stores

Because of the need for increased parking space in relation to shopping area in suburban stores and shopping centers, the multiple-level store is especially appealing to retailers. Even supermarkets have experimented with this type of design. Properly carried out, a multilevel facility offers the merchant a means of both expanding the selling area and separating areas from one another. It also gives an overall feeling of unity to the store. One of the problems with multilevel facilities is that of "pulling people" through the store. Careful attention has to be paid to which merchandise is in high demand so that it can be placed on the upper levels. In the process of seeking it out customers will move through the store. Putting a restaurant on the top level, for example, helps this pulling process.

An example of a multiple-level store would be Marshall Field in Chicago. It is situated in a mall called The Atrium, which is part of Water Tower Place. The shopping mall is one city block square and eight levels high. The department store uses one entire side of this center and all eight levels.

The bottom line is that the exterior design provides the first view a potential customer has of the store. It's difficult to change first impressions. This is especially true in retailing, where a store rarely has the opportunity because customers with poor impressions from the exterior rarely enter the store.

While the exterior of the store is vitally important, it is insufficient by itself. Getting the customer inside is only the first step in what should be a long and profitable relationship. Once the customer is inside, it is important that the interior continue to convey the intended image. So it is vital that the exterior not only give a potential customer a good impression but also unite with the interior of the store in conveying a singular image.

INTERIOR STORE DESIGN AND LAYOUT

The interior design of the store determines the way the merchandise is stored and offered for sale. The design should allow easy access to merchandise for the customer. There are several layout patterns that enhance the customer's access to goods. The interior also projects an image to the shopper that should be consistent with that conveyed by the store's promotion, price, and merchandise and with the exterior design. The store interior must make the customer comfortable and encourage shopping.

The objective of layout management is to obtain the maximum benefits from the space available. There are issues that retail managers should consider when they make layout decisions: (1) value of space, (2) space utilization and allocation, (3) customer traffic flow, (4) the types of goods, (5) complementary merchandise proximity, (6) the desired store image.

A store layout is not a one-time challenge for the retailer. While a complete layout plan must be developed during the opening, expanding, or remodeling of a store, each day offers layout opportunities. Promotional, seasonal, clearance, and new merchandise must be constantly and properly positioned.

Value of Space

The value of space, depending on the location within the store, is expressed in sales per square foot of floor space, sales per linear foot of shelf space, sales per square foot of exposure space, and sales per cubic foot of cubic space.[14] **Sales per square foot** is the typical measure for a store, department, or freestanding display. A display, for example, may generate sales of $1,500 per square foot,[15] whereas a retailer like Sam's will generate sales per square foot of $500 across the entire store. **Sales per linear foot** is the common measure of shelf space for items like groceries, pet foods, and health and beauty aids. An emerging method of calculating space value on the shelf is **sales per square foot of exposure space.** This is calculated by a length times height measure of vertical space. Space has height value in addition to linear value. **Sales per cubic foot** is a relevant measure for freezer and refrigerator cases.

The first and perhaps the most significant element in planning a store layout is the fact that store space varies in value. Some parts of the store are visited by more people than other parts. Therefore, it is easier to make sales along the routes traveled by customers. This means that the value of the space is higher along the more highly traveled routes.

Not surprisingly, the area closest to the entrance of the store is the most valuable. The space nearest the front ranks second in value, and so on to the back of the store. By the same line of reasoning, store space is less valuable in parts of the store that are difficult to reach. One would also expect variations in sales and profits on different floors of the same store. As height from the ground floor increases, the difficulty of attracting customers becomes greater. Consequently, space on the upper floors or in the basement has less value than space on the main floor. In general, what this means is that obtaining complete customer circulation throughout all parts of the store can be a problem. Knowing this, retailers should assign space to departments in such a way that the sales volume per square foot of selling area is maximized across the total store.

Space Utilization and Allocation

The available space in the store is divided into selling and nonselling areas. The nonselling space includes administrative offices, storage, and customer amenities, such as rest rooms. These are all critical requirements for a store. Box 7.3 presents an ethical dilemma faced in adding nonselling space. The

7.3 AN ETHICAL DILEMMA: SINGLE PARENTS, THE RETAILER, AND STORE DESIGN

Twenty-seven percent of families are headed by a single parent, usually a mother. And the percentage is increasing. In another 58 percent, both parents are wage earners, leaving only 15 percent of the families consisting of both parents but only one wage earner.

When a wage-earner parent spends time with his or her children, there is less of a tendency for a child to join a gang, drop out of school, rob, sell drugs, or become involved with other unlawful or antisocial activities that cause all of us growing concern. Retailers employ about 20 million people out of the national workforce of about 125 million. Retailing probably employs the largest percentage of single, head-of-household females, yet few employers do much to assist their single-parent workers in rearing their children and in seeing that they complete high school, go on to higher education, or resist the attractiveness of gangs. Nor do they take other action to help employees rear productive members of society—who, hopefully, will become customers.

Robert Kahn suggests there are many ways a retailer could help to provide a better family atmosphere. For instance, the first day in school is probably the most frightening in the life of a child. One company lets the mother have paid time off to take her children to school on the first day and be together with them for the remainder of the day.

Many stores are in large shopping centers—500,000, 750,000, or even more than a million square feet—where 50 to 150 retailers employ thousands of people, many of whom are single, head-of-household parents. Retailers could provide day-care centers with the "day" extending into evening hours. Imagine how relieved employees would be knowing that their children are well cared for and nearby in case of a problem. A day-care center would also relieve the pressure on employees from taking their children to outside facilities, perhaps at a remote location, and then getting themselves to work on time.

Since many single parents are employed on a part-time basis, retailers could arrange their hours so that the parent could drop off the child at school on the way to work and pick up the child when school lets out.

Questions

Do retailers have an ethical responsibility to provide the services suggested by Kahn? What are the ethical pros and cons? What about the economic and store design issues associated with each suggestion? Senior retail management comes largely from the two-parent, single-wage-earner group. Do they really understand the needs of their employees?

Source: Adapted with permission from Robert Kahn, "Single Parents and the Retailer," *Retailing Today,* February 1995, p. 3.

6543217

desire to minimize nonselling space has led to several innovative operating procedures. Among them is the restocking of inventory. Many retailers have begun using quick response (QR) inventory systems, where inventory arrives from vendors or a distribution center as it is needed on the selling floor. Many retailers lack the partnering relationships with vendors required for QR.

There are several different methods of determining the amount of space a department or product class should receive. Among the most popular is space allocation by historical sales, gross margin contribution, industry averages, or strategic objectives.

Some departments command a higher gross margin and/or higher sales volume per square foot than others. Because departments such as jewelry, candy, and toys can pay their way in the high-value locations of the store, they can be placed in the more valuable areas. Some merchandise has better display potential than others and is capable of generating higher sales per square foot. A leather goods department, for example, lends itself to an interesting and dramatic display. Therefore, departments with such capabilities should receive choice locations.

Allocation by historical sales.
The amount of space that a department or product is allocated is sometimes based on the proportional sales of the product. For example, if apparel traditionally accounts for half of the store sales, it would receive half of the space. A minor problem with this method is that it can lead to under or overallocation of space over time. For example, if space is allocated each year and a department has decreasing sales, the space of that department is decreased. This could lead to a greater decrease in sales, which in turn will lead to a continuing decrease in space. Another potential problem is the overallocation of space on high-priced items. A jewelry department may have very high sales compared to shoes; however, jewelry requires less space because of its physical size. Competition may mean that some volume-selling seasonal goods have much lower margins. This can lead to a great deal of space given to a less profitable item. However, with a little common sense and care, the allocation method based on sales is both simple and appropriate. Critics indicate that the major shortcoming is that it may give little space to highly profitable items and a great deal to items that sell well, but contribute proportionately less.

Allocation by gross margin.
One way around the problem of allocating space by sales is to allocate it by gross margin. You remember that gross margin is sales less cost of goods sold. The same method as sales is used except that space allocation is based on the proportion of a margin. For example, assume an electronics department has 10 percent of the sales but contributes only 8 percent of the total gross margin for the store. The department would receive only 8 percent of the space. Programs such as the Spaceman family of software by Nielsen and SpaceMax by MarketMax have become important tools in the effort to maximize space allocation in the store. On the basis of

financial criteria, these programs recommend how much space each category of products should have and a specific product mix that will enable the retailer to maximize profits.

Allocation by industry averages. Stores sometimes allocate space based on competitive pressures. They allocate the same proportion of space to a particular item as the competition or a similar store. Trade associations provide these kinds of data. This allows the retailer not to appear weak in a particular department. However, it also creates a "me too" atmosphere that may not differentiate the store from competitors.

Allocation by strategic objective. Often a store will wish to build up sales in a particular product line. The manager will allocate the product more space than is justified by its previous sales. For instance, if shoes are not selling well but they are important to the image of the retailer, a manager may give more space to the shoe department so that more varieties in types and styles and a greater assortment of colors and sizes are available for sale. Store managers may also use this method for short-term promotion to build up sales of a new product line. Thus, this is sometimes referred to as the "build up" method.

Storage of Stock

There are three accepted ways to handle storage in designing a retail store. The first way is to use **direct selling storage**—either exposed in showcases, counters, and drawers, or concealed behind cabinet doors. The second way to provide for storage is through **stockrooms** directly behind the selling area and in the perimeters. The third way is through a **central storage** location. In general, central storage is best located next to receiving and marking areas and as close as possible to selling areas. The trend is to reduce inventory levels by more frequent delivery and better forecasting of sales. It has become easier to display a greater percentage of the store's stock, leaving as little in concealed areas as possible.

Some store formats, like Service Merchandise, do not sell the stock on display. The goods are stored on floors above the selling area and then sent to a receiving area for customer pickup. Furniture, carpet, and appliance stores often stock merchandise off-premises in less expensive warehouse space because delivery to the home is required. There is no reason for valuable selling space to be devoted to duplicate items on the selling floor.

Exposed merchandise has great appeal. Recently, there has been a movement toward **open storage,** displaying all the inventory on hand and eliminating dead space. The trend toward self-service selection has made it practical to display most of the stock. Furthermore, stocking and stock maintenance time is reduced.

Customer Traffic Flow

Merchants use three basic types of layout patterns to control traffic flow in a store. The first type is known as the **grid pattern.** See Figure 7.4. This arrangement has main, secondary, and tertiary aisles. The layout often maximizes the amount of selling space. It has an advantage in lower costs because of the possibility of standardizing construction and fixture requirements.

The second major type of layout design is the **free flow pattern.** See Figure 7.5. The free flow arrangement provides for flexibility in a layout. It reduces to a minimum the structural elements that form the fixed shell of the building, such as columns and fixed partitions. Counters are arranged to give maximum visual interest and customer attention to each merchandise department. Counters can be positioned so that their angles will literally capture customers in a department. The use of "cross aisles" by Drug Emporium is an effort to make shopping easier, make the aisles wider, and increase the number of endcaps (displays at the end of rows) from sixteen to thirty-two.[16]

The third type, the **"shop" concept** or **boutique pattern,** is a natural extension of the free flow layout arrangement. See Figure 7.6. The idea behind the shop is to create departments that sell related merchandise. A ski shop, for example, sells products traditionally carried by the shoe department (ski boots), the sweater department (ski sweaters), the sporting goods department (skis), and so on. Shops must be presented to the public so that they stand out from other departments and become small, intimate specialty stores within themselves. The free flow layout patterns make this easy to do.

Stores should be laid out so that customers can get to various parts conveniently and with little effort. Some aisles are made larger and are designed

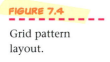

FIGURE 7.4

Grid pattern layout.

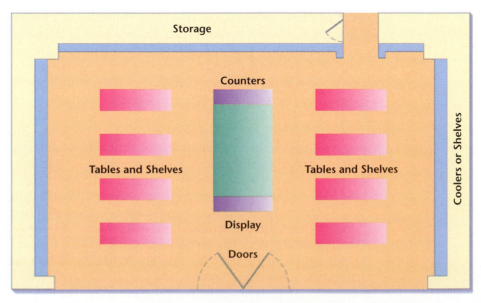

FIGURE 7.5

Free flow layout pattern.

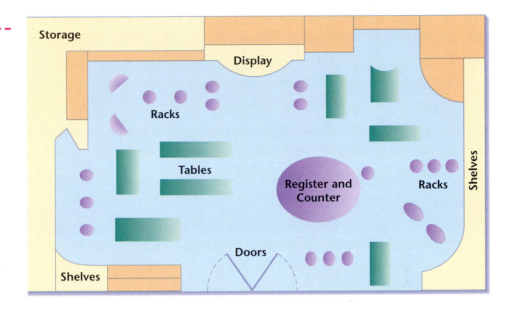

FIGURE 7.6

Boutique layout.

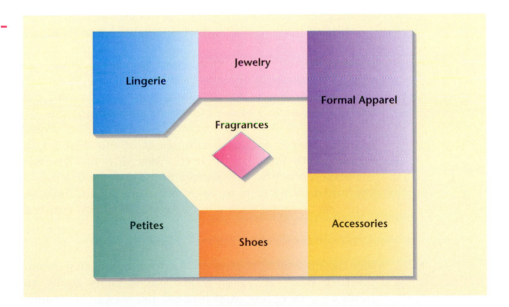

to accommodate a higher traffic count than others. In general, aisles should be wide if the merchandise adjoining the aisle is the type that customers like to look at for a long time before purchasing; if there tends to be a large concentration of customers, such as at entrances and escalators and before promotional merchandise displays; or if the retailer is attempting to control traffic to maximize customer exposure to various merchandise departments.

The right-hand-conditioned reflex will cause most customers to turn to the right when met by barriers. This makes the right-hand wall inside the store a good location for a high concentration of impulse goods. It will also cause a counterclockwise flow of traffic in many stores, particularly supermarkets. Likewise, merchandise shelved on the right side of the counterclockwise flow may get more customer attention.

One way of gauging the effectiveness of a store layout is to "map" the flow of customers as they move throughout the store. In developing a customer flow map, each customer's movements are charted on store layout replicas. A separate layout sheet is used for each customer. As selected customers move throughout the store, their movements are recorded. The information on each layout sheet is then transferred to a single master sheet.

The master sheet representing the layout of a pharmacy is presented in Figure 7.7. Observations of the density of customer traffic throughout different areas of the store reveal that customer flow is unequal. Management would certainly wish to correct this situation. Alternatives might be to relocate merchandise, improve positions of displays and signs, and reposition counters. The results should improve customer flow and generate greater sales per customer. Shoppers cannot buy what they do not see. In addition to recording traffic flow, observations could also be made on customer characteristics, time spent in the store, the dollars spent, and the types of purchases.

One of the key challenges managers have in dealing with a store layout is understanding customer flow. In addition to simple observation, electronic tracking efforts have included the Videocart.[17] Pioneered by Wal-Mart and used by stores like Schnuck's grocery chain, the Videocart is a shopping cart with a video screen attached. Small sensors suspended from the store ceiling record the pathway of the cart for future flow analysis.

Consistent with our philosophy of continuous quality improvement, quantification is a critical component of our analyses. Managers of Marsh Supermarkets quantified their customer flow by department, aisles, days of the week, dollars by day, average transaction by day, sales volume by time of day, and sales by store to improve a store layout, improve product presentation, and fine-tune staffing schedules to optimize customer satisfaction.[18]

Types of Goods

Merchandise can be broken up into four major categories: impulse goods, convenience goods, shopping goods, and specialty goods. **Impulse goods** are goods customers buy as unplanned purchases. An example might be candy sold at the checkout counter, a corkscrew in the wine section, or videotape in the electronics section.

Convenience goods are those that consumers put a minimum amount of thought into, usually purchasing a known brand or whatever is available. Examples are newspapers and batteries. **Shopping goods** are those for which a customer is willing to search and compare. There may or may not be a brand preference. If a customer is looking for a specific brand, such as a Sony

FIGURE 7.7

Traffic flow in a neighborhood pharmacy.

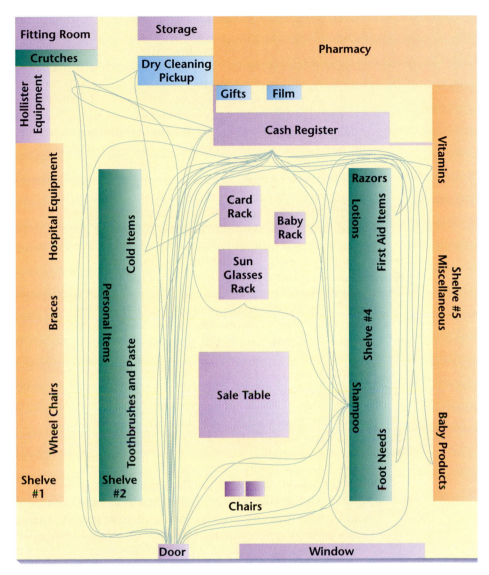

Tritron TV, the shopping may be for the best price or service. A customer will likely make a trip to different stores seeking just the right goods. **Specialty goods** are those for which customers have a preconceived need and for which they make a specific effort to come to the store to purchase. Consumers usually will not accept a substitute for a specialty good and will sometimes go to extraordinary effort to purchase such an item. If a man wears an Allan Edmond size 11B wing-tip shoe and he will accept no substitute, dress shoes are a specialty good for him.

Impulse and convenience goods benefit by being located in high-traffic areas where customers, as they pass by the displays, are likely to pick up an item for purchase. In many stores the checkout counter will be crowded with impulse goods such as candies, batteries, and miscellaneous odds and ends. Shopping goods, on the other hand, because of the preconceived need, may be situated in more remote areas of the store. In most grocery stores, the meat is located at the back. This encourages customers to pass through other aisles and increases the possibility of a higher number of purchases. Specialty goods are unique in that they can create customer traffic. Often a store selling specialty goods can locate in a less expensive site.

The type of merchandise is an important consideration in a store layout. Think about how all four types of goods might influence a layout in a discount drugstore. For a particular customer a prescription could be a specialty good, and the customer would travel through a maze to get to the pharmacy. While going to the pharmacy a lot of convenience goods such as health and beauty aids may be picked up for purchase. While in the store the customer could seek out the area where a shopping good like a home vaporizer was located and do some brand and price comparisons for a future purchase. In the checkout area an unplanned purchase of film could be made. The key to using the type of good concept for layout is to understand how the store's target market shops for the goods that are going to be offered.

Complementary merchandise placement. The layout must also take into consideration the nature of complementary merchandise that is interrelated: A sale of an item prompts the sale of another item. For example, the sale of a shirt could logically lead to the sale of a tie, which in turn could lead to the sale of a tiepin. Because of these additional sales possibilities, it is appropriate to plan the interior design so that related merchandise is in close proximity.

In general, merchandise should be grouped in some manner that makes it easy for the customer to find it. The two most common methods of grouping merchandise are product class and customer. It is common to have product classes grouped together. For example, condiments like ketchup, mustard, and mayonnaise would not be found in separate sections of the grocery store. Alternatively, products can be grouped by customer type. Most apparel stores are grouped into men's, women's, and children's sections.

Seasonal departments. Some departments need considerable space during particular times of the year. Seasonal departments such as toys, lawn and garden, and greeting cards are examples. Because these departments must expand and contract during certain times of the year, provision must be made to accommodate these seasonal changes. To accomplish this, departments with offsetting seasonal peaks in sales should be placed next to one another or in place of one another.

Other considerations that may be important in developing a workable layout plan for the store include using the least desirable space for employee, stock, and customer service areas. In addition, departments that have extensive stock requirements such as shoes may be placed close to stock areas. Departments that require refrigeration, cooking facilities, and many fixtures, or that contain large bulky items, all require special consideration.

INTERIOR DESIGN ELEMENTS

With basic decisions made as to layout type, aisle width, and space allocation, management can turn its attention to the various interior design elements. The elements of design can be used to create an image that matches the desired customer profile.

Fixtures

A major consideration in developing an appropriate store design involves the use of fixtures. They are used to display merchandise, to help sell it, to guard it, and to provide a storage space for it. They should be attractive and focus customers' attention and interest on the merchandise. Figure 7.8 shows a design developed by The Store Decor Company for a new PetsMart store. Notice how a traditional fixture, a cage for holding animals, has been integrated into a total design that directs the customer to the store area and displays the merchandise for sale.

One way to bring the cost of fixtures down is standardization; customization is expensive, and construction budgets today allow this luxury only where specialty departments can justify the cost. Some stores are trying to keep a lid on fixture costs with walls that don't reach the ceiling but instead begin two feet down. Besides being cheaper and faster to put up, they don't affect sprinklers, lighting, heating ventilation and air conditioning (HVAC), and other ceiling ducts.

Most stores are moving toward smaller and less dense fixtures than what they previously used, which is another way to control costs. But even more significantly, the trend reflects the reduction in many stores' inventory levels. Glass cubes that once consisted of sixteen-inch and eighteen-inch high bins may now be housed in twelve-inch bins. This way, although there are fewer items in each unit, it still looks full. Another trend is a renewed

FIGURE 7.8

Fixtures to display the merchandise are only one element of the overall display in this luv-a-pet adoption center being constructed in a new PetsMart store. (*Source:* The Store Decor Co. Inc., RETAILGRAPHICS, Dallas, Texas.)

demand for wood and glass, which in recent years were overshadowed by the more affordable clear plastic.

Displays

Displays play an important role in a retail store. An attractive and informative display can help sell goods. Poorly designed displays can ruin the store's atmosphere and create an uncomfortable setting. Since displays often take up premium space within the store, they carry a heavy burden of productivity in terms of creating sales.

There are several principles or rules of displays that help ensure their effectiveness: They should achieve balance, provide a dominant point, create eye movement, allow for a gradation, adjust merchandise to proper height, group the merchandise in the display, generate sales appeal, keep merchandise in proper order, and display names of products and the store name. Displays should also be simple and not chaotic or congested. Figure 7.9 illustrates these basic concepts.

Balance. In building a display, it is important to make sure that it appears balanced to the viewer. This is achieved by arranging products in a symmetric manner. Displays may have formal or informal balance. **Formal balance** is achieved by placing similar items equal distance from the center. **Informal balance** is achieved by placing different sized goods or objects away from the center based on their relative size. For example, an object that is twice the size of another would be put half the distance from the center of

FIGURE 7.9

Basic display concepts.

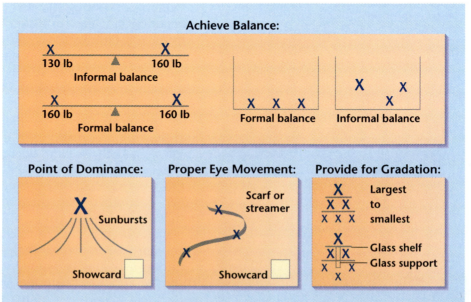

the display. The effects of informal balance are less peaceful and less obvious, but often more interesting as well.

Dominance. All displays should have a central point that will attract the viewer's eye. The point may be achieved by using a prominent piece of merchandise, such as a diamond pendant, using dramatic colors, such as a bright scarf, or using streamers arranged toward the center of the display. A point of dominance acts as a focal point on which the viewer's eyes rest and from which the eyes move to other parts of the display.

Eye movement. Displays should direct the eyes away from the point of dominance in a systematic fashion, instead of encouraging them to jump from one end to the other. If the viewer's eyes move indiscriminately around the display, the shopper will miss some of the merchandise and will not get the full message intended.

Gradation. The gradation is the sequence in which items are arranged. For example, small items are usually placed at the front of the display, medium items farther back, and large items at the rear. This creates harmony and an appealing illusion.

Height of merchandise. Merchandise that has the greatest effect should be placed at the eye level of the customer. Because viewers tend to look straight ahead, merchandise placed at eye level is most likely to be seen.

Grouping merchandise. Too many retailers place one item after another in a long row. Shoe stores, jewelry stores, and mass merchandisers tend to do this. Stores with large amounts of one item or with one line of goods are likely to build longer displays. Instead of creating long displays where the customer has problems picking out merchandise, retailers should group items so that the customer's eyes cannot travel from group to group but stop and focus on particular products.

Sales appeal. Displays should always show the best merchandise that the retailer has to offer. As discussed above, displays take up some of the most valuable space in the store. Using slow-moving items for display is a waste. One way to generate sales appeal is to choose the most important feature of the merchandise being displayed and focus on it. Another way is to create a theme that already exists within the consumer's mind, such as Valentine's Day, Christmas, or back to school. Customers relate best when they can grasp the total picture.

Keeping it simple. Since displays take up a great deal of valuable space, there is a tendency to get as much into them as possible. While the idea of more is better may be true for chocolate, it is not true for displays. Too many items in a display distract and confuse the consumer, and they tend to create

FIGURE 7.10

Displays may consist of a simple and attractive arrangement of merchandise. What appear to be light fixtures in this store are actually skylights. (*Source:* The Store Decor Co. Inc., RETAILGRAPHICS, Dallas, Texas.)

an atmosphere of chaos or congestion. Look at Figure 7.10. In the case of the wheelbarrows, the merchandise becomes its own display. Notice how the paint display is set off in a clean, crisp environment. Below we discuss store lighting. Figure 7.10 also illustrates an advance in this area. What appear to be overhead light fixtures are actually skylights. Motorized mirrors track the sun through the day to maximize the amount of natural light in the store. The strip fluorescent lights are sensor-activated so that they are on only when needed.

Color

The psychological effect of color continues to be important to retailers. For example, the $3 billion renovation undertaken by Kmart included reducing the use of bold colors in many departments and moving to softer pastels. This is not a universal movement, however. Drug Emporium's new "vibrant" decor package features purple, teal, and fuchsia.[19] Color is also important in warehouse-type stores because of the vast open area of the interior. Bold colors are frequently used to highlight merchandise sections or departments and to reduce attention to what is typically an open-girder ceiling.

The use of color and lighting can be very effective during various selling seasons. For example, red and green can be used during Christmas, orange during Halloween and Thanksgiving, and pastels to emphasize Easter and Mother's Day. Retailers are becoming especially appreciative of the fact that color, probably more than any other factor except price, is the "stopper" that catches the customer's attention. Clearly, intelligent use of color is important in store design. Since people are drawn to warm colors, yellow and red can help draw customers into the store through the entrance. Cool colors such as blues and greens tend to calm people and are useful in areas where customers need time to deliberate over the purchase decision.[20]

Lighting

Proper lighting is one of the most important considerations in retail design. At one point in time the function of lighting was to provide customers with a means of finding their way through the store. Today, lighting has become a display medium. It is an integral part of the store's interior and exterior design. Lighting should match the mood the retailer is attempting to create with the rest of the store decor and should complement, rather than detract from, the merchandise.

A lighting management program helps the firm derive maximum benefits from lighting energy resources. Lighting can help achieve the overall image that the store is trying to project. The level of electric illumination can create environments that enhance displays. For example, it can highlight racks of impulse-purchase goods no matter where they are located. The outdoor system can identify the store at night to passersby and reduce shoppers' apprehensions about parking-lot crime.[21]

General illumination is needed throughout the store. However, most stores need additional localized lighting to highlight special displays and showcases, help bring out colors, and relieve the monotony of even, overall light. Too much or too little lighting, or even the wrong type of lighting, can create false impressions about the merchandise on display. Incandescent lighting used alone, for example, accents yellow and red. Fluorescent lights frequently build up blues and purple. Therefore, retailers must use a lighting combination that gives a correct impression of the merchandise while deemphasizing the source of the light itself.

Energy efficiency is another consideration when lighting a store of 1,000 square feet or one of more than 100,000. Lighting consumes approximately 60 percent of the utilities used by a retail store.[22] In addition to using energy to light the store, the cooling system must absorb the additional heat generated by older or less efficient lighting systems.

Ceilings

Ceilings represent a potentially important element of interior design. In older stores, ceilings of twelve to sixteen feet are still common, but most department store ceilings are now in the nine- to ten-foot range. Remember, the higher the ceiling, the more space to heat and cool at increasing energy rates. Ceiling heights are becoming much less standardized within stores. Designers are making use of varied ceiling drops to create distinct identities for different departments within a store.

Ceiling colors continue for the most part to be somewhat muted, with dark gray and beige tones predominating. The idea is to not call attention to the ceiling because no merchandise is sold up there. But there are currently two new trends. The $6 million renovation of the main floor of Bloomingdale's flagship store in New York City is a good example of the trend toward somewhat theatrical merchandise displays. A network of ceiling drops is used to define specific areas and create the appearance of several individual shops within the store. They set off such high-volume departments as cosmetics and perfume. The other trend is toward an overall well-lighted look with little "action" above the sales floor. The ceilings are simple, and even with different ceiling heights, they do not distract from the merchandise on display.

As you shop in many of the discount warehouse stores, you will notice that the ceiling is the roof. High open-girder construction has become quite common in the high-volume discount superstores. Shoppers are quite willing to give up ambience in favor of wider selection and lower price.

One of the latest technologies in ceiling construction is metal.[23] Being used by boutiques, mass retailers, and even prisons, the new ceiling technology absorbs 80 percent of the noise, compared to 50 to 60 percent for traditional acoustic ceiling tiles. Although these metal panels offer retailers a bold, contemporary look, their cost currently runs about four times that of fiber-based acoustic ceiling panels.

Flooring

Retailers are taking a sophisticated "return on investment" approach to flooring decisions. Firms are willing to pay higher up-front installation costs for more expensive materials if they see a return in greater durability and reduced maintenance expenses. Additionally, firms like Kmart see carpeting as reflecting a "higher image" that will translate into increased customer pull and, possibly, higher price-point merchandise.

Flooring choices are important because the coverings can be used to separate departments, muffle noise in high-traffic areas, and strengthen the store image. The range of choices for floor coverings is endless: Carpeting, wood, terrazzo, quarry tile, and vinyl composition all have applications in different settings. Generally speaking, given the broad spectrum of styles, colors, fabrics, and cuts, carpet is often the best choice for both discounters and upscale stores.[24]

Shelving

The material used for shelving as well as its design must be compatible with the merchandising strategy and the overall image desired. Stainless steel shelving creates an entirely different effect than the painted wood cubes in the County Seat or the typical metal shelving seen in a general merchandise store. Glass shelving, framed in fine woods, creates an element of elegance difficult to achieve otherwise. General shelving considerations and merchandise display are discussed in the next section.

Planograms and Shelf Layout and Design

One of the key tools of modern shelf and layout planning is the **planogram.** This is a graphical representation that visually shows the space to be allocated by describing where every stockkeeping unit (SKU) within a space is physically located. As you will see in Chapter 10, every product has its own SKU. The planogram produces a map for the length, height, and depth of shelves with the number and location of the SKU. These computer-driven databased electronic shelf management systems offer reduced time and labor for shelf sets, easier resets, increased units and dollar sales, increased return on inventory investment, and reduced out-of-stocks.[25] Software, such as Spaceman Orbitor, allows the retailer to create the planograms to increase the efficiency of space use. It also allows financial input to be incorporated into planograms to reflect actual product performance.[26]

With a planogram, space allocation can be made in a variety of means. For example, retailers could allocate shelf space on the basis of item profitability (allocating the most shelf space to items with the highest profit margins), item velocity (assigning shelf space on the basis of item movement), or gross margin return on inventory investment (GMROI). Allocating shelf space on the basis of GMROI is an attempt to balance item profitability and item velocity. GMROI will be explained in Chapter 9.

Merchandise arrangement can also follow many different schemes: by brand, by size, by product, or by a combination of all three. In a grocery store, for example, a coffee section is normally divided by product (instant coffee, vacuum-packed coffee, regular, decaffeinated, conventional, or gourmet products), by size (some stores keep all products of the same size on the same shelf), and by brand (all Hills Bros. or all Taster's Choice together).

Since shelf arrangements are vertical as well as horizontal, retailers must consider what to put on the bottom and what goes on the top. Often retailers allocate the bottom shelves to the high-volume items and the easier-to-reach shelves to high-margin items. The top shelves are often dedicated to specialty-type products. Horizontal arrangement of items is still another concern. In order for shoppers to be exposed to new products, they need to "shop" the whole section. The human eye tends to scan from left to right. Also, the mind tends to retain the last object seen by the eye. To take advantage of this left-to-right shopping pattern, retailers often place products they have less interest in promoting (such as items with lower profit margins or items that cut into private-label volume) on the extreme left. Also, the small size of each item is put on the left. Since most customers are right-handed, they will tend to take the size on the right instead of reaching across their body to take the smaller size.

One more issue faced by shelf space planners is the notion of color break. Manufacturers spend large sums of money to differentiate their product's packaging from that of others. Retailers want to take advantage of natural color breaks between products. They believe this reduces confusion for customers and adds to their shopping ease. Unfortunately, when retailers use color blocks to separate different brands, the section could develop a "checkerboard," which most retailers want to avoid. Occasionally a product must receive more or less shelf space than it deserves in order for a retailer to maintain a "color block." Figure 7.11 illustrates a planogram developed with the Apollo Shelf Management System.

These planograms may be generated at the store level, at the region level, by the store buyer, by the vendor, or using a retailer-vendor partnership. Sears, for example, finds that about 90 pecent of planograms can be designed by

FIGURE 7.11
– –

Planogram with category schematic for three shelves in a cooler with detail for a portion of shelf 2. (*Source:* Keith Prazar, Tower Marketing, Dallas, Texas. Produced with Apollo Shelf Management System.)

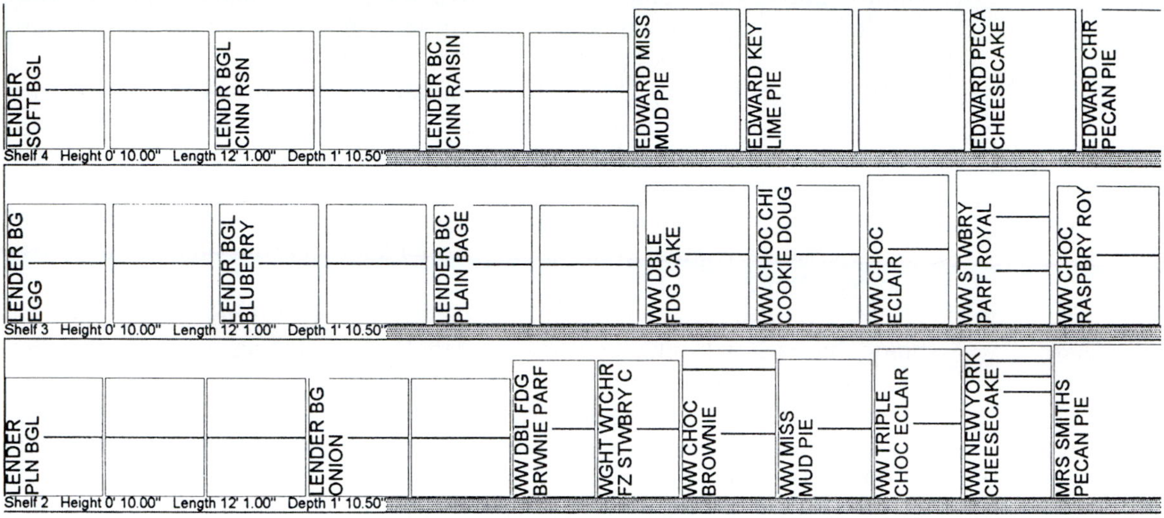

Category Schematic for 20-D 5 Door Desserts and Breads

Position	UPC	Long Description	Size	UOM	Facings
Shelf: 2, Length: 12' 1.00", Height: 0' 10.00", Depth: 1' 10.50", Product: 12' 0.94"					
1	768000001	LENDERS PLAIN BAGEL	12.00	oz	2
2	768000001	LENDERS ONION BAGEL	12.00	oz	2
3	258000234	W.W. DOUBLE FUDGE BROWNIE P	5.30	oz	1
4	258000196	W.W. STRAWBERRY CHEESECAKE	8.00	oz	1
5	258000205	W.W. CHOCOLATE BROWNIE	3.75	oz	1
6	258000223	W.W. MISSISSIPPI MUD PIE	6.75	oz	1
7	258000233	W.W. TRIPLE CHOCOLATE ECLAIR	6.40	oz	1
8	258000235	W.W. NEW YORK CHEESECAKE	5.00	oz	1
9	277001502	MRS. SMITH'S PECAN PIE	36.00	oz	1
10	277001300	MRS. SMITH'S NAT JCE APPLE	37.00	oz	2

the buyers with the fine-tuning done at the district level.[27] A final consideration of planograms is change. The planogram must be updated as soon as new data are added to the database. This is a constant challenge that can generate numerous planograms. The British chain Tesco, for example, believes that one planogram has a useful life of one to six weeks, and they produce more than 2 million planograms each year![28]

Other Considerations

There are other considerations that can round out the image and atmosphere created by the interior design elements. For example, the type and sound level of music can be focused on a given market segment. Scents can be used to help identify with a market group or create a feeling about being in the store. The level of maintenance and cleanliness also sets a tone. In-store signing is another element of interior design. When planning in-store signing, it is advisable to do so in moderation. Dillard department stores classify in-store signing into three categories: location, vendors, and merchandise.[29] Location signing includes perimeter and interior signs and is used to identify major departments. Because the Dillard customer is brand-conscious, the store makes a special effort to identify major vendors. In fact, like many other retailers, Dillard has special vendor departments (e.g., Polo). The final category includes point-of-sale signs. These indicate "sales," "markdowns," or "new arrival" merchandise within the store.

KMART—REVISITED: GLOBAL EXPANSION AND SUPER KMARTS

In 1993, Kmart's restructuring plan was slowed while the company integrated the Super Kmart centers into the plan and opened fourteen of the new stores. The Super K stores have between 160,000 and 180,000 square feet and feature full lines of Kmart general merchandise and groceries. Food covers about one-third of the area. There are also a variety of services including dry cleaning, hair care, optical, and floral shops.

In addition, larger format (116,500 square feet) discount stores were integrated in the plan, which also closed 503 additional stores and called for expanding and refurbishing another 500. The managers at Kmart believe that there is the potential to open 450 Super Kmart centers.

New Super K prototype stores opened in Norfolk and Virginia Beach, Virginia, in 1996. The prototype features produce and other perishables at the front of the store. (They were previously placed at the rear to pull customers through the store and to avoid carrying messy fruits and vegetables while shopping.) The stores also have two gourmet food kiosks at the front of the food side. Visual merchandising is used to set off areas from the aisle, making the departments easier to access with shopping carts.[30]

Interestingly, the Super Kmart concept is not Kmart's first experiment in the grocery business. In the 1960s, Allied Supermarkets Inc. operated for a time within Kmart stores. Another attempt in 1987, in a joint venture with Bruno's department stores, ended after five years. Both supermarket partners cited huge losses as the reason for discontinuing the relationships.

Remodeling existing stores and adding Super Kmart centers are just two dimensions of Kmart's plans for the future. These plans also include a thrust into the international arena and divestiture of some specialty store groups in an effort to focus on the core discount business.

Internationally, Kmart has operations in Canada, the Czech Republic, and Slovakia. There are more than 120 stores in Canada, and 13 department stores in the Czech Republic and Slovakia were purchased in 1992. Kmart is modernizing and remodeling stores in these countries and streamlining operations. Of particular importance is the development of advanced distribution systems and training to increase merchandising skills. The company has joint ventures in Mexico and Singapore. A significant ownership position in Coles Myer Ltd., Australia's largest retailer, was sold in 1994.

Kmart took a close look at the profitability of its specialty store groups. In an attempt to return to its core discount business, Borders and Waldenbooks, the retail office products superstore Office-Max, and The Sports Authority were spun off as separate companies through an initial public offering. Kmart has sold its Payless Drug Stores and PACE membership warehouse stores. The firm is also seeking a buyer for Builders Square, the category killer entry in the home improvements and home building business.

Kmart continued to lose money, and in 1995 Chairman Joseph Antonini was ousted by the Board. In 1996, after suffering from three years of disappointing earnings, the discount retailer began laying off people, closing money-losing stores, and revitalizing product offerings. In an attempt to differentiate itself, the company began a search for a strategic partner in an advertising agency. Market leader Wal-Mart is positioned as the value leader, and Target is positioned as more trendy, but Kmart was seen as having no defined image.[31]

1. **How would you design a store with all of the products and services that are in a Super Kmart center?**
2. **Why might Kmart have purchased the stores in Eastern Europe? What are the advantages and disadvantages that you see from a store design and layout point of view?**

SUMMARY

The layout and design of a retail store communicate a significant amount of information about the retailer to the consumer. Store design is the architectural character or decorative style of the store. Obviously, the retailer's goal is to have an appearance that is pleasing and inviting to the customers.

Whether the retailer is building a new location or renovating existing facilities, exterior design decisions will play a key role in the store design. Areas that need to be addressed include building codes, color and materials, signs, windows, and the store entrance, to name a few.

The main restriction on interior store design and layout is quite clearly the amount of space in the location. Interior store design and layout must maximize the value of the space in an order that is logical to both the retailer and the customer. Other factors that will impact the layout are the storage of stock, the traffic flow of customers, and the type of goods carried by the retailer.

Along with the general exterior and interior design, there are many interior design elements that will influence how a customer shops in the store and the opinion a customer has of the retailer. These elements include fixtures, displays, color, lighting, ceilings, and flooring.

One of the main elements that retailers use to attract customers to their stores is display. An effective display should achieve balance, provide a dominant point, create customer eye movement, generate sales appeal, and be kept simple.

A key tool of modern shelf and layout design is the planogram, which is a graphical representation of how products should be placed and arranged within an allotted space. With the advancement of computers, planograms have become more common in retailing today as businesses experience firsthand their effectiveness in reducing time and labor and increasing return on inventory investment. Retailers today understand the importance of external store design, interior store design, and design elements to communicate an integrated image of the store to their customers.

KEY TERMS AND CONCEPTS

Boutique pattern, 272
Central storage, 271
Convenience goods, 274
Direct selling storage, 271
Formal balance, 278
Free flow pattern, 272
Grid pattern, 272

Impulse goods, 274
Informal balance, 278
Open storage, 271
Planogram, 282
Sales per cubic foot, 268
Sales per linear foot, 268
Sales per square foot, 268

Sales per square foot of exposure space, 268
Shop concept, 272
Shopping goods, 274
Specialty goods, 275
Stockroom, 271
Store design, 256

QUESTIONS

1. In your opinion, should space be allocated to products on the basis of sales, on the basis of gross margin, or on some other basis? Would your answer vary according to the type of store under discussion?

2. In store layout, how do you resolve the dilemma of finding the right location for a department when today's stores may have several entrances?

3. A store design and layout result as much from management considerations as from customer considerations. Comment.

4. What do you think are current and future trends in store design and layout?

5. Why are customers' first impressions of a store so vital to the success or failure of a store? How will this affect buying habits? What factors create this impression?

6. How could improper store design affect a business's image? Its ability to serve customers?

7. Discuss the trends that you see in display window arrangement. Do you think these will have any impact on consumer buying habits? If so, why?

8. When and why would awnings be considered a drawback to a store's appearance?

9. What factors must a retailer consider when deciding on a sign for the business? How can these factors affect the retailer's decision?

10. How have the changes in ceilings and flooring helped retailers' budgets? How have they hurt them?

SITUATIONS

1. You are the manager of a downtown gift shop. In recent months you have become aware of how old and drab your store seems to be in comparison with the stores in the new strip shopping center and regional mall. You especially notice your store's high ceilings, high windows, drab colors, and old fixtures. You wish to remodel with an absolute minimum of expense, and yet you want to create a new look. What can you do?

2. You are the manager of a surplus store that handles everything from sporting goods to clothing items and from paint to hardware. It is located in an old section of town and occupies an old building. Your store has enjoyed phenomenal success. It is the type of establishment that people like to come into and browse around in; many spend a half-hour to an hour merely walking through the aisles. Recently, a new discount house has come into town, and you are already beginning to suffer decreased sales. Consequently, you are evaluating your total operation, especially layout, to determine whether improvements can be made. It has been your philosophy that a store such as yours should carry a great deal of merchandise, like sporting goods, located in four or five different places in the store. You have made the counters high, reaching up to about six feet; and you have staggered the counters throughout the store so that there is not one continuous aisle. Will you make any changes in the layout? If so, why? If not, why?

3. You hire an interior designer to change your window displays to increase traffic in your store, which is located in a small town. You look at the finished windows and find them ghastly looking. Should you tear them down?

4. The committee on downtown rejuvenation has decided to turn the business district into a theme area to attract more traffic. They have decided on an old west theme. You sell high-fashion clothing and feel that this theme is contradictory with your product line. What should you do?

CASES

CASE 7A
Lloyd's Ltd. Fine Men's Wear

Before making his final site decision (Case 6B) for his new store, Mr. Tanner decided to do a preliminary design and layout for each of the two alternatives. He has asked you to help him with these designs. A dimensional floor plan for both is shown in Figure 7.12.

The proposed layouts should contain at the least the following areas: suits, sport coats, dress slacks, casual slacks, dress shirts, casual shirts, ties, belts, socks, underwear, and accessories.

1. *What design and layout factors do you consider critical for each of the sites?*

2. *On graph paper, sketch your concept of a layout for each site.*

CASE 7B
Section Planogram[32]

Gary Kitchens worked through high school and college as customer service manager in a major store of the Massive Mart national grocery chain.

Upon graduation he applied for a position as assistant grocery manager in one of the new Massive Mart stores. His responsibilities as assistant manager would include employee scheduling, buying for chain advertisements, and writing section planograms. In the past, manufacturers' sales representatives were responsible for designing these. However, with the downsizing of sales forces, some grocery chains were once again assuming the responsibility. Unlike many chains that wrote planograms at headquarters, this chain required assistant managers to write their own in accordance with local market taste, but with some guidelines from the national headquarters. As part of Gary's interview, he was required to draw up a planogram for a vacuum-packed coffee section.

1. *What factor should Gary consider in developing his planogram?*

FIGURE 7.12

Dimensional floor plans for layouts.

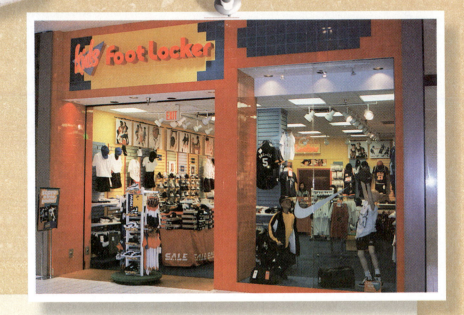

Chapter Goals

After reading this chapter, you should be able to:

- Understand the basic skills required by retail supervisors.
- Define and apply the management concepts that affect retail supervision.
- Know the fundamental responsibilities of a retail supervisor along with the different approaches to motivating employees.
- Understand the retailing organizational structures.
- Explain the legal environment in which labor and management operate.
- Discuss the future organizational challenges for human resource management in the retailing industry.

HUMAN RESOURCE MANAGEMENT AND STORE ORGANIZATION

WOOLWORTH CORPORATION:[1] COMPETING WITH STORE FORMATS

Foot Locker, Northern Reflections, Kinney Shoes, After Thoughts, and Champs Sports—few people would recognize these stores as some of the approximately forty different formats operated by the Woolworth Corporation. Many people think of downtown five-and-dime variety stores when the name Woolworth is mentioned. Today's Woolworth Corporation is an example of the complexity of retail organizations. The company has more than 8,200 specialty and general merchandise stores.

In 1982, the Woolworth Corporation was facing financial difficulties and decided to reposition itself as a group of specialty retailers. The company actively pursued both established and new specialty formats. Most of the formats focus on leisure lifestyles. Throughout the 1980s Woolworth's earnings grew at a compound rate of 15 percent. However, in the 1990s earnings began to fall dramatically even though sales continued to rise.

Roger N. Farah is the new chairman of the board and CEO. His strategic plan is based on accelerating growth in formats where the company is already strong, fixing what does not work, and disposing of those businesses that do not provide a return on investment that exceeds the cost of capital. They will strive to be number one or number two in the markets in which those businesses operate. His plan to strengthen and rebuild the company includes strengthening the financial position by reducing and restructuring company debt, building a top-notch management team and delayering the organization, lowering the expense structure, and reducing inventories substantially and improving their quality.

Mr. Farah plans to continue to develop new business strategies. The company projects that more than 75 percent of profits will be derived from specialty stores, which are more profitable than general merchandise stores. Retailers have been criticized for the fact that there are comparatively few women in senior management positions in most firms. Woolworth Corporation is committed to building an outstanding management team by attracting from outside the company high-caliber retail executives with proven track records to serve in key positions. For example, Carol Greer is president and chief executive officer of the newly formed specialty Footwear Division, which includes Kinney Shoe stores, Footquarters branded shoe stores, and the company's manufacturing facilities. Marty Nealon, vice president and general manager, has responsibility for merchandising and operations for more than 850 After Thoughts and Carimar stores, which specialize in moderately priced jewelry and accessories. Maryann M. McGeorge joined the company as vice president of merchandise planning and systems. She is responsible for the design and development of consistent corporatewide merchandise planning and reporting information processes. Virginia Harris is a new senior vice president and general merchandise manager responsible for men's, women's, and children's apparel; women's accessories; cosmetics; and health and beauty aids at the F. W. Woolworth general merchandise division.

The company has instituted regular performance reviews and organization development programs, including training, succession planning, and recruiting. Sales associates are given special training about the items they sell in order to better assist customers in selecting the merchandise that is best for them. The programs give associates the power to make "on the spot" decisions so that each customer's shopping experience will be more positive. The company has implemented a compensation system that ties pay more closely to individual performance as well as stock appreciation.

Woolworth won an American Spirit Award from the National Retail Federation (NRF) for its documentary film on hiring qualified persons with developmental disabilities for a variety of jobs and integrating them into the workplace.[2] The Americans with Disabilities Act (ADA) makes such efforts more important than ever before. The ADA guarantees disabled individuals equal access to employment as well as to all public buildings, transportation, and telecommunications. Woolworth, like all merchants, has had to review its hiring practices and methods of operation as well as examine its building structures because of the ADA.[3] The difficulties in managing a large and diverse organization are demonstrated by the company's continuing struggle to make a profit on more than $8 billion in sales.

1. **How do you think a company with numerous different kinds of stores should organize itself? By geography? By function? By store type?**
2. **What are some of the fundamental challenges in human resource management facing businesses today?**

INTRODUCTION

In this chapter we will examine the concept of supervision of employees, followed by an exploration of the management functions all supervisors must perform: planning, organizing, staffing, directing, and controlling. We then present an overview of the typical types of retail establishments and some basic concepts of retail store organization and specific management techniques. A review of the labor-management legal environment is followed by a look at the challenges and changes in organizations as retailers prepare for the twenty-first century.

RETAIL SUPERVISION

Retailers by their very nature play a boundary spanning role in the distribution channel. They deal with businesses from which they obtain goods as well as the market to which they sell goods. Retail employees are the "face" the customers and the vendors see. Often the only thing that differentiates one store from another is employee service. It is often the sales associates that deal directly with consumers. Their actions affect every aspect of success. A customer who receives poor service will not only refuse to return but in most cases tell friends and acquaintances about the bad experience. It is the retail supervisor's responsibility to make sure that each customer is treated well. In manufacturing, if an employee fails to do something properly, it can usually be caught and repaired before leaving the assembly line. In retailing, little can be done to correct poor service after a customer has left the store.

All supervisory jobs in retailing involve working with people. Nonselling employees are usually responsible for materials and equipment. Although sales employees work with people, they are not responsible for the actions and the performances of these people. Supervisors, on the other hand, are responsible for achieving goals by motivating and directing employees. As we have said before, retailing has become more and more directed toward customer satisfaction through the fulfillment of people's needs. In many cases a big part of meeting those needs requires knowledgeable and caring sales associates. The viewpoint that the primary role of the supervisor is to control the behavior of subordinates has been replaced; today the primary concern of the supervisor is to develop the self-directing capacities of subordinates so that they can enhance the customer's experience. Management training is designed to enable supervisors to serve as resource persons for subordinates and as facilitator for their continuing self-development. In order to accomplish these roles a supervisor must have certain skills.

Management Skills

The art of leading people has been a fascinating topic throughout history. Although an endless number of theories have been proposed to explain why some people are good leaders while others fail miserably, all the theories possess a common theme: Successful leadership depends on one's ability to influence others for a specific purpose. It is the ability to induce psychological or behavioral change.

The qualifications for supervisory success can be viewed as positive answers to the questions raised in Box 8.1. Necessity dictates that a supervi-

BOX 8.1 CAN YOU QUALIFY AS A RETAIL SUPERVISOR?[4]

Do you like to deal with people? Of prime importance to success is the ability to get along with people. Leaders must be able to cooperate with all of their superiors and receive needed cooperation from all of their subordinates. Their job does involve gaining group cooperation so that an integrated effort can be made to accomplish goals.

Have you mastered your job? Before people can expect to be promoted to a higher level, they must have performed to the best of their ability and at a high level of competence at their present position.

Do you look for better methods? Supervisors must be alert to possibilities of improving company image, enhancing employer-employee relations, decreasing costs, increasing quality, saving time, and so on.

Do you reach out for responsibility? Supervisors must be able to assume the responsibilities of their job in terms of their own performance and the performances of subordinates. They must be able to delegate duties to others and share knowledge and experience with coworkers. Training subordinates is an important supervisory function.

Are you willing to keep learning? Whether one manages a large store or a corner newsstand, all jobs require up-to-date knowledge. Supervisors must constantly gain current information about their store, its products, its competition, customer needs, and the marketplace.

How do you react to criticism? Successful supervisors must be able to accept failure without anger or resentment and not let pride sway their judgment.

Do you express yourself clearly? If supervisors cannot get ideas across and communicate them effectively, their ability will be severely hampered.

Do you think positively? Although every problem has both good and bad aspects, supervisors cannot let themselves develop pessimistic attitudes. If workers see their "leader" with a negative attitude, they will develop one too.

Do you thrive on competition? By the nature of the job, supervisors must thrive on competition. They are constantly competing with others for their jobs, their workers, and their products.

6543217

sor must deal with others in the work environment. Effective supervisors need to understand their authority and responsibilities. Developing a policy of honesty and integrity, dealing with problems immediately, and explaining procedures and changes with subordinates are good management tools that can be applied to a variety of retailing situations. Supervisors must have a good understanding of the goods and services they sell. It is hard to lead others if a person has no knowledge base. Supervisors need to recognize that subordinates like consistency and order, and want to see the mistakes or wrongdoing of others corrected. Otherwise, they lose the incentive to do a good job themselves. Several specific skills are needed; among them are leadership, staffing, directing, training, motivating, and controlling.

Leadership Skills

To be an effective supervisor, a person must constantly work at developing and improving his or her leadership skills. The success of the supervisor's leadership will be measured by ability to influence others to accomplish organizational goals. Supervisors must be motivated to learn everything they can about their jobs, the needs and activities of their subordinates, and the overall activities of the firm. Learning to be a supervisor, therefore, should involve development of the skills necessary for leadership. There are basically three types: human skills, technical skills, and conceptual skills.

Human skills. Human skills involve the ability to work with people. Supervisors must understand human relations. They must be able to motivate people, satisfy their needs, and promote cooperation between and among them so that the goals of the organization can be accomplished. They have to be able to "sell" an idea to their employees and coordinate their activities. Box 8.2 illustrates some of the ways in which supervisors must work with people.

Retail supervisors must have human, technical, and conceptual skills to be effective managers. Successful supervisors take a nonauthoritarian, consultative approach with employees. Seasonal departments may have a number of part-time workers who must have some technical knowledge as well as an understanding of store policies and sales principles. The ultimate measure of a supervisor is customer satisfaction.

BOX 8.2 "PEOPLE WORKING WITH PEOPLE"[5]

The actions of supervisors are at least as important as their intentions. The adage that actions speak louder than words never held truer. In discharging their duties, good supervisors:

- Demonstrate organized thinking
- Know what and when to delegate
- Are fair
- Give recognition
- Let their people know how they are doing
- Answer questions honestly and fully
- Set goals and build work schedules
- Accept changes
- Treat everyone as individuals
- Do not pass the buck

For the most part, poor performance can be attributed to employee discontent, which can stem from a variety of causes:

- Failure to receive credit for ideas and suggestions
- Not knowing where one stands with regard to one's performance
- Not being kept informed on changes, procedures, and so on
- Failure to have grievances recognized or acted on
- Favoritism
- Being criticized in the presence of others
- Having a supervisor who is too aloof and does not accept the opinion of others
- Not being held accountable

6543217

Technical skills. Technical skills involve the ability to perform the specific duties and tasks required by the position. Knowledge of specific job processes and administrative duties is essential if the supervisor is to do the job well. Take, for example, the manager of a small grocery store. This supervisor must know the specific managerial requirements of the position, as well as the duties performed by the employees. A store manager must know what to order, when to avoid being out of stock, how to price the merchandise, how to display it, how departments should be set up, and how much space should be given to various products. For a large grocery chain like Safeway, decisions about many of these issues would be made at the corporate or division level. The greatest responsibility would be staffing and other operations issues such as store maintenance and theft reduction.

Conceptual skills. In addition to human and technical skills, every supervisor must have conceptual skills. These skills may be viewed as the ability to see the "big picture." Supervisors must be able to visualize how their particular department or division relates to the overall organization. If supervisors see their department as the entire store rather than a portion of it, serious problems can arise. Those who "see trees instead of the forest" lack the perspective to make a real contribution to the firm.

BASIC MANAGEMENT CONCEPTS

Retail supervisors must understand seven basic management concepts: division of labor, authority, responsibility, delegation of authority, unity of command, span of control, and line and staff functions.

Division of Labor

Division of labor is job specialization aimed at increasing efficiency. As an organization grows, the tasks to be performed become more and more complicated. It is more efficient to have employees work at only part of a task than to have each employee perform a whole task. Take, for example, a couple who opens a small convenience store. When they first went into business, they were the only employees; they ordered, stocked, and sold the goods. When the town grew, sales volume increased, and ordering, stocking, and selling became more and more complex. They decided they could work more efficiently if they hired a stock person and a salesclerk. In hiring these employees, the store owner divided the labor and introduced job specialization. This not only freed the owners to take care of management responsibilities but also allowed the employees to concentrate on tasks that they could accomplish efficiently.

Authority

Authority is the right to give directions and to expect employees to carry them out. There are three types of authority: formal, technical, and personal. **Formal authority** is the authority conferred on the retail supervisor by the organizational hierarchy. This is the right to rule based on position. For instance, a store manager must have the formal authority to direct the salespeople. **Technical authority** is the authority that comes from the knowledge and skills of the supervisor. Often employees will ask for direction from a more senior coworker because they realize that he or she has the knowledge required to do the job. This may be something as simple as asking where to stock a particular item or more complex, such as assisting in determining proper markdowns to reduce inventory levels. **Personal or charismatic authority** is based on leadership ability and depends more on personal characteristics than position. However, supervisors have none of these kinds of authority unless employees recognize that they have the right to give orders.

Supervisors can delegate a large amount of authority and can possess outstanding leadership qualities, but unless their employees acknowledge and accept their authority, they actually have little.

Retail supervisors delegate authority because they cannot perform all tasks themselves. There are many different tasks that need to be done in a retail organization, including buying, stocking, pricing, selling, and merchandising. In most cases, it is impossible for the manager to complete all the tasks required to successfully operate a store. Delegating authority helps employees gain experience in supervising. It improves morale, because employees' attitudes improve when they believe they are making vital contributions to a firm's success.

Eileen Fisher, president of the $50 million Eileen Fisher Inc., is one of many women who have taken the entrepreneurial route to breaking the glass ceiling. Fashion designer, manufacturer, and retailer, Fisher has her own stores from Boston and New York to Florida; and more than 200 department stores and boutiques carry her clothes. Her fashions work with most body shapes and are targeted to women with careers and families who are not interested in building a trendy wardrobe.

Unity of Command

Unity of command means that employees should have one and only one supervisor. At one time this was a basic organization concept. With today's flattened organization and emphasis on teamwork, the concept of unity of command has been blurred. However, it is problematic to have more than one supervisor. For example, if stockers are responsible to several department heads, they are likely to run into conflicting jobs. Each department will wish to be restocked on a constant basis. This leaves the stocker in the unenviable position of having to be in several departments at the same time.

Beyond the store level, today's complex organizations must account for the fact that all employees need to know their reporting relationships. The May Department Stores Company is the largest department store retailer in the country. It operates eight regional companies nationwide. Each company has its own chairman, chief executive officer, and president so that authority and responsibility are defined for the store employees. There are thirty corporate executives at the vice presidential level and above in areas ranging from data processing and strategic planning to risk management and insurance. These areas support the primary function of getting goods sold in the stores.

Span of Control

Span of control refers to the number of employees a supervisor can manage effectively. Some experts say that no supervisor can control more than seven employees and must have control over at least three to keep busy. This, of course, depends on the characteristics of the supervisor, the characteristics of the employees, and the business situation. If employees depend greatly on the skills and knowledge of the supervisor, there must be considerable interaction between them. Therefore, a narrow span of control is required. If supervisors work according to stringent time schedules, the span of control should be narrow. If the employee's work is complex, close control is required; if the work is repetitive, the span of control can be wide. If employees are highly skilled and proficient at their jobs, a wider span of control can be used. For example, the span of control for sales people is a function of the amount of service they are expected to give. A retail supervisor can effectively manage many cashiers; however, commission salespeople may take considerably more time, especially in the areas of training and new product knowledge.

Let's go back to the example of thirty executives in corporate management at the May Department Stores Company. There are four individuals at the president and chairman level, two executive vice presidents, seven senior vice presidents, and seventeen vice presidents. Notice the wider span of control as the sphere of responsibility decreases. By the way, how many of the senior management personnel at the corporate and store level do you suppose are women? Three!

FUNCTIONS OF THE RETAIL SUPERVISOR

Retail supervisors are responsible for the conduct of others in the achievement of a particular task, the maintenance of performance standards, and the protection and care of merchandise. Their job is to integrate and coordinate these responsibilities so that the store's overall objectives are met. They ensure a smooth flow of work activity by implementing decisions made by people above them and by making decisions themselves. Among the responsibilities of the retail supervisor are staffing, directing, training, motivating, communicating, and controlling.

Staffing

The staffing activities of a retail supervisor involve the recruitment and selection of employees. The human resources of a retail firm are its most important asset. Success and failure are determined mainly by the caliber of the workforce and the effort it exerts. Therefore, the policies and methods a retail firm adopts to meet its staffing needs are of vital significance.

It is very costly to hire new employees. This cost is, in fact, an investment amortized over the length of time the person is employed by the company. Personnel turnover is very expensive. If a wrong selection is made and a replacement must be found, the increased costs of training may signficantly affect the store's financial picture. For example, it may cost about $5,000 to recruit a new college graduate for a management training position, but to recruit a buyer at the corporate level, costs may reach as high as $50,000. The true cost of turnover is addressed in Box 8.3.

BOX 8.3 TURNOVER: THE TRUE COST[6]

1. Recruiting and selecting employees
2. Costs of training new employees
3. Pay and benefits during the time employees are in training before full productivity is reached
4. Lower initial productivity for new employees
5. Lost sales and unhappy customers because of lower staffing levels during training time
6. Mistakes made by inexperienced employees
7. Loss of customers loyal to former employees
8. Loss of knowledge and experience obtained by employees who quit
9. Possible damaged relationships with suppliers
10. Low overall employee morale because of high turnover
11. Customer perceptions of poor attitude associated with low morale

Source: Adapted from Terri Kabachnick, *Arthur Andersen Retailing Issues Letter,* September 1995, p. 3.

6543217

Determining staff needs. Before carrying out staffing functions, a firm must identify its needs in terms of what tasks people will perform and then prepare a job description. To obtain the information for a job description, firms conduct a **job analysis,** a report giving pertinent information on a specific position. A job analysis usually provides answers to questions like these: 1) What specific work should be accomplished? 2) How much work is expected? 3) What quality of work is expected? 4) What are the best ways to accomplish the expected work? 5) What do the working conditions involve? For example, is physical effort necessary? Are physical hazards involved? 6) What responsibilities are associated with the position? 7) What authority is associated with the position? 8) What characteristics should an employee have to fill the position? a) Experience and training? b) Attitude? c) Mental abilities? d) Leadership qualities? The **job description** is a written record of the duties, responsibilities, and requirements of a particular position. An example of a job description is shown in Box 8.4. The job description has several important uses. It is a guide for testing and selecting prospective employees. It describes exactly what is expected of them, and it provides standards of performance by which they can be judged.

Some large retail firms use the information obtained from job analysis not only to develop job descriptions but also to make job evaluations. A **job evaluation** determines the value of a job in relation to other jobs. It establishes minimum and maximum salaries for a job, based on its relative value.

8.4 JOB DESCRIPTION FOR WESTERN WEAR RETAILER

Job title: Department supervisor
Status: Nonexempt
GENERAL SUMMARY:
Supports the assistant store manager by supervising the daily operational aspects of the department.
ESSENTIAL FUNCTIONS:
Assists customers in determining needs and locating the merchandise to fill those needs.
Supervises and trains sales associates.
Opens/closes the store as per company policy (key carrier).
Completes floor moves and maintains floor standards as directed by the assistant store manager.
OTHER RESPONSIBILITIES:
Processes paperwork and merchandise for price changes, transfers, charge-backs, and so on.
Handles merchandising and stocking of the sales floor.
Operates the cash register.
Performs authorization responsibilities for checks and refunds as per company policy.
Handles customer objections to the customer's satisfaction.
Assists with store cash balancing, deposits, and reports.
KNOWLEDGE, SKILLS, AND ABILITIES:
Thorough knowledge of merchandise and fashion trends.
Good math skills.
Knowledge of the computer information system and the ability to read sales reports.
Good communication and interpersonal skills. Must work well with customers and other employees.
Ability to communicate ideas and concepts to senior management.
Active listening skills.
Ability to work independently with particular attention to details and accuracy.
Flexible schedule. Must be available to work any hours and on weekends.
Good judgment and a balanced perspective on issues.
Ability to move fixtures and lift twenty-five to thirty pounds of merchandise.
College degree required.
Willing to relocate.
WORKING CONDITIONS:
Nonsmoking environment, with little exposure to excessive noise, dust, temperature changes, and the like.
This job description in no way states or implies that these are the only activities to be performed by the employee occupying this position. Employees will be required to follow any other job-related instructions and to perform any other job-related responsibilities requested by their supervisor.

APPROVED: _____   _____ _____
                          DIRECTOR OF HUMAN RESOURCES   DATE

6543217

Jobs are graded and classified according to the skills and knowledge needed to perform them, and salary ranges are established according to these classifications.

Compensation and benefits. Proper staffing requires an understanding of the compensation and benefit packages to be offered to employees. As noted, the job description and job analysis should be the basis for determining the compensation and benefits package. In addition to the salary or hourly wage, benefits such as retirement programs, health insurance, sick leave, vacation days, and child care are an important consideration for most employees.

Historically, retailers have had a reputation for paying very low wages and hiring part-time workers to avoid paying benefits. However, many retailers realize that to retain quality employees, an adequate compensation and benefits package is critical. In fact, when recruiting, training, and productivity issues are considered, a better package is often good business. Home Depot is a company that believes the best way to create wealth is to share it. Through various employee stock ownership plans, all employees are able to own a piece of the company. Their benefits and compensation package is also considered one of the best in the industry.[7] Another example of forward thinking comes from The Limited Inc. The company sponsors a defined contribution retirement plan. Company contributions to the plan are based on a percentage of the associates' annual compensation. Contributions total about $30 million each year.

Recruiting employees. Several widely used sources are available to employers who are seeking applicants for retailing jobs. All searches for employees must be in compliance with affirmative action plans, as described later in this chapter. One such source is local trade and high schools. Alert supervisors talk to school principals and guidance counselors in secondary schools and inform them of job opportunities and employment practices in their firms. There is also large-scale recruiting at junior colleges, four-year colleges, and universities. Such institutions are excellent sources of potential management trainees and personnel for specialized positions. We have discussed how the number of stores has declined. Along with this, the size of stores has increased as well as the proportion of corporate ownership. These factors require skilled management personnel. Corporations are turning to colleges to find them. Pay and working conditions now attract highly qualified college graduates.

Employment agencies are another source for recruitment. Every state has an employment service with offices in cities and large towns. Employers may place job orders by telephone or in person. There are also large numbers of privately operated employment agencies. Many of these do a careful job of interviewing, testing, counseling, and screening applicants to meet employer specifications.

Newspaper and trade magazine advertising is another widely used method of recruiting. The most common type of advertising is the placement of classified ads in newspapers. In placing such ads, supervisors should remember that advertising for personnel is no different from other kinds of advertising. Jobs must be sold in the same way products and merchandise are sold. When placing an ad, it is important to spend enough money to give complete information about the job opening. One of the dangers of newspaper want ads is getting too many unqualified applicants. For example, a department store in Springfield, Missouri, advertised: "Needed—photographer for store newspaper for employees. Little or no experience necessary." As a result, the store had a line of 197 applicants applying for the job. It actually disrupted business, and applicants were angry when told that others had more experience. A better advertisement might have said: "Experienced freelance photographer needed."

Most retailers rely, to some extent, on people who walk into the store and fill out applications. This source of personnel is uncertain because the candidates display a wide range of abilities. If, however, a company has demonstrated that it treats employees well, pays adequate wages, and has fair personnel practices, qualified applicants will be attracted to the firm. Another source for recruiting is the store's own personnel. If an employee suggests a person who is subsequently hired, it is common to award a bonus to that employee.

Equal opportunity.   Most retailers today have a commitment to providing equal employment and advancement for women and minorities. Such policies and practices are not only the law but good business in today's multicultural and multiracial customer and employee environment. See Box 8.5. Wal-Mart states that its equal opportunity commitment is ingrained in the company's philosophy of respecting the individual. Because of the importance of this issue Wal-Mart communicates to all applicants and employees its unyielding commitment and regularly monitors programs and performance regarding hiring and advancement to ensure that the company's actions match its words.[8]

Employee diversity.   You recognize how diverse the customer base for most retailers has become. To be able to serve that customer base the store employee mix would ideally mirror it as closely as possible. Minority hiring practice for most retailers now means that ethnicity, race, gender, age, and disability must not be a deterrent to job placement or advancement.

In the professions, the ranks of women have increased from 10 percent in 1970 to a critical mass of 30 to 50 percent in fields such as banking, accounting, and computers. Women are starting new businesses twice as fast as men. Although not true for retailing, women hold 40 percent of the nearly 15 million executive, administrative, and management jobs. The signs of this emerging trend appear to be taking place in developed countries around the

8.5 AN ETHICAL DILEMMA: WOMEN AT THE TOP

onsultant Robert Kahn has studied the annual reports of retailers doing more than $1 billion of business a year and has found, with few exceptions, that these companies show between one and zero women listed as corporate officers and have about the same number of women among their directors. Yet retailers recognize the skill of women as executives as evidenced by the large number who are buyers or merchandise managers.

Dr. Lawrence Pfaff of Lawrence A. Pfaff and Associates, Kalamazoo, Michigan, has published a report entitled "Study Reveals Gender Differences in Management and Leadership Skills." Pfaff surveyed 9,000 people of which 1,050 were managers (676 males and 384 females) from 211 organizations.

There are three relationships based on twenty factors in the Pfaff study, or a total of sixty factors. In fifty-two cases, women were rated higher. In forty-one of these cases, the higher rating of women was at a level that was statistically significant. Put

another way, two out of three ratings favoring women were significantly better than the rating for men.

The women beat the men by more than the Cowboys beat the Steelers in the 1996 Super Bowl! All of the Cowboys received a gold ring. In retailing, the female winners, in many cases, receive discrimination, harassment, or an office under a "glass ceiling." Retailers employ more women than any other segment of our economy, but are failing to use their competence.

Questions

In retailing, success, if not survival, in the next century will depend on management, leadership, systems, and efficiency. What are the ethical issues involved in retailers hindering themselves, perhaps even to the point of business failure, by underutilizing the talent of women? Are there any legal issues? What would you suggest in an attempt to change the existing situation?

Source: Adapted with permission from Robert Kahn, "For Retailers with Few or No Women among Their Top Officers," *Retailing Today,* April 1995, pp. 2,3.

6543217

world, even in Japan, where the number of women in administrative positions has doubled in ten years and where a woman (Takao Doi) heads the major opposition political power.[9]

Selection of employees. After applicants have been recruited, selections must be made. This involves evaluation of an applicant's capabilities in relation to the requirements stated in the job description. A resume may be the starting point for the evaluation. See Box 8.6. Most stores have potential employees complete an application form. A well-designed application form

8.6 SAMPLE RESUME

VALERIE K. REYNOLD
2204 Georgetown Circle
St. Louis, Missouri 89554
Telephone: 808/492-3894

OBJECTIVE

Seeking an entry-level position in retail merchandising that will lead to an opportunity in store management.

EDUCATION

Bachelor of Business Administration, May 1997
University of Missouri, St. Louis, Missouri
Field of concentration: Retailing
Major GPA: 3.5/4.0 Overall GPA: 3.3/4.0

WORK EXPERIENCE

Russell's Department Store, St. Louis, Missouri

Retail Salesclerk
Summer 1996 and midterm breaks of 1994 and 1995
- Sold merchandise.
- Arranged, stocked, and assisted with inventory of merchandise.
- Assisted store manager in training new personnel.
- Involved in customer relations as a result of sales position.

University of Missouri Bookstore, St. Louis, Missouri

Salesclerk
May 1993 to July 1994
- Sold merchandise.
- Participated in stocking and inventory work.
- Handled customer inquiries.

Jeans West—North Star Mall, St. Louis, Missouri

Retail Salesclerk
Summer 1992
- Involved in all aspects of retail sales including operation of the store when the manager was absent.
- Named Employee of the Month in August.

ACTIVITIES

Dean's Honor Roll—two semesters
Fashion Group—Merchandising Association
Sigma Phi Epsilon little sister
Big Brothers and Sisters of St. Louis—Secretary

REFERENCES

Furnished upon request.

6543217

Store operations include hiring and training employees. This human resource function is a critical support area for the strategic operations of the store. Recruiting, interviewing, and training are time-consuming and expensive. Management knows how to treat customers. It should think of employees as customers as well, for they are purchasing a career from the company. If treated poorly, they have many alternatives.

provides information on an applicant's personal and family history, education and work experience, types of work the applicant desires, and the reason the applicant wants to work for a particular firm.

Interviews provide additional information about applicants and give prospective employees an opportunity to learn what is involved in the job to be filled. The interviewer can explore the areas covered on the application by asking why the applicant left a previous position or why some of the lines on the application form were left blank. Interviewers can evaluate personal appearances, self-confidence, and speaking ability. Many firms follow up on initial prescreening interviews by giving the applicant tests that evaluate skills, aptitudes, and sometimes personality traits.

Directing

The purpose of giving directions is to orient employee behavior toward accomplishment of organizational goals. In short, directions tell the employee what the supervisor wants done. Whether a direction is specific or general depends on the preference of the supervisor, the ability to foresee the consequences of the order, and the response made by the employee. If supervisors want employees to participate in the decision-making process, they give general rather than specific orders. General orders permit employees to use imagination and initiative to determine how to accomplish a task. General directions are also given when the employee who is to perform a task is not in personal contact with the supervisor or when the supervisor cannot possibly foresee all the contingencies that may arise. In almost all circumstances, general directions are preferable to specific ones because employee participation enhances implementation of directions (assuming high skill level). If employees show initiative, possess the skills and experience required, and are willing to accept the responsibility for their actions, they should be permitted to act as independently as possible.

When retailers recruit better qualified people and train them better, the employees can be empowered to make more decisions without seeking direction from supervisors. At stores like Electronics Boutique, a national chain of computer and video software shops, college graduates can be promoted to store manager in less than two years. They receive merchandising and pricing directives from the corporate staff, but they are expected to be able to run the store without close supervision and direction.

Training

One activity that requires supervisors to apply all their human, technical, and conceptual skills is training. Retail training should emphasize the need for commonsense thinking and evaluation of a situation. The effectiveness of a training program is limited in part by the suitability of the trainees to their respective positions. Certain questions pertaining to prior experience, aspirations, and ability to work with others should be considered before hiring and training potential personnel.

Training may occur as part of the on-the-job working experience of the employee, in formal classrooms run by the store itself, or in schools and colleges. And, of course, training can take the form of self-study on the part of the employee. Training must go on continuously and must be implemented when a new employee is hired, a job operation is changed, new equipment is introduced, or new procedures are to be used. It is the supervisors' skills and abilities that determine the success of the company. The extremely important function of training increases the basic skills and abilities of all employees, and therefore increases efficiency in all store operations. The importance of training is illustrated by some of the activities at Kmart. The company annually provides about 360 hours of information and training associates via its satellite-based Kmart News Network. In addition the company runs a Leadership Conference that prepares assistant managers for additional responsibilities. The training program emphasizes teamwork, leadership, motivation, and customer service.[10]

Increasing the basic skills and abilities of employees through training is difficult. There are no definite rules to follow because each employee is different. There are, however, some guidelines as presented in Box 8.7 that will apply to most employees in retail training situations.

Department stores have found that they must increase service to compete with general merchandise discounters. This service includes having courteous and well-trained employees at the point-of-sale. Another important dimension in providing service is product knowledge. Many stores use satellite systems to provide product information and selling suggestions for employees.

8.7 GUIDELINES FOR EMPLOYEE TRAINING

Guideline 1
People learn when they are ready and willing to learn. Supervisors will find it difficult to teach employees unless they are ready and willing. Because learning is difficult and requires attention and concentration, supervisors should always try to provide an environment that is conducive to learning.

Guideline 2
Employees learn when they see a need to know that which is being taught. The desire to learn must be present in employees before they will learn. Supervisors must create a situation in which employees will see a direct personal value in learning and recognize that the new knowledge and skills will help them satisfy a personal need in the job.

Guideline 3
Learning requires both involvement and thinking. Depending on what they are attempting to teach, supervisors should try to use as many training techniques as possible. In this way, they will be able to adjust to the individual differences of the trainees.

It is important to recognize that the more senses involved, the greater the comprehension and retention of what is presented.

Guideline 4
Employees learn by participating. There can never be any lasting effects from the training process unless the employee actively participates. In on-the-job training, employees must follow the presentation mentally as well as physically. In classroom training, employees must be forced to use their powers of reasoning to integrate their new knowledge and skills with those they already possess.

Guideline 5
Employees learn through associations and impressions. Supervisors should try to find out about the interests and past experiences of employees and relate what is being taught to what they already know. When working with an experienced employee, an "as you know" approach can be used; this indicates that the employee already knows the material and needs only to be made conscious of it once again.

6543217

Technology has provided both good and bad with regard to training. Technology-based systems have made it more difficult to train employees because they must deal with increasingly complex and advanced equipment. For example, training for a salesclerk to scan products at the point-of-purchase must include sufficient explanations. The employer must recognize that employees often reduce their workload by scanning only one product of a particular price and entering the total number of products. If soup is always $0.98, then the salesclerk must be aware that scanning only one can of soup and entering the total number of cans (regardless of kind) will result in inaccuracies in the inventories of the various kinds.

The capability of technology has also increased with the demand for better training systems. Many of the more advanced POS installations have a tutorial, much like you will find with most software products on the market. This allows the employees to learn the system in a step-by-step process paced by computers. With VCRs, employees can now be taught without constant and immediate supervision. For example, salespeople can learn to identify potential shoplifters by watching videotapes.

Motivating Employees

If supervisors are to lead, they must be able to motivate employees to perform tasks that are asked of them. Employees sometimes have to do things that are boring and have little interest or challenge. In spite of the monotony, however, the tasks must be performed. It is the supervisor's job to motivate employees to perform all their duties. Motivating involves guiding employees' efforts toward the accomplishment of the firm's objectives. Success depends on managers' ability to know employees on a personal basis, and to know and understand the nature and sources of job satisfaction.

Retailers use many approaches to get employees moving in ways beneficial to the organization. Some shout, others coax, some have contests, others give time off from work, and some praise while others threaten. These and other possible methods can be categorized into three alternative approaches to motivation: the human need approach, the authority approach, and the financial approach.

The human need approach.
The human need approach to motivation is based on the premise that the most effective motivators are those that act as satisfiers of employee needs and goals. It is important that the supervisor recognize two assumptions underlying this view. First, each individual may have different needs. Second, different motivational devices may satisfy the same need for different individuals.

Job enlargement and job enrichment have gained much recent attention as ways to motivate employees by meeting their human needs. **Job enlargement** increases the number of tasks an employee performs. For example, a job structured to incorporate two tasks would be redesigned to include four. In this way the satisfaction of the employee would be increased by the added stimulation of the additional tasks and the overall variety of the tasks included in the job. **Job enrichment** includes building into people's jobs greater possibilities for individual advancement and growth through more challenging and responsible work. For example, a salesperson may be given additional responsibilities of choosing, ordering, and displaying merchandise in the department rather than simply waiting on customers.

The authority approach.
The authority approach is based on the assumption that the supervisor's authority and position are the only factors necessary to motivate subordinates. Authority is the right to take action and

the right to expect others to perform. In other words, subordinates will do the assigned tasks because they are told to do them and because they fear the consequences of doing otherwise. This is really a negative view of motivation. It is doubtful that negative incentives such as loss of a job are motivation devices in the true sense of the concept. They may cause an employee to do an adequate job, but seldom will they inspire a person to perform to the best of his or her ability.

The financial approach. The financial approach to motivation is based on the assumption that employees work to maximize their economic position. Today we know that money is only one of many factors important to the employee. When much of the work environment becomes depersonalized, other intrinsic rewards, such as social and higher-level ego needs, may be more important than additional money. Supervisors have many motivational tools available to them: pay increases, promotions, prizes, paid vacations, insurance plans, praise, recognition, and added responsibility for deserving individuals.

The key to successful motivation is to use one or a combination of the above tools. Unfortunately, supervisors may at times be forced to use negative incentives. They also can use competition to motivate. Most people have a strong desire to win, and this can be channeled into a motivational device. It is amazing how monotonous jobs gain appeal and excitement when people are in competition with their peers.

Communication

Communication is the key to understanding others. It is only through communication that individuals are able to interact and relate to each other. If supervisors are to be effective leaders, they must be able to communicate.

Forms of communication. Although communication is usually written or spoken, there are other alternatives. Lack of communication is one of them. In many situations, nothing communicates better than dead silence. In oral communication, a person's voice inflections can indicate feelings. One of the best communicators is facial expression. Physical appearance and "body language" also serve as communication tools. A person's actions are one of the most effective forms of communication. The saying "Actions speak louder than words" is true.

Barriers to communication. There are barriers to communication, and supervisors must overcome them if they are to be effective leaders. There is, for example, the poorly expressed message in which the supervisor uses words or illustrations that have no meaning to the employee. There are the semantic and cultural differences that arise when words have different meanings to different individuals. There are the role expectation differences between superior and subordinate. Subordinates, for example, may not like confrontation or do not want to be the bearers of bad news; they just tell the supervisor what he or she wants to hear. Or subordinates may have little skill in expressing themselves, whereas supervisors, because of the nature of their jobs, have considerable experience in communication.

Supervisors must first make a conscious attempt to break the barriers created by their organizational role. By transmitting ideas frankly and by encouraging employees to make suggestions and offer opinions, supervisors can greatly reduce organizational tensions. Encouraging employee participation and feedback can enhance communication flow and reduce status and role tensions. Second, supervisors can greatly increase understanding if they transmit messages in the employee's frame of reference. By viewing the world as their employees do, supervisors can make their messages more effective. Third, if supervisors are to communicate effectively, they must listen so that they understand what is being said.

Controlling

Supervisors must follow up to make sure work is being carried out in the proper manner. To do this, they must establish standards of performance. Then they can measure actual performance and compare it with planned performance to determine whether work is progressing according to schedule. If the system is not under control, the supervisor can isolate the trouble spot.

In a way, supervisors maintain control much like a thermostat. If performance is not according to plan, the supervisor can expend additional resources or change activities to bring the performance back to a desirable level. One way to help keep things under control is by operating on the **exception principle.** This means that routine matters should be handled at the lowest management level possible. An executive spending time cleaning a receiving area represents a misallocation of resources. At the same time the executive needs to spend time on the sales floor in order to be in touch with both employee and customer needs and concerns. To the extent that executives can concentrate on more fundamental, difficult, and abstract issues, they can better manage the organization.

Employee Scheduling

Retailers are constantly trying to balance labor costs without compromising customer service. More and more they are turning to sophisticated and automated scheduling technology. Automated applications can produce schedules that meet budget, service, and employee requirements in a fraction of the time it takes managers to do this by hand.[11] Two major types of systems exist: time and attendance (T&A) and scheduling systems. T&A systems such as Kronos' Timekeeper Central allow retailers to develop budget and staffing parameters. Automated time accounting has resulted in the impartial application of pay rules and policies.[12] Software systems that improve the scheduling and planning of employee effort are continually improving.

Evaluation of Employees

It is always difficult to appraise an employee's contribution to the store. Traditionally, this has been done by having the manager evaluate the employee's work habits and attitude. For salespeople, managers can quickly and accurately measure the value that a specific employee adds to the store's sales. Currently POS systems can give the manager information on how much a salesperson has sold, the number and speed of transactions for checkers, as well as more specific measures like the amount of add-on sales by employees.

Today managers seek approaches that emphasize better leadership, motivation, and communication as a way of achieving store goals and objectives. Systems of management whereby superior and subordinate work together to identify common goals are critical to define each worker's major area of responsibility in terms of results expected of that worker. Results measures are used as guides for operating the unit and assessing the contribution of each of its members.

THE LABOR-MANAGEMENT LEGAL ENVIRONMENT

Let's turn now to the legal environment in which retail organization supervision exists. Many state, municipal, and federal statutes impact the retailer's relations with employees. Failure to comply with these regulations can result in fines, civil lawsuits, and business closure. These statutes are usually concerned with job discrimination; labor-management relations; and wages, hours, and working conditions.

At the forefront in the popular press are the laws affecting job discrimination. These laws continue to cause a great deal of social debate. Only time will tell how society handles the issue of trying giving everyone equal opportunity and being sure that discrimination does not come into play in the hiring and promotion of individuals. See Box 8.8. The fact that the issue is not settled is reflected in the passage of a referendum in California to deny social service benefits to immigrants who are not legally residing in this country. The U.S. Supreme Court also continues to hear cases addressing affirmative action issues.

Job Discrimination

The federal government, most state governments, and many city governments have passed legislation designed to prevent discrimination in the selection, discharge, promotion, and pay of employees. Discrimination because of race, color, creed, sex, national origin, and sometimes age is expressly forbidden.

8.8 AN ETHICAL DILEMMA: HIRING ISSUES AND DISCRIMINATION

andall Smyth is the owner/manager for an Iowa-based department store. He recently attended a seminar in Chicago. Part of the program required the participants to discuss a number of retailing practices and to judge whether they were ethical or unethical. Three of the situations are presented below.

- During a golf match a store owner learned from a health care professional that a longtime employee, his controller at the store, has AIDS. He knows that it is probably illegal to fire the worker. Because he feared the premiums on his small group health insurance policy would increase, he decided to outsource the accounting function and hired an outside firm. He then eliminated the position of controller and released the employee.

- A firm had an opening in the merchandising department. One of two qualified applicants appeared to be about five months pregnant. Because of the requirements of the Family Leave Act, the decision was made not to hire her.

- The flagship store of a Chicago chain contains three restaurants. A number of the restaurant employees are nonnative English speakers. The corporate human resource manager sent an auditor to examine the preemployment documents required before anyone can be hired. The federal I-9 Employment Eligibility Verification requires two documents to establish the right to work in the United States. The auditor reported that all the documents were in the personnel files. However, she stated that she believed some of the documents were forged.

Questions

Are there ethical issues in these three situations? How would you have handled each?

6543217

The most well known of these laws is the **Civil Rights Act of 1964,** which declared it illegal for an employer to discriminate in matters of compensation against any person otherwise qualified because of race, creed, color, national origin, or ancestry. As a result, equal employment opportunity became a civil right. The Civil Rights Act requires the retailer to be responsible in hiring, promoting, and firing employees. There are seven areas employers must watch to make sure they are complying with the intent of the law: recruitment sources, application forms, interviewing, testing, hiring, training, and promotion. Many retailers have established specific affirmative action policies.

The Equal Pay Act of 1963 prohibits gender discrimination in salaries and fringe benefits. It provides that a man and a woman working for the same employer under similar conditions in jobs requiring substantially equivalent skills, effort, and responsibility must be paid equally even when job titles and assignments are not identical.

The Age Discrimination in Employment Act of 1967 makes it illegal for an employer to refuse to hire or to discharge any individual because of the person's age. The law extends to compensation, as well as to the terms and conditions of employment.

The Rehabilitation Act Amendments of 1974 provide that no qualified disabled person should be subjected to discrimination in employment. Disabilities covered may be physical or mental and may limit major life activity such as hearing, seeing, or walking. The purpose of the law is to ensure that only job qualifications are used to decide who is employed.

The **Equal Employment Opportunity Act** of 1972 permits the **Equal Employment Opportunity Commission (EEOC)** to bring legal action against any employer who does not comply with the provisions of civil rights legislation. In order to abide by the law, retailers must be consistent in the application and enforcement of personnel policies and make sure personnel policies and actions are based on reasonable and valid points that can be supported in economic terms.

The Americans with Disabilities Act (ADA) of 1992 requires employers to make reasonable accommodations to hire all persons regardless of mental or physical disability. This act extends the protection provided in the Civil Rights Act, Equal Pay Act, and Age Discrimination Act so that the mentally and physically disabled cannot be discriminated against.

Management-Labor Relations

In the area of management-labor relations there are several laws that affect retailers. **The National Labor Relations Act,** also referred to as the **Wagner Act,** was passed in 1935. It is applicable to all retail concerns that have

The Americans with Disabilities Act extended the laws regarding discrimination against individuals with physical and mental disabilities. It has also enhanced the sensitivity of retailers to the special needs of these individuals. Visually impaired customers can read the new braille signs on the front of every retail store in the Barton Creek Mall in Austin, Texas.

yearly gross sales of $500,000 or more. The act contains two basic provisions. First, employees have the right to organize and bargain collectively through representatives of their own choosing, and will be free from the interference, restraint, or coercion of their employers.

Second, no employee and no one seeking employment will be required as a condition of employment to join any company union or to refrain from joining, organizing, or assisting a labor organization of his own choosing. In other words, employers cannot interfere with the efforts of employees to form, join, or assist labor organizations. Neither can they discriminate against employees because of such actions. Furthermore, they must bargain collectively with a duly designated representative of their employees. The **Labor-Management Relations Act (Taft-Hartley Act) (1947)** and the **Labor-Management Reporting Disclosure Act (1959)** clarified certain areas of the previously discussed legislation.

The **Occupational Safety and Health Act (OSHA)** of 1970 provides employees with a wide scope of protection regarding their working environment. Places of employment are required to provide safe working conditions. This has translated into various specific regulations that cover things such as chemical usage and storage, maintenance conditions in the workplace, equipment safety, and many other areas that affect a retailer.

Wages and Hours

There is significant federal legislation dealing with employee wages and hours. **The Fair Labor Standards Act of 1938** deals with minimum wages, equal pay, maximum hours, overtime pay provisions, record keeping, and child labor. This law has been amended in some form by almost every new Congress. There are some exemptions to minimum wage and overtime provisions, including executive, administrative, and professional employees, as well as outside salespeople.

As retailers seek increased productivity from employees, they are experimenting with various new pay plans. Bonuses are replacing base wage increases, and commission pay incentives are once again entering department stores.[13] Even retailers that are very successful and progressive with employment practices can run afoul of labor laws as they seek greater productivity. Nordstrom's sales associates are given the freedom to do almost anything to satisfy shoppers. They are paid on commission and earn much more than the typical retail salesperson. However, in the early 1990s Nordstrom Inc. was sued for millions of dollars in back pay by its employees; it was charged by the Washington State Department of Labor and Industry with unfair labor practices and faced claims by the National Labor Relations Board that it had violated federal labor laws. Among other things, it was alleged that workers never got paid for attending meetings, writing thank-you notes to customers, and other tasks they performed "off the clock" on their own time. In 1993 the company settled the lawsuit, agreeing to pay an estimated $40 million to thousands of employees.[14]

All states have enacted *workmen's compensation and unemployment benefit laws* to provide medical expenses for employees who are accidentally injured at work or who suffer from occupational diseases. Compensation laws also make provision for payments to the families of workers who die as a result of their employment.

In addition to the mandatory contributions for retirement and disability, the **Social Security Act of 1935** provides a national unemployment insurance plan. A tax is placed in the employer's fund, and former employees, if they qualify, can receive unemployment benefits when they are out of work. To qualify, an employee must usually be fired or laid off. The amounts of the benefits and the length of time they can be drawn vary among states.

The Family Maternity Leave Act (1993) requires employers to allow eligible employees unpaid leave of up to twelve weeks for the employee's own serious illness, the birth or adoption of a child, or the care of a seriously ill child, spouse, or parent. This regulation applies only to employers with more than fifty full-time workers.

It is easy to see that the legal environment touches nearly every aspect of retailing. A major part of retail supervision is making sure that employee rights and employer responsibilities are well understood throughout the organization. We have looked at the basic supervisory management concepts and the legal environment of the employee/employer relationship. In the next section of the chapter we examine the topic of store and firm organization.

THE RETAILING ORGANIZATION

Organizations establish relationships among people, materials, and other resources to get a job done. There are two organizations in the retail firm. One is the **formal organization**—the planned structure created by management. The formal organization will be our primary concern. The **informal organization** is the structure that arises naturally out of the activities and interactions of personnel. It is the natural flow of authority and communication that develops as people work together. These flows may or may not be the same as those on the formal organization chart, but they exist in every firm. The informal organization can be a powerful force, and it can work for or against a company. If supervisors understand and utilize the informal organization, they can greatly increase work performance. One way of working with the informal organization is to recognize its existence and cultivate its support.

Before we examine the various types of formal organizations in retailing, we will look first at some of the elements of all formal systems. Retail stores usually develop organization charts illustrating the formal structure of the firm. These charts show the formal lines of responsibility and authority existing within the firm.

Levels of Organization

With retailers growing both internationally and into a variety of store formats, they have had to organize in different structures than in the past. The size of many retailers requires organization at three major levels: parent corporation, subsidiary, and the individual store.

Parent Corporation

Today the majority of businesses in every retail sector except hardware are chain stores or franchises. Chain stores are groups of the same basic retail outlets linked by centralized management and common ownership. Chain store organizations are generally larger and more complex than department store organizations, although the same basic functions of merchandising, promotion, operations, and control are carried out. Additional functions such as real estate and construction, warehousing, and legal matters may also be needed.

Centralization is the major difference between chain store and single store organization; major responsibility and authority are centralized. Store managers are responsible for the selling functions only in a particular outlet. The chain store organization must link decision centers, economic resources, and personnel in an efficient system. This network of supervision and control is designed to allow for accountability and performance standards to be tied to each of the units, while providing central management with constant information. Many large retailers are divided into several subsidiary corporations. For instance, Gap Inc. is divided by both geography and product/store format. See Figure 8.1. As you can see, there are four major store formats that are different parts of the organization: Gap, Banana Republic, GapKids, and Old Navy Clothing Co. Gap Inc. is divided geographically into domestic and international operations.

FIGURE 8.1
- - - - - - - - - -

Gap Inc. is organized first by geography and then by store format.

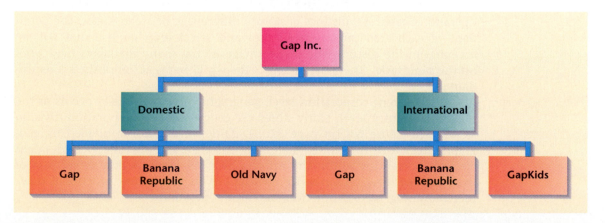

Subsidiary level. Because of the increasing size of retailers, many are organized at the subsidiary level. Here there are three major types of organization parameters: organizational function, product class, and geography. Large retail corporations may also organize according to their mission statement. The organizational structure for Wal-Mart depicted in Figure 8.2 shows that the first level (executive vice president) is based on store type (i.e., Wal-Mart versus Sam's Club). However, the second (senior vice president) and third (vice president) levels are based on organizational functions. The senior vice presidents represent the functions of store planning, legal (general counsel), and distribution. The vice presidents represent the financial (controller), information, loss prevention, marketing, international, risk management, and human resource (benefits) functions. The only exception to this functional structure is the vice president of international operations.

The advantage of this type of organization is that managers can focus their specialized skills on specific problems. For instance, an advertising manager would not attempt to operate and update an information system or reorganize the merchandise in the stores. The disadvantage is that it assumes one system works well in every environment in which the stores operate. However, the marketing mix may differ widely between different regions of the United States and countries throughout the world.

Product class organization. At the corporate level, few retailers are structured around the goods that they sell. However, at both the parent corporate level and the store level, many retailers are divided into departments or corporations based on the goods sold. Toys 'R' Us is structured into various corporations based on three categories of goods: children's clothing (Kids 'R' Us), toys and infants'/children's apparel (Toys 'R' Us), and books (Books 'R' Us). This division also occurs at the store level, as is noted later. Toys 'R' Us is also divided into corporations depending on country or world region.

Geographic organization. Many firms like Toys 'R' Us are organized at least in part by geography. This has become even more common as retailers expand overseas. Geographic organization has the benefits of separating operations based on distinct customer differences between areas. The president of each area can operate stores and select merchandise that will be accepted in the district. The disadvantage is that many managers may work on the same tasks. Therefore, much of the work that is accomplished is redundant.

At the parent corporation level, geographic division usually occurs at the region or country level. Many stores use geography as a corporation division as well. In Figure 8.3 on page 320, Dillard Corporation is divided by geographic region in the United States. For instance, the Phoenix vice president controls operations within the Arizona area. As shown in the lower part of the figure, each region has a vice president in charge of three functional areas: merchandising, sales promotion, and store operations.

Wal-Mart Organizational Chart

Wal-Mart Corp.

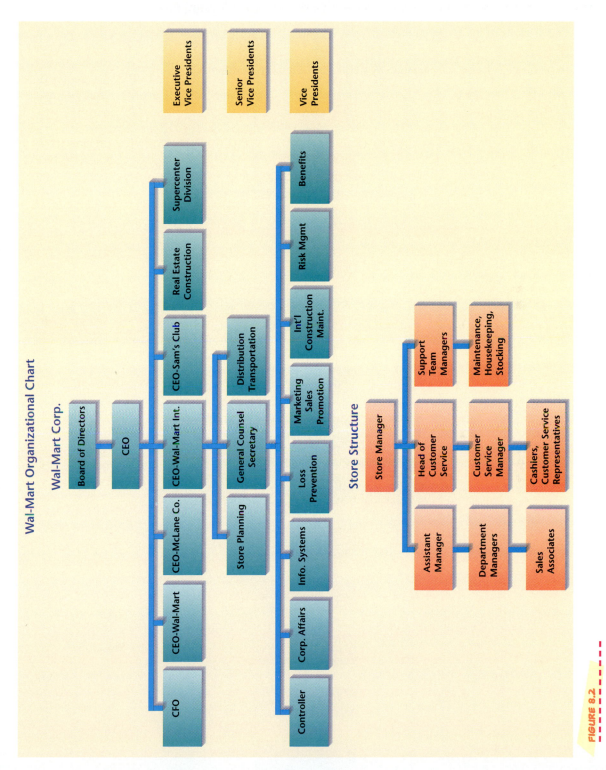

Executive Vice Presidents

Senior Vice Presidents

Vice Presidents

Board of Directors

CEO

CFO

CEO-Wal-Mart

CEO-McLane Co.

CEO-Wal-Mart Int.

CEO-Sam's Club

Real Estate Construction

Supercenter Division

Store Planning

General Counsel Secretary

Distribution Transportation

Controller

Corp. Affairs

Info. Systems

Loss Prevention

Marketing Sales Promotion

Int'l Construction Maint.

Risk Mgmt

Benefits

Store Structure

Store Manager

Assistant Manager

Head of Customer Service

Support Team Managers

Department Managers

Customer Service Manager

Maintenance, Housekeeping, Stocking

Sales Associates

Cashiers, Customer Service Representatives

Most large retailers have a central corporate management organization. The store organization is very simple.

FIGURE 8.3

Dillard Department Stores—Organization by geographic region and function.

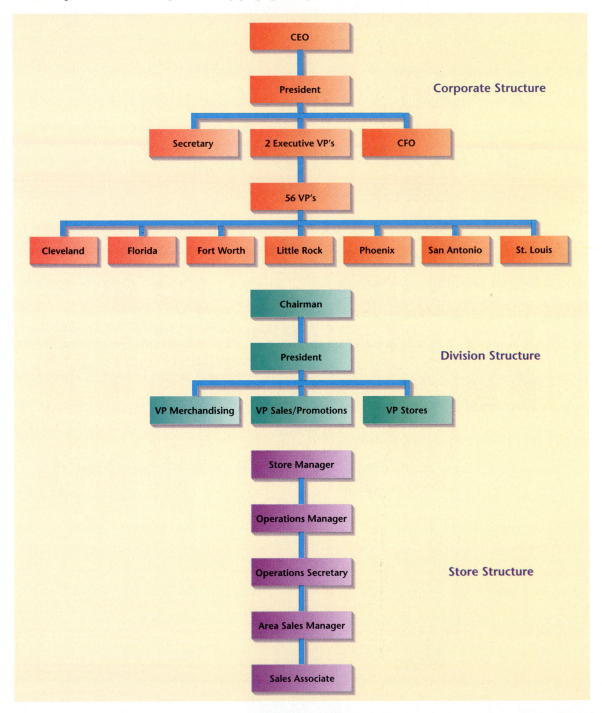

Function/Process Organization

In 1927, Paul Mazur[15] suggested that retailers organize according to their major functions. He defined these as merchandising, marketing, management, and accounting/finance. This basic organization by functions is still used widely today. However, it is usually adapted to the size of the organization. Another way to describe the four main functions of the retail organization is in terms of merchandising, promotion, operations, and control. These functions must be performed in both small and large stores regardless of the organizational structure. Let's look for a moment at the four functions.

Merchandising. The merchandising department is usually organized into the merchandise lines a department store carries. This allows for merchandising specialization. The merchandising department is responsible for buying the goods, vendor relations, planning assortments, and working with the promotion department in planning special events and advertising campaigns. More specifically, this department implements the merchandising policies of the company's management while directing its specialized managers in the formulation of a consistent store image through the products offered to the public. It has a more direct relationship to the profit-producing sales activities than the other departments, which serve in supporting roles.

Promotion. The promotion department's job is to attract people into the store and influence them to buy items offered for sale. With the exception of personal sales, all selling activities—such as advertising, window or interior displays, and special events like autographing sessions and product demonstrations—are functions of this department. The promotion manager in a large department store may have several assistants. A separate assistant may be needed for television, radio, newspapers, displays, and special events. The promotion manager needs to supervise and coordinate these assistants and their activities while working closely with the merchandising department.

Operations. The operations manager usually will be responsible for a variety of activities related to providing and maintaining suitable facilities for selling, for customer service functions, and for employee staffing. In many organizations the store manager serves primarily as the head of operations because buying, pricing, and promotion are handled at the corporate level.

Control. The control department's main function lies in the area of financial affairs. The preparing of financial data and records, expense budgeting and control, company credits and collections control, and the firm's compliance with city, state, and federal regulations are among its responsibilities.

The controller usually heads this department. The increasing use of computerized information systems, making more data readily available, and the growing complexities of government regulations have increased the size and importance of this department. Specialized assistants, responsible to the department manager, may be needed to meet the needs of the organization.

In the past, many of the large tasks such as buying, advertising, promotion, and merchandising were done by each individual store. Today, many of these activities are done by the home office with the store manager mainly concerned with keeping the store stocked and in order. For example, Wal-Mart purchases 95 percent of its merchandise out of the home office. Store managers, however, have significant latitudes in selecting merchandise from assortments developed by corporate buyers. A store manager in Corpus Christi, Texas, or St. Petersburg, Florida, would select a wide variety and assortment of ocean fishing equipment in the winter while those in the Midwest are selecting an assortment of snow shovels and ice fishing gear.

Departmentalization, the dividing up of merchandise and services into separate but related groups, helps an organization cope with the problems of size and the associated complexity of work. Department stores without a multiple-store central organization generally separate the functions of operation, promotion, merchandising, and control under different managers. These departments and managers have separate duties, and their activities are coordinated by the general manager. Figure 8.4 shows the organization chart for a very large family-owned department store.

Leased Departments

One dimension of the store organization that is little recognized by customers but widely used by retailers is the **leased department.** Department stores, discount stores, and supermarkets often lease space within the store for a specialized department to be operated by someone other than the management of the store itself. Leased departments can be seen in many stores as banking, hair care, laundry and dry cleaning, travel services, and video rental outlets vie for high-traffic space. For example, Silo, the discount home electronics retailer, leases space in Marshall Field's stores in Chicago to supplement its twenty-four freestanding locations in the market,[16] and McDonald's is leasing space in Wal-Mart stores.[17]

The firm that leases the space is responsible for management and merchandising within the particular department. The store typically charges a flat rental fee per square foot, a percentage of the gross sales, or a combination of the two. These relationships continue to evolve.

Leasing to an expert retail vendor can provide the store with an additional dimension for its customers in terms of specialized products, services, and experienced management. Stores will often lease departments such as jewelry, cameras, restaurants, or snack bars. The store, however, typically loses significant control over pricing, promotion, and selling within the leased department.

Individual Store Level Organization

With complex corporate organizational structure, individual stores often now consist of a store manager, assistant manager, department manager, and sales personnel. Even in small store chains like Spencer's Gifts, a store manager, an

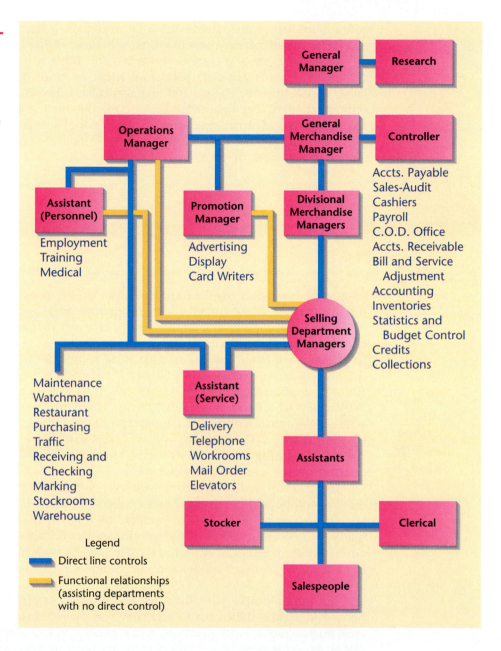

FIGURE 8.4

The store organization for this single-unit downtown department store reflects each of the major retailing functions.

assistant manager, a sales supervisor, and sales personnel constitute the local organizational structure. In the past, stores had more positions to handle the different operations.

The trend today is to flatten the organizational structure with fewer managers handling more responsibility. Although the flattening has reduced some of the bureaucracy associated with large structures, it has increased the stress level of many managers and subordinates because of the increased workload.

Small stores usually carry fewer items, and there is less need for specialization. Employees generally perform a wider range of duties than those in larger establishments. The general manager often is involved in operating and selling activities. The organization is simple but no less important than for any other type of store, regardless of size. Before leaving the area of human resource management and organization, let's look at some additional challenges and changes that managers are facing.

ORGANIZATIONAL CHALLENGES AND CHANGE

Managing the global retail enterprise of the twenty-first century will require retailers to overcome unprecedented organizational challenges. This will necessitate developing and implementing changes that seem almost inconceivable today. To understand this, imagine the expertise needed to manage the future retail enterprise. Many more retail companies will span several continents, countries, and cultures. Some of the markets where the retailer has stores or divisions will be stable, while others will be highly volatile. In each market, several different formats will exist. These may range from highly specialized, lifestyle-oriented stores to electronic shopping channels, and everything in between. Competition will be fierce, with more players throughout the world chasing fewer dollars, yens, rubles, and marks. Consumers will demand quality, choice, and value.

The makeup of the workforce will vary widely. In a few countries, the workers will be highly educated and customer-friendly, but there will be relatively few people available for retailers to hire. In other countries where many people are available, the workforce will be less educated and less attuned to the concept of customer satisfaction. A key challenge will be adopting a common business model and merchandising approach to different cultures.

Motivating people with different backgrounds, aspirations, desires, and needs will require skilled managers. They will operate in a complex world of local bureaucracies, work practices, and regulations. The only solution for the global retailer will be hiring and developing local managers.

Managing Diversity

Managing diversity means fostering an environment in which workers of all kinds—men, women, whites, blacks, Hispanics, Asians, Native Americans, the disabled, homosexuals, heterosexuals, the elderly—can flourish and, given opportunities to reach their full potential and contribute at the highest level, can give top performance to a company.[18] Managing diversity offers a competitive advantage in problem solving, meeting customer demands, and hiring and retraining quality employees. To achieve this advantage, retailers must have a diverse workforce to match the demographics of the customer base.

There has also been evidence that diverse groups are more effective at solving problems. They have a richer variety of ideas, greater creativity, and a better, more flexible understanding of diverse markets.[19] One study showed that diverse student teams viewed situations from a broader range of perspectives and produced more innovative solutions to problems than homogeneous teams.[20]

Retailers can learn lessons from other types of firms. A study of Fortune 500 companies found the following strategies for managing diversity: Avon encourages cultural networks, Apple computer has a manager of multicultural and affirmative action programs and mentors minority employees, and Xerox managers are held accountable for the number of minorities in each division.[21]

Empowerment

To achieve the lowest cost structure retailers will have to be continually rethinking their business, striving to eliminate costs and non-value-added functions as Wal-Mart has so successfully done. Being an efficient, low-cost provider can lead to a competitive advantage because it is so difficult to achieve.

Empowerment is a concept that is relevant for any organization wishing to become more efficient. **Empowerment** refers to allowing subordinates to have decision-making power that was usually only in the hands of the managers. It is especially important in retailing because the greatest amount of customer contact occurs at the lowest level in the organization. This makes it critically important to empower the person serving the customer to make the appropriate decisions to satisfy that customer.

Focus on Core Competency

Because of functional divisions in the merchandising and operations areas, decisions regarding how much merchandise is needed, how it will travel, what it should travel in, how quickly it must be moved, and how it will be stored are usually made independent of one another.

In traditional organizational structures each functional area seeks to optimize its own performance, not the performance of the entire supply chain. This can result in delays, misunderstandings, and errors. Ultimately costs may increase while service levels decline. These problems can be avoided. The first step required is to identify the core processes that drive the business.

The *core competency* is what the company does best and where its real competitive advantage lies. Examples of a retailer's core competency may be "providing superior service," or "better and cheaper supply chain management." For instance, The Limited's core competency is "faster and better product development." The company is more successful than the competition at doing this because it is the "king of testing." Rather than deciding to initially commit to huge quantities of an item, The Limited begins by testing a few of them within selected stores. Several weeks later, merchants check sales levels. On the basis of these results they may then place larger orders, which are received in the stores in four weeks or less.

Heightened Cultural Sensitivity

Before moving into a new country, geographical region, or even neighborhood, retailers must thoroughly assess the culture in that location and what impact it may have, not only on merchandise assortments but also on staffing and organizational structure. All too often retailers entering new markets failed because they underestimated the effect that these cultural differences would have on their business. As was stated above, to help overcome some of these problems, having a local management team in place is critical. At the global level, the good news is that while today few American retail executives have international experience, the opposite is becoming true as sources of supply and channels of distribution become more international.

The Team Construct

As retailers in the twenty-first century focus their business around core competencies, many activities will occur within a **team construct.** Organizational structures will become looser and more networked. Multifunctional teams will set plans, make decisions, and monitor performance.

John Martin, the chairman and CEO of Taco Bell, writes that the company has extended the notion of ownership and broad responsibility to the employees who interact with the 50 million customers served each week. Many of the restaurants operate without the need of a full-time unit manager. Instead, crew people team together to handle nearly all the activities required to run a restaurant from the moment it opens to the time it closes. The individual unit managers have become general managers who oversee more than one restaurant and become more of a coach and counselor for employees. Instead of being told what to do, team members now take full responsibility for accomplishing tasks such as tracking and ordering inventory, hiring and training other team members, and handling customer requests.[22]

The use of teams will continue to increase. See Box 8.9. Teams will comprise individuals who have a "total business" perspective, but who possess some of the knowledge of a specialist as well. The definition of team roles and responsibilities will replace traditional organizational functions such as merchandising, operations, and marketing. For instance, teams will be charged with the goal of getting the lowest cost product to the customer in the least costly way.

Using technology, teams will be able to simulate movement of products through the supply chain, identify inefficiencies, and adjust the supply chain model accordingly. The team will share incentives, risks, and rewards. Teams

| 8.9 | CHANGE IN BUYER'S JOB |

Today a buyer's job includes many tedious activities. For instance, a buyer may need to visit vendors to view merchandise, to write orders, or to negotiate for better terms. Buyers may spend part of their day analyzing stacks of reports containing sales, gross margin, and markdown budget data. They may also get involved in issuing price changes. Buyers spend time visiting stores, remerchandising the selling floor, digging through the stockroom, and talking with sales associates and management. Part of the day may be spent on the phone with the distribution center to locate lost or late merchandise. There is often considerable strife between buyers and the distribution center, with arguments over conflicting priorities. Examples of disharmony are endless and frequently reduce productivity.

The job of a "buyer," as it is defined today, is disappearing. The functions (assessing the customer base, evaluating consumer segments, analyzing trends, developing the product mix, budgeting, forecasting, and acquiring merchandise) are being taken over by a team transformed and empowered by technology, by process improvements, and by new performance measures. The team is directed by a category manager who "owns" the process of getting the right product to the customer.

6543217

will also audit merchandise displays and check selling floor conditions within stores daily via video. Video conferencing allows teams to meet face-to-face with management as well as with customers.

Rightsizing the Organization

"Rightsizing" is the term being used to explain the current trend of finding the right number of employees to run a successful organization. Global competition, outsourcing, and technological advances are forcing organizations to take a harder look at their structure and size.

Not long ago, companies looked at growth as a positive sign and paid little attention to the process. Those companies that failed to look at the long-term effects of unplanned growth are now facing the dilemma of downsizing the number of employees. Before downsizing, companies should look at the following alternatives: training employees, maximizing effectiveness and efficiency, and use of new technology.

Companies usually decide to downsize when productivity is low or when technological advances make current operations obsolete. This means that successful companies downsize also. However, research shows that downsizing alone is not an effective solution to cost and productivity problems.

WOOLWORTH—REVISITED: ORGANIZATION COMPLEXITY FOR THE GLOBAL RETAILER

Woolworth is the largest international specialty store retailer. They see great growth opportunities in their athletic businesses. They plan to aggressively expand the Lady Foot Locker, Kids Footlocker, and Champs Sports chains in the United States. Although U.S. retailers represent a very small proportion of retailers in Europe, Woolworth is the leader among U.S. retailers with more than 300 general merchandise stores and nearly as many specialty shops in seven European countries.

In an attempt to increase profitability, the company is taking a number of organizational actions as part of its worldwide repositioning strategy.

The global expansion plan includes opening additional Foot Locker stores in Asia following customer acceptance in Hong Kong. The Foot Locker chain also opened more stores in Europe, Mexico, and Australia. The company opened its first Champs Sports store, the first Kids Foot Locker, and the first Carimar boutique in Mexico City in the mid-1990s.

The company believes that its success at "exporting" formats across national borders reflects the wide appeal of merchandising concepts as well as responsiveness to the special needs of the local customers.

The power of having a worldwide chain is best illustrated by the success of the Foot Locker format. Its 2,800 outlets have 23 percent of the athletic shoe sales in the United States alone. Foot Locker's power in the marketplace allows it to demand exclusive styles, preferred deliveries, and earlier input into marketing plans.[23]

In its attempt to become a low-cost, customer-driven organization, and to support its global business, the company is conducting a review of its logistics processes. Logistics activities such as transportation, warehousing, storage, shipping, and receiving are a major component of a retailer's cost structure and are critical to any firm's ability to serve customers. Effective management of logistics processes can keep its stores well stocked with fresh and competitively priced merchandise. By effectively scheduling merchandise deliveries and improving stockroom technology, Woolworth can reduce stockroom size, increase stockroom productivity, and add to a store's selling area.

1. What are the special organizational issues that occur for a global retailer? What are the personnel issues?

Summary

In retailing, people are the lifeblood of the business—whether they are customers or employees. People sell the goods and people buy the goods. A successful manager must possess skills regarding employees and store operations. Management, human, technical, and conceptual skills are needed in retail supervision.

Many management concepts can be applied to retailing. Among these are the division of labor, the concept of authority, unity of command, and span of control.

Fundamental responsibilities of a retail supervisor include staffing, directing, training, motivating, communicating, and controlling. Motivating employees involves guiding their efforts to accomplish the retailer's goals. Different approaches are used, including the human need, authority, and financial approach.

Retail organizations have formal and informal structures. The formal organization is divided into different levels and can be organized by product class, geography, and/or function.

Many federal, state, and local laws impact how a retailer interacts with employees. Failure by the retailer to understand both the spirit and the letter of the law may result in fines, civil action, punitive damages, or business closure. Major categories of laws that affect human resource management are job discrimination, labor-management relations, and compensation legislation.

As retailing becomes more competitive and global, it is imperative that retailers increase the productivity of their assets. By becoming more efficient and focusing on processes, the retail organization can do more with fewer resources. Focusing on core competencies, empowerment of employees, and developing cultural sensitivity should be goals of a successful retail organization.

Key Terms and Concepts

Authority, 297

Civil Rights Act of 1964, 313

Division of labor, 297

Empowerment, 325

Equal Employment Opportunity Act, 314

Equal Employment Opportunity Commission (EEOC), 314

Exception principle, 311

Formal authority, 297

Formal organization, 316

Informal organization, 316

Job analysis, 300

Job description, 300

Job enlargement, 309

Job enrichment, 309

Job evaluation, 300

Labor-Management Relations Act (Taft-Hartley Act) of 1947, 315

Labor-Management Reporting Disclosure Act (1959), 315

Leased department, 322

Occupational Safety and Health Act (OSHA), 315

Personal or charismatic authority, 297

Social Security Act of 1935, 316

Span of control, 298

Team construct, 326

Technical authority, 297

The Age Discrimination in Employment Act of 1967, 314

The Americans with Disabilities Act (ADA) of 1992, 314

The Equal Pay Act of 1963, 313

The Fair Labor Standards Act of 1938, 315

The Family Maternity Leave Act, 316

The National Labor Relations Act (Wagner Act), 314

The Rehabilitation Act Amendments of 1974, 314

Unity of command, 298

QUESTIONS

1. How might supervisors gain and improve their human, technical, and conceptual skills?

2. How is the process of decision making related to the supervisory function of planning? How is it related to the training situation?

3. Are the guidelines for training consistent with your formal educational experience?

4. Should different motivational devices be used for the new employee and the veteran employee? Why or why not?

5. Why do you think most people are poor communicators?

6. What is the distinction between the formal and the informal organization?

7. Discuss the relative value of different sources for recruiting applicants for buyers, for salespeople in specific departments (for example, the camera or toy department), and for assistant store manager trainees.

8. Are there advantages in giving directions in the form of suggestions instead of orders? If so, what are they? Are there potential problems? Does the type of authority affect this?

9. Which of the more recent federal laws do you think will be the most difficult for retailers to implement? How can they overcome the difficulties you have identified?

SITUATIONS

1. You are the assistant to the merchandise manager for a large general merchandise store doing $4 million of business a year. You are asked to take the responsibility for conducting the yearly white goods sale. Every January this store makes an all-out effort to sell (or promote) sheets, pillowcases, and bedspreads. In the past some unusual and interesting ideas have been successfully used to motivate employees to work for bigger and better sales. How would you proceed to obtain the total involvement of all employees?

2. You are the newly appointed personnel manager. One of the first problems you face is a request by a department head to dismiss an employee. The employee has been with the firm for eighteen years and until a year and a half ago was very productive. Recently, however, he has frequently been late for work, and his absenteeism is increasing. The department manager's report suggests that he may have family problems and/or an alcohol problem. How will you proceed? What will you do?

3. You are the manager of a high-fashion men's clothing store. Because of the location, your customer base consists of very high income white males. The past employment practice has been to hire only white males as salespeople. Some research suggests that customers respond better to salespeople of the same background. Does this justify continuing this hiring practice?

Cases

CASE 8A
Massive Mart (A)

Massive Market, a modern supermarket, contains a number of product departments: dry grocery, frozen foods, refrigerated foods, produce, meat, delicatessen, bakery, nonfoods, pharmacy, and liquor. Each department has its own manager who reports directly to the store director. These departments would be considered line departments in an organizational structure. Functional staff departments are office administration, front end (cashiers and sackers), stocking crew (stock dry groceries and nonfoods at night), customer service, receiving, and Universal Product Code (UPC) pricing coordinators (responsible for maintaining shelf and scanner pricing). In an attempt to implement TQM (total quality management), the store's unit director, Chuck Burg, is developing an organization chart. He hopes to use this to identify the store's internal customers (the employees served by other employees).

1. *Design an organization chart for Chuck's store.*

2. *Which departments are the internal customers within the store?*

3. *Which departments are providers to the internal customers you have identified?*

CASE 8B
Lee Hardware's Minority Hiring Practices[24]

Lee Hardware is a profitable building and supply company that was founded in 1945 and is still operating at its original downtown location in a Southwestern community of 40,000. The population is growing slowly with several new manufacturing firms (including a plant that produces disposable diapers), growth in the dairy industry, and slow growth at Southwestern State College, which enrolls about 3,500 students. Approximately 25 percent of the population is Hispanic, and 14 percent is African American. Lee Hardware has seen many businesses leave downtown along with the gradual deterioration of a once flourishing business area. Ten years ago the local chamber of commerce began actively working to revitalize the downtown area by bringing in new businesses. An old movie theater has been renovated for the community fine arts performances; law offices, three restaurants, and an antique minimall have also been added. The owners of Lee Hardware decided not to leave and are now looking forward to continued improvements in the downtown area.

Five years ago Lee Hardware received an award from LULAC (League of United Latin American Citizens) for its fair minority hiring and work practices. Recently, however, resentment seems to be building among the company's Hispanic employees. Bill Smith, the present manager of Lee Hardware, spoke to them to try to discover the source of the problem. Two months earlier, Lee Hardware had announced six part-time openings, five of which were filled by Hispanic applicants. The employees felt that Lee Hardware should have hired two or three full-time workers who would be able to receive benefits rather than part-timers without benefits. When Smith visited an instructor at the local college, he discovered that recent research has found that within Hispanic communities, hiring part-time workers in order to not pay the benefits accorded to full-time positions is often perceived as "unethical."

1. *What actions could Bill Smith take in regard to his current situation? What are the social and business consequences of each possibility?*

2. *What actions could be taken in order to avoid such problems in the future?*

Chapter Goals

After reading this chapter, you should be able to:

- Understand financial, sales, and merchandise inventory records.

- Analyze a retailer's financial position.

- Understand the different aspects of a balance sheet: assets, liabilities, and net worth. Comprehend profit and loss statements.

- Perform ratio analysis to assess performance.

- Calculate gross margin return on investment, return on space, and return on labor.

- Use the retail profit margin accelerator concept to target strategies for improving financial performance.

- Understand the financial issues in the global market.

FINANCIAL ANALYSIS AND MANAGEMENT

DILLARD DEPARTMENT STORES:[1]
COMPETING WITH EXPENSE CONTROL

Founded by William Dillard in 1938, Dillard Department Stores is one of the most successful retail chains in the United States with over 240 stores in 21 states and sales of nearly $6 billion. Dillard's has established a pattern of growth by building, buying, integrating, and upgrading store properties throughout the Southeast, Southwest, and Midwest. The company seeks to offer a full line of fashion brand apparel and home furnishings that will appeal to what the company sees as "value conscious" consumers.

Dillard's family-based management has four main areas of emphasis: cost control, innovative merchandising philosophies, expansion through acquisition and new store construction, and increased productivity through highly efficient operations.

Dillard's programs and systems have a goal of making the firm a leader in low operating expenses. Part of its success in expense control results from buying smaller department store groups, often for not much more than the value of the real estate. Management believes that ownership of real estate as opposed to leasing allows the firm to control real estate costs, an important retailing expense.

The company expands in areas where it can be a leader in the community. A market dominance location strategy helps expense control by providing promotion and distribution efficiency. Dillard's operates seven state-of-the-art, highly automated distribution centers that have dramatically reduced distribution costs, which in turn contributes to its low-cost position. Merchandise now takes an average of eight days, as compared to a previous thirteen, to complete the distribution process from the vendor to the store. With the distribution centers, the merchandise moves on a two-day turnaround.

Dillard's is committed to investing the capital necessary to support its goals of efficiency and growth. Each year the company invests over $300 million on capital improvements in existing stores.

The company's merchandising strategy is centered on delivering high value. This high-value strategy requires aggressively pricing merchandise with an everyday fair pricing policy (EDFP) that is designed to build customer loyalty. In the first three years after adopting this strategy, Dillard's gained additional market share in its major trading areas. EDFP can put real pressure on gross margins, making the low-cost expense structure even more important.

Adopting EDFP has allowed a minimal promotion schedule with all storewide sales eliminated except for two anniversary events per year. Promotional dollars previously spent on television and general distribution sale circulars have been redirected to specialty catalogs aimed at specific customer groups.

Highly accurate mailing is based on the company's proprietary database that contains very specific information on customer buying habits. The right audience is reached for each offering, thus avoiding unnecessary mailing costs.

The merchandise marketing strategy has moved steadily toward more upscale product lines with an emphasis on private-label as well as exclusive-label items from top vendors. The private-label merchandise program began in 1990 with the introduction of Roundtree & Yorke, a premium label in men's fashions. The exclusive-label program incorporates the lower cost of a private label with the value of a well-known brand name.

1. **How many business elements are involved in Dillard's overall planning for efficiency and growth?**

INTRODUCTION

In virtually any conversation where the nature of retailing is being discussed, you will hear store managers, buyers, merchandisers, and salespeople say, "Retailing is a numbers-driven business." In previous chapters you have seen the importance of numerical analysis to define markets and locate stores. Retailing is too complex, competition too keen, and products too numerous for a merchant to lose sight of the details of the business.

Overwhelming evidence shows that managers who operate with less than complete information are the ones whose businesses are most likely to fail. In fact, a study has shown that in the records of one U.S. District Court, 90 percent of the firms adjudged bankrupt failed to keep adequate records. Therefore, a retailer must be able to compile, understand, and use records effectively. For most of us, working with records is not the most exciting or glamorous part of running a retail business. In fact, it can be both boring and confusing. Even if you have good accountants, you must understand the financial side of the business to make good operating and merchandising decisions.

FINANCIAL RECORDS

We begin with a discussion of the minimum set of records that should be kept by any retail business, along with an explanation on how to use them. We then explore the financial analysis of the operation with information developed from these records.

Records are the basis for guiding and controlling the operations of a retail organization. They tell how much is owed to employees, the government, and suppliers. They tell whether the business is making a profit. They tell when, how much, and what type of merchandise are needed in the store. And they help the merchant make plans for the future. Records are the tools of the trade, providing information to make decisions. To fulfill their functions, records must be timely, accurate, complete, and convenient to use.

What constitutes an adequate set of records depends on several variables:

1. The type of retail business being conducted
2. The financial and human resources available to the firm
3. The type and extent of the manager's informational needs
4. The manager's ability to make good use of the information in the records
5. The information necessary to assess the business's tax liability

There are, however, three areas in which it is absolutely essential to keep records: sales, merchandise inventory, and expenses. There are numerous other possibilities. See Table 9.1.

Sales Records

Managers should receive on a regular basis three different types of sales information—store cash and charge sales, department sales, and sales by individual salespeople. Managers who record less information cannot find out what is contributing to the business.

With sales information available, managers can compare last year's sales with this year's. They have one of the essential pieces of information necessary for the preparation of profit and loss statements. They can forecast needs for personnel, inventory, and facilities.

Cash and charge sales.
Electronic cash registers have the ability to record both cash and charge sales. Some stores may use sales tickets to keep track of this, as well as to record sales per individual or department. This

TABLE 9.1

Examples of Records Kept by Retail Stores

Allowances given customers	Salaries and wages and benefits	buying goods
Allowances received from suppliers	Rent	Notes paid by merchant
Sales by:	Light, heat, water	when due
Store	Telephone	Notes—part payment to
Departments	Losses from bad debts	merchant, with interest
Salespeople	Depreciation	and renewal
Cash sales	Delivery	Notes renewed by mer-
Charge sales	Repairs	chant and interest paid
Checks written	Equipment rentals	Other income
C.O.D.s	Donations	Outstanding charge
Customer count	Services purchased	accounts of customers
Delivery equipment bought and sold	Insurance	Refunds (paid out)
Departmental information	Freight and express reimbursements	Returns by customers for
Sales	Furniture and fixtures bought and	credit
Expenses	sold	Returns to wholesalers
Profits	Inventory	Salespeople's sales
Deposits made	Invoices paid and received	Shortages and overages
Discounts earned	Layaways	Taxes paid
Discounts given customers	Merchandise purchased	Sales
Discounts given employees	Money borrowed	Income
Employees' employment and earnings	Money drawn from business	Excise
Expenses	Money received on accounts	Property
Advertising	Notes given by merchant when	Taxes withheld

method is practical only when total unit sales per day are relatively small, as in appliance stores or a boat dealer's shop.

Department sales. Receiving a breakdown of sales by department or product is a necessity. It is impossible for a manager to keep abreast of the performance of each department or all the merchandise within one department without some systematic method. A manager who lacks knowledge of a department's performance frequently misses sales opportunities and, as you will see in Chapters 10 and 11, cannot do an adequate job of buying merchandise.

Cash registers can key sales to individual departments; sales may be further divided into merchandise categories. By scanning bar codes, each SKU (stockkeeping unit) can be tracked.

Employee sales. Notwithstanding the impact of self-service on today's retailing, personal customer contact still plays a dominant role. It is often personal contact that alienates or retains customers. In the absence of self-service, it is the salesperson who brings in the dollars. Therefore, managers should determine whether they are obtaining maximum performance from their salespeople. Because payroll expenses in a retail store are often greater than all other operating expenses combined, managers must be concerned with individual sales employee performance.

One of the many ways to assess each salesperson's performance over a particular period of time is by establishing a system to code each transaction with an employee name or number.

Merchandise Inventory Records

The largest investment in most retail businesses is in merchandise available for sale. Since retail firms often have 60 to 70 percent of total assets invested in their stock, it is important that managers keep informed of the merchandise inventory situation. This includes (1) knowing what purchases have been received and (2) keeping an accounting of the in-stock inventory.

It is more difficult to keep track of the in-stock situation. Yet this knowledge is fundamental to management's appraisal of a retail store. The in-stock situation provides information on the store's investment in inventory and on its **gross margin position.** Remember that gross margin is equal to net sales minus the cost of goods sold. To know the amount of profit a firm is making, expenses are subtracted from gross margin.

Cost of goods sold is the difference between the cost of the total merchandise handled during a period (beginning inventory plus purchases—all the goods that have been in the store at one time or another during the period) and the cost of the ending inventory (what is left at the end of the period). If a manager knows how much merchandise was handled during a period and how much was left at the end of the period, he or she can calculate the difference between the two to determine how much was sold. Note, however, that the value of the merchandise must be calculated at cost prices, not retail prices, because gross margin is figured by subtracting the cost of goods sold from retail sales.

The following illustration shows again how gross margin is calculated:

Beginning inventory	$400 —cost
Purchases	+ 600 —cost
Total merchandise handled =	$1,000 —cost
Less ending inventory	− 300 —cost
Cost of goods sold =	$700 —cost
Sales	$1,000 —retail
Less cost of goods sold	− 700
Gross margin =	$ 300

You will see later how transportation costs increase the cost of goods sold. Also, cash discounts increase gross margin, and alteration costs decrease gross margin. To obtain the figure for total merchandise handled, one must keep records of the beginning inventory plus all purchases received at cost price. Ending inventory may be found by taking a physical count, at cost prices, of the inventory in stock. Exact gross margin can be determined only if a physical inventory is taken. Most firms take a complete count of their goods only once a year, which is required by the Internal Revenue Service. Since managers need to know the inventory position on a regular basis so that they can buy carefully as well as track gross margin and profit performance, they must have a method of estimating the inventory position at any given time. There are three ways of doing this: the cost method, the book method, and the retail method. Each of these will be explained in detail in Chapter 10.

Cash Outflow Records

Cash flows out of the store for a variety of reasons. Expenses must be paid, merchandise must be purchased, debt payments must be made, and equipment must be bought.

Expense records. In department and specialty stores, operating expenses may run as high as 33 percent of sales. For each dollar of merchandise sold, then, 33 cents is spent on operating expenses. Interestingly enough, in the same department and specialty stores, 64 cents out of each dollar of sales is spent to pay for the merchandise. The 33 cents for operating expenses and 64 cents for cost of goods sold leave a net profit of only 3 cents after taxes. It is obvious that good records are a must; it is not possible to be a sloppy merchant and still make money.

Some items in the expense list can be controlled by the store manager, a department manager, or a buyer. These **controllable expenses** are also called **direct expenses** and are those that could be eliminated in the short run if the unit or department were eliminated. For example, payroll, advertising, and supplies could stop quickly. **Uncontrollable** or **indirect expenses** are those that would continue for a time even if a store were closed or a department eliminated. For example, closing a store would not necessarily end rent payments.

Management should frequently check and analyze expenses, because they directly affect profits. A comparison of the expenses of one's own store with those of other stores or a comparison of last year's expenses with this year's provides a basis for analysis. Since it is important to compare one's own business with similar kinds of businesses, the retailer should use generally accepted expense classifications. Trade associations and suppliers are good sources of information, as is the *Retail Accounting Manual* published by the National Retail Federation.

Merchandising records. The major cash outflow goes to pay for the goods purchased for sale. Careful record keeping requires recording merchandise when it is received and making sure the merchandise on the invoice is what is received. Invoices should be checked against purchase orders before payment is made.

In addition to payments for goods and expenses, outflows may also go toward reducing the principal on borrowed funds. (The interest on these funds is an expense.) Borrowed funds may be needed periodically to purchase fixtures, equipment, vehicles, and other items necessary to operate the store. Adequate records ensure that payment is made correctly and on time.

In summary, a successful retail business depends on good records. Modern cash registers, electronic scanning system bar codes on merchandise, and computers give information on sales and inventory. Expenses are captured through normal accounting processes.

The Financial Position

Management can use the information found in records to make profit and loss and balance sheet statements that assess the financial position of the business. Management uses budgets to plan its operations and, therefore, can adapt to change instead of simply reacting to it.

To determine how well a business is doing, management needs certain information: It needs to know if it can pay its bills, if it is making a profit, and if it can live with its net worth position. Businesses differ in many ways. From a financial standpoint, however, some things are common to all businesses. Typically, these things are expressed in terms of ratios—that is, a numerical relationship between one figure and another. The profit and loss statement and/or the balance sheet statement provide the figures for computation.

Let's examine the development of profit and loss statements and balance sheets. Then we can show how information gathered can be used to evaluate financial performance through financial ratios. We also explore the concepts of financial inventory control through stock turnover and gross margin planning to increase profitability. Finally, we explain financial planning through budgets.

FINANCIAL STATEMENTS

An evaluation of the financial condition of a retail store should tell four things: whether the store can pay its bills on time, whether it is making a profit, whether it has a healthy balance between debt funds and ownership funds, and whether its assets are productive.

Profit and Loss Statements

The **profit and loss (P&L) statement** (often called the income statement) shows how successful the buying and selling of goods has been and how well operating expenses have been controlled over a period of time. In summarizing sales and expenses, it reflects the profit situation. As noted above, gross margin is the difference between net sales and cost of goods sold. If gross margin exceeds expenses, a profit is made; if not, a loss is generated. A sample retail profit and loss statement is shown in Table 9.2.

The P&L statement shown here tells how much profit was made, how much gross margin was earned, and how much was spent on total expenses. Notice also that accounts are represented in terms of both dollars and percentages. Percentages in Table 9.2 are calculated by using net sales as the base, or the 100 percent. For example:

$$\frac{\text{Rent}}{\text{Net sales}} = \frac{\$1,250,000}{\$18,000,000} = 6.94\%$$

$$\frac{\text{Profits}}{\text{Net sales}} = \frac{\$1,050,000}{\$18,000,000} = 5.83\%$$

The percentage figures establish relationships that show the effect of management's decisions on various operating accounts. The relationship of accounts such as cost of goods sold, operating expenses, and profits to the

TABLE 9.2

Profit and Loss Statement

			Percent
Gross sales	$19,000,000		
Sales returns and allowances	1,000,000		
Net sales	18,000,000		100%
Cost of goods sold			
Inventory	$15,000,000		
Purchases	30,000,000		
Total merchandise handled	45,000,000		
Less ending inventory	−35,000,000		
Total cost of goods sold		10,000,000	55.56%
Gross margin		8,000,000	44.44%
Operating expenses			
Payroll	3,770,000		
Rent	1,250,000		
Advertising	600,000		
Other	900,000		
Total expenses		6,520,000	36.11%
Net profit before taxes		1,500,000	8.33%
Income taxes (30)%		450,000	
Net profit after taxes		1,050,000	5.83%

net sales figure permits managers to compare their store's performance with its performance in previous years or with the performance of similar stores. (Percentage figures make comparisons much easier than dollar amounts.) Managers may use this information to make adjustments that affect operations.

The Balance Sheet

A **balance sheet** tells management how efficiently the business is operating by showing whether the firm is overcommitted or undercommitted in asset holdings or is too far in debt. It gives the value of all assets, debts, and the net worth of the business at a particular time. See Table 9.3. In other words, it shows (1) everything a business owns, called **total assets;** (2) everything a business owes, called **total liabilities;** and (3) **net worth (owner's equity).**

Retailing can be a very capital intensive business. It is not unusual for the investment in inventory, equipment, accounts receivable, real estate, and buildings to exceed $40 million, with $10 million in owner's equity and the rest borrowed. If a merchant nets 2 percent on sales of $60 million, the store will have a return on owner's equity of 12 percent. That is less than the return from long-term stock market investments.

Assets. Assets are broken down into current and fixed. Current assets are those that will be converted into cash during the normal operation of the business within an accounting period, usually one year. Cash, accounts receivable, and merchandise inventories represent such assets.

Other types of assets include land, equipment, fixtures, and buildings—assets that are retained and used in operating the business. They are considered fixed assets because they will not be converted into cash in the normal yearly operations. Other assets such as deferred charges (for example, prepaid insurance) and goodwill are found in many retail balance sheets, but for our purposes they are of little significance.

TABLE 9.3

Balance Sheet

Current assets			Current liabilities		
Cash	$	300,000	Accounts payable	$	1,500,000
Accounts receivable		1,500,000	Accrued payable		300,000
Inventory		3,500,000	Notes payable		3,000,000
Fixed assets			Long-term liabilities		
Land		900,000	Long-term debt		7,200,000
Fixtures & equipment (less depreciation)		1,500,000	Net worth		2,500,000
Buildings (less depreciation)		4,100,000	Total liabilities and net worth		**$11,800,000**
Total assets		**$11,800,000**			

Liabilities. Liabilities show the amount of money a company owes its creditors that will be due within a year and debts that will mature in a longer period of time. As is true of asset accounts, liabilities that mature within a year are called current liabilities; they include items such as accounts payable, notes payable, accrued taxes, and salaries payable. Long-term debt liabilities include obligations such as payments on the mortgage of the building and long-term bonds.

Net worth. The net worth of a business is simply the difference between total assets and total liabilities. Net worth is often referred to as *owner's equity.* In a large retail firm, net worth may include preferred stock, common stock, earnings retained in the business, and reserves set aside from earnings for special purposes. The net worth of a small retail firm is usually the owner's capital. In any event, whether net worth includes many accounts or only one, it is still the difference between the value of assets and the liabilities.

 Ratio analysis

The use of financial ratios allows the retailer to evaluate the financial performance of the store. The trends of the ratios are as important as the values of the ratios themselves. Industry ratios are compiled by a number of organizations. The industry norms provide benchmark figures against which the business's ratios can be compared.

Strategic Profit Model

The information in the P&L and the balance sheet allows the development of a **strategic profit model (SPM),** which lets the retailer calculate the return on net worth and evaluate the performance of the main areas of financial management as they impact the return on net worth: profitability on net sales, asset utilization, financial leverage, liquidity, working capital, and debt to net worth. Each of these areas has a direct impact on the profitability of the business.

The calculations on page 344 show that every dollar invested by the owners earned an exceptional 41.6 cents in return on net worth compared to the net profit after taxes of 5.83 percent. See Table 9.2. If the store had a 6 percent return on net worth and it was possible to receive 8 percent on an investment in commercial bonds, the owner might want to consider getting out of the business.

The SPM can be seen graphically in Figure 9.1. In formula form it is as follows:

FIGURE 9.1

Understanding the strategic profit model.

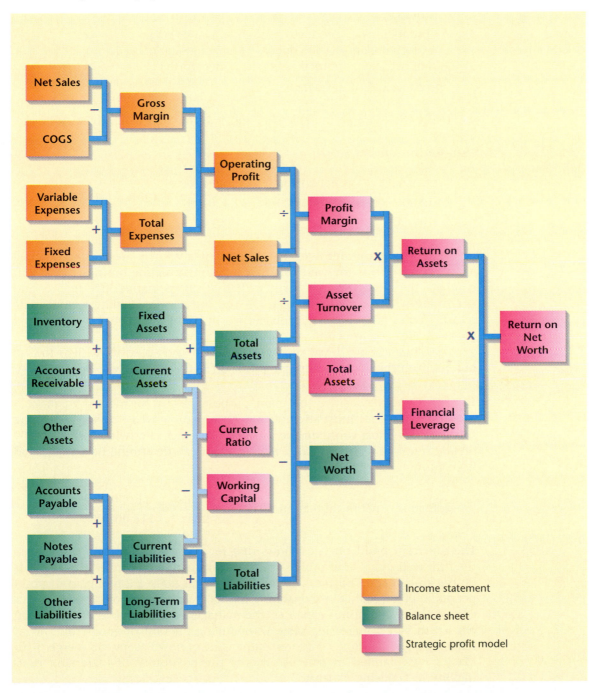

Return on net worth =

$$\frac{\text{profit}}{\text{net sales}} \times \frac{\text{net sales}}{\text{total assets}} \times \frac{\text{total assets}}{\text{net worth}} \times 100\% =$$

profitability   productivity   financial leverage
of each dollar   of each dollar   for each dollar of
of net sale   of total assets   net worth

profit as a % of net worth

Using the example in Tables 9.2 and 9.3, the SPM would be as follows:

Return on net worth =

$$\frac{\$1,050,000}{\$18,000,000} \times \frac{\$18,000,000}{\$11,800,000} \times \frac{\$11,800,000}{\$2,500,000} \times 100\% = 41.6\% = 0.416\%$$

0.058   ×   1.52   ×   4.72

The **return on net worth** is the number owners are most concerned about. Net worth is the value of their investment in the business. They can compare the return on net worth with that of alternative investments and determine whether the investment in the business is yielding an adequate return. You can see that return on net worth in the SPM becomes simply net profit divided by net worth.

Let's look at how the retailer could evaluate each part of the SPM to find out what can be done to improve profit on net worth.

Profit analysis.   Since the main purpose of any business is to make a profit, management must attempt to determine how well it is accomplishing this goal. The most common way is to compare net sales with net profits. By dividing net profits by net sales, management can determine how well it has been running the business.

$$\text{Profitability (net profit margin \%)} = \frac{\text{net profits}}{\text{net sales}} = \frac{\$1,050,000}{\$18,000,000} = 5.8\%$$

The 4 percent profit on sales shows that for every dollar's worth of business the firm realizes a 4-cent profit. Again, the evaluation of percentages depends on the kind of retail business. Usually, retail firms make a 2 to 3 percent profit per dollar of net sales. Since operating profits are a function of net sales minus cost of goods sold minus expenses, the manager could improve the return on net worth by (1) increasing sales, (2) reducing the cost of goods sold, or (3) reducing expenses. Box 9.1 addresses the issue of how Federated's merger with Macy's was planned in part because of the possibility of increasing profitability by reducing expenses.

BOX

9.1 FEDERATED/MACY'S PLANS INCLUDE REDUCING COSTS[2]

Laura Bird, writing for *The Wall Street Journal*, notes that the $4.2 billion Federated Department Stores Inc. spent to acquire R. H. Macy & Co. from bankruptcy was well timed. The deal created the nation's largest traditional department store retailer, with more than $13 billion in revenue from 300 stores. Federated predicts that the combination with Macy's will eliminate $500 million in operating costs, buying and management functions, and information systems by 1999. Federated's new eight department store divisions, ranging from Bloomingdale's and Macy's to Lazarus and Stern's, will be organized into three store price levels to reach affluent, middle-market, and value-conscious shoppers. "The question we must constantly ask is, how do we get our cost of operations down so we can offer better value to our customers?" says Federated's CEO. "Our prices don't have to be the lowest in the world, but they have to be seen as the best value." Federated will have tremendous buying power to ensure quantity discounts, preferred shipping dates, and unique products manufactured for them.

6543217

Asset utilization. The second component of the SPM looks at the productivity of the assets of the store. Asset utilization is important to the retailer. The goal is to generate the highest level of sales possible for a specific amount of assets. Declining productivity would indicate that the retailer has too much invested in the business's assets for the sales level that is being produced. Higher productivity ratios point to better asset utilization in the generation of net sales.

The total asset turnover ratio is computed by dividing net sales by total assets. This ratio indicates how many dollars of net sales are created per dollar of total assets. The higher the ratio, the more productive the assets. For example:

$$\text{Total asset turnover} = \frac{\text{net sales}}{\text{assets}} = \frac{\$1,800,000}{\$11,800,000} = 1.5 \; times$$

In this illustration, $1.50 in net sales is being produced for every $1.00 of total assets. Every type of business has a different asset productivity level. A range of 1.5 times to 3.5 times is typical for a retail business. The higher the ratio, the more effectively the business is managing its total assets.

Financial leverage. The **financial leverage ratio,** sometimes referred to as the equity multiplier ratio, is computed by dividing the business's total assets by its net worth. The higher the ratio's value, the more leverage the retail business is using.

$$\text{Financial leverage ratio} = \frac{\text{total assets}}{\text{net worth}} = \frac{\$11,800,000}{\$2,500,000} = 4.72 \text{ times}$$

A ratio of 4.72 times indicates that the retailer's assets are heavily funded by debt. Debt is almost 5 times the value of what the owners have invested in the business, the net worth. This would be considered unacceptable for nearly all firms. Retail stores often grow by increasing the amount of debt, which is all right to a point. But debt can put the store at risk if profits decline and principal and interest payments cannot be made.

Liquidity. Many other ratios may be used in the evaluation of the financial performance of a retail business. Some of the most important are measures of liquidity. **Liquidity** is a firm's ability to meet its cash obligations as they become due. **Insolvency** exists when a firm cannot pay its bills on time. Obviously, firms that become overextended are the most likely to become insolvent and wind up in bankruptcy. Although the ratios must be considered in conjunction with other variables, they do give some indication of the financial soundness of a firm and can help management determine future policies. To compile these ratios, both the profit and loss statement and the balance sheet again must be used (see Tables 9.2 and 9.3).

The **current ratio** evaluates the ability of the business to pay its current liabilities with its current assets.

$$\text{Current ratio} = \frac{\text{current assets}}{\text{current liabilities}} = \frac{\$5,300,000}{\$4,800,000} = 1.1 \text{ times}$$

A current ratio of 1.1 times indicates that for every dollar of current liabilities, the firm has only $1.10 of current assets with which to make payment. Because cash is usually generated through the turnover of merchandise inventory and the collection of accounts receivable, it is desirable to have more current assets than current liabilities. For a retail firm, a current ratio of 2.0 is considered satisfactory.

Net working capital. The financial leverage ratio we calculated above shows one measure of the capital structure of the firm, the relationship of total assets to net worth. Another ratio that reflects capital structure divides the net sales by the net working capital of the store. **Net working capital** is defined as current assets minus current liabilities. The financial leverage ratio shows how many dollars of net sales are generated per dollar of net working capital. The higher the ratio, the more productive the net working capital. However, too high a ratio may indicate a lack of net working capital and a loss of liquidity. Current assets ($5,300,000) minus current liabilities ($2,100,000) = $3,200,000.

$$\text{Financial leverage} = \frac{\text{net sales}}{\text{net working capital}} = \frac{\$18,000,000}{\$3,200,000} = 5.56 \text{ times}$$

The typical retailer has a value of about 6.00 times for this ratio.

Net worth position. A store's net worth position influences both the ease with which management can finance its operations and the cost of financing. The usual way of assessing a firm's net worth position is to compute the ratio of the firm's **total debt to net worth.** This is done by dividing total debt by net worth.

$$\frac{\text{Total debt}}{\text{Net worth}} = \frac{\$9,300,000}{\$2,500,000} = 3.72$$

The percentage shows the financial relationship between creditors and owners. A general rule of thumb for a retail firm is that owners should have as much invested in the business as creditors; in other words, there should be a 1 to 1 relationship. Firms that have a small amount of ownership funds compared to debt funds are less likely to weather periods of stress. In other words, when sales drop and inventories pile up, the firm has to count on its permanent source of ownership funds to see it through. In the example shown, 3.72 indicates that the firm's total debt is 372 percent of its net worth and is therefore seriously high. Table 9.4 shows the ratios of retailing as prepared by the Dun & Bradstreet Corporation.

This concludes our study of ratio analysis and how it helps in assessing the performance of the stores. We now turn to the topic of gross margin analysis.

TABLE 9.4

Ratios of Retailing: Performance for the Median Quartile of Selected Retail Businesses

Line of Business	Current Ratio (times)	Assets to Net Worth (%)	Net Sales to Inventory (times)	Total Assets to Net Sales (%)	Return on Net Sales (%)	Return on Total Assets (%)	Return on Net Worth (%)
Grocery stores	1.9	54.7	18.3	17.7	1.3	6.0	14.2
Department stores	3.4	21.5	4.5	48.7	1.7	3.6	6.5
Radio, television, and electronics	2.1	33.4	6.5	33.3	3.2	6.5	17.6
Furniture stores	2.9	18.5	4.9	46.4	3.2	4.9	9.1
Family clothing	5.2	14.9	3.9	50.8	4.3	6.7	12.3
Men's and boys' clothing	3.4	15.2	3.7	47.5	4.2	6.5	12.3
Women's clothing	3.8	18.8	5.0	37.2	4.0	7.6	12.9

Source: "Ratios of Retailing," *Industry Norms and Key Business Ratios. Desktop Edition.* Copyright © 1994 Dun & Bradstreet Information Services, a company of the Dun & Bradstreet Corporation, pp. 162–180.

GROSS MARGIN ANALYSIS

Recently a buyer for better dresses at a Midwest department store made a comment: "I don't feel like a buyer anymore. I'm just an investment manager for the company." Today's emphasis on financial performance makes many retailers feel like this buyer. At the same time, buyers are on the front line of decisions about many other aspects of the business. See Box 9.2. Gross margin analysis is an important means of tracking financial performance. There are three primary gross margin measures: gross margin return on investment (GMROI), gross margin return on space (GMROS), gross margin return on labor (GMROL). The formulation for each is shown in Table 9.5.

Gross Margin Return on Investment

GMROI measures how many gross margin dollars are returned for each dollar invested in inventory. Assume that management gave a buyer an average of $150,000 for merchandise in several stores. Sales for the year were $800,000, and the gross margin was 25 percent. Therefore the gross margin dollars were $200,000. With the average inventory of $150,000, the GMROI was 1.33. So the buyer returned $1.33 for every dollar invested in inventory. The GMROI can be used by comparing results to the industry, the corporation, the department, other merchandise classifications, or the individual SKU. It is a good tool to use to compare the performance of different vendors of similar goods.

TABLE 9.5

Strategic Resource Allocation Analysis

Gross margin % × net sales = gross margin $

$$\frac{\text{Gross Margin \$}}{\text{Average inventory at cost}} = \text{gross margin return on investment} = \text{GMROI}$$

$$\frac{\text{Gross Margin \$}}{\text{Sq ft of selling space}} = \text{gross margin return on space} = \text{GMROS}$$

$$\frac{\text{Gross Margin \$}}{\text{Employee payroll \$}} = \text{gross margin on labor} = \text{GMROL}$$

Measurement comparisons:

GMROI: Industry, corporation, market, store, department, merchandise classification, SKU, vendor

GMROS: Corporation, market, store, department, merchandise classification

GMROL: Corporation, market, store, department

348

BOX 9.2 AN ETHICAL DILEMMA: FINANCIAL PERFORMANCE VERSUS COMPANY POLICY

Judy Johnson is the regional salesperson for a computer software vendor. She calls on corporate buyers for chains as well as owners/managers of independent stores. The following is a copy of her most recent performance review.

Six-Month Performance Review

To: FASTCO National Sales Regional Manager
From: District 14 Sales Manager
Re: Six-Month Performance Review for Judy Johnson

Sales Performance:
Judy has slightly exceeded the sales quota assigned to her. She has sold a mix of products to a mix of customers and shows no inclination to excessively favor one product/customer mix over another. Overall, I'd say she's done a good job.

Customer Relations:
As Judy's supervisor, I have queried a few of her customers. Most seem to like Judy and believe she is providing excellent service to them especially for a newly assigned salesperson. Interestingly, two of the buyers at major computer warehouse stores that I spoke to mentioned how much they enjoyed the NFL football tickets she dropped off recently. Since gift giving is against company policy, I discussed this matter with Judy. Although she is aware of our policy, Judy claims that the accounts pressured her to "sweeten" the deal.

Other Comments:
I have not yet taken any action on the matter of the football tickets, but I did tell Judy that I would have to forward this information on to you and confer with you regarding appropriate courses of action.

Questions

Is there an ethical issue here for the retailer? If you are Judy's manager for the vendor, what action would you take given Judy's violation of the company gift giving policy? If you are the retailer's divisional merchandise manager and it is your corporate buyers who have been pressuring Judy to "sweeten" the deal, what action do you think would be appropriate?

6543217

Gross Margin Return on Space

The GMROS is seldom used to evaluate buyers because they don't control the space allocation. It is, however, a valuable tool for store managers to use to allocate space. Assume a department has net sales of $300,000 and occupies

Drug Emporium owns and operates more than 130 company-controlled stores with sales of about $750 million. The company is a category dominant, value-added retailer selling health and beauty aids, over-the-counter medication, prescription drugs, and cosmetics. Drug Emporium had several years of significant losses from restructuring and store closure expenses. Gross margins exceeded selling, administrative, and occupancy expenses. Therefore, the stores made a profit from operations.

1,200 square feet. If the department achieved a 40 percent gross margin, the gross margin dollars would be $120,000. With 1,200 square feet, the GMROS would be $100 ($120,000/1,200). This number can be compared to others across the store or among stores.

Gross Margin Return on Labor

GMROL can assist management in allocating payroll dollars to departments or to stores. It is also valuable in looking at staffing levels by time of day or day of the week. The process simply requires calculating gross margin dollars for a given period of time and dividing by employee payroll cost for that period of time. For example, if weekly sales in a department were $100,000 with a gross margin of 36 percent and the weekly payroll was $16,000, then the GMROL would be 2.25 ($100,000 × 0.36/$16,000). Each dollar of labor returned $2.25 in gross margin dollars.

INVENTORY CONTROL AND PROFITABILITY: STOCK TURNOVER

A major key to profitability and a sound balance sheet is inventory control. As you know from previous chapters, there are disadvantages to having an inventory that is either too large or too small. Having too much merchandise may lead to excessive markdowns if all the goods cannot be sold or if they become soiled or obsolete before people can buy them. The cost of carrying excessive inventory creates a major interest expense. Overstocking is also expensive because of increased handling, storage, and insurance costs. On the other hand, having an inventory that is too small leads to lost sales because items are not in stock when customers ask for them.

One way to measure whether there is too little or too much invested in inventory is to compute the number of times stock turns over in a given period, which is called the **rate of stock turnover.** Chapter 10 will illustrate how this rate is critical for the buyer in merchandise planning. It is also critical in financial analysis, so we introduce the concept here. Stock turnover may be found in three ways, each of which involves the calculation of average inventory. **Average inventory** is calculated by adding the inventory at the beginning of the period and the inventory at the end of the period and dividing by two.

1. Annual rate of stock turnover in retail dollars:

$$\frac{\text{Net yearly sales in retail dollars}}{\text{Average inventory on hand in retail dollars}}$$

2. Annual rate of stock turnover at cost:

$$\frac{\text{Cost of goods sold during the year}}{\text{Average inventory on hand at cost}}$$

3. Annual rate of stock turnover in units:

$$\frac{\text{Number of units sold during the year}}{\text{Average inventory on hand in units}}$$

Calculation of stock turnover can be illustrated using the first formula. Suppose, for example, that net sales for one year were $100,000. On January 1, inventory was $40,000; and on December 31, inventory was $60,000. The rate of stock turnover is determined in the following manner:

$$\text{Average inventory} = \frac{\$40,000 + \$60,000}{2} = \$50,000$$

$$\text{Rate of stock turnover} = \frac{\text{net sales}}{\text{average inventory at retail}}$$

$$\text{Rate of stock turnover} = \frac{\$100,000}{\$\ 50,000} = 2$$

Whether a stock turnover of 2 is good or bad depends on the type of retail business. Some retail businesses, such as supermarkets, operate at turnover rates as high as 18; others, such as clothing stores, operate at turnover rates as low as 3.

The reason for differences in stock turnover rates should be obvious. Supermarket sales may be very rapid. (How long, for example, does it take to sell 300 cans of green beans?) Markets must replenish stock as often as twice a week. (Imagine how much space and investment would be necessary if stores were to stock for several months!) Supermarket suppliers ship quickly and constantly from nearby distribution points, and merchants do not have to keep too much stock on hand. The fast turnover, therefore, is caused by small in-stock inventories and large volume of sales. The situation in clothing stores is different. First, customers demand extensive choice; they want to examine different styles, colors, and sizes before they buy even one item. Second, the system for manufacturing and distributing clothing forces most merchants to order the bulk of their merchandise as few as four times a year. Therefore, it is necessary to carry backup stock, and backup stocks slow down the rate of stock turnover.

Table 9.6 lists some sample stock turnover rates for selected retail stores. But to a large extent, total store turnover rates are of limited use to managers in making operational decisions. The turnover rates of departmental stock or, in some cases, of different kinds of merchandise are much more useful than figures for the store as a whole. In determining stock turnover, it is important to understand that the rates for particular stores and departments are compared to the so-called average stock turnover rate for that kind of store or department. Obviously, allowances must be made for businesses that operate in ways significantly different from the average. A retailer should examine stock turnover rates in relation to the store's clientele and overall operating policy. It is useful, however, to monitor changes in stock turnover and compare them to those of other stores.

Several things can be done to increase stock turnover. One is to carry minimum inventory of slow-selling lines (or items) or eliminate them altogether.

TABLE 9.6

Sample Stock Turnover Rates by SIC

Line of Business	UQ	MED	LQ
Food stores	29.9	18.9	12.1
Department stores	6.2	4.5	3.1
Radio, television, and electronics stores	10.4	6.5	4.3
Furniture stores	7.5	4.9	3.3
Family clothing stores	6.1	3.9	2.5
Shoe stores	5.0	3.4	2.3
Men's and boys' clothing	7.7	5.0	3.3
Women's clothing stores	7.7	5.0	3.3

Source: "Ratios of Retailing," *Industry Norms and Key Business Ratios, Desktop Edition.* Copyright © 1994 Dun & Bradstreet Information Services, a company of the Dun & Bradstreet Corporation, pp. 162–180.

Efficient buying from reliable distributors who make fast deliveries can help reduce average inventories. A retailer may also be willing to live with a higher out-of-stock situation. Finally, prices can be lowered or promotion increased, with the goal of an increased level of sales from the same amount of inventory. However, actions that increase turnover may in fact reduce profitability. Lower prices shrink gross margins, and higher promotion increases expenses. Being out of stock may mean losing a customer. At the same time, increasing turnover by reducing average inventory can cause serious problems. It can result in stock outages, higher transportation cost, increased handling costs, and the loss of quantity discounts.

FINANCIAL PLANNING

An integral part of a retailer's overall strategy is the development of a plan that projects the financial performance of the business. The plan will aid management in determining its future liquidity position, its profit potential, and its growth limitations. A complete financial plan is made up of the following components:

- Balance sheet: situation at the start of the planning period.
- Expense budget: estimates of expenses during the planning period.
- Cash budget: estimates of cash inflows and outflows during the planning period.
- Pro forma income statement: estimates of revenues, expenses, taxes, and profits for the planning period.
- Pro forma balance sheet: estimates of assets, liabilities, and equities at the end of the planning period.

All firms must plan for the future. Good managers start by utilizing the information found in current income statements, balance sheets, and expense summaries.

Expense Budgets

Expense budgets are plans of operation that increase efficiency. Only by using an expense budget can management plan to conserve resources, establish the proper relationship between income and expenses, and identify trends in time to adjust to them before money is lost. If a retail store is to be profitable, managers must spend time on details and have definite goals in mind.

The budget should include all the expenses expected during the planning period. These should also be stated as a percentage of net sales.

Cash Budgets

Another budget commonly used in retailing is a cash budget, which may be referred to as a cash flow analysis. It is one of the best ways to avoid becoming overextended. A **cash budget** forecasts on a week-to-week or month-to-month basis all cash receipts and disbursements expected during the period. The purpose of a cash budget is to pinpoint *in advance* the timing and amount of any surpluses or shortages so that plans for taking care of them may be made.

Cash inflows. The majority of cash inflows are directly related to level of sales volume. The percentage of sales that are cash sales and the timing of the collection of credit sales must be projected in order to determine the amount of cash inflows. The store's credit policy affects estimates of collection of accounts receivable. Since revenue projections are so influential in the establishment of cash inflows, a cash budget should be developed only after all prospective revenues have been determined. The ability to obtain cash from other sources, such as a bank loan or the addition of more equity, should also be included.

Cash outflows. Cash outflows are also affected by sales projections. Once sales levels have been estimated, purchasing and inventory plans can be developed. Subsequently, the necessary items can be projected and the payments predicted. Then all other cash disbursements, for expense items as well as nonexpense items, should be projected. The timing of cash disbursements depends on management decisions and/or company policy with regard to payment schedules for the various cash outflow categories.

Cash flow budget analysis. After cash inflows and outflows are estimated for each time period, the need for cash or the excess of cash becomes evident. The following steps are then taken to determine the liquidity situation.

1. Find net cash flow for the period by subtracting disbursements from receipts.
2. Add the beginning cash balance to net cash flow to find the ending cash balance.
3. Assuming it is necessary to maintain a minimum balance in the cash account, adjust the funds accordingly.

Only cash inflows and outflows are recorded in the cash budget. For example, if a cash budget is prepared by month (a typical approach), only the cash expected to go in or out of the business in a particular month is entered.

The cash budget allows the retailer to evaluate the liquidity of the firm and to determine whether that liquidity will be impaired during the planning period. Furthermore, the need for short-term financing, and the duration and amount of that need, can be calculated. Retailers must realize that the cash budget is merely an approximation of the movement of funds. Changes may occur in cash inflows and outflows or in their timing no matter how diligently the budget is prepared. Despite the possibility for error, however, the cash budget remains a valuable tool for retailers.

Pro Forma Statements

The pro forma statements consist of an income statement and a balance sheet. These statements reflect the impact of the proposed cash budget and related noncash expenses on the future financial status of the business. Pro forma statements present estimates of the future revenues, expenses, income, assets, liabilities, and equities of the company, based on information from the current balance sheet and the proposed cash budget. The cash flow budget, in conjunction with the pro forma statements, coordinates the flow of funds and products within the firm, as well as between firm, customers, and suppliers.

The pro forma income statement.

The **pro forma income statement** projects the future profits of the firm from the plan proposed by management in the cash budget. The data used to create the pro forma income statement consist of the cash budget for the period and management estimates of noncash budget items. After the development of the pro forma income statement, the pro forma balance sheet can be made up.

The pro forma balance sheet.

The **pro forma balance sheet** shows the assets, liabilities, and equities that would result from the proposed cash budget. The data reflect the financing mix used to support the plan. The liquidity of the retail firm appears clearly in the pro forma balance sheet. The information is derived from the current balance sheet, the cash budget, and the pro forma income statement.

RETAIL PROFIT MARGIN ACCELERATORS

Not long ago a recruiter for a major retailer made the following statement: "Students don't seem to really understand what goes into maintaining gross margins and the importance of doing so." The retail profit margin accelerators (RPMA) concept forces merchants to make their analyses and decisions in the context of potential impact on profitability. The use of RPMA reinforces the importance of understanding how small changes in operating results can create dramatic changes in profits.

Four accelerators are used in the RPMA concept: (1) an increase in unit volume, (2) an increase in price, (3) a decrease in the cost of goods sold (COGS), and (4) a decrease in expenses. We will explain the RPMA concept through an illustration. Let's use the following data:

Base Period	
Sales	200,000 units
Average price	$5
Average unit cost	$3.50
Expenses	$280,000

Increase in Volume

Now hold everything the same as the base period except for unit volume, which is increased by 5 percent. Notice in Table 9.7 that a 5 percent increase in unit volume increased profitability by $15,000, or 75 percent. An increase in volume without increasing expenses might be achieved in a number of ways, including more effective and productive salespeople, better training, more targeted and efficient use of promotion, control over stockouts with a good inventory system, and just plain better attention to good buying.

Increase in Price

This time hold everything the same as the base period except for a 5 percent increase in prices. Note the dramatic increase in gross margin (Table 9.7) and therefore profitability if it is possible to increase the average price per unit by 5 percent. It might be tough to do without hurting volume or increasing expenses, but for a 250 percent increase in profit, it could be worth trying.

TABLE 9.7

Retail Profit Margin Accelerators: Increase in Unit Volume

	Base Period	Increase Unit Volume 5%	Increase Prices 5%	Decrease COGS 5%	Decrease Expenses 5%
Sales (dollars)	$1,000,000	$1,050,000	$1,050,000	$1,000,000	$1,000,000
Cost of goods sold	700,000	735,000	700,000	665,000	700,000
Gross margin	300,000	315,000	350,000	335,000	300,000
Expenses	280,000	280,000	280,000	280,000	266,000
Profit	20,000	35,000	70,000	55,000	34,000
Profit increase $	X	$ 15,000	$ 50,000	$ 35,000	$ 14,000
Profit increase %	X	75%	250%	175%	70%

First, especially in inflationary times, a retailer should constantly monitor prices to be sure they are consistent with levels of service offered and the competition. It is easy to let prices fall behind. Second, salespeople can help sustain higher levels by being trained to accentuate features, benefits, and services. Third, careful buying with an eye to reducing markdowns produces the same effect on net sales as an actual increase in list prices.

Decrease in COGS

Hold everything the same as the base period except for a 5 percent decrease in the cost of goods sold. As illustrated in Table 9.7, this decrease can also make dramatic improvements in profitability. It can be attempted by several means: (1) the retailer can check suppliers and vendors regularly for the best prices on staple merchandise, (2) careful planning may allow for an increase in quantity discounts, and (3) freight costs should be studied and alternative shipping means and closer suppliers considered.

Decrease in Expenses

Hold everything the same as the base period except for a 5 percent decrease in expenses. In our example (Table 9.7), reducing expenses has the least impact on profitability. However, the effect is substantial and well worth attention from management. Lower expenses may result from actions that range from reducing shoplifting and employee theft to better scheduling of employee time on the selling floor. It is a good practice to examine each expense category regularly to look for cost savings.

Malibu Beachwear sells upscale fashions and accessories for the beach. Small high-value items make stores the target of customer theft, and the impact is tremendous. Consider that if theft is 3 percent of sales and profit is 5 percent of sales, reducing theft to 1 percent would increase profits by 40 percent (0.02 is 40 percent of 0.05). This shows that a reduction in any expense can mean a major increase in profits.

TABLE 9.8

Retail Profit Margin Accelerators: Changes Necessary to Achieve 25 Percent Increase in Profits

	Base Period	Change Unit Volume	Change Prices	Change COGS	Change Expenses
Sales (dollars)	$1,000,000	$1,016,666	$1,005,000	$1,000,000	$1,000,000
Cost of goods sold	700,000	711,666	700,000	695,000	700,000
Gross margin	300,000	305,000	305,000	305,000	300,000
Expenses	280,000	280,000	280,000	280,000	275,000
Profit	20,000	25,000	25,000	25,000	25,000
Dollar change in factor		$ 16,666	$ 5,000	$ 5,000	$ 5,000
Percent change in factor		1.6%	0.5%	0.7%	1.78%

Using RPMA Analysis

One way the manager can use the RPMA concept in financial planning is to analyze the operation by looking for ways to achieve a targeted increase in profits. Let's examine Table 9.8 to see what changes would achieve a 25 percent increase in profits over the base period.

To achieve our targeted increase, we need to do *one* of the following:

1. Increase unit sales by 1.6 percent.

2. Increase prices by 0.5 percent.

3. Decrease cost of goods sold by 0.7 percent.

4. Decrease expenses by 1.78 percent.

This illustration vividly demonstrates how very small changes may create major improvements in profitability.

FINANCIAL MANAGEMENT IN THE GLOBAL ENVIRONMENT

Financial analysis and management are increasingly important for many retail organizations as they expand their global presence. Retailers are already discovering that the complexity of global financing issues requires that their finance staff be involved in the development of overall operating plans.

Many retailers are sourcing at least part of their product line internationally. When all transactions are conducted in U.S. dollars, exposure to foreign economies and foreign currencies occurs. International suppliers may be willing to accept dollars in payment for goods manufactured overseas, but customers and sales staffs in foreign stores want their local currency.

The many international financial issues facing global retailers can be broken down into four major categories:

1. **Foreign exchange issues:** What are the risks inherent in dealing in multiple currencies, and how can they be minimized?

2. **Transaction issues:** How should day-to-day cash management issues be handled to make certain that the money is available where and when it is needed?

3. **Technology issues:** What technology is available to monitor and control global financial management?

4. **Strategic issues:** How should foreign operations be financed, and how should the balance sheet of foreign subsidiaries be structured? How and when should profits be repatriated (returned to the home country)?

Foreign Exchange Risk

There are different types of foreign exchange risk including transaction risk and economic risk.

Transaction risk relates to the fact that foreign exchange rates may change, either positively or negatively, between the time a transaction is booked and the time it is settled. For example, a retailer sells $100 of merchandise in Mexico for the equivalent amount of pesos. Before the pesos can be converted into dollars, the dollar strengthens and the pesos are worth only

French-headquartered Printemps is part of a global retailing, distribution, financial services, and manufacturing firm. With sales exceeding FF 63.3 billion, sophisticated global money management keeps the company functioning. Retail stores in Europe and the Far East convey a strong, attractive image with high-quality fun clothing, home and leisure goods, perfumes and beauty products, books, and music CDs.

McDonald's is one of the world's best performing service retailers. Gross sales exceed $10 billion. Operating costs and expenses total about 20 percent; net income is 15 percent of sales after taxes. McDonald's manages changes in foreign currencies to minimize the business risk. Weak foreign currencies in some years have had a significant negative impact on earnings. Stores in developing countries, such as this one in Beijing, are a particular challenge.

$98. The $2 difference represents a transaction loss that directly affects the bottom line.

Economic risk is the long-term effect of transaction exposure on the retailer's cash flow. Overall changes in foreign exchange rates can affect the competitive relationship between two companies that are sourcing and/or selling in different countries with different currencies.

A prime example of this is what has occurred in the automotive industry. In the past decade the dollar has weakened dramatically against the yen. Cars manufactured in Japan and sold in the United States reaped an economic advantage over cars both manufactured and sold in the United States when the yen was 280 to the dollar. However, as a result of changes in the relative strengths of the two economies, cars manufactured in Japan are now at an economic disadvantage to those manufactured in the United States. The Japanese manufacturer gets less than 100 yen for 1 dollar in U.S. sales. It is because of this economic shift that Japanese auto manufacturers are now building cars in the United States.

Transaction Issues

U.S. retailers have come to depend on, and often take for granted, a sophisticated banking system with well understood rules. They use this system to collect on customers' checks, concentrate receipts, pay vendors, and handle a host of additional functions.

While banking systems in other markets can be just as sophisticated and effective as those of the United States, each country's banking system has different rules, regulations, capabilities, and products. The complexity of the different systems may make it difficult for a retailer to collect, concentrate, and disburse cash on a day-to-day basis.

For example, in many European countries, banks use "value dating" to process checks. Under this system, a bank grants credit for checks deposited and charges for checks written according to internal rules, often based on the date the check is written instead of the actual deposit or clearing date.

The situation becomes more complex when checks or transactions need to be cleared across national borders. Cross-border transactions typically involve currency conversions that result in transaction risk as well as added processing fees. The time period involved for foreign collections can stretch to weeks or months instead of days. And unless the retailer knows how to issue the proper instructions to the settling banks, funds may end up in the wrong account in the wrong location.

Technology Issues

As financial transaction and information needs expand, retailers must have easy access to cash management, securities, and foreign exchange services. Ideally, access is combined into one system providing the global retailer a single source for all international treasury information, from current exchange rates to current balances, in all bank accounts worldwide.

Most major retailers have already invested time and effort in modernizing and integrating their POS, inventory management, and forecasting systems. Retailers must also integrate their global financial management systems into the same framework. It's not enough to report total and projected sales in domestic currency. The information needs to be available on a country-by-country and currency basis so that retailers can plan their transactions while minimizing foreign exchange exposure. In addition, traditional international financing practices such as international letters of credit can be significantly enhanced using modern technology and information system capabilities.

Major international banks have already spent time and money to develop the technology that retailers need. Rather than reinvent the wheel, companies are turning to their banks as partners in their global expansion. When a global retailer teams with a global bank, it can create a win-win situation for both.

Strategic Issues

In addition to the day-to-day issues of international cash management, global retailers need to be concerned with a number of longer term strategic issues as they plan for their entry into new markets.

Chapter 16 discusses the pros and cons of using various methods such as organic growth, acquisition, or franchising to enter a market. Each method raises issues as to how the new market entry would be financed. The complexity of global capital markets, investment restrictions and regulations, and international tax issues makes the decision especially difficult. Whether financing should come from the parent company or local borrowing depends on expected rates of return, anticipated inflation rates, relative strengths of the economies involved, and the availability of credit in various markets.

The answers to these and other questions are complex and depend on a large number of factors: local currency and tax laws, expected rates of return, anticipated exchange rates, local borrowing rates, and local availability of funds, to name a few. In each case the best answer requires the retailer to evaluate the specifics of the situation and usually calls for a team effort to examine all the financial, legal, and marketing issues involved.

Toys 'R' Us is a retailer that understands the complexity of global finance. One of the keys to its success is the ability to provide its store management with a large amount of local autonomy while encouraging good communications and while keeping key systems, including money management, centralized. The combination of good communication and centralized money management allows Toys 'R' Us to focus on retailing issues while avoiding most of the risks of global financing. The company finances all foreign subsidiaries in the U.S. commercial paper market, where it gets excellent rates.

Recognizing that domestic funding of foreign operations could result in currency risk and potential losses or gains, Toys 'R' Us insures against this by automatically **hedging** all foreign transactions. This means that when it sends funds to a foreign subsidiary, it simultaneously purchases the needed currency in the financial market. This protects it against rate swings in the value of currencies.

DILLARD DEPARTMENT STORES—REVISITED[3]

illard's is constantly looking for ways to provide more streamlined and efficient operations. Dillard's low-cost structure has significantly reduced operation expenses, which in turn supports the company's merchandising and expansion strategies.

The foundation of this efficient structure is an advanced information system that enables Dillard's to monitor merchandise flows and maximize in-stock positions. Using this system, which gathers information at the point-of-sale, also provides knowledge of peak selling periods, so that labor schedules are established to give optimum customer service and avoid excess labor costs.

Data from the point-of-sale also keep management aware of exactly which lines of merchandise are selling. Consequently, shelves are fully stocked, early buying trends are spotted, and the products more nearly match customer needs.

Dillard's also uses information technology to provide sales associates with high-quality training. The company regularly broadcasts programs over its own private satellite network, simultaneously reaching training sites throughout the country. These broadcasts are often conducted in conjunction with merchandise vendors. This high-tech approach allows salespeople to receive the latest information on products and key company developments. Equally important, it also reduces the time and expense ordinarily incurred with site visits. Dillard's also uses the satellite network to train managers on other aspects of the information systems, so that technology is more widely understood and used by employees.

Besides providing top-notch technology-based training, Dillard's keeps sales associates highly motivated through performance-based compensation and employee stock ownership programs. Together these factors contribute to one of the highest levels of employee productivity in the retail industry: approximately $144,000 per year in contrast to an industry average of $100,000.

The company sees additional opportunities for cost savings through technology advancements. For example, a new computer system simultaneously scans external packaging bar codes and package contents to ensure error-free order acceptance.

Dillard's has a corporate structure that combines the strengths of centralized and decentralized functions. Centralized, highly computerized functions such as credit, accounting, legal, data processing, and real estate offer obvious economies of scale. Alternatively, having certain functions such as merchandise buying decentralized to the local and divisional level, closer to the customer, allows store managers to spot trends and capitalize on them quickly.

1. **What contributes to Dillard's net income/sales exceeding 5.4 percent?**

Summary

Accounting records provide information for a financial analysis of any retailer. Financial records, sales records, and merchandise inventory records are valuable information sources. The profit and loss statement summarizes sales and expenses of the retailer and reflects the profit situation for a given period of time. The balance sheet provides the value of assets and debts along with the net worth.

Financial records are utilized to evaluate a store's performance. Measures of a retailer's ability to meet its cash obligations include the average collection period of accounts receivable and the stock turnover rate. Productivity is evaluated by the total asset turnover rate and the ratio of net sales to working capital. A store should evaluate profitability in terms of net profit to sales, total assets, and net worth. Gross margin analysis is another tool for tracking financial performance.

A retailer should develop a financial plan that projects the performance of the business.

Such a plan helps retailers anticipate the future by determining growth and profit potential. Information for developing a financial plan comes from current financial records and management goals.

The global economy will continue to have a major impact on retailers. There are numerous risks inherent in global operations. Fortunately, many tools of global finance are available to assist retailers entering new markets. Financial analysis in the global arena requires new skills to be honed and developed as the retailer faces new competition and new challenges.

KEY TERMS AND CONCEPTS

Average inventory, 351

Balance sheet, 341

Cash budget, 354

Controllable expenses (direct expenses), 338

Cost of goods sold, 337

Currency hedging, 362

Current ratio, 346

Economic risk, 360

Expense budget, 353

Financial leverage ratio, 345

Gross margin position, 337

Insolvency, 346

Liquidity, 346

Net working capital, 346

Net worth (owner's equity), 341

Pro forma balance sheet, 355

Pro forma income statement, 355

Profit and loss (P&L) statement, 339

Rate of stock turnover, 351

Return on net worth, 344

Strategic profit model (SPM), 342

Total assets, 341

Total debt to net worth, 347

Total liabilities, 341

Transaction risk, 359

Uncontrollable expenses (indirect expenses), 338

QUESTIONS

1. What factors are necessary to determine the amount of profit a firm is making?

2. Why is it so important to receive a breakdown of sales by department or product? How can this be done in the best way in a shoe store?

3. What are the major categories in an income statement? In a balance sheet?

4. What are the key financial ratios, and what does each show?

5. Why is financial planning important?

6. What are the types of budgets? Give specific examples where each could be used.

7. Financial statements and cash budgets are interrelated. What are some of the interrelationships, as you see them?

8. Explain the difference between long-term liabilities and current liabilities. What constitutes each?

9. Explain the concept of cash flow. Why is it important?

10. What major components make up the SPM formula of profitability?

11. Most retailers face financial issues raised by the global sourcing of merchandise. Explain how they can address each issue.

12. Why is the RPMA concept important? What items make up the RPMA, and how can each be used?

13. If a retailer had $20 million in profits in 1996, did it do well?

SITUATIONS

1. You have recently established a small pet store. One of your initial problems is to determine the minimum set of records you should keep for your business. You are aware that the Internal Revenue Service has an interest in the records of retail businesses. What is the absolute minimum set of records that will satisfy the IRS? What additional records might you want to maintain to satisfy your need for management information?

2. You have been asked to prepare a cash budget for the Whoopee Cowboy Shop for the period January 1 to March 31. Given the following information, will there be enough cash available during the period to pay bills?

   Sales are 80 percent cash, 20 percent on open account.

   Credit sales are collected in the first month following the sale.

   Gross margin on sales is 40 percent.

   Cash on hand January 1 is $1,000.

   Sales are forecasted at $7,000, $4,000, and $10,000 for January, February, and March, respectively.

   Expenses are $2,700 each month.

3. You are the department manager in a large retail store. You have been given a goal of increasing profit by 5 percent. According to the following information, and based on the RPMA, what alternatives are open to you?

Sales	$80,000
Average price	10
Average cost	6
Expenses	15,000

4. You are the manager of a local drugstore that is part of a large chain. Recently you have been receiving pressure from your district manager to raise your gross margin, which is 30 percent. Other stores in the district have gross margins of almost 32 percent. The district manager argues that your store should also earn 32 percent. Can you give reasons for the differences in gross margin? Explain.

CASES

CASE 9A
Rag Tag Dresses: Expense Allocation and Planning

Maggie McWay, the owner of Rag Tag Dresses, is considering opening a branch store. She estimates the following expenses:

Three-year lease at an annual rent of	$19,800
Equipment lease	3,300
Bad debts	4,950
Professional services	4,125
Advertising	8,580
Selling expenses	36,300
Supplies	1,650
Telephone	660
Utilities	3,465
Insurance	1,320

1. *Ms. McWay plans for an operating expense figure of 32 percent. What would be the total dollar net sales figure necessary to meet total operating expenses?*

2. *Ms. McWay desires a before-tax profit of $60,000 to justify her investment in the new store. If the cost of goods was $342,000, what gross margin percentage would be necessary?*

CASE 9B
Carters: Departmental Contributions

A store manager for Carters was interested in doing a productivity analysis of the performance of various departments. The data in Table 9.9 are supplied by the accounting department.

1. *Rank each department's performance on the basis of:*
   a. GMROI
   b. GMROS
   c. GMROL

2. *How does the manager's evaluation change based on the choice of productivity measure?*

TABLE 9.9

Departmental Performance

Department	Selling Area Square Feet	Net Sales	Gross Margin	Average Inventory at Cost	Payroll
Men's wear	2,000	400,000	38%	$50,000	$44,000
Junior sportswear	2,400	500,000	43	45,000	40,000
Intimate apparel	1,200	180,000	46	28,000	10,000
Boys' wear	3,500	300,000	41	60,000	15,000
Infants' wear	2,000	200,000	46	14,000	8,000
Women's wear	2,500	300,000	41	60,000	15,000
Housewares	4,000	400,000	39	125,000	20,000
Cosmetics	3,000	800,000	40	48,000	96,000
Appliances	1,500	450,000	22	140,000	45,000
Electronics	1,000	280,000	30	100,000	28,000

CASE 9C
Soho's: Plans to Increase Productivity

Ronda Sims is a manager for a small appliance store. Her store is located in a growing Western community of 80,000. Her plan for the coming year calls for an operating profit increase of 20 percent. The following data show current year operating results:

Net sales	$650,000
Cost of goods sold	460,000
Average price of goods	390
Expenses	
Rent	20,000
Payroll	60,000
Advertising	36,000
Supplies	5,000
Utilities	13,000
Insurance	4,000
Bad debts	3,000
Depreciation	15,000
Professional services	2,000

1. What alternatives should Ronda explore to meet the profit goal?

2. What constraints does each alternative have?

3. What do you recommend? Why?

4. Use RPMA calculations. Does this put a different light on your analysis?

RETAIL MERCHANDISING AND PRICING

CHAPTER

10

Chapter Goals

After reading this chapter, you should be able to:

- Develop a merchandise budget for planned purchases.
- Calculate a planned sales figure from estimated sales.
- Explain the impact of planned reductions (markdowns, shrinkage, employee discounts) on merchandise budgets.
- Illustrate how to plan for beginning and ending inventories.
- Use the planned initial markup percentage to calculate planned purchases at cost.
- Manage merchandise using open-to-buy.
- Understand the cost, retail, and book methods for determining the value of inventory.

PLANNING MERCHANDISE NEEDS AND MERCHANDISE BUDGETS

Specialty apparel retailers enjoyed great success in the 1980s with growth far outpacing the general economy. Firms like The Limited Inc., Gap, and Ann Taylor had aggregate sales of over $100 billion, up 65 percent from 1980. Much of the increase in sales for specialty apparel stores was obtained by taking market share from department stores, not from a larger total pie.

THE LIMITED, INC.

Perhaps the best example of the specialty explosion was The Limited Inc. It was hailed in the eighties as the most successful innovator in its industry. The company grew by adding formats that appealed to specific market niches in both the women's apparel and the non-women's apparel business sectors. The Limited was also an innovator in the development of larger specialty stores, which were far less dependent on mall traffic for survival.

By the early 1990s, The Limited's women's store businesses included Express, Limited Stores, Lerner, Lane Bryant, Henri Bendel, Victoria's Secret Catalog, Structure (men's apparel), Bath & Body Works, Abercrombie & Fitch Co., Cacique and Penhaligon's, and Limited Too (girls' apparel). Some hailed Lerner, among others as "the new champions of retailing."[1]

Things were looking good for The Limited. However, trends in the early nineties indicated that growth and profitability might be difficult to maintain. The first sign of trouble appeared when reports showed that the average percentage of merchandise sold at a markdown for the industry had increased from 25.7 percent in 1986 to 28.6 percent in 1990. At the same time, gross margin returns on dollars invested in inventory (GMROI) fell from $3.80 to $2.60. Specialty apparel retailers saw inventory turnover fall from 3.8 to 2.9.[2] The specialty market declines were attributed to changing customer preferences and increased competition from department stores and discount merchants.

In 1991, specialty retailers failed to increase their share of the apparel market for the first time in a decade. Customers became increasingly price-conscious. As the baby boomer generation matured, they were no longer as concerned with buying particular labels. Men and women who once bought branded merchandise from Gap, The Limited, and other large specialty retailers started seeking unbranded items perceived to be of the same quality at general merchandise discount stores. These consumers also started cross-shopping, that is, shopping for their basics at less expensive stores and purchasing expensive accessories from more upscale retailers.[3]

Competition became even more fierce when stores such as Kmart, Wal-Mart, and Target quickly copied fashion trends. With information systems that are real-time responsive, these retailers can obtain fashions for their stores in minimal turnaround time. Retailing consultant Alan Millstein commented, "For ten years the country has been Gapped and Limited to the max; there's been a proliferation of boredom. So customers are starting to buy their look-alikes at Wal-Mart or Lands' End instead of The Limited."[4] Competition also increased from department stores as they attempted to regain their traditional markets. J. C. Penney remodeled and reorganized its stores to appeal to the more quality- and fashion-conscious consumer. Sears instituted a high-budget promotion, "the softer side of Sears," to regain market share in the apparel business.

1. **What merchandising problems may have accompanied The Limited's difficulties in the early nineties?**
2. **What is the impact on merchandise budgets when stock turnover increases? When stock-to-sales ratios increase?**

INTRODUCTION

"What makes you think you're a buyer?" an angry manager was overheard saying to an assistant after reviewing the inventory position of the employee's department. Markdowns were too high, too much of the wrong merchandise was still in stock, and there were too many out-of-season items. Each of these problems directly take their toll on gross margins and therefore profits. The job seemed to have gotten away from the assistant.

Some people appear to have a flair for buying. They seem to be able to distinguish significant fashion trends and assemble a stock of merchandise that appeals to their customers, and they can predict the merchandising potential of various items offered for sale. Buyers who possess this ability, however, are the first to say that their knack comes from the ability to "step into the shoes of their customers" and anticipate their needs. We need to remember the Neiman Marcus philosophy: "There is never a good sale for Neiman Marcus unless it's a good buy for the customer."

Today's focus on *customer satisfaction* and *continuous quality improvement* makes it necessary for the buyer to do more. In fact, to miss customer needs and have markdowns increase by one or two percentage points can mean a change in the "bottom line" of 50 percent or more. The critical responsibility of the buyer's budgeting process has been highlighted in a McKinsey report.[5] Researchers found that three key factors were critical to the success of retail business in the 1990s: simplifying the merchandising process; focusing on assortment performance; and integrating buying, selling, and distribution.

The budgeting function of the buyer relates directly to fulfilling these identified needs. It is the budget that drives the merchandising process and the final assortment. A clear recognition of the need to integrate buying, selling, and distribution implicitly falls on the shoulders of the buyer. In other words, the buyer must be extremely sensitive to matching the *who, what, when, why,* and *where* of the consumer's buying habits and choices.

The "who" refers to the demographic descriptions that provide a profile of the potential customers. The "what" refers to the types of merchandise these potential customers want to buy and, therefore, want the retailer to stock. The "when" refers to the part of the year when the customers make their purchases. The "why" refers to the characteristics of the customers that reflect their varied lifestyles and the projection of these lifestyles into purchasing habits. The "where" refers to the trading area from which the retailer attracts its customers.

The central responsibility of the buyer is merchandising: having the right products, at the right prices, in the right quantity, at the right time, and in the right place to satisfy today's value-conscious consumer. Basic to all merchandising is to first answer the where, who, what, when, and why customer satisfaction questions suggested above. Answers to these basic questions lead to further questions: What will be our rate of sale on what we're buying? How long does it take to replenish stock? How large an assortment will we need?

Ben Franklin Retail Stores is a franchisor of variety and craft shops providing world-class customer service, quality merchandise at attractive prices, and a setting that offers an enjoyable shopping experience. Buyers must match the merchandise offering to customer needs, wants, and buying habits for the 50,000 items that are maintained at distribution centers. More that 150,000 products are shipped directly to stores from vendors.

FIGURE 10.1

The elements of the buying function.

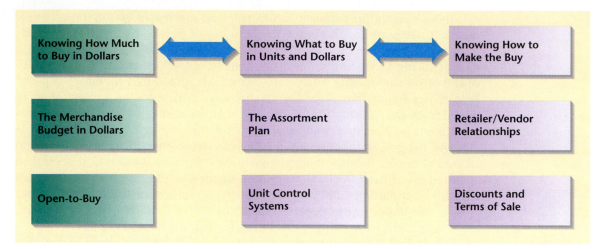

Which manufacturers supply the best merchandise for our customers? At what price can we sell the merchandise most efficiently? How will we promote the merchandise we buy?

Our answers to the above questions will say a great deal about what merchandise we buy and how much money we have to spend. The merchandise budget is the plan that specifies the amount of money to spend for the merchandise we buy. It provides the means for controlling merchandise expenditures. The assortment plan (Chapter 11) tells what to buy in units. Knowledge of how to make the buy and understanding the terms of sale are all a part of a buyer's responsibility. See Figure 10.1. Today's retailing reality is that the buyer must develop a comprehensive merchandise budget that is part of the firm's financial plan and matches the needs of its retail target market.

MERCHANDISE BUDGET

The objective of the merchandise budget planning process is to quantify the financial considerations required of the merchandise side of the store. The **merchandise budget** is the amount of purchases (in dollars) that will be made for an upcoming selling season. It is not a complete **buying plan** because it does not tell the buyer what kind of merchandise to purchase or in what quantities; the merchandise budget only indicates dollars. The assortment plan covered in Chapter 11 will specify the actual goods. Because the merchandise budget imposes a dollar figure for the money spent on inventory, it is referred to as "top-down planning."

Balanced Inventory Investment versus Stockout

Failure to impose limits on merchandise expenditures leads to overstocking. While this increases consumer choice in the store, it also increases the retailer's costs. It is important to maintain a level of inventory in the store to meet customer expectations and demands. While many people concentrate on imposing upper limits on stock, it is just as important to impose lower limits. Thus a manager should be just as concerned about being under budget as over budget with regard to merchandise. See Figure 10.2.

Planned Purchases in Dollars

Developing a merchandise budget allows the retailer to calculate the number of dollars that can be invested in inventory within a given period of time. As noted, the merchandise budget is a master control plan based on a top-down approach. As such, it places a **dollar control** on how much can be spent for merchandise inventory within a given period. The overall objective is to allocate the proper amount of money in inventory to meet financial requirements and customer needs. Achieving this balanced inventory level is a continuing effort. For many stores, the merchandise budget will specify the dollars to be spent, not just at the store level but also for every department and merchandise category within the department. The merchandise budget may specify dollar expenditures down to the individual stockkeeping unit (SKU). SKUs are unique to each item. For example, an SKU can identify that the item is a blue long-sleeve silk shirt in size 15. Each SKU will have its own universal product code (UPC) to identify it.

FIGURE 10.2

Balancing investment in inventory.

Problems of Too Much Merchandise	Problems of Not Enough Merchandise
1. Inventory investment dollars are not productive.	1. Stockouts cause irritation and loss of customers.
2. Merchandise stale, shopworn, and out of fashion.	2. Opportunity cost of profit that could have been made.
3. Excessive markdowns.	3. Degrades store atmosphere and appearance.
4. High inventory maintenance: interest, insurance, and warehousing costs.	

Developing a merchandise budget requires planning that allows calculation of planned purchases:

- Planned sales
- Planned reductions
- Planned ending inventory
- Planned beginning inventory

The dollar value of the merchandise in a store for a specific period must equal the planned sales for the period, plus planned reductions, plus the amount of merchandise the buyer wants left in the store at the end of the period. In the following section you will see that planned reductions include markdowns, employee discounts, and shortages. If we know our expected beginning inventory, we can calculate planned purchases. Since our planning is done in retail dollars we have to convert them to our cost so that we know the actual amount we have to spend for merchandise when we place an order. Before we go through an example and explain each factor in detail, let's describe the process in equation form.

Total merchandise needed must account for sales, reductions, and having enough merchandise at the end of the period so that you will have goods to sell for the next period. While reductions are not desirable, they do represent a loss in the dollar investment in inventory in the store, and if not anticipated, the planned gross margin cannot be obtained. Therefore:

Planned total merchandise needed (at retail) = planned sales
+ planned reductions + planned ending inventory

Given that we determined total needs above, we must also account for the fact that in any given time period we start with some of the needed inventory in the store. Anything we need that is not already in the store must be purchased. Therefore:

Planned purchases (at the retail price) = planned total merchandise needed
− expected beginning inventory

To maintain a continual account of what must be purchased during a period, we must remove that which has *already* been purchased. This can be in the form of merchandise on order (referred to as O.O.) for delivery during the period or merchandise received during the period. If we subtract these from what we initially planned to purchase, the result is what is still needed. Therefore:

Open-to-buy (at retail) = planned purchases
− merchandise on order for the period
− merchandise received during the period

So far all of the equations have dealt with inventory at retail value. However, the retail buyer purchases at cost. In order to know the actual dollars to be spent, the inventory dollars needed at retail must be converted to dollars the buyer actually has to spend.

Planned purchases (at cost) = planned purchases at retail
times (1 − planned markup percentage)

(Note that 1 − planned markup is the *complement* of the markup. If the markup is 25 percent of the planned purchases at retail selling prices, the *complement* is 75 percent.)

A Brief Example

Look at the example illustrated in Table 10.1. This buyer anticipates needing $75,000 of inventory *at retail* for the period to meet sales projections. Retail reductions of $3,000 and $47,000 in inventory on hand are planned for the end of the budget period so that the store will not be empty when the next season begins. To meet these conditions, the total merchandise needed is $125,000. A $40,000 inventory will be available at the beginning of the budget period. (*Note:* The beginning of period inventory for this period is the same value as the ending inventory for the previous period.) Therefore, $85,000 worth of merchandise will have to be bought during the period ($125,000 − $40,000). We must remember that the $85,000 planned purchases estimate is *at retail*.

To determine the actual dollars *at cost* available to the buyer to spend for merchandise, we multiply the $75,000 by 1 *minus* the appropriate markon percentage (calculated as a percentage of the retail price). If the markon

TABLE 10.1
- - - - - - - - - -

Simplified Merchandise Budget, August 1–January 31

Planned sales	=	$ 75,000
Less planned reductions	=	3,000
Planned end of period inventory	=	47,000
Total merchandise needed	=	$125,000
Less: Planned beginning of the period inventory	=	40,000
Planned purchases	=	$ 85,000
If initial markon percentage is 30%, then the complement is 70		
percent so: 0.7 of planned purchases	=	$ 56,500
Less: On order for delivery this period	=	$ 10,000
Less: Received during this period	=	$ 20,000
Open-to-buy at cost	=	$ 26,500

percentage was 30 percent, for example, the dollars available to purchase merchandise would be $75,000 \times (1 - 0.3) = $52,500$. If we subtract merchandise on order for delivery during the period ($10,000) or items already received during the period ($20,000), we have what is called open-to-buy (OTB) ($26,500).

This example illustrates how the merchandise budget and OTB planning control the dollar investment in inventory. As long as buyers know their OTB, they will not exceed their projected inventory investment and they will know the extent to which they need to be in the market. In fact, a plan that is properly constructed and followed is essential to control the inventory investment.[6]

THE PLANNING PROCESS

While the above gives a brief example of an open-to-buy situation, the planning process itself involves much greater detail. One of the important aspects of planning is to have the items in stock when the customers want to buy them. This implies going into the market to buy the goods early enough to ensure delivery to the store at the proper time. For example, for BabySuperstores to ensure on-time delivery of children's Easter clothing, orders must be placed and budget commitments made by the previous September. Buying for a retail store requires advanced planning to determine the merchandise needs for each month and then placing the order commitments to ensure proper lead time. Because retailers offer new fashion items on sale months before the actual calendar date for the beginning of the new season, it is imperative that your merchandise budget be formulated early enough to allow for intelligent buying without any last-minute panic purchases. An additional consideration is that many manufacturers today are as concerned about excess inventories as retailers. Consequently, your ability to "go late into the market" for prime merchandise is becoming increasingly difficult.

The first six-month plan includes February-March-April (spring) and May-June-July (summer). The spring plan is usually prepared and finalized by the previous August to permit early buying of imports and other long lead time merchandise. The second six-month plan includes August-September-October (fall) and November-December-January (winter). Similar to the spring plan, the fall plan is typically prepared and finalized by the previous February.

The main reason for what frequently appears to be an early offering of new items is because the retailer regards the **calendar date** for the beginning of the new season as the **merchandise date** for the end of the old season. For example, March 21, from a merchandising viewpoint, is the end of the spring season; June 21 is the end of the summer season; and December 21 the end of the winter. The period following the calendar date for the beginning of the season is used by the retailer to sell closeouts, job lots, imperfections, irregularities, seconds, distress merchandise, off-season purchases, and markdowns from regular stock. By establishing merchandise dates relative to calendar dates, department managers and buyers can plan displays, promotions, sales, and markdowns more efficiently.

The next section will be devoted to understanding the actual process of planning merchandise needs and open-to-buy. This process requires seven steps as illustrated in Table 10.2.

Step 1: Develop a Sales Plan

The first step in developing our merchandise budget is planning for sales volume in the upcoming budget period. A buyer should never proceed without first making a sales estimate for the period. It is most often a six-month plan, but there can be time frame variations depending on the merchandise. This is particularly true for lines with short "seasons" like the Fourth of July, back to school, or Mother's Day.

Estimating sales. There are probably as many different ways of planning for a store's sales volume as there are retailers. However, estimates of future sales require using one or all of the following factors:

TABLE 10.2

The Process of Planning Merchandise Needs and Open-to-Buy

Develop a sales plan	→	Estimate planned sales
Plan reductions	→	Shrinkage Markdowns Employee discounts
Develop a stock plan	→	Beginning inventory Ending inventory
Plan merchandise needs	→	Add together estimated sales, reductions, and ending inventory.
Calculate planned purchases	→	Merchandise needed less the beginning inventory. Subtract merchandise ordered to get open-to-buy at retail.
Plan an initial markup percentage	→	Planned gross margin plus retail reductions divided by the total of planned sales plus retail reductions
Plan the open-to-buy at cost	→	Multiply the complement of the initial markup percentage by open-to-buy at retail.

- Last year's sales volume
- Last two months' sales volume trends
- Local and national economic conditions
- Fashion trends
- An assessment of competitive forces
- Sales promotions planned for the store
- Wholesale and retail price changes
- Local employment conditions
- Changes in store policy
- The effect of payday in the community (some months may have three paydays for people who are paid every two weeks)
- The number of weekends, four or five, between Thanksgiving and Christmas

Considering all of these methods separately would be a difficult task for most buyers. However, they can be grouped into two major categories: historical analysis or industry analysis. In general, stores tend to use industry analysis either to adjust plans that have been estimated using historical analysis or to develop a plan when the store has no history (i.e., a new store).

A retailer who can assess the impact of economic conditions, employment, and fashion trends on retail sales will modify the planned sales figures accordingly. Most likely, assessments will be made in qualitative terms rather than attempting to assign numerical values to them. Regardless of the types of data you use for your forecast, whether internal or external, be sure that they are accurate and apply to your marketplace.[7] An experienced buyer for

For buyers of high-fashion goods, a difficult task is forecasting sales months before the merchandise reaches the selling floor. The open-to-buy is dependent on the accuracy of the sales forecasts incorporated into the calculations. The purpose of regularly calculating the open-to-buy is to control purchases so that inventories are maintained at the levels planned in the merchandise budget. The objective of this system is to keep the inventory investment and sales in harmony so that financial objectives are achieved.

TABLE 10.3

Joyce's Shoe Department: An Example of Planned Sales

Joyce is the shoe buyer for a medium-sized department store in the Midwest. Her previous year's sales were:

Spring	$ 300,000	30%
Summer	250,000	25
Fall	300,000	30
Winter	150,000	15
Total	$1,000,000	100%

An analysis of trends in her department led Joyce to estimate sales of $1,210,000 for this year, a 21 percent increase. Therefore, she estimates sales for spring to be $363,000 (0.30 × $1,210,000).

a retailer that has been in operation for a number of years is likely to look at last year's sales volume for the forecast period and adjust it up or down given sales performance over the last two months to forecast sales for the forthcoming period. The assumption is that sales in the forthcoming period will follow recent sales trends fairly closely. In other words, if the store has recently experienced a 10 percent increase in sales, it is reasonable to assume that in the forthcoming period there will be an increase of 10 percent over the same period a year ago. The buyer would want to examine sales levels and growth for each department and for each category within the department. Sales might well increase 10 percent in one department while decreasing a similar amount in another. It is important to look at seasonal[8] and year-to-year trends[9] in making the sales forecasts. See Table 10.3.

Your merchandise budget should be available for each season and subdivided into months. Sales may be planned by recording last year's results. Then the overall or monthly plans can be made based on percentage increases occurring in previous months, an assessment of economic conditions and competition, and whether or not significantly more or less effort or resources will be committed to the department. The spreadsheet must also provide a column for revisions if changes occur during the period, plus a column to record actual results. By keeping *planned, adjusted,* and *actual* sales in different columns, you will be able to analyze actual results against both planned and adjusted amounts.

The **selling plan** is more than a simple estimate of the dollars anticipated for monthly sales. It should also detail when:

● The market should be visited to see, examine, and study the new offerings for the coming season

● Commitments should be placed

● The first delivery should be received at the store

- The items should be promoted through advertising, window, and interior displays
- The inventory should be peaked
- Reorders should no longer be placed
- Markdowns from regular stock should be taken
- The item should no longer be in stock

At the very least, the buyer must determine when merchandise will be purchased, when it should be displayed, when it should be reordered, when it should be marked down, and when it should be removed from stock.

Step 2: Plan Reductions

The second section of our merchandise budget calls for estimating planned reductions. **Planned reductions** refer to a lowering of the retail value of the inventory for reasons other than sales to final customers. These reductions are caused by planned markdowns, shrinkage, employee discounts, and other individual or group discounts. Because reductions cause the retail value of your inventory at the end of a period to be lower than it was at the beginning of the period, they must be included in your merchandise budget.

All retailers would like to maintain very low levels of reductions. While employee discounts may be favorable to the retailer, the other two categories, markdowns and shrinkage, are to be avoided when possible. However, a retailer must realize that no matter how well the store attempts to minimize reductions, they will still occur. Thus retailers must plan for a certain percentage of them. See Box 10.1.

Markdowns.   The retail value of merchandise in the store is lowered when the retail price is reduced (marked down). When markdowns are taken, merchandise dollars go out of the store. Markdowns are a normal part of operations, though retailers strive to minimize them. **Markdowns** occur because

Too much inventory means higher markdowns, reducing the gross margin and profits. Too little inventory reduces sales. Every day, sales tell what is good and bad in the inventory, and buying decisions should be made accordingly. Products have different shelf lives, and allowing inventory to age beyond its prime selling time without markdowns is the first step toward inventory mismanagement.

10.1 AN ETHICAL DILEMMA: PROSECUTING AND REPORTING EMPLOYEE THIEVES

Planning for shortages from theft, both employee and customer, is essential in developing the merchandise budget. Reducing shortages can make a tremendous difference in store profitability. The *National Home Center News* devoted considerable space in its March 20, 1995, issue to the problem of shortages from employee theft. An article raised the question, "If Builders Square fires a store employee because of theft, how will a Lowe's store manager across the street know when the innocent faced employee applies for a job in his store?"

The problem is that unless the store has successfully prosecuted the employee for theft and the court decision is a matter of public record (some reports on minors are not available to the public), no one will probably know. The most a store can generally ask of a former employer would be, "Is this person eligible for rehiring?" Some former employers will answer this question, and some will not. Sometimes, the hesitation on the other end of the phone call is the answer.

Robert Kahn, editor of *Retailing Today,* says that stores should establish a policy of prosecuting thieves and post signs in employee areas setting forth this policy. Then, compare the total cost for the signs, and the investigation and prosecution costs, with the savings resulting from lower shrinkage. According to Bob Oberosler, vice president of loss prevention and safety for Lowe's Companies, "Most prosecutions don't give an adequate return on investment of the investigator's time." In the opinion of the authors, this is a shortsighted view of the problem. The costs saved on one nonprosecution may encourage several thieves-at-heart to begin or to reactivate a career of stealing. A policy of prosecuting cases of proven employee theft sends a strong message that is clearly understood by most employees. If there is no such message, a thief-at-heart may think he or she is merely playing a game, pitting his or her skill at stealing against the store's skill at detection.

Question

If someone calls you for a reference, do you see an ethical issue in reporting an incident of employee theft leading to a firing but not prosecution? What would you do?

Source: Adapted with permission from Robert Kahn, "Home Center News on Employee-Thieves," *Retailing Today,* June 1995, p. 2.

of promotions and special sales during a period; because goods have become shopworn, soiled, or damaged; because of competition or manufacturers' adjustments; because of obsolescence of the goods; or simply because customers won't buy the items unless the price is lowered. See Box 10.2.

Shrinkage. **Shrinkage** is defined as the difference between the amount of merchandise listed on the books and what is on the shelves. The difference in value is due to shoplifting, employee theft, vendor overbilling,

10.2 MARKDOWNS OCCUR BECAUSE OF FOUR TYPES OF PRODUCT OBSOLESCENCE

1. **Fashion.** Trends in consumer preferences and buying habits no longer make the product desirable (solids and pastels replace plaids and earth tones).

2. **Physical.** Products get shopworn or damaged as a result of handling or time (bright colors that quickly fade).

3. **Technological.** Improvements in the product make the older designs decline in value (Pentium Pro multimedia computer).

4. **Product.** New and improved products replace the old ones (yearly model changes).

6543217

distributor theft, paperwork errors, breakage, and spoilage. Again, the effect of shrinkage is to reduce the total retail value of merchandise in the store. In effect, your merchandise walks out the back, goes out the front door, or is thrown out with the trash. Typically, shrinkage will vary by department. Because of this, you need to make planned shrinkage adjustments to your budget on a by-department basis. For example, shrinkage has been reported in drugstores to be as high as nearly 40 percent in women's fragrances and less than 3 percent in cough syrups.[10] On average, retail shrinkage was estimated to be 2.08 percent of retail sales, with customer theft accounting for approximately 60 percent.[11]

Employee discounts. Discounts given to employees also reduce the total retail value for merchandise in the store. If an employee takes a $10 item to the cash register and receives a discount of 20 percent, the sale will be recorded at $8. **Employee discounts,** however, should not be seen as unfavorable. However, store inventory will have been reduced by the $10 even though sales were recorded at $8. This will leave a shortage of $2 in the retailer's records if it is not accounted for. Many stores offer special discounts to senior citizens, church groups, public aid recipients, and/or students. These discounts, too, must become part of the adjustments in your merchandise budget. The buyer must plan for discounts by increasing the planned reductions, which increases the total merchandise needed figure. Reductions can often best be estimated by using last year's percentages. See Table 10.4.

Step 3: Develop a Stock Plan

Having established planned sales and planned reductions for the merchandise budget period, the retailer should plan how much stock should be in inventory at the beginning and end of the budget period. A retail store must contain inventory to be sold at the beginning of each selling period and must also contain inventory at the end of the budget period. In this way, mer-

TABLE 10.4

Joyce's Shoe Department: An Example of Estimating Reductions

Joyce's reductions for last year were:		
Period	*Dollars*	*Percentage of Sales*
Spring	$ 75,000	25%
Summer	15,000	15
Fall	40,000	10
Winter	40,000	20
Total	$170,000	17%

As stated earlier, Joyce expects sales of $363,000 for this spring. Therefore, she estimates reductions for spring to be $90,750 (0.25 × $363,000).

chandise will be in ample supply on a constant basis. It is the buyer's responsibility to anticipate these inventory needs.

Stock turnover. Planning beginning and ending inventory requires the use of a planned turnover figure to calculate a stock-to-sales ratio or a week's supply of goods. A well-run store or department will maintain a satisfactory **stock turnover rate,** which is determined by dividing average inventory at retail into the net sales. As we said before, a satisfactory stock turnover rate is important because too much inventory on hand ties up capital, and therefore unnecessarily increases the cost of doing business. On the other hand, having too little inventory leads to out-of-stock situations on merchandise needed by customers and results in lost sales.

Retailers should remember that capital is a commodity and costs money. For example, for a retailer who borrows from a bank, an investment of $100,000 in inventory would cost $12,000 a year in interest payments if interest rates were 12 percent (0.12 × $100,000). Consequently, if reductions in inventory can be made, say from $100,000 to $80,000, without losing sales, the cost of doing business would decrease by $2,400.

Today, the reality for corporate buyers in large retail organizations is that a planned turnover number is given to them by corporate managers. Since the inventory investment can be as much as 70 percent of current assets, management wants the maximum return of sales and gross margin dollars for every dollar invested in inventory. Recently a buyer for better women's dresses lamented that she had achieved a turnover of 2.8 last year and management had given her a target for this year of 3.0.

Unfortunately, even though buyers know they are being evaluated on a particular stock turnover performance, they often do not know how to plan for satisfactory results. Let's look again at the simplified merchandise budget previously shown for the period August 1 to January 31 in Table 10.1.

We have already learned that stock turnover is derived by dividing average inventory at retail into net sales. Using the figures in Table 10.1 as an illustration, we can determine the average inventory at retail for the period—the first step in solving for stock turnover rate. Because average inventory is found by adding the beginning and ending inventory figures and dividing by their number, it is possible to add $40,000 and $47,000 and then divide by 2 to arrive at an average inventory at retail of $43,500. Subsequently, if the average inventory figure ($43,500) is divided into the planned sales figure ($75,000), the stock turnover can be derived for the budget period. The stock turnover rate is 1.72 for the six-month period. The annual stock turnover would be 3.44 (1.72 × 2).

$$\text{Average inventory at retail} = \frac{\text{beginning} + \text{ending inventories}}{2}$$

$$= \frac{\$40,000 + \$47,000}{2}$$

$$= \$43,500$$

$$\text{Stock turnover rate} = \frac{\text{net sales}}{\text{average inventory at retail}}$$

$$= \frac{\$75,000}{\$43,500}$$

$$= 1.72$$

Now let us assume for the moment that a stock turnover rate of 1.72 is unsatisfactory and that, in fact, management has decreed that a satisfactory level of performance for a department for the upcoming six-month period would be a rate of 2. The manager of the department will have to make adjustments in the plan in order to realize this figure.

To achieve a particular stock turnover rate, department managers may adjust the planned sales figure or the average inventory figure. If department managers have done an acceptable job of determining customer wants, it is unrealistic for them to adjust planned sales figures merely to obtain a given stock turnover rate. Therefore, they usually realize a given stock turnover rate by making adjustments in planned stock levels. The following calculations show how department managers do this with the 1.72 number.

First, divide the buyer's stock turnover by management's stock turnover as the basis for adjusting beginning and ending inventories:

$$\frac{\text{Buyer's stock turnover}}{\text{Management's stock turnover}} = \frac{1.72}{2.00} = 0.86 \text{ inventory adjustment factor}$$

Next, adjust the buyer's beginning and ending planned inventories:

$47,000
$\times$ 0.86
$40,420$ new end of season inventory

$40,000
$\times$ 0.86
$34,400$ new beginning of season inventory

Recalculate the average inventory with stock turnover of 2.0:

$$\text{New average inventory} = \frac{\$40,420 + \$34,400}{2} = \frac{\$74,820}{2} = \$37,410$$

$$\frac{\text{Net sales}}{\text{Average inventory}} = \frac{\$75,000}{\$37,410} = 2.0 \text{ (rounded)}$$

In merchandise budget planning, beginning of the period inventory has been bought during a prior budget period and represents inventory available for sale in the current period. The section entitled Methods for Determining Inventory Valuation at the end of this chapter describes in detail how the value of the inventory at the beginning of the period can be calculated. It is not necessary to buy all of this inventory for the current period because some inventory will be left over from the previous period. On the other hand, end of the period inventories are inventories that must be on hand at the end of the current budget period and must be bought during this period.

You may still wonder, however, how the buyer arrives at a planned retail inventory level. Plans are formulated several months before the merchandise budget period. If plans are made in this way, how can the buyer know how many dollars of inventory will be on hand at the beginning and at the end of the upcoming budget period? Actually, buyers cannot be sure of their exact dollar position, but they should try to make estimates that will not be too far off the mark. A buyer can use several methods to plan the inventory level, including stock-sales ratios, last year's stock, and the basic stock method.

Stock-sales ratios.   One of the most important ways to arrive at planned stock figures is to establish a **stock-to-sales ratio.** Usually, this relationship will vary depending on the size of the store; the nature of the goods being carried; and whether the goods are seasonal, staple, or fashion items.

The stock turnover rate is found by dividing net sales by average inventory at retail. If you had an average of $250,000 in inventory and net sales for the year of $1,000,000, the stock turnover rate for the year would be 4. There is a direct relationship between the stock-sales ratio and the stock turnover rate:

$$\text{Stock-sales ratio} = \frac{12 \text{ (number of months in year)}}{\text{planned turnover for the year}}$$

Therefore, if the stock turnover rate is 4, the stock-sales ratio is 3 (12 ÷ 4). So $3 in inventory is needed to support each $1 in sales. You can see that stock-sales ratios can be very helpful in planning inventory needs. Using this kind of analysis, management can establish its stock levels on a basis consistent with the amount of sales anticipated for the department. Again, the turnover rate and therefore the stock-sales ratio may come from experience in the store, from trade data that show what other firms in the industry are doing, or from goals set by management based on financial planning.

The stock-to-sales ratio can be used to plan inventory for each period's planned sales. The relationship is established by dividing the planned sales for the month or period into the beginning of the month or period's stock:

$$\text{Stock-sales ratio} = \frac{\text{beginning of the month stock}}{\text{sales for the month}}$$

For example, suppose management has determined that for a particular month (January) a department had sales of $50,000 last year and had a beginning of the month (January) inventory of $250,000. This information suggests that it took $5 in backup stock to generate $1 in sales. If management plans to do $60,000 worth of business for the same month this year and the stock-sales ratio has been 5, management must plan for a beginning inventory of $300,000 in order to generate $60,000 in sales, as shown below.

Calculating last year's stock-to-sales ratio:

$$\text{Stock-sales ratio} = \frac{\$300,000 \text{ (beginning of month inventory last year)}}{\$60,000 \text{ (sales)}} = 5{:}1$$

Calculating this year's beginning of the month (BOM) inventory:

$$5 = \frac{\text{BOM inventory}}{\$70,000 \text{ estimated sales}} = \$70,000 \times 5 = \$350,000 = \begin{array}{l}\text{beginning of} \\ \text{the month} \\ \text{inventory}\end{array}$$

Using this kind of analysis, management can establish its stock levels on a basis consistent with the amount of sales anticipated for the department.

Notice carefully. If we look at last year's sales and inventory numbers to determine our stock-to-sales ratio, we also have a basis for calculating the annual turnover.

$$\text{Stock-to-sales ratio} = \frac{12}{\text{turnover}} \quad \text{therefore:}$$

$$\text{Turnover} = \frac{12}{\text{Stock-to-sales}} = \frac{12}{5} = 2.4$$

Notice how the stock-to-sales ratio allows the calculation of the beginning and ending inventory levels. See Table 10.5.

TABLE 10.5

Joyce's Shoe Department: An Example of Determining Inventory Needs

Joyce's sales and stock-to-sales ratios for last year were:

Period	Sales	% of Sales	Stock to Sales
Spring	$300,000	30	2.85
Summer	250,000	25	3.25
Fall	300,000	30	3.00
Winter	150,000	15	3.00

As stated earlier, she expects sales of $363,000 for this spring. Therefore, she estimates BOM stock balance for spring to be $1,034,550 = (2.85 × $363,000) and for summer to be $983,125 = [3.25 × ($250,000 × 1.21)].

Last year's stock. Another way to arrive at planned inventory positions is to use last year's stock position at the same point in time and project current needs from that figure. For example, if the beginning of the period last year showed a $100,000 stock inventory, it is reasonable to assume that this year's stock will amount to $100,000, plus or minus any projected increase or decrease in sales. If sales are expected to increase by 10 percent (and the stock-to-sales ratio is 3), then this year's BOM stock would be:

$$(\$100,000) + (\$100,000)(30\%) = \$130,000$$

Basic stock method. One method of planning the inventory level is called the **basic stock method.** It requires buying adequate goods to begin the month so there is inventory that exceeds the planned monthly sales by a basic stock amount. The basic stock method should not be used if the stock turnover rate is 6. It will tend to overstock the store. The basic stock amount is a minimum stock level below which inventory is not allowed to fall. It is calculated in this way:

Basic stock amount = planned average stock for the season
− planned average monthly sales for the season

For example, if the average monthly inventory for the fall season of September, October, and November is $80,000, and average monthly sales for the three months are $50,000, the basic stock amount is $30,000.

Planned average stock for the season	$80,000
− planned average monthly sales for the season	−50,000
= basic stock amount	$30,000

The beginning of month (BOM) inventory for any given month becomes:

BOM = estimated sales for the month + basic stock amount

Therefore, if sales were estimated to be $45,000, the beginning inventory would be $75,000.

$$BOM = \$45,000 + (\$80,000 - \$50,000) = \$75,000$$

The week's supply method. This method is used to plan beginning inventory where it is desirable to cover sales planned on the basis of a number of weeks instead of monthly. This method is useful for staple merchandise but not fashion items, where sales may vary significantly by season and month. The week's supply is calculated by:

$$\text{Week's supply} = \frac{52 \text{ (weeks)}}{\text{turnover}}$$

For example, in the staple grocery department of a supermarket, the stock turnover might be 21. The inventory level then should equal about 2.47 weeks' supply (52 ÷ 21 = 2.47). The beginning inventory therefore equals the estimated sales for a predetermined number of coming weeks. The inventory is regularly replaced with enough goods to cover the same number of future weeks.

You should now have a better idea of how the retailer can determine planned sales, planned reductions, and planned inventory levels so that planned purchases and OTB can be calculated.

Step 4: Plan Merchandise Needs

The information in the previous steps allows us to figure the amount of inventory that will be needed during a period of time. This is referred to as *total merchandise needed*. It is calculated as:

Total merchandise needed (at retail) = planned sales
+ planned reductions + planned ending inventory

Total merchandise needs represent all the uses of inventory for a given time period. If sales or reduction estimates are off, then the ending inventory will either exceed or fall short of what is needed for the next period and must be adjusted. See Table 10.6.

Step 5: Calculate Planned Purchases

Information from steps 3 and 4 allows us to calculate how much inventory we need to purchase during a season or time frame. The total amount of inventory at retail that needs to be purchased is referred to as **planned purchases.** This can be calculated as follows:

$$\text{Planned purchases (retail)} = \text{total merchandise needs}$$
$$- \text{expected beginning inventory}$$

The only difference between planned purchases and total merchandise needs is the beginning inventory. This is because we need to purchase only what we do not already have.

Once the planned purchases are calculated, the buyer can then derive an open-to-buy figure at any given time. OTB is a running account that tells the buyer how much inventory will be needed at any moment. It can be calculated as:

$$\text{Open-to-buy (retail)} = \text{planned purchases} - \text{merchandise on order}$$
$$- \text{merchandise received}$$

TABLE 10.6

Joyce's Shoe Department: An Example of Estimating Merchandise Needs

Joyce must calculate the total merchandise needs for her store. In Table 10.5 she expects spring sales of $363,000; an ending inventory of $983,125 (note that ending of spring inventory is the same as beginning of summer); and reductions of $90,750 for this spring. Therefore, she can estimate her total merchandise needed for spring to be:

$$\$363,000 + \$90,750 + \$983,125 = \$1,436,875$$

The members of the Sporting Goods Manufacturer's Association who exhibit at the Annual Super Show in Atlanta hope that an abundance of new products will attract retailers with a big open-to-buy (OTB). OTB is the amount of inventory a retailer can buy during a specific time period without exceeding the budgeted purchases.

Joyce's Shoe Department: An Example of Planned Purchases and Open-to-Buy

Joyce has decided to go to market and purchase goods for her store. She calculates her planned purchases nearly six months before spring. She uses her previous estimates to calculate:

Total merchandise needed	=	$1,436,875
Less: BOM inventory spring	=	1,034,550
Planned purchases	=	$ 402,325

During October Joyce placed orders for $125,000 worth of merchandise for delivery during February. Thus she calculates the remaining open-to-buy to be:

Planned purchases	=	$402,325
Less: Merchandise ordered	=	−125,000
Open-to-buy	=	$277,325

All this says is that your open-to-buy is reduced by inventory that has already been purchased for the period. This is necessary so that buyers have a running total of what is needed versus what has already been purchased. The open-to-buy makes sure that buyers do not make repeat purchases by mistake. See Table 10.7.

Step 6: Plan an Initial Markup Percentage

The planned purchases figure tells us how much inventory, in retail dollars, we need to buy during that period. Open-to-buy represents the portion of this that remains to be purchased. However, if the open-to-buy is $277,325, a buyer cannot simply go to market and purchase $277,325 of merchandise from a vendor. The $277,325 amount represents a *retail* value, while buyers purchase at *cost*. Therefore, the figure must be converted into a cost value.

As we have seen, having a **planned initial markup percentage** will allow us to determine the dollar amount that we can spend for merchandise during that period. The initial markup percentage is frequently called *original markup* or *cumulative markon percentage*.

Retailers should attempt to buy merchandise that may be sold at a price consistent with planned gross margin. **Gross margin** (in dollars) is equal to the retail selling price minus the cost of goods sold. To calculate the gross margin, firms adjust the cost of goods sold by decreasing the invoice price by the amount of cash discount earned by paying the invoice before it is due and by increasing the cost of goods sold by the amount of the cost of alterations or workroom costs such as assembly. The markup percentage achieved from simply selling the goods is referred to as the *maintained markup*. Note that the gross margin calculation is the maintained markup decreased by cost of alterations and increased by the amount of cash discounts. When we calculate the planned initial markup below using gross margin, we account for alterations and cash discounts. Therefore if:

Net sales	=	$100,000	100%
COGS	=	70,000	70
Maintained markup	=	$ 30,000	30
Less: Alterations	=	3,000	
Plus: Cash discounts	=	2,000	
Gross margin	=	$ 29,000	29

The gross margin should cover expenses and a profit. To achieve a specific gross margin, retailers must price their goods so that all expenses, profits, and expected reductions are covered. This means that retailers, before going to the market and making any purchases, should determine the average planned markup they need to achieve on the goods they buy. The markup will likely differ depending on the kind of merchandise, but this will help them decide which item to buy and which to ignore.

Determining a planned initial markup percentage. Once planned purchases have been calculated, this retail figure must be reduced to a cost figure. Again to arrive at the cost value, it will be necessary to apply an initial markup percentage. In other words, this markup figure will provide the basis for buying and for pricing merchandise. You should not expect all merchandise to be consistent with your planned markup. On average, it is

Pricing that gives good value is a consumer expectation worldwide. A growing percentage of goods are private labels that can be priced lower and yield higher gross margins than branded goods. Private labels are 30 percent of sales in Europe and 20 percent in the United States. Marks & Spencer in the United Kingdom and Migros in Switzerland sell many private labels, such as Migros' "Aproz" mineral waters. (Roach, Loretta, "A Global View: 32 Million Retail Outlets in 1995," *Discount Merchandiser,* May 1995, p. 97.)

critical that you plan a merchandise mix such that the markups on individual lines or items will yield to overall average planned markup.

In establishing a planned markup figure for a department or category of goods, it is necessary to follow four stages:

1. Establish a planned sales volume for the period. Because the planned sales figure has already been used in other ways in the management of the business, this value is readily available from the merchandise budget.

2. Determine the operating expenses for the period. This estimate can be projected from last year's figures. It should not be difficult for managers to determine how much money will be spent in the forthcoming period on rent, salaries, heat, and so on.

3. Determine the retail reductions. You need to estimate the markdowns, discounts to employees, and stock shortages that are expected for the upcoming period. Again, figures for previous years yield a reliable approximation of the reductions expected and are a part of the merchandise budget.

4. Establish a net profit goal. This estimate may be based on an attempt to equal last year's performance, to better last year's performance, to obtain a particular rate of return on investment, or to equal the competition's profits.

In other words, retailers should average out markups on the goods purchased for the period so that they can meet expenses, take necessary retail reductions, achieve a requisite profit level, and attain desired retail sales goals.

Business operating performance does not simply happen: It is planned. A formula for the relationships indicated above may be expressed as follows: Planned markup equals expenses plus profit plus retail reductions divided by net sales plus retail reductions. (Remember that expenses + profit = gross margin.) Therefore if:

Planned sales	$100,000
Planned expenses	20,000
Planned profits	10,000
Planned retail reductions	10,000

$$\text{Initial markup \%} = \frac{\text{\$ gross margin} + \text{\$ retail reductions}}{\text{\$ planned sales} + \text{\$ retail reductions}}$$

Or, since gross margin covers expense and profit:

$$\text{Initial markup \%} = \frac{\text{expenses} + \text{profit} + \text{retail reductions}}{\text{sales} + \text{retail reductions}}$$

$$= \frac{\$\,30,000 + \$10,000}{\$100,000 + \$10,000}$$

$$= 36.36\%$$

In percentages, the formula would be expressed as:

$$\text{Initial markup \%} = \frac{\text{gross margin \% + retail reductions \%}}{100 \text{ percent + retail reductions \%}}$$

or

$$\frac{30\% + 10\%}{100\% + 10\%} = \frac{4}{1.1} = 36.36\%$$

Step 7: Plan the Open-to-Buy at Cost

A buyer with an OTB figure at retail and a planned markup percentage can know exactly the amount of the buying budget. (See Table 10.8.) In Chapter 12 on pricing we discuss how to convert a percentage on selling price to a percentage on cost. But for now, note that 36.36 percent on retail is equal to 57.13 percent on cost. Either approach will yield the same markup in dollars.

If:

Markup percentage on retail	= 36.36%
Selling price	= $100
Less: Markup $	= $36.36 (0.3636 × $100)
= cost of goods	= $63.64

If:

Cost of goods	= $63.64
Markup on cost	= 57.13%
Markup $	= $36.36 (0.5713 × $63.64)
Selling price	= $100 ($63.64 + $36.36)

Making Multiple Purchases

Before leaving the subject of buying against a planned markup, let's go one step further. Suppose that you go to market and plan to spend all of your open-to-buy on this buying trip. Also, suppose that you had done some

TABLE 10.8

Joyce's Shoe Department: An Example of Open-to-Buy at Cost

Joyce had an open-to-buy of $277,325. If she had an initial markon of 36 percent, she would have $177,488 to actually spend at market.

Open-to-buy	=	$277,325
Less: Initial markup $(0.36 × $277,325)	=	99,837
Dollars available to spend	=	$177,488

preliminary planning before going to market and you decided you would have to buy merchandise that, on the average, would yield an initial planned markup of 36 percent. Assume that with the first vendor you approached, you placed an order (at cost) for 20 percent of your open-to-buy for merchandise with retail prices that would yield you a markup of 25 percent. The vendor's merchandise was good, and you felt you could sell it easily. Unfortunately, you thought that sales would be jeopardized if you priced the goods to give more than a 25 percent markup.

The problem now becomes one of buying the remaining goods so that the overall markup obtained on all items purchased averages out to your planned initial markup percentage. Intuitively, you know that the remaining 75 percent of your open-to-buy must be spent on merchandise that will yield more than the initial markup percentage.

To determine the markup percentage to be obtained on the goods yet to be purchased, divide the dollar markup required of the goods left to be bought by the retail value of the goods left to be bought. See Table 10.9.

You see that because Joyce's first order yielded a 25 percent markup, if she purchases the remaining goods to yield a 38.75 percent markup, total purchases should permit her to achieve the planned markup of 36 percent. She will then realize her planned gross margin figure.

In reality, everything may not come out as perfectly as we have shown. It is important, however, to do a thorough job of controlling purchases.

The number of items in all stock plans is multiplied by the price line to arrive at the dollar value of the planned inventory. Adjustments in the stock plan may be necessary if the financial constraints preclude an ambitious stock assortment. Knowledgeable buyers generally commit 50 to 75 percent of the planned purchase figure in order to allow funds for reorders, to anticipate fill-ins, and to take advantage of unexpected marketing opportunities.

TABLE 10.9

Joyce's Shoe Department: An Example of Open-to-Buy at Cost—Multiple Purchases

Joyce had an open-to-buy at retail of $277,325 and $177,488 to spend at cost since the planned initial markup was 36 percent. She would then achieve $99,837 initial markup dollars. If she purchased 20 percent of her goods with an initial markup of 25 percent, she would have to achieve an initial markup percentage of 38.75 on the remaining 75 percent of the goods.

Original open-to-buy	= $277,325
Purchased 20%	= 55,465
Left to buy	= $221,860
Initial markup $ received on first purchase (0.25 × $55,465)	= 13,866
Initial markup $ planned (0.36 × $227,325)	= 99,837
Initial markup $ still needed ($99,837 − $13,866)	= $85,971
Initial markup % needed on remaining goods: $85,971/$221,860 =	38.75%

One last thought should be added about your merchandise budget. With the lag that exists between the time plans are prepared and the day the actual selling season begins, you can well imagine that the figures planned in August may not materialize in February. Generally, management expects this, but hopefully the two sets of figures will not be too far apart. If they are, an adjustment in plans may have to be made.

METHODS FOR DETERMINING INVENTORY VALUATION

The largest investment in most retail businesses is in merchandise inventory. Retail firms often have 60 to 70 percent of total assets invested there.

Knowing one's merchandise inventory situation includes keeping an accounting of in-stock or on-hand inventory and knowing what purchases have been received. For firms with computer merchandise information systems the value of the inventory in stock in the store at any given time can be rapidly determined if an estimate of shortages is made.

To know the amount of profit a firm is making, it is necessary to know the amount of gross margin. The number of sales made and the cost of goods sold are its two components.

Cost of goods sold is the difference between the cost of the total merchandise handled during a period (beginning inventory plus purchases—all the goods that have been in the store at one time or another during the period). If you know how much merchandise was available during a period and how much was left at the end of the period, you can calculate the difference between the two to determine how much was sold. Note, however, that you have to calculate the merchandise at cost prices, not retail prices, because gross margin is figured by subtracting the cost of goods sold from retail sales.

The following illustration that you saw in Chapter 9 clarifies how gross margin is calculated:

Beginning inventory	$ 400	—cost
Purchases	+ 600	—cost
Total merchandise handled	$1,000	—cost
Ending inventory	− 300	—cost
Cost of goods sold	$ 700	—cost
Sales	$1,000	—retail
Cost of goods sold	− 700	—cost
Gross margin	$ 300	

To obtain the figure for total merchandise handled, one must keep records of the beginning inventory plus all purchases received at cost prices. Ending inventory can be found by taking a physical count, at cost prices, of the inventory in stock, or by using the retail method of inventory discussed below. Exact gross margin can be determined only if a physical inventory is taken. The Internal Revenue requires a complete count of goods at least once a year.

Checking and Marking Inventory

Whether goods come directly from the vendor or through a distribution center, they have to be received, checked, and possibly price-marked.

Traditionally the receiving function involved checking the condition and quantity of the goods using a manual method. In order to know that the shipment contained what was ordered, employees physically counted the merchandise and compared the count with a paper copy of the invoice.

The manual method takes a great deal of labor and is expensive. Much of this activity has been automated to improve efficiency and avoid mistakes. The advent of scanning technology and computers have led to great gains in labor productivity in this area. It is now possible to read bar codes from goods with handheld scanners as the items arrive in the store, often premarked with bar codes by the vendor. A computer can then automatically check for and report discrepancies with the original order to ensure accuracy.

The items are then placed on the shelf, thus bypassing the marking process. The price may also be labeled on the shelf, appropriately called *shelf marking,* instead of on each good. The shelf tag tells the customer the price, and the bar code can be read at the point-of-sale to ring up the purchase.

Scanners also assist in the physical inventory process. Instead of counting each item and marking it on paper that is aggregated at the end, an employee simply scans the shelf tag and inputs the number of products on the shelf. Another advance in handling inventory is *vendor marking,* where the vendor takes the responsibility for marking the merchandise before it reaches the retailer. This allows the retailer to move the merchandise directly to the sales floor.

Assigning a Value to Inventory

Fundamental to the taking of inventory is the assignment of some value to each item. If inventory values are recorded at the cost price (what was actually paid for the goods), the assumption is that present in-stock items have the same worth as they had when they were bought. This, of course, is not always the case. Inventories can depreciate in value.

For example, a motor bike bought for $200 and priced at $300 might have to be sold for $250 if it were still on the floor when new models appeared. In this case, the merchant would not want to value the motor bike at its original cost but at some lower value—probably at one that would give the same markup planned for the $300 price. The inventory value of the bike could be determined in the following manner:

$$\text{Cost} + \text{markup} = \text{retail price}$$
$$\text{Old pricing } \$200 + \$100 = \$300$$
$$\text{New pricing } \$167 + \$83 = \$250$$

where retail multiplied by a desired markup of 33⅓ percent would equal the new dollar markup. In other words, the bike would now be valued at $167 at cost.

Goods may become soiled or damaged, wholesale prices may move downward after goods are bought, or customers may lose interest in particular items. Any one of these reasons makes the goods less valuable to the retailer. To value items at their original cost despite these considerations is to overvalue the inventory, and this inflates profits.

In accounting for inventory, it is possible to show unearned profits. That is why inventories are usually valued at cost or market value, whichever is lower. Thus, any inventory loss is recognized and accepted in the period in which it occurs.

For example, let's assume that two store managers operate in exactly the same way except that they carry their inventories differently. Manager A always carries his inventory at the cost he originally paid for the goods. Manager B carries her inventory at the original cost or at a cost (market value) that she would pay for the goods if she were to buy them today. Manager A's ending inventory, then, is in general higher than manager B's. The following illustration shows how gross margin is affected by the different ways of valuing inventories.

	Store A	Store B
Beginning inventory	$ 50	$ 50
Purchases	+50	+50
Total merchandise handled	$100	$100
Ending inventory	−60	−50
Cost of goods sold	$ 40	$ 50
Sales	$100	$100
Cost of goods sold	−40	−50
Gross margin	$ 60	$ 50

The only difference between store A and store B is that store B's ending inventory was justifiably depreciated, because the goods were no longer worth their original cost value.

To summarize, a valuation of inventory at cost or market, whichever is lower, reduces the value of the ending inventory. This in turn increases the cost of goods sold, which reduces gross margin. Because the amount of gross margin earned has a direct bearing on the amount of taxes paid, a reduction in gross margin reduces taxes and saves cash for the firm.

Accounting for Inventory: The Cost Method

The underlying assumption of the cost method of inventory is that all goods are recorded at cost and that ending inventory values are determined by actually counting the goods in stock and recording values at cost prices. This tells the manager (1) how much money is invested in inventory and (2) the firm's gross margin position. Recall that if ending inventories are not figured at cost, it is impossible to calculate the cost of goods sold—a necessary step in formulating gross margin.

In using the cost method of inventory, it is important to realize that calculations of inventory investment and gross margin are impossible unless a physical count of goods in stock is made. If a business and its inventory stock are small, management may be able to keep abreast of its inventory investment and its profit situation through observation and the taking of inventory once or twice a year.

Large stores, however, face different problems. Obviously, stores stocking thousands of items cannot actually count the total inventory very often. Merchants, however, may want to make regular assessments of inventory investment and gross margin so that they can take corrective action if necessary.

Accounting for Inventory: The Book Method

The book method provides a way of recording inventories so that a person may, at any time, look at the books to obtain information on the amount of merchandise handled and sold. No physical counting is required. The book method is a *running*, or more properly a *perpetual*, inventory.

In recording information for a book inventory, values may be entered at either cost or retail prices. Firms that employ the book method usually use retail prices. The illustration below shows that beginning inventory and purchases have been recorded at retail prices and added to yield a total figure for the merchandise handled. Since the amount of inventory handled during the period is known, it is necessary to know only the amount sold to determine the amount remaining in inventory at the end of the period. The store's sales record shows how much was sold.

	At Retail
Beginning inventory	$ 700
Purchases	+ 500
Total merchandise handled	$1,200
Sales	−1,000
Ending inventory	$ 200

Once again, a knowledge of the ending inventory position helps the firm to evaluate how well it is handling its inventory. The retail book method provides a means of obtaining this information without taking a physical count.

Using the book method at retail prices to obtain information on gross margin is a different matter, however. In fact, it can't be done unless cost information on inventory is recorded at the time of sale.

Information on inventory investment and gross margin may be obtained without counting through the use of the book method at cost prices. The procedure for recording information is essentially the same as that for the book method at retail prices, except that cost prices are used. The illustration below shows the same format that was used above.

	At Cost
Beginning inventory	$200
Purchases	+300
Total merchandise handled	$500
Less cost of goods sold	−400 ←
Ending inventory	$100

The problem with this method arises at the point designated by the arrow. To obtain the figure for the cost of goods sold, every time a sale is made, the cost of the goods must be entered on the sales ticket. Such a procedure is cumbersome when many sales are made each day. Therefore, stores that sell high-ticket items such as automobiles, appliances, and furs usually benefit most from the book method at cost prices.

Accounting for Inventory: The Retail Method

The third way of evaluating inventory is through the use of the retail method. The advantage of this method is that it provides information on both inventory investment and gross margin but does not require a physical count. It combines elements of the cost method with those of the book method at retail prices.

The retail method may best be understood by going through a basic illustration, step by step. The following procedure was used to arrive at the $240 gross margin figure.

Step 1. Crucial to the steps underlying the retail method of inventory is the recording of component parts of total merchandise handled at *cost* and *retail* prices, as illustrated below.

	At Cost	At Retail
Beginning inventory	$180	$300
Purchases	+300	+500
Total merchandise handled	$480	$800

Step 2. Compute the average markup percentage, called *cumulative markup*, for total merchandise handled.

$$\text{Cumulative markup} = \frac{\text{markup}}{\text{retail}} = \frac{\$320}{\$800} = 40\%$$

Step 3. Subtract the net sales from the retail value of total merchandise handled to compute ending inventory at retail.

$$\text{Total merchandise handled} - \text{net sales} = \text{ending inventory}$$
$$\$800 - \$600 = \$200$$

Step 4. Convert the ending inventory at retail to cost by using the percentage figure derived from the cost and retail figures of total merchandise handled.

Ending inventory at retail	$200
× cumulative markup (%)	×40%
= cumulative markup ($)	$ 80
Ending inventory at retail	$200
− cumulative markup ($)	−80
= ending inventory at cost	$120

Step 5. Subtract ending inventory at cost from the cost value of total merchandise handled to compute the cost of goods sold.

Total merchandise handled at cost	$480
− ending inventory at cost	−120
= cost of goods sold	$360

Step 6. Subtract cost of goods sold from net sales to compute gross margin.

Sales	$600
Less cost of goods sold	−360
Equals gross margin	$240

Notice that the total merchandise handled was recorded at retail prices (as in the book method at retail prices) and again at cost prices (as in the cost method of inventory). Immediately, it is possible to determine that with a cost of $480 and a retail of $800 yielding a markup of $320 ($800 − $480), the average markup on all the goods handled during the period would be 40 percent.

Step 3 calls for a deduction of the net sales figure from the total merchandise handled at retail to compute ending inventory at retail.

If, on the average, the total merchandise handled reflects a markup of 40 percent, any inventory left in stock should also have an average markup of 40 percent. Applying this average markup to the ending inventory at retail permits us to compute the ending inventory at cost and ultimately the gross margin figure. All this may be done without a physical count. The difference between what is actually in the store and what is calculated using the retail method is adjusted when the annual physical inventory required by the IRS is taken.

An extension of the retail method involves adding factors such as freight-in and net additional markups to total merchandise handled. Net markdowns, employee discounts, and a provision for shortages are included, along with net sales, as total deductions from the retail figure of total merchandise handled. Accounting for alteration costs and cash discounts is also illustrated. Look at the following table:

	At Cost	At Retail	
Beginning inventory	$125	$200	
Gross purchases	250	440	
Less returns to vendors	−25	−40	
Transportation costs	16		
Net additional markups	____	10	
Total merchandise handled	$366	$610	
Cost multiplier/cumulative markon %			$366/$610 = 60%/40%
Gross sales		$210	
Less customer returns		10	
Net sales		200	
Net markdowns		−20	
Employee discounts		−10	
Estimated shortages		−15	
Total retail deductions		$246	
Ending inventory at retail		$364	
Ending inventory at cost	$218		364 × 0.6
Maintained markup		52	52/200 = 26%
Less: Alteration costs		−3	
Plus: Cash discounts		5	
Gross margin		54	54/200 = 27%
Less operating expenses		46	
Net profit before taxes		$ 8	8/200 = 4%

The procedure is similar to the one previously described, in that beginning inventory and purchases are entered at both cost and retail figures. Then freight-in (entered at cost) and net additional markups (entered at retail) are added to beginning inventory and purchases to arrive at total merchandise handled for both cost and retail columns.

You will learn that net additional markups include markups (price changes upward after goods have been originally priced) less markup cancellations (additional markups that have been canceled). At this point, the cumulative markup is calculated.

To obtain the value of the inventory at the end of the period, total retail deductions are subtracted from total merchandise handled at retail. Total retail deductions are the sum of (1) the net sales figure; (2) net markdowns, which include markdowns (prices changed downward after goods have been originally priced) less markdown cancellations (markdowns that have been canceled); (3) employee discounts; and (4) estimated shortages. If a physical inventory is taken, shortages (or overages) do not have to be estimated, but are known as a result of a discrepancy between physical and book figures.

The cost of the ending inventory is found by multiplying the cumulative markup percentage times the ending inventory figure at retail and subtracting the product from the ending inventory at retail. Subtracting the ending inventory at cost from the total merchandise handled at cost gives you the cost of goods sold. Net sales less the COGS gives you the maintained markup

FIGURE 10.3

The retail method of inventory.

Calculations	Items	Cost	Retail	Percent
A	Beginning inventory	$ 60,000	$ 105,000	
B	Gross purchases	$ 316,000	$ 345,000	
C	Less: Returns to vendor	$(9,000)	$(14,100)	
D	Transfers-in	$ 3,000	$ 4,800	
E	Less: Transfers-out	$(4,500)	$(7,200)	
F	Transportation costs	$ 4,500	XXXXXXXXXXXXX	
G	Additional markups		$ 2,100	
H	Less: Cancellations		$(600)	
Add columns from rows A - H	Total merchandise handled (TMH)	$ 270,000	$ 435,000	
Divide TMH (cost) by TMH (retail)	Cost multiplier			62.07 %
(1 - cost multiplier)	Cumm. markon			37.93 %
I	Gross sales		$ 309,000	Net sales in dollars
J Net = gross - returns	Less: Customer returns		$(9,000)	$ 300,000
K	Gross markdowns		$ 12,000	Percents based on net sales
L	Less: cancellations		$(1,500)	Net markdowns 3.5 %
M	Employee discounts		$ 1,500	.50 %
N $ shortages = % shortages × net sales	Estimated shortages		$ 2,250	.75 %
Add retail column for rows I-N	Total retail deductions		$ 314,250	
Tot merchandise handled − Tot retail deductions	Closing book inventory & retail		$ 120,750	
Closing book at retail × cost multiplier	Closing book inventory & cost	$ 74,948		
Tot merchandise handled − Closing book (cost)	Gross cost of goods sold (COGS)	$ 195,052		
Net sales - COGS	Maintained markup	$ 104,948		34.98 %
O	Less: Alteration costs	$(3,000)		1.00 %
P	Add: Cash discounts	$ 6,000		2.00 %
Maint markup − O + P	Gross margin	$ 107,948		35.98 %

in dollars divided by the net sales. The maintained markup less alteration cost, plus cash discounts, is the gross margin. The gross margin less operating expenses is the net profit before taxes.

Now look at Figure 10.3 and see if you can work your way through the complete illustration.

Advantages of the retail method.   The advantages of using the retail method of inventory are significant, especially for larger stores. First, since a physical inventory is taken at retail prices, fewer errors occur. Also, it can be done in less time than taking inventory at unmarked or coded cost prices (as under the cost method). Second, it serves as a management device. Since markups, markdowns, and so on, are regularly compiled, these figures can be compared with industry norms or past company performance and thus give management a basis for control. Third, at some time the merchandise in the entire store must be physically counted. It is highly unlikely that a count will show agreement between the book inventory and the physical inventory. If the book inventory exceeds the physical inventory, there is a shortage. If the reverse occurs, there is an overage. Differences between the two figures result from clerical errors and/or loss of merchandise.

THE LIMITED—REVISITED: FOCUSED MERCHANDISING AND GLOBAL SOURCING

In the early 1980s The Limited Inc. could do no wrong. Each of its new retailing ideas developed into an instant success story. It expanded rapidly by developing different formats. But some were too similar to the existing ones. The Limited divisions and the Lerner stores started cannibalizing each other's sales. This happened as Lerner abandoned its traditional clientele and attempted to move more upscale, while at the same time Limited stores attempted to change from moderate-priced sportswear to higher-priced career clothes.

The Limited has tried to regain its former growth and dynamics with an inter-

THE LIMITED, INC.

esting program. Limited's president is working to boost the retailer's quality and to differentiate it from the competitors. Gross fired 70 percent of the merchandising team and hired top merchants from Saks Fifth Avenue and R. H. Macy. He has also started finding factories in Italy and the Orient that manufacture clothes for upscale designers.

In an attempt to reverse the company's fortunes, the management approved a restructuring plan that focused on the enhancement of core retail operations and the utilization of underperforming retail assets of the business. This plan included:

1. An emphasis on the mature baby boomer in Limited's stores
2. Acceleration of store remodeling
3. Downsizing and closing Limited stores and Lerner divisions that are not performing well
4. Refocusing the merchandising strategy at other divisions

Other ideas the company is considering include catalogs for a business like Express or Abercrombie & Fitch Co., expansion into international retailing of a business like Bath & Body Works or Victoria's Secret, and better global sourcing that will utilize the best resources worldwide and give the companies a competitive advantage in both quality and value.

The company president stated "[We] are very focused on our women's businesses, and are doing our best to get them back on track. . . . You already know that we've based all of our growth on providing fresh and new fashion ideas, with the quality our customers demand and the values they deserve."[12]

The restructuring did not accomplish all that was hoped. In late 1995 The Limited Inc. created a new company, Intimate Brands, by separating out the Victoria's Secret, the Victoria's Secret Catalog, and Bath & Body Works. These operations accounted for 29 percent of that year's sales of $7.32 billion.[13]

1. **What problems in planning merchandising budgets are made more difficult with global sourcing?**

SUMMARY

Retail buying is part art and part science. The needs and wants of the consumer influence what merchandise the retailer carries and how much. Retailers strive for a delicate balance between the amount of inventory investment and the risk of not having the right product at the right time in the right amount.

A merchandise budget allows the retailer to calculate how much will need to be invested in inventory within a given time frame. To accomplish this, the retailer must have an accurate estimate of what the planned sales figure will be. Planned sales estimates are determined by industry or historical analysis.

Reductions will cause the retail value of inventory to be lower than expected at the end of the month; therefore, any planning process must take into account estimated values of markdowns, shrinkage, and employee discounts.

The amount of merchandise needed, the amount of open-to-buy, estimated beginning and ending inventories, and initial markon percentages are all part of the merchandise planning process. As competition and markets become more complex, the issues and decisions that retailers will need to address concerning merchandise planning will become more intricate and challenging.

KEY TERMS AND CONCEPTS

Basic stock method, 389
Buying plan, 374
Calendar date, 378
Dollar control, 375
Employee discounts, 384
Gross margin, 392
Markdown, 382

Merchandise budget, 374
Merchandise date, 378
Planned initial markup percentage, 392
Planned purchases, 391
Planned reductions, 382
Selling plan, 381

Shrinkage, 383
Stock-to-sales ratio, 387
Stock turnover rate, 385
The week's supply method, 390

QUESTIONS

1. Of what value are merchandise planning and control to the manager?

2. Why is inventory turnover of great importance to retail managers? How can managers achieve a planned inventory turnover?

3. Suppose that stock for January 1 is planned at $15,000 at retail, and sales for January are planned at $2,000 with retail reductions planned at 2 percent. Stock for February 1 is planned at $12,000. What is the open-to-buy figure for January? Would proper merchandise planning permit an alteration of the OTB figure? Explain.

4. Why is inventory such an important asset to plan for? How could a poorly planned inventory hurt a business?

5. If a manager calculates open-to-buy in retail dollars, can he or she go out and spend this amount on inventory?

6. What effect does shrinkage have on how much retailers order?

7. What are the effects of having too much inventory? What about too little inventory?

8. Initial markon percentage includes the shrinkage figure. Why? What would happen if it didn't?

9. Is a department store buyer likely to purposely overvalue or undervalue the inventory at the end of the year? Why or why not?

10. Discuss the three methods of valuing inventory. Give specific examples of circumstances in which each would be used.

SITUATIONS

1. The assistant manager of the Outlet Shoe Store is directed to set up the inventory-taking procedure for a business doing $420,000 yearly. This is a family shoe store with both counter and backroom stock. One of the things at issue is whether to use a cost or book inventory method, or both. Analyze these methods, and then set up steps in the

inventory-taking procedure you would choose.

2. You are the manager of a gift shop. You have $250 (at cost) of open-to-buy left for the current period. A vendor calls and tells you that he has a special deal on glass plates, but you must purchase the entire lot for $1,500. You believe that you can sell these for a high markup, but simply do not have the money in your open-to-buy to make the purchase. What do you do?

3. You are the buyer for a chain of record and tape stores in the western United States. Lately there has been a problem because all the Pearl Jam recordings and merchandise are selling out, first in one town and then in a nearby city the next week. This has been going on for several weeks. You decide to order more of their recordings and related merchandise for all of your stores. Now some are overstocked, and others are still understocked. What are the potential underlying problems?

CASES

CASE 10A
Ready-to-Wear

Kim East is a new assistant buyer for ladies' ready-to-wear. She has just completed the store's training course in inventory valuation. Her buyer requested the following information for the children's department:

1. Closing book inventory at retail

2. Closing book inventory at cost

3. Gross cost of goods sold

4. Estimated shortages

5. Gross margin in dollars and percentage

6. Net profit in dollars and percentage

Kim has the following information available for departmental analysis. Complete the buyer's request as though it had been made of you.

The department had an opening inventory of $157,500 at retail that had a cumulative markup of 40 percent. Gross purchases of $120,000 at cost had been placed into inventory with a markup of 35 percent. Merchandise valued at $12,000 retail and $7,500 cost had been returned to vendors during the period. Transportation charges paid during the period totaled

3 percent of the cost of gross purchases. Because of rising demand for some items, additional markups of $15,000 were taken. Because of competition, additional markup cancellations totaled $4,500. Gross sales for the department during the period were $232,500 with sales returns and allowances totaling $9,000. During a sale, markdowns of $24,000 were made, but markdown cancellations of $10,500 occurred. Employee discounts amounted to $6,750. The departmental operating expenses were $57,000. A physical inventory showed an ending stock of $102,000 at retail.

CASE 10B
Developing a Merchandise Plan

J. Johnson is the buyer for a women's apparel specialty store. It is the store's policy to prepare a merchandise plan based on a department's turnover. In Johnson's department the turnover is four times a year, so the planning period is three months for turning the average inventory.

However, in addition, a monthly purchase plan is prepared regardless of the number of turns a year. This allows the buyer to know how much open-to-buy remains for the balance of the month on a week-to-week basis and ensures that there is available money to place additional orders for merchandise. J. Johnson makes it a policy to not commit more than half of planned purchases to initial purchases. This allows adequate dollars for reorders on fast-moving items, fill-ins on style or seasonal merchandise, and off-price purchases for promotions. Assume you are J. Johnson and have been given the following information as of September 8 (all figures are at retail):

Needed (planned three months)

Net sales	$175,000
End of month inventory	90,000
Markdowns	4,000
Planned markup %	40%

Available

Beginning of month inventory	$72,000
Receipts to date (Sept. 8)	16,500
Outstanding orders (Sept. 1)	45,000

Actual transactions to date (Sept. 1 to Sept. 8)

Net sales	$16,500
Markdowns	1,400

Find the dollar values for the balance of September for:

1. Outstanding orders
2. Net sales
3. Markdowns
4. Merchandise needed
5. Merchandise available
6. Purchases
7. Open-to-buy at retail
8. Open-to-buy at cost

Chapter Goals

After reading this chapter, you should be able to:

- Understand and apply the concept of assortment planning.
- Explain the aspects of a model stock plan.
- Describe the different unit control systems.
- Explain how to reorder merchandise.
- Distinguish between the five types of buying offices.
- Comprehend the relationships between retailers, vendors, and suppliers.
- Illustrate different merchandising systems.
- Understand the legal environment affecting vendor relations and merchandising.

Assortment Planning, Buying, and Vendor Relations

RUSSELL-NEWMAN INC.:[1]
POWER BUYERS—POWER VENDORS

In 1992, a *Business Week* story forecast that by the beginning of the twenty-first century retailers who accounted for half of all retail sales in the United States would be gone.[2] Department store closings, mergers, and acquisitions, such as that triggered by the bankruptcy of the R. H. Macy Co. and its subsequent purchase by Federated Department Stores, had concentrated power in fewer and fewer department store chains. These "power buyers" have consolidated to bring costs down and remain competitive.[3]

The "power buyers" require "power vendors" that can deliver the volume of goods necessary to supply hundreds of stores and support the margins they demand. To be on a chain's most favored list the vendor must have short cycles for making and delivering merchandise, which typically require computerized inventory systems. Apparel vendors with sales of less than $10 million can seldom survive today.[4]

One of the emerging power vendors is Russell-Newman Inc. with sales in

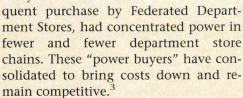

excess of $80 million. The company manufactures and distributes ladies' robes and sleepwear. According to James Martino, president, the firm is seeing annual sales gains of more than 20 percent with its private-label and branded business. The firm markets to mass merchandisers under the Club Bed and Pinx labels. Its Cypress label robes are sold exclusively to department stores.[5]

Russell-Newman imports approximately 80 percent of its merchandise, which is just the reverse of what it was as late as 1989 when virtually all merchandise was made in the United States. The dramatic change in direction has occurred because—as Steve Speck, vice president of sales, indicates—retailing has changed the way the manufacturers must do business. The big are getting bigger, and the small retailer is struggling to survive. Ten years ago Russell-Newman's business was comprised of 60 to 70 percent sales to specialty stores; today it is less than 5 percent. The specialty stores simply did not change quickly enough to meet new competition.

Instead of "specializing"—offering new and innovative items, something different, something better—the specialty store tried to compete on price. As Herb Kelleher, president of Southwest Airlines, says in the company television advertisements, "If you try to compete in price against Southwest, you're going to get nuked." The small specialty stores got nuked!

The business from the manufacturer's viewpoint continues to evolve dramatically. The playing field is different, and the rules are certainly different. No longer is it "enough" to deliver a quality product, at a fair price, on time. Now the manufacturer has to be concerned with the retailer's sell through, inventory turn, margins, and profitability. Consequently, both the manufacturer and the retailer are forming "partnerships" that are equitable and profitable for both.

How do these partnerships work, and what are the benefits? The manufacturer gives the retailer choice of deliveries and schedules production accordingly. The retailer in turn gives the manufacturer commitments early so that production "downtime" can be utilized. This assures the retailer of getting the best price, it keeps costs low, and it aids in obtaining targeted gross margins. It also ensures optimum deliveries, which can help increase inventory turns. The manufacturer can now produce based on actual orders by style, size, and color, and thus inventory markdowns are kept to a minimum. Negotiations of this magnitude occur twelve to fifteen months prior to any merchandise being delivered. The financial stability of both the manufacturer and the retailer is an integral part of the partnership.

1. **How has buying changed in the new world of power vendors and power buyers?**
2. **What risks does a vendor face as the number of retailers declines?**
3. **What risks does a retailer face as the number of vendors declines?**

INTRODUCTION

Knowing how much to buy and knowing what to buy are operationally inseparable concepts. A buyer must simultaneously consider what merchandise will fit customer needs and how many dollars can be specified in the merchandise budget. Chapter 10 described the dollar planning necessary to develop the merchandise budget. This chapter discusses the importance of planning just how the dollars will be spent for specific merchandise. Also discussed is the choice of specific items in assortment planning. Finally, the considerations involved in making the buy are examined.

Knowing *what to buy* requires knowledge of the wants and needs of the market. It sounds simple enough, but in execution, difficulties arise. Information systems that provide the store with a continuous profile of what customers are buying are nearly a necessity. In this regard the buying function is dynamic. Changing customer interests, buying habits, and motivations must also be given consideration.

In earlier chapters we discussed the idea of market segmentation and target markets. Assortment planning must mesh with the overall strategy. For example, the Men's Wearhouse targets a customer group that seeks name brand suits and accessories at a lower price in exchange for reduced breadth and depth of selection, while Brooks Brothers' customers expect depth of merchandise and greater personal attention. Buyers in both stores must build an assortment plan of merchandise that earns day-in and day-out acceptance by their targeted customer groups. This means that the assortment plan should eliminate doubt about what the store stands for and to whom it appeals.

ASSORTMENT PLANNING

In the previous chapter, we examined the merchandise budget in detail, which is a top-down approach to merchandise planning that results in a lump sum dollar amount to be spent for inventory. Assortment plans call for dollar and unit purchases by item or groups of items. See Figure 11.1. Merchandise needs are classified in narrow categories, such as guns in a sporting goods

FIGURE 11.1

The elements of the buying function.

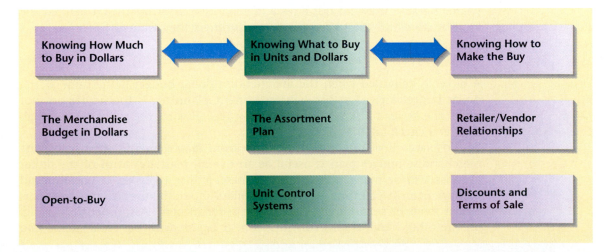

Knowing How Much to Buy in Dollars	Knowing What to Buy in Units and Dollars	Knowing How to Make the Buy
The Merchandise Budget in Dollars	The Assortment Plan	Retailer/Vendor Relationships
Open-to-Buy	Unit Control Systems	Discounts and Terms of Sale

Competing in today's environment is difficult when the merchandise looks the same regardless of the store. Benetton attempts to offer clothes not found on the shelves of any other store in town. It concentrates on finding the best designs and the coolest colors and dyes. A huge distribution center in Italy uses robots to get the latest fashions out to company stores in 120 countries in twelve days. (Rapoport, Carla, "Retailers Go Global," *Fortune,* February 20, 1995, pp. 102–108.)

department and wide-brimmed hats in an accessories department. After determining the categories of merchandise the store will stock (men's clothing, stationery, costume jewelry, etc.), the retailer divides the broad categories into smaller ones called classifications (e.g., men's suits, tuxedos, raincoats). In turn, the classifications are divided into subclassifications (single-breasted, double-breasted). A unit plan of the number of items to be stocked in each SKU (stockkeeping unit) is then prepared. The purpose of this approach is to ensure that the stock will present an assortment of items that will satisfy the wants and needs of the majority of targeted consumers.

Assortment planning helps the buyer in two ways. First, it forces development of a plan, the thrust of which is to ensure a balanced stock in terms of units and retail dollars. In achieving this stock balance, the buyer is influenced by (1) the kinds of goods typically carried in the department or store, (2) the space available for inventory, and (3) the sales and profit potential of the merchandise. Crucial to all operational decisions is the need to achieve stock balance in the context of a well-defined store image. Thousands of retailers ranging from department stores to convenience stores have disappeared because they did not have a merchandise assortment that defined the kind of store and the target group of customers they wanted to serve.

Merchandise Budget/Assortment Planning Comparison

A buyer is delighted when the merchandise dollar budget is the same as the dollar budget arrived at through assortment planning. If the figures are not close, the buyer must reconcile them by reevaluating the plans. One procedure is a check on the other.

To place all of this into perspective from management's standpoint, the merchandise budget plan is useful as an overall master control of the dollar purchases to be made within a broad merchandise category. It does not aid management in planning how many dollars should be used to purchase particular items or small groups of items in a department. Assortment planning, on the other hand, fulfills this function. It begins with particular items and small groups of items and builds up to a total purchase figure. An advantage of assortment planning is that early in the planning process, particularly before going to market, a buyer must think in terms of a balanced assortment of items (in units).

Basic stock lists. One way to approach assortment planning for staple merchandise is to use **basic stock lists.** These represent merchandise for which there is a fairly constant demand and where fashion plays a relatively unimportant role. The demand for cigarettes, toothpaste, white athletic socks, and many other items is fairly constant—not varying significantly from season to season.

A basic stock list is usually developed for goods of this kind. Such a list is a precise statement of the items to be carried in stock. It includes the name of each item and its description by style number, size, price, color, weight, and brand. Sometimes a picture of the item is listed for easy identification. Basic stock lists should contain room for the buyer to record the inventory position on each item (see Figure 11.2).

The merchandise is expressed in terms of specific units and the dollars to be invested in these units. Following through on the information provided in Figure 11.2, the buyer has apparently decided to have the department covered for the forthcoming budget period in the following way:

1. Toothpaste will be carried in two brands (Crest and Gleem). Crest will be carried in two sizes, economy and regular. Crest mint flavored will be carried in regular, and Gleem in one size, regular (column 1).

FIGURE 11.2

Basic Stock List

Column 1	Column 2	Column 3				Col. 4	Column 5					
			Price	Sales		Project Dollar Sales	Jan. Sales		Feb. Sales		Mar. Sales	
Merchandise Description and Stock Number	Packing	Cost	Retail	Last Year	This Year		Last Year	This Year	Last Year	This Year	Last Year	This Year
287 Crest toothpaste economy size	1 doz.											
288 Crest toothpaste regular size	1 doz.											
289 Crest toothpaste regular size mint flavored	1 doz.											
293 Gleem toothpaste regular size	1 doz.											

2. Minimum packing units are one dozen (column 2).

3. From last year's unit sales, this year's sales can be projected (column 3).

4. Given the retail price of the item (column 3) and projected unit sales (column 3), total dollar sales can be projected (column 4).

5. Column 5 will contain projections for each month of the budget period. The total dollar sales built via a bottom-up approach (assortment planning) should yield the same number of dollars achieved by using the top-down approach (OTB planning). They both tell the buyer how much to spend on inventory for the budget period.

Model Stock Plans

Model stock is an assortment of seasonal or fashion goods that seems to best fit the needs of the store's customers. Model stock is expressed in terms of the important features of the assortment such as price lines, styles, colors, materials, and sizes.

The **model stock plan** is a breakdown of the merchandise a store plans to stock. Once the plan is developed, the store buys the appropriate quantities. These quantities are determined on the basis of planned sales.

Recall that the basic stock list also provides a breakdown of expected stock. However, in the basic stock list, the breakdown was definitive. It described each item to be carried. A model stock plan also describes the stock to be carried, but items are identified by general characteristics, not by specific details.

In assortment planning, the model stock plan is used for stocking of seasonal and fashion items. Plans are made to purchase by common characteristics, such as sizes and price lines. In other words, when health and beauty aid buyers go to market, they know, for example, that they will buy sixteen cases of Crest toothpaste, regular size. Dress buyers, on the other hand, know only that they can buy so many dozen dresses to be priced at $89.95, in assorted sizes. They have no way of knowing the style they will purchase until they see the suppliers' offerings.

Developing a model stock plan requires a particular sensitivity to fashion trends. Buyers frequently say that if they could only gauge the fashion picture correctly, success would be certain. To some extent, this is an accurate picture of the importance of fashion in retailing. However, this may also be an exaggeration of the realities of merchandise buying.

It is necessary to define two words that are frequently used interchangeably, "fashion" and "style." In the world of retailing, there is an important distinction. *Style* is a characteristic or distinctive mode or method of expression, presentation, or conception in the field of art. *Fashion* is the currently accepted, or popular, style in a given field. In other words, a V-neck cardigan sweater, because of its distinctive characteristic, is a style. It may not be a fashion if few people are willing to buy it. Whether a style becomes fashionable will depend on its ability to satisfy consumers' desire for change.

Many buying offices have people responsible for anticipating what merchandise will be popular in coming seasons. Representatives travel to important fashion houses in Europe and Asia to purchase the items outright or buy the rights to copy the designs. They then return and present lectures and slides to various retail customers. Smart merchants rely on their expertise.

The model stock plan must be flexible enough to react to the fashion trends in terms of style, color, and fabric, yet at the same time maintain a balanced assortment of sizes and types of merchandise.

Model Stock Example

Illustrative of a model stock plan is one developed by a department manager prior to making buys for the six-month selling season beginning in February and ending in July. The department was men's shirts, and the merchandise classification was men's sport shirts. In planning to purchase sport shirts, the department manager worked from a model stock plan, because each season and each year the merchandise was different and the styles were new. On the other hand, the department manager set up an assortment plan for men's dress and men's work shirts, a merchandise classification that the department also stocked, through the use of basic stock lists. Dress and work shirts are staple items with style and size numbers that are carried from season to season.

In working up the model stock plan for sport shirts, the buyer was influenced by the following facts:

1. The general characteristics of sport shirts:
   a. Long and short sleeves
   b. Plain and fancy styles
   c. Small to extra-large sizes
   d. Regular and tall lengths
2. The department currently carried $18, $25, and $32 price lines.

The buyer's worksheet for the model stock plan is shown in Figure 11.3. As you can see, it is designed to enable buying according to price line, type of shirt, size, and the "Remarks" given on the spreadsheet.

The percentages for price lines were based on those the buyer had found to be satisfactory in past years. After an analysis of last year's sales of sport shirts, the buyer had found that the following percentages prevailed:

Price Lines	Last Year's Sales	% of Sales
$18.00	$11,000	22%
25.00	14,000	28
32.00	25,000	50
	$50,000	100%

Because he believed last year's assortment of each price line was adequate, he based his assortment plan on this information. The same rationale was

FIGURE 11.3

Model stock planning work sheet.

Price Line	Remarks	Budgeted $50,000					
				Size			
$18	Buy even assortment of 0 and 1 pocket.	**Plain**	**S**	**M**	**L**	**XL**	**Total**
22%		20% $2,200	20% $490	40% $880	30% $660	10% $220	100% $2,200
	Buy 10% long sleeve.	122 units	25 units	50 units	35 units	12 units	122 units
$11,000	Go light in the pastels	**Fancy**					
		80% $8,800	20% $1,760	40% $3,520	30% $2,640	10% $880	100% $8,800
611 units		489 units	98 units	195 units	147 units	49 units	489 units
$25	Buy even assortment of 0 and 1 pocket.						
28%							
$14,000	Buy 2 patterns in talls.						
560 units							
$32							
50%	Buy 3 patterns in talls.						
$25,000							
781 units							

Additional information: *This year's best colors: hunter green, navy, burgundy.*

used to further break down the assortments into plain and fancy styles and lengths. Carefully follow the steps the buyer went through to arrive at the other calculations in Figure 11.3's model stock plan:

Step 1. The buyer arrived at the total dollar retail value of inventory he should stock in men's sport shirts for the budget period from the merchandise budget. Figure 11.3 shows this amount to be $50,000 (top of the right-hand column). This figure was arrived at by taking last year's sales in men's sport shirts and projecting this year's sales.

Step 2. The buyer selected the general characteristics that might be used to describe men's sport shirts—characteristics he will look for when he makes his buys. As we said, these characteristics are usually determined by the way customers buy the merchandise. It is important to have enough but not too much detail (characteristics). The buyer cannot afford and does not need to plan for every purchase eventuality. Therefore, he selected *major* characteristics that showed a balanced assortment. Figure 11.3 shows that the buyer decided to stock men's sport shirts by price lines, kinds (plain and fancy), and sizes.

Step 3. The buyer planned how many units and dollars to stock in the price lines, kinds, and sizes chosen to represent the assortment. Checking last year's sales and the assortments needed to back up these sales, he arrived at the percentages and established proportional relationships for the current totals. This is exactly what we did earlier, when we calculated the proportion of last year's sales realized in each of the three price lines.

Step 4. The buyer calculated the dollar and unit amounts in the following way:

a. He calculated the amount of stock to be carried at the $18 price line as $11,000 ($50,000 × 22 percent). The dollar values of the $25 and the $32 price lines were derived in the same way.

b. Using the percentages on the assortments to be carried in the plain and fancy shirts at the $18 price line, the buyer calculated that $2,200 should be carried in the plain shirts ($11,000 × 20 percent) and $8,800 should be carried in the fancy ones ($11,000 × 80 percent). Again, the same method was used for the plain and fancy shirts at both the $25 and $32 price lines.

c. The percentage figures given for size distributions were applied against the dollar value of the types of shirts by price lines. In other words, in the $18 plain shirts, small size, the firm would stock $440 worth (20 percent × $2,200).

d. Finally, the buyer calculated the number of units to be carried in stock by dividing the dollar totals by their price lines. The buyer, for example, planned to spend $11,000 on the $18 shirts; therefore, he planned to buy about 611 shirts ($11,000 divided by $18 = 611.1). The same procedure was used to derive the remaining stock.

How Much Stock Is Enough?

Obviously, it is necessary to have enough stock to accommodate the needs of customers. This does not mean, however, that a store should attempt to satisfy all needs. To do so would require an unacceptable investment in inventory.

Take, for example, men's dress shirts. It is possible to stock men's dress shirts from a neck size of 14 to a size 20. It is also possible to stock them in sleeve lengths from 29 to 36. The bulk of sales will be made in and around the 15½ neck, 33 length sleeve. The distribution of sales and sizes is such that 12 percent of all dress shirt sales will probably be in 15½ neck, 33 sleeve. Only one shirt will probably be sold in 14½ neck, 29 sleeve.

Shirts are bought in lots of three. A buyer who stocks 14½ neck, 29 sleeve with the expectation of selling only one shirt would have an overstock of two shirts. Overstocking leads to the tying up of funds in investment and the risk of having to take markdowns on inventory because of slow movement, possible deterioration, and obsolescence. The natural reaction, then, would be not to stock for this one sale and, in fact, be out of stock in the 14½ neck, 29 sleeve shirts.

This returns us to the original question, "How much stock is enough?" The answer is, "Large enough to serve *most* potential customers." The following are guidelines for maintaining a satisfactory stock turnover rate by keeping a small but ample stock level:

1. Carry a few brand styles and price lines for which there is a steady demand.

2. Carry a complete assortment of these brand styles and price lines.

3. Carry the items you know will sell in your store, and beware of putting too much emphasis on what goes well in someone else's store.

4. Do not buy all the unusual lines some vendors would like to sell you.

5. Do not be persuaded into purchasing excessive quantities by the lure of extra discounts.

6. Order only items that are needed rather than placing orders across the board, which leads to duplication of similar items already in stock.

UNIT CONTROL SYSTEMS

Before concluding our discussion of assortment planning and how to know what to buy, we want to look at another aspect of the subject. Successful merchants must also have some knowledge of **unit control.** This is a system of recording units of stock on hand, on order, and sold in a given period. It indicates the degree of customer acceptance of a particular item of merchandise. Unlike dollar control, which is used for the financial investment in inventory, unit control keeps track of the number of items and pieces in inventory. Like dollar control, however, unit control provides information that helps buyers know how much to purchase.

The Unit Control Plan

To maintain an in-stock position of wanted items and to dispose of those not wanted, it is necessary to establish an adequate form of control over the merchandise on order and the items in stock. Computer systems can provide a regular report of the unit inventory position. For the small retailer there are many simple, inexpensive forms of unit control. For example:

1. Visual control enables the retailer to examine the inventory visually to determine if additional items are required.

2. A daily physical count of a small portion of the inventory ensures that each segment is counted on a regular basis.

3. Stub control enables the retailer to retain a portion of the price ticket when the item is sold. The retailer can then use the stub to record which items were purchased.

4. Click sheet control enables the retailer to record the item sold (at the cash register) on paper. The information is then used for reorder purposes.

For the small retailer, information on units in stock may be kept on unit control cards. Typically, information contained on the card includes classes, stock on order and on hand, style number, size, color, price, merchandise received, and any other characteristic that the store wishes to follow. Figure 11.4 shows the front of a unit control card. The back of this card would show the distribution of shoes by size and width.

FIGURE 11.4

Unit control card, side A.

DATE OF ORDER	PAIRS ORDERED	MONTH	ON HAND	REC'D FROM MFR.	TOTAL	RET. TO MFR.	SALES	TOTAL	BALANCE END.	STOCK COUNT
		Jan. 1-15								
		16-31								
		Feb. 1-15								

DESCRIPTION _____ PATTERN _____ STOCK NO. _____

HEEL _____ COLOR _____ MATERIAL _____ MFR. _____

RETAIL / COST / MARK-UP

Periodic versus Perpetual Control Systems

One kind of unit control, called a **periodic control system,** involves counting inventories periodically. Another kind of unit control, called a **perpetual control system,** involves keeping track of inventory changes continually through accurate computer or manual records.

Periodic control.

Periodic control is the basic system used for staple, low-value products. Because these items enjoy a continuous demand, there is less of a necessity to take markdowns.

Periodic control of staple merchandise is accomplished by monthly, weekly, or even daily inventory counts. In the absence of a computerized system, counting too often is time-consuming and expensive; however, failure to count often enough may not achieve the level of control desired. A merchant must have a system that (1) makes certain merchandise is ordered as needed, (2) accounts for the speed with which different items are selling, and (3) accounts for the replenishment time required from the vendor to ensure stock levels.

An informal way of making periodic counts is an inspection. The **inspection system** involves looking over the stock from time to time, noting the quantities on hand, and ordering as needed. Some stores place labels on the front of the shelves or on top of counter boards to indicate the minimum quantities of stock that should be on hand. If an inspection reveals that the count is at or below the minimum, a buy is made to bring the stock up to the maximum.

Perpetual control.

The other kind of unit control is the perpetual inventory system. Perpetual controls have historically been used for merchandise that is of high unit value, that is sold in a short selling season, or that is extremely vulnerable to obsolescence. In these cases, merchandise markdowns are more frequent because quick action must be taken to liquidate slow sellers. Just as important, quick action is needed to reorder best-sellers.

Today nearly all the larger retailers use perpetual control because of the advantages provided by sophisticated computer hardware and software. Under perpetual control, retailers receive continuous feedback on how the merchandise is moving. Because they receive this information on a weekly or even daily basis, they can adust inventory levels when necessary. To get this information, stores must establish a method of recording all sales, the receipt of all merchandise, and the number of merchandise returns in units. Computer technology allows the capture of the needed data much more rapidly than is possible with the manual systems still used by some retailers. Electronic cash registers with optical scanning systems capture the data for perpetual inventory computer software from the bar code tags on the merchandise.

Merchandise Reorders

Reorders of merchandise depend heavily on unit control information. Buyers are confronted with the problem of reordering merchandise frequently. Especially in the case of basic stocks, buyers forecast sales based on information from unit control records and current records on stock in inventory. In figuring the amount of merchandise to be reordered, buyers start with the notion of **maximum operating stock.** This is the amount represented by a **minimum selection stock** (basic low stock and a safety) plus the stock needed to cover the **buying period** (reorder interval and the delivery time). Between deliveries, stock on hand should fluctuate between minimum selection stock and maximum operating stock. After maximum operating stock has been determined, stock in inventory should be subtracted to arrive at the open-to-buy in units that can be purchased.

Before giving an illustration of how to compute reorder stocks, look at the terms in Box 11.1. The following example illustrates how to calculate merchandise reorders. If:

Time from order to received	Lead time (2 weeks)
Normal sales	+ Basic stock (1 week)
Backup for emergencies	+ Safety stock (1 week)

Therefore the order point is 4 weeks (2 + 1 + 1). The order should be placed at least when stock level reaches the point of four weeks' supply.

BOX 11.1 TERMS TO UNDERSTAND IN COMPUTING REORDER STOCKS

Basic low stock. Lowest level of stock permissible without losing sales because of an out-of-stock condition

Safety or reserve stock. Protection stock as a hedge against unanticipated surge in demand

Minimum selection stock. Quantity of a given item below which inventory would ordinarily not be permitted to drop (basic low stock plus cushion)

Reorder interval. Elapsed time between two consecutive reviews of an item (or the stock needed to cover this period of time)

Delivery or lead time. The stock needed to cover normal time between executing an order and receipt of the merchandise

Buying period. Equal to reorder period and delivery time

Maximum operating stock. Sum of minimum selection stock and the stock needed to cover the buying period

6543217

One example might be the situation where a buyer needs to reorder a certain style of women's key chain. Stock control records show that the store sells an average of 10 units a week and that sales are generally stable throughout the year. Periodic stock counts on this item are taken every four weeks. Deliveries are received within three weeks of placing the order. The buyer tries to provide a safety stock of one week's sales and to maintain a basic low stock of 12 units. Assuming that this period's stock count equaled 20 units and stock on order was 15 units, what amounts should the buyer reorder? In other words, what is the open-to-buy in units?

Minimum selection stock	
Basic low stock	12
Safety (sales for one week)	10
	22 units
Stock needed during buying period	
Reorder interval (four weeks' sales)	40
Delivery time (three weeks' sales)	30
	70 units
Maximum operating stock	92 units
Total stock available	
Stock count	20
Stock on order	15
	35 units
OTB = 92 − 35 =	57 units

In this situation, if the stock on hand had exceeded the maximum operating stock, the buyer would have been overbought and would not have needed to reorder.

Assortment Planning—A Summary

To know what to buy, a retailer must make a detailed analysis of customer wants by getting information from many different sources, including the customers themselves, store records, and the trade. Each of these sources helps buyers decide what kinds of staple and fashion merchandise to purchase. Additional knowledge of what to buy comes from unit control systems, which help retailers decide how much and what kind of merchandise to stock. Even with great planning, a buyer will make mistakes. See Box 11.2.

BUYING

In addition to knowing how much and what to buy, retailers must have some knowledge of how to make a buy. See Figure 11.1. To purchase merchandise the buyer must be familiar with the thousands of old and new products

11.2   FINAL SALE! STORES UNLOAD BUYERS' ERRORS[6]

Approaching the cashier, Susanne Lemberger can hardly carry all the designer dresses, jackets, and shoes she has picked out. But the price is light—about $200. "It almost seems like a mistake," she says. It is, and Dillard Department Stores is paying for it. Ms. Lemberger is shopping the Dillard clearance center in Kansas City, Kansas. At its half-dozen centers, Dillard unloads some merchandise for less than wholesale. The full retail price of Ms. Lemberger's purchases exceeded $1,000.

The existence of these centers shows that department store retailing remains an art—despite predictions that technology would make it a science. Dillard's computer system tracks every purchase and informs company officials which items aren't selling and need promotion and which are selling out and need replenishing. But as yet, computers can't predict consumer tastes.

"This isn't retailing; it's getting some money out of the goods and washing your hands of it," says Sidney Doolittle, a Chicago retail consultant. That's a fine distinction for customers who find a Ralph Lauren sweater just as handsome at $29.99 as at $165—and who are willing to buy it in August. "It's the only Dillard's I'll shop," says Jeanne Young, a Missouri schoolteacher who drove forty miles to the Dillard clearance center, past full-price Dillard's as well as factory outlet centers. Few discount stores or factory outlets can beat the clearance centers' prices.

Predicting consumers' behavior is the job of retail buyers; for them, clearance centers are halls of shame. "Walking in and seeing those 1,000 green sweaters you bought isn't pleasant," says Kay Winzenried, a Dallas retail consultant whose seventeen-year career at the Neiman Marcus chain included a stint as buyer.

At Neiman Marcus, whose clearance centers are named Last Call, buyers are required to "visit their mistakes" twice a year, says Ms. Winzenried, adding that any buyer whose goods consistently land there won't survive. But she and others say that any buyer whose choices never enter a clearance center may be buying too little. "Not having what the customer wants is the biggest mistake," Ms. Winzenried says. Nor should a buyer apologize, she and others say, for taking risks. In an age of complaints about department store homogeneity, "buyers should be encouraged to seek novelties, and novelty makes the gamble greater," says Stanley Marcus, the former chief executive of Neiman Marcus who advises retailers on buying matters.

6543217

offered for sale as well as the testing, evaluating, and retesting of products that have been purchased. There may be many vendors around the world who could potentially supply the desired merchandise, and they must be evaluated as to their financial ability to meet the needs of the store.

Discount Store News (August 1995, p. 21) reported that Oshman's, a sporting goods retailer, discovered through consumer research that the company was perceived as "jockish, uncool, expensive, upscale, and narrow." The company wanted to achieve a young and hip image. To do so, buyers selected merchandise for their model stocks to reflect the new "look." Oshman's new mega-stores are characterized by golf playing areas, synthetic ice arenas, rollerblading lanes, basketball areas, as well as knowledgeable salespeople.

Preparing to Buy

One requirement of working with the details of buying is a system for getting the most out of trips to the market, where merchandise is bought, or for use in direct negotiations with vendors and manufacturers. Whether one buys from a firm across town or on the other side of the world, a buyer must be prepared before beginning the purchasing process.

For many types of merchandise, the biggest part of the buying is still done on these "trips to the market." However, partnership alliances with manufacturers and importers require that buying be done in plants around the world, at the buying office, at the store, or at the retailer's headquarters.

Many large cities have a Merchandise Mart where manufacturers of various goods display them periodically. One such market is the Chicago Apparel Mart. It is set up like a shopping mall, with representatives of large manufacturers staffing displays where buyers can inspect their merchandise lines. In Dallas, the Apparel Mart, the World Trade Center, and the InfoMart each occupy large buildings with space for hundreds of vendors. Many more are located in the nearby "design district." In addition, national shows such as the January housewares show in Chicago, the July electronics show in Las Vegas, and the furniture show in Dallas are major buying opportunities for retailers. At the market it would be easier for buyers to purchase only in preparation for the beginning of a new season. However, they must constantly add merchandise to their initial purchases throughout the period.

The number of visits to a market depends on the distance involved, departmental sales volume, market conditions, whether the store has resident buyers (agents permanently located at the market), and store policy.

Industry trade shows for everything from toys to hardware are major buying opportunities for retailers. One of the nation's largest is the Comdex show in Las Vegas. More than 200,000 attendees view the latest in computer hardware and software and other new technology. Millions of dollars in business for the coming year is written in just a few days.

Market Influences on Buying

Retail buyers are confronted by conditions in the market that often are not under their control. If circumstances were always the same, any changes would be reasonably predictable and their job certainly would be simplified. Unfortunately, the buyer must be prepared to adjust to the changing supply and demand conditions in the marketplace.

Smart buyers have repeatedly emphasized the need for flexibility in the buying function. For example, if the economic picture begins to show a downturn or if important merchandise cannot be purchased, buyers must be prepared to enter or get out of the market in a short time. Having this information plus knowing in general terms how to enter a market and how much merchandise to commit oneself to is important to intelligent buying.

A buyer may be initially concerned with **basic stocks** for which the retailer can anticipate fairly accurately the needs for the forthcoming season. Part of the model stock may be allocated for **test stocks,** which are purchased for the purpose of gauging customer reactions to merchandise before large orders are placed. Retailers may be uncertain as to which fashions their customers will respond to during the season; they must be particularly alert to hot items. Usually, however, if an item proves to be hot in one store, it is likely to receive similar responses in others. By that time, manufacturers may be hard-pressed to supply the rush of orders they receive.

Before the season begins, retailers must commit themselves to stocking merchandise in depth to ensure that inventory will be adequate at the height of consumer buying. To do this, they must engage in **forward buying**— that is, buying ahead of needs, constantly checking with resources, and generally looking for goods or substitutable items that can be counted on for delivery. It is at this time that the retailer's supplier relationships go a long way in ensuring that it receives preferential treatment.

Late season planning dictates that a conscious effort be made to work stocks down before demand for products decreases. To be unprepared for this will result in an overstock position. Sometimes, to support demand late in the season, retailers will offer special promotions to rekindle customer interest. Markdowns can also serve to keep interest alive. Substantial markdowns and clearance sales are often used to move merchandise out of stock at the end of the season.

The Central Buying Office

Only larger companies can afford a staff in the merchandise markets to offer research, expertise, information, and other services to the store's management. For this reason, many department and specialty stores make use of the services and facilities of resident buying offices, which work for a group of noncompeting stores.

There are several types of buying offices. The most common is the **independent office,** from which a group of noncompeting client stores purchase professional services. The stores and the office are separate entities, and neither has any control over the other. Some, like the Independent Retailers Syndicate, deal with all kinds of merchandise that would be found in full-line department stores. Others focus on the merchandise and operations of specialty stores.

A second major type is **cooperatively owned** and controlled by the stores that are members of that particular buying office. Examples are Associated Merchandising Corporation and Specialty Stores Association. A buying office may also be a division of a corporation that operates a group of retail companies, and such an office serves only the members of the corporation.

Another major type of buying office is the one owned by and designed for only one company. There are also **commission buying offices.** These receive their income from commissions paid to them by manufacturers on orders placed, rather than from fees or commissions paid by retailers, as is the case with other types of buying offices.

Services of a Buying Office

The services provided by a resident buying office include those that assist the store in buying merchandise, services associated with selling and promotion of merchandise, and information and services for operations and general management.

Buying services. The primary service of the buying office is market coverage. The representative visits the vendors and gathers information on fashion, color, and fabric trends; new resources; hot items; prices; delivery dates;

and best-sellers. This information is available to the store buyers through a variety of reports, including bulletins, market reports, vendor lists, and catalogs. An important function of a buying office is to alert the retailer to items that give evidence of strong potential.

Buying offices also assist in group buying for a number of stores. Benefits include lower prices, better selection, and better delivery dates because of the purchase of large amounts of merchandise at any one time.

Selling services. Buying offices may have a sales promotion staff that provides assistance in planning promotions, advertising, displays, and special events. It may serve as a clearinghouse for the exchange of outstanding promotional ideas. Some offices offer a direct mail service that plans and distributes catalogs for the stores. Store merchants work with office staff to select the merchandise to be included. An example would be a Christmas catalog prepared by buying offices and available to participating stores.

Management services. Management services offered by buying offices may be numerous, such as providing the latest information on government regulations, training methods, and management techniques, as well as executive recruiting. A purchasing service may offer information on prices, availability of supplies, and new equipment. The office may make available information on new techniques and sources of supply and act as a clearinghouse for the exchange of ideas among stores concerning physical operations. The buying office may also operate an exchange of sales and expense statistics. This allows stores to compare their own performance with that of others. Some buying offices provide information on selection of the proper equipment and creation of the systems needed to process information.

Visiting the market. When going to market, buyers may first contact their resident buyer to expedite their purchases. The resident buyer has been preparing for the visit and probably has identified key resources worth investigating and may even have established a clinic where buyers can exchange opinions on fashion, merchandise, and markets. Resident buyers will be on call to schedule appointments with suppliers.

Evaluating suppliers. Some retailers attempt to evaluate their suppliers in a systematic fashion. This evaluation may take the form of periodically assessing the supplier's performance by determining the average gross margin obtained on goods purchased through this source, the markdowns taken, customer complaints, store returns and adjustments, speed and dependability of delivery, and other systems and/or concessions supplied.

To make such an evaluation, retailers must establish a system for collecting the necessary information. Having done this, they may judge their suppliers and decide whether to continue doing business with them. They may also decide in which situations it is best to use different suppliers. A sample resource evaluation form is found in Figure 11.5.

Resource Evaluation

Manufacturer/Jobber _____ Dept. No. _____

Address _____ Date _____

History of the Line:

Buyer Contacts – State peculiarities or special handling required by:
  a. Sales Office
  b. Factory

Rating – Dun & Bradstreet or Moodys

Manufacturer's Ethics

Position in Industry

Vendor Importance to Store

Store Importance to Vendor

Record of All Arrangements (Terms, Trade Discounts, Cash Discounts, etc.)

Markdowns

Adjustments History

Customer Credits, Complaints, and Adjustments

Speed and Dependability of Delivery of Goods

Cooperative Advertising, Demonstrators, Prepackaging

Other Services

Remarks (Additional information that will guide any member of our
organization who may have to deal with this resource)

Evaluator _____

Buying and Tracking Inventory

Major technological advances in buying have occurred over the last decade. Retailers are using computers to communicate with their vendors in order to improve the ordering process. Through **electronic data interchange (EDI)** and **quick response (QR) systems,** retailers can now track and control inventory from order to manufacture to shipment and final delivery. You remember that EDI is a system that allows the retailer's computer to communicate directly with the vendor's computer and share data on transactions. QR is a delivery system based on shipping smaller inventory units in accordance with sales data from the store. For example, Russell-Newman receives from Dillard's a sales report of its merchandise each week. Russell-Newman automatically replenishes stock from its own distribution center to match what Dillard's sold. Both EDI and QR systems involve a commitment to share data between retailers and vendor. This allows the vendor to review stock positions in the store and sometimes even process reorders without the retailer's involvement. Retailers can send orders electronically and then track them throughout the distribution chain.

EDI and QR systems have several positive results for the retailer and vendor alike. The vendor's position is improved by knowing exactly what to produce or stock at any given time. This reduces downtime and allows better planning for production and warehousing facilities, thus reducing costs for the vendor. These cost reductions are often shared between the vendor, through higher profits, and the retailer, through lower cost of goods sold.

Retailers are the major beneficiaries of EDI and QR systems. They can increase customer service with fewer stockouts, fresher merchandise, faster service, and fewer returns. Also, both inventory levels and the risk of goods perishing on the shelves can be reduced. See Box 11.3 for an outline of how The Limited Stores used EDI and QR to be more competitive.

Using EDI and QR not only decreases inventory carrying costs but also allows the retailer to reduce stockroom space and instead use it as selling space. These systems also enable faster check-in of merchandise and inventory evaluation. Often the vendor will premark items with bar codes, saving

BOX 11.3   HOW THE LIMITED CUTS THE FASHION CYCLE TO SIXTY DAYS[6a]

1. From point-of-sale computers, daily reports on what is selling flow to headquarters of The Limited in Columbus, Ohio.

2. To restock, the company sends orders by satellite to plants in the United States, Hong Kong, South Korea, and Sri Lanka.

3. The goods are hustled back to Columbus from Hong Kong aboard a chartered Boeing 747 that makes four flights a week.

4. At a highly automated distribution center in Columbus, apparel is sorted, priced, and prepared for shipment—all within forty-eight hours.

5. By truck and plane, the apparel moves out to The Limited's 3,200 stores.

6. Within sixty days of the order, the apparel goes on sale. Most competitors still place orders six months or more in advance.

6543217

the retailer this effort and allowing the merchandise to proceed directly to the sales floor once it is checked in. Retailers want the bar code data to reflect the initial price.

RETAILER/VENDOR RELATIONSHIPS

It was not long ago that an adversarial relationship existed between the suppliers of goods and the buyers. Companies and consumers sought the lowest price and highest quality through the bidding process and "shopping around." Suppliers were continually played against each other in an attempt by the buyer to obtain the best possible deal. This was necessary for the buyer because the manufacturer usually had the greater power in the negotiating process. The size of most retailers was dwarfed by that of the vendor. Also, many vendors had power in the market because customers wanted the vendor's brand. This led to the attitude that the buying and selling of merchandise was a zero sum game where one party must lose for the other to gain.

Several changes in both the external and the internal environments of retailing caused a shift in attitudes. Among these changes were increased competition among suppliers, the introduction of new management techniques from other countries, increases in the market power of large retailers, and the introduction of strategic partnerships by innovative retailers and vendors.

The simultaneous increase of competition between suppliers and the relative growth in the size of retailers changed the power structure of the buyer-seller relationship. Large retailers of merchandise ranging from toys to books and women's apparel to building supplies started buying vast quantities of items to supply their stores nationwide. These accounts were heavily sought after by vendors. As a result, retailers dictated the terms of sale to a much greater extent than in the past. Also, these retailers now had the volume and market power to skip over intermediaries and buy directly from the manufacturers. Large orders required the suppliers to hold high levels of inventory or be prepared to produce large orders on short notice. In order to facilitate the process, large retailers started to set up longer term contracts with the manufacturers. This helped the vendors to better respond to the retailers' needs. As a matter of efficiency, the retailers started sharing sales and ordering information with regular suppliers. This sharing of information and trust quickly had an effect on the relationship between the retailers and vendors and was central to the retailers' desire to develop strategic partnerships.

Using Key Suppliers

Many retailers have found it advantageous to do the bulk of their business with a few suppliers, as indicated on their preferred vendor list. There are several reasons for doing this. First, there are a large number of suppliers in the market, and since each handles a large number of lines, it is confusing to work with too many of them. Second, retailers who purchase from only a few suppliers reduce the amount of time they must devote to buying. Using a few suppliers reduces the number of contacts retailers must make; not only do they spend less time actually making buys, but they also spend less time making adjustments that arise from shipping errors. Third, consolidating orders may bring advantages in credit terms, delivery, price breaks, and service arrangements, such as liberal adjustment policies. Fourth, suppliers are usually able to give considerable attention to retailers who account for a significant portion of their business.

On the other hand, buyers would be negligent if they did not attempt to get acquainted with resources new to them. Buyers need to be continually looking for new merchandise. Small firms are particularly useful in producing the unusual item that can give distinction to a department. In addition, looking at potential new suppliers gives the buyer an opportunity to assess the appropriateness of the buying decisions she has made or is about to make.

The desire of both manufacturers and retailers to become more integrated led to the development of strategic partnerships. A higher degree of coordination was required to ensure the timing and delivery of merchandise from the manufacturer to the retailer. Because of the effort required to initiate delivery on reoccurring schedules, these relationships were developed on a longer term basis. No longer could a retailer or vendor afford to switch between partners to obtain temporary discounts or premiums.

Strategic Partnerships and Relationship Marketing

Large retailers were at the leading edge of the creation and maintenance of **strategic partnerships.** The advent of computers and information transfer technologies allowed coordination between retailers and vendors to reach a degree never before possible. Relatively recent reductions in the cost of this

The Rocky Mountain Chocolate Factory sells high-quality chocolate candies and caramel apples. Many candies are made in the store, sending marvelous aromas throughout the area. The franchisees purchase some prepared candies from the franchisor. They also purchase items such as material to make gift baskets direct from vendors approved by the franchisor and at market from an approved vendor list.

technology have allowed smaller and midsized retailers to take advantage of such systems. While the transfer of information is critical to the relationship between retailers and vendors, it is by no means sufficient to maintain a long-term partnership, which must include an attitude by both parties to work together to achieve a common goal. The common goal of the retailer and vendor is the distribution of the right product to the end consumer at the right price, right time, and right place. All of these requirements demand a great deal of coordination and sacrifice by both parties. However, the end result is a satisfied customer, which in turn leads to profits.

Vendor/retailer partnerships have focused on getting the products to the retailer at the right time. Orders are filled with greater accuracy using computer-based electronic systems. There is less worry about receiving the products ordered and getting them on time. Many partnerships are rapidly expanding. Manufacturers such as Leslie Fay now assist their retail accounts in the development of merchandising and assortment plans. Russell-Newman will take a buyer to sewing plants in foreign countries where they will work together on quality and delivery issues.

Partnerships also include a give-and-take component that cannot be overlooked. Manufacturers and retailers have started what is referred to as *margin sharing*. This is where the manufacturer will share losses of margin incurred by the retailer under certain conditions. The retailer may agree to devote prime space and/or more space to a manufacturer's product under these terms. Figure 11.6 shows an actual case of a retailer's calculations for margin sharing with the vendor. Note at the bottom the $ variance at cost. In this case the department achieved $3,900 more than the planned gross margin of $58,700. This vendor agrees to split any shortfall 50/50 with the store.

Retailers like to buy in small lots, at low prices, and with frequent deliveries. Suppliers desire just the opposite. Today, they are forming "partnerships" based on a commitment to meet customer needs while squeezing costs out of the supply chain. Levi Strauss's "quick response" partnerships with retailers use information technology to improve ordering, physical distribution, assortment planning, inventory control, sales forecasting, and production scheduling.

FIGURE 11.6

Calculations by a department store to arrive at gross margin sharing with a vendor.

GROSS MARGIN CALCULATION*

RESOURCE ___S W Imports - Men's Robes___

	COST	RETAIL
purchases	92.0	196.0
freight	1.6	
retail MUs		(6.5)
accum cost	93.6	

MARKUP % 48.9
(retail purch+ retail MUs - accum cost) / retail purch

SALES $	148.2
MD $	22.2
MD %	14.9
COST %	51.1
MARKUP %	48.9

minus
MD % MARGIN
14.9 **x** 51.1   7.6
MD % x Cost %
plus
DISCOUNT % SALES
1.5 / 148.2   1.0
cash disct / sales

GROSS MARGIN %   42.3

GROSS MARGIN $ CALCULATION
42.3 **x** 148.2   62.6
GM % X SALES = GM $
39.6 **x** 148.2   58.7
DEPT GM % X SALES = GM $

VARIANCE AT COST   3.9
($ allowance needed to perform at dept trend)
***$ X** 100

The popularity of private brands has taken market share away from large manufacturing companies such as Procter & Gamble. This has become a strain on relations between large discount retailers and manufacturers at a time when retail sales are stagnant in many categories. While carrying the private labels helps the retailer maintain sales, manufacturers are having to make adjustments in pricing and promotional strategies to stay competitive.

Vendor Relations in the Global Environment

Whether learning how to more efficiently source products throughout the world or physically expanding into foreign markets, globalization is having a major impact on how retailers define **supply chain management.** Because of distance, language, culture, and government regulations among countries, the challenge for supply chain management is how to optimize inventory investment, customer service, and logistics activities when operating stores and/or sourcing products throughout the world. The challenge often creates new dilemmas. See Box 11.4.

BOX 11.4 AN ETHICAL DILEMMA: RETAILERS AND THEIR GLOBAL VENDORS

Milton Friedman's statement that the only social responsibility of business is to make a profit is one dimension of the debate on ethical and social responsibilities of business. Others argue that behaving ethically and in a socially responsible manner is good business sense because customers respect such firms and reward them with their business.

We have a global economy. Retailers are looking worldwide for customers. To meet consumer merchandise needs retailers may contract with sometimes hundreds of suppliers for goods. Many of these contractors subcontract with factories around the world. The vendor must be able to provide the highest quality goods at the lowest possible price. The pressure to exploit labor in developing countries with very low wages, long hours, and poor working conditions is enormous. To put the situation into perspective, consider that a leather worker in the United States might make $2,500 a month, in Mexico the worker would earn the equivalent of $700, and in China it would be $70.[7]

Bob Ortega, writing for the *Wall Street Journal,* notes that many American retailers require suppliers to sign a code of conduct forbidding any violation of local labor laws. J. C. Penney Co. makes vendors agree to a code of conduct that forbids violation of local labor laws including using underage workers. "Virtually everyone applauds the intent of the codes, and the stated penalty for violations—immediate [cancellation] of the contract."[8]

Ortega further explains that some manufacturers and retailers try hard to enforce their codes. For example, Levi Strauss & Co. employs inspectors to monitor working conditions in developing countries, but because they try to avoid offending factory owners, they don't probe too deeply.

Questions

Retailers say they can't realistically enforce the codes because the number of contractors and factories may literally be in the thousands. They have to depend on the contractors to police themselves. Do you agree with the retailers' position? Why or why not? How might retailers be more proactive in improving working conditions? Is this an ethical issue for them?

6543217

Supply chain participants, ranging from the raw materials supplier to the final consumer, will be more involved in partnering arrangements. Similar efforts will be undertaken by retailers and other members of the supply chain in foreign markets, with unique approaches being developed in order to overcome specific challenges in individual countries.

For example, three leading food retailers—Argyll (United Kingdom), Ahold (Netherlands), and Casino (France)—banded together to form the European Retail Alliance (ERA).

Rather than functioning only as a buying group, AMS is actually a strategic alliance, with collaboration extending to areas related to business development and the exchange of information and skills. Buying groups are more prevalent today among European retailers in all industry segments than among those in the United States. Their activities include the exchange of market information and coordination of promotions. They also work together in the area of packaging development and improvements, assortment/development of products, and the distribution and logistics functions of transportation, storage, and warehousing.

Through the creation of all-encompassing partnerships, no matter what specific approach is taken, companies around the globe are working toward the common objective of lower costs and improved customer relationships. Retailers are taking greater control of all aspects of the supply chain, minimizing costs at every point in order to become the low-cost provider in their retail category.

Sourcing will move closer to demand. As retailers rethink traditional concepts of supply chain management, they will view product sourcing in a new way. With global resources to draw upon, the optimum location for product manufacturing will depend on many factors, including quality standards, cost, and proximity to the final customer. Political stability and the overall economic attractiveness of the source country are major factors in evaluating global sources of supply.

In general, though, cross-border retailers will service neighboring countries through logistics networks established in their home countries. Existing networks will be expanded as needed to reach outlying stores, with ease of movement facilitated by the continued breaking down of trade barriers. Retailers may approach their markets by centralizing core inventory in one location and servicing their stores by air, while bulk or specialty items could be sourced locally and shipped directly to stores.

For example, although the Swedish specialty retailer Hennes & Mauritz has warehouses in each of the eight countries in which it operates stores, it has recently established an "all Europe" warehouse in Germany. This is serving as a duty-free zone for receipt of goods shipped from all over the world, earmarked for its European stores.

Greater use of foreign trade zones. More and more retailers will take advantage of foreign trade zones for warehousing imports from countries where trade agreements do not exist. Ross Perot's Alliance Airport near Dallas is designed as a cargo-only facility. Retailers and manufacturers have established operations in the foreign trade zone there. This zone enables them to delay paying duties on imports, avoid duties on exports, and reduce duties paid on goods processed from imported parts. They are also able to more closely monitor foreign supply sources and avoid paying duties on rejected imports.

Transportation companies will take a broader role. Multimodal, full-service transportation companies are available now to satisfy retailers who want it "faster, better, and cheaper." Partnerships will develop between retailers and those carriers, and retail customers will demand one-stop shopping for all their transportation needs.

Many transportation companies have moved into the third-party arena and manage the entire logistics function, providing all the necessary services from the point of origin to the point of destination. Carriers not only transport goods but are moving toward facilitating the exchange of information. Purchase order data are being integrated with delivery schedules to expedite the receiving process.

INFORMATION AND MERCHANDISE FLOWS

The world of retailer/vendor relationships allows information technology to increase the efficiency of nearly every aspect of the business. New technologies provide buyers with greater and faster access to information than ever before, shifting the emphasis away from the inventory itself. Technology now allows real-time communications between all the participants in the supply chain: the manufacturer, wholesaler, importers, warehousers, and shippers.

Demand communication will be key to efficient supply chain management. Technology will facilitate communication of consumer demand data back through the supply chain to all participants including the raw materials suppliers. This will make possible as close to a one-to-one merchandise replenishment as economically feasible. The retailer's efforts are being facilitated by the growth of **just-in-time manufacturing,** which supports the retailer's desire for **just-in-time delivery.**

Communications systems will allow the retailer to adjust supply and product flow to actual demand. ENCOMPASS, for example, was developed as a joint venture by American Airlines and the carrier CSX to provide a globally integrated, multimodal cargo trade system. This allows shippers, consignees, forwarders, and carriers to electronically communicate through a single window on the world. It increases customer service capabilities, provides a higher level of intelligence and management over inventory, and makes possible pipeline visibility across the entire supply chain.

Merchandise Systems

Figure 11.7 offers an illustration of **information flow** and **merchandise flow** within the retailing/vendor merchandise system. It should not be forgotten that the final intent is to provide the customer with merchandise that fits his or her wants and needs.

Merchandise flow.   As discussed earlier, the retailer must provide the customer with the right merchandise, at the right place, in the right quantity, at the right price, and at the right time. In order to accomplish this, the buyer

FIGURE 11.7

Flow of information and merchandise within the retailer/vendor system.

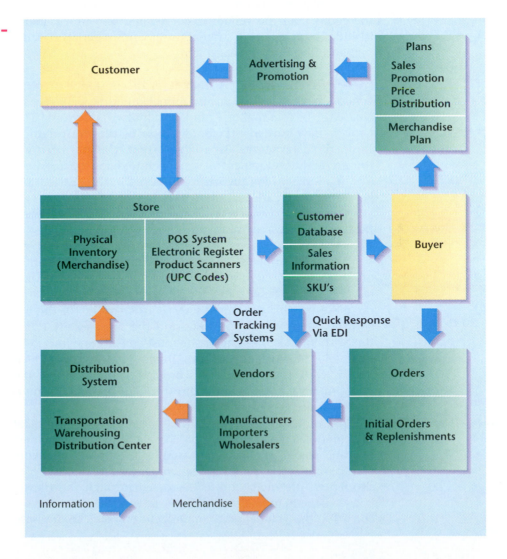

must be familiar with the physical distribution of merchandise from the producer to the consumer, including the role the retailer plays. Failure to properly account for the physical distribution of the merchandise can result in receiving products late or not at all, incurring excessive distribution charges by warehouses and transporters, and improper delivery of the merchandise.

Merchandise can be ordered directly from the manufacturer or from other companies such as importers or wholesalers. Larger retailers often order directly from the manufacturer, while small retailers typically order merchandise from importers or wholesalers. Firms that provide merchandise to retailers are referred to as **vendors,** regardless of whether they are manufacturers, wholesalers, or importers.

Merchandise must be physically transferred from the vendor to the retailer in an efficient manner. The purpose of **logistics** is to physically move the goods from the vendor to the retailer in a timely manner. This function includes transportation, warehousing, and materials handling, order processing, and inventory management.

Information flow. A high level of coordination between retailers and vendors is necessary to ensure proper ordering, delivery, and receipt of merchandise. Firms ranging from The Limited and Home Depot to Associated Grocers have turned the coordination of their distribution function into a competitive advantage. To a large extent, this has been established through the use and development of new technologies to increase the flow of useful information between the parties involved in the distribution process. The single arrows in Figure 11.7 show the flow of information within the system.

The primary source of all information for the retailer is the consumer. Retailers also receive information from vendors and statistical sources. **Point-of-sale (POS) systems** are the heart of capturing consumer data.

The traditional use of customer and sales information is to determine orders in the short run and a merchandising plan for the longer term. The buyer is usually responsible for interpreting the sales data and placing orders for more merchandise. As discussed in Chapter 10, the buyer develops and controls the planned purchases and the open-to-buy (OTB). In order to do this with any accuracy, he or she must consult previous POS sales data to estimate sales for the future and to obtain EOM inventory levels. After developing an OTB, the buyer places orders with the appropriate manufacturers. These manufacturers then obtain (through production, inventory, or buying) the necessary goods for shipment.

EDI allows access to a retailer's sales and inventory database by the manufacturer. The replenishment order is developed directly by the computer system and placed with the manufacturer through the network. Quick response systems allow the time between ordering and receiving to be dramatically shortened. The merchandise is ordered through the transfer of information between the manufacturer and the retail store. In order to maintain stricter controls, the retailer and manufacturer often share information on the progress of filling orders. This is accomplished through the use of an order tracking system (OTS).

Although EDI decreases the workload of buyers, it certainly does not eliminate the position. Buyers are still responsible for developing and maintaining merchandise plans, creating initial orders, and maintaining the integrity of the EDI system through continuing audits. They may also be responsible for the larger replenishment orders. As buyers prepare to face the challenges of the twenty-first century, competitive pressures will continue to force them to be more accurate with buying plans.

Buyers transfer information to those who conduct planning functions. These include development of merchandise plans, which are, in turn, used to generate sales, promotion, price, and distribution plans. Usually, the buyer is responsible for the development of the merchandise plan, although in most large organizations a separate department develops the merchandise budget and ties it together with pricing and promotion plans.

The last step in the information flow process is communicating to customers through advertising and promotion. This keeps them informed on the availability of products and services that fit their needs.

To effectively and efficiently do their jobs, buyers must understand discounts and terms of sale. Let's look now at this important area.

DISCOUNTS AND TERMS OF SALE

Buyers going to market with a dollar open-to-buy at cost and retail must understand discount and invoice terms. A *discount* is a reduction in price given to retailers by their suppliers. An *invoice* is a bill sent by suppliers; it calls for payment for merchandise delivered.

Our treatment of discounts and invoice terms is divided into two parts: terms of sale and terms of payment. *Terms of sale* are the conditions under which merchandise is sold. The terms specify the trade, quantity, and seasonal discounts offered retailers. Terms of payment are the conditions under which retailers must make payment. They indicate the permissible discounts and describe the circumstances under which payment must be made.

Terms of Sale

Terms of sale include trade, quantity, and seasonal discounts.

Trade discounts. A **trade discount** is a reduction in price available to some classes of buyers, such as wholesalers and retailers. Trade discounts are usually quoted in a series and are expressed as a percentage reduction from a supplier's list or suggested retail price: "Less 40%–10%." When trade discounts are used, only the retail price is listed on the invoice. All other invoices show the cost price to retailers. The rate of discount is determined by operating expenses in the trade. For example, some toy manufacturers give discounts of 12, 6, and 4 percent to wholesale customers; the 12 percent is for handling and credit costs, the 6 percent for selling effort, and the 4 percent for profit. Footwear manufacturers give 40 percent and 10 percent discounts to their retailer customers; the 40 percent is for the retailer's operating expenses and profit, and the 10 percent is given if the retailer assumes the functions of a middleman.

There are two reasons why suppliers use trade discounts. First, they offer a simple way of adjusting prices to a rising or falling market. When suppliers increase or decrease prices, they merely publish a change in the discount rate, rather than change the price on each individual item. Second, trade discounts enable suppliers to exert some control over the suggested retail price. They specify the price on the invoice and then set up a series of discounts so that retailers can make a given margin.

In calculating a trade discount, assume that you have an invoice similar to the one shown in Box 11.5. Notice that this invoice carries a total list price of $20,300 with trade discounts of "less 30-10." The percentages should be applied to the list price in the order they appear. They are *not* added to create, in this case, a 40 percent discount. Thus, 30 percent is taken off the list price, and 10 percent is taken off the balance:

A. $20,300 × 0.30 (discount) $ 6,090	C. $14,210 × 0.10 (discount) $ 1,421
B. $20,300 − 6,090 (discount) $14,210	D. $14,210 − 1,421 (discount) $12,789

If no other discounts are given, the cost price to the retailer is $12,789. So, the total reduction from the selling price is 37 percent ($6,090 + $1,421 = $7,511; $7,511/$20,300 = 0.37).

Quantity discounts. A **quantity discount** is offered to retailers who buy a given quantity. Box 11.5 shows that a 5 percent quantity discount was earned by the retailer, which is figured after the trade discount has been calculated. In this case, the cost of the merchandise (after the trade discount was taken) was $12,789; an additional 5 percent discount yields a revised cost calculated in the following manner:

$12,789 × 0.05 (quantity discount) $639.45	$ 12,789 − 639.45 $12,149.55

BOX

11.5   INVOICE FOR GOODS RECEIVED ON 9/20/97

Fashion Apparel
1427 LeForge
Ypsilanti, Michigan

Invoice No. B-67341

Terms:
Trade discount Less: 30–10. Quantity discount: 5 percent. Cash discount: 2/10, n/30.

Date: 5/6/97

Sold to: Engblon's
1258 W. Prospect
Detroit, Michigan

Customer Order No. V29775

Air Freight: Prepaid 6201 F.O.B. factory

Stock	Description	Quantity	Price	Amount
56211	Pant suits	105	$150.00	$15,750.00
56210	Slacks	40	40.00	1,600.00
56301	Blouses	50	35.00	1,750.00
56270	Skirts	30	35.50	1,065.00
				$20,165.00
Transportation				135.00
Total				$20,300.00

Received 5/7/97 Mark Smith, Buyer

6543217

Some manufacturers and wholesalers use **cumulative** quantity discounts. The values of all orders in a period are added together. If the order values exceed a specified amount, the discount is applied. Otherwise, a noncumulative quantity discount is applied to each order.

Seasonal discounts.   A seasonal, or early order, discount is one that retailers earn by ordering or taking delivery of merchandise before the normal selling period has begun. It is the suppliers' inducement to encourage retailers to buy early, and it helps suppliers obtain business during slack periods.

For example, ski equipment retailers may not need an inventory of skis until early October, because they don't want to tie up dollars in inventory prior to the time they begin to sell the equipment. Their suppliers may have completed production of skis by mid-July, and because they want to minimize storage facilities, they may wish to get the skis out of their plants as soon as possible. As an inducement to retailers to buy the skis early, they may not require payment on the goods until mid-December. Seasonal discounts, then, give retailers a reduction in price and time in which to receive money from sales before they must make payment on the goods.

Terms of Payment

Terms of payment show the conditions under which retailers must make payment and reflect the cash discounts allowed.

Cash discounts. *Cash discounts* are a reduction in price given by suppliers in return for prompt payment of the invoice. Look back at Box 11.5. On this invoice, the retailer was offered a 2 percent discount, which is shown as 2/10, n/30. The 2 represents the amount of the discount, and the 10 represents the number of days within which the retailer must make payment. If the retailer had cash available, payment would be made within 10 days of the invoice date, or May 16 (May 6 plus 10 days). At that time, the retailer would write a check for $11,906.56. If the bill is paid after the 10 days, $12,149.55 would be due by June 6.

A. $12,149.55	B. $12,149.55
$\times$ 0.02 (cash discount)	$-$ 242.99 (cash discount)
$ 242.99	$11,906.56

Payment Requirements

Some terms establish the conditions under which invoices must be paid. They may be identified as ordinary terms or advanced dating.

Ordinary terms. There are five major types of terms given to retailers when purchasing goods: net, F.O.B., F.A.S., C.I.F., and C.O.D. These are discussed below.

1. **Net.** Terms such as *net 30* mean that payment of the invoice must be made within 30 days of the invoice date.

2. **F.O.B. (free on board).** This means that merchandise is placed on board a truck, a railroad car, or an airplane. Title to the goods passes from seller to buyer at the F.O.B. point. The merchandise is the responsibility of the supplier until then. For example, in the case of F.O.B. factory, the supplier ceases to assume responsibility after the merchandise leaves the factory dock. In the case of F.O.B. destination, the supplier assumes responsibility until the merchandise reaches the docking point of the retailer.

3. **F.A.S. (free alongside ship)** at a named port means that the seller quotes a price for the goods, including charges for delivery alongside a vessel. The seller handles the cost of loading. The cost of unloading, ocean transportation, and insurance is paid by the buyer.

4. **C.I.F. (cost, insurance, and freight)** to a named destination means that the seller quotes a price including all transportation, insurance, and miscellaneous expenses.

5. **C.O.D. (cash on delivery).** These terms may be used when the supplier is unfamiliar with the retailer or when the retailer may be a poor credit risk. In essence, the supplier is saying to the retailer that it is taking no chances—first the payment, then the goods.

Advanced dating. Sometimes in order to encourage a retailer to purchase goods early or to entice it to purchase their goods, vendors will use advanced dating. This gives the retailer extra time in which to pay the bill. It allows the retailer to save inventory costs because the vendor is actually carrying the cost of the inventory for a period of time.

1. **Extra dating.** One type of extra dating is expressed as 2/10-60x n/30 (x stands for extra). In this case, the retailer has 70 days from the date of the invoice in which to take the discount (10 days + 60 days) or 90 days in total in which to pay the bill. Notice that the retailer has 60 extra days before the ordinary dating of 2/10, n/30 begins. If in Box 11.5, 2/10 60x n/30 appeared in place of 2/10, n/30, then for the purpose of taking the discount, the invoice date would change from May 6 to July 6.

2. **EOM (end of month) dating.** Under EOM dating, the ordinary period does not begin until the end of the month of the date shown on the invoice. For example, an invoice dated September 2, with terms of 2/10 EOM n/30, would mean that the cash discount could be taken through October 10. In other words, for purposes of taking the discount, the new invoice date becomes September 30 (EOM), and the retailer is given another 10 days beyond that. Because the net date calls for 30 days, the bill would have to be paid by October 30. The cutoff point for EOM dating is the 26th of the month. Any date on or after the 26th is treated as though the goods were received in the following month.

3. **ROG (receipt of goods) dating.** Under ROG dating, the terms of the discount do not begin until the goods are received in the store. For example, if an invoice were dated September 2, showing 2/10 ROG n/30, and if the goods were received by September 10, the store could take the discount if it paid any time before September 20. If the retailer chose not to take the discount, the bill would have to be paid by October 5, because the net period is measured from the date of the invoice.

4. **Anticipation discount.** Under the dating policies just described, the retailer has no incentive to pay an invoice until the last day of the discount period. Anticipation discounts are given by some vendors as an incentive for early payment in the form of a percentage rate per year. For example, terms are 2/10-60x, n/30 EOM, 12 percent anticipation on an invoice for $900 dated September 18. Note that the 60 extra days start

on October 1 (EOM) and end on November 29. The invoice is due December 8 if the cash discount is taken and due in full on December 28. What would be the amount due if the invoice was paid on October 1?

$$\text{Cash discount} = \$900 \times 0.02 = \$18$$
$$\text{Invoice less discount} = \$900 - \$18 = \$882$$

The anticipation is 12 percent per year. The invoice is paid 90 days before it is due. Therefore:

$$\text{Anticipation} = \$882 \times 0.12/4 \text{ (90 days early/360 days per year gives the four for the denominator)} = \$26.46$$
$$\text{Net invoice} = \$882 - \$26.46 = \$855.54$$

We conclude this chapter with a look at the legal environment of vendor relationships and merchandising.

THE LEGAL ENVIRONMENT OF VENDOR RELATIONS

Antitrust Laws and the *Uniform Commercial Code*

There are several important dimensions to the legal environment of vendor relations including aspects of antitrust laws and the **Uniform Commercial Code.**

Exclusive dealing. **Exclusive dealing** occurs when a retailer agrees with a supplier not to sell its competitor's product. Under Section 3 of the Sherman Act, this practice is only illegal when it creates a monopoly or substantially lessens competition. However, often a weak manufacturer has to offer one-way exclusive dealing arrangements to get shelf space at the retail level. This occurred when Ben & Jerry's was a new ice cream company trying to break into the market and Häagen-Dazs blocked some of the deals Ben & Jerry's was trying to make with different retailers. Arrangements in which there is no expectation of reciprocal favors are legal. Exclusive dealing agreements, when done in good faith, can help both the retailer and the supplier. However, these arrangements are illegal if the agreement prevents competitive products from gaining a larger share of the market.

Exclusive territories and restricted distribution. A supplier may grant a retailer an exclusive right to sell the supplier's product within a specified geographic area. Essentially this leads to a geographic monopoly for the retailer. The courts have tended to hold **exclusive territories** illegal when other retailers have no access to similar products and therefore cannot compete. Recognize that territorial agreements among competing retailers are almost always a restraint of trade and illegal under the Sherman Act.

Tying contracts. In a **tying contract,** the supplier allows the retailer to purchase a product or products only on the condition that the retailer also buys other specific items from the supplier. Sometimes, to carry one or two of the supplier's products, retailers are required to handle the full line. Tying arrangements have been found to be in violation of Section 3 of the Clayton Act, Section 1 and 3 of the Sherman Act, and Section 5 of the FTC Act.

Refusal to deal. Normally, both a supplier and a retailer have the right to deal or **refuse to deal** with anyone those choose. However, there are exceptions to this general rule when there is evidence of anticompetitive conduct. A supplier may refuse to sell to a particular retailer, but it cannot do so for the sole purpose of benefiting a competing retailer.

The Legal Environment Affecting Merchandise

The *Uniform Commercial Code* defines retailers' rights and responsibilities with respect to product warranties. It states that in the sale of goods, the **warranty** is an obligation of the seller with respect to the products that have been sold. Retailers are responsible for selling merchandise that has a good title, is of proper quality, and is free from defects.

Implied warranties. Under the **warranty of merchantability,** goods must be adequate for the ordinary purposes for which they are used. If a retailer knows this purpose and if the customer is dependent on the retailer's skill and judgment to select goods suitable for that particular use, an implied **warranty of fitness for a particular purpose** is created. **Warranty of title** is an implied warranty. In any sale, buyers expect retailers to convey a good title to them, and they expect retailers to have the right to sell goods.

Express warranties. When retailers make statements of fact or promises about a product and buyers might reasonably rely on these facts or promises, an **express warranty** is created. There is a fine line between statements of fact or promises and mere sales talk about value. Often the distinction is made on the basis of whether or not the statements made during a sale are an expression of opinion or fact.

The Magnuson-Moss Warranty Act. Passed in 1975 this act is designed to ensure that consumers have accurate, understandable, and readily available information about product warranties. Retailers are required to give this information to customers before they buy a product. The terms of the warranty must be disclosed by retailers in a clear manner. They also must provide a procedure for handling complaints by customers.

Product liability. Concern for the safety of consumers places an increasing burden on both manufacturers and retailers. Firms are being forced to find ways of increasing the safety of their products and of giving warnings of dangers involved in using them. Retailers under Section 15 of the **Consumer Products Safety Act** have a specific responsibility to monitor the safety of the products they sell. They have a duty to warn consumers whenever they have knowledge of a product's dangerous condition and when it appears likely that consumers may not discover the danger for themselves. Retailers may be liable for injuries caused by defective products.

If reasonable care is not exercised in the manufacture and sale of products and in the issuance of warnings about them, a seller may be liable on the basis of **negligence.** If an injury is sustained by a customer who uses a product and the court rules that the retailer should have foreseen the possibility of injury, the retailer can be held liable. Retailers may publicly misrepresent a product through advertising, selling, or labeling. If so, they are subject to liability for any physical damage sustained by customers who rely on the **misrepresentation.** In most states, suits can be brought because of a **breach of implied or expressed warranties** based only on proof that the product was defective and was the proximate cause of injury. Statements and promises made in advertising may constitute an express warranty.

There are numerous other laws dealing with the sale of different kinds of products ranging from guns to alcohol to pesticides and pharmaceuticals. For example, a Florida jury recently ordered Kmart to pay a woman $12.5 million who was shot by her former boyfriend with a firearm purchased at a Kmart store.[9] The jury found that the firm was negligent when it sold the weapon because the individual was so drunk he could not legibly fill out the form required by law of all gun purchasers. The form was completed by a clerk.

RUSSELL-NEWMAN—REVISITED: PARTNERSHIPS AND RELATIONSHIP MARKETING

To grow and prosper in the highly competitive global retailing environment of the next century, retailers and vendors alike must change and adapt or die. Dun & Bradstreet Corporation reported that in one year, 562 apparel and textile firms went out of business. Like other vendors, Russell-Newman is pursuing several initiatives to grow and prosper.

The company has both manufactured and distributed ladies' apparel to every major department store and discounter in the United States and Mexico. It entered a new segment of the business in 1994 with the formation of a men's division that produces men's robes under the

Cypress label. The robe line includes updated traditional styles in cotton terry cloth fabrics. James Martino, president, predicted that the company would do $4 million worth of business at wholesale its first year. Men's robes are targeted to be sold to moderate-priced and better department stores nationwide.[10]

The company continues to seek manufacturing relationships with textile mills worldwide in an effort to remain a low-cost producer. It was named importer of the year by the International Trade Association of Dallas–Fort Worth.[11] Merchandise is now imported from Brazil, Turkey, Egypt, China, Pakistan, Honduras, and Guatemala. Mr. Martino says that the company is looking to add Mexican opeations to its existing sources in Central America.[12] The North American Free Trade Agreement (NAFTA) makes investment in manufacturing in Mexico more convenient and easier and also opens the possibility of new markets.

Finding new accounts and new markets is another avenue to survival for vendors. In 1995 Tony Hilfiger Corporation licensed Russell-Newman's Cypress Apparel Group to manufacture and distribute men's robes, loungewear, and sleepwear under the Hilfiger label. Cypress targets the line to current Hilfiger department store and specialty store accounts. The president of Cypress's Hilfiger Division expected to pick up some 400 of these retailers.[13]

The company will continue to seek partnership arrangements that work to the benefit of both retailer and vendor. For example, Russell-Newman is very proud of the partnership it has developed with Dillard Department Stores, which is based in Little Rock, Arkansas. Since 1990 the company has been the exclusive supplier of women's terry cloth robes to the giant retailer. Every year and in the truest sense of partnership, margins have increased significantly on the line for both companies as each has lived up to the "partnership agreement." In October, these two firms sit down and map out their strategies together for the following fall and holiday season months before the first delivery of merchandise.

1. **What other strategies for growth and profitability would you suggest for Russell-Newman Inc.?**

Summary

Retailers should be able to understand what specific merchandise should be carried to satisfy the needs and wants of the consumer. Assortment planning consists of the dollar or unit purchases by item or by groups of items. Merchandise budgeting and assortment planning figures should produce similar results.

While the basic stock list gives a breakdown of staple merchandise, the model stock plan is used for purchasing seasonal and fashion items. Retailers keep track of what has and has not sold by using either periodic control or perpetual control systems. When and how much inventory a retailer reorders depends heavily on the control system.

Retail buyers use information technology to help provide data about products, vendors, and forward buying choices. To save time and money, buying offices are used by most medium-sized and small retailers. The most common type is the independent office from which a group of noncompeting client stores purchase professional services.

Large and small retailers are now developing strategic partnerships with suppliers in order to deliver the right product to the retailer at the right time. These changes are partly the result of advances in computer technology and the increasing relative power of large retailers.

Not only must the retailer and supplier agree on the price and amount of merchandise to be bought or sold, but the terms of sale and terms of payment must be agreed on as well. Discounts offered by the supplier affect the actual price paid by the retailer.

Globalization has altered retail supply channels in an effort to optimize inventory investment and customer service in an international market. Supply chain strategies are being developed that have global capacities but are tailored to specific markets. Along with all the changes in assortment planning and vendor relations, retailers must also pay close attention to the legal environment surrounding vendor relationships and merchandising. Exclusive dealings, tying contracts, and warranties are major legal issues.

KEY TERMS AND CONCEPTS

Anticipation discount, 445

Basic low stock, 423

Basic stock, 427

Basic stock list, 415

Breach of warranty, 448

Buying period, 423

Buying services, 428

Central buying office, 428

C.I.F., 445

C.O.D., 445

Commission buying office, 428

Consumer Products Safety Act, 448

Cooperatively owned office, 428

Cumulative discount, 443

Delivery or lead time, 423

Demand communication, 438

Electronic data interchange (EDI), 430

EOM, 445

Exclusive dealing, 446

Exclusive territories (restricted distribution), 446

Express warranty, 447

F.A.S., 444

F.O.B., 444

Forward buying, 427

Independent office, 428

Information flow, 439

Inspection system, 422

Just-in-time delivery, 438

Just-in-time manufacturing, 438

Logistics, 440

Management services, 429

Maximum operating stock, 423

Merchandise flow, 439

Merchandise systems, 439

Minimum selection stock, 423

Misrepresentation, 448

Model stock plan, 416

Negligence, 448

Periodic control system, 422

Perpetual control system, 422

Point-of-sale (POS) system, 440

Product liability, 448

Quantity discounts, 442

Quick response (QR) systems, 430

QUESTIONS

1. What would be the characteristics of an assortment plan for men's hats? Give the characteristics for power hand tools.

2. Discuss a store's image in relation to the selection of merchandise by buyers.

3. What is the basis for merchandise classification? Why is it done this way?

4. What are the implications of the implied warranties of the warranty of merchantability, warranty of title, and express warranties? Explain each.

5. What are the components of supply chain management? Why is it such an important factor for retailers?

6. Some merchants shun the use of any type of unit control system. Under what conditions, if any, do you think this is justified? Which kind of unit control system best fits the various retail inventory situations (for example, consumer electronics, nuts and bolts, stoves, dresses, and so on)?

7. Describe the process that allows a clothing retailer to know what to buy at market. What factors may make her pass up the current styles?

8. Compare the periodic control system to the perpetual control system. How do they differ? How are they similar?

9. How could a supplier salesperson be more helpful to a retailer than a trip to market?

10. What preparations should a retailer make before going to market? What are his major considerations? What role do salespeople and consumers play in the choices?

SITUATIONS

1. You have recently been hired to manage a Western wear shop doing $640,000 of sales a year. Because your experience has been with a large chain operation, you feel that the store needs to improve its merchandise planning and control. Specifically, you want to initiate open-to-buy and assortment planning. Before implementing your ideas, you ask the owner for his opinion. To your surprise, he is against your ideas, feeling that

your system is unnecessarily elaborate for a store of this size. Describe the merchandise plan you think is appropriate.

2. You are the buyer for a large retail store. A vendor has offered you the choice of the following terms of sale on July 2, with a delivery date of July 20:

5/10 n/30 EOM;

2/20 n/30 with trade discounts of 1 percent and 3 percent;

3/10 n/30 ROG with trade discounts of 1 percent and 2 percent; or

2/20 n/30 with trade discounts of 2 percent and 4 percent.

Which should you choose, and when would you pay?

CASES

CASE 11A
Planet Shoes

Assume this is February 28, and you are the shoe buyer for Thompson's, a suburban branch store of a major department chain in the Midwest. Thompson's has recently become an authorized dealership for the "Planet Shoes" line. Planet Shoes are a new concept in footwear, designed to improve and correct posture. Sales have been extremely good in one of the four styles you are carrying. You project an increasing demand based on past sales. Your merchandise manager has just given you the following unit figures about your hot-selling style. From the information below, determine the open-to-buy in units for March.

February on order	85 units
1/31 end of month inventory	180 units
2/28 planned EOM stock	240 units
Transfers-in	6 units
Returns from customers	3 units
Transfers-out	9 units
Planned sales	125 units
January stock turn	5

1. *What is the OTB for March?*

2. *Now that you have an open-to-buy in units, develop a buying plan from the following*

information: You carry this Planet Shoe style in full and half sizes, from 7½ to 11. Your width assortment is B, C, D, and E. Your past sales have indicated the following percentages within sizes: The most popular size has been 9½, which represents 19 percent of past sales. Sizes 9 and 10 followed closely, each accounting for 16 percent of total sales. About 12 percent of sales were in size 10½, and 11 percent in size 8½. Sizes 11, 8, and 7½ accounted for the remaining 26 percent of sales, with 7½ being the least popular size. In terms of percentage of sales attributed to widths, D is the least popular with 49 percent, and C width accounts for 30 percent. Because the owner has a B width shoe, he has made it a policy to carry at least two pairs of shoes in B width for every size. Now that you have made your assortment plan, you are almost ready to order. Your vendor sells the shoes to you at $75 per unit. Shipping terms are F.O.B. destination. Cost of shipping per unit is $1.05.

3. *What is your true total cost per unit?*

4. *What is your open-to-buy in dollars?*

5. *Your initial markup for Planet Shoes is 52 percent. What is your unit retail selling*

price, if your retail price ending policy calls for even or half-dollar amounts?

6. On the basis of your answer to question 5, what is the total retail value of your open-to-buy?

7. It is now the middle of April. You have to begin planning for summer stock. Sales for this style of Planet Shoes have been less than your projections. You need to turn over 33 percent of your remaining stock. What is your plan for reducing stock and increasing your open-to-buy? Formulate a plan of action, and be prepared to justify it to your divisional merchandise manager.

CASE 11B
Engblon's Inc.

Engblon's policy is to take advantage of every discount available. The invoice shown in Box 11.6 describes a transaction between the retailer and a vendor. Assume that Engblon's makes a payment on October 5.

1. For what amount will the payment check be written?

2. On which day may payment be made with no interest penalty charged to Engblon's?

11.6 INVOICE FOR ENGBLON'S INC.

Fashion Apparel
1427 LeForge
Ypsilanti, Michigan

Invoice No. B8928

Terms:
Trade discount Less: 40-10. Quantity discount: 3 percent. Cash discount: 3/10 EOM net 30.

Date: 9/16/97

Sold to: Engblon's
1258 W. Prospect
Detroit, Michigan

Customer Order No. V6372

Air Freight: 8203 F.O.B. factory

Stock	Description	Quantity	Price	Amount
56211	Pant suits	226	$150.00	$33,900.00
56210	Slacks	71	40.00	2,840.00
56301	Blouses	89	35.00	3,115.00
56270	Skirts	42	35.50	1,491.00
				$41,346.00
Transportation				265.00
Total				$41,611.00

Received 9/20/97 Mark Smith, Buyer

6543217

CHAPTER

12

Chapter Goals

After reading this chapter, you should be able to:

- Define price.
- Understand the concept of elasticity and supply and demand curves.
- Describe market structures facing retailers.
- Explain the importance of pricing.
- Comprehend the fundamental pricing strategy alternatives.
- Understand markdown strategies and psychological pricing.
- Perform pricing calculations.
- Explain the federal legal environment of pricing.

Pricing Merchandise

TOYS 'R' US: COMPETING WITH EVERYDAY LOW PRICE

In today's retail environment, it is essential that a merchant obtain and maintain a competitive advantage. One retailer that has been particularly successful in doing this is Toys 'R' Us. The company began with the premise that customers wanted value for their dollar. In response, Toys 'R' Us was one of the pioneers of the everyday low price (EDLP) policy. However, unlike some other retailers that followed an EDLP strategy, Toys 'R' Us maintained consistently high quality with recognizable brands. The strategy was to assure customers that the everyday price would be 10 to 15 percent below that of other retailers carrying the same brands.

In thirty years, Toys 'R' Us grew from an idea to over 800 toy stores, 300 children's book shops, and 200 children's clothing stores. Today, the dominance of Toys 'R' Us in its category is indicated by the fact that it sells over 20 percent of all toys in the United States. The company has recorded fifteen years of consecutive sales and earnings growth, averaging over 25 percent compounded annually.

Toys 'R' Us concentrates on providing value to customers by focusing on the products and services that are important to them. For instance, the EDLP strategy simplifies the decision-making process. Consumers are assured that the products Toys 'R' Us carries are competitively priced, and this saves the customer time in gathering information about competing retailers and shopping time as well. However, price is only one component of value, which also consists of product features, service, and shopping convenience. Service and price are foremost in consumers' minds today, partly because product quality is very similar and many retailers handle the same brands.[1] Having a wide variety and deep assortments in one place adds to the value equation for Toys 'R' Us. The EDLP strategy includes using promotions linked to coupons, free-with-purchase offers, and heavy merchandising efforts to stimulate sales, particularly during holiday seasons.

The company continues to expand at a rapid pace. The expansion includes not only Toys 'R' Us stores but other formats such as Books 'R' Us children's book shops within Toys 'R' Us and Kids 'R' Us children's clothing stores. Toys 'R' Us expects to open new stores in the United States at a significant pace for the next five years.[2] It also expects to experiment with new formats, such as it has done with Books 'R' Us, including construction toys, stuffed animals, and large outdoor playsets. Finally, Toys 'R' Us is implementing a new idea in retailing, the kids-only strip center. Plans in Johnson City, New York, call for adding 80,000 feet of floor space and two related retailers to an existing center that has a Toys 'R' Us and a Kids 'R' Us store.

Toys 'R' Us has been successful by concentrating on a single market and strategy that has taken it to a dominant position its its category. Management is committed to continued expansion through both existing and new formats that target children's products.

1. **What is the future of price as a key motivator for customer buying?**
2. **What elements combine with price to make Toys 'R' Us successful?**
3. **Contrast an EDLP strategy to one that focuses on full margin pricing with regular or seasonal reduced price sales.**

INTRODUCTION

Retailers have had to adapt to changing consumer expectations and values in the 1990s. Customers today are much more value-conscious than they were in the 1980s. Quality, selection, and availability, all at the *best price,* form today's new value equation. Competition is growing more intense as retailers engage in a fierce battle for market share and consumer loyalty. In the absence of market expansion from population growth or increasing personal income, sales increases for individual retailers can come only by taking business away from the competition.[3] With price as a major success factor, who will win the battle? Most likely it will be those that cut costs without cutting service and that use technology intelligently to support buying, distribution, and transportation systems to allow them to turn the product faster. In addition, successful retailers will develop profitable partnerships with vendors and manufacturers worldwide allowing merchandise cost control. Many will look to international markets for opportunities where price competition might not be as intense.

Most industry observers believe that consumers will remain cautious into the next century. In addition, customers often now see shopping as time-consuming and frustrating.[4] Today's consumers are spending less time shopping than they did in 1990. One-stop shopping is in vogue, as is shopping at outlet malls. Because of the desire for value, narrow-line price-oriented stores will face intense competition from traditional broad-line retailers that adopt lower price strategies. Recent sales gains by these retailers are attributed largely to value pricing. Similarly, supermarkets and department stores are finding ways to compete with the price-oriented warehouse clubs. Supermarkets offer larger packages of goods at lower unit prices, and department stores offer more value-based private-label merchandise.[5]

Price Is Important

For years, many retailers did not consider pricing as important as other major aspects of the business. Buying, advertising, and administrative and control decisions were given higher priority. This reluctance to give price its proper due resulted in part from retailers' inability to understand the role of price. If, for example, retailers did a more effective job of advertising than their competitors, they knew they could anticipate increased sales volume.

Merchants, however, were not sure they could increase sales by using the same kind of decision making in pricing. It was easy for competitors to respond to price changes in a way that often had adverse effects on their own businesses. When competitors responded by meeting price changes, nobody had an advantage; and if price changes resulted in retail price wars, all merchants suffered.

Today price is a major strategic weapon for many retailers. The pricing decision is a complex one. Basic economic concepts provide an important foundation for fundamental pricing strategies. The retailer must also establish markdown strategies and decide what psychological price concepts might be considered. Finally, an understanding of the mechanics of making pricing calculations is critical. See Figure 12.1.

Part of the reason pricing has a new role as an important variable in decision making is because today's consumers are very price-conscious. Even though many people have more money than they have had at any other time in their lives, they look for good buys. Bargain-conscious behavior seems to be acceptable at all income levels. It has become almost a status symbol to be able to say, "I got it on sale!" Bargain consciousness—together with increases in mobility, sophistication, and education—has produced such price-discriminating consumers that the idea of a list price may be obsolete. For a number of years now, consumers have been bombarded with price as the leading product and/or store feature, and they have been conditioned to look for price first. In the 1980s Sears' customers learned they had only to wait a few weeks and their choice of product would be on sale; consequently, margins plummeted as sales at original markup shrank. At the same time stores like Toys 'R' Us offered greatly increased selections and low price, while Kmart and Wal-Mart taught us all that if we wanted to accept less service, convenience, and selection, a lower price was available.

FIGURE 12.1

Many factors go
into the pricing
decision.

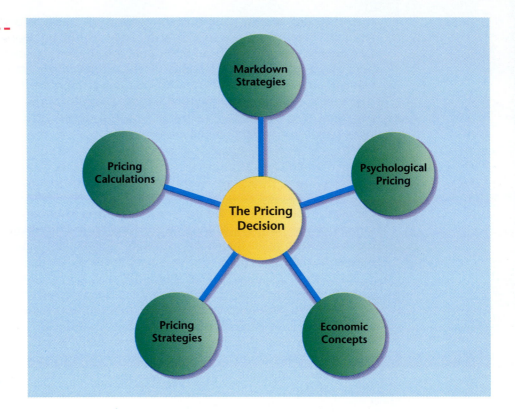

Obviously, not everyone buys by price. Many stores, particularly those offering more exclusive goods or those perceived as being of higher quality, are able to attract customers despite a higher than usual markup. The store's name, the services offered, location, and other considerations come into play. Furthermore, some kinds of merchandise are less susceptible to being purchased on the basis of price. The point, however, is that retailers can no longer set prices in the traditional way; today, a manager cannot afford to adopt a passive attitude toward price and concentrate only on promotion, services, displays, and layouts.

Pricing strategies and policies for most retail stores depend on store image, targeted customers, competition, general level of prices, cost and kind of merchandise, and their advertising and personal selling programs. For example, if the store has an image of selling medium- to high-quality merchandise at full price and the clientele expects and purchases this quality of product along with exceptional service, it could be disastrous to attempt to sell at low prices. The customers would reject the merchandise, causing a shift in the image of the store. The reverse is also true. If the retailer "trades up" to a point at which customers object because they cannot afford the new prices, the store's image will change, causing a downturn in sales. Retailers in Manhattan like

Gimbel's, Bonwit Teller, and Korvette's once drew millions of shoppers, but over the years they went out of business as consumers' tastes changed and Manhattan's real estate became more expensive.[6]

New dimensions of price. To understand that price has assumed new dimensions for retailers, one has only to observe the number of advertisements giving prices before, during, and after a season; or witness the dramatic inroads to the sales and profits of more traditional retailers made by discount merchandisers, category killer stores, and warehouse clubs that compete primarily on a price basis. Furthermore, when one adds price reductions resulting from factors such as profit reductions, promotional giveaways, and decreased services, one understands even better why retailing is as competitive as it is. For example, as personal computers became more standard, consumers started looking for better prices and value, and the name-brand manufacturers and their vendors had little choice but to respond. Not only did prices fall, but the margins were low, which meant that prices stayed low even as the technologies changed and as features and services were improved. As gross margins fell and the difference between retail price and the cost of supplies got smaller, many retailers were forced to leave the business.[7]

Price Defined

By definition, **price** is the value assigned to something bought, sold, or offered for sale expressed in terms of monetary units. In pricing merchandise, retailers must price goods such that:

- They sell at a satisfactory rate
- Inventory costs and expenses are covered
- A desired profit is made
- Customers are treated fairly
- They can be competitive with stores attempting to serve the same target market

Costco Wholesale Corporation and The Price Company combined to form Price Costco, a major player in the membership warehouse format. The strategy of this format is to stock relatively few SKUs, have very low prices, and require bulk purchases for lower-priced items. The company is looking to international expansion. In addition to operations in Canada, it has formed joint ventures in Korea and Taiwan.

ECONOMIC CONCEPTS

Retail managers rely a great deal on their knowledge of customers and their previous experience in pricing merchandise. In addition to this, an understanding of fundamental pricing principles is essential. We begin with a look at some basic economic concepts.

Supply and Demand Concepts

One way that prices in the marketplace can be understood is by reference to the concepts of supply and demand. *Supply* is the amount of goods offered for sale at various prices. *Demand* is the amount of goods that people will be willing to buy at various prices. In the long run the price of a product will be at the point where the amount offered for sale at a given price equals the amount demanded at the same price. This idea is the basis for supply and demand curves, as shown in Figure 12.2. It is characteristic of a supply curve that the higher the price at which customers are willing to purchase a product, the greater the amount of the product retailers will be willing to provide. In the case of a demand curve, the lower the price at which retailers are willing to provide a product, the more of the product the customers will want. In our example, at a market price for the unit at $60, the retailer would be willing to supply 145 units, but customers would buy only 115. When Wal-Mart advertises "falling prices," it is attempting to increase volume. Its esti-

FIGURE 12.2

Supply and demand curves.

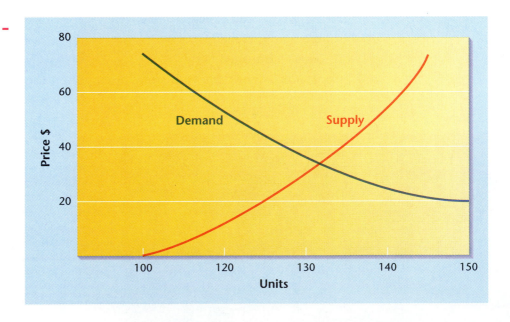

mate of the shape of the demand curve would determine the additional sales forecasted. In the above example, lowering the price from $60 to $20 would increase units demanded to 150. Except the retailer would be willing to supply only 115 units at the lower price. So, total revenue would fall from $6,900 ($60 × 115 units) to $3,000 ($20 × 150 units). See Figure 12.2. This would indicate that the demand curve is inelastic as explained next.

Elasticity of demand. The idea of price sensitivity provides a way of thinking about how demand affects pricing. The sensitivity of demand to changes in price can be described as either inelastic or elastic. Demand is said to be **inelastic** when a large percentage change in price brings about a relatively small percentage change in sales. On the other hand, demand is said to be **elastic** when a small percentage change in price brings about a relatively large percentage change in sales. We can more easily see the difference by closely examining Figure 12.3.

FIGURE 12.3 ELASTIC AND INELASTIC DEMAND CURVES.

The formula for determining elasticity is as follows (*E* stands for *elasticity*, *Q* stands for *quantity*, and *P* stands for *price*):

$$E = \frac{\% \text{ change in } Q}{\% \text{ change in } P}$$

Unitary elasticity exists if the formula yields *E* = 1. If *E* > 1, demand is said to be elastic, and if *E* < 1, it is inelastic.

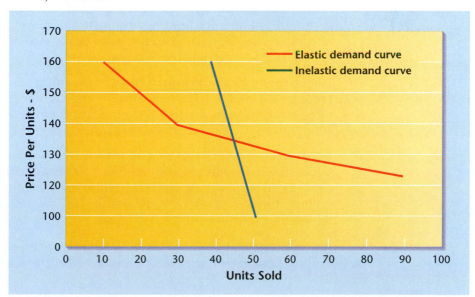

Let us discuss the implications of these figures with respect to the home electronics industry. Figure 12.3 shows that if an inelastic curve described the demand for home electronics, then no matter how the price of the products changed, there would be little change in the quantities sold. Circuit City knows there would be no reason to lower price because volume would not increase. However, raising price would not lower demand very much. However, if the demand for home electronics is elastic, then if the price of the products changed even a small amount, the quantity demanded would change quite a bit. Common sense tells us that more elastic accurately reflects the demand for home electronics. For example, as the price of video camcorders has fallen, demand from consumers at all income levels has increased dramatically.

Retailers that face elastic demand curves are competing in situations where demand is significantly sensitive to the price of their products. That is the case faced by most retailers. The major factors that influence the degree of price sensitivity include:

- **Availability of substitutes** (if good substitutes are available, the demand for a given product can be very sensitive to price changes). If the price goes up, many consumers will seek a substitute. The availability of substitutes applies as much to stores as it does to products within the store. If a customer wants a Weber grill and the price is higher in one store than in another, the customer does not have to select a substitute product.

- **Relative price of the product** (the higher the price of the product, the greater the tendency toward price sensitivity—greater elasticity). The retailer might raise the price of a pen from $0.89 to $0.98 (a 10% percent increase) and not meet much resistance. However, raising the price of a camcorder $890 to $980, the same percentage increase, might completely kill the possibility of selling the item.

- **Importance of the product to the consumer** (the greater the importance of the product, the less sensitive the consumer will be to price—more inelastic). A pharmacy selling medical equipment may find less sensitivity to its equipment than to over-the-counter medications.

- **Income characteristics of the purchasers** (if purchasers come from a high-income group, the consumer demand is more likely to be less sensitive to price changes than if the purchasers came from a lower-income group). However, many consumers with high income are very value-conscious and pay close attention to price.

Products that typically have elastic industry demand curves include home electronics, automobiles, and jewelry. On the other hand, staple groceries and gasoline have inelastic demand curves.

PRICE STRATEGIES

To set prices effectively, a retailer must determine the role price will play in the business. A store that does not have clear expectations for pricing policies continually fights shadows. A policy of reacting to other merchants' price strategies causes a retailer to lose money and confuses customers. Fundamental to establishing a strategy is deciding how the store will position itself with respect to pricing and the market. There are three fundamental pricing strategies that a store can take: pricing under the market, above the market, or at the market. The retailer's choice can be significantly influenced by the strategy of the manufacturers of the goods the retailer carries. See Box 12.1.

Pricing under the Market

Most merchants have preconceived ideas of the role of price. Some use it to encourage customers to come into their stores. In other words, they appeal to bargain-conscious shoppers by pricing their products **under the market.**

BOX 12.1   MANUFACTURER'S PRODUCT INTRODUCTION PRICING: SKIMMING VERSUS PENETRATION

Just as stores think about the impact of below the market, at the market, or above the market prices, when manufacturers decide to introduce a new product, they have to set a price policy. An examination of the demand curve may suggest that a high price may lead to higher profit from each sale, but to fewer units sold. Conversely, a lower price might appeal to a larger group of customers and result in a higher level of unit sales. A *skimming price policy* is more attractive if the demand is inelastic and the manufacturer wants to "skim the cream off the top" of the demand curve by selling at a high price before lowering it to appeal to more price-sensitive customers. However, the retailer may see that there are real advantages in selling the new product at as low a price as possible to capture market share from other stores.

In other cases, the manufacturer may want to price the product as low as possible in order to attract many initial customers. This is called a *penetration pricing policy*. It has the advantage of creating large market share and may keep competitors from entering the market. Again, the retailer might not want to carry products that have low margins or ones that all other stores have in stock and are advertising at a low price. It might not be seen as in the best interest of the retailer if the store is trying to attract customers with above the market pricing and a high level of service.

6543217

Furthermore, they advertise prices and promote their stores on the basis of price. There are many who believe that retailers have moved too far in their attempt to draw customers with an undermarket price strategy.

Retail prices have declined for a number of years in real dollars. As suggested above, retailers have contributed to the downward shift in prices by discounting their goods rather than balancing product features, services, and convenience in response to the market reality of value-conscious consumers, increasing competition, and a slow-growth economy. A fear of job loss associated with corporate downsizing has lowered discretionary income and consumer confidence, making customers even more value-conscious. Retailers have used off-price promotions so much that they have made consumers expect to pay less than the initial price. Price, not product features or service, has become the primary message of advertisements.[8] Some department stores sell less than 10 percent of women's apparel at the original ticketed price.

There are three ways merchants convey the image of a price store. One involves pricing goods for a lower than usual markup. This is the traditional method of discounters ranging from T. J. Maxx to Price/Costco. They accept low markups in return for increased volume coupled with concentration on expense control. A second way to convey this image is to run many sales before, during, and after selling seasons. The managers of stores who operate in this way frequently offer *leader merchandise*—products that are appealing enough to attract customers to the store. They take a low markup on these goods to generate business. A third way is with an *everyday low price (EDLP) policy.* This is based on establishing a price level that is below what the consumer might expect for the merchandise but not a level that might be associated with a discount store. A key factor in the EDLP strategy is that few price reductions are offered that customers do not wait to "shop the sales." Promotion expenses may also be lower, which allows the store to operate on a reduced margin. Dillard Department Stores is one of the companies that has been able to effectively implement the EDLP policy.

Pricing above the Market

Some retailers consistently price merchandise **above the market.** Stores that do this appeal to people who are willing to pay for exclusivity, quality, convenience, and/or service. It takes a well-conceived concept such as that of Nordstrom and Talbots in the apparel sector, Laura Ashley in home furnishings, and Brookstone in housewares to successfully carry off a strategy of pricing above the market.

Pricing at the Market

Merchants who price **at the market** believe that a significant number of customers neither look for the lowest prices nor are willing to pay the highest prices. When making a purchase, these consumers consider the convenience and attractiveness of the store, the expertise and attitude of the sales personnel, and the number and kind of services offered, as well as the price of merchandise.

After making the fundamental decision of where to price with respect to the market, managers should establish strategies that help make pricing decisions as easy and routine as possible.

Pricing to Cover Costs

Regardless of the strategy followed, all retailers hope to set prices high enough to cover costs and make a reasonable profit. The common ways of accomplishing this objective are the standard markup percentage, the cost-plus approach, and the dollar margin approach.

Standard markup percentages. Retailers in the past often relied on standard markup percentages compiled by trade associations. The U.S. Census of Retailing also publishes markup data by kind of store. The markup, for example, was usually 33⅓ percent on electric appliances, 40 percent on shoes, and 50 percent on clothing. When retailers bought goods at a standard cost and used a standard markup, they could expect that other retailers, buying the same goods and using a similar markup, would arrive at the same retail price. The effect, of course, was to reduce the role price played in retail management.

Suppliers also helped to standardize prices so that merchants could apply standard markup percentages and arrive at a sound retail price. For example, a shoe importer might offer one line of children's rubber footwear at $12.00 so that retailers could apply a standard 40 percent markup and charge about $19.95—a reasonable price for the shoes. Suppliers also encouraged price standardization by providing suggested retail prices.

Albertson's cost control and distribution efficiency allow it to compete with an everyday low-price strategy in big, clean, beautiful stores. Being a low-price leader is difficult to sustain with numerous competitors, including new store types. Kmart, Target, and Wal-Mart superstores are aggressive competitors attracting shoppers for food purchases along with general merchandise.

Over two decades of success by general merchandise discount stores and the evidence of the category dominant formats have made retail pricing more volatile. A large segment of consumers have been educated by retailers to seek low prices. To maintain market share, branded goods manufacturers have engaged retailers in discount price efforts. When a bitter price war in the competitive pet food market was consuming profits, the top U.S. pet food marketers unleashed every tactic available to keep retail prices as low as possible. They used massive trade promotion spending to encourage retailers to discount prices while quietly downsizing products to avoid wholesale price increases. The vice president of marketing for Heinz Pet Products noted that pricing for profit became a problem for everyone, and even so-called premium pet foods could no longer command premium prices.[9]

Cost-plus pricing. The **cost-plus approach** is designed to provide a floor beneath which prices cannot fall. Because a product has its cost and its expenses, any price set below the sum of the two outlays causes a loss on each item sold.

In the past, a standard markup percentage seemed justifiable and gave retailers the security of knowing that if they used this percentage correctly, they could at least cover costs and expenses and would, if expenses were controlled, probably make a profit. Increasing costs and competition have led retailers to begin to question this method of pricing. Some now believe that strict adherence to a standard markup percentage forces them to rely unduly on making a definite percentage profit on each item sold. They argue that this is an inflexible approach that leaves them vulnerable to competitors.

Dollar margin approach. An alternative to the standard percentage markup and cost-plus pricing is the **dollar margin concept.** Retailers who use this do not price to achieve a given profit on each item. Instead, they price on the basis of demand, appeal, and competition. They consider cost only when deciding whether they will buy an item. Price is set on the basis of "what the market will bear," which to retailers simply means that a given item has some particular value to customers. Sometimes this value permits retailers to make a profit; sometimes it does not. From a pricing standpoint, whether retailers do or do not make a profit on a particular item is immaterial. Their sole concern is to price the product so that it moves out of the store in a reasonable period of time. They carry some items that do not make money, otherwise known as **loss leaders,** to offer customers a complete merchandise selection. Of course, for every item that does not make money, there is the expectation that many others will.

The long-held practice of pricing some items as loss leaders was called into question in 1993. Wal-Mart Stores Inc. has, of course, an aggressive low-pricing philosophy. A state court in Arkansas ruled that the company engaged in **predatory pricing** by selling pharmacy products below cost. In Arkansas, *cost* is defined as the invoice price plus overhead. Twenty-two states have

Unfair Trade Practices Acts similar to those in Arkansas. In 1995 an appeals court overturned the Arkansas state court decision.

Probably the best way to price to cover full costs is to follow the practice of most retail chains, which operate on both a dollar margin basis and a dollar profit goal. Keeping a watchful eye on the monthly cumulative markup percentage (an indication of the success of achieving a planned percentage profit) and the dollar gross margin (an indication of the success of achieving a planned dollar profit) helps management compete realistically. It makes prices consistent with the competition's prices, customer needs, and the economics of running a business.

PSYCHOLOGICAL PRICING

Many retailers feel that consumers can be influenced by the way prices are quoted. Common use of psychology in pricing revolves around policies associated with one-price selling, the price-quality relationship, odd-number pricing, multiple-unit pricing, and oddball pricing.

The used car business has traditionally been one where the retailer had low credibility with the consumer. CarMax in Richmond, Virginia, set out to change that image with its superstore. Included in its strategy was a one-price, no-haggle, below-book-price policy. Low mileage, less than five-year-old cars, a five-day return privilege guarantee, and hundreds of cars in inventory completed the strategy.

One-Price Selling

This is the practice of selling to all customers at the same price. In some kinds of stores—such as pawnshops, used furniture stores, and flea markets—and in some countries—such as Mexico and Morocco—retailers pursue variable pricing policies, as opposed to offering merchandise at a take-it-or-leave-it price. However, most retail firms in the United States today follow a one-price policy. It is even catching on in the auto industry. New car pricing has traditionally been a mystery to consumers, with negotiating skills being the determining factor in the price the customer paid. The Saturn Division of General Motors introduced the one-price policy for its cars, and the idea has rapidly caught on among other new and used auto and boat retailers.[10] Although the one-price policy is not universally accepted,[11] from an operational standpoint, this practice saves many retailers money. Imagine, for example, the vast amounts of time salespeople have to spend bargaining with customers in the absence of a one-price policy. Additional time is spent when shelf and floor displays must be rearranged and repriced as items go on and off sale. Imagine, too, the extra training that is required to teach salespeople to be effective bargainers. Looking at it from the consumer standpoint, customers probably do not save an appreciable amount of money when they have the chance to bargain.

Price-Quality Relationship

For some consumers the decision as to whether or not a product is superior or inferior is strongly influenced by price. Such customers are suspicious of low prices and presume that high prices indicate high quality. Retailers must be aware of the possibility of consumers associating price with quality especially in some businesses where customers tend to rely on price when they are unable to judge the quality of the goods they are purchasing, such as carpets and jewelry, or when fashion is an important consideration.

It is also essential to remember that there is a bottom price for some merchandise, and no price should be set below it. If, for example, hair spray usually sells at $3.49 a can and a retailer purchases hair spray that can sell at $0.77 a can, customers may react with disbelief. They may feel that the $0.77 hair spray cannot be as effective as others. A price closer to $3.49 may, in fact, generate a greater number of sales.

Odd-Number Pricing

Odd-number pricing is the practice of ending a price in an odd number. For example, some traditional department stores end their prices with a "5," that is, $25.95, $30.95, and so on. Most New York Fifth Avenue fashion retailers use the whole dollar figure, such as $200, $300, $650. On the other hand, many discounters end their prices with a "99." The image of the store usually plays a part in determining which type to use. American retailers began to use odd prices for two reasons. First, they felt that customers were more likely to buy an item at, for example, $4.99 than at $5.00 because the first price seems less than the second. Furthermore, merchants wanted to force salespeople to use the cash register to make change, therefore limiting their opportunity to avoid ringing up a sale in order to pocket the money. Today, neither argument seems very convincing, although the practice is still in general use. There is no conclusive evidence that customers are more likely to purchase goods because of odd prices. And the argument for using odd pricing to force salespeople to make change from the cash register isn't relevant because of the practice of collecting sales taxes.

Multiple-Unit Pricing

Bundling or **multiple-unit pricing** is the practice of combining two units of a product and selling them as one; for example, two tubes of toothpaste, each retaining at $1.39, may be packaged together and sold for $2.69 in the expectation that packaging them together with a small price savings would increase sales.

Oddball Pricing

The practice of selling an assortment (related merchandise) at the same price is referred to as **oddball pricing.** For example, several different gift items may be placed on a table and priced at $78 each. The price is oddball because it bears no direct relationship to cost, desired markup, or traditional selling price of any of the items. The policy gives the illusion of low prices and consequently sells merchandise. If, as some people think, bargain-conscious customers look at the average price they spend for items rather than the price of each item, merchants can put a full line of related items together to sell at the same oddball price.

Price-Line Pricing

Another policy used by many merchants in setting retail prices is the use of price lines. **Price lines** enable retailers to offer merchandise at a limited number of prices and make it easier for customers to compare products. For example, fishing lures could be offered at $1.29, $1.39, $1.50, $2.00, $2.98, $3.49, $3.50, and so on. A retailer who chooses to carry an inventory of fishing lures at each of these prices would have three problems: (1) Too much capital could be tied up in inventory, without the necessary depth of stock, (2) salespeople could not logically justify a quality difference between lures priced so close together, and (3) consumers would be confused trying to figure out the differences. To avoid these problems lures of similar types may be priced at $3.99 for the recognizable branded goods and perhaps $2.45 for the knock-off brands.

Products that lend themselves to price lining are items that offer an adequate assortment and yet allow for significant differences in price. Clothing and furniture, for example, are frequently sold by price lines.

As a practical matter, most retailers use price-line zones. Men's sport coats may, for example, fall within three zones (a $75 to $100 zone, a $150 to $175 zone, and a $225 to $275 zone) to represent good, better, and best. Using price-line zones permits merchants to reap the advantages of price lining: providing depth of assortment along with less confusion for the customers. The price lines allow significant differences in style or quality among groups of merchandise.

Hitting the appropriate price line or zone is often critical to success. In the early 1990s the outerwear business was dominated by the active looks category. Regardless of geographical differences, retailers reported that business was driven by mixed-media designs, iridescent nylon outer shells, fur trims, and parka- and stadium-length

The Stamp of Oxford Ltd. located on High Street in Oxford, England, carries a limited line of clothing accessories in just a few price lines as well as cards for the tourists. The small boutique's owner typically visits designers to select her merchandise. The key to her success is knowing her customers very well. She often buys with a specific customer in mind and may call and offer to take an item to the customer's home on approval.

jackets. All this diversity, combined with prices that hovered in the range of $99.99 to $149.99 for most of the season, enhanced the perceived value of the product, making casual jackets the most sought-after outerwear option.[12]

There are two disadvantages of price lining. To live with supplier price increases while maintaining stable retail prices, merchants must accept decreases in gross margins. The other alternatives are to lower the quality of merchandise offered while maintaining gross margin and prices or to adjust price lines upward. Changing price lines too often creates confusion among customers, who then no longer know what price level is used by the store.

The second disadvantage of price lining concerns markdowns. Suppose, for example, that a merchant sets one price line at $65 but feels that a 10 percent markdown would move a $65 item out of the store at a satisfactory rate. If the next lowest price line is $50, the merchant has a problem. The alternatives are to segregate all sale merchandise from regular stock and price it so that it moves, run the stock in with regular merchandise and clearly indicate on the price ticket that a particular article is a sale item, or mark down to the next lowest price line.

Additional Pricing Issues

Several additional pricing issues that concern retailers include how to price new regular merchandise, pricing sale merchandise, special event pricing, and price matching policies.

Pricing new regular merchandise.
It seems as though regular price decisions should be made routinely, and to a large extent they are. A discount store manager who has thousands of items to price cannot devote too much time to any one of them. Therefore, he or she depends on a routine procedure such as the standard markup percentage.

In using the standard markup, retailers first look at costs. Gross margin percentage performance is so integral to pricing that retailers start with the cost of an article and then apply an average markup to arrive at the retail price. In other words, if a furniture retailer purchases some goods at a cost of $300 and usually receives a 40 percent markup on retail, the goods would be priced at $500. Realistically, the retailer might decrease or increase the price slightly to conform to established price lines or standard industry prices.

Some retailers are unwilling to routinize the pricing procedure, particularly those that work from a planned markup; those that sell high-priced, highly competitive, fashion-oriented goods; and those that operate small stores. Such retailers are likely to base price on their knowledge of the value customers will place on the goods.

Actually, it is unlikely that any retailers price all goods in a routine manner or price all goods individually in a completely random manner. Most use both techniques. What usually happens is that once retailers have used the standard markup percentage to give an estimate of price, they generally rely on their judgment and evaluate that price against these factors:

- The prices of the same or similar merchandise offered by competitors
- The effect of price differences on demand
- The merchandise's appeal to consumers
- The manufacturer's suggested retail price
- The price history of the merchandise
- The kind of image they want the store to maintain

Pricing sale merchandise. Many stores bring in new merchandise to sell at sale prices. The intent is to stimulate sales by attracting customers to the store. Once there, the customers may buy regular merchandise at nonsale prices. Legitimate retailers offering sale merchandise will usually price it so that they realize decreased margins and give customers greater than usual value. One retail store bought sport shirts and placed them on sale with only 7 percent markup. This was hardly enough to cover the expenses of selling the shirts, but the bargain attracted many customers to the store.

Some kinds of items make better sale, or promotional, merchandise than others. You have probably noticed that the same kinds of products are regularly offered in advertisements run by a retailer. Because customers' basic needs are similar each season, the items run in last year's ad are probably being run again this year.

Items currently selling well make the best sale merchandise. Seasonal goods, products that are well-known and/or well-advertised brands, and goods that are price-sensitive or bought frequently also make attractive sale items. Retailers try to find such traffic builders for every department of the store.

Special event pricing. Retailers often schedule special events to generate store traffic and to increase customer enthusiasm for a product category or new product. Events might range from a cooking demonstration or fashion show to a book signing. In such cases, tie-in products might have lower prices that would contribute to the overall event. The merchant typically would not attribute the lower prices to a sale, but rather would identify them as special event prices.

At the other end of the spectrum, certain events might lead to premium prices. On the weekend that Pink Floyd is in town for a concert, special merchandise—T-shirts, mugs, and the like—might be premium priced.

Price matching plans. In the 1980s retailers were forced to respond to the growing bargain consciousness of consumers, who compared prices often and waited for sales to make purchases, thus increasing competition. One way to respond was to institute price matching policies. The policies typically require customers to have a competitor's advertisement showing a lower price for an identical item.

Some stores also offer to match or beat their competitor's advertised prices for thirty days after a purchase.[13] Few consumers collect on the price guarantees. This may be because prices are truly competitive or more likely because most customers don't go to the trouble to do the research to get what they believe will be only a small price difference.

Advertising a price matching policy has been found to work to the advantage of the retailer. One research study concluded that offering to match a competitor's price made a store seem more attractive to as many as two out of three customers. However, some question the fairness of a policy that allows retailers to have a special price only for those who are careful comparison shoppers.

MARKDOWN STRATEGIES

Because merchandise is not always bought correctly, markdowns are common. Furthermore, new products arrive frequently from manufacturers, and retailers must move old stocks out, via markdowns, to make room for incoming items.

When and How Much?

In taking markdowns, retailers must consider both the timing and the amount. Timing is important because minimal markdowns may be sufficient if they are taken at an appropriate time. There is no standard rule one can apply to decide how much of a markdown to take. However, retailers generally feel that to activate demand, the first markdown on staple goods should be at least 10 percent. They also feel that reductions greater than 25 percent unnecessarily eat into profits. For fashion goods anything less than an initial markdown of 20 or 25 percent may not stimulate customer demand. It often takes at least a 50 percent markdown to move goods at the end of the season.

Markdowns should be taken when sales have peaked and appear to be softening. At this time, there is probably still enough demand for the item to move well with only a slight markdown. That is why markdowns in summer ready-to-wear clothing are taken as early as mid-July—at a time when most of us feel summer is only beginning. Retailers know that consumers have already bought a

Markdowns can be used to generate traffic and increase sales. The markdown is much more effective when combined with other elements of the retail mix. Product knowledge used by a salesperson to explain customer benefits, a recognized brand name, and a trusted store combined with sale pricing are powerful sales tools.

12.2 MARKDOWN REMINDER CARD[14]

1. Balanced buying
Do you:

Strive to maintain an open-to-buy position in all classifications?

Know what your customers want?

Know the best styles, colors, prices, fabrics, and patterns?

Know stock on hand and on order?

Study information on rate of sale?

2. Careful promotional buying
Check the following:

Is it in the best selling price line or below?

Is it in the best selling sizes?

Is it in the best selling colors and styles?

Is the quality right?

Is the timing for promotion correct?

After the sale, will the merchandise fit into regular stock?

3. Well-timed deliveries
Do you:

Check delivery dates?

Work closely with manufacturers?

Buy early enough to ensure merchandise arrival when needed?

Know the selling season for each item?

Know when to stop reorders?

4. Good selling
Do you:

Check to see that items are on the selling floor?

Keep salespeople well informed through weekly meetings?

Check location of merchandise and its presentation by salespeople?

6543217

substantial portion of their summer clothes by then, so they offer new or promotional merchandise and begin to prepare for the fall season.

Controlling Markdowns

Equally important to recognizing when to take markdowns and in what amount is finding ways to control them. To control markdowns means first understanding why they occur. Box 12.2 analyzes how markdowns can be controlled.

Retaliation to a Special Sale

In today's competitive world, retailers are constantly emphasizing price in newspapers, in handouts, on radio, and in other media. Almost every week, merchants can see a competitor advertising a special sale in which there is a price reduction on products identical to their own. The problem facing retailers is to decide whether to retaliate by meeting or bettering the advertised price.

As a matter of policy, most retailers are inclined to permit competitors to have their sales and hope that competitors will permit them to have theirs. There is some justification for doing business this way, considering the disadvantages of price retaliation: Most customers shop for individual sale items at all stores offering them but tend to give continued patronage to a store on the basis of overall strategies relative to price, buying, and promotions. However, store loyalty has decayed for a myriad of reasons, including bank credit cards, customer mobility, and self-service.

End-of-Season Pricing

Anyone in retailing knows that toward the end of a selling season old merchandise hangs heavy on one's hands. For example, imagine that you are in women's shoes and have been selling light colors and whites during the last few months. Around the first of July, the store receives its first fall offerings, which are suedes, in rich oranges, browns, and blues. You find this merchandise exciting, new, and clean. Your customers' reaction to the shoes will probably be the same as your own. Suddenly, the light colors and whites seem less attractive, and you stop showing them to customers, who are beginning to demand the new merchandise. Retailers must be alert to this eventuality and begin moving products early by taking slight markdowns and using whatever promotional methods are necessary. When movement has lost substantial momentum and consumers are uninterested in buying the merchandise, only large markdowns will generate sales. In the apparel business it is not unusual for half of the merchandise to be sold at a 50 percent markdown. But old goods simply tie up inventory dollars and will not move without a major price reduction.

MARKUPS AND MARKDOWNS USED IN SETTING PRICES

We have discussed the concepts and terms involved in retail pricing. To really understand them it is important for you to know the mechanics of pricing calculations. This section leads you through the basics. You will recognize the terms from the above discussion.

Students of retailing are often confused by two groups of terms. Those in the first group shown below concern the marking up and marking down of merchandise and the actual setting of prices. These terms include *original markup, additional markup, markup cancellation,* and *net markdown.* The terms in the second group also concern markup, but they are used specifically in planning for and analyzing markup performance. These terms include *planned markup* and *cumulative markup*.

Group 1 *(Used in Pricing)*	*Group 2* *(Used in Planning Pricing)*
Original markup	Planned markup (initial markon or original markup)
Additional markup	Cumulative markup
Markup cancellation	
Markdown	
Markdown cancellation	

Initial Markup or Original Markup

By definition, *markup* is the difference between the selling price of an article and the cost. In making all markup calculations, one must know only one formula: Cost + markup = retail. In other words, if merchants buy scarves at a cost of $25 and price them at $35, they are pricing at a markup of $10. This markup is frequently called *original markup* or *initial markup,* and it is placed on goods when they are first priced for sale. For example:

$$\text{Cost} + \text{markup} = \text{retail price}$$
$$\$25 + \$10 = \$35$$

Initial markup is illustrated in Figure 12.4.

Markup as a percentage of retail.
Markup may be expressed as a percentage so that year-to-year comparisons can be made in performance by tracking the changes that occur. More importantly, percentages give the retailers a common frame of reference over time. Markups may be expressed as a percentage of retail or as a percentage of cost. To determine markup as a

FIGURE 12.4

Initial markup.

$35 First Retail Price $10 Markup

$25 Cost of Goods

percentage of retail, we divide the markup (in dollars) by the retail price. In so doing, we determine what percentage of the retail price is represented by the markup. For example, if the cost of an article is $25, the markup $10, and the retail price $35, we find the markup as a percentage of retail in the following manner:

$$\frac{\text{Markup}}{\text{Retail}} = \frac{\$10}{\$35} = 28.57\% \text{ of the retail price}$$

Now we can express the formula in percentage if we wish. We have already determined that the markup based on retail is 28.57 percent. The retail price is the base figure, or 100 percent. To complete the formula, we obtain 71.43 percent. We then look at the total formula and verify the results by adding 71.43 and 28.57:

$$\text{Cost} \quad + \text{ markup} = \text{retail}$$
$$71.43\% \ + \ 28.57\% \ = \ 100\%$$

Markup as a percentage of cost. As we said earlier, it is also possible to express markup as a percentage of cost. To do this, we divide the markup by the cost. Using the previous example, we divide $10 by $25:

$$\frac{\text{Markup}}{\text{Cost}} = \frac{\$10}{\$25} = 40\% \text{ of the cost price}$$

Note that the only difference in determining markup percentage based on retail and markup percentage based on cost is that in the latter case cost replaces retail in the divisor.

It is also possible to show this formula in percentages. We have already arrived at a markup of 40 percent. We know that our cost figure is 100 percent because in this example we are working with a markup based on cost. Thus, we incorporate these two percentages in our formula:

$$\text{Cost } + \text{ markup} = \text{retail price}$$
$$100\% + \ 40\% \quad = \ 140\%$$

Most retailers express markup as a percentage of retail to make their markup comparable to other percentage calculations, such as percentage of profit, percentage of gross margin, and percentage of expenses. All these calculations are based on retail rather than cost figures.

Table 12.1 shows some markup percentages based on retail with equivalent markup percentages based on cost. Do you understand why the markup percentage on retail is always smaller than the equivalent markup percentage on cost? Is it possible to have a 200 percent markup on retail? On cost?

TABLE 12.1

Frequently Employed Markups, Based on Retail and Cost

Markup Percentage on Selling Price Is Equivalent to (Retail)	Markup Percentage (on Cost)	Markup Percentage on Selling Price Is Equivalent to (Retail)	Markup Percentage (on Cost)
20.0	25.0	35.0	53.9
22.0	28.2	38.0	61.3
25.0	33.3	40.0	66.7
28.0	39.0	42.0	72.4
30.0	42.9	47.5	90.0
33.3	50.0	50.0	100.0

There are four remaining ways in which you may have to work with markup:

1. Cost is $25 and markup is 28.57 percent of retail. Find retail.
2. Retail is $35 and markup is 28.57 percent of retail. Find cost.
3. Retail is $35 and markup is 40 percent of cost. Find cost.
4. Cost is $25 and markup is 40 percent of retail. Find retail.

Situation 1. Working with our standard formula we substitute the known numbers:

$$\text{Cost} + \text{markup} = \text{retail}$$
$$\$25 + 28.57r = r$$

We also know that retail is 100 percent, because we were told that markup is a percentage of retail. Therefore, we can substitute further, using the decimal equivalents of 28.57 percent and 100 percent:

$$\text{Cost} + \text{markup} = \text{retail}$$
$$\$25 + 0.2857r = 1.00r$$

Since we have like unknowns, r, on both sides of the equation, we must transfer them to the same side. The algebraic procedure, you may recall, is to subtract the unknown that we wish to move from both sides of the equation:

$$\$25 + 0.2857r - 0.2857r = 1.00r - 0.2857r$$
$$\$25 = 0.7143r$$
$$\$35 = r$$

To find r, we divided $25 by 0.7143.

Situation 2. We substitute our known information into the formula:

$$\begin{aligned} \text{Cost} + \text{markup} &= \text{retail} \\ c + 0.2857r &= \$35 \end{aligned}$$

We know that the markup is 28.5 percent of the retail price. From elementary algebra, you may recall that 28.5 percent is interpreted as 28.5 percent times r, or in decimals as 0.285 times r. We know r to be $35. Thus, the markup (in dollars) is calculated as follows:

$$0.285 \times \$35 = \$10 \text{ markup}$$

To find the cost, we simply subtract the markup from the retail:

$$\begin{aligned} \text{Retail} - \text{markup} &= \text{cost} \\ \$35 \quad - \quad \$10 \quad &= \$25 \end{aligned}$$

Situation 3. We substitute the known information into the formula:

$$\begin{aligned} \text{Cost} + \text{markup} &= \text{retail} \\ c + 0.40c &= \$35 \end{aligned}$$

We also know that cost is 100 percent because we were told that markup is a percentage of cost. Therefore, we can substitute further:

$$1.00c + 0.40c = \$35$$

Next, we simply solve for c:

$$\begin{aligned} \text{Cost} + \text{markup} &= \text{retail} \\ 1.00c + 0.40c &= \$35 \\ 1.40c &= \$35 \\ c &= \$25 \end{aligned}$$

Situation 4. We substitute the known into the formula:

$$\begin{aligned} \text{Cost} + \text{markup} &= \text{retail} \\ \$25 + 0.40r &= \text{retail} \end{aligned}$$

Next, we simply solve for r:

$$\begin{aligned} \$25 \qquad\qquad &= .6r \\ \frac{\$25}{.6} \qquad\qquad &= \$41.66 \\ \$25 + \$16.66 &= \$41.66 \end{aligned}$$

We then add cost to markup to arrive at an answer for retail:

$$\text{Cost} + \text{markup} = \text{retail}$$
$$\$25 + \$10 \quad = \$35$$

Additional markup. We have looked closely at original markup. We now turn to the other pricing terms. An *additional markup* is a price increase made in addition to the original markup. If an article was originally priced at $35 and an increase made the price $45, as illustrated in Figure 12.5, an additional markup of $10 was taken. The selling price of goods is increased for different reasons:

1. A higher price may make an article more attractive to customers (not outside the realm of possibility).

2. A retailer whose inventory costs have gone up may want to take an inventory profit. *Inventory profits* are sometimes made when the cost of an item is raised by the manufacturer and the retailer then raises the retail price. However, the retailer may have items in stock paid for at the original cost. On these items, the retailer makes an inventory profit.

3. A retailer must meet competitors' prices.

4. An article has become scarce.

Markup cancellation. A *markup cancellation* is a price reduction in any additional markup already taken. If the article in Figure 12.6 were to be repriced downward from $45 to $40, a markup cancellation of $5 would have to be made. *Net additional markup* is additional markup minus markup cancellation. Thus, in Figure 12.6 the net additional markup would be $10 − $5, or $5.

Markdown. A *markdown* is a reduction in the original retail price of an article. Markdowns occur as a result of the following factors: (1) special sale events, (2) the desire to meet competition, or (3) the need to clear out

FIGURE 12.5

Additional markup.

$45 Second Retail Price	$10 Additional Markup
$35 First Retail Price	$10 Markup
	$25 Cost of Goods

Markup cancel-
lation.

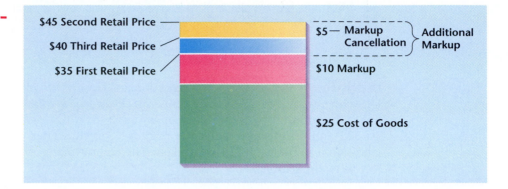

Markdown.

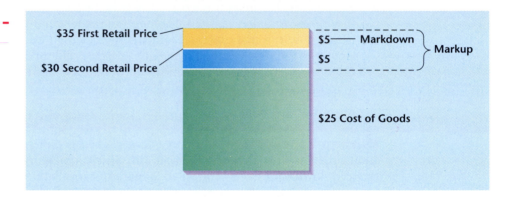

merchandise that has deteriorated, has become obsolete, or is part of a broken assortment. A markdown of $5 is illustrated in Figure 12.7.

Retailers account for markdowns as a percentage of *net sales*. To analyze
operating results, the price reduction of the items is stated as a percentage of
the lower price, which is the actual selling price. So for the above example,
we have:

$$\text{Markdown percentage} = \frac{\text{dollar markdown}}{\text{actual selling price}} \times 100$$

$$\text{Markdown percentage} = \frac{\$5}{\$30} = 16.6\%$$

The relationship of the markdown reduction to the first or original retail price
is called the *off-retail percentage*.

$$\text{Off-retail percentage} = \frac{\text{dollar markdown}}{\text{original price}} = \frac{\$5}{\$35} = 14.3\%$$

As far as the customer is concerned, the markdown is only 14.3 percent, and this off-retail percentage reduction is the only one marked or advertised to the customer. The markdown percentage is used by the retailer to control and monitor operating results.

Markdown cancellation. A *markdown cancellation* is a price increase in any markdown already taken. If the article in Figure 12.7 were to be repriced at anywhere from $30 to $35 (the original price), a markdown cancellation would have to be made. *Net markdown* is the difference between markdowns and markdown cancellations. Thus, in Figure 12.8, the net markdown is $5 − $5, or 0.

Pricing formulas. A summary of the retailing pricing formulas is presented in Table 12.2.

Planning Prices

In planning for prices or analyzing the prices set on all items, the concepts of planned markup and cumulative markup are important. These concepts are used in overall planning and analysis of operations. These markups are usually expressed in terms of percentages.

Planned markup. Planned markups were discussed previously in connection with buying merchandise and may be referred to as original markup or initial markup. Retailers should attempt to buy merchandise that may be sold at a price consistent with a planned gross margin. To achieve a specific gross margin, retailers must plan to price goods so that all expenses, profits, and expected retail reductions are covered:

$$\text{Planned markup} = \frac{\text{expenses} + \text{profit} + \text{retail reductions}}{\text{sales} + \text{retail reductions}}$$

The prices set for individual items must average out to be consistent with the planned markup.

FIGURE 12.8

Markdown cancellation.

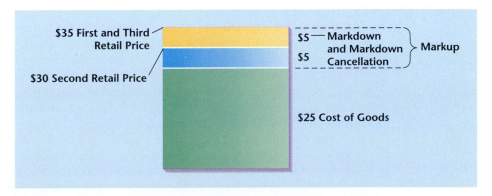

TABLE 12.2

Summary of Pricing Formulas

Cost + markup = retail

Original markup or initial markup $= \dfrac{\text{expenses + profit + reductions}}{\text{sales + reductions}}$

Maintained markup percentage $= \dfrac{\text{expenses + profit}}{\text{sales}}$

Gross margin % $= \dfrac{\text{expenses + cash discounts − alterations + profit}}{\text{sales}}$

Original retail price = cost + initial markup

Markup percentage on retail $= \dfrac{\$ \text{ markup}}{\$ \text{ retail}}$

Markup percentage on cost $= \dfrac{\$ \text{ markup}}{\$ \text{ cost}}$

Markup percentage on cost $= \dfrac{\text{markup percentage on retail}}{100\% - \text{markup percentage on retail}}$

Markup percentage on retail $= \dfrac{\text{markup percentage on cost}}{100\% - \text{markup percentage on cost}}$

\$ retail $= \dfrac{\text{cost}}{100\% - \text{retail markup percentage}}$

\$ retail markup = percent retail markup $\times$ \$ retail

\$ cost $= \dfrac{\$\text{retail}}{100\% + \text{cost markup percentage}}$

Cumulative markup. Cumulative markup is the difference between total merchandise handled at cost and total merchandise handled at retail. It shows merchants whether their goods have, on the average, been priced to yield a given markup. In Chapter 10 when we discussed the retail method of inventory, you discovered that the cumulative markup is the average markup on all goods in stock; the cost complement of cumulative markup (percentage) is used to calculate the ending inventory at a cost.

The cumulative markup also serves as a yardstick for measuring whether a store is moving smoothly toward its gross margin objective. Any erosion of the cumulative markup should be of concern to a retailer. Obviously, a retailer whose planned markup was 40 percent would stand a slim chance of achieving the planned gross margin if the cumulative markup was running at 30 percent. If retailers can receive cumulative markup information frequently from the computer, they can adjust their buying and/or pricing, when necessary.

Figure 12.9 is a form used by a major department store to analyze the results of stocking each vendor's goods. You can see many of the pricing terms we have used reflected in just this one analysis form.

FIGURE 12.9

Calculating gross margin results.

Midwest Department Stores *Cleveland, Ohio* **Store**

Dept: _283_   Resource: _New Line_   Season/Year: _9 96_   Date: _1-2-97_

Purchases:	Cost	Retail	Retail	MU %	Cost
Actual:	29093	59061			
+ Projection:	____	____			
1. Total Purchases			59061	50.7	29093

Reductions:

2. Sales	Actual:	21985		
	+ Projection:	1682		
	Total Sales:		23667	

3. Markdowns	Actual:	8353		
	+ Projection:	5304		
	Total Markdown:		13657	

	Retail	MU %	Cost
4. Total Reductions (#2 + #3):	37324		
5. Ending Stock at Retail (#1 Minus #4):	21737		
6. Cumulative MU% Complement:		49.3	
7. Ending Stock at Cost (#6 × #5):			10716

Gross Margin Analysis

	Cost
8. Purchases at Cost (#1):	29093
9. Less Ending Stock at Cost (#7):	10716
10. Cost of Goods Sold (#8 minus #9):	18377

	Retail	MU %
A. Sales (#2):	23667	
B. - Cost of Goods Sold (#10):	18377	
C. = Maintained Margin $: %:	5,290	22.3 %
D. + Cash Discount:	2313	
E. = Adjusted Gross Margin $: %:	7603	32.1 %

THE LEGAL ENVIRONMENT OF RETAIL PRICING

Before we leave the topic of pricing, it is appropriate to examine some legal issues. Today, the federal regulation of price competition affects retailers primarily through the Robinson-Patman Act. In Chapter 3 you learned about horizontal and vertical price fixing and predatory pricing. Retailers also may be faced with state laws regulating minimum prices.

The Robinson-Patman Act

In 1936 the Robinson-Patman Act amended Section 2 of the Clayton Act. Its purpose was to eliminate price discrimination by ensuring equality of treatment to all buyers from a seller. The **Robinson-Patman Act** prohibits price discrimination in interstate commerce among different purchasers of products of like grade and quality when the effect is to lessen or prevent competition or to tend to create a monopoly. In other words, retailers who are competitors are entitled to pay the same price when they buy the same merchandise in the same quantity from the same supplier. For instance, smaller independent supermarket chains are entitled to purchase Cheerios from General Mills at the same price as a large national chain. Other provisions include:

1. Price differences are permissible for "differentials which make only due allowance for differences in the cost of manufacture, sale, or delivery resulting from differing methods or quantities in which such commodities are sold or delivered." An exception is also made for seasonal obsolescence and physical deterioration. So, General Mills could sell Cheerios to the large supermarket chain at a lesser price than that charged to the small chain if it could be shown that a quantity purchase resulted in lower costs for the manufacturer.

2. Buyers are as guilty as sellers if they knowingly induce or receive an unlawful price discrimination. A large retailer like Best Buy cannot have an agreement with General Electric to purchase laundry appliances at a lower price than that paid by one of its competitors except for differences as noted above.

3. Promotional allowances must be given to all competing buyers on proportionally equal terms. If one retailer receives a $2 a case promotion allowance, the same or a proportionally equal allowance must be given to competing retailers.

4. It is unlawful for a seller to pay, or a buyer to receive, brokerage payments except for services rendered. In many industries it is the norm for brokers to represent manufacturers and sell products to retailers. The manufacturer pays the broker a commission. In some cases a retailer might want to purchase direct from the manufacturer and receive the equiva-

Business districts may take on a special shopping character. The Ginza district in Tokyo has stores from all over the world targeting the affluent Japanese consumer. Lights, signs, store architecture, and merchandise create a vibrant and exciting shopping environment where price is not the issue. Japan has a different legal environment regarding the role of price, which restricts competition.

lent of the broker's commission in the form of a lower price or a direct payment. This provision of the act makes this practice illegal.

You can see that the underlying principle behind the Robinson-Patman Act was to help the small retailer compete on price with the large retailer by having access to goods at competitive terms of sale. To ensure compliance with the Robinson-Patman Act, retailers should observe the following guidelines: (1) Make no promises to abide by a vendor's pricing policy, (2) hold no group meetings with other retailers or vendors at which pricing policies are discussed, and (3) have no discussions with the vendor concerning other retailers' resale prices.

Horizontal Price Fixing

Horizontal price fixing occurs when competing retailers agree to set a common price. Price fixing in this manner is always illegal. In other words Best Buy and Circuit City cannot get together and agree on the prices they charge for Sony TVs. Price collusion between competing retailers is illegal under the Sherman Act and the Federal Trade Commission Act.

Vertical Price Fixing

Vertical price fixing is often referred to as price maintenance. This occurs when vendors or manufacturers set minimum prices for the sale of their products by retailers. The fact that such vertical price fixing is illegal under the Sherman Act is well established in case law when it impedes free trade and when there is an express or implied agreement between dealer and supplier.[15] However, many manufacturers emphasize suggested retail prices instead of maintaining a minimum price.

Predatory Pricing

Predatory pricing is the practice of setting prices to try to deliberately drive competition out of business. As mentioned before, in 1992 three independent drugstores accused Wal-Mart of selling more than 100 products below cost with the intent of hurting rivals and destroying competition. The group also claimed that Wal-Mart and several other retailers were violating antitrust laws by trying to deal directly with manufacturers so that they could earn the third-party brokerage fee, which, as you remember, is illegal under the Robinson-Patman Act. Complaints and investigations of predatory pricing are handled by the Federal Trade Commission.

TOYS 'R' US—REVISITED: PRICING IN THE GLOBAL ENVIRONMENT

In an attempt to further increase the market for Toys 'R' Us, the company has been rapidly expanding overseas, where over 20 percent of its stores are currently located. Toys 'R' Us owns and operates stores in Puerto Rico, Canada, the United Kingdom, Germany, France, Spain, Austria, Switzerland, the Netherlands, Belgium, Portugal, Japan, Hong Kong, Singapore, Malaysia, Taiwan, and Australia. It is currently expanding into Denmark, Sweden, the United Arab Emirates, Qatar, Bahrain, Oman, and Kuwait. In recent years, Toys 'R' Us opened more stores in foreign countries than in the United States. This trend is expected to continue.

Many retailers have found that their strategies and concepts do not transfer to overseas markets. Managers must carefully consider not only the economics of other countries but the "fit" between the concepts that they use to sell products in the United States and the culture of different areas. Some concepts are difficult to transfer from culture to culture even when there is a perceived market for the merchandise. Toys 'R' Us has done a good job of familiarizing itself with the culture and economies it has targeted. Its success is partly the result of the fact that consumer lifestyles, needs, and aspirations of developed markets in Europe and Asia are converging with those of the U.S. consumer.[16]

Toys 'R' Us has been successful in most countries because the idea of value is nearly universal, as are children and toys, and its strategy of everyday low price with vast selection has proved very profitable. However, the company has had problems with its stores in some Asian markets. In Malaysia in particular, Toys 'R' Us has not yet received the response that it has experienced elsewhere. Also, some problems were encountered in Japan, where toy shopping is much different than in the United States because the children make the choice of which product they want as opposed to the parents choosing the item.

The global expansion plans of Toys 'R' Us are constrained by the fact that many countries have laws that limit the amount of foreign ownership of companies. To overcome this, Toys 'R' Us has started to grant franchises for the first time. Most of these will be located in the Middle East. This allows Toys 'R' Us mar-ket access to countries that were previously closed.

1. **Will the concept of everyday low price work in other countries as well as it has in the United States?**
2. **What additional pricing or merchandising problems do retailers such as Toys 'R' Us face when entering new international markets?**

 SUMMARY

Consumers today are much more value-conscious; they demand the best price along with quality, selection, and availability. Price is the value assigned to something bought, sold, or offered for sale expressed in monetary units. Pricing decisions are one of the most important aspects of competition.

Basic economic concepts help the retailer understand the pricing decision. One important piece of information is the supply and demand for the store's goods and the elasticity or inelasticity of a product's demand curve. Major factors that influence the degree of price sensitivity include availability of substitutes, relative price of the product, importance of the product to consumers, and the income characteristics of the purchaser.

Market structure in which a retailer operates impacts the demand curves of its products. The market structure is defined by the kind and amount of competition facing the retailer. In relation to market structure and demand curves, retailers have three strategies to choose from in pricing products: at the market, below the market, and above the market. Retailers utilize different pricing strategies depending on the store image, the type of product offered, the target market, and other competitive and market influences.

The retailer also has to make decisions regarding the use of psychological pricing and markdown strategies. Fundamental to pricing strategy are the pricing concepts of original markup, markup as a percentage of retail, markup as a percentage of cost, and markdowns. Retailers are also affected by laws governing the pricing of merchandise. Issues such as price discrimination, horizontal and vertical price fixing, and predatory pricing greatly influence retail pricing strategies.

KEY TERMS AND CONCEPTS

QUESTIONS

1. Do discount stores always charge lower prices than other stores? Explain.

2. Pricing is more of an art than a science. Do you agree? Why or why not?

3. One pricing method is based on ability to exchange markup for gross margin. Explain.

4. Suppose that you, as a retailer, bought a style of shoes at $8.95, giving you a gross margin of 43 percent. Suppose also that after you received the shoes, you believed you could charge $10.50. Would you do this? Describe the consequences of your decision.

5. Discuss trends in retail pricing. What has caused the changes that have occurred?

6. Can pricing merchandise above the market draw customers? How could it prove to have a negative effect?

7. Which to you, as a consumer, is more advantageous: the cost-plus approach or the dollar margin approach?

8. How does the principle of one-price selling compare to bargaining? Which would you prefer as a customer? As a retailer? Why?

9. How should you, as a manager of a major discount store, price items or lines of items that sell quickly?

10. Does odd-number pricing work? How well?

SITUATIONS

1. You are the manager of a small automotive parts store in a small town. The practice of most stores like yours is not to mark prices on displayed merchandise because the automotive replacement parts business sets different price levels for different customers. In other words, retail customers pay one price, machine shop customers pay another, highway construction customers pay still another price, and schools, hospitals, and other institutions pay yet another. You have been following this practice, and recently you have noticed that many of your retail customers are reluctant to purchase merchandise because they cannot readily determine the price. Should you do anything about the situation? If so, what alternatives do you have?

2. You are the manager of a women's wear boutique. You are preparing to go to market to do your semiannual buying. During the preceding season, you bought, among other things, head scarves that were to retail at $2.98, $3.19, $3.29, $3.98, $5.50, $5.98, $7.50, $8.00, $10.50, $11.50, $13.00, $13.50, and $15.95. Unfortunately, this merchandise has not moved as satisfactorily as you had hoped. What steps should you take to make better purchasing decisions than in the past? What kinds of problems should you have anticipated before you bought the scarves?

MARKUP SITUATIONS

1. The purchase price of two gross of dress skirts is $4,500 to the wholesaler. Handling costs of these items are 6 percent of purchase price, which is passed to the retailer. The wholesaler also desires a 16 percent gross margin. What will be the selling price to the retailer?

2. The Equality Market, a local shop, has adopted a new line of posters. The purchase price per 50 posters is $145.00, with terms of 10/10 net 30. The selling price per poster has been set at $8.95. Assuming that the Equality Market pays for the posters within 10 days of the invoice date, what is the percentage of markup, based on selling price?

3. A buyer purchased goods at $150. The total markup was $50. What is the percentage markup on cost? On selling price?

4. A line of skis has been offered at $125 per pair. Half a gross was purchased at this price from a wholesale distributor in Colorado. The markup on these skis is 30 percent of their selling price by the retailer. What is the total markup in dollars?

5. At the end of the summer one retailer found herself overstocked with swimsuits. They had cost her $16 per suit for the 23 suits she had left. In order to make room for ski incidentals she decided to sell the suits at a 5 percent markup on cost. These suits were selling for $24 during the summer, and 8.5 percent of the selling price was going to cover handling costs. Does the retailer realize any profit on the sale of these last 23 suits?

6. A markup of 30 percent of cost is equivalent to what percentage of the selling price?

7. A markup of 45 percent of retail is equivalent to what percentage of the cost of the goods?

8. Your fifteen-year-old brother has ordered 25 gross of firecrackers to sell for the Fourth of July. They cost $0.10 a dozen. He asked you what he should price them at. You tell him to use a 50 percent markup. You notice that he is selling them for $0.15 a dozen, when you intended for him to sell them at $0.20 a dozen. Explain in simple language the difference between the two prices. What is the difference in gross margin?

9. If the cost is $20 and a 100 percent markup on cost is used, what is the final price?

10. You purchase 100 dozen roses for $500. You mark them up 150 percent of cost. What is the price for a single rose?

11. You are an employee of an apparel shop. The standard markup for pants is 75 percent of cost. The cost of the pants is $17.50. As an employee, you can receive your choice of a 20 percent discount off the retail price or a 40 percent discount on cost. Which will you choose?

12. As a retail buyer, you notice that china plates cost $2.25 each. You will need a 75 percent markup on cost to make it worth buying them. You figure that you can sell 500 at $4.50; 1,000 at $4.00; or 2,000 at $3.75. How many, if any, should you purchase?

13. You advertise a $320 computer printer at 20 percent off. The printer originally cost you $175. What is your final markup at retail on the computer if you sell it at this special price?

14. As the manager of a sporting goods store you have sold 150 winter jackets at $120 each. These cost you $76. However, it is now spring and you must sell the remaining 25 jackets. You need to have an overall achieved gross margin on this item of 25 percent. At what price should you mark the rest of the jackets?

PART 5

COMMUNICATING WITH THE RETAIL CUSTOMER

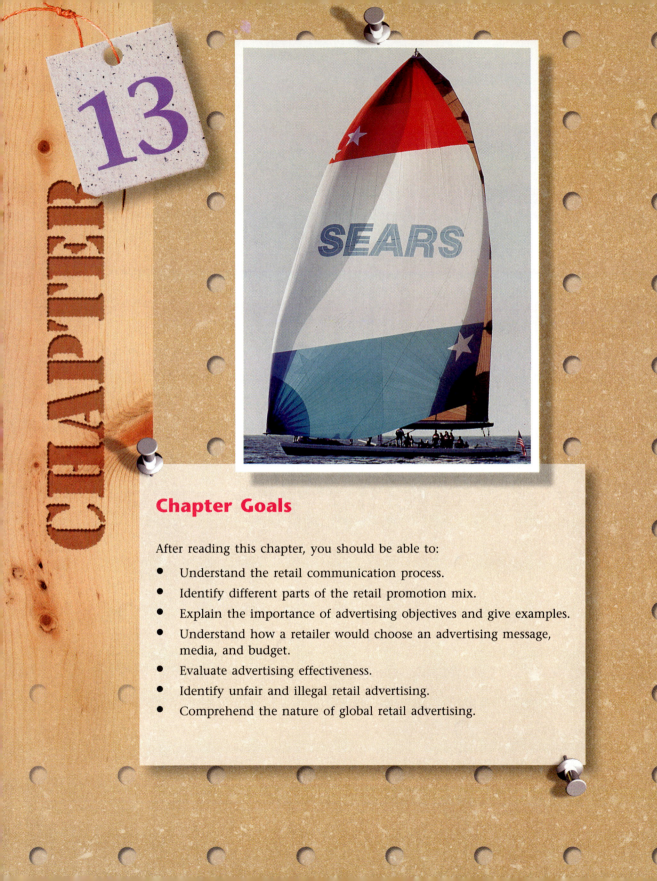

CHAPTER 13

Chapter Goals

After reading this chapter, you should be able to:

- Understand the retail communication process.
- Identify different parts of the retail promotion mix.
- Explain the importance of advertising objectives and give examples.
- Understand how a retailer would choose an advertising message, media, and budget.
- Evaluate advertising effectiveness.
- Identify unfair and illegal retail advertising.
- Comprehend the nature of global retail advertising.

RETAIL ADVERTISING

SEARS: COMPETING WITH EFFECTIVE ADVERTISING

At one time, Sears was the largest retailer in the world. In 1990, it lost this position to Kmart. It soon became the third largest behind Kmart as Wal-Mart passed both of them in sales. The rocky road of the last two decades taught the company important lessons about consumer perceptions. In 1992, Arthur Martinez, then vice chairman at Saks Fifth Avenue, was recruited to take over retailing operations.[1] The company took a pretax charge of $2.65 billion for restructuring related to discontinuing its domestic catalog operations, closing 113 unprofitable retail stores, streamlining unprofitable merchandise lines, and slashing 50,000 jobs. In addition, the company spent $4 billion to renovate stores, build more freestanding hardware operations, and move furniture into separate emporiums.

With nearly a hundred years of history, Sears decided that it could no longer afford its catalog business, which had been losing $140 million a year. Many saw the loss as a historical event. The "big book" had served Sears' customers for ninety-seven years with products that varied from tools and apparel to chicken eggs and homes.

The image of Sears was related to its strength in hard goods. Concentration on its Craftsman tools and Kenmore appliances created perceptions consistent with a hardware store, instead of the famous department store. Central to Sears' restructuring plans were new advertising and promotion.

Like most retailers, Sears traditionally advertised in the local newspapers. Although newspapers remain a staple media, Sears has started shifting into national television ads. The first several themes in the new advertising campaign targeted the traditional middle-class clientele. The slogans "Sears: You Can Count On Me" and "Sears: Where America Shops" were mostly unsuccessful. They targeted a shrinking segment of the middle market that was no longer interested in shopping in the traditional department store.

In addition, Sears ran into various legal problems with its advertising and promotion attempts. The company was investigated when it started to advertise new low prices. After a promotional blitz and the temporary closing of stores to lower prices, customers expressed dissatisfaction because of the lack of noticeable price changes. Also, Sears received some bad publicity after several states investigated practices at its auto centers.[2]

Sears spent $40 million on an advertising campaign based on extensive consumer research.[3] The purpose was to rebuild Sears' declining image by decreasing the emphasis on store-branded hard goods, such as Kenmore, and concentrating on national-branded apparel and other soft goods. The campaign was built around the theme "The Softer Side of Sears." The promotion was successful in improving Sears' image among women and significantly increased the sales of apparel. For the winter holiday season, Sears uses a takeoff on the campaign with "The Merry Side of Sears."

Store images are extremely difficult to change. However, with a billion-dollar marketing budget that is growing at approximately 9 percent a year, Sears has both the financial ability and a focused direction necessary for change. Sears' $190 million apparel marketing budget supports advertising concentrated on highly visible television events.[4] By 1996 Sears was again the number two retailer with sales surpassing Kmart.

1. Why do you think that Sears' new campaign, "The Softer Side of Sears," helped change its image and increase profitability?
2. While a large advertising budget obviously assists in changing a store's image, is it enough?

INTRODUCTION

We had to eliminate the polyester image," said Peter Hirsch, creative director, about Kmart's image turnaround efforts.[5] In today's competitive marketplace, image promises to play an ever increasing role in differentiating one retailer from another. Advertising plays a major part in communicating the desired image to the target market.

Retailers work hard to provide customers a facility that is attractive and convenient. They try to develop an assortment of products and services that will be desirable to potential purchasers with prices at a level they will see as reflecting true value. However, regardless of the quality of merchandise, the completeness of lines, or the helpfulness of sales associates, effective promotion is central to success. To encourage prospects and customers to visit the store and make purchases, messages must be designed that accurately portray products, prices, and store image. In this chapter we explore the role that communication plays in the retailing process, introduce the promotion mix, and suggest ways to manage communication efforts. The chapter concludes with some thoughts about retail advertising in the global environment.

Retail Advertising Is Big Business

Continued growth and expansion of huge retail firms, buyouts, and mergers have left fewer retailers controlling ever larger markets.[6] As noted in Chapter 8, the current organizational structure of these large multistore retail firms takes much of the promotion activity and decision making out of the hands of the local store. Individuals at the corporate level select the strategy and control the implementation of the message and the media. For example, RadioShack has an in-house advertising agency responsible for a wide range of advertising and promotion activities. The local store executes what comes from the corporate office.

With today's corporate structure, the advertising dollars controlled by major retailers are enormous. Total U.S. advertising by retailers in measured media exceeds $8 billion. **Measured media** refers to *national* ad expenditures. For example, the newspaper dollars are only for space in 203 newspapers in the top 40 markets. Box 13.1 shows the advertising expenditures for 8 retail organizations that are among the 75 leading national advertisers. It is particularly interesting to see the expenditures for the **unmeasured media**. These estimates are compiled by *Advertising Age* and include direct

BOX 13.1 ADVERTISING EXPENDITURE DOLLARS AND PERCENTAGE OF SALES FOR SELECTED RETAILERS

Retailer	Total U.S. Advertising Spending	Unmeasured Spending	Total Measured Media	Measured Magazine and Newspaper	Measured TV, Cable, and Radio	Advertising-to-Sales Ratio (%)
Circuit City	308.5	46.3	262.2	210.8	51.5	9.43
Dayton-Hudson	266.7	55.9	210.8	145.0	64.9	1.39
J. C. Penney	585.2	319.4	265.8	101.7	164.1	2.99
Kmart	558.2	264.2	294.0	153.4	140.1	1.52
May Dept. Stores	403.6	40.4	363.2	317.5	45.7	3.50
McDonald's	736.6	325.9	410.7	8.6	387.9	9.94
Sears	$1,310.7	714.2	596.5	222.1	374.3	2.55
Wal-Mart	251.9	145.4	106.5	19.1	87.3	0.45

Source: Kevin Brown, R. Craig Endicott, Susan Taras, Cecilia Ramirez, and Kenneth Wyle, "The Advertising Fact Book," *Advertising Age*, Jan. 2, 1995, p. 12.

6543217

Toys 'R' Us inserts an eighty-four-page holiday catalog in Sunday newspapers with sixteen pages of coupons. The message is "lower prices—bigger selection guaranteed." The eighty coupons expire November 29. The firm hopes the coupon price and wide selection will stimulate purchases early in the holiday season. The use of measured media (newspaper) and unmeasured media (coupons) is typical practice for retailers.

mail, promotions, cooperative advertising, couponing, and special events as well as numerous other categories such as the Yellow Pages.[7] Box 13.1 also shows the percentage of sales each of the retailers spent for advertising. What factors might account for the large differences? What might account for the differing proportions spent in measured and unmeasured media?

The magnitude of change in the nature of advertising is illustrated by the case of Avon, the highly successful direct retailer of personal care products. Avon's U.S. ad budget is about $33 million. It uses fifteen-second network television commercials and national print advertisements, not to sell products but to encourage ordering from an Avon catalog via an 800 number, by fax, by mail, or from a traditional Avon sales representative.[8] The trend of spending less on media advertising and more on promotion and direct mail will likely continue.[9]

The centralization of advertising does not mean that the local stores have no say in this area, but roles may be very limited. At the same time, there are still hundreds of thousands of small retailers who are responsible for their advertising and promotion efforts. In any case, the planning and thinking for successful retail advertising are the same whether centralized or local.

THE ROLE OF RETAIL COMMUNICATIONS

Customers need and desire a constant flow of factual information to use as a basis for making need-satisfying purchase decisions. They want to know store hours, what specials are being run, what styles are in fashion, product features, and a host of other things. Information alone, however, is seldom sufficient to motivate consumers to purchase. Because retailers desire to influence their customers to take a desired course of action, retail communications must be well organized and designed so that each message contains the appropriate balance of **information** and **persuasion.** A good example is the award-winning campaign by Target Stores. Its advertisement entitled "Which Would You Rather Depend On in an Emergency?" clearly presented the information outlining the benefits of cellular phones and pagers in the context of personal safety.

The Communication Process

The transmission of a promotional message from the retailer to the customer is a complex process. For any promotional effort to be effective, the retailer must gain the attention of the customer and persuasively communicate the desired ideas. The communication process is facilitated and affected by many factors. Your knowledge of this process will help you understand how communication occurs and what factors are important in promoting your store and your products effectively.

Figure 13.1 diagrams the information flow in the basic retail communication model. The figure shows an *idea* being communicated by a source (retailer) to a receiver (customer). As you can see, the **source** is the originator or possessor of an idea that it desires to communicate to a receiver. The idea is the thought, concept, or relationship the source wishes the receiver to know. The **receiver** is the individual toward whom the idea is being communicated. For example, in a local newspaper advertisement the source could be a neighborhood bank, the receiver would be a resident of the neighborhood within which a new branch bank has been located, and the idea is that "a new drive-in branch banking location is opening near your home." To initiate the communications process, the retailer must encode the idea to produce a message. **Encoding** is the process of translating an idea into signs and symbols that have meaning for the receiver. Words, pictures, color patterns, and music are some of the signs and symbol systems we have developed to represent ideas or objects. The banker may choose words in the English language, show a picture of the new branch, or place a map in a newspaper in an effort to communicate the idea.

Once encoded, the message must be carried to a receiver via some communication channel. The **communication channel** is the element of the promotion mix that carries a message to the receiver such as a telephone, a sales associate, a coupon, the product label, or even the air. For example, The Great American Cookie Company circulates the aroma from its baking ovens into the counter area of its mall locations. The idea of fresh chocolate chip cookies is encoded as aromas and transmitted via the communication channel of air. The receiver must decode the message into an interpretation. The process of **decoding** occurs when the receiver interprets the original idea from the signs and symbols into which it was encoded. If the thought pat-

FIGURE 13.1

The basic retail communications process.

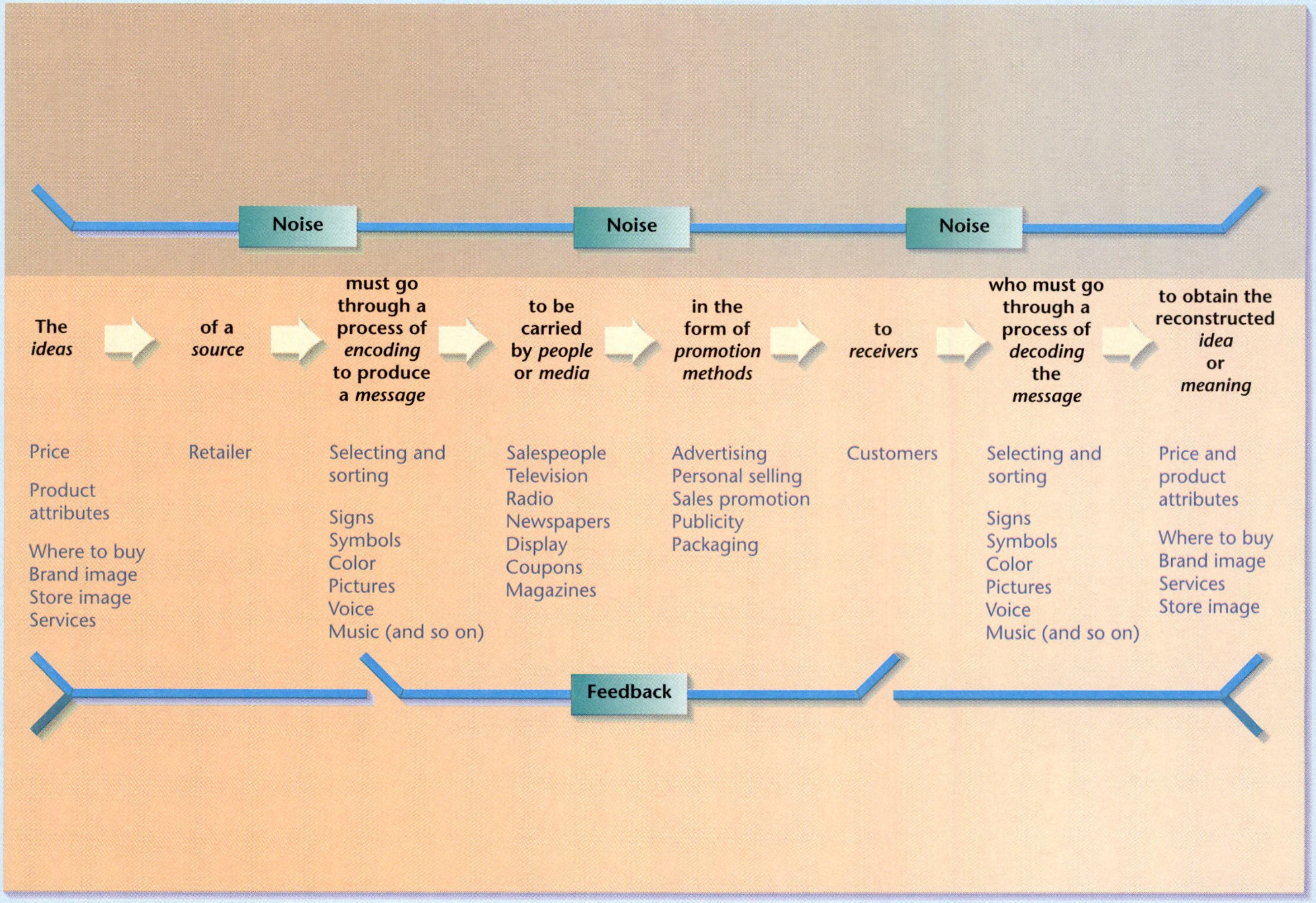

The ideas — of a **source** — must go through a process of **encoding to produce a message** — to be carried **by people or media** — in the form of **promotion methods** — to **receivers** — who must go through a process of **decoding the message** — to obtain the reconstructed **idea or meaning**

The ideas:
Price
Product attributes
Where to buy
Brand image
Store image
Services

of a source:
Retailer

encoding to produce a message:
Selecting and sorting
Signs
Symbols
Color
Pictures
Voice
Music (and so on)

carried by people or media:
Salespeople
Television
Radio
Newspapers
Display
Coupons
Magazines

in the form of promotion methods:
Advertising
Personal selling
Sales promotion
Publicity
Packaging

to receivers:
Customers

decoding the message:
Selecting and sorting
Signs
Symbols
Color
Pictures
Voice
Music (and so on)

to obtain the reconstructed idea or meaning:
Price and product attributes
Where to buy
Brand image
Services
Store image

Noise   Noise   Noise

Feedback

Mike's developed a taste for

Salsa!

plus the latest British pop music, contemporary jazz from Moscow, and worldbeat sounds from the Pacific Rim.

With a Science Fair® shortwave radio he put together himself, Mike's discovering a world he never dreamed of. New music, new languages, new ideas. From places like London, Tokyo and Rio. Parents would say it's educational, but Mike would say "It's hot!"

What'll it be tonight? If conditions are right, Mike just might tune in the latest hits from Helsinki—definitely cool!

Radio Shack
You've got questions. We've got answers.™

A store should communicate its competitive advantage with a focus that is important to the customer and has leverage over the competition. RadioShack determined that a large segment of the home electronics market is confused by sophisticated technology. It wanted to demystify the technology with knowledgeable salespeople. The theme—"You've Got Questions, We've Got Answers"—positions the stores in mind of the customer.

terns, backgrounds, and experiences of the source and of the receiver are not similar, the signs and symbols may have different meanings for each. Under such conditions, it is very likely that the source's idea will not be interpreted accurately by the receiver.

Figure 13.1 also shows that the communication process can be altered or disturbed by noise. **Noise** is any interference during the communication process that arises from situational disturbances, physical or technological problems, cultural and social differences, or problems associated with semantics such as a poor choice of words.

Finally, Figure 13.1 illustrates that no communication process is complete without feedback. **Feedback** is the reverse flow of information from the receiver back to the sender from which the success of the communication effort can be judged. Feedback helps a sales associate, a manager, or a retail communications specialist determine how well customers are understanding their respective efforts. While a sales associate gets immediate feedback from the words, facial expressions, and actions of a customer, obtaining feedback from an advertising campaign is much more difficult. In fact, the retailer will often use measures like store traffic, sales by product line, or number of telephone inquiries to judge the effectiveness of a retail advertisement.

RETAIL PROMOTION MIX

Retail communication should be designed to stimulate and enhance demand. In large part, retail communications determine how potential customers perceive prices, products, and services. In the case of merchandise or services that are sold by in-store associates, their job will be made easier by a well-informed

FIGURE 13.2

The communications channels.

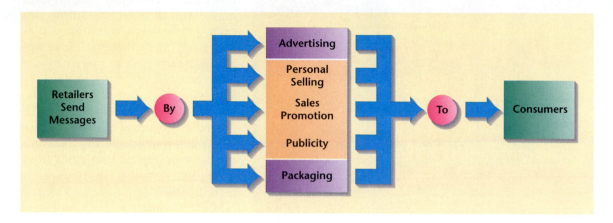

clientele. The group of methods available for communicating with people in the market is called the retail promotion mix.

The **retail promotion mix** is the set of controllable elements that a retailer can use to communicate ideas. These elements include advertising, sales promotion, personal selling, public relations, and packaging. The primary communication elements used by retailers, and the ones over which they have direct control, include advertising, sales promotion, and personal selling. The secondary elements used by retailers, and the ones over which they have less control, include packaging and public relations. From a retail management point of view, these elements should be viewed as interdependent communication channels through which the retailer's message can be transmitted to customers (see Figure 13.2).

ADVERTISING

Advertising is a paid presentation of a message on behalf of a product, service, or idea by an identified sponsor to a mass audience. Advertising messages can be transmitted over the radio, by television, on the Internet, in the newspaper, or many other ways. Clearly, in each of these choices of media, many people see the same message for the product or service and see the store or brand sponsoring the message.

When a retailer considers the use of advertising, a number of questions must be answered. The answers will tell the retailer whether any advertising should be done and, if so, in what manner it should be carried out. The questions are:

1. To whom will you direct your advertising?
2. What do you want to accomplish?
3. What will you advertise?
4. What will you say?
5. Where will you place your advertisement?
6. How often will you advertise?
7. How much will you spend?

These questions must be answered by all retailers whether they are developing a total advertising program for the store, working up a promotional campaign, or considering running a single ad. Although more effort is spent on developing an advertising program than on the running of a single advertisement, the same considerations apply.

To Whom Will You Direct Your Advertising?

When making any advertising decision, the first step is to analyze your retail market and the demand within it. As suggested in previous chapters, a retail market should be analyzed in terms of population, income characteristics, and the motivating influences that form the basis for purchasing behavior. Without such an analysis, store policies concerning merchandise offerings, pricing, and advertising will be ineffective. If you look at a newspaper, you can't help noticing the lack of true market identification revealed in many ads.

Most retailers like to think they do a fairly good job of defining their market and then tailoring their retail mix to best hit that market. By and large, this is true. However, there is one activity that is frequently given less attention than others—identification of the people the advertising is directed toward. Retailers will, for example, direct ads for household furnishings toward particular consumer segments. However, they often do not determine who does the buying, who makes purchasing decisions, who reads or listens to the advertisements, and who influences purchases. For example, many retailers overlook the fact that ethnic minorities now represent about 25 percent of the U.S. population and about 40 percent of the population in the largest ten cities. However, a number of retailers are now hiring ethnic specialists in the corporate advertising departments. But advertising to a particular ethnic segment is not enough; merchandise selections and visual displays must be in line with the target group's very diverse needs and wants.[10]

What Do You Want to Accomplish?

After carefully analyzing and defining the market, a retailer must define the objective for a promotion campaign or single advertisement. This will help the retailer choose among media alternatives and provide a standard against which performance can be measured. When developing their advertising objectives, retailers should consider two things. First, they must determine what stage in the purchase decision process consumers are in. For example, impulse items, seasonal goods, or sale merchandise will draw quicker response to advertising than major appliances or automobiles. If the consumer is at the search phase of the decision process, it may be several weeks or months before a "purchase" will occur. Similarly, an advertisement for a "sale" during the July–August "back to school" season can be expected to draw an immediate response. To accommodate for these differences, objectives need to be separated into two groups: indirect action and direct action. **Indirect action objectives** are associated with promotional efforts that seek to impart knowledge or create favorable attitudes, but unlike **direct action objectives** they are not expected to produce immediate sales-oriented results.

Second, retail managers must determine whether the objective provides a method of measuring performance quantitatively. Indirect action objectives should be evaluated using such measures as awareness, attitude change, or purchase likelihood. Direct action objectives should be measured using sales-oriented results. For example, sales in dollars may be a useful measure for self-service goods. Store traffic, however, may be a better measure than sales for products that are sold by in-store personnel. This is because promotional efforts may have brought customers into the store, as was intended, but sales may have actually been lost by poorly trained or overworked employees.

Examples of objectives.   Consumers may be in one of several situations as far as making a purchasing decision. Naturally, the specific advertising objective you select will be influenced by the number of consumers in each of the different situations:

● **Situation 1.** Consumers may not know the store exists or the nature of its products and services. The advertising objective might then be to stimulate **awareness.**

● **Situation 2.** Consumers are in the initial stages of the purchase decision and are beginning to obtain market information; only now are they becoming aware of various merchandise offerings. The advertising objective might be to increase the disposition to buy.

● **Situation 3.** Consumers have made a tentative decision to purchase and have begun to search in earnest for the right product or service. The advertising objective might be to provide both information and persuasion. Its intent would be to gain an immediate sale. In this case, price might be emphasized.

● **Situation 4.** Consumers are buying merchandise routinely, out of habit. The advertising objective might be to remind or reinforce an existing preference and, therefore, retain patronage.

- **Situation 5.** When special promotion events are planned, such as a "red tag" sale, the advertising objective may simply be to provide an announcement.

- **Situation 6.** Rather than a particular product or event, the emphasis may be on brands, services, or other patronage advantages designed to create or enhance a store image.

- **Situation 7.** Much retail advertising is tied to manufacturer advertising for a particular brand. In this case the retailer's ad seeks to direct traffic to the store.

A well-defined objective for a total advertising program, a campaign, or even a single ad depends on the retailer's knowledge of what should be communicated to consumers. Fundamental to this knowledge is an understanding of where consumers stand in making a purchase decision. Retailers selling some products, for example, facial soap, would find that few of their customers would ever be in the first two situations. (Most would be in the third or fourth.) On the other hand, those selling products like the RCA Digital Satellite System for home TVs would find that most of their customers are, at least at the beginning, in the first situation.

Stating advertising objectives and performance measurement.

After an advertising objective has been defined in terms of "how far along the consumer is in making the purchasing decision," the objective should be stated in precise terms containing five specific elements:

1. Specific product/service identification[a]
2. Specific goals[b]
3. Audience/market identification[c]
4. Benchmark (reference point) levels[d]
5. Time horizons[e]

Applying these specific elements, an objective statement might read something like this: "Per-store quarterly sales of children's toys[a] will increase from $50,000[d] to $70,000[b] in our seventeen Tennessee and Kentucky[c] stores by December 1995.[e]" Note the reference to each element from the above list with superscripts.

Suppose, for another example, that a store carries the Botany 500 line of men's suits. The advertising objective might be stated as follows: "To communicate to the maximum number of customers that we carry a complete line of Botany 500 men's suits." You probably noticed that there are a few flaws in this statement. First, no market segment is specified, and therefore, there is no way to select a communication channel that would best reach the market. Second, there is no indication of the number of potential customers who are already aware that this line is carried. Third, there is no standard by which advertising effectiveness could be measured after implementation. Finally, there is no target or benchmark sales level specified.

What Will You Advertise?

Decisions about what to advertise are partially made when objectives are defined. Retailers may, however, use definite criteria.

Best-sellers.
First, it is a good idea to promote best-sellers or, at the very least, advertise products that have the potential of being best-sellers. Too often, retailers try to use promotion to rectify mistakes in buying. Promotion, however, cannot make customers buy what they do not want. In fact, a small reduction or markdown on a "hot" item will produce far greater results than a half-price reduction on a "dog." Even in storewide sales, where the assortment is mixed, customers tend to select the best items first and bypass the less valuable ones.

When deciding whether a product will be a best-seller, retailers should take several factors into consideration. The wants of people in the market have a bearing on what will sell and what will not. Seasonal occurrences such as holidays, leisure activities, and school sessions influence what sells. Products that are heavily promoted by manufacturers and suppliers may be best-sellers as well as products that attract immediate interest and that may be easily illustrated and written about. Ace Hardware advertises outdoor barbecue grills prior to the Fourth of July because it is the right product at the right time.

Special events.
Advertising at particular times of the year and for special events is effective because customs and tradition have made some occasions and times major shopping periods for Americans. The event should coincide with and attempt to accelerate the customers' mood to buy. Retailers can use Mother's Day, back-to-school, Easter, special purchase, anniversary sale, end-of-the-month clearance, preseason sale, or any kind of special attraction.

When retailers decide what products or services to advertise, they should also consider communicating the unique aspects of the store to enhance its reputation and its image.

What Will You Say?

After defining the market, stating precise objectives, and choosing what to advertise, a retailer must consider the structure of the appeal for the advertising message. Each appeal should match customer motives with the benefits of the products and service offerings. The matching process is done by someone, often a copywriter, who can look at the offering from both the retailer's and the customer's point of view. The message should be completely true. See Box 13.2.

A recent case illustrates how carefully the advertising message must be crafted. Wal-Mart was told by an advertising industry board to stop using the slogan "Always the Low Price." The company agreed to change it to read

BOX 13.2   A "FINE WAY" TO GET HONEST ADVERTISING

You may not want to expand into Canada after you read this item from the *Montreal Gazette:* "A Dorval-based retailer in blinds, drapes, and other interior accessories was fined $40,000 [Canadian] . . . after pleading guilty in court to eight charges of engaging in false or misleading advertising." The company had advertised prices for certain vertical blinds as being "20% to 40% off," or at "50% savings," or at "half price," when they were actually the regular prices.

Source: Adapted with permission from Robert Kahn, "Why Customers Doubt Sale Prices," *Retailing Today,* June 1995, pp. 1, 2.

6543217

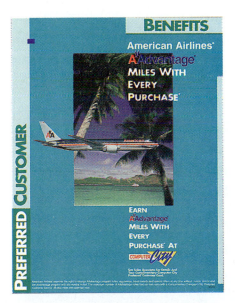

You can buy virtually the same computer at the lowest price guaranteed at CompUSA, Best Buy, Montgomery Ward, OfficeMax, Office Depot, and many other places. Retailers struggle to find ways to get a customer to choose their store. For example, Computer City has introduced a promotion to "get one American Airlines AAdvantage mile for each dollar in purchases."

"Always Low Prices." Target Stores had complained to the Council of Better Business Bureaus that the word *the* in the slogan created an objective statement that couldn't be substantiated. Wal-Mart agreed to immediately begin using "Always Low Prices" in its newspaper and television advertisements and began a program of placing the new slogan on trucks and stores.[11]

Facts about the product, its features, and benefits must be considered when structuring an appeal. The information is obtained through careful product analysis and by asking questions like:

1. What is it made of?
2. How well is it made?
3. What does it do?
4. How does it compare with the competition's product?
5. How much does it cost?
6. How can it be identified?[12]

From the many product facts, it is necessary to select those few that will be of real interest to the customer. From the seller's point of view, these facts become the features, or the selling points, of the product. Typically, they will be facts that make the product unique, define it as a special value, or fill a clearly defined need. From the buyer's point of view, these facts become benefits.

The concept of customer benefits is important to retailers. Customers buy benefits, not products. If a benefit satisfies a need, the retailer can make a successful appeal. To pinpoint the features that may be considered benefits, retailers must examine those aspects of the product (derived from the product analysis) they think will be most important to consumers. By expressing product facts in terms of their features, the retailer focuses on the benefits desired by the consumer. One way to focus on benefits is to ask these kinds of questions about the product. What product features will:

● Make the buyer feel more important?

● Make the buyer happier?

● Make the buyer more comfortable?

● Make the buyer more prosperous?

● Make work easier for the buyer?

● Give the buyer more security?

● Make the buyer more attractive or better liked?

● Give the buyer some distinction?

● Improve, protect, or maintain the buyer's health?[13]

As we have seen, then, retailers decide what to say in their advertisements by bringing together a product analysis and a market analysis (see Figure 13.3). The appeal—what is said—results from a matching of product features to customer motives. It is this matching that highlights the benefits, which should be the basis of an advertisement, event, or promotion.

Another approach to selecting an advertising appeal, particularly one that is to define the store's image, is illustrated in Figure 13.4. Along the edge of the figure are listed six choices that could be the store's strengths. There could be others. Across the top are four evaluation criteria. A method as simple as a *yes* or *no* in each box could lead a retailer in the direction of an appeal. The key is to define the firm's strengths and then pick a single focus consistent with other strategies that will define the store in the mind of the customer.

Where Will You Place Your Advertisement?

The function of media is to provide a means for transmitting advertising messages to the market. Clearly a retailer cannot develop an effective appeal without understanding the medium that is going to carry it. At the same time,

FIGURE 13.3

The advertising message should focus on consumer benefits.

Product Analysis → Product and Store Features → Benefits ← Customer Motives ← Market Analysis

FIGURE 13.4

A retailer should pick a single focus for advertising that will position the store in the minds of customers. A *yes* should go in each box that defines a store strength. From the "yes" boxes a single focus can be selected.

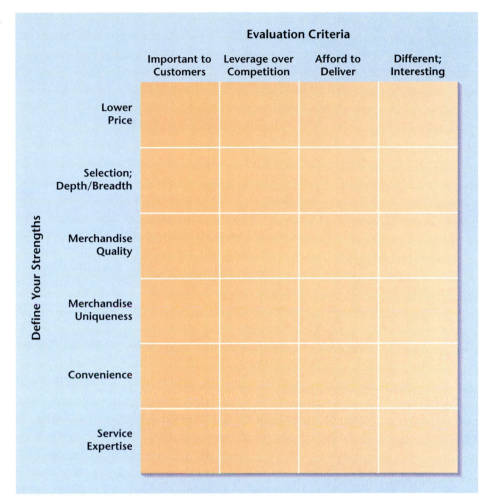

Evaluation Criteria

	Important to Customers	Leverage over Competition	Afford to Deliver	Different; Interesting
Lower Price				
Selection; Depth/Breadth				
Merchandise Quality				
Merchandise Uniqueness				
Convenience				
Service Expertise				

Define Your Strengths

the nature of the message influences the choice of medium. For example, if a product demonstration is critical to the message, radio may not be an appropriate choice.

Although retailers have traditionally been heavy users of newspapers, there are many threats to the growth of the print media, both newspapers and magazines. On-line computer service bulletin boards and advertisements, point-of-purchase displays, expansion of cable TV infomercials, expanded coupon distribution, catalogs, and direct mail all compete to carry the message.[14]

There are four primary kinds of media:

1. Printed media
    a. Direct mail
    b. Leaflets, handbills, and circulars
    c. Newspapers

      d. Magazines

      e. Yellow Pages

2. Broadcast media

      a. Radio

      b. Television

3. Traffic media

      a. Outdoor advertising—billboards

      b. Signs

4. Computer media

      a. The Internet

      b. Computer on-line services

      c. CD ROM and disks

Although it is difficult to choose which medium to use, the following is a list of questions that can help managers make selections.[15] Note that in answering these questions, a manager must already have made decisions about the market, objectives, and appeal.

1. Does the media reach the largest number of prospects at the lowest cost per prospect?

2. Does the media provide an opportunity for an adequate selling message, or does it make possible only the briefest of copy?

3. Does the media provide opportunity to illustrate the products or services being sold?

4. Does advertising in the media present any difficult, time-consuming, or creative problems?

5. Does the media actually sell products or services or merely announce them?

6. What is the media's flexibility? Can the message be changed easily?

7. Does the media provide opportunities to repeat the selling message?

8. Does the media provide excitement for special promotions?

9. Does the media fit my type of store in prestige and distinction?

10. Does the media cover my entire market area with minimum waste coverage of areas outside my trading zone?

11. Is the cost of advertising in the media within my financial capacity?

Media source guides.   A publication such as SRDS provides basic information on the media. SRDS publishes multiple volumes on a regular basis that give a great deal of information the retailer can use in evaluating media. Each broadcast station, newspaper, and magazine is included. A general description of the audience reached and the rates charged is provided.

Obviously, no one media is likely to provide perfect solutions to all the problems raised. Retailers have to find the media mix through which they

TABLE 13.1

Strong and Weak Points of the Various Media

	Strong Points	*Weak Points*
Newspaper	Permits product illustration Frequent publication Some flexibility in responding to sudden change Regularly used as a shopping guide Some geographical selectivity Immediacy Traditional advertising medium	Poor color reproduction Short life of individual issues Poor qualitative selectivity— everyone reads the paper Many competing ads
Radio	Personal—human voice can often be more persuasive than print Flexible—permits sudden change in message Particular stations may appeal to selective audience because of program content Relatively inexpensive	Audio only—may make less impact than visual media Can't use illustrations Short life of message Needs consistent use to be most valuable in achieving recognition
Television	Combines sound, sight, and motion to convey the message Some flexibility in responding to sudden change Gives a sense of immediacy	Expensive for small- or middle-sized retailer Message is short-lived Time and production costs are high
Outdoor advertising	Costs are low per person reached Low cost per impression delivered Frequent repetition of the message Good reinforcement media Good geographical selectivity	Poor qualitative selectivity Extreme copy limitations, message must be simple
Direct mail	Reaches a select market with precision Can be used on a limited budget Flexible in timing and message Can add a personal touch	High cost per person per message
Computer	Can be very interactive. New and modern. Reaches an upscale audience with well-defined demographics. Excellent graphics. Easily changed.	Effectiveness is unproven. Reaches a comparatively small market.

can best communicate. It is important, however, for retailers to understand the strengths and weaknesses of each (see Table 13.1). These may also be social issues involved in the selection of media. See Box 13.3. Let's look in more detail at selected media.

BOX

13.3   AN ETHICAL DILEMMA: DIVERSITY—SORT OF!

Retail advertisers spend millions of dollars to provide information to customers in an attempt to persuade them to shop at their particular store. *Ebony* is a national magazine that targets the African-American female as its primary audience. African Americans constitute 13 percent of the U.S. population. *Ebony*, in celebrating its fiftieth year, published "The *Ebony* Honor Roll," a list of "great companies" that have marketed their products through the magazine. The list of companies totaled 270. The few retailers included were:

Amway Corporation	J. C. Penney Company
Avon Products	Publix Supermarkets
Eckerd Drug	Sears, Roebuck and Co.
Edison Brothers Stores	The Southland Corporation
Franklin Mint	Spiegel, Inc.
Grolier Enterprises	T. J. Maxx Stores
Kmart	Toys 'R' Us
Thom McAn	U.S. Shoe
Benjamin Moore Paints	Walgreen Company
Nordstrom	Wal-Mart Stores, Inc.
PayLess Shoes	Zale Corporation

Only 22 retailers out of a total of 270 companies, or 7.8 percent, were represented on the list. Publix Supermarkets is listed, but where are Kroger, Safeway, and American Stores? Nordstrom is listed, but where are Federated Department Stores, May Department Stores, and even Dayton-Hudson? Eckerd and Walgreen are listed, but where are the other large drug chains? Sears and J. C. Penney are listed, but where is Montgomery Ward? Kmart and Wal-Mart are listed, but where is Target?

The primary source of revenue for magazines is from advertising. Subscription fees seldom do much more than pay the cost of delivery and some of the production costs.

Questions

Do you see an ethical issue here? What reasons might retailers have for not using a magazine as a print media for delivering their message? What reasons, or excuses, might they give for not selecting *Ebony* for their advertising? What would be your position?

Source: Adapted with permission from Robert Kahn, "Diversity—Sort of!" *Retailing Today*, August 1995, p. 1.

6543217

Newspapers.   Most advertising in daily newspapers is for local retailers. In weekly newspapers and neighborhood shoppers, the advertising is almost entirely local as well. These weeklies, together with dailies in small- and medium-sized cities and suburbs, are especially good media for retail and service advertising. Newspapers are good for retail advertisers for several reasons.

(1) People want local news. Many now depend on radio and television for news of national and international events. They also want news closer to home and of more personal interest. For this, they turn to their local newspapers. Many big city dailies are responding to the desire for local news by issuing zone and suburban editions.

(2) Newspapers have something for everybody. People of all ages, both sexes, every educational and income level, and varied cultural and recreational interests find something to read in newspapers. Regardless of what is sold, advertising in a newspaper will reach people who live near the store and are logical customers.

(3) Newspaper advertising is flexible. The paper can insert an advertisement wherever there is a place for it ("run of paper," or ROP), or the ad can be put on a special-interest page that preselects readers. There are society pages and sports pages, pages for real estate, automobiles, boating, gardening, and other special interests. There is flexibility, too, in the size and frequencies of the advertisement. A newspaper ad can illustrate what is offered and describe it in as much detail as desired.

(4) Newspaper advertising brings a quick response. Results will often continue to show up for as long as a week.

(5) Short lead times make quick changes possible. An ad can be submitted only two or three days before the publication date, or even later. This means that if the store sells food and a hot spell strikes, it can switch advertising to feature cold beverages and ice cream. If the store sells antifreeze or snow tires, it can inform a newspaper to run an ad as soon as the temperature drops to a specified degree or the snow is so many inches deep.

(6) Newspaper advertising gives intensive coverage. Most of its readers live in a well-defined, compact geographical area.

(7) Newspapers offer frequency of contact. This is true even if the only available newspaper is a weekly. Some advertisers in daily newspapers find that they get satisfactory results from once-a-week insertions.

Large general merchandise discounters, the membership warehouse stores, and the category dominant retailers have supplanted many of the traditional department stores whose ads supplied a majority of the newspaper advertising revenue. The newspapers have had to counter with strategies that appeal to the smaller secondary retailers, such as publishing neighborhood editions and supplements.[16]

Yellow Page directories. The majority of Yellow Page advertising, about 90 percent of revenues, is strictly local. The ads allow residents to find specific products at a specific location ("Let your fingers do the walking"). To test the pulling power of Yellow Pages the producers are now selling advertisements in the directory that are actually coupons. The retailer has no trouble identifying the source and thus has at least one measure of effectiveness. In a community of 70,000 people a quarter-page ad with one color would cost about $475 monthly. In a metropolitan area of 500,000, the cost could exceed $1,500 monthly.

Direct mail. **Direct mail** by retailers is expanding throughout the world, with growth in Europe rivaling that of the United States. Direct mail's share of the retailer's advertising budget is also growing. This topic is covered in depth in Chapter 15, "The Virtual Store and Retail Database Marketing."

Newspapers have been the primary advertising medium for retailers. The number of national chains and demographics are causing a shift to TV. In a recent two-year holiday period, TV advertising increased more than 60 percent while newspaper ads fell. Because of higher costs and fewer people reading newspapers, Pier 1 Imports cut its print advertising budget 75 percent. TV advertising brought in younger customers, and sales increased. (Lee, Louise, "Retailers Pin Holiday Hopes on TV Ads," *Wall Street Journal*, November 20, 1995, p. B5.)

Radio and television.

Radio and television are carrying an increasing volume of retail advertising. The time people spend reading is typically a fraction of the hours they spend listening to and viewing electronic media. To reach them, managers often find it necessary to augment print advertisements with radio or television ads.

Radio advertising, of course, has long been a workhorse for local business. Radio is a quick attention-getter that can introduce a store and its image to uninitiated customers, while generating enthusiasm and emotional response.[17] Radio advertising has been gaining favor among retailers as the media world has become more and more fractionalized.[18] With numerous AM and FM stations targeting niche markets, radio often offers a relatively low-cost way to speak to a variety of specific customer segments.

Television as a national medium is too expensive for most small retailers. On a local level, it can be beneficial and efficient relative to the size of the audience reached, particularly for multistore outlets that are located throughout a city. Radio and television allow accurate aim at an advertising target. Both have the flexibility to appeal to specific types of prospects: teenagers, home workers, young adults, or whoever your target customers are.

When shopping, do you ever turn around and wonder which store you are in because it looks like so many others? Not only is there intense price competition for many categories including apparel, home furnishings, consumer electronics, and food, but there is a great deal of similarity in brands, products, merchandising, and positioning. As a result of this "sameness" aggressive advertising has become essential. *The Wall Street Journal* reports that advertising on television by retailers is increasing while newspaper advertising is declining. In a recent two-year period, holiday ads increased 68 percent on the networks and 61 percent on local TV.

The human voice over the air can establish a friendly rapport with listeners. It can be more persuasive than print. For example, a female announcer can impart a feminine touch to commercials for products of special interest to women. Some advertisers broadcast their own commercials to give them a special personal sincerity. The human voice can also convey urgency. For an immediate response, the advertising message can end with a suggestion that listeners phone right away. Spoken in a conversational manner and repeated frequently, broadcast advertising is remembered. Television advertising is the closest of all to personal selling. Because it combines sight, color, motion, and sound, it can explain and demonstrate what is being sold in thousands of homes simultaneously.

Radio and television do have their disadvantages. If potential customers are not listening or watching during those seconds when the message is being transmitted, even the most creative advertisement is useless. The broadcast media lack permanence. The audience cannot cut out a radio ad and take it to the store with them. A television commercial cannot lie on the coffee table for a week waiting for someone to see it. That is why repetition is important. Repeating the message, of course, costs money. Many advertisers with limited budgets often use broadcast ads to supplement and call attention to their advertising in print media, often with excellent results. Finally, radio and television are limited to brief copy. The message typically lasts no more than a minute.

Cable television. The continuing growth of cable television has offered new opportunities to retailers. There are so many highly targeted programs that a retailer can select one that reaches a very specific audience. For example, The Bass House, a bait and tackle shop, sponsors a Saturday morning fishing show. New technology continually splits the TV audience into smaller and smaller segments. The digital satellite system (DSS) offers nearly 200 channels. Some cable companies are installing systems that will provide 500 channels, many of them interactive.

The role of cable television in retail advertising seems to be changing almost daily. Time-Warner has a product called ShopperVision that was being tested in the mid-1990s in Orlando, Florida. About 4,000 cable subscribers are linked together by the ShopperVision technology through their television sets to a database of supermarket and drugstore items. These items can be ordered directly by consumers through the network.[19]

Traffic media. Although not a major part of the media mix, retailers do use traffic media when frequent repetition of a message is desired. There are some 390,000 billboards in the United States, and the advertising revenue exceeds $1.5 billion. Technology is offering possibilities for making outdoor advertising easier and more convenient to use. Computer-generated graphics now allow advertisers the opportunity to see what their ads will look like on a billboard or carcard mounted on a bus, taxi, or company vehicle. Video technology is also being used to monitor how a given billboard looks in its environment without the retailer having to actually visit the location.[20]

Computer media. The rapidly expanding area of computer media includes delivery of the message via the Internet, services such as America Online, and CD ROM. Computer media is a topic of Chapter 15.

How Often Will You Advertise?

Customers are exposed to hundreds of commercial messages every day. Each successive message tends to make customers forget those received earlier. The frequency with which a retailer advertises depends on how often customers should be reminded and informed about the store's image, products, prices, and services.

Major events and sales benefit from advertising regularly. They will not be isolated occurrences but will seem part of the day-to-day business of the store. Continuity and consistency in communication are necessary to convey an image and to capture and retain customer interest.

While the size of individual ads is related to their frequency and the funds available, there are other factors to be considered as well. If the store features price discounts and other bargain offers, it will need to advertise often and will probably require large advertisements. How large a specific ad will be depends on how many products are to be mentioned, how large the illustrations are, how many words of description there are, and how bold the headlines are going to be.

Because the demand for what sells often varies with the season, the store should set up the size and frequency of ads that make people conscious of their needs. This would be the case for air conditioners, electric fans, heaters, antifreeze, and many other products. Christmas, Easter, Mother's Day, Father's Day, and other special occasions call for advertising if the products carried fit these special demands.

The newspaper often has special editions that should be planned for—back-to-school, heating, home remodeling, fashion, and so on. True, increased advertising in those issues will appear side by side with the increased advertising of competitors, but the fact that special pages are devoted to a specific type of product will focus the attention of buyers on their needs in that area. Whether the store or its competitors get the order will depend on which one makes the most attractive offer and on how well the offer is presented.

For some products, Wednesdays, Thursdays, and Fridays are heavy advertising days because of the approaching weekend. These days may also coincide with paydays. Similarly, most food ads will appear on the days when food is on the minds of many shoppers: usually before the weekend, a holiday, or a special event.

On the other hand (depending on what is sold), the day of the week may not be important in your advertising. Or the store may want to build up sales early in the week. If you believe consumers will make the effort to shop on Mondays and Tuesdays, when there is usually less advertising in the papers, these could be the logical days on which to schedule ads. However, they will not likely be remembered on the Saturday shopping trip.

How Much Will You Spend?

Many retailers try to spend as little as possible on advertising. They probably consider it to be an expense. However, it is more realistic and much more positive to consider advertising expenditures as an investment in sales, customer information, and positive attitudes. Many retailers don't want to take the time to do a good job of planning and advertising. They take an "all I can afford" approach or "whatever the competition seems to be doing." Neither is an example of good management. How much, then, should be spent on advertising?

Two methods are frequently used to provide an adequate advertising budget: the percentage of sales method and the objective and task method.

Percentage of sales method.
To budget based on a **percentage of sales,** you can use last year's sales or the current year's anticipated sales, together with average industry percentages. Although some retailers base their advertising budgets on last year's sales, this is not realistic. At the very least, it doesn't allow for changing conditions. A prudent manager should not base future action only on past results.

Typically, a budget based on a percentage of sales is constructed by using average industry percentages. These are easily obtained through the trade associations that serve the retailing industry. The firm may also use its own historical percentages.

Some retailers take the average percentage of net sales spent for advertising and apply the figure to past or anticipated sales. Even with its disadvantages, the percentage of sales method is practical and easy to use.

In every case the unique aspects of a particular store must be considered. Modifications in industry average or store experience percentages can be made on the basis of several factors:

1. Location—more promotion is needed for a store in a less favorable area.
2. Competition—new or strong competition may require additional expenditures.
3. New stores require additional expenditures until awareness is created and a trade is developed.
4. Stores with a strong price appeal usually require below average levels of promotion.
5. Special dates and events that offer sales opportunities may require additional expenditures.

Objective and task method.
An alternative or supplement to the percentage of sales approach is provided by the **objective and task method.** This is based on the premise that advertising should be budgeted to accomplish specific goals. In practice, the retailer will establish specific dollar sales objectives for the store or its product lines for the forthcoming event, season,

or year and will budget the amount to be spent on advertising to accomplish the objective. In developing the final budget, the retailer makes an estimate of how much will be needed to promote shopping events and how much will be required for regular advertising. In addition to making estimates for the store as a whole, the retailer may make budget estimates for merchandise lines or departments.

During the budget period, the sales picture is reviewed at regular intervals. Such reviews provide an opportunity to adjust the advertising budget if sales objectives are not being met or are being exceeded. Some retailers find the careful figuring, the constant watching, and the necessity to make changes a great burden and therefore do not use the task and objective method. It is, however, a logical and effective approach in planning advertising expenditures.

Even those retailers who use the objective and task method rely, to some extent, on the percentage of sales approach as a useful control device. Using average industry percentages provides a warning to managers who plan advertising budgets significantly smaller or larger than those used by competitive stores.

Reach and frequency. Many retailers advertise in low-cost media because they can "get more for less." However, the old axiom "You get what you pay for" is more often true than not. This issue can be examined by using the concepts of reach and frequency. The **reach** of an advertisement is defined as the total number of people who are exposed to the ad at least one time. The **frequency** of an advertisement is the average number of times that the ad is seen by the audience.

Retailers are using as many as 400,000 interactive multimedia self-service kiosks to provide information to consumers at lower costs. In a home electronics store a customer can see full-motion video clips that demonstrate TV resolution and the impact of motion control on their camcorder. In a sporting goods store the kiosk can communicate what is on the shelf, product features, and where to find the item.

TABLE 13.2

Example of Calculation of Cost of Reaching 1,000 People with Various Media

Media	Total Cost of a Single Ad	Reach (Audience or Circulation)	Cost per Thousand (CPM)
Local newspapers	$120	60,000	$2/M
Radio	100	20,000	5/M
Television	150	10,000	15/M

Advertising prices can be examined and compared using the cost per thousand (CPM) concept, which indicates how much it costs to reach 1,000 people. For example, Table 13.2 shows the relative price of several types of hypothetical ads.

Table 13.2 shows that even though the radio ad is the least expensive, the newspaper cost is less when considering the number of people that the ad reaches. However, it should also be recognized that different media have different levels of ability to persuade. Obviously, cost alone is not enough to make an informed decision on which media to choose, although it does allow for comparisons.

A relatively new concept, **effective reach,** refers to the number of target market members who have received enough exposures for the advertising to have the desired effect. Usually effectiveness is defined as having been exposed to the ad at least three times. However, the effective media reach measure does not distinguish between differing media vehicles and actual exposure levels.[21]

COOPERATIVE ADVERTISING

Cooperative advertising is a process whereby manufacturers or distributors share the cost of local ads with retailers. It currently represents over $15 billion a year in potential advertising support. Cooperative support comes largely from consumer goods manufacturers. In some local markets or shopping center programs, the merchants collectively contribute to each other's advertising. Consequently, we can classify it as either vertical or horizontal. **Vertical cooperative advertising** occurs when advertising support dollars for a retailer flow from either the manufacturer or the wholesaler. **Horizontal cooperative advertising** occurs when advertising support dollars for one retailer flow from another. Many franchisors require franchisees to contribute 1 or 2 percent of sales to a cooperative advertising fund that is supplemented by the franchisor.

Cooperative support is most commonly seen as a percentage contribution for print display advertising on behalf of the retailer. It is not uncommon for the manufacturer to pay up to 50 percent of the ad cost. For example, if May's Appliances placed a one-half-page advertisement featuring Maytag washing machines in the *Newton Chronicle* that cost $400, Maytag Corporation would "refund" May's Appliances $200. In addition to the financial support, Maytag Corporation will supply to the retailer much of the "camera ready" materials that are needed to design and construct a professional-looking retail ad. These items are often composed by an advertising agency or the manufacturer's ad staff and are usually better than what the retailer could produce alone. All the retailer has to do is add the store's name and address in the appropriate place. The ad is ready to print!

Another way that cooperative support is awarded is based on current dollar-value purchases or as credit against past purchases. Such methods are designed either to build current inventories and promote aggressive selling or to reward the retailer on past selling performance. A key stipulation is that the money awarded for cooperative advertising must be spent in that way. Failure on the part of either a manufacturer or a distributor to make cooperative awards available to all competing resellers on a proportionately equal basis is a violation of the 1936 Robinson-Patman Act.

Manufacturers are willing to spend money for cooperative support for several reasons. In some cases, they are willing to pay to increase local exposure for the product or product line. In other cases, the manufacturer wants to have the product or product line associated with the retailer and enjoy the benefits of the retailer's name or prestige. One of the principal motivators is money. It remains a common practice to offer local retailers significant discounts on newspaper advertising rates relative to national advertisers. In other words, the May's Appliance–Maytag alliance saved Maytag Corporation $400 by having May's, the local retailer, place the ad. By advertising cooperatively the way they did, both firms saved money. Specifically, May's saved $200 by Maytag paying half the cost, and Maytag saved $400 because May's paid the local rate rather than the national rate of $800.

Cooperative advertising can offer a significant promotion advantage as long as retailers are careful in selecting opportunities. One of the first questions regarding the selection of cooperative sponsors is, "How is the merchandise sold?" If, for example, the product line offering co-op is personally sold, then the use of the co-op to generate store traffic is a key benefit of participation. In fact, under such circumstances, you may or may not be overly concerned if the sponsored product is a high-margin item since customers can be cross-sold additional products. Conversely, if your merchandise assortment is largely self-service, then the selection of co-op partners should center on fast-moving, high-margin products. Some manufacturers permit the retailer to feature only those products manufactured by that single firm. In other cases, directly competing products cannot be featured, but items that "round out" a product line can be.

As you can see, the decision to use co-op support is not always an easy one. Overall, items should fit the image of the store, be timely, generally sell on their own, and bring enough profit to the store to offset the cost of advertising. It is important that a retailer not be lured into advertising for the sole purpose of generating co-op support from a manufacturer or distributor. At the same time, cooperative advertising does offer retailers a way to maximize the investment in positioning and promoting their merchandise. Yet millions of co-op advertising dollars go unspent.[22]

EVALUATING ADVERTISING EFFECTIVENESS

The retailer's efforts to establish a budget are guided by comparing the cost of promotion with the expected return. This is no different from the decision-making process used in building a new parking lot, setting up a window display, or investing more merchandise in inventory. The retailer is going to spend money on advertising because of the expectation that the expenditure will be more than offset by additional sales and ultimately profits. Whether the decision affects the store image, immediate sales, or number of customers, the alternatives to advertising or promotion are as difficult to evaluate as advertising effectiveness. Ideally, the retailer spends money on advertising so that sales are increased and the additional profits generated exceed the expenditure on the advertising effort.

To spend money on advertising so that profits are maximized, one must know (1) how sales are related to advertising expenditures and (2) how profits are related to sales. Measurement problems make it difficult to understand these relationships. Finding the relationship between sales and advertising is difficult because the way people have responded to a particular ad can never be definitely known. They may have responded to a message, or to the medium presenting the message, or because of the number of times they were exposed to the message. Retailers never know for certain what caused a particular sale.

Finding the profit generated by sales that may have been produced by advertising presents the same kind of problem. A customer who has been persuaded by advertising to purchase a sale item may become a regular customer and make many purchases in the future. In this case, which profits should be measured against which sales?

As an alternative to measuring sales relationships directly, a retailer may attempt to measure through survey research such factors as attitudes toward the store or recall of the store's name and products. For advertisements designed to stimulate immediate response, retailers rely on a simple tool to help them find out what sales were generated through the advertising. They

FIGURE 13.5

Calculating the sales results from an advertisement.

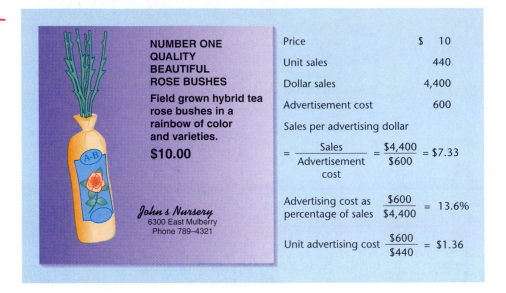

keep track of the number of units they sell during the time the ad is in effect. Then managers compute the retail value of these units and divide it by the advertising cost for the item. This gives them an idea of how many dollars of sales they received from each dollar spent on advertising.

For example, say a plant nursery ran the ad shown in Figure 13.5. That weekend sales of roses were $4,400. If the total cost of the ad was $600, the retailer would divide $4,400 by $600 to find that this ad produced $7.33 of sales for every dollar of advertising spent. However, if the weekend sales of roses this time of the year usually ran $2,000, the retailer might conclude that the $600 advertisement contributed only $2,400, the difference between the $4,400 and $2,000. The ad then contributed $4.00 in sales for each advertising dollar spent. Now note that if the gross margins were only 25 percent, the retailer merely broke even on the ad ($2,400 in additional sales times 25 percent equals $600, which was the cost of the advertisement). The retailer examines the results of the rose offering and has a basis for (1) deciding whether to run a similar ad again and/or (2) determining whether more or less money should be spent if roses were to be repeated in an ad.

THE LEGAL ENVIRONMENT OF ADVERTISING

The **Federal Trade Commission** (FTC), created by Congress in 1914, is the agency that enforces most sections of the Clayton Act and its amendments, including the **Wheeler-Lea Act,** which was passed in 1938.

The Wheeler-Lea Act of 1938

The Wheeler-Lea makes "unfair methods of competition and unfair or deceptive acts or practices in commerce unlawful." False or deceptive advertising for merchandise sold in interstate commerce is an unfair method of competition. The FTC jurisdiction includes ads placed through the media, promotion items sent through the mail, price lists, and similar promotional material.

In fulfilling its responsibility to determine what methods, acts, or practices are deceptive or unfair, the FTC, as the enforcement agency, has in recent years prosecuted many retailers and manufacturers for deceptive advertising. In particular, it has been concerned with deceptive advertising involving food and drugs. Furthermore, retailers and manufacturers have, in increasing numbers, been ordered to cease and desist from technically misrepresenting products in advertising and from using list prices to advertise low prices when the advertised merchandise is commonly available at prices below list.

Bait and switch. In **bait and switch,** products are advertised at an unusually attractive price. The retailer has no intention of selling the low-priced merchandise but instead wants to build store traffic. Once the customers contact the retailer, they are told that the goods or services are out of stock or of inferior quality. Then the retailer attempts to "switch" the consumer to a higher-priced product. This tactic of understocking advertised merchandise falls under the jurisdiction of the FTC. Recently, several states have passed laws requiring retailers to give "rain checks" for sold-out advertised specials. This guarantees the advertised product at the advertised price when the stock is replenished.

Advertising substantiation. In 1971, the FTC initiated a program for substantiation of advertising claims. An advertiser may be required to submit data to support claims of product safety, performance, quality, or comparative prices. The program is intended to provide information that will allow consumers to make more rational decisions and to discourage advertisers from making unsupported claims. *Discount Merchandiser* warns that modest transgressions in price claims are costing retailers thousands of dollars in court settlements.[23] It is recommended that retailers carefully substantiate claims, including comparative prices, before advertising.

Corrective advertisements. The FTC has used the **corrective advertisement** as a remedy designed to overcome the effects that misleading advertising may have had on the consumer. If a firm is found to have run deliberately misleading ads, it may be required to devote a percentage of its advertising budget to running FTC-approved advertisements for a certain period of time.

In general, the courts have ruled that retailers' advertisements are only invitations to customers; that is, they are not offers of contracts. This means that retailers cannot be held liable if they do not meet the terms in advertisements that contain mistakes in prices or descriptions.

Deceptive Advertising

Any advertising that contains a false statement about or misrepresents a product or service is deceptive and therefore unlawful. **Deceptive advertising** can take different forms: It can be an intentionally false or misleading claim by the advertiser, or it may be true in a literal sense but may leave some consumers with a false or misleading impression.

Price comparison.   A common practice of retailers is to compare the price of merchandise offered for sale with a higher "regular" price or a manufacturer's list price. This practice, known as **price comparison,** may be a good strategy since it gives customers a price comparison point. The Better Business Bureau guidelines state that proof of a retailer offering a product at a prior price for a reasonable period of time is enough to satisfy the law. Retailers should keep records documenting the price and the evidence of meaningful sales at that price before claiming a reduction. Documentation is also needed before advertising a comparison between a retailer's prices and the current price of identical merchandise at competitors' stores. Furthermore, the FTC ruled that it is deceptive to refer to the manufacturer's list price unless it was the ordinary and customary retail sales price of the merchandise in that area.

Puffery.   Simply exaggerating the benefits of a product is considered **puffery.** The use of puffery in advertising is common and generally allowable. The FTC has taken the position that consumers expect exaggeration or inflated claims in advertising and that puffery is recognizable by them and will not lead to deception since it is not believed.

THINK GLOBALLY—ADVERTISE LOCALLY

Global retailers face the classical international marketer dilemma: How does a company think globally in terms of sourcing, financing, concept, and format, and yet at the same time act locally with location, merchandise mix, and advertising? In each country, retailers must understand and take advantage of local market distinctions, social trends, and environments to capture market share.

It's obvious, as you have seen throughout the text, that strong retail concepts and formats are rapidly being adapted across national boundaries. In less than ten years, Aldi, the German food discounter, has opened over 3,000

Have a good gulp! Sapporo beer can be purchased in your local supermarket, at a sidewalk café in Europe, or in a convenience store in the Tokyo subway. Manufacturers with global brands support retailers with advertising tailored to the local market. Manufacturer advertising says, "Buy my brand." Retail advertising says, "Buy it at my store, at this price, now."

stores in European countries from Spain to Norway. The European furniture industry is dominated by the Swedish retailer IKEA, which is also opening stores in former Soviet Union countries. Benetton, the Italian women's fashion retailer, is expanding rapidly and becoming a market leader in Europe. Both IKEA and Benetton have a significant presence in the United States.[24]At the same time Japanese retailers are expanding into China, while Tiffany's and Toys 'R' Us are moving quickly into Japan and Southeast Asia. Wal-Mart and Pier One Imports have targeted Mexico. Advertising by these and all global retailers requires varying degrees of cross-country adaptation.

There are some critical issues that retail managers can start with as they think about advertising in a global environment. The framework for their planning requires answering the same questions asked throughout the chapters, beginning with a study of the market. The market study, however, requires a careful analysis of cultural differences. Retailers must understand customs, etiquette, values, and the characteristics of the dominant religions. Potential areas of difference include the role of family members, the perception of time, personal space, individuality versus group identity, and individual achievement versus personal relationships.[25]

Worldwide Standardization

Concurrent with a study of the markets, a policy question regarding worldwide standardization versus country customization has to be answered. The answer typically revolves first around an analysis of how different cultures might lead to the need for a different message or media.

Culture directly affects the way advertising communicates to customers because culture shapes attitudes, beliefs, perceptions, and value systems.[26]

This chapter has pointed out that an advertising message must use the language, signs, and symbols that have meaning to the customer in terms of the individual's environment and experience, of which culture is a major part.

Specialists in international marketing note that the degree to which advertising is adapted or standardized to the local culture is a significant policy issue.[27] Arguments for a more standardized approach include the fact that global consumers have similar needs and wants, particularly the more affluent customers typically targeted by the global retailer.

Proponents for customized country advertising policy would argue that each country must be seen as a special case because customers have significant differences in the way products and services satisfy needs, wants, and desires. The more customization, the greater the coordination problems in establishing a global image for the retailer.

Pattern Advertising

Retailers can resolve the conflict by establishing a policy of what is called pattern advertising. **Pattern advertising** is a global strategy with a standardized basic message that also allows some degree of adaptation to local situations.[28] A company entering Mexico would have to recognize that Americans are very time-sensitive while Hispanics are more flexible in this area. A pattern advertising campaign for dishwashers might be developed around the product's time-saving features. In the United States, the appeal might be implemented around the desire to "be at work on time." A cultural adaptation reflecting Mexicans' strong sense of family might emphasize the desire to "have more time for your children."

Language, Legal, and Media Differences

An understanding of the cultural environment forms the basis for the retailer to plan the advertising message. Language, legal, and media differences complicate the advertising effort. In India, for example, at least fourteen different languages and dialects make standardization difficult, even within the country. Similar situations exist elsewhere.

The legal environment can limit what is said as well as what media are used. For example, comparative advertising is restricted in Belgium, Luxembourg, and Germany.[29] Laws forbidding vulgarity or the use of sexual themes and restrictions on advertising of products such as alcohol are prevalent in Middle East countries. In Egypt, advertising is not allowed on television.

In selecting media, the global retailer faces significant differences in availability, cost, frequency, and reach across countries. In addition, consumers have significant media consumption patterns. For example, in Mexico, only about 18 percent of advertising expenditures are in print media, while nearly 50 percent are in television. In contrast, over 50 percent of the expenditures in New Zealand are in print media, while television expenditures are about 28 percent.[30]

SEARS—REVISITED: UNORTHODOX? PROMOTIONS

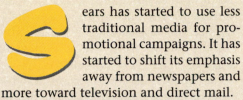

ears has started to use less traditional media for promotional campaigns. It has started to shift its emphasis away from newspapers and more toward television and direct mail.

In 1994 Sears agreed to support a yacht racing team and formed a $3 million agreement to partially sponsor Dennis Conner's *Stars and Stripes* boat in the America's Cup race.[31] The agreement allows Sears to use the "Stars and Stripes" label on sportswear and shoes. It was the first time the company involved itself in something of this nature on a large scale.

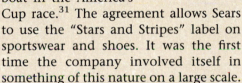

Sears also agreed to exclusively sponsor Phil Collins' thirty-city North America concert tour, hoping to increase its name recognition with the younger generation. This is a radical change from the middle-income family that has been Sears' traditional customer. Sears put up banners near the stage and posters throughout the stadium. It sold Collins'

album "Both Sides" at its Brand Central departments. It was the first time that CDs were sold at Sears. Initial sales of the release during the first seven weeks were about 500,000 units.[32]

Many analysts applaud the initiative and the choice Sears made by sponsoring Phil Collins. The rock star is one of the few who has appeal across age groups. Also, Mr. Collins is a fairly safe bet in an unstable industry. It is not expected that he will cause the problems that Pepsi ran into when it sponsored Madonna and Michael Jackson.

As it became comfortable with the idea of nontraditional formats, Sears began to experiment even further. King World Productions Inc. has produced several "infomercials" for Sears.[33] The first thirty-minute commercial promoted the $350 Kenmore Wispertone II vacuum cleaner. A smaller two-minute segment was produced for a pair of Sears pliers called RoboGrip.

1. **Will sponsoring a rock concert help or hurt Sears with its traditional customers?**
2. **What impact might it have on the potentially new market from a younger generation?**
3. **What are the risks associated with identifying with celebrities in store promotions?**
4. **Do you think infomercials will be a viable way for retailers to sell products?**

Summary

Effective communication between retailers and consumers is a central factor in the success or failure of a retail store. Successful promotion and advertising require that the retailer grab the attention of the consumer while delivering the relevant message.

The retail promotion mix consists primarily of advertising, sales promotion, personal selling, public relations, and packaging.

Advertising objectives are set by the retailer and depend on what stage in the decision process consumers are in and whether the objective provides a method of quantitatively measuring performance. An advertising objective should contain a specific product/service identification, specific goals, audience/market identification, benchmark levels, and a time horizon.

After defining the market, setting precise objectives, and selecting what to advertise, decisions must be made concerning the advertising message, media, and budget. Each media has unique advantages and disadvantages that must be weighed before deciding which one is best for the message. Advertising budgets are normally set by using the percentage of sales or the objective and task method.

Evaluating advertising effectiveness is a difficult task for retailers because of the problem in measuring the exact influence of advertising on sales. Measures such as reach, frequency, and cost per thousand provide some assessment of advertising efficiency.

There are many state and federal laws that regulate retail advertising. In the international market, there are many country-specific laws that affect the advertising message and media choices. Global retail expansion has given rise to many debates concerning issues of culture and standardization versus customization in retail advertising.

Key terms and concepts

Advertising, 500
Awareness objective, 502
Bait and switch, 521
Communication channel, 497
Cooperative advertising, 517
Corrective advertisement, 521
Deceptive advertising, 522
Decoding, 497
Direct action objectives, 502
Direct mail, 511
Effective reach, 517
Encoding, 497

Federal Trade Commission, 520
Feedback, 499
Frequency, 516
Horizontal cooperative advertising, 517
Indirect action objectives, 502
Information, 497
Measured media, 495
Noise, 499
Objective and task method, 515
Pattern advertising, 524

Percentage of sales budget, 515
Persuasion, 497
Price comparison, 522
Puffery, 522
Reach, 516
Receiver, 497
Retail promotion mix, 500
Source, 497
The Wheeler-Lea Act, 520
Unmeasured media, 495
Vertical cooperative advertising, 517

QUESTIONS

1. Does the relative importance of advertising vary among a supermarket, a discount store, and a specialty store? What factors cause the differences?

2. Explain why choice of media influences the nature of the advertising message and vice versa.

3. From your local newspaper, select an advertisement for men's or women's wear. Can you identify the target market? Can you determine what the retailer was trying to accomplish?

4. Why do retailers usually employ several media in their advertisement programs?

5. Discuss the process of encoding. How can it be altered or disturbed?

6. Why do most retailers use newspapers for their advertising?

7. Why would a retailer wish to advertise on cable TV instead of network programs?

8. Which is the best way to determine an advertising budget?

9. Which advertising media has the highest reach? Which has the highest frequency?

10. Should all retailers use cooperative advertising?

11. What is bait and switch? Is it illegal?

12. Should international retailers standardize their advertising message? What are the advantages and disadvantages?

13. Is the practice of exaggerating claims about products or stores legal? Is it ethical?

SITUATIONS

1. You are the promotion manager in a large metropolitan department store. Last week you attended a meeting of consumers and retailers sponsored by the Mall Merchants Association. You were surprised by the ferocity of the outcry against advertising directed toward small children—particularly advertising associated with toys and food products. Because your firm has been using co-op advertising with a toy manufacturer to sponsor a children's action show on Saturday morning television, you initiated a check of your firm's letters of complaint. Criticism of this type of promotion activity seems to have been increasing dramatically. These are selected quotations:

"I deplore your firm's callous manipulation of children for your own profit-oriented purposes."

"Who do you think you are? Have you no conscience, morals, or sense of decency?"

"Our organization opposes commercial exploitation of small children. Because industry has been unable to clean up its own house, we will concentrate our efforts on passage of strict laws prohibiting this activity. We believe that this is a sensitive political issue. Victory is expected."

"Because of your advertising program, our family will no longer buy your products."

What kind of response will you make to consumer groups that are concerned because you are advertising children's toys on TV?

2. You are the owner-manager of a pet shop in a community of 50,000. Recently, a group of interested citizens gathered to develop what they considered to be an appropriate sign code for the city. As a result of their meetings, they have called for legislation that would prohibit the use of any signs not attached to the building and that would limit the size of signs to no larger than 3 feet by 5 feet. In addition, they are proposing that revolving signs and signs with blinking lights be forbidden. Your store is located in a block with many other retail stores. You have recently paid $5,000 for a new sign, which in your estimation makes it easier for people to see your store and know what services you offer. What position will you take?

CASES

CASE 13A
Law Firm Advertising

Monty Miller and Dori Jenkins recently formed a law firm in a city of 150,000 on the East Coast. Monty specializes in consumer cases and Dori in real estate and contract law. Because business had been slow in developing, they were considering doing some advertising. Ever since the Supreme Court's 1977 approval of law firm advertising, nearly all those that advertise have directed their appeals to middle-income consumers looking for counsel for divorces, wills, personal injury, and other common problems. Some lawyers are shedding their "budget clinic" image to attract more clients, including beginning businesses.

For example, one competitive firm is preparing ads aimed at small businesses and at professionals who need help with state licensing agencies. Another firm that chases bad debts has begun to pitch corporate clients with ads in a local business-oriented newspaper. A poll by the American Bar Association in mid-1991 showed that 27 percent of all lawyers had advertised at least once. The percentage, says an ABA official, has reached a plateau since then.

1. *What are the pros and cons Monty and Dori should consider in deciding whether or not to advertise?*

2. *Assuming they decide to advertise, what message and media alternatives would you recommend? Why?*

CASE 13B
Second City Bank

Lamar Lewis was the vice president for the Second City Bank, located in a town of 85,000 people. Lewis saw the bank primarily as a retailer of financial services. The city was growing fairly fast. The local university was also growing and contributing to the thriving economy. Lewis had recently read a report confirming his suspicions that few people change banks once they make an initial decision. He concluded that the major avenue of growth open to the bank was to attract new customers as they moved into the community. Because he had little information as to why people make a particular choice, he commissioned a local research firm to conduct a study for him. A summary of the report follows:

One hundred and two personal interviews were conducted.

Using house value or apartment rent as a proxy for income, First National seems to draw a proportionally greater share of customers from the upper-income groups. This variable does not seem to influence choice of Second City or other banks.

In terms of percentages, First National draws proportionally more customers from the white-collar and student ranks, while Second City does better in the blue-collar segment.

Location appears to be important for all occupational groups. The second most often mentioned basis for choosing a bank was recommendation by friends and coworkers.

A breakdown suggests that a bank's location is most important in relation to place of employment, followed by the location in relation to residence and in relation to a regularly traveled route.

For selecting a bank, the recommendations of friends and relatives far outweigh the advice of business associates, but the recommendations of coworkers were more important to white-collar employees than to blue-collar workers.

Other considerations for bank selection included bank advertisements, bank literature, full-service banking, and drive-in capabilities.

Only 18 percent of the respondents said they spent more than one day collecting, formulating, and studying information in order to make a banking decision. Most people open a bank account within just a few days of moving into town.

1. *Given the results of the study, what advertising would you recommend to Lewis?*

14

Chapter Goals

After reading this chapter, you should be able to:

- Understand the roles of personal selling, publicity, and sales promotion.

- Explain the duties and responsibilities of a salesperson.

- Comprehend the retail selling process.

- Demonstrate how to manage salespeople and improve employee productivity.

- Identify the forms of employee compensation.

- Distinguish between the various types and uses of sales promotion activities.

- Understand the different aspects of publicity.

RETAIL SELLING, SALES PROMOTION, AND PUBLICITY

NORDSTROM: COMPETING WITH SALESPERSON SERVICE

Nordstrom is an upscale specialty fashion retailer whose unique format has allowed it to achieve higher sales per square foot than any other similar store. Nordstrom has expanded well beyond its traditional West Coast base with phenomenal success, much of which is attributed to a unique culture and organizational style that concentrates on customer satisfaction.[1]

A Commitment to Service

While other retailers have attempted to copy Nordstrom's format, none has yet succeeded. Nordstrom has turned the traditional pyramid organizational chart upside down, literally. This inverted pyramid puts the customers at the top, with "top" management on the bottom. It underscores the idea that the manager's job is to support the sales floor in dealing with customers' needs. The bottom-up design has allowed for greater degrees of autonomy on the sales floor and in the buying process.

Unlike traditional retailers that have one buyer for three to five stores, Nordstrom often has a buyer for each department in the store. This is especially true for its shoe departments, which have led the market in sales. Although having many buyers presents some logistical problems for vendors (i.e., dealing with many individuals making smaller purchases), the company believes it allows the buyers to purchase specific merchandise for their markets and to respond to the unique idiosyncrasies of each market by being closer to salespeople and customers. The buying process has traditionally been very personalized and low-tech.

Nordstrom has incorporated technology only when it would be an added benefit to its customers. This lack of technology made the merchandising systems in the stores archaic compared to those of other retailers. However, in the last several years this situation has changed, and Nordstrom has started to adopt higher-tech systems. The late entry into the technology game has allowed the stores to capitalize on the latest developments and continually falling costs. The company has insisted that new technology enhances its current

NORDSTROM

operating structure and does not change it. This has allowed for a successful marriage of technology and culture that is unique in the retail industry.

Nordstrom maintains exceptional customer service. In fact, the results of Frequency Marketing Inc.'s retail satisfaction index ranked Nordstrom highest among seventy retail department and discount stores in overall customer satisfaction.[2] The salespeople help deliver exceptional service through activities such as handwriting thank-you notes to customers and personally calling them to announce new product arrivals or impending promotional sales. Also, it's not unknown for a Nordstrom salesperson to call and remind customers of a spouse's birthday or special events such as anniversaries. New computer software allows salespeople to keep customer information in a readily accessible database.

1. **What are the competitive advantages that Nordstrom has over other retailers?**

INTRODUCTION

As discussed in the previous chapter, the **promotion mix** includes personal selling, sales promotion, publicity, and advertising. This chapter will discuss the first three. Each is a necessary component of the promotion mix (see Figure 14.1). A retailer should strive to use all parts of the promotion mix to create a single image in the mind of the consumer. Treating these aspects separately often results in confusion.

PERSONAL SELLING

Personal selling involves the individual, face-to-face communication between a sales associate and a customer. Effective personal selling is often the most important element in retail communications. In a retail setting personal selling really occurs any time a store employee interacts with a customer. Whether the customer is ordering a soft drink over a remote speaker in a Hardee's drive-through or negotiating terms for a new Lexus, personal selling is taking place.

FIGURE 14.1

Personal selling, sales promotion, and publicity are important communications channels for the retailer.

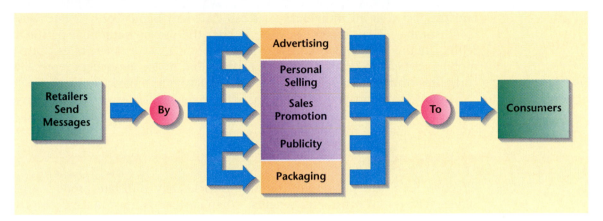

As retailing becomes increasingly dominated by large chains and super-sized low-cost discounters, cost control, flexibility, self-service, and low price will dominate many retail environments. Heavy manufacturer promotion budgets, deep discounting, and keen competition have reduced the need for personal selling in many formats. Not only has the structure of retailing changed dramatically, but the retail personnel pool is growing increasingly diverse. Consequently, because personal service usually requires the time of relatively expensive employees, it is critical that these encounters result in the sale of high-margin goods or ones requiring high levels of customer service.[3]

Diversity, the blending of many ethnic and demographic groups, also promises to offer numerous opportunities and challenges for today's retail manager. As the hiring, training, scheduling, advancement, and termination of sales associates become increasingly complex, so will the opportunities to match the individual skills of sales personnel to a pool of customers with constantly changing needs. While this chapter is dedicated to explaining the role of personal selling in today's retail setting, it is incumbent upon us to constantly think in terms of how changes in our society will create challenges and opportunities in the retail sales force.

The Economics of Retail Personal Selling

Today's high-volume low-margin orientation to retailing has prompted some managers to employ personnel whose primary responsibilities are to restock shelves, arrange merchandise, complete transactions at checkout, and provide assistance in helping customers find merchandise. These individuals are not asked to spend a lot of time with each customer or to help them buy. Rather, the retail associate must quickly and professionally show the customer the desired merchandise and move on to the next customer. Full-service selling is not an economic option in many sectors of today's retail economy.

The extraordinarily low retail margins available on most consumer goods and the fact that an individual sales associate can handle only a relatively fixed number of customers per hour restrict the use of traditional personal selling in the retail environment to high-margin low-turnover items. Automobiles, expensive fashions, suits, furniture, and major appliances represent categories of items where personal selling could be economically viable.

Despite this apparent inability to "afford" retail sales associates in many settings, the importance of selection and training remains a critical ingredient in the retailing mix.

Effective Selling

Effective retail salespeople are communicators. They translate product and service features into customer benefits. When customers must make decisions about brand, style, quality, price, color, and size, it is often the sales associate who skillfully guides the purchase decision. Not surprisingly, sales associates become the permanent representatives of the store. Figure 14.2 illustrates the importance RadioShack places on the role of the sales associate.

You may have a "favorite" sales associate in a shoe, suit, accessory, or jewelry department. This individual is someone with whom you have established a rapport and feel comfortable. As a result of initial and long-run interactions with one or more salespeople, customers judge a store, in large measure, by the impressions given by its sales staff. When customers make a purchase, they buy not only the product but also a set of psychological satisfactions provided by the salesperson, the retailer, and the manufacturer. It is important, therefore, that retail managers devote a significant level of energy to hiring, training, and rewarding sales associates.

Because there are an increasing number of self-service stores and because manufacturers are attempting to presell merchandise through extensive adver-

FIGURE 14.2

Stores like RadioShack give personal selling a significant stragetic role. (*Source:* Used with permission of RadioShack. Statement by Mr. Leonard H. Roberts on his first day as president of RadioShack.)

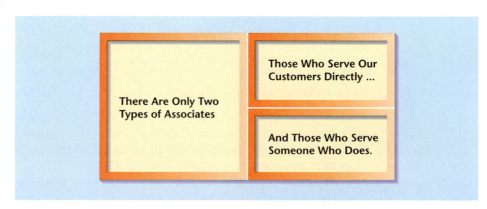

There Are Only Two Types of Associates

Those Who Serve Our Customers Directly ...

And Those Who Serve Someone Who Does.

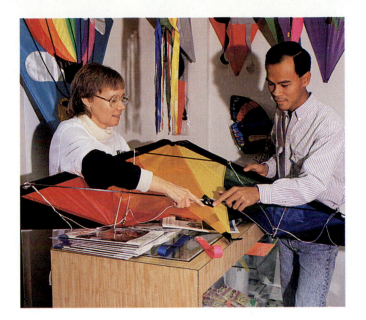

The difference between stores often comes down to customer service by sales associates who know what is expected of them. A National Retail Federation report outlines the keys to high performance in personalized customer service: Give the customer appropriate greeting, determine the customer's need by listening and asking questions, make the shopping experience enjoyable, direct customers to traditional services, and refer customers to another department. (Reda, Susan, "Blueprint for Retail Skill," *Stores*, February 1995, pp. 24–26.)

tising, it might be argued that personal selling is losing some of its importance. Even in these situations, however, the people on the floor are important to sales because customers ask them for information and advice. Supermarkets, for example, are models of self-service. Yet many people ask for help in the bakery, produce, and meat departments.

Personal Selling and Communication

One essential part of effective communication is feedback. Only in personal selling does the potential for a clear feedback channel exist. Checkout personnel and cashiers are "salespeople" in the sense that they convey a message to the customer and are in a position to help the shopper solve problems.

As salespeople talk with customers, they not only hear verbal responses but also see smiles, frowns, and nods. The verbal responses and the nonverbal reactions provide feedback that helps salespeople tailor the sales message to the specific needs of the customer. This feedback also helps salespeople provide additional information of the kind most likely to reduce customer uncertainty. Likewise, customers receive feedback from salespeople. Nonverbal reactions from the sales staff—a helpful manner, pride in the products and the store, and friendliness—may increase the customer's receptivity to the salesperson's verbal message.

Unquestionably, advertising can call attention to products, create interest in them, and (in many cases) even convince customers to buy them. However, only in the face-to-face communication that takes place in the personal selling situation can retailers (1) clearly identify the individual customer's problems, (2) pinpoint the customer's uncertainties about purchasing and provide knowledge and information to reduce these uncertainties, and (3) provide specific reasons that help the customer make a purchasing decision.

Personal Selling in the Retail Promotion Mix

The role of personal selling in the retail promotion mix varies widely by type of store, merchandise, price policy, and customer. The strategy that management takes to position the store is the determining factor in the role established for personal selling.

At the most basic level sales associates can simply help consumers complete a transaction. At a higher level information is provided to customers to assist them in making purchases. At the highest level associates persuade customers to make purchases that have benefits matching the shopper's needs and wants. At every level the sales staff must help maintain customer satisfaction and service. They may also play a key role in handling returns and dealing with customer concerns and complaints. See Figure 14.3.

Through effective face-to-face communication, salespeople translate product features into benefits and satisfactions that solve customers' problems and fill their needs. To be successful, salespeople must know their merchandise,

FIGURE 14.3

The hierarchy of responsibilities in differing roles for personal selling.

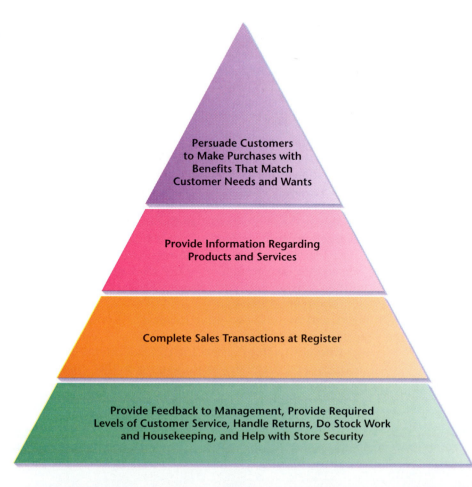

Persuade Customers to Make Purchases with Benefits That Match Customer Needs and Wants

Provide Information Regarding Products and Services

Complete Sales Transactions at Register

Provide Feedback to Management, Provide Required Levels of Customer Service, Handle Returns, Do Stock Work and Housekeeping, and Help with Store Security find out what their customers want and why they want it, and use selling techniques designed to produce satisfaction.

Retail selling is a difficult job that involves long hours of standing and working with customers who may not always be pleasant. The salesperson has to keep up with what is new in an environment where there are more and more items, and where the sales features of each product are varied and often technically complicated. The sales staff must perform a number of different functions, including customer contact, stock work, housekeeping, and security.

Customer contact. Once the retail salesperson has greeted the shopper promptly and courteously, he or she may first be involved in simply making a transaction. In this case, the customer has a specific product purchase in mind and the salesperson's job is to write a sales ticket, arrange for payment or credit, and possibly wrap the item and prepare it for delivery. Accuracy is very important in handling these transaction functions.

The second element of customer contact involves creative selling: identifying the customer's problems, responding to questions, answering objections, or showing how a particular product may meet the customer's needs. A creative salesperson generates sales by providing the kind of information particular customers require. For example, one shopper looking for a large appliance may need information about the availability of financing, warranties and guarantees, delivery arrangements, and other service-related questions; a second customer may seek information about the technical nature of the product—its construction and its component parts. A creative and effective salesperson can modify a presentation to satisfy both types of shoppers.

The third element of customer contact may involve handling complaints. There are times when service is unsatisfactory or products do not work, and it is these times when the salesperson will encounter the irate or unhappy shopper. The salesperson must start with the premise that the customer is always right and do whatever is possible in line with store policies to make sure that an unhappy customer is not turned into a permanently lost one. Rather, the object is to have a shopper who is more loyal to the store than before because a complaint has been satisfactorily handled. Salespeople are also responsible for providing after-sale service, such as product operating instructions or information about maintenance, as well as for handling returns and exchanges.

Finally, salespeople have responsibilities to their customers in seeing that they make the best possible product decision in light of needs and financial resources. It is the responsibility of salespeople to help educate consumers to be wiser shoppers.

Housekeeping and stock work. Some of the salesperson's time must be involved in keeping the store and the selling areas clean, and arranging the merchandise and displays. Working the shelves is another continuous task. As goods are sold, the shelves must be refilled.

Security. The store's best protection against the shoplifter is the retail sales-person. The sales staff has a responsibility to the store to be vigilant and aware of the techniques shoplifters may use. Ross Stores, for example, have an award system for sales associates that includes earning points for deterring and apprehending shoplifters. Greeters and close personal attention have also proved to be effective in reducing the incidence of theft.

How Should a Salesperson Sell?

Almost all views of the selling process fall into one of three categories: (1) the stimulus-response approach, (2) the selling formula approach, or (3) the problem-solving–need-satisfaction approach. All three require salespeople to be aware of legal and ethical issues. See Box 14.1.

The key to selling is merchandise knowledge. There is absolutely no way people can effectively sell a product or service they know nothing or little about. Many salespeople do not even know the store has an ad in the local paper the day it runs.

The **stimulus-response approach** is based on the premise that for a given stimulus there is a particular response. You may be familiar with the work of the Russian scientist Pavlov, who conditioned dogs to salivate (response) at the sound of a bell (stimulus). This approach suggests that if salespeople have a series of things to do or say (stimuli), and if they say and do them correctly, they will obtain the desired response (buying). However, customers differ: What pleases one may or may not please another.

The **formula approach** is based on a standard sales presentation containing statements that lead the customer through stages to a purchase. One frequently used formula is **AIDA:** attract attention, arouse interest, create desire, and obtain action. Like the stimulus-response approach, the formula method is based on the assumption that all customers can be persuaded by the same message. The approach does not take into consideration customer questions and individual needs.

The **problem-solving–need-satisfaction approach** differs from the previous two methods in that it stresses the importance of being genuinely concerned about individual customer needs. In the previous two cases, sales-people dominated the conversation, presenting a message designed to per-suade the customer. The problem-solving–need-satisfaction approach is ori-ented toward the individual. Notice in Box 14.2 what Saks Fifth Avenue says about the customer.

In the initial phase of the selling situation, salespeople are encouraged to ask questions designed to clarify or to define the customer's problem. Care-ful questioning, with the customer doing most of the talking, helps the sales-person find out what the shopper's needs are and how he or she will use the product. Once salespeople have pinpointed customers' needs, they can select the appropriate combination of features of the product or service. The sales-person's role, then, is one of translating the product's features into benefits

BOX 14.1 AN ETHICAL DILEMMA: WHAT WOULD YOU DO IF YOU RECEIVED THIS LETTER?

Robert Kahn, editor of *Retailing Today*, reports that the following letter was written by one of his readers to the manager of operations at a large supermarket chain.

Attached find a cash register receipt from your store in . . .

The customer immediately before me was a girl who I surmise was less than 18 years old. She purchased a pack of Marlboro Light cigarettes. I commented to your cashier, Laurie B., that I believed her less than 18. She stated that she thought the girl more than 18. I told her that I thought it was irresponsible to treat this in such a casual manner. The customer was not out of the store, and if Laurie wanted to, she could have had the manager check the girl's I.D., but she didn't.

The supermarket is directly across the street from a high school, and I have seen lots of students in the store from time to time. It is vacation time now; however, I think I can recognize a high schooler as well as most.

I play handball with an agent from ATF [U.S. Bureau of Alcohol, Tobacco and Firearms]. Had he been with me in the store at the moment, I feel confident that he would have stopped the girl, showed her his badge, and asked to see her identification. If she was under 18, he would have closed your supermarket on the spot.

Questions

If the law states that there are to be no sales of any specific product to a person below a certain age, what responsibility does the store have to be sure salespeople follow the law? Do you have an ethical responsiblity in this situation regardless of the law? What would you say in a letter replying to this customer? What excuses might a manager make in the situation? How about, "We thought he (or she) was over eighteen." "Everybody sells to underage kids." "Cigarettes are high-margin items, and we need the money."

Source: Robert Kahn, "What Would You Do If You Received This Letter?" *Retailing Today,* September 1995, p. 3

6543217

and advantages. Notice that this process is no different from that used in constructing a good advertising message, except that in personal selling the message can be tailored to the individual customer.

The problem-solving–need-satisfaction approach requires that salespeople have a thorough knowledge of merchandise, stock, store policies, services, promotion, and competition. They must be able to take cues from the customer, to listen well, and to talk about merchandise in specific terms, that is, in terms of how it will help the customer.

BOX

14.2 ELEVEN COMMANDMENTS OF GOOD BUSINESS: A CUSTOMER IS . . .

A customer is the most important person in any business.

A customer is not dependent on us—we are dependent on her.

A customer is not an interruption of our work—he is the purpose of it.

A customer does us a favor when she calls—we are not doing her a favor by serving her.

A customer is part of our business—not an outsider.

A customer is not a cold statistic—he is a flesh and blood human being with feelings and emotions like our own.

A customer is not someone to argue with but to help.

A customer is a person who brings us her needs, and it is our job to fill those needs.

A customer is deserving of the most courteous and attentive treatment we can give him.

A customer is the person who makes it possible for us to earn our salary.

A customer is the lifeblood of our business.

Source: Courtesy of Saks Fifth Avenue.

6543217

THE RETAIL SELLING PROCESS

Let's take a brief look at the selling process. It cannot, in practice, be divided into separate actions, although there are at least five parts: (1) approaching the customer, (2) determining customer needs and wants, (3) the selling presentation, (4) closing the sale, and (5) following up after the sale.

Approaching the Customer

Many retail sales are made in the first few moments after the customer arrives in the sales area. If the salesperson displays a courteous, helpful attitude, an excellent start is made. However, the sale will be difficult if the customer is neglected and treated in an unfriendly manner.

The initial greeting to the customer is very important. Many salespeople repeat the worn phrases "May I help you?" or "Can I help you?" This is an overworked and ineffective approach because the standard response is "No, thank you" or "Thanks, but I'm just looking." Once the customer says this, the salesperson must leave or possibly make the customer uncomfortable by staying nearby.

Phrases that do not allow for a "No, thank you" are better to use, such as "What size are you looking for?" "What size (color, style) of refrigerator did you have in mind?" or "May I show you the sale merchandise featured in today's newspaper advertisement?" The retail salesperson who uses this approach offers assistance without the customer having to request it and does not invite the negative reply. The key is for the salesperson to show concern for the customer's interests, be willing to provide information, and give customer assistance while making the individual feel important.

Determining Customer Needs and Wants

In order to make an effective sales presentation, the salesperson must strive to identify the individual's wants. As was pointed out in the chapter on understanding the retail customer, this is a difficult task because of the variety of consumer tastes and interests. To determine customer needs, the salesperson first must learn to listen. Concentrating on what the customer is trying to say is important because some may have difficulty in expressing their needs in terms of specific product characteristics.

Complementary to listening is learning to ask questions designed to help the customer formulate and express specific needs. Questions such as "Who will use the merchandise?" "How will it be used?" "Is it a gift?" all may guide the salesperson in identifying needs. If there is any doubt, ask the customer. Finally, the salesperson must be alert. Observing the customer's behavior, manner of dress, and facial expressons can provide necessary clues.

The Selling Presentation

The selling presentation may involve a number of elements. It starts with an explanation of the product and its benefits as they are related to the needs, wants, and problems the customer may have. An actual demonstration of the product always adds impact to the presentation. Stimulating the senses through feeling the texture or weight of a fabric, smelling an aftershave lotion, or seeing how the shoes look when tried on may take the customer a major step closer to purchasing the product.

In cases where the exact product or brand is not carried, or when another item may suffice or clearly offers better satisfaction for the customer's needs, **substitute selling** may be used. The salesperson may suggest another brand of the same item or an alternative product. There is sometimes the opportunity to trade up. This involves the customer buying a more expensive item or a larger quantity of a product than originally intended. Both trading up and substitute selling should be approached with caution. Ill will for the store will obviously result if the customer is dissatisfied with the alternative merchandise or feels that he or she has been pressured by the seller into accepting an unsatisfactory alternative.

Another important part of the presentation is known as **suggestion selling.** This consists of suggesting a tie to go with a shirt, a pair of earrings to go with a certain outfit, or a handbag to go with the shoes. Suggestion selling will really add to the sales volume if done with the customer's taste and wants in mind.

Closing the Sale

Closing the retail sale may occur almost as soon as the shopper walks into the store. The customer may know exactly what she wants, what brand, and the price she expects to pay. In this case, the salesperson's job, in terms of closing, is simply to complete the transaction. But often the retail selling process requires a creative closing effort in order to bring the customer to the actual decision to buy.

Without the close there is no sale, so it is important for the salesperson to learn when to close and how to do it. The **close** is the process by which the salesperson gets the customer to make a commitment. First, the salesperson must learn when the customer appears to be ready. Obviously, those who attempt to close too quickly will appear overly aggressive. By the same token, the customer who is ready to buy does not want to hear much additional selling information.

There are a number of closing techniques that a good salesperson can learn to use. Many are variations on questions such as "What particular features are you looking for in a chair?" to obtain responses that will determine how far the customer has gone in making up his or her mind about what is desired. If the customer replies with an answer identifying features similar to those the salesperson has presented, it is time for another question, such as "Will that be cash or charge?" "Do you want us to deliver it?" or "Do you want to take it with you?" All the questions should be designed to determine if the customer has all the information needed and has made a decision. Box 14.3 makes additional suggestions to keep from losing sales.

Following Up after the Sale

Following up is an important part of the selling process. For big-ticket items the salesperson typically has an address and phone number. A simple thank-you note can go a long way to help the customer feel good about a transaction. More importantly, a phone call can reveal possible areas of potential concern that the customer has about the product or the service received. Firms or individuals can put customer information into a database (Chapter 15) for regular follow up with greeting cards at appropriate times, announcements of new merchandise, product recalls, and so forth.

14.3 WHY SALES ARE LOST

Very often sales are lost through carelessness or indifference on the salesperson's part. Here are some reasons why:

1. **Disinterest.** Don't conduct a conversation with a fellow employee or another customer while waiting on someone. Give the customer your complete attention.

2. **Mistakes.** If you show the wrong item or make a mistake in change, acknowledge it and make the customer feel you are genuinely sorry.

3. **Appearing too anxious.** Show customers you want to serve their interests. Overinsistence and high-pressure tactics are objectionable to customers.

4. **Talking down other brands.** Talk up the brand you want to sell. Do not make unfair remarks about a competitive brand.

5. **Arguing.** Never argue with a customer. There's little profit in winning an argument and losing the sale. If a customer makes an absurd statement, don't laugh or argue. You may anger the customer, and an angry customer is a lost customer.

6. **Being too long-winded.** A flood of words doesn't make many sales. Some people take time to make up their minds, and silence at the right time allows the customer to think and decide. Being a good listener often makes more sales than being a fast talker.

7. **Lack of courtesy.** Discourteous salespeople rarely last long on a job; they lose too many customers.

8. **Showing favoritism.** Never wait on your friends or favorite customers before taking care of customers who were there first.

9. **Being too hurried.** Take time to find out what a customer wants and then take time to show the merchandise properly.

10. **Embarrassing the customer.** Never laugh at a person who speaks with a foreign accent or correct a person who mispronounces words or product names.

11. **Misrepresenting merchandise.** Never guarantee any cures or make any claims for products that cannot be backed up by facts.

12. **Lack of product information.** Salespeople who are not well informed cannot expect to build a steady clientele for their store.

13. **Wasting customers' time.** When a customer is in a hurry, finish the sale as quickly as possible.

14. **Getting too personal.** Assume a professional attitude. Be sincere and friendly, but keep a touch of dignity and formality in all customer contacts.

6543217

MANAGING SALESPEOPLE

Management of retail personnel is discussed in detail in Chapter 8. Because of their unique positions, salespeople are often treated differently than other employees. The following section describes some of these differences.

Motivation

The most important job for managers is to communicate with and motivate their salespeople. Motivation has the dual role of retaining employees and stimulating productivity. Most people can be positively motivated if they are given good reasons for doing good work. Among the reasons, the following have been suggested: (1) Some salespeople will work better and harder in anticipation of money rewards for seniority and for above-average performance in sales and service. (2) They may be stimulated to greater effort by quota bonuses and by commissions, provided the rewards are substantial, attainable, and promptly paid. (3) Another effective management tool is to offer **sales incentives.**

These incentives may run from contests to premiums to gifts or special allowances for the person who achieves or exceeds a sales target figure. One traditional way of motivating a salesperson to sell a particular item is through what is called push-money or a spiff. **Push-money** is a cash bonus received by the salesperson for selling particular items. The customer assumes that the item is being sold because of the enthusiasm the salesperson has for the product and not necessarily because there is an extra incentive in the form of a money reward. Of course, the push-money does create record keeping problems, and there could be an ethical dilemma if the salesperson misrepresents the item because of the extra incentive for selling a particular product or brand. Push-money is often used for high-margin or low-demand merchandise and for cosmetics. The store or the manufacturer may offer push-money to encourage the salespeople to try to sell slow-moving items, such as shoes at the end of a season.

An incentive system that furnishes the opportunity for promotion can be an effective motivator. Promotion to supervisory or executive jobs should also be possible; potential among all employees should be recognized and cultivated. Everyone needs spoken approval for good performance. Many salespeople need **praise** so much that they completely lose interest in the job when it is not given.

People will work hard at a job they like. The goals of a store should be consistently presented to employees in terms of consumer benefits whose importance they can recognize. It is essential to fit job assignments to employees' special interests, if at all possible. People will meet standards and observe rules when they are known, reasonable, and enforced. They are more productive when they know for certain that rules will be enforced equitably and consistently.

Staffing

If there are too many salespeople, wage costs are misspent. If there are too few, customers must wait and service is inadequate. Either of these situations results from an uneven flow of customers into the store. Since salespeople's salaries are one of the largest expenses for most retailers, it is important to keep the number at a level consistent with demand and customer service requirements. This, however, is not easy to do, because several variables must be taken into consideration:

1. Customer arrival time and frequency
2. The number of contacts made with customers
3. The number and length of actual sales transactions
4. Store expense constraints

Frequently, managers simply set an upper limit on expenses, expressed as a percentage of projected sales. They then hire as many salespeople as they consider necessary until they exceed their dollar limit. This procedure does not indicate the mix of part-time and full-time employees, nor does it state how many employees should be working at any given time of day. However, many managers, by using their experience and by considering the variables previously listed, seem to do a satisfactory job of meeting customer requirements while keeping sales expenses in line.

Training

The basic purpose of training is to increase employee productivity by providing product information and knowledge of sales techniques. Every store, large or small, should have a training program for new salespeople and a continuing program for everyone. It should include a full explanation of store policies concerning employees, returned merchandise, credit handling, and filling out sales slips. The most important training is for customer contact and product information.

Insufficient formal training causes high employee turnover, low employee morale, and loss of sales and customers. Without training, a salesperson may antagonize customers by being abrasive, curt, unable to explain the use of merchandise, and unfamiliar with company policies on returns or credit.

Most large stores have special staffs that conduct continuing in-store training programs. Some use the **sponsor system** in which an experienced employee is given the responsibility for introducing the trainee to other workers, explaining departmental procedures, giving product information, showing the location of stock, and helping to improve the trainee's selling techniques. It is the sponsor's job periodically to evaluate and motivate the new employee. Such stores usually have their own training manuals, materials, and visual aids. Small stores that do not have specialists to plan and direct training can rely on experienced salespeople and can use training materials provided by manufacturers and suppliers.

Customer service training and product knowledge are essential for sales associates at Crate & Barrel stores. The beautiful housewares and home furnishings stores feature unique and exciting products and displays. The company strives to educate customers through the continuing training of its staff, and service in the store is marvelous.

Before salespeople can begin to do their jobs effectively, they must be able to translate product features into customer benefits. Knowledge about the customer provides answers to objections, but product knowledge provides the self-confidence necessary to convince the customer of the solution to the problem. There are a great number of sources a salesperson can investigate for information pertaining to the merchandise she or he is selling. One source is the buyer. Others include the manager, vendor salespeople, vendor aids such as brochures and lectures, and merchandise tags and labels.

Training for effective, creative selling involves teaching techniques on the approach, on how to determine customer needs, on the sales presentation, and on how to overcome objections and close a sale. The approach must gain the customer's attention and make the person interested in hearing more. By listening to the customer and asking questions, noticing the customer's interest, and respecting the customer's preferences, effective salespeople focus on the needs of the particular individual. Only then is a salesperson in a position to make a presentation of merchandise and select the quality, quantity, and price range the customer may want to examine. Explaining the value of the goods and demonstrating them may be necessary to increase the salesperson's effectiveness and meet objections. Finally, the salesperson should be trained to know when and how to close a sale.

Improving Sales Associate Productivity

Improving productivity of the personal selling function involves (1) establishing performance standards, (2) measuring and evaluating performance, and (3) providing training and motivation when performance falls below the standard. However, not all of a salesperson's time is spent in selling. In fact, it is estimated that as little as 25 percent of the time may be spent in this way. Another 25 percent may be spent on stock work and other activities associated with selling, and as much as 50 percent may be spent awaiting customer arrivals. Standards for performance may be established on the basis of several factors:

1. Dollar volume of sales
2. Units sold

3.   Number of completed transactions

4.   Gross margin contributed

By measuring such factors as number of contacts and store traffic, retailers may calculate ratios that can be used to set standards of performance as well as to analyze the factors affecting performance. For example, dividing the number of customer contacts by the number of transactions gives the percentage of customers who bought merchandise. Dividing the units sold by the number of customers produces a traffic productivity ratio.

Regardless of the standards set for evaluating performance, it is vital that they be thoroughly understood by every salesperson and that they be fair, reasonable, and easy to measure and calculate. Table 14.1 contains the results of a recent survey showing the factors used by retailers to evaluate employees.

As you can see in Table 14.1, general attitudinal measures are still the most commonly used. However, the financial and customer interaction measures are close behind. Regardless of the standards set, productivity improvement is a key to retail profitability.

Productivity starts with effective recruiting, selection, and hiring practices. If qualified people are hired, then training in selling techniques, product knowledge, and customer service can improve productivity. Technology ranging from point-of-purchase scanners and satellite systems to CD ROM product demonstrations are also used for training purposes, which increase productivity.

Compensation

Salespeople are usually compensated by one of four methods: (1) straight salary, (2) straight commission, (3) salary plus commission, or (4) salary plus quota bonus.

TABLE 14.1

Measures Used by Retailers to Evaluate Performance

Measure	*Percentage of Sample Indicating Use*
Sales per time period	49.9%
Gross margin attained	21.1
Profit added	31.5
Number of transactions	37.0
Number of customer contacts	63.9
Fulfilling expected behavior	37.0
Attitude measures	73.5
Other	9.8

Most retailers indicated the use of multiple measures

Straight salary is the most commonly used method of compensation for salespeople. A specified amount is earned for each pay period. Similar to the straight salary is the hourly wage, where the amount paid varies only by the number of hours worked.

Straight commission is a method where salespeople are paid on the basis of the total number of sales they make. At the end of the pay period, total sales are multiplied by a commission rate to determine earnings. A straight commission is often used in conjunction with a drawing account. Here payments are made to employees at regular intervals and are then charged against commissions earned at the end of the month. For instance, if a salesperson has a $1,000 draw and only makes $800 on commission, the $200 difference would come out of the next period's earnings.

Straight salary plus a small commission provides an incentive to make sales. This is a compromise that attempts to combine the best features of the straight salary and the straight commission plans. The **salary plus quota bonus** is another compromise. Here salespeople are paid a fixed amount for the pay period, and a sales quota is established. At the end of the period a bonus is paid on the amount by which sales exceed the quota.

In addition to the regularly scheduled paycheck, store personnel are usually provided with a program of fringe benefits that supplement the dollars received in their paychecks. The fringe benefit programs of many firms cost up to 40 percent of the actual salaries, wages, and commissions paid. All or part of the following may be included:

1. Employee discounts for merchandise purchased in the store
2. Social security and unemployment insurance contributions
3. Medical and life insurance
4. Retirement savings plans
5. Profit sharing

We now turn to sales promotion and its role in the promotion mix.

SALES PROMOTION

Sales promotion consists of a broad set of activities designed to induce some immediate response or provide a novel way to transmit a message (see Figure 14.4). For example, many sales promotion programs are designed to encourage a customer to visit the store for an immediate one-time sale, while others have long-term goals like building customer loyalty or salesperson morale. Promotion programs include elements like displays, fashion shows, coupons, and trading stamps. The toy in the McDonald's "Happy Meal," the

FIGURE 14.4

Sales promotion
takes many forms.

chance to win a trip for two to the Bahamas offered by a retail chain, and the Gold Toe Hosiery Club, where the member gets a free pair of men's hosiery after buying twelve pairs at full price, are all typical examples of sales promotions.

Sales promotion includes a broad array of marketing activities that are designed to increase the basic value of the product or service being sold. Each year more than $170 billion is spent on consumer and trade sales promotion.[4] Of this total, some $60 billion is spent in the consumer area. Clearly, sales promotion is a major element of the retailer's marketing tool kit, and most retailers consider it an important part of the total communication effort. To be effective, a decision to use one or more sales promotion methods must be made with specific communications or behavioral objectives in mind.

Sales promotion offers the retailer a way to accomplish one or more of the following objectives:

- Generating immediate sales
- Attracting customers into the store
- Building customer loyalty
- Increasing the customer's level of product/service knowledge
- Building the retailer's or the manufacturer's database
- Promoting goodwill for the product line, service, or store

When achieving these objectives, sales promotion efforts can be designed to stimulate an immediate response or to build a pattern of behavior over time. Similarly, we can classify a specific sales promotion effort as being either a single-event or a continuity promotion. A **single-event promotion** is designed to encourage the retail customer to engage in a single purchase or trial of goods or services with the hope that future purchases will follow. Receipt of the inducement (e.g., cash, goods, services) by the customer is contingent only on a single purchase, usually within a specified time period, for example, a "$2 off" coupon for any T-shirt in the store. As you have undoubtedly seen, cents-off coupons are usually accompanied by an expiration date to motivate consumers to move quickly toward making their purchase.

A **continuity promotion** program is designed to encourage the customer to engage in multiple purchases or trials of goods or services over a period of time. The inducement of cash, goods, or services is contingent on the retail customer making repeated purchases within a specified time period, thus building continuity of purchasing behavior and hopefully continuing loyalty to the store. An offer by 7-Eleven to give you a free Big Gulp after you have purchased four Big Gulps at full retail price is an example of a continuity program. Continuity promotions are designed to build a routine shopping pattern for customers and reward them for doing so.

The purchase of a specific product is not the only benefit of sales promotion to the retailer. In the convenience store example above, the outcome was not only the sale of four Big Gulps, but the store visits necessary to make these purchases. These visits allowed the retailer the opportunity to make additional sales. The generation of store traffic is a profitable by-product of both single-event and continuity promotion efforts.

There are numerous types of sales promotions. We are going to discuss several of the most popular and easily implemented methods for building awareness, stimulating store traffic, generating sales, and fostering goodwill.

Advertising Specialties

Advertising specialties are items offered to consumers without charge to build brand name or distributor name awareness and recall. The key feature of a specialty item is that no purchase is required to receive it. Advertising specialties can be used by either trade or retail sellers, and over $5 billion was spent on them in 1992.[5] Ad specialties are often used by retailers because they can maintain close control over both selection and distribution. Anything that can be imprinted with the name of the retailer can be used.

Many specialty items are physically small and allow only a limited amount of advertising space. An imprint can seldom tell more than who you are, what you sell, and where you are. Even so, the primary use of specialty items as a reminder advertising media makes them an effective tool. Their use can be supplemented with ads in other media, or they can be an advertising effort in their own right.

Ad specialties can be effective in keeping customers and in bringing in new business. They are especially useful as ways of showing appreciation for patronage and as an invitation to continue to buy. Their value as an advertising media depends a great deal on selection and distribution.

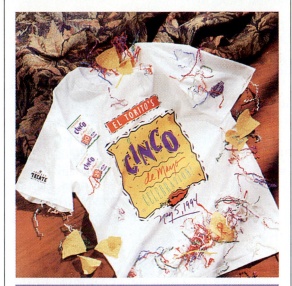

Consumer Promotions/Less than $10 Per Recipient
El Torito Mexican Restaurant

Objective:
To increase guest counts and food sales and position the restaurant as the ideal place to celebrate festive occasions.

Strategy & Execution:
Commemorating the victory of Cinco de Mayo seemed to be a very logical holiday for the Mexican restaurant to celebrate with a grand fiesta. To build momentum and attract guests, the advertiser developed a countdown theme which was executed with a colorful button that included a miniature pad of peel-off numbers descending from 30 (days away) to "It's Here!" In addition to the buttons restaurant employees also wore theme imprinted T-shirts, and banners were prominently displayed to build excitement among the staff and increase awareness among patrons. Contests also were held during the May holiday celebration so customers could win one of the promotion T-shirts as a souvenir.

Results:
El Torito's marketing manager reported a 2% increase in guest counts and 12% more in sales of food and liquor during the May 5 celebration.

Commemorating the victory of Cinco de Mayo was a great way for El Torito Mexican Restaurant to celebrate with a grand fiesta. Imprinted T-shirts and banners built excitement among the staff and increased customer awareness of the holiday. Contests were held during May so that customers could win a promotion T-shirt as a souvenir.

Guide for selecting specialties. Two guides to use in selecting advertising specialties are:

1. Select something unusual: It will probably be valued and used more often than items other advertisers give, competitors or not.

2. Something related to the business is likely to be a better reminder than an item that is only novel. For example, a thermometer has a logical tie-in with anything that has to do with cooling and heating, whether an air conditioner or a furnace.

Premiums

Premiums represent a powerful and significant element in the marketing of consumer goods and services. Spending on free and self-liquidating premiums exceeded $4 billion in 1992.[6] A **premium** is a complementary or stand-alone product that is offered as an inducement to the consumer to purchase a particular item. The premium product can be offered without any additional payment, or it may require the purchaser to help defray part of the cost. Specifically, an incentive is called a free premium when the item being awarded requires no further payment by the purchaser. When the managers at Kellogg's Corn Flakes offer free baseball cards in specially marked cereal boxes or McDonald's offers a free toy inside each Happy Meal, these are illustrations of free premiums.

On the other hand, a **self-liquidating premium** requires the payment of additional money. For example, when Pizza Hut offers a Holiday's Spirit glass for $1.49 with the purchase of any large pizza and a soft drink, part or all of the cost of the glass to Pizza Hut is being defrayed by the customer.

Coupons

Coupons benefit retailers by building total sales volume and store traffic, as well as by encouraging the sale of the particular product(s) featured on the coupon. It is hoped that the price reduction will entice customers to try the product and become regular users. Another benefit of the coupon is that it serves as its own reminder to the customer to purchase the product.

Couponing is a huge business. Over $7 billion is spent annually by manufacturers on coupon promotions with more than 300 billion coupons distributed to U.S. households.[7] Formally defined, *coupons* are certificates redeemable for services, merchandise, or cash when offered as partial payment for goods or services. These "manufacturer sponsored" or "retailer sponsored" coupons may be offered solo or co-branded. Solo coupons are ones that are offered to consumers by a single manufacturer or a single retailer. For example, Ace Hardware may print a coupon book for its franchise stores offering discounts on numerous products.

Sometimes there may be cooperation between manufacturers and retailers. For example, shoppers may receive $1 off when they purchase a specific brand of breakfast cereal and a half-gallon of a store brand of milk. In this way, the cereal producer and store have teamed up to extend the offer jointly; the two products are co-branded.

Coupon distribution.   Store coupons can be distributed in magazine advertisements, newspaper ads, free-standing inserts, direct mail, or in-store handouts. Of these methods, free-standing inserts accounted for 80 percent of the total coupon distribution volume. Retailers also distribute coupons on the store shelves, using dispensers attached to the shelf near the product. A relatively recent trend is to distribute store coupons at the checkout by using the back of the sales receipt.

Contests and Sweepstakes

Contests and sweepstakes are participative events whereby consumers have the opportunity to receive something of value for little or no personal investment. Not surprisingly, these forms of promotion are quite popular. Games and contests rank second among all forms of consumer promotion spending with 18.2 percent of total expenditures, or just under $900 million. Spending in this category exceeds $1 billion.[8]

The difference between these two forms of promotion is that contests stipulate that skill is required to participate. For example, radio call-in programs where the caller must identify a particular song or artist are contests. On the other hand, when managers of American Family Publishers design a promotion whereby names will be drawn randomly from among all of the received entries and millions of dollars will be awarded to the winners, this is a sweepstakes. All that is necessary in this situation is for the consumer to mail the form: No skill is required. The effectiveness of both of these types of promotions is rooted in a desire by consumers "to get something for nothing."

Pet Food Warehouse stores average 18,000 square feet and carry more than 10,000 items. The company uses several marketing tools such as events and promotions to build community relations and generate store traffic. Pet Tricks competitions, portrait sittings, and costume contests are annual events.

Special Events

Many retailers use special events to promote goodwill and increase customer education, as well as to stimulate sales. The nature and extent of the special events used by stores depend on the kind of store and the size of its operations. Fashion shows are a popular device used by both large and small clothing and department stores to obtain goodwill. Only incidentally do fashion shows produce immediate business.

Some products require instruction if customers are to acquire skill in using them. When this is so, retailers provide schools and classes in which present and future customers are taught to use the product. Stores that do this reap obvious benefits: When customers buy associated merchandise, goodwill and traffic may be substantially increased.

Although other special events such as parades, art exhibits, and lecture series may be tied to specific merchandise sales, most of these programs are intended to attract people to the store and create goodwill by promoting the idea that the retailer is a kind of community center that supports cultural and athletic programs. A noteworthy example of such special events is the annual Macy's Thanksgiving Day Parade, marking the opening of the Christmas shopping season. Other retailers support local bowling teams or the Little League, sponsor art exhibits or lecture series, and participate in local athletic events (e.g., 10-Ks, Special Olympics, Senior Olympics).

The International Events Group of Chicago suggests that there are eight major reasons why a firm would want to become a sponsor. They include:

- Increasing awareness of the company or product name
- Identifying with a particular lifestyle

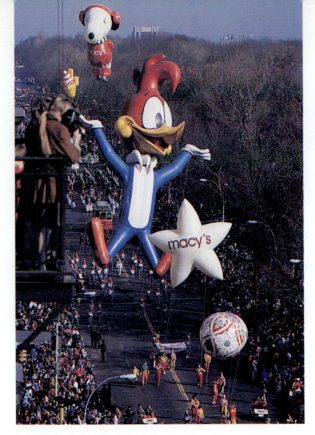

Public relations events can be key components of an overall communications mix. They can be as complex and long-lasting as the Ronald McDonald House. The Macy's Thanksgiving Day Parade is enjoyed by millions of people and focuses attention on the store at the critical phase of the holiday shopping season.

- Differentiating your store or product line from those of competitors
- Enhancing commitment to a community or ethnic group
- Entertaining key customers
- Enhancing merchandising opportunities
- Shaping or reinforcing public perceptions
- Improving the "bottom line"[9]

Point-of-Purchase Sales Promotions

Sales promotion at the point of purchase ranges from product demonstrations and samples to in-store displays, shelf talkers, and coupon dispensers.

In-store displays are usually designed to encourage customers to try a product. This is done by attracting attention to the item and by providing facts and information. Well-designed interior displays are very effective in creating product awareness and stimulating unplanned purchasing. They can also be profitable. The window coverings maker Curton Curtains, Inc., for example, shows merchants how they can generate an average of $1,500 in sales per square foot with their displays.[10] Many stores also use them to create department-specific themes or enhance the atmosphere.

Manufacturers frequently supply retailers with display or point-of-purchase (POP) material. POP is so popular that $15 billion is spent on this form of promotion each year.[11] POP displays vary in size and complexity. Examples range from a wire rack displaying razor blades at a checkout counter to a twelve-foot motorized carousel in a supermarket promoting a new soft drink.

If retailers are tempted to use these materials because they are free, they should remember the opportunity costs associated with using the floor space, together with the costs for building or assembling and maintaining a display.

End caps. Stacks of merchandise or displays constructed at the ends of aisles are called **end caps.** Space at end caps is extremely valuable for the retailer and for the manufacturer whose products are displayed there. Quite frequently, manufacturers pay the retailer for the opportunity to have items on an end cap. Until recently, the purchase of an end cap assured the manufacturer of an exclusive display. Supermarkets, however, no longer make such guarantees, and you will now see a private-label brand from the same product category placed in the center of the manufacturer's end cap.

J-hooks and clip strips. **J-hooks** are the metal or plastic rods that attach to the retail shelf on which small items can be hung for display. **Clip strips** are the metal or plastic strips that attach to the retail shelf on which small items can be clipped for display. J-hooks and clip strips can be used effectively to promote a complementary item. They also offer an effective way to display unrelated products that are frequently purchased on impulse.

Shelf extenders are wire baskets or lips that attach to the stationary shelf to support impulse items associated with the primary product being displayed. For example, a shelf extender may be used to promote dip and salsa in front of a potato chip display.

Shelf talkers are any type of printed matter that has been attached to a display shelf for the purpose of attracting attention to a brand or product category. Shelf talkers can communicate price information, distribute coupons, or suggest ways to use the featured product.

Collateral materials include any printed matter distributed to customers from either a point-of-purchase display or a sales associate. A prominent example of collateral materials is seen on or near the cosmetics counter in a department store, where small brochures or leaflets may promote the uniqueness or benefits of a particular product. Among the many benefits of collateral materials to the retailer, the principal ones include attracting attention to the display, providing sales support for self-service items, providing materials to aid sales associates when describing products, and enhancing the professional appearance of in-store displays.

Demonstrations and Samples

Each product in a store is competing with every other product for the attention of the customer. Both manufacturers and retailers hire individuals to conduct in-store demonstrations for products as diverse as vacuum cleaners, satellite systems, and multimedia computers. The goal is to encourage purchase by letting the consumer see the product in use and by offering an opportunity to ask questions. For example, in a toy store recently a manufacturer was demonstrating radio-controlled vehicles to moms and dads.

We are used to seeing product samples, particularly for new food items. Initial trial allows the product itself to communicate benefits and encourage purchase. Samples may be delivered outside the store by manufacturers and/or retailers. A coupon delivered by mail, redeemable for a free bag of microwavable popcorn with the rental of a video movie, is an example of a manufacturer and retailer cooperating to encourage trial of a product as well as to motivate customers to visit the store.

PUBLICITY

We now turn to another element of the retail promotion mix. The public relations function within the retailing mix includes publicity as its principal component. **Publicity** is any news-related event that broadcast or print media run on behalf of the store, products, services, or personnel. Three factors distinguish publicity from advertising: cost, control, and sponsorship identification. When a newspaper, magazine, television station, or radio program features a retailer's store, personnel, products, or events as a news story or special-interest item, the retailer receives publicity. Although this exposure to the public is free, the retailer cannot control when the message is heard, the duration of the message, or the content.

In this section of the chapter we discuss the retailer's use of public relations and publicity as part of the total communications mix. Publicity is distinguished from advertising and other elements by the fact that it is not paid for directly by the retailer. The message is run by the media because of some newsworthy event or because a company press release is deemed interesting by an editor. This does not mean that the message is free. A great deal of effort and sometimes money is spent on getting favorable publicity for the store. Some public relations activities worthy of coverage by the media are relatively inexpensive for retailers, large and small, and enable the store to get noticed and remembered by customers. Sought intelligently and creatively, publicity, though not absolutely free, may help save some advertising dollars. In today's competitive environment, the retailer must use every possible avenue to communicate with the customer.

Public relations is often thought of as "the projection of a desired image." The same principles used by large firms to project their image to millions of people can be employed by the corner video rental store to communicate its image to neighbors down the street.

Selecting an Image

In developing your public relations program, the first step is to make sure that you have defined an image and that your public relations activities are consistent with the total communications mix. Is your store a "local" grocery store? Is your firm's inventory "more complete"? Your staff "better trained"? Does your firm offer "dependable service"? Has it been in operation "longer"? Your store's image should reflect something unique about your business, something that makes it different from your competition.

Retailers should ask, "What do I want my customers to think of my business?" Decide on an overall image you would like people to have of your company and write it down. This will place it clearly in focus. Remember, the image chosen for publicity must be tied to the overall promotion program of the business. There should be complete consistency between that image and the one projected in advertising and in personal selling. The retailer must have one image based on the defined mission of the store.

Selecting a Target Audience

Everyone may not need or even be interested in the particular services or products offered by the retailer. You must select a specific audience toward whom the store wants to communicate its image.

Just as with advertising, retailers should ask, "Who are my present customers? Who are my past customers? Who are my potential customers? Who are the other people who should know about my business?" This last question is often overlooked. The concept of "opinion leadership" is well understood and used by communications experts and can be valuable to the retailer. *Opinion leaders* include people who influence the opinions and attitudes of others. The mayor, city council, business leaders, legislative representatives, civic club leaders, area media representatives, school board members, teachers, and student representatives are examples. These people may never have a need for the store's products or services, but they will influence others.

Choosing a Media

Next, choose the media through which the store attempts to gain favorable coverage. Just as with advertising, the choice of an appropriate media is important. Ask "Where do my customers and others get information?" A sample listing could include television, newspapers, radio, brochures, special events, slide presentations, speeches, personal letters, and meetings. A discussion of the various media will shed further light on which one to use.

Newspapers.
The local newspaper offers many opportunities for publicity. First, get to know the editor, news editor, or city desk editor. Find out who this person is and introduce yourself. Try to get some idea of what the editor regards as newsworthy.

The best way to provide information to an editor is through a news release or fact sheet. Standard practice is to ask yourself the who, what, where, when, why, and how of the event or topic and answer these questions in the news story. For a grand opening, mention the more important items first, such as what is happening, where, when, and to whom. Also include information about the store, that is, where the owner is from, the amount of experience he or she has in the business, the major types of services or products sold, size of the staff, and so on.

For retailers who feel uncomfortable writing a news story, a simple fact sheet can serve the same purpose. List on the left side of the paper the topics or questions you will answer: who, what, where, when, why, how, and so on. To the right of each, include a short explanation. Some of the items you might write about include new personnel announcements, opening of branch stores, introduction of new product lines, new construction, anniversaries, announcements of major sales, product success stories, charity gifts, employee awards, or any other newsworthy event that can contribute to the image of the store. A photograph of the event, product, or person involved may also be of interest to the newspaper.

Television and radio. Most television and radio stations have morning or afternoon talk shows on which a host or hostess discusses topics of interest. Various salespeople may be particularly knowledgeable in fashion, home repair, or some other area that relates closely to your products or services. Contact the show host and explain what could be discussed or demonstrated that might be of interest to viewers. These shows cannot be a commercial advertisement for the firm, but they can deal with topics of general interest. For example, demonstrate painting tips if the store sells paints, explain points to remember in taking care of a car if it has a service department, or discuss plant care hints if green plants are sold.

A special event, product, or service demonstration at the store may be of interest to television news departments. They may also be interested in the new, unique, and different projects, hobbies, or outside interests of managers or associates. Through activities like these, people will soon think of store personnel as leaders or experts in a particular field and may very well seek them out.

Community Involvement, Speeches, and Demonstrations

A valuable way to become recognized as an opinion leader in an area of business is through speeches and "how to" demonstrations. Store personnel can select a topic of interest to business owners, high school students, science teachers, agriculture students, and so on. Managers must be cautious, however, because it is easy to become overly involved in community activities. Select only those clubs, organizations, or projects that will gain proper exposure to opinion leaders and to the specific people who can be potential users of the store's products or services.

Special Events

Open houses, store anniversary celebrations, demonstrations, displays, special commemorative days, holidays, dedications, contests, competitions, and so on, if planned thoroughly, can be useful means of gaining exposure for the store. In and of themselves, many of these events are newsworthy. The key to success lies in selecting an event that fits the store's personality or image and then planning all the details to match the needs of the target audience.

Organizing Your Plan of Action

After you choose your image, identify your audience, and select your media, the next step is to organize a plan of action. This should include specific long- and short-range goals, definite time limits, and methods of acquiring feedback from the people involved so that you can evaluate your plan.

Dealing with the Effects of Unintended Publicity

This section has concentrated on the attempt to gain favorable media coverage. However, it sometimes happens that coverage will be unintended and often derogatory to the retailer. Witness the example in Chapter 3, when Food Lion suffered from unfavorable coverage. Contrast this with the response of Sears to news items that accused it of unethical actions in its auto repair centers. Food Lion ran a huge advertising campaign arguing that it was wrongfully accused; whereas, Sears settled the cases with the states and changed its policies that were causing the problems. Although neither store admitted fault, their actions dealt with the unfavorable coverage in very different ways.

NORDSTROM—REVISITED: CAN CUSTOMER SERVICE BE MAINTAINED?

Although Nordstrom stores have excelled in high sales, they have also suffered from low earnings. Much of this has been attributed to the high costs of buying merchandise and building maintenance. In order to correct these problems, Nordstrom's management has concentrated on improving the efficiency of its operations. This includes restructuring the buying and delivery processes and expansion into more and different services. Also, Nordstrom has installed a computerized inventory system that allows for better information availability and control by managers and buyers. Enhancements continue to be added to the system. Finally, Nordstrom hopes to improve its delivery system by switching operations to more modern facilities.

The company has also entered other retail formats. It began opening off-price stores, called the Nordstrom Rack, to sell older inventory, and it has also started a mail-order catalog.

No business is without its bumps. In 1990 Nordstrom ran into legal problems with its employees and agreed to a multi-million-dollar settlement. Payments have been made to current and former personnel, particularly commission salespeople, who allege that they were not paid for attending work meetings, writing thank-you notes to customers, and other nonselling tasks that were completed off the clock.[12]

1. Can Nordstrom continue to offer extremely high levels of service and still remain competitive?
2. Where should Nordstrom strive for more improvement?

Summary

Retailers employ personal selling, publicity, and sales promotion to help create a single image positioned in the mind of the consumer. Personal selling involves face-to-face contact between the consumer and a salesperson. A salesperson must know the products offered, discover what the shopper wants, and then apply selling techniques to match the product with the customer. Most of a salesperson's time is devoted to customer contact, although some of it is spent in stock work and security.

A retail manager must be able to effectively motivate and train sales staff. The manager must set the appropriate measurement standards for the salespeople in order to evaluate their performance. Employee compensation can be straight salary, straight commission, or salary plus commission.

Sales promotion consists of a broad set of activities designed to induce an immediate response or provide a novel way to transmit a message. Objectives of sales promotion may be to generate immediate sales, attract customers to the store, or increase the customer's level of knowledge about the product. Types of sales promotion include price reductions, advertising specialties, premiums, coupons, contests and sweepstakes, special events, and in-store displays.

Publicity is any news-related event that is broadcast on behalf of the store, products, personnel, or services. Unlike the other areas of promotion, the retailer has little control over when or how the message is presented or even what message is used. Public relations personnel must also be prepared to deal with the effects of unintended publicity.

Key Terms and Concepts

Advertising specialties, 550
AIDA, 538
Clip strips, 555
Close, 542
Collateral materials, 555
Continuity promotion, 550
End caps, 554
Formula approach, 538
J-hooks, 555
Personal selling, 532
Praise, 544

Premium, 551
Problem-solving–need-satisfaction approach, 538
Promotion mix, 532
Publicity, 556
Push-money (spiff), 544
Salary plus quota bonus, 548
Sales incentives, 544
Sales promotion, 548
Self-liquidating premium, 551

Shelf extender, 555
Shelf talker, 555
Single-event promotion, 550
Sponsor system, 545
Stimulus-response approach, 538
Straight commission, 548
Straight salary, 548
Substitute selling, 541
Suggestion selling, 542

QUESTIONS

1. Frequently, each of two salespeople may consider the same customer to be his "personal trade." When salespeople are paid on commission, this can create considerable animosity. What problems does a department manager face in trying to handle this situation?

2. What problems does a department manager face in trying to reduce the nonselling time of salespeople?

3. Does the relative importance of personal selling, publicity, and sales promotion vary among a supermarket, a discount store, and a specialty store? What factors cause the difference?

4. What roles does a salesperson play in dealing with customers? Are salespeople even needed? Why or why not? Give examples of each argument.

5. How could a salesperson aid in maintaining security within the store? Is it important to involve the salesperson in store security? Why or why not?

6. How does the stimulus-response approach to selling differ from the formula approach and the problem-solving–need-satisfaction approach?

7. Explain why it is important that all elements of the promotion effort be coordinated.

8. How can sales promotion efforts be made effective?

9. What type of advertising specialties are most appropriate for retailers? Does your answer depend on the type of retailer?

10. Retailers should always be involved in their community. Discuss this statement.

11. Is a public relations program possible for a small independent retailer?

SITUATIONS

1. You are entering a sales position in a family-oriented shoe store. You had previously worked in a stock position where you had no contact with customers. After talking to several of your coworkers, who each use a different sales tactic, you aren't sure how to approach customers. Your shy personality is the first thing you must overcome. Which approach would you use? Why? Does the type of store you are working in have influence on your choice? The type of customer?

2. You are the manager of a local supermarket. You think manufacturer coupons are valuable for stimulating initial purchase activity, and you have tried very hard to cooperate with your suppliers when they are running a coupon campaign. Recently, however, several of your competitors have started giving customers the "cents off" on their orders even when the coupon product is not purchased. You know this action violates the manufacturer's agreement with the stores.

What should you do? What can you do? What problems are involved?

3. You are the manager of a Greek restaurant. The local paper has just completed a review of your service and food, which it found to be lacking. You don't feel the assessment was fair because the local critic is known not to like Greek food. What should you do about the situation?

CASES

CASE 14A
Sales Promotion for Foothills Mall Expansion: Hot-Air Balloon Race

The Foothills Fashion Mall had just completed a major expansion. Ann Griffith, the mall promotion manager, had planned a major sales promotion event for the grand opening. Beginning about three years ago, the original mall, which is made up of three major department stores and fifty-three mall tenants, was fully leased and experiencing demand for additional space. The decision was made to expand the mall to include twenty-two additional shops and a fourth major department store.

The expansion area—including retail, service, mall, and department stores—has approximately 131,011 square feet, bringing the total building footage to just over half a million.

Ann explained her plans for the opening this way:

The Grand Opening for this expansion area begins Saturday morning, August 27, with the Foothills Sertoma Club serving a pancake breakfast. Balloon races, with thirty-two hot-air balloons, will begin approximately at 7:00 a.m. The local high school band will provide music prior to the opening ceremony.

Sunday morning, August 28, will again feature balloon races and a Rotary Club breakfast. The thirty-two hot-air balloons will be launched two miles outside the site and will attempt to fly to the mall and grab a set of car keys for a new Ford Explorer. The keys will be suspended on a sixty-foot pole above the mall roof. The successful balloonist will win the new vehicle!

During Grand Opening week, civic groups, clubs, and schools will participate in activities in the mall to celebrate the opening. The following exhibits [Boxes 14.4 and 14.5] explain promotion and activities in more detail. Note that the hot-air balloon prize paid for itself through sponsor fees.

---

1. *Richard Callous owns a family shoe store in the old part of the mall. He invested the following in the expansion Grand Opening:*

$0.25/sq ft × 2,500 sq ft = $ 625
Sponsor of a balloon   = 1,000
Full page in tabloid   =   600
Total   = $2,225

This was 12 percent of his total promotion budget for the year. How should he evaluate the effectiveness of the expenditure? Are there quantitative methods he could use? How many promotion and publicity activities can you identify?

BOX

14.4 GRAND OPENING: FOOTHILLS FASHION MALL

Foothills Fashion Mall
100 Foothill Way
New Plateau, NM 55566

July 2, 1997

RE: *Special Assessment for Grand Opening of the*
     Foothills Fashion Mall Expansion

Dear Merchant,

Last week, a meeting of the Merchant's Association, Inc., of Foothills Fashion Mall was held for the election of officers, the presentation of the Grand Opening plans, and a vote on a special assessment by existing tenants for Grand Opening purposes.

Section #7 of this Merchant's Association By-Laws provides for special assessments to be taken to the General Membership when approved by two-thirds majority of the Board of Directors. The Directors passed an assessment at their meeting of $0.25 per square foot. The assessment was passed with no dissenting votes at the General Meeting.

In addition to other Grand Opening promotional costs, the assessment will be used to circulate 101,000 Grand Opening tabloids to the Mall Trade Area through insertion in various area newspapers and direct mail by zip codes (see the supplementary information on the tabloid in this folder).

Attached is the statement of amount now due on the Special Assessment.

Sincerely,

Darlyne K. Pierce, President
Foothills Fashion Mall Merchant's Association

6543217

BOX 14.5 SPONSORSHIP MEMO TO MERCHANTS

Balloon Race and Parachute Drop

Twenty merchants have already sponsored the balloon race. There are still eleven balloons left. The cost for a split sponsorship (one day) is $1,000 plus $40 for the banner. The sponsorship entitles you or a person of your choice to ride in the balloon with the pilot plus a banner with your store's name.

There will be a balloon pilot and sponsor "Get Acquainted" Party at the Holiday Inn, Friday, August 26, at 7:30 p.m. Plan to attend and meet your pilot. Also all sponsors are invited to a picnic at Ray Roberts State Park on Saturday, August 27, starting at 12:00 p.m. On Sunday, August 28, there will be a Pilot's Brunch at Act I, with trophies and cash prizes awarded. All sponsors are invited.

Picture the crowd watching the launching of over thirty hot-air balloons. Imagine the excitement as they each drop ten parachutes filled with coupons for free gifts from the merchants at Foothills Fashion Mall.

Please support this Parachute Drop by donating giveaways from your store. No discount coupons please, only freebies. Parachutes will be dropped on Saturday, August 27, only.

All you need to do is handwrite on a small piece of paper (as many as you can give away) your store name and the gift and watch those people come into your stores. We need all coupons by Friday, August 19, at the Management Offices.

CASE 14B
Neiman Marcus: Technology versus Customer Service?

Neiman Marcus stores are upscale specialty operations catering to a clientele that demands the ultimate in personal service and unique, high-quality products. The company operates on the philosophy that customer service by all its people is directly linked to bottom-line performance.

Neiman Marcus was one of the first companies to engage in relationship marketing—even before the term became popular in business. Sales associates are expected to keep personal logs that contain buying habits, preferences, and special dates for each of their customers. They often call to suggest gifts for special occasions such as birthdays or anniversaries and contact their customers when new merchandise arrives at the store.

Neiman Marcus ran into a unique problem with its relationship marketing system: If the sales associate left, so did the customer information. Not only that, many of the customers were loyal to the sales associate, not the store. They shopped at Neiman's because they could count on the personal service.

In the early 1990s, Neiman Marcus began to integrate technology to improve customer data. A customer database contains all the information that sales associates previously kept in notebooks. The system automates and updates record keeping for each member of the sales staff. Productivity gains were expected because sales personnel would have less paperwork and more time to spend with the customer.[13]

While the system received rave reviews from both management and the business press, it has not been universally appealing to the sales staff. The older sales associates are nearly indispensable with their little black books. They are the backbone of the customer service on which Neiman's depends for a competitive advantage. As the database grows, the sales associates become replaceable. This has led to some resistance from the older staff members, who now see their individual advantages disappearing.

The new Neiman Marcus computer system collects information from its frequent buyer pro-gram, called InCircle. To become a member, customers need only use their NM credit card for purchases. They receive a point for each dollar spent. After 3,000 points, they receive their own InCircle Frequent Shopper card.[14] As points accumulate, the customer may use them for discounts or prizes. They also obtain benefits such as free gift wrapping, magazine subscriptions, and travel certificates. The program has been a big success. It not only encourages repeat shopping but allows the database to be expanded to further personalize service for the customer.[15] The loyalty programs pay off in increased customer lifetime value.

1. *Will technology dilute the competitive advantage that sales associates have given Neiman Marcus?*

PART **6**

RETAILING CHALLENGES AND CHANGES

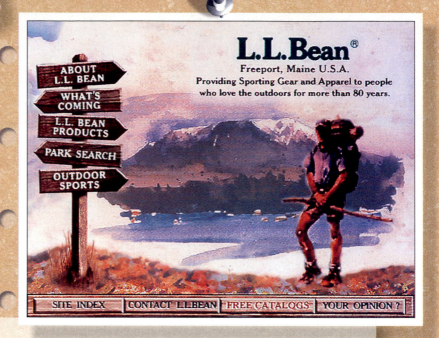

CHAPTER 15

L.L.Bean®
Freeport, Maine U.S.A.
Providing Sporting Gear and Apparel to people
who love the outdoors for more than 80 years.

ABOUT
L.L. BEAN

WHAT'S
COMING

L.L. BEAN
PRODUCTS

PARK SEARCH

OUTDOOR
SPORTS

SITE INDEX   CONTACT L.L.BEAN   FREE CATALOGS   YOUR OPINION ?

Chapter Goals

After reading this chapter, you should be able to:

- Understand how technology is affecting retail communications.
- Discuss how the Internet will change retailing.
- Compare the features, advantages, and disadvantages of interactive television shopping and electronic kiosk retailing.
- Describe how to capture data and maintain a customer database.
- Explain the uses of a "personalized shopper database."
- Describe database marketing.
- Discuss how the retailer can profitably use direct mail.
- Analyze micromarketing opportunities.

The Virtual Store and Retail Database Marketing

L. L. BEAN: COMPETING WITH CATALOGS AND THE INTERNET

A privately held, Maine-based retailer, L. L. Bean sells sporting goods and outdoor clothing primarily through direct response media. A large retail store is located in Freeport as is the company's outlet store. L. L. Bean has sales of about three-quarters of a billion dollars and more than 3,000 employees. Access to product descriptions, services, company data, and ordering information is available on the Internet at its World Wide Web site: http:\\www.llbean.com. However, orders are not placed via the Internet; the customer must call an 800 number. The company believes it is important to have person-to-person contact and for customers to have full detailed descriptions provided in a catalog.

Many consumers are hesitant to buy products from catalogs. This is especially true with apparel, where it is difficult to judge the quality and fit of an item from a picture and a catalog description. In order to overcome this concern, L. L. Bean helped pioneer the tradition of accepting returns without question, even when the item was purchased several years earlier.[1] This policy, along with superior products and exemplary service, has established trust and confidence among customers.

L. L. Bean has several characteristics that make it a success in the highly competitive catalog business. It has developed its own unique sizing system for apparel to make sure that the garments fit right the first time. Its catalog is well designed with simple and logical order forms and the L. L. Bean "size guidelines." The guarantee is often presented on the first few pages, while the rest of the catalog contains detailed descriptions to make sure customers have adequate knowledge about the selection of merchandise.[2] The company has won several industry awards, including the American Catalog Awards' Silver Award and the *Personnel Journal*'s Optima Award for managing change.[3]

The company has been instrumental in implementing a total quality management (TQM) approach to dealing with customers. TQM at L. L. Bean concentrates on improving the employee, not the process. This allows employees to be better trained and informed, which in turn creates better customer service, particularly in receiving and filling orders.[4] The TQM system is a success in increasing consumer satisfaction.

Before caller ID became widely used, L. L. Bean instituted a caller identification system known as PC Connection in order to further increase customer service. The system recognizes the incoming telephone number and displays prior ordering information on the monitor. It allows the salesperson to avoid time-consuming paperwork and increases accu-racy, especially for name and address information. Caller ID systems are increasingly popular with both individuals and businesses. After a reporter aired grievances over privacy concerns of the system, L. L. Bean instituted a policy of allowing customers to be blocked from identification.[5] Also, a statement of the company policy concerning customers' privacy with respect to the mailing list is prominently displayed in the catalog.[6]

1. **What expanded role could (should) retailing on the World Wide Web play in L. L. Bean's operation?**

INTRODUCTION

Retailers often refer to the store building as the "box." A few years ago, a short video was shown at a national retailing symposium entitled "Joshua in the Box."[7] Joshua, a cartoon character that looks somewhat like Barney the Dinosaur, is trying to get out of a box. After a struggle, he creates a crack and manages to get out. Joshua looks around at his new surroundings with a smile. In just a few minutes a tear runs down his cheek as he becomes aware of his new environment. Beginning to cry profusely, Joshua opens his mouth wide enough to turn himself inside out and he winds up back in the box. The point the speaker was making, of course, was that retailers must consider **getting "out of the box"** and looking for opportunities to sell to customers who do not come to the store. But, like Joshua, being "out of the box" can be scary for the traditional retailer. In this chapter, we are going to examine how advanced technology is creating and expanding new opportunities for retailing out of the store.

In the past decade, every facet of operations has been affected by information technology developments. One way to visualize this impact is illus-

FIGURE 15.1

Information technology is freeing consumers from the time and location constraints of traditional retailers.

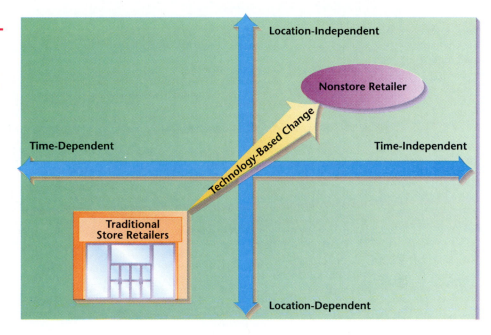

trated in Figure 15.1. Traditional stores limit consumers' options. They must go where the store is and must shop when the store is open. Thus, customers are location-dependent and time-dependent. However, the information technologies discussed in this chapter allow the consumer to be independent of the time and location constraints of traditional retailers. This independence already accounts for as much as $300 billion in sales. Consumers can shop or "consume" advertising when they have the desire, time, and energy. They can access a virtual store on the Internet at 3 a.m. or view an infomercial in their home or at the office while on break. With a credit card, an 800 phone number, and UPS delivery, the customer can complete the retail transaction anytime, anywhere.

In a presentation entitled *Retail . . . Vision of the Future,* Tom Doddridge, then at AT&T Global Solutions, now NCR Corporation, outlined several factors that he believed would define the future of retailing. Two of those factors, cyberspace retailing and retail database marketing, are the topic of this chapter. Chapter 16 will focus on three other factors: globalization, changing retail formats, and new formats. Figure 15.2 illustrates the many factors that will motivate changes in the retail industry. Those factors not discussed in Chapters 15 and 16 have been presented previously in the text.

The bottom line in the *Retail . . . Vision of the Future* presentation was that embracing change will be fundamental to retailers obtaining and retaining a competitive advantage.

FIGURE 15.2

The changing retail industry: Embracing change = competitive advantage.

In the past decade, every facet of store operations has been affected by technological developments. Today, more than ever, technology offers retailers opportunities to expand the way they communicate with and sell to customers, which is our focus in this chapter.

There are thousands of nonstore retailers. Some are catalog operations like Spiegel. Other firms like Columbia House, which retails music and video products, use mailing lists to reach individual customers with regular offerings. Still others like the Virtual Vineyard sell only on the Internet. Many retailers such as L. L. Bean have stores but primarily sell out of the box. At the same time a department store chain like J. C. Penney has a major catalog operation. Retailers sell all kinds of goods with infomercials and on TV shopper networks. The whole field of nonstore retailing is growing dramatically. The major reasons are outlined in Box 15.1. In this chapter we discuss two major topics: the virtual store and database retailing. See Figure 15.3.

One of the meanings of the word *virtual* is "implied." So virtual reality is implied reality. We define the **virtual store** as any communications and selling retail format that relies on electronic technology to interact with a potential customer. A store is virtual because it is implied by the description,

15.1 PRESSURES ON TRADITIONAL IN-STORE SHOPPING[8]

1. Fifty percent of consumers say they feel too time-pressured to enjoy on-site shopping.
2. Advertising clutter has produced ad-weary buyers. The typical retail promotion or advertisement just adds more confusion.
3. Consumers complain that they've left a store after selecting a purchase because they couldn't get good service or information.
4. Shopping alternatives such as catalogs, mail, video shopping channels, and computer on-line networks are growing in number and competitive strength.
5. New technologies are simplifying the out-of-store shopping experience and making it faster and more convenient.

FIGURE 15.3

The multiple dimensions of electronic nonstore retailing.

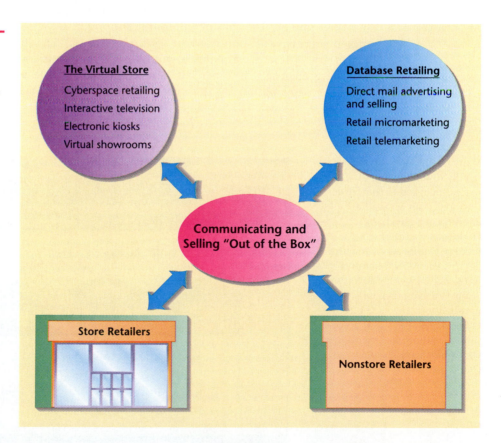

promotion, and offering of merchandise and/or services through electronic means. We will discuss retailing in cyberspace on the Internet, interactive television, electronic kiosk retailing, and the virtual showroom.

Our discussion of database retailing focuses on the idea of developing and managing a personalized customer database that can be used in numerous ways by store and nonstore retailers. You are most familiar with **direct mail selling** and advertising. A database can also be used in retail micromarketing and retail telemarketing.

THE VIRTUAL STORE

After years of speculation concerning whether or not consumers would ever accept electronic shopping, the answer can no longer be in doubt. The cable home shopping industry generates sales of about $3 billion. Furthermore, infomercials, unheard of just a few years ago, generate an additional $1 billion. It is estimated that as many as 80 percent of American adults have viewed television shopping, and 19 percent of these viewers purchased a product they saw on TV. On-line computer shopping services, still meeting with mixed success, will soon account for an additional $1 billion in sales. There are many different estimates about growth, but one source expects home shopping channels, infomercials, and computer on-line services to reach as much as $100 billion by the year 2000.[9] Bill Gates, in an address to food

Many retailers are moving rapidly toward adding the cyberspace dimension to their store. Customers can access the offerings of a merchant worldwide via Internet MCI, Prodigy, CompuServe, America Online, and MSN (Microsoft Network). OfficeMax advertises, "Now you can purchase hundreds of items direct from OfficeMax Online." It is accessed through the services mentioned. On CompuServe it's as easy as GO: OFCMAX.

industry executives, said, "Electronic retailing will grow rapidly, because potential operational efficiencies, convenience, and direct access to the consumer, regardless of geography, guarantee success with certain products and customer sets."[10]

Cyberspace Retailing on the World Wide Web

Cyberspace is a popularized term that refers to the world of computer electronics where we cannot see what is taking place but we know that somewhere, somehow we are linked together and can communicate. The most obvious possibility for expanding electronic shopping is via the Internet's **World Wide Web.** The **Internet** is a global computer network; the graphical portion is the Web, which is connected with **hypertext links** (hyperlinks). The opening "http" in an Internet address stands for "hypertext transport protocol" and tells the computer you want to seek out material displayed in graphical form. Hyperlinks enable the users to instantly skip from information place to information place. It is the hyperlink capability that allows you to search and browse on the Web. Netscape Navigator Software is the most popular means for doing this.

The information superhighway.   The Internet has been referred to as an "**information superhighway,**" which is a catchall name for a high-speed digital communications system that can handle computer data as well as TV and telephone signals. See Box 15.2.

BOX 15.2   THE FUTURE OF THE INFORMATION HIGHWAY

More than 100 million computers allow us to manipulate, store, and transmit information in digital form. Bill Gates, in his book *The Road Ahead*, says that "in the future computers will allow access to almost any information in the world."[11] Today's Internet is just a shadow of what the information superhighway will be like.

According to Gates, "You will be able to conduct business, study, explore the world and its cultures, call up any great entertainment, make friends, attend neighborhood markets, and show pictures to distant relatives—without leaving your desk or armchair."[12] We will have a global marketplace of information combining all the ways that goods, services, and ideas are exchanged to create an information society.

There will be some costs and concerns along with the benefits. Dislocations will force worker retraining. New concerns about individual privacy, confidentiality of business transactions, and national security will emerge. And perhaps, most important, will be a concern about how everyone will be served by the information society, not just the technically advanced and economically privileged.[13]

6543217

Many different hardware and software components will make up the future information superhighway.

The Information Superhighway

FIGURE 15.4

When compared to its potential, it is still a system of small country lanes. Your personal computer, telephone lines, and the Internet network form the hardware base for the information "lane." Adding interactive multimedia CD ROMS, high-capacity cable television networks, Digital Satellite Systems, fiber-optic cable networks, very high speed modems, and wireless cellular and digital telephones will turn the country lanes into "roads." Fast and inexpensive software that makes it easy to navigate, ensures user security, and allows applications to work together will turn the roads into "highways." When there are effective ways for users to pay for these services, the developers of large databases will make a world of information available on the Web, and all the components together will create the information "superhighway" (see Figure 15.4). It will certainly be a reality before 2005.[14]

Searching the store. Search "engines" enable individuals to sit at their computer and seek out information by store, product, topic, key word, author, or source. The World Wide Web allows merchants, or any firm or individual, to have an electronic address and home page. Merchants can offer goods for sale, and software is built into home Web pages so customers can search the electronic store. One music store's Web site is designed to allow shoppers to search by music type, label, artist, and song title.[15] New tools to improve the Web allow for sound, animation, and 3D,[16] as well as enhanced color.

There have been complaints by stores that computers are not fast enough and that security software is not perfected. However, there are more than 60,000 vendors on the World Wide Web, and the number is growing every day. See Box 15.3. When Wal-Mart announced in 1996 that it was entering a venture with Microsoft Corporation to go on-line with a virtual retail operation, the stakes in cyberspace retailing were raised to a new level. Microsoft chairman Bill Gates said, "Our goal is to provide the tools necessary to easily create and manage an on-line store so that merchants can focus on merchandising, branding, and differentiation of their products and services in a cost-effective way." [17] In addition to the customer segment that will use it for convenience, many may come to the Web if the virtual stores pass on the lower cost of doing business electronically. Going shopping on the Web also may be attractive because it puts the individual in control. It doesn't just make shopping time and location independent of the retailer, as discussed above—the individual has real control over other uncontrollable factors. Bad experiences with salespeople, traffic, parking, and crowds can be exchanged for a controlled environment where what pleases the individual is the driving factor. Customers will search the Web for information, advertising, entertainment, and shopping, all of which will have to be a part of the successful retailer's virtual store.

Virtual money. One of the persistent problems with conducting business over the Internet has been the lack of a secure manner of transferring money.

BOX 15.3 CUC INTERNATIONAL: A VIRTUAL STORE

CUC International sells everything from cars, computers, and home electronics to airline tickets by phone and on-line. Operators and customers search a database of 250,000 name-brand products, which are shipped directly from the more than 600 manufacturers and distributors to the customer. The most surprising fact is that with $1.3 billion in sales in 1995 and profits of more than $100 million, this retailer has no warehouses, no stores, and no inventory. CUC adds 7 percent to the costs of products to cover expenses for telephone calls, electronic ordering, and UPS shipping. Thirty-four mil-lion members pay $29 each to buy from CUC. Seventy-five percent renew their membership each year.[18] A significant portion of its revenue is from membership fees, so the firm doesn't care if potential customers log on simply to check prices before they go shopping. CUC is now also selling over the Internet. The true genius of the idea is that most retailers suffer from the high cost of fixed assets, land and building, and inventory. In contrast, CUC is dealing with assets such as computers, databases, and telecommunications equipment, which are becoming cheaper.[19]

6543217

Companies such as CompuServe and Check Free Corp. are making available a new electronic wallet. CyberCash Inc. has a joint venture with Check Free to support secure, real-time payments over the Internet using credit cards, debit cards, checks, and cash. The companies argue that their innovations will make it safer and more convenient to shop on the Internet than in the local mall. Some contend that the risks and equipment needed to gain access to credit card numbers simply aren't worth the time or effort. They argue that to gain access to any encrypted number a thief would need nearly $1 million worth of equipment, much too high a price to pay to obtain a card number with a $25,000 credit limit.[20] Once customers believe that their credit card numbers are secure, many predict that shopping on the Web will increase dramatically.

Advertising on the Web. Retailers who are selling on the Web can measure the results directly. A larger issue involves using the Web simply as an advertising media. If a firm believes that a target segment includes customers who regularly surf on the Internet, placing electronic advertisements may be considered. A number of firms are doing research on ways to measure who and how many individuals look at these ads. "Hits" are a count of the number of times a Web page is accessed. However, one person could visit the page a great number of times. Nielsen Media Research, Yankelovich Partners, and ASI Marketing Research are teaming up to measure the total number of visitors and the depth of consumer interactivity.[21] Regardless of the problems, the impact of cyberspace on the retail industry will continue.

Richard Falls of Technology Service Solutions estimates that the number of Internet users doubles every year and that 1 billion people will be using the technology by the year 2000.[22] An *Internet Demographic Survey* by Dun & Bradstreet's Nielsen Media Research and CommerceNet estimates that advertising expenditures could reach as much as $4 billion by the end of the decade.[23]

Costs on the Web. The Internet is a relatively inexpensive way to advertise. The most expensive manner to create a site on the Web involves starting a node. This costs approximately $10,000 for a Windows NT workstation, $5,000 to $7,000 for design work, and about $30 to $100 a month in connection fees. Large companies have been known to spend as much as $1 million to create a Web site. For the small retailer, renting is often the best alternative. A dial-up account large enough for a Web page with an Internet service provider costs approximately $100 to $400 per month. With an additional $100 to $500 per page for design, maintenance, and updates, this is often less than the cost of a one-time ad in the local newspaper.[24]

By creating a home page on the Web, small retailers can reach potential customers from around the world. When first approached about advertising on the Web, Mike McCoy, president of McCoy's Fine Cigars, had just one question: "The what?" After he initiated a home page, 3,500 potential customers started visiting each day. Given the increase in advertising costs, McCoy stated that it's the first form of advertising he's had that's paid for itself. Patricia Nail, the owner of Pretend Like Fashions, a Dallas-based retailer, says, "I would have been lucky to reach Oklahoma with my advertising budget. . . . The exposure has been phenomenal."[25]

Selling on the Web. Why is interest in selling and advertising on the World Wide Web so great? The Internet audience, even though it is less than 5 percent of the U.S. population, is potentially very important to businesses. The *Internet Demographic Survey* profiles the Internet audience: Users average over five hours each week on the Web, 25 percent have incomes greater than $80,000, 50 percent are in professional/managerial occupations, and 64 percent have at least some college education.

For a retailer who wants to go beyond advertising, the steps are fairly straightforward, but not necessarily easy. The store would begin with a home page that would have words or icons to hyperlink the user to additional pages.

The Virtual Vineyard retails fine specialty wines and foods such as Alta Valtellina's jams from the Italian Alps on the Internet. Unique products, fast service, and free advice for both consumers and restaurants create a sustainable competitive advantage. Yearly sales may reach $20 million by the year 2000. The Web site cost $300,000 to develop. Address: http://www.virtualvin.com.

Suppose you wanted to open the "Grandparent T-Shirt Shop." You silkscreen Edge Gear T-shirts with slogans and pictures. You have ten best-sellers including *The Bank of Grandpa* (with a sign hanging off the word *Bank* that says *Sorry Insolvent*) and *I'm Spending My Children's Inheritance So They Won't Fight over It.* Your price is $19.95 plus $4.00 for UPS shipping.

You would need pages with item numbers, titles, and pictures. An order page would contain the item numbers, size, quantity, and color. Still another page would include shipping information, and another would have payment methods, either on-line with virtual money or credit cards. Options might include off-line ordering by mail, fax, phone, or E-mail. With your Web site designed and programmed you would go to an Internet access provider so that your site would be available to everyone worldwide who is connected with their personal computer. This includes a rapidly growing number of senior citizens.

To initiate an order, customers would complete all the information on each page of the form and click on *PLACE ORDER*. Potential customers might find your site as they browse using key word searches. You might also advertise with direct mail and *Money Magazine* and include your WWW address.

Once an order is received, you face the same situation as all direct retailers. To be successful you must provide fast and accurate order fulfillment with provision for returns, guarantees, and so forth.

Interactive Television

In the words of *Business Week,* "Retailing Will Never Be the Same."[26] In May of 1993 Saks Fifth Avenue sold almost $600,000 of its private-label merchandise on the Quality Value Channel (QVC) network, 50 percent more sales than expected. Even though both the company and the concept later had major difficulties, in June Macy's announced plans for a twenty-four-hour shopping channel.[27] Innovative technologies, combined with the growth of cable television, are opening up new ways of shopping for the consumer. Video shopping is allowing the retail customer to buy a wide variety of merchandise direct from both store and nonstore offerings.

You often hear interactive TV referred to as **direct response television** (DRTV). As the name suggests, DRTV allows a customer to respond to a message on television by making a direct purchase. We use **interactive television** as a more encompassing term because of the future capability to do more than pick up a phone and place an order, including selecting on demand the product to be viewed and controlling and participating in the product demonstration. We will discuss both shopping networks and infomercials.

Cable television has grown to the point where 70 percent of America's 100 million homes have cable. Today, technological advances in two-way or interactive television make shopping at home, including video catalogs and merchandise demonstrations, more and more feasible. As the number of items offered grows, and the costs of satellite time and cable installations decrease, the unit cost of purchases should go down.

The outlook for interactive TV is phenomenal. See Box 15.4. High growth will result from increased entertainment and educational programming driven by advanced technology that will reduce costs. Just as cellular phones create communications without wire, satellites are bringing hundreds of channels to viewers worldwide, also without wire. For example, DirectTV is already reaching millions of people with 175 channels. Just as important, the entry of major firms into multimedia services provides increased quality of programs including interactive CD ROM catalogers and product demonstrations.

Using digital compression technology, up to 500 channels can be squeezed on existing cables. With so many options, a Quality Value Channel (QVC) or Home Shopping Network (HSN) program can target a small audience, and viewers can also order video on demand. Already the technology is being used to allow PCs to tie into the TV cable and give far greater speed than is possible over a telephone line.

Video shopping has a great deal of appeal for retailers. In recent years traditional stores have been faced with rising costs and flat sales. Many see direct retailing as one of the few bright spots in the industry. In fact, sales from coupons, direct mail, radio and TV offers, and catalogs are rising nearly 15 percent per year, which is twice the rate of increase for retail sales.

Shopping networks. A typical cable "shopping channel" provides a nearly continuous advertising television program. In a typical application, a ten-minute product demonstration is repeated several times during the month. In addition to retailers, national firms such as Maytag, Encyclopedia Britannica, Walt Disney, and Procter & Gamble have all experimented with various home shopping shows. In most of today's applications, viewers order displayed merchandise by calling a toll-free number. The spread of interactive

---

BOX 15.4 INTERACTIVE TELEVISION BENEFITS TO THE RETAILER

On-demand, interactive TV will bring numerous benefits to retailers as current and potential customers access a multimedia CD ROM catalog and place orders.

- Interactive TV in essence extends the store into the home. It can allow the retailer to offer better targeted products with high levels of convenience and comfort.

- To the extent that sales can be increased without significant increases in the costs

of selling space, promotion and advertising costs, and the costs of personal selling, interactive TV leverages the retailer's use of resources.

- By being a part of the interactive TV revolution, a retailer conveys the perception that it is up to date and striving to provide the highest levels of customer service.

6543217

two-way cable will speed up the growth of video shopping. Instead of telephoning, viewers will soon be able to order goods with a handheld calculator device (resembling a TV/VCR remote control) linked to a central database by cable or telephone wires. Customers will be able to summon up on the TV screen a description of what they want to buy and see it demonstrated. In fact, a number of companies have already moved toward putting their traditional merchandise catalogs on video. Sears has moved in this direction, as has J. C. Penney.

QVC and HSN are the industry leaders in home shopping. Their rate of repeat customers is nearing 60 percent, with the average repeater spending ten times more per year than the one-time customer. Yet problems remain, including those related to image, high return rates, and shipping costs.

Toll-free response numbers. Toll-free response numbers are standard tools for direct response television and database marketing. In fact, the Direct Marketing Educational Foundation reported that over half of all advertising expenditures include a direct response mechanism such as toll-free numbers. Because of their popularity, America is quickly running out of 800 numbers. In an effort to avoid depletion, beginning in 1996, the FCC activated new toll-free area codes, beginning with 888 and continuing with 877 and 866.

Expanded electronic shopping options. Much of the current attention that television shopping is receiving focuses on the outlook for niche and upscale extensions of the core product mix and target audiences. Saks Fifth Avenue's sellout indicates a market for more upscale merchandise—a market already being pursued by Nordstrom and Bloomingdales.

In addition, shopping programs targeting consumers who share similar interests would be a natural complement to existing informational programs. For example, these might focus on home improvement with Home Depot or IKEA coupled with "Our House," or The Kitchen Store linked with "Julia Child" or the "Frugal Gourmet."

Consumers, perhaps even sooner than they think, will be able to view a far richer selection of home shopping options than what's currently available, along with having access to an expanded array of services, teleticketing, and pay-per-view offerings.

International expansion. Through a series of alliances, the U.S. cable home shopping industry is looking to expand its core programming concept throughout Europe and Latin America. For example, QVC has announced a joint venture with Grupo Televisa, the $1.3 billion Mexican media conglomerate, to develop a home shopping program. This will debut first in Mexico and then expand into other Spanish- and Portuguese-speaking countries throughout Latin America and Europe. With more than 350 million people throughout the world using Spanish as their first language, the Mexico-based venture obviously has significant sales potential. QVC's European entry strategy includes a 50-50 joint venture with Britain's SkyTV satellite television network to develop a live broadcast home shopping channel targeting all European countries except Spain and Portugal.

Kinnevik ("TV Shop") is another European player that is well entrenched in Scandinavia and recently began penetration of the German market, enhancing its effort by acquiring the Telekauf home shopping operator. A Japanese example is illustrated in Box 15.5.

Challenges and problems.   Potential problems with home shopping have appeared. The joint venture between Spiegel and Time Warner, Catalog 1 cable shopping network, had to cut back on programming hours. Scheduled twenty-four hours a day, seven days a week, Catalog 1 scaled back to two hours on Saturday. The reason given for the change was the limited availability of cable channels. However, several analysts suggest that production problems, as well as problems in developing programs for young upscale shoppers, were the reasons for the cutback. The joint venture is now concentrating on offering goods over the Internet.[28]

Infomercials.   Another dimension to direct response television shopping channels is the infomercial. An *infomercial* is a longer version (typically ten to thirty minutes) of a conventional commercial that uses product demonstrations and information in an attempt to persuade potential customers to

BOX 15.5   JAPAN'S "WORLD SHOPPING THEATER"

Japan's "World Shopping Theater" is aired twice monthly for two hours at midnight. The top rated program in its time slot, the show targets upscale adult males and reaches 3 million households. Advertising rates rival those of U.S. late night talk shows. The format is similar to a combination of "Lifestyles of the Rich and Famous," "Saturday Night Live," and game shows such as "guess this product's use."

The midnight broadcast attracts a young adult cult following, à la "Saturday Night Live" or David Letterman. The program's angle is unique: featuring a combination of entertainment, information, and shopping for products and services targeted to upscale consumers; and selling image and prestige as much as the product itself. "World Shopping Theater" moves more than $2 million worth of merchandise per episode at retail prices. Ninety percent of the orders are C.O.D.; the remainder are by credit card. Telephone lines remain open four days after the program to accommodate late orders. The show is produced by Fujisankei, Japan's largest communications conglomerate, and is broadcast on the company's network, Fuji TV. Conveniently, Fujisankei publishes the country's largest direct mail catalog, which reaches about 2.5 million households. Annual sales total some $500 million. Companies that sell their products through the shopping show are also offered an opportunity to have them featured in the catalog.

6543217

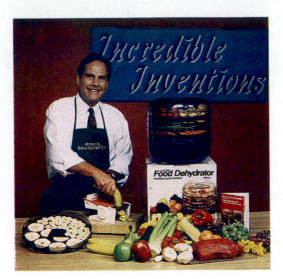

Ron Popeil sold $1.25 million worth of pasta makers in twelve minutes on QVC. Credited with creating the infomercial industry, he sells $50 million of merchandise a year. He often goes to a county fair to see if people want to buy the product and what they are willing to pay. The program must be about entertainment as well as selling. (Hall, Cheryl, "The Pitch-O-Matic Man," *Dallas Morning News*, November 12, 1995, p. H1.)

make a direct response purchase. The infomercial attempts to combine the elements of entertainment to maintain attention with a persuasive product demonstration. Only one in eight products sold via infomercial generates a steady stream of sales. Yet that is enough to total over $1 billion each year.[29]

Whether it is Sears producing infomercials to sell vacuum cleaners, your local nursery buying thirty minutes on late night TV to demonstrate and sell roses, or a nonstore retailer selling fitness equipment, the fundamentals are the same. Information and product demonstrations along with a request for an immediate purchase response are presented to the viewer. The interactive device is typically the telephone, although E-mail on the Internet or regular mail at the U.S. Post Office may be used. The infomercial may be on cable or broadcast channels or on closed-circuit TV in a store. Order fulfillment is via mail or private carrier such as FedEx or UPS. In the case of in-store infomercials, the desired response is to have customers walk down the aisle, pick up the product, and purchase it.

There are a number of federal legal requirements for infomercials.[30] Objective factual claims must be substantiated on a "reasonable basis" including evidence to support a specific claim. Health, nutrition, or safety claims for products or services require a high level of substantiation. Endorsements must be based on the opinion, findings, or experience of the endorser. The endorser must also be a bona fide user if such use is represented. If a money-back guarantee does not include a refund of shipping and handling, that fact must be clearly stated. Just as with other advertisements, price statements must be truthful. Additional costs such as shipping and handling must be disclosed. If the claim of a sale or savings over an alternative source is made, significant sales must have been made at the represented higher price. In addition, if "free goods" are offered, government rules say that the offer cannot be made for more than six months in a twelve-month period and no more than three offers can be made in the same period. Just as important, substantial sales of the product must have been made at the offered price without the "free goods."

Electronic Kiosk Retailing

A third dimension of our virtual store involves **electronic kiosk** retailing. Today, the kiosks you see are typically stationary and usually feature a single application such as travel information in an airport or your ATM machine.

The year 2000 may see more than 2 million kiosks featuring real-time information and interactive multimedia linked to global satellite networks. The kiosks may be located in stores, throughout malls, in businesses and schools, and nearly anywhere else consumers are gathered.

Electronic kiosks offer retailers an additional medium to personally communicate with customers. They can be used to inform, educate, train, persuade, or perform information-based transactions.[31] They not only offer customer communications but also sell. Kiosks can be a personal "shopping assistant" for the customer. For example, in the area of consumer electronics, detailed information about complicated products can be provided in an environment without sales associates. Best Buy's Concept III stores include as many as a dozen interactive multimedia kiosks known as Answer Centers. The content includes thousands of photos and video clips. Customers can learn details about product features and prices without help from salespeople. The data on the kiosks are updated frequently from a centralized database.[32] There are many ways both consumers and retailers can benefit from their use. See Box 15.6.

A **"smart card"** the size of a credit card containing a microcomputer processor can store large amounts of information about customers. In Europe, smart cards are being integrated into customer loyalty programs to track and reward shoppers based on purchasing behavior. Visualize a customer carrying a smart card. It has all kinds of demographic and economic data about the individual as well as information about family and friends. You will be able to go to a kiosk, insert your smart card, and indicate your desire to purchase a fiftieth wedding anniversary present for Granddad and Grandmother. Your

BOX 15.6 THE CONSUMER AND RETAILER VIEW OF KIOSKS[33]

Customers use electronic kiosks to:

- Obtain detailed product information
- Compare different products and services
- Determine if a product is in stock
- View photos and videos of the products
- Obtain suggestions about substitutes if an item is not available
- Order and pay for a product

For retailers an electronic kiosk can:

- Offer twenty-four-hour shopping in numerous in-store and nonstore locations
- Collect consumer information
- Offer a wider range of products than they can stock in a store
- Provide continuous communications near the point of product display
- Analyze the information consumers seek
- Identify the products considered but rejected as well as those ordered

6543217

smart card knows their ages, where they live, and even what they like. The kiosk interacts with its retailer databases and comes back with recommendations that are demonstrated with motion and sound. You make a selection, click on a few icons, and your order is placed, charged to your bank account or credit card, and shipped direct via UPS.

One of the real advantages of the electronic kiosk is its ability to expand the product lines offered in a store without the cost of space and inventory. Michael Ricker Pewter is sold in many gift shops, but a typical retailer can carry a limited number of the 3,000 works of art available. A touch screen multimedia kiosk that takes up only 22 inches by 30 inches of floor space contains a PC, a laser disk player, a receipt printer, a credit card capture device, stereo speakers, an audio amplifier, and a high-speed modem. Customers can browse and order items at the kiosk that are not stocked in the store.[34]

A kiosk can also improve customer service. Lee Apparel has an interactive kiosk it calls Fit Finder, which helps customers in department stores select the best fitting jeans.[35] The largest single use of kiosks is for registering gift selections for weddings, baby showers, and the like. Many national retailers, such as Target and Dillard, offer kiosks that contain the gift preferences the future bride and groom have selected and then keep track of whether or not each selection has been purchased as a gift. Kiosks are also used for interactive in-store advertising.

Virtual Simulations and Showrooms

The same microcomputer technology that is having such an impact in expanding electronic shopping is also making itself felt in the store. Whether it is in-store systems such as **point-of-sale couponing, liquid crystal display (LCD) shelf tags, self-service scanning checkouts,** or credit processing systems, customer convenience is being driven by technology. One of the most exciting new developments involves **virtual reality simulations and showrooms.**

Simulation Research has created what it refers to as the Visionary Shopper.[36] This allows a retailer to duplicate the shopping experience without the expense of using a real store. Although its current application is for **virtual reality marketing research,** the potential for home shopping via interactive TV or on the Internet is tremendous. As reported by *Marketing Week,* through computer simulation the firm can test price promotions, store layout, and product positioning, as well as new products. A "shopper" sits at a computer screen and watches images of genuine three-dimensional products. With a trackball, the "shopper" moves up and down retail aisles, zooming in and out on any shelf and picking out products to examine. The items can then be placed in a virtual shopping cart.

In a similar application of virtual reality technology, the British manufacturer of Electrolux kitchen appliances has developed a virtual reality kitchen. It uses 3D images linked to a personal computer. Consumers can build their own virtual kitchen by selecting the equipment from a catalog.

The kitchen can be customized by changing appliances, positions, and colors. Consumers can even open the virtual refrigerator or use the washing machine. The system should allow smaller inventories and increased sales.[37]

We now turn to our second major topic of the chapter.

RETAIL DATABASE MARKETING

In order to respond to customers, retailers must determine their needs and wants. As explained in Chapter 5, marketing research is often used to try to understand the consumer. However, retailers also have the opportunity to capture data about their customers from their contact with them. In this section we discuss retail database marketing, which is defined as the retailer's use of any "marketing process in which useful, behavioral, psychographic or demographic information about prospects or customers is stored in the company's database and is used to enhance or prolong the relationship or to stimulate sales."[38]

Retailers are in a unique position to know their customers. Years ago this was easy. There were relatively few people shopping at small neighborhood stores. Owners and clerks could know their clientele on a personal basis. Today, operating in this manner is impossible for most retailers, even though many individual sales associates keep a notebook of information about their customers. Instead of gathering knowledge from personal contact, retailers capture, compile, and store information about their customers in a consumer database.

The Personalized Shopper Database

A **personalized shopper database (PSD)** can be developed by capturing every piece of information possible about individual customers. Think about the potential. The detail of every customer transaction includes what was purchased by SKU, when and where it was purchased, how it was paid for, and possibly who purchased it. Other useful information may include voice prints or thumb prints for identification and customer image data for computer-generated mannequins. Spiegel uses an in-house computer-assisted telephone interviewing system for research to gather customer information. The data are merged with the customer database to constantly monitor the tastes, needs, and purchase motivation of shoppers.[39]

The opportunities for a retailer to increase customer service and expand sales with a personalized shopper database are tremendous. We will examine direct mail advertising and selling, including catalogs. We will also look at micromarketing, including sales associate support. More information about the shopper allows better matching of products and services to customer desires as well as cross-selling opportunities. Think about the advantages of associates being able to communicate at very low cost with the shopper, because the database also contains Internet E-mail addresses. Retail micro-marketing will also make possible store-specific merchandise assortments.

As the number of items in the store, the number of store locations, and the number of shoppers have increased, more sophisticated methods to keep customer records have developed. Today, firms like Service Merchandise link each store to the home office computer via satellite. Transactions are recorded on the network each time a customer makes a purchase at any store throughout the United States. In fact, Service Merchandise has collected data on more than 20 million households.[40] Pizza Hut keeps an on-line database of more than 9 million customers. Increasingly, computerized **database retailing** is becoming synonymous with both store-based as well as nonstore merchandising. While database retailing has its roots in direct marketing, it's not just for direct marketers anymore. It can become a critical ingredient in building individual customer relationships for large and small retailers. When embarking on this effort, the first task is database design.

Developing the Database

Customer information is gathered from a variety of sources, the most reliable of which are often from within the store. The database needs to be designed so that it will:

- Improve sales interactions
- Improve checkout interactions
- Precisely identify customers
- Track overall purchases by dollar value
- Track dollar value of purchases by promotional vehicle
- Perform these tasks quickly and efficiently

Point-of-sale data capture. A POS system uses a computer in conjunction with a bar code scanner, credit and check authorization system, and cash register to improve the accuracy and shorten the time for checkout. Today, a **wireless POS system** is not only used at the cash register but allows the sales associate to go to where the customer is, for example, setting up a checkout at a sidewalk sale. Portable wireless systems are also used for receiving in the back room and for taking physical inventory on the sales floor.

As customers buy goods, scanners at the POS collect information from the bar codes on the product. The data collected at the POS are then stored in customer and sales databases. Collecting and storing information is only the first of several steps in the process. Using information such as zip codes, customers can be grouped with data gathered from secondary sources, such as the *Retail Census of Trade,* for the demographics of the surrounding area.

Collecting and storing information at checkout can substantially increase customer service. Pizza Hut's database is organized by their customers' phone numbers. Sales staff no longer need to ask many questions regarding where to deliver a pizza. Instead they ask the customers for their phone number or obtain it by caller ID, and the rest of the information is provided by the computer including what the customer has purchased frequently. A salesperson may ask, "Would you like a large supreme with four large Pepsis again today?" Customers are rightly concerned about privacy issues when retailers collect so much information. See Figure 15.5.

The POS system—which can collect information from checks, credit cards, and/or other ID such as a social security number—can be used to identify a consumer. This data can then be compiled with purchase information—such as size, style, color, model, brand, and frequency of purchase—and stored in the database. There are a number of software programs that help analyze the data. Efficient consumer response (ECR) is a computer-based technology used to decide which goods to move to which place at what time.

Preferred customer programs.   Many retailers have begun using **frequent purchase** or **preferred customer programs.** These are similar to frequent flyer programs in that they give awards/prizes or discounts for shopping at a store more often. For example, Neiman's "InCircle" club members can receive a ten-day vacation for spending $3,000 in the store. When applying for the membership program, customers record valuable information that can be correlated with the purchase data. Customers are identified by a program ID number, regardless of whether they use credit, check, or cash. This allows the retailer to keep an accurate record on each customer in the program, including the content and timing of purchases. The membership application for the Valley View center in Dallas asks for names and dates of birth

WE RESPECT YOUR PRIVACY

I've heard customers ask, "Why does RadioShack need my name and address?"

Simply put, we value you as our customer! We add you to our private mailing list in order to inform you of upcoming sale events and special offers, and to send you important product updates. Printing your name and address on every receipt also helps to speed up warranty work, returns, and adjustments.

Rest assured that this information is held in strictest confidence. Our mailing list is never sold to other companies.

We want you to think of RadioShack as more than just a store! Thanks for helping us serve you better.

Leonard Roberts
President, RadioShack

of each member of the household. Information is also requested regarding race, marital status, homeowner/renter, combined household income, and education levels.[41]

Prospecting for new customers.

One key factor in developing the database is having a system for adding qualified names. **Prospecting** begins with knowing the characteristics of current customers. To prospect effectively, you profile your best customers on demographic, behavioral, and purchasing characteristics and then try to obtain lists of similar types of people.

There are numerous sources for new prospects including in-store lists, broker lists, and affinity lists. The names of past customers, if available, may also be added to the prospect database. The availability and future profitability of prospects from each of these sources will vary. For example, a past customer may be more likely to respond to an offer than prospects from a broker.

When sourcing from a **broker list**, people can be selected by gender, age, income, educational level, occupation, recreational interests, or almost any other characteristic desired. To be of value, the list must be made up of people who can use what you sell, who can buy it, or who can influence the purchase. Let's consider an example. You want to hold a pre-Valentine "Men's Shopping Night." You might buy a list of 10,000 names of men living in zip codes 75207 to 75212 who have an income greater than $40,000 and who are married. You would probably pay about 10 cents a name for a one-time use. If you used a device such as a door prize drawing form, you could add to the database the names of the individuals who responded to an announcement mailing.

A **store list** is a listing of people who are not currently customers but whose names have been collected by store personnel. The store list may consist of names, addresses, and phone numbers of people who responded to a contest, a sweepstakes offer, or some other promotion effort intended to solicit prospects. The lists may also be developed from names turned in by salespeople; telephone directories; city directories; inquiries received from advertising in other media; newspaper birth, engagement, marriage, wedding anniversary, and death announcements; and permits for new buildings, additions, remodeling, or repairs. For example, to announce the opening of a frame shop a flyer was sent to art instructors and students at area colleges and to the individuals listed in the directory of the church the new owners attend.

Retailers may also be able to obtain names from companies that are not competitors but have one or more characteristics in common. Such an **affinity list** is collected because the purchase behavior of its members is similar to that of the current customer list. For example, the owner of an upscale high-fashion apparel boutique and the owner of a women's shoe store who both cater to a similar clientele might profitably exchange mailing lists because their customers have an affinity connection: They are upscale and fashion-conscious. We may or may not care whether the customers match on a set of demographic characteristics.

A relatively new source of database information is from the use of coupons. Coupons Online (COL) will distribute promotion incentives for several retailers through on-line services such as CompuServe, Prodigy, and its own World Wide Web site. Coupons, rebates, refund offers, mail-order forms, recipes, and product information are available from COL for customers to download and print at their home PC. Dual bar coding will identify users by household and build customer histories. The household ID code will also be used to minimize the potential for mass redemption fraud. At the manufacturer's clearinghouse, coupons will be scanned and audit data will be captured along with the household ID.[42]

Managing the Database

Determining lifetime value; knowing recency, frequency, and monetary value; and merge/purge functions are key elements in managing the database. To begin, knowing the lifetime value of a single customer or group of customers is a fundamental unit of analysis in the database management process.

Lifetime value.   You may recall that we established an annual dollar value for customers within our retail trade area in Chapter 6. Determining the lifetime value of a group of customers is critical as you make decisions about obtaining or maintaining their stream of purchases. For example, it may require six catalog mailings before a prospect becomes a customer. If it costs $40 to mail the catalogs and handle the first order, you need to know if it was all worth it. If a certain profile of customer tends to place twenty-five orders over a four-year period and each order is larger than the previous one, then this is a shopper with a high lifetime value that you will want to cultivate.

Recency, frequency, monetary value.   A point of analysis similar to lifetime value is the **recency, frequency, and monetary value (RFM)** of a customer. RFM lets you know when their last order was placed, how frequently (on average) the customer places orders, and what the monetary value is of the average sale to that customer. By knowing the RFM of a set of customers, you will be able to evaluate which of them have greater value to the organization; how often to mail offers, have the sales associates make calls, or send invitations for special events; and how much money can be spent on developing a customer group.

Merge and purge.   You will need to add and delete names from lists as you obtain new customers and eliminate those who move or are no longer important to the customer profile. Some of these additions will be from lists purchased from brokers and others will be from your own name-gathering efforts. **Merging** activities occur when you add a new prospect or customer to the existing database. It is common for current customers to also be included in the new lists that you purchase or compile yourself. To ensure that these individuals do not receive two mailings or other forms of contact, it is desirable to remove all but one of their entries from your final list. **Purging** is the process of deleting duplicate names.

USING THE DATABASE FOR DIRECT MAIL

One of the major uses of a customer list is direct mail promotion, through either advertising or sending catalogs. Direct mail by retailers is growing throughout the world, with expansion in Europe rivaling that of the United States. Direct mail's share of the retailer's advertising budget is also growing.

BOX 15.7 AN ETHICAL DILEMMA: USING TECHNOLOGY TO COMPLY WITH THE LAW

Far too many individuals and firms have engaged in scams that rip customers off by selling them shoddy merchandise, overcharging, failing to honor warranties, and sometimes never delivering the goods at all. Legislators have been particularly concerned about this situation in the case of nonstore retailing, such as mail order and telemarketing.

In 1985, federal legislation led to a rule stating that mail-order retailers must ship merchandise ordered by mail or phone within the time set in the ad; if no time limit is indicated, shipment must be within thirty days. The merchant must also notify the customer about any delay and offer the *option* of agreeing to the delay or canceling the order.

Neiman Marcus has a very successful mail-order retail business. However, recently the FTC alleged that in numerous instances since 1991, when Neiman Marcus was unable to ship within the applicable time, it failed to offer customers the required options. The FTC also alleged that the firm failed to notify the customer that if he or she did not reply, Neiman Marcus considered the customer's failure to act as a consent to the delay set forth in the notice. Neiman Marcus paid an $85,000 fine for violating the rule. Today's technology can track order fulfillment processes, determine the status of orders, and contact customers automatically. Hundreds of mail-order firms know and comply with this ruling with very little difficulty.

Questions

Do you see an ethical issue here? Are there economic or business reasons that would lead Neiman Marcus to risk fines, bad publicity, and customer dissatisfaction over this issue?

Source: Adapted with permission from Robert Kahn, "Neiman Marcus Group Pays $85,000," *Retailing Today, Feature Report,* March 1995, p. 1.

Retailers must be sure their operations comply with the appropriate laws. See Box 15.7.

The degree to which a retailer's advertisement is seen as "junk" is directly related to how well the merchant utilizes the database. Retailers have less interest in sending out junk mail than consumers have in receiving it. For the retailer, sending out direct mail is an expensive proposition. By carefully maintaining and cultivating an up-to-date database that can be sorted by a number of factors, retailers can minimize sending out junk mail and instead transmit information that potential customers find useful.

Uses of Direct Mail

If retailers doubt that they are reaching all customers and prospects through other advertising media, direct mail gives them another chance. If they are already reaching them, direct mail can add to the impact. Box 15.8 offers suggestions for using direct mail advertising.

Direct mail is the most selective and flexible of all the retail media. The merchant selects individuals who would have a use for the product or service. It can be confined to a small area, such as a few city blocks, or distributed throughout the world. Direct retail advertising is flexible because the sizes and shapes of the ad and the presentation can be simple or elaborate.

Another advantage is that the reader is not distracted by other advertising. For a moment, at least, there is undivided attention. At the same time there is no editorial or entertainment support to keep the reader exposed to the ad. Direct mail has to be good, both in what it offers and in how the offer is presented.

BOX 15.8 DIRECT MAIL ADVERTISING HAS MANY USES FOR RETAILERS

- To solicit mail-order or phone-order business
- To announce new models, new designs, new lines, new items, or changes in products or services
- To notify customers of price increases or decreases
- To welcome new customers
- To help regain lost customers
- To thank all customers for their business at least once a year

- To create an image for the business
- To remind customers and prospects of seasonal or periodic needs
- To make the most of special events such as product use classes
- To take advantage of printed advertising materials supplied by manufacturers
- To provide customers with information concerning new locations

6543217

SAVE 20%–41% ON FINE CASHMERE SWEATERS.

The communications strategy for a retailer requires decisions about reach, frequency, content, and image that are illustrated in this page from the Lands' End winter sale catalog. Direct mail can reach a high portion of the targeted customer base. The winter sale catalog has a low frequency: once each year. This page is content-oriented with product detail and price. At the same time the quality image desired by the company is conveyed through the use of color, quality graphics, paper, and white space.

The Mailing Piece

Direct mail advertising in its simplest form is a postcard with a message handwritten on it. It can be simple or elaborate, a self-mailer or an envelope with numerous enclosures.

Direct mail advertising is sometimes used for announcements, but usually retailers try to elicit action by persuading the recipients to come to the store or to phone or mail in an order. The message can be mailed solo, co-op, or as a bill stuffer.

A *solo mailing* occurs when a single firm mails a postcard, flyer, letter, brochure, or catalog. Some retailers, however, may choose to pool their funds with others and be one of several sponsors of a mailing piece. A *co-op mailing* occurs when at least two retailers share the cost. The key advantage is a lower cost per targeted household to each of the individual advertisers than they would have paid doing a solo mailing of a similar quality message.

Bill stuffers are sales letters, brochures, small samples, or flyers that are inserted with a retailer's routine monthly billing statement. Customers regularly receive bill stuffers inside their monthly department store or credit card bills. One of the advantages for the retailer of using bill stuffers is that the recipient is almost certain to open the envelope.

The Cost of Direct Mail

Direct mail is the most costly advertising media in terms of dollars spent per household or individual. The true measure of the cost of advertising is the amount per inquiry or per sale. A store can get some idea of what a mailing will cost by estimating the expenses of all the elements involved in the mailout: postage, printing, production, and employee time. Estimates can then be made on a per piece basis and multiplied by the number of people it will take to get one response. One way to control costs is to carefully target the direct mail. See Box 15.9.

Alternative delivery. Competition for the U.S. Post Office has developed in response to increased postage costs. *Alternative delivery* refers to a company that delivers a packet of promotional information to the specific households you request. These services are being provided by the local telephone company, the local newspaper, as well as firms specializing in this area.

Retail Catalogs

As retail direct marketing increased in popularity during the 1980s and made inroads into traditional store-based sales, traditional retailers began to strike back. Merchants can use catalogs to build sales or to replace parts of their business eroded by national catalogers or local competitors. Catalogs are being used by store retailers ranging from Service Merchandise to Victoria's Secret and L. L. Bean. The list grows daily.

Catalog selling permits the retailer to make sales beyond the immediate geographic trade area of the store(s). It allows the retailer to "carry" items that cannot be easily accommodated within the store because of individual size, assortment, price, or space. It also permits people who do not have the time or desire to travel and shop in the store the opportunity to order by phone, mail, or computer. These advantages are not without their costs, however. Designing, printing, and mailing a catalog are an expensive undertaking.

15.9   TARGETING DEMOGRAPHIC GROUPS WITH DIRECT MAIL

Retailers are finding it much more difficult to compete for the consumer's attention with direct mail. The average customer receives 350 pieces a year. However, some retailers are finding ways to better identify their targets. Montgomery Ward is a retailer that has targeted Hispanic consumers for its direct mail campaigns. The U.S. Hispanic market consists of more than 26 million people with a purchasing power of some $200 billion. The population will be 35 million by the year 2000.[43]

It is estimated that Hispanic households receive less than two dozen Spanish-language pieces of direct mail annually. Since Hispanics receive fewer direct mailings and have common media consumption habits, direct marketing programs can be more cost-effective. The president of HispanAmerica, a Hoboken, New Jersey–based direct marketing shop, recently said, "Because the [Hispanic] consumer is so under-solicited, if they get anything in Spanish they will read it."

Order fulfillment is equally important. Rick Blume, vice president of Database Management, says, "Nothing is worse than having Hispanic prospects call your toll-free customer service line with questions or comments and having them greeted with an English-speaking operator. Prospects can't communicate their messages, and you lose both sales and integrity."[44]

6543217

In addition, the maintenance of a catalog database, the fulfillment operation, and returned-goods handling are expensive.

The catalog decision is not an easy one. It can permit a retailer to increase sales, but care must be taken that the net contribution margin is acceptable. The total costs associated with producing and distributing a catalog may far outweigh any benefits. The decision to use catalogs is an effort to increase market share, growth rate, profit, and stability by sharing the operating costs of two businesses in a synergistic arrangement.[45]

Fingerhut is one of the most successful catalog retailers. According to its CEO, the firm's future depends on nurturing the company's relationships with its customers and what he terms the "world's most sophisticated" database of more than 25 million potential customers. Fingerhut sends out nearly 500 million pieces of mail each year. The company has 7 million regular customers.[46]

An old idea with a new twist.   Ask a person to describe a catalog and you're likely to get a response that depicts either the large printed book of a department store, such as J. C. Penney, or a smaller specialty catalog, such as Victoria's Secret. The latest trend involves putting the information on computer media for access by a home PC or interactive TV.

Apple Computer has put catalogs on compact disks. The compact disk is a tool for inexpensive storage and distribution of very large databases. Digital files of images also have the potential to create an exciting multimedia catalog format.[47] In one test, approximately 30,000 households with Apple Computers received a free single CD containing nearly two dozen catalogs. The program is called El Passant. The CD program allows customers to order from all the retailers through a single toll-free number. In the future, Apple hopes to offer ordering direct from the computer screen by using a modem.

El Passant allows the user to compare competing products side by side and search for products by catalog or department. The customer not only examines products but sets up reminders to make purchases for specific occasions. The program also makes use of the power of today's PC computers. The user can examine an article of clothing and, with a click of the mouse, change the colors of the products. It also allows the user to overlay images. For example, if the user wishes to see how a particular tie matches a shirt, he can put them together on the computer screen.

USING THE DATABASE FOR RETAIL TELEMARKETING

What does the word **telemarketing** conjure up in your mind? A call at dinnertime with an offer to buy the latest and best burial plot or solicitation for a credit card deal? Most retailers do not use outbound telephone solicitation from their databases to the extent that they might find profitable. However, the use of the telephone for response via 800 or 900 numbers in support of other retailing efforts is common. For example, Dell Computer Corporation is a $2 billion company that has been built selling personal computers by tele-marketing to both individuals and businesses. The heart of the operation is a database of more than 1 million customer records to which 20 million pieces of direct mail are sent. The company uses the direct mail, direct response print ads, and catalogs to generate inbound telephone calls. The print ads are used to build awareness and generate sales leads. The calls are handled by 600 tele-phone representatives who take some 22,000 calls each day.[48]

Inbound Telephone Calls

There are numerous ways retailers use inbound telephone calling. Customer service call centers are much more common with manufacturers than retail-ers, but many merchants are setting them up to stay in closer contact with customers. Consumers can call to find the location of the nearest store, check an in-stock situation, get warranty information, and so on. A hotline can also let customers respond to promotional activities.[49]

Catalog retailing and video shopping are dependent on the convenience of the telephone. J.C. Penney handles an average of 70 million long-distance phone calls a year in support of its catalog operation. The company has four-teen telemarketing centers located throughout the country.[50]

You call. You listen. You like. You Buy.[SM] A noncatalog retailer using an 800 number for potential customers to place an order employs an advertising message to reach them via some alternative medium. In the case of 1-800 MUSIC NOW,[SM] the retailer has a co-branded offer with The GM Gold Card that was included as a bill stuffer with the monthly statement. The advertisement encourages use of the GM Card in making 1-800 MUSIC NOW purchases. (© 1996 MCI and General Motors Corporation. All rights reserved. The GM Card is a registered trademark of General Motors Corporation.)

Estimates are that sales of information, entertainment, and products via 900 numbers exceed $3 billion. There are a number of information items that certain customers are willing to pay to receive. MTV, for example, uses the 900 number to interact with its millions of eighteen- to twenty-four-year-old viewers who pay for catalogs and order forms. Retailers may find situations in which customers will pay for the phone call to order or to receive helpful information.[51]

Outbound Telemarketing

Even though relatively few traditional retailers have ventured into using their databases for outbound telemarketing, numerous sales associates do call their customers to inform them of new products or promotional events and to remind them of special occasions. With a well-designed database, outbound telemarketing holds opportunity for most situations listed for direct mail in Box 15.8 above.

The Maintenance Warehouse is a cataloger that carries many of the items found at traditional retailers like Home Depot. In fact, Home Depot uses a direct mail program that targets the same customer profile. Maintenance Warehouse has a database of 100,000 customers and 200,000 prospects. The company has an order-taking staff of thirty and an outbound telemarketing staff of ten.[52]

Outbound telemarketing is finding some possibilities in the foreign markets of developed countries, particularly in Europe. Japan, however, is a different story. Japan's retail trade is highly centralized and serviced by multilevel wholesalers who are difficult to circumvent. Alternative distribution including direct mail, door-to-door selling, and telemarketing, offers possible opportunities. However, Japanese consumers resent being called at home, so it will likely take a long time to change their attitude.[53]

Micromarketing assortments that match the demographics of local store customers have become a major emphasis of supermarkets' merchandising approach to meats and produce. The amount of space devoted to various items varies by market, as do price points. This selection of fancy produce in a New York City supermarket is targeted to the neighborhood's upscale customers.

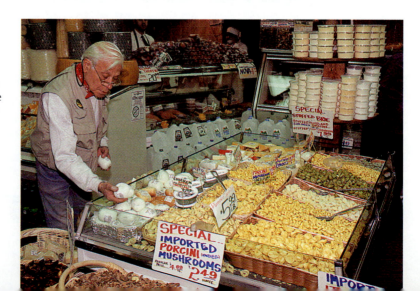

RETAIL MICROMARKETING

Micromarketing involves identifying the needs and wants of the local marketplace and customizing marketing efforts at the store and the individual level, allowing the retailer and manufacturer to capitalize on differences in consumers and competition. "The underlying motivation of micromarketing is simple: Give the consumers more of what they value highly and less of what they do not value."[54] Statistical methods and relational database programs give retailers the ability to identify underlying patterns and relationships in data. Efforts may include buying and merchandising for a specific store, salesperson support, promotions, and preferred customer programs.

Store-Specific Merchandise

Even if a retailer does not currently have a catalog or engage in direct mail promotions, it can benefit by applying the principles of database marketing. The information about sales trends in a database can be used by the buyer to determine what styles are hot and what customers want. The idea is to build customer relations and store traffic by carefully developing the buying and merchandising programs around the customers of the given store. By knowing the shopping habits and preferences of their customers, buyers can plan better for merchandise and service offerings. They will be able to segment their customers and make informed decisions about the introduction of new products or services. For example, in the greeting card industry retailers and vendors have worked together to share data on what specifically is selling in each store, productivity per square foot, profit per foot, and space sale per square foot. At Gibson Greetings, Inc., a team uses a demographic package to develop the proper product mix by title of greeting card, party goods, and gift wrap that matches a store's specific customer base. A retailer can scan the card pockets that need refilling and transmit the order electronically by telephone. The order is shipped the next morning, bringing what is selling right back into the store.[55]

Salesperson Support

One way micromarketing can be implemented is through salesperson support. A good example is Max Grassfield's men's clothing operation in Denver, Colorado. All the store's customers are in a database, and each is linked to a personal salesperson. A personalized mailing is created for each member of the sales staff: one for birthdays, one for those who haven't stopped in for a while, and one for wives, who do 50 percent of the shopping for men's clothes. For example, 3,115 notes were mailed to wives with a $20 gift certificate. Exactly 154 customers came in and spent an average of $392, more than $60,000 in additional business.[56]

Debit cards, smart cards, customer profiling systems, and loyalty programs used at the point-of-sale are helping sales associates to quickly recognize the characteristics of individual customers and build closer relationships with them.

Preferred Customer Programs

Earlier in the chapter we mentioned that the application form for a preferred customer or loyalty program, as it is often called, is a valuable source of information for building a database. The members of these programs are logical targets for micromarketing efforts.

Information from preferred customer programs can be used to anticipate the shopper's needs and wants. For instance, the customer can be reminded of family birthdays and can also receive assistance in buying based on the previous purchases the family member has made. The husband no longer has to say "My wife is about the same size as you" to a sales associate. Instead, the salesperson simply looks up the spouse's size and preferences in the computer. Not only does the wife get the right size, but the item is in a style consistent with her tastes. In another application, Saks sales associates can call customers with updates on new merchandise or make regular shipments of staple goods.[57] This not only encourages shopper loyalty but also increases the store's information about its best consumers. Initial studies indicate that members' spending may increase by 15 to 20 percent through such a program.[58]

In order to take full advantage of preferred customer incentives, retailers such as Bloomingdales, Saks Fifth Avenue, and Kroger are offering co-branded credit cards with VISA or MasterCard. Stores can keep a transaction history for each customer and get limited access to information on what the customers purchase from competitors when the credit card is used.[59]

Shopping malls are also becoming more involved in database marketing. This allows not only the large stores that have proprietary or co-branded credit cards to get information but the smaller, nonanchor stores as well. Softouch infoCenters has a program called "Mall Rewards!" for customers who frequently shop at the stores in a mall. The customers receive a card that gives them certain patronage benefits including a computerized interactive directory of goods and services, discounts, and announcements of special events. Stores benefit from increased customer loyalty and traffic.

Mall stores are also realizing the advantages of cross-selling opportunities through these programs. Consumers who purchase products at one store can be targeted for promotions by other stores in the mall that carry complementary products. University Town Center in San Diego created The Added Value Club to capitalize on database marketing efforts. Purchases by members are more than three times that of nonmembers. In order to further capitalize on this trend, a Web site has been created, called CyberShop (http://www.cybershop.com). Cyber savings and special store discounts and coupon programs are used to generate names for the database. The use of Cybershop requires customers to fill out extensive registrations and surveys that are shared with feature manufacturers. The database is used for direct promotions such as E-mail.[60]

L. L. BEAN—REVISITED: SEEKING INTERNATIONAL OPPORTUNITIES

In the early 1990s, L. L. Bean started to run into the same problems as many other retailers. The recession and increasing competition were shrinking its sales. L. L. Bean and competitors such as Lands' End, Patagonia, and Eddie Bauer were fighting for market shares. Sales between 1981 and 1988 grew at an average of nearly 20 percent. In 1989, this dropped to 3 percent and stagnated during the 1990s. Along with many other companies, L. L. Bean started to downsize. Within three years it laid off 200 employees and abandoned a project to build a new distribution center in Maine.[61] In an attempt to curb slow growth, the company started to concentrate more on its overseas markets.

L. L. Bean mails catalogs to 146 countries. Nearly 70 percent of its foreign sales are from Japan with another 20 percent from Canada and 6 percent from the United Kingdom.[62] Obviously the Japanese market is an important one for the company. The $14 billion Japanese mail-order business has been growing at about 12 percent per year. However, the newness of the mail-order industry in Japan has made entry difficult. Estimates are that Japanese mail-order sales will reach $50 billion by the end of the decade.[63]

L. L. Bean has also entered into high-tech marketing with Apple Computer, Redgate, and Electronic Data Systems. Apple computer has put L. L. Bean catalogs, among others, on compact disks for a test market. Digital files of images also have the potential to create an exciting multimedia catalog format.[64] CD ROM electronic catalogs from retailers like L. L. Bean can be available to computer users worldwide through America Online[65] and other computer networks.

1. What are the potential problems associated with L. L. Bean's strategy of using mail order as an entry into the world markets?
2. What are the advantages of using a CD ROM instead of a printed catalog?
3. How does being on the Internet broaden L. L. Bean's global strategy?

Summary

Advances in technology are rapidly changing the way retailers do business. Merchants have learned that the proper use of technology can improve efficiency in many areas. Consumers have greatly benefited from better customer service, increased customer convenience, improved employee service, reduced costs, and better selections.

Nowhere is change happening faster than in the arena we have called the virtual store. Retailers will find many opportunities in advertising and selling on the Internet's World Wide Web. As the information superhighway evolves, it will be open to new kinds of competitors and retail formats.

Electronic kiosks offer opportunities to better communicate with the customer and expand the retailer's offerings. Interactive TV will also bring new opportunities as well as new competitors. Virtual reality for research and actual shopping is another retailing frontier.

Many merchants are actively using customer databases to help understand consumer needs and buying habits. Information from database systems can be gathered through many internal and external sources. Point-of-sale systems and membership programs are popular. Customer quality can be measured through the RFM (recency, frequency, and monetary) value.

Of equal importance, should merchants decide to engage in some form of direct retailing, they will know who their current profitable customers are and be able to attract similar individuals when they decide to enlarge their customer base. Additionally, they will be in a position to know what merchandise to include in an offer to any given set of customers. Clearly, retail database marketing provides managers and associates with a valuable tool for improving consumer satisfaction.

Key terms and concepts

Affinity list, 590

Broker list, 590

Catalog selling, 595

Cyberspace retailing, 575

Database retailing, 588

Direct mail advertising, 594

Direct mail selling, 574

Direct response television, 580

Electronic kiosks, 584

Frequent purchase programs, 589

Getting "out of the box," 570

Hypertext links, 575

Information superhighway, 575

Interactive television, 580

Internet, 575

Liquid crystal display (LCD) shelf tags, 586

Merging, 591

Micromarketing, 599

Personalized shopper database (PSD), 587

Point-of-sale couponing, 586

Preferred customer programs, 589

Prospecting, 590

Purging, 592

QUESTIONS

1. What are the pressures on traditional in-store retailing?

2. How might a small retailer use infomercials to reach a new audience?

3. Are there any disadvantages of placing a manufacturer's kiosk in a retail store?

4. What is the importance of maintaining a customer database?

5. What are the ethical dimensions of maintaining a database on customers? Is the information too intrusive? Should retailers be allowed to maintain and sell information about their customers' purchase patterns?

6. How will the issues of privacy and security on the Internet be overcome?

7. How can the economically disadvantaged be brought into the information superhighway?

8. How might a retailer effectively use telemarketing and micromarketing? What are the advantages and disadvantages?

SITUATIONS

1. You are hired as the manager for an apparel store that has been in business for eighty-five years. The owners have run the store for three generations but have decided to retire and hire a professional manager (you). The store operates in nearly the same manner as it has since the beginning. A cash drawer and calculator are used to ring up purchases. The owners explain that they have survived for generations by offering the customer a personalized service that cannot be found anywhere else. They believe that updating the store would displace its ambience and make it less personalized. You realize that their customer base consists mostly of older people who have been shopping there for years and are very loyal. You would like to buy a computerized point-of-sale system and start building a personalized shopper database. Could you convince the owners of these changes? How?

CASES

CASE 15A
Kiosks Replace the Salesperson[66]

How many times have you walked into a store and been asked by a salesperson "Can I help you?" Your typical response is "No thanks, I'm just looking."

Technologies in the form of interactive multimedia kiosks are providing one solution to this dilemma. Customers shopping at authorized General Electric appliance dealerships are utilizing the kiosks to allow them to research products they are interested in and to obtain instant credit approval. Shoppers are able to view pictures and videos of GE appliances through the custom-designed touch screen. Full-scale kitchen mockups allow customers to "walk through" a kitchen stocked with GE appliances. They have the ability to change the colors of the kitchen cabinets and flooring to match what is in their own homes. They can also choose different colors for the appliances to find out what works best with their kitchens. Dimensions and features of each appliance can be printed out for the customer to take home.

The Minnesota Twins sell tickets to games at interactive kiosks located in supermarkets around the Minneapolis–St. Paul metro area. Information kiosks are also available through the Internet covering everything from college selection to software development.

Other examples are becoming more numerous. Sara Lee Intimates, which makes the Bali line of bras and underwear, has the Bali Solution Center to help women select the right size and type of intimate apparel. The system allows virtually real-time on-line access from a kiosk, providing Sara Lee with point-of-sale information such as what styles and colors customers requested and what on-line videos were accessed the most. And if the retail store does not have the right style in stock, the customer can order any of the products listed and have them shipped directly to their home.

1. *As a customer, when might you use a kiosk?*

2. *What type of customers do you think would be more likely to use a kiosk?*

3. *For what retailers would a kiosk be an effective retailing tool?*

CASE 15B
Door-to-Door Technology

Avon Products, Inc., is a company well positioned to be proactive in the expected increase in direct selling and home delivery systems. Through either home or office delivery the company already sells cosmetics, fragrances, gifts, and videos in 107 countries.

While Avon has had considerable success in developed markets (including the United States), where it most excels is in countries with a weak retail infrastructure. For example, in China, Avon Products expect to generate sales in excess of $500 million by the end of the century.

Technology is playing a major role in facilitating Avon's global expansion. For example, in the United States, where 750 million items are distributed per year, the filling of orders has been mechanized and automated through specialized picking technology. The company's computer system also calculates its complex commission and incentive formulas as it generates the representatives' product invoices.

Avon concentrates on building relationships with its representatives because they are the link to its customers—the final consumers who use most of its products (the representatives themselves are, of course, also users). To facilitate the actual "order taking" 15,000 representatives in the United States carry a handheld device known as POET (portable order-entry terminal). They input the orders directly into this system, which electronically sends them through to the shipping locations. The representatives will also soon be able to receive information through the terminal. For those without POET, orders are written on special forms that are later imaged into the system.

The development of a new electronic client-server program allows Avon to produce the world's largest circulation four-color marketing brochures. Countries participating in this graphics product setup include the United States, the United Kingdom, Germany, and Australia. By facilitating almost instant transfer of images, proof turnaround time has been reduced from two weeks to four minutes—a critical factor, because in the United States the company introduces a new promotional campaign every two weeks.

1. *Is technology a help or a problem in the global environment?*

2. *What role could cyberspace retailing have for Avon?*

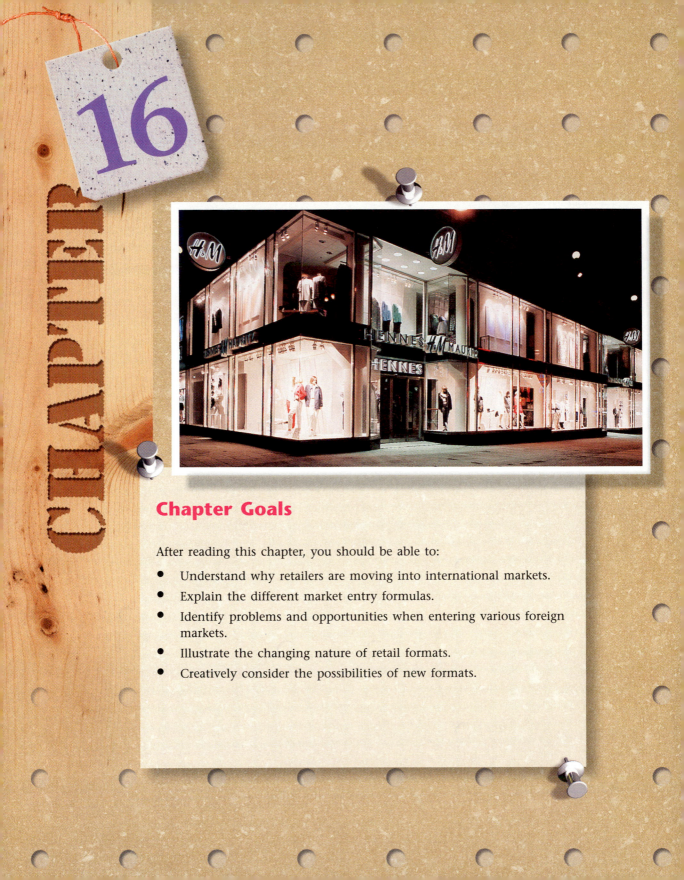

Chapter Goals

After reading this chapter, you should be able to:

- Understand why retailers are moving into international markets.
- Explain the different market entry formulas.
- Identify problems and opportunities when entering various foreign markets.
- Illustrate the changing nature of retail formats.
- Creatively consider the possibilities of new formats.

GLOBALIZATION AND CHANGING RETAIL FORMATS

HENNES & MAURITZ: THE "MTV" OF FASHION

Hennes & Mauritz (H&M) is a fashion-forward specialty store handling apparel, shoes, intimate wear, and cosmetics. It is known for offering color- and look-coordinated collections of good-quality merchandise at very reasonable prices, which is a relatively unusual occurrence for companies in this fashion-forward niche.

The strategy is to offer the latest fashion at the lowest price in the best locations. The company considers itself the "MTV" of the fashion world. In Sweden, its home country, the firm operates full-assortment stores under the name H&M Hennes & Mauritz. These stores average 15,000 square feet in size.

In addition, the company also operates a broad range of single-assortment stores in Sweden: Mauritz for men, Hennes for women, Impulse for teenagers, H&M Children's Wear for the younger set, and H&M Cosmetics.

The company began expanding internationally relatively early in its history. With 275 stores at the beginning of the decade, the firm had approximately 350

stores operating in eight different European countries five years later.[1] It was founded in Sweden in 1947 but made its first cross-border move into Norway in 1960. After Norway, the company entered Denmark, the United Kingdom, Switzerland, Germany, Holland, Belgium, and Austria. Sales exceed 8.5 billion Swedish krona ($1.2 billion), and net income is over 600 million krona. Plans call for sales in Germany to exceed those in Sweden well before the turn of the century. The retailer is one of Europe's most profitable companies.[2]

H&M has been opening about forty new stores each year outside of Sweden. The company reports that its profitability has been approximately the same in all countries in which it does business, primarily because two of the largest expense components (rent and salaries) tend to be relatively similar in all nine countries in which it operates. When H&M enters a new location, it pursues a market dominance strategy. For example, in Geneva, a typical market saturation situation, there are now six H&M stores in the city, with three of them near each other on the main shopping street.[3]

H&M also operates a discount format known as Galne Gunnar Stores, with nineteen facilities in Sweden only. These operations allow H&M to take advantage of opportunistic buys on overruns, canceled goods, end-of-season merchandise, and closeouts. In addition, in Sweden and Norway the company operates H&M Rowells, a mail-order firm that carries the H&M merchandise.

The company competes largely by being a very innovative merchant with both a keen interpretive eye for "new" fashions and considerable creativity in developing "new" and niche departments. Recent innovations include a "Mommy" department, which features fashion-forward, funky clothes for pregnant women, the look of which is so different that it seems inappropriate to refer to it as "maternity wear." A "Big Is Beautiful" department showcases fashion-forward merchandise for the large-sized female customer. A better-wear collection called BK brings a fashionable twist to career apparel.

H&M stores operate as a self-service concept, with the layout of the stores, groupings of collections, mix and match presentation of different items, and graphic messages constituting a "silent service" that informs and assists customers in making choices without having a salesperson present.

1. **How can a retailer be on the forefront of fashion when operating in nine different countries?**

INTRODUCTION

In Chapter 15 we introduced a graphic from the presentation entitled *Retail . . . Vision of The Future* where Tom Doddridge outlined his view of the changing retail industry. As we said, he argues that in order for retailers to obtain and retain a competitive advantage, they must embrace change. See Figure 16.1.

We begin this chapter with a discussion of why retailers are moving into international markets. We will then look at how U.S. investments in foreign retailing operations exceed $10 billion and are increasing rapidly. Retailer expenditures exceeded $5 billion on new stores in foreign countries in 1995 and 1996.[4] Choices range from exportation of new or existing retail concepts, purchase of existing retail companies, joint ventures, and franchising to licensing agreements. We also examine the nature of the market in selected countries. The trend toward globalization has a direct impact on how retail-

FIGURE 16.1

The changing retail industry: Embracing change = competitive advantage.

ers are structured and will play a major role in the changes ahead. The chapter next explores changing and new retail formats.

Why Globalization?

The United States retail market is one of the most competitive in the world. Competition is tough, and the only way to obtain growth is to take market share from others. There are 32 million stores worldwide.[5] None of them are going to be anxious to give up sales to anyone.

The greatest opportunity for retail growth will come from outside the United States in countries that have greater population and/or income growth rates. Some of the most successful retailers in the United States are "banging their head against the wall of expansion" at home, including Gap, Office Depot, Staples, Home Depot, Wal-Mart, and Toys 'R' Us. To maintain a growth rate, investors feel they have no choice but to expand.[6]

It is not new for retailers to look outside their home country. Woolworth opened its first store outside the United States in Liverpool, England, in 1909. C&A, a Dutch clothing store chain, entered England in 1911 and Germany in the 1920s.[7] As shown in Box 16.1 not all efforts have been successful by any means.

BOX

16.1 RETAILER'S INTERNATIONAL EXPANSION CAN CRASH

Foreign retailing can be a mystery: for example, both J. C. Penney and Sears, Roebuck in the '70s and '80s lost considerable amounts of money—J. C. Penney in Italy and Sears in Belgium."[8] Penney opened apparel and home furnishings stores but was unaware that Italian law restricted new retail space in order to protect existing small shops. Sears had bought a medium-range department store chain in Belgium. Noticing how inefficiently the workforce was being used, Sears thought it could become profitable by reducing personnel costs. But it couldn't do anything about it because of restrictive Belgian law.

In another example, U.S. retailers have underestimated the impact of rules and regulations in Canada. George J. Kosich, CEO and president of Hudson's Bay Company, says, "The cost of doing business is 30 percent higher and in terms of taxes, it's 300 percent higher. And, because we are a highly taxed country, discretionary income is less than the U.S. Woolco sold out to Wal-Mart after losing market share to Canadian-owned Zellers, Russell Athletic has closed its stores, Eagle Hardware left, Petstuff has gone back to the U.S., and Safeway has restricted its expansion plans."[9]

Toys 'R' Us has a well-deserved reputation as one of the most successful global retailers. Yet it is often forgotten that the company had troubled times initially. Following its move into Europe in 1984, profitability suffered considerably. It took a long time for the company to recover.[10]

6543217

Retailers are expanding internationally to take advantage of volume discounts from manufacturers, logistics efficiencies, faster turnover, and lower corporate overhead. IKEA of Sweden targets price-conscious consumers who are willing to take home and assemble stylish contemporary furniture to save money and who enjoy the creative involvement. IKEA has expanded throughout Europe and North America with catalog and store operations.

16.2 RETAILING: THE GLOBAL MANDATE[11]

Larry R. Katzen says, "I asked my audiences the question, 'What are you thinking about?' Many U.S. retailers articulated self-imposed barriers. Here are a few that I heard frequently:"

- **"It didn't work in the past."** Pointing to past failures—of J. C. Penney in Europe or Sears in South America—retailers fear to tread outside home territory.

- **"It's too complex."** Political, economic, and cultural differences—as well as the different business practices and the challenges of travel—appear to reinforce the appeal of simple and manageable operations on home turf.

- **"There's still untapped market potential here."** This appears in the annual reports of companies like The Limited. The argument goes, "Why squander precious financial and human resources elsewhere?"

- **"It will dilute our management focus."** American business schools have taught well the risks of distracting management.

- **"Real estate is too expensive."** This is also heard as "It's too expensive" or "It doesn't fit our economic model."

6543217

Growing countries assure retailers of greater markets to serve in the future. Nearly all national markets are less competitive than in the United States, and foreign retailers are generally less efficient. Less competition usually means higher margins, which can lead to higher profits. Despite the opportunities, Larry R. Katzen, who is the managing partner of the Arthur Andersen & Co. World Wide Industry Practice, believes that the imperative to "go global" is more talk than action for many retailers. See Box 16.2.

THE ROAD TO SUCCESS

Among the factors that are important in achieving success in international expansion are timing, understanding the environment, paying attention to core competencies, and balancing standardization and local market differentiation.

Timing

Timing is often a critical element in international expansion. A retailer does not always have to be the first in a new market, but there is often a narrow window when there is a well-defined opportunity. Failure to take advantage of the window can lead to other retailers staking out a dominant position in the market. At the same time entering too early may mean a market is not developed enough to support the format.

Understanding the Environment

The lack of success of many retailers is often tied to failure to fully understand the environment in which they will be operating. There are some retail formats that clearly work in different consumer and business environments. They have a universal appeal that can shape consumer behavior and even create demand. Toys 'R' Us and The Body Shop are examples of companies that have been very successful in exporting their formats, with comparatively little change, to overseas markets.

Core Competencies

International retailers must build on their core competencies. There must be clear advantages that will be difficult for local competitors to replicate. Retailers who establish themselves as low-cost providers must drive inefficiencies out of the business and pass savings on to customers. Category dominant retailers like Staples or OfficeMax have to build on volume purchasing, work with suppliers to keep costs down, and offer customers broad selections at the best prices.

Balancing Standardization and Differentiation

Retailers who have expanded internationally have learned to take advantage of **economies of scale,** from purchasing to customer delivery. For example, McDonald's achieves cost advantages by investing heavily in training franchisees to use standardized production processes and operating procedures, providing consistency and a high degree of efficiency.

However, there exists a balance between taking advantage of common factors and keeping in touch with the local culture. There has been a great deal of debate on the degree to which marketing can be standardized across countries. Standardization reduces costs and creates superior performance, yet complete standardization ignores the customers and the fact that marketing efforts often must be differentiated to suit the local area. A balance must maximize the advantages of operating between countries while allowing for flexibility to meet customer differences.

Toys 'R' Us has been successful in achieving this balance. Its basic premise is that toys are universally loved. Enjoyment of Barney, Legos, Power Rangers, or Barbie does not depend on nationality. Adaptations are still necessary to satisfy local consumer tastes. At the same time, efficient warehousing, distribution, and careful buying allow Toys 'R' Us to be a low-cost provider.

Another firm that has been successful in achieving a balance between cost reduction by standardization and adapting to local conditions is The Body Shop. It uses the same format, facade, and logo at its units worldwide. The company manages operations locally with franchisees always selected from the host country. The Body Shop also makes modifications in its merchandise mix to meet differing local skin and hair types and local fragrance preferences.

THE INTERNATIONAL RETAILERS

Until the early 1980s, the retail industry worldwide was generally a localized business. Products, services, and methods of operation reflected the wide diversity of consumer demands and business environments.

Since the mid-1980s there has been much more **internationalization.** In fact, in some retail sectors globalization is the dominant force for change. Retailers moving into new countries may face new ethical dilemmas. See Box 16.3. This section examines retailers in various regions of the world.

BOX 16.3 AN ETHICAL DILEMMA: GLOBAL SOCIAL ISSUES

Milton Friedman's statement that the only social responsibility of business is to make a profit is one dimension of the debate on ethical and social responsibility. Others argue that behaving ethically is good business sense because customers respect such firms and reward them with their patronage.

David Swindley,[12] a professor at Manchester Polytechnic in England, argues that retailers need to define their ethical and social obligations at local, national, and international levels. He proposes areas where retailers could make a difference.

The starvation, deprivation, and poverty experienced by 1 billion people are a pressing global issue. One cause is exploitation and cultivation of land used to grow tea, coffee, tobacco, and bananas, and to harvest timber. Land used for cash export crops is not available to feed the native population, nor is the income sufficient for the labor force to exist above the subsistence level.

Swindley also notes that the British government has not implemented a European Economic Community directive that would limit pesticide applications to food crops and pesticides in water. Food retailers and customers have been blamed for insisting on blemish-free produce. They have been slow to accept biodegradable products including toilet cleaners, washing products, and detergents.

In the 1970s it was discovered that chlorofluorocarbons (CFCs) released into the atmosphere may be a threat to the ozone layer, leading to increased solar radiation with a possible link to skin cancer, plant and animal mutations, and global warming. It has been suggested that retailers could have been influential in reducing such releases if they had informed vendors that they would refuse to stock products containing CFCs.

Questions
Do you see these global concerns as ethical issues facing retailers? Are there other such issues? What actions are available to retailers if they want to be proactive in dealing with global social concerns?

6543217

European Retailers

European retailers were the first to make major moves internationally. They started by expanding beyond the saturated northern European markets and today are looking for growth opportunities in Spain and Italy. For example, since Spain's entry into the European Community in 1986, retail operations in the major cities have become dominated by the French hypermarket groups like Carrefour/Euromarche. Foreign retailers such as GIB (Belgium) and Bauhaus (Germany) have also moved aggressively into the area. Simplification of store development and licensing procedures has been an important factor in Italy, where French hypermarket groups are also moving quickly.

European retailers who did not have unique formats decided to acquire existing chains. British merchants have been reluctant in the past to move into Continental Europe, and thus looked to the United States instead. A change in attitudes is seen in Kingfisher's acquisition of Darty, France's number one consumer electronics retailer, and Tesco's acquisition of Catteau, a leading regional grocer with stores in northern France.

Some of Europe's specialty retailers are taking their formats into other countries. Benetton of Italy and Hennes & Mauritz of Sweden are examples. In the food business, Tengelmann (Germany), Ahold (the Netherlands), and Delhaize Le Lion (Belgium) derive more than 50 percent of their total sales from businesses they have bought in the United States.

Other examples of international expansion by Europeans include Carrefour (France) and Metro (Germany/Switzerland) in Taiwan. In the Czech Republic, grocery retailers Ahold, from the Netherlands, and Tengelmann, from Germany, have established a significant presence. Also, Benetton has opened stores in China as has Cartier, the luxury jeweler and watchmaker.

Japanese Retailers

Japanese-based retailers have moved into Singapore, Hong Kong, and China, as well as into other Asian countries. Japanese retailers have acquired a number of U.S. stores instead of exporting their own formats. Jusco's owns Talbots, Isetan's invested in Barney's New York department stores, and Ito Yokado's acquired the Southland Corporation and the 7-Eleven Stores. The Japanese have also acquired European retailers. For example, the Aeon Group purchased a 15 percent stake in Laura Ashley.

The Japanese have kept their eye on opportunities in China. Yaohan International opened the first Japanese-owned department store in Shenzen, and then followed with stores in Beijing and Shanghai. Japan's Ayomama, a discount clothing retailer, has announced plans to open stores in both Shenzen and Shanghai.

North American Retailers

Until recently, the international activities of U.S. retailers were largely confined to Mexico and Canada. Remember the exit of J. C. Penney and Sears from Europe? Today J. C. Penney and Dillard Department Stores have developed a presence in Mexico as have Wal-Mart and Price Club. Wal-Mart is also established in Canada. With some success, U.S. retailers are seeking new opportunities in the apparel business. Gap has made a successful entry into the United Kingdom, France, and Germany. Woolworth's Foot Locker is an important player in Europe.

The U.S. warehouse club operator Costco has moved into the United Kingdom, bringing a completely different format to the country with its emphasis on value pricing, self-service, and bulk buying. Kmart's purchase of the Maj department stores in the Czech and Slovak republics reflects a strategy of establishing a major presence in Eastern Europe, where there may be significant economic growth.

MARKET ENTRY FORMULAS

For the remainder of the 1990s and beyond, many more retailers will expand their operations to become global players. In doing so, they will have to determine the most appropriate "entry formula." This will require an evaluation of a number of factors:

- Cost versus control
- Desired rate of market penetration
- Legal barriers
- Market knowledge required
- Availability of good locations
- Uniqueness of the format
- Financial strength of the firm
- Recognition of store name and brands
- Performance objectives

For example, the formula for market entry will have to balance the trade-off between cost of entry and amount of control, while taking each of the other factors into account as well. The various options are summarized in Box 16.4 and discussed here.

The developers of the Mall of America implemented the concept of retailing as theater by combining an actual entertainment experience with store, cart, and kiosk retailing. The 4.2-million-square-foot mall features Camp Snoopy as an amusement center attraction. Dozens of eating places, arcades, movie theaters, and interactive retailers help draw customers to the mall and keep them there.

BOX

16.4 DEFINING FORMULAS FOR ENTRY INTO FOREIGN MARKETS

Going it alone: Maximum control but the greatest cost. The company introduces its format into new markets. This is called "organic growth."

Acquisition: Lower risk but at a high cost. The company benefits from success of the existing format.

Joint ventures: Partners share risks, but the firms lose some control.

Franchising: Small capital investment. Others operate the store in a defined market area.

Concessions: Low risk and low cost. But there is some loss of control from leasing a space within a larger store.

Licensing: Smallest capital investment with the least amount of control.

6543217

Going It Alone

Going at it alone, called "**organic growth,**" provides maximum control in the targeted country. This can be an attractive alternative if the retailer has a distinct format and the culture, legislative climate, and business environment are favorable. The retailer is able to control management selection, merchandising, advertising, promotion, and store design. Organic growth requires substantial investment in capital and time, as well as an understanding of the market.

Acquisitions

Acquisition or a merger may be the way to gain desirable retail sites, acquire access to market knowledge, and obtain buying expertise and new sources of supply. Acquisition is a viable alternative when the retailer's concept is not sufficiently different from that of local competitors to achieve success, but the country offers an open business and legal environment.

Joint Ventures

Joint ventures are an expansion option when a country has a restrictive business environment. If barriers to entry are high, a joint venture allows a retailer to achieve market knowledge and expertise through partnership with a local operator. The barrier in some countries is the requirement that the majority of ownership be by citizens.

As an example, Sears PLC in the United Kingdom (no relation to the U.S. based Sears) and Groupe Andre in France created a 50-50 joint venture. The Sears Andre Retail Group (SARG) operates almost 500 shops. In this case, both companies were already active outside their own national markets but formed an alliance to continue international expansion.

Franchising

A franchisee can own and operate a store using the franchisor's brand name and benefiting from its operational structure and buying expertise. **Franchising** allows a local entrepreneur to start with a proven format.

The benefit for the franchisor is that the investment risk is carried by the franchisee. Franchisors are able to increase their penetration of new markets with relatively low capital investment. McDonald's is one of the most well-known global businesses. Almost 70 percent of McDonald's locations are owned by franchisees.

Concessions

Concessions are a low-risk and low-cost form of entry that usually involves leasing a space within a store. It provides an opportunity to move into a country such as Japan, where entry is restricted. American fashion manufacturers and designers operate concessions in a number of Japanese department stores. In Russia, where market entry is extremely risky, concessions are a viable option. Karstadt, Germany's largest department store chain, has a concession in the GUM, Mowcow's largest department store. Karstadt trains the staff and advises on merchandise selection, while the Russians order and sell the goods.

Licensing

Licensing requires the smallest capital investment but provides the lowest level of control. In a licensing agreement a company typically gets access to the store name, products, or operating methods for royalty payments. L. L. Bean licenses its name to The Seiyu Ltd., one of Japan's general merchandisers, to take advantage of the expanding demand for outdoor products, particularly apparel.

INTERNATIONAL MARKET OPPORTUNITIES

Regardless of the entry formula, moving into specific markets can be very complex. In this section we examine the characteristics of countries where opportunities might exist.

In developed markets, the first group we will discuss, consumers will be more demanding and expect a higher level of service, convenience, and value. The second group of countries are characterized largely by the entry barriers their governments have erected. The third group will offer opportunities, but

The Level of Economic Development, the Political/Economic Investment Risk, the Extent of Government Regulation, and the Size and Growth of Population Help Categorize the Markets Represented by Different Countries

Highly Developed Markets	Difficult Entry Markets	Markets with Economic Volatility	High-Risk Markets
United States	Japan	Turkey	Brazil
Canada	Republic of Korea	Mexico	Russia
United Kingdom	Italy	Argentina	China
France			India
Germany			
Spain			

may have political and economic volatility as they adjust to rapid economic growth. The final group will present retailers with great potential but high risks. See Table 16.1. Retailers will have to consider the competition, the economy, and the political and investment risks associated with a given market.

The Highly Developed Markets

In the highly developed retail markets competition will be fierce. The United States, Canada, the United Kingdom, France, Germany, and Spain will not be very attractive targets for expansion for most retailers. Major chains already control key segments in the market. Foreign retailers will not find it easy to face Wal-Mart in the United States, Sainsbury in the United Kingdom, Carrefour in France, or Karstadt in Germany.

United States. Consumers are financially pressured because of increased taxes, health care costs, low savings rates, and high credit card debt. There will be some opportunities for niche specialty concepts, for lifestyle-oriented formats, and in the area of new electronic/home shopping technology.

Canada. Canada probably faces significant political instability, as the 1995 secession election in Quebec demonstrated. Canadian consumers are also suffering from an unfavorable exchange rate that makes imported goods very expensive. In addition, taxes are very high. The market has intense price competition, which is likely to continue as U.S. retailers such as Wal-Mart expand.

United Kingdom. Department stores in the United Kingdom have enjoyed comparatively little competition and large gross margins. They are now being challenged by new formats including warehouse clubs, discounters, and outlet malls.[13] The United Kingdom is an attractive entry point for companies seeking to move into Western Europe. Retailers considering the U.K. markets are using joint ventures or acquisitions to get around existing competition and entry barriers.

Germany. Rapid retail development in the former East Germany is creating opportunities for new specialty formats as incomes rise. Examples are the activities of the Swiss-German Metro group and the German subsidiary of the Swedish retail clothing group H&M.[14] Joint ventures with German firms make entry less difficult in the highly regulated environment. Local authorities can keep new stores out if they believe existing ones will suffer. Additional regulations limit store hours and Sunday opening. Retailers can hold a sale only twice a year and are not allowed to discount food items.[15]

France. Retailing in France is generally concentrated in the hands of a few firms. Price competition is intense. The French consumer likes high-quality apparel and food, which means that companies like Gap have further opportunities to carve out a niche.

Spain. Spain has benefited from a growing economy and consumption-oriented consumers. Membership in the European Community has expanded trade and manufacturing. In Spain, entry by numerous European retailers means that the level of concentration in food and hard goods will approach that of the United States, thus limiting opportunities.

Difficult Entry Markets

In Japan, the Republic of Korea, and Italy, retail opportunities will come slowly because of governmental interference, strong cultural values, and the structure of the economy. Still, some significant possibilities will exist in these markets for those companies that can successively navigate through this complex environment.

Italy. Barriers to development exist in Italy. Legal constraints are slowly easing in this country of "1 million shops." The government recognizes that more efficiency in the retail sector will enable productivity gains across the economy, from the more economically prosperous north to the poorer south. Joint ventures are a means of circumventing strict regulations.

Republic of Korea. Foreign firms have been allowed to own real estate in the Republic of Korea since 1993. Restraints on the retail sector will be lifted after the year 2000, allowing foreign firms to operate freely. Many local retailers have already imported foreign formats into their market. With a growing population and increased disposable income, consumption will create opportunities.

Japan. The market in Japan will become increasingly consumer-driven as economic growth slows and the number of senior citizens increases. Barriers to new retail development will ease slowly because of political pressure. As a result of efforts by Toys 'R' Us, the Large Retail Store Law, which limited store size, was relaxed in 1991. The multilayered distribution system is breaking down as consumers seek lower prices, which in turn encourages the development of discount formats. Joint ventures and franchising will remain the primary methods of entry for foreigners because of ownership restrictions and the inherent complexity of the economy. Typical is the fact that local merchants can legally demand concessions when new stores enter their market. Stores must close for twenty-four holidays a year, and regulations govern the importing of goods.[16] Opportunities will exist in specialty stores, limited-line discount stores, and category dominant retailing. Electronic shopping and catalog merchandising will be increasingly attractive to the Japanese consumer.

Markets with Economic Volatility

Mexico, Turkey, and Argentina are attractive to foreign firms even though they have volatile economies. Prospects for long-term economic expansion will result in opportunities for sales and market share growth if a company can weather storms like the 1995 crash in the value of the Mexican peso.

Turkey. Turkey has well-educated consumers who are very Western in outlook. The increasing, affluent population has a strong work ethic. The retail structure is highly fragmented, with "mom and pop" stores within a block or two in every neighborhood. The country does not have the distribution and communication infrastructure to support large retail formats. As the infrastructure develops, there will be opportunities for department stores, supermarkets, and some specialty formats. During the next two decades discount stores and category dominant retailers will find opportunities in the major cities of Ankara, Istanbul, and Adana.

Mexico. Mexico has relaxed foreign ownership laws, franchising restrictions, and import duties, which for non-North American products, such as goods from China, can be as high as 1,000 percent. Economic growth will attract new competitors that are willing to take a long-term view. As import duties are lowered, global sourcing can occur. Economic growth and a growing middle class will create opportunities, particularly for department stores, supermarkets, discount formats, and category dominant retailers.

Argentina. As economic reforms take hold, Argentina's economy is becoming more stable. It has a larger middle class than other Latin American countries; 97 percent of the households have television sets, 3 million with cable. The retailing industry is fragmented, and small "mom and pop" stores dominate the market. Opportunities for supermarkets, department stores, and some specialty offerings will exist as the economy continues to mature.

High-Risk Markets

Improvements in infrastructure and an easing of government regulations and entry barriers will enhance the attractiveness of high-risk markets in Brazil, Russia, China, and India over the next two decades. Still, significant political and economic risks will continue.

Brazil. Changes have made the country more open to foreign retailers. Many important restrictions have been eliminated including quotas on nearly 2,000 goods. Brazil has the sixth largest population in the world with 200 million people, including 80 million urban adults. It has one of the youngest populations, with 33 percent under fourteen years of age. Limiting opportunity for some types of retailers is the fact that the top 10 percent of the population controls 50 percent of the income and 20 percent of the people live in abject poverty. Also, a high rate of inflation, intricate tax structure, and import tariffs exist.

Retailing is concentrated in the cities of Sao Paulo and Rio de Janeiro, where over 70 percent of the merchants operate. Consumers are very value-conscious, and with universal access to media and extensive advertising, shoppers have a huge appetite for American products. In the cities, a rapid decline in disposable income is creating price-conscious but still relatively sophisticated consumers. Supermarkets, discount stores, and specialty retailers have been successful. The unknown management variable is Brazil's unstable political situation.

When retailers move across national boundaries, fundamental decisions about the degree to which the concept will be standardized or customized must be made. McDonald's maintains the basic concept of value pricing and fast service in a convenient and clean environment. It customizes foods to match the market customs and habits: McLobster in Maine, McRib in Texas, Bolshoi Mac in Moscow. This is the newest of three stores in Moscow.

Russia. The breakup of the former Soviet Union left Russia's economy and retailing industry in turmoil. Consumers shop daily because they have limited incomes. With insufficient refrigeration space at home, they also have to buy fresh meat and produce daily. Existing stores are badly located. They are in disrepair and supported by a primitive infrastructure. Wholesale and distribution systems suffer from inefficiency and are plagued by vandalism and theft.

McDonald's successful entry into Russia was made possible only because it developed sources of supply and its own distribution system within the country. Many Russian women make exceptional incomes selling Mary Kay Cosmetics. The direct retailing approach may be a possibility for other merchants to get around some of the infrastructure limitations. In the long term there is a potentially tremendous market for goods and services if the free market reforms are allowed to work so that incomes rise.

Market entry is very difficult. Foreigners can own stores in Russia, but joint ventures must receive authorization from the Ministry of Finance.

China.   China has a population of more than 1.2 billion. There are some 300 million urban adults in ninety-five cities, four times more than in Brazil or Russia. Chinese children spend $5.7 billion a year on themselves, almost as much as U.S. children. "The prospect that such a huge segment of the world's consumers is still more than a decade short of its peak spending years is enough to make any retailer reach for an Atlas. This is why Wal-Mart and Carrefour are willing to build huge buildings and wait for their customers' income to grow."[17] See Box 16.5.

Reforms have improved the distribution system. Multiple channels now exist, and less than one-half of all retail sales take place through state-owned outlets. However, obstacles are still significant; the economic and political situation remains unstable. The infrastructure, including energy sources and distribution, is underdeveloped. The same is true for the legal and business environment. The government bureaucracy is very challenging. It does not value retailing as highly as construction or industrial ventures deemed necessary for the country's development needs, so it has been reluctant to grant approvals

BOX 16.5   WAL-MART GOES TO HONG KONG, LOOKS AT CHINA[18]

Retailers in the northeastern United States have tried to keep Wal-Mart out of their towns. In contrast, Hong Kong retailers haven't paid much attention to the fact that Wal-Mart is opening Value Clubs that resemble small Sam's Clubs. They don't seem to see a retail/wholesale cash-and-carry membership warehouse operation as a sales threat. Hong Kong shoppers are very price-sensitive. However, the difficulty of carrying purchases home makes them value convenience as much as lower prices.

As the world's largest retailer, Wal-Mart has tremendous financial resources that it can bring to the marketplace. Hong Kong retailers might have a reason for concern. Wal-Mart is committed to being the low-price leader and will continue this strategy as it serves the price-sensitive Hong Kong consumer. The company has been able to implement changes in its marketing mix that please customers, while keeping costs of operation very low.

The key to understanding Wal-Mart's long-range interest in Hong Kong may lie just across the border in China, where the household income has been growing 8.5 percent annually for the last ten years.

Wal-Mart has an Asian partner, a subsidiary of C. P. Pokphand, which has extensive experience with joint ventures and a track record of doing business in China. Wal-Mart will learn about satisfying Chinese consumers with its Value Clubs in Hong Kong.

6543217

for retail activities and has limited the scope of foreign involvement.[19] Merchants need strong local business partners to share risks and help deal with the system if they are to take advantage of long-term prospects in China.

India.   With a population of 850 million, India is the second largest consumer market in the world. In the next twenty years the number of people will reach 1.1 billion. Although the absolute size of the population is staggering, many live in abject poverty. There are some 200 million consumers that can be defined as "middle class."

Retailing is dominated by family-owned shops and open-air booths serving local neighborhoods. Each specializes in selling a single product category such as textiles, household items, shoes, or spices. More than half of expenditures are for food, beverages, and tobacco.

A poor infrastructure, regulated prices, and labor laws that are unfriendly to business will challenge retailers. Also tariffs are high and imports are restricted, which makes sourcing goods worldwide very difficult. Even so, India's potential is the reason many international firms have entered the market. Franchised retailers such as Benetton are bringing ready-to-wear clothing to markets that are used to made-to-order garments. A survey found that thirty-seven of the top sixty-two brands in India are foreign-owned. If the economy continues to improve, the best way for global companies to enter the market is to target the premium segments.[20]

CHANGING RETAIL FORMATS

The globalization of retailing will accelerate changes in store formats as merchants focus on the local target markets. Many existing formats will evolve in terms of merchandise mix, size, location strategy, and channels of distribution. Changes in consumer needs and tastes, as well as new market entrants, will make possible the success of formats yet to be developed. Let's examine some changes that will likely occur over the balance of this decade and into the twenty-first century.

Traditional Department Stores

Although it will undergo major changes, the traditional department store will continue to be a viable format. Elderly consumers appreciate the convenience of shopping for multiple products in a single store, and many have sufficient discretionary income to afford the higher quality merchandise department stores offer.

Those stores that survive will become a "destination" for customers in a wider trading area. Restaurants, groceries, and prepared foods will become a

It truly is a global village! A Spanish named restaurant (The Crazy Chicken), located in Japan, featuring spices from India (curry), in California style. Whatever the format, retailers will likely find adaptation across national boundaries somewhat easier as consumers are exposed to global concepts and brands. Global mass media ranging from CNN to MTV has accelerated the blurring of cultural differences.

more important part of the department store format, as they already are in European countries and Japan.

Some retailers may decide to function primarily as landlords. Manufacturers will design and operate their own stores within the department store buildings. The definition of *store* will expand to be more than simply a building where products can be found. Retailers are developing new channels of distribution through electronic home shopping networks and catalogs. Some department stores may actually become merchandise depots. Customers who purchase products offered by retailers through interactive TV or on the Internet may come to these depots to pick up their merchandise.

Food and General Merchandise

Combination food and general merchandise retail formats will become more prevalent throughout the world. European hypermarkets and supercenters will be battling U.S. firms for this business.

The supermarket will continue to be a viable format. It will compete with food and general merchandise superstores, with an emphasis on service. In developing countries, supermarkets will be a key format in meeting consumer needs for convenience and basic goods. Expansion of membership warehouse stores, however, may be limited because of their large size requirements.

Convenience Stores

The consumer's need for convenience and a scarcity of time mean that convenience stores should be well positioned to be a winning global format. Some will continue to focus on food, expanding their product offerings to better meet the requirements of time-pressured shoppers. Time-starved two-career households will appear throughout the world as more and more women join the workforce.

Other "convenience" stores will break down traditional merchandise classifications. For example, office building "newsstands" will sell basic grocery products, health and beauty aids, and basic clothing to meet the needs of office workers. Service retailers such as drycleaners, barber shops, and health clubs will extend their presence in office buildings and apartment complexes.

Discount Stores

Europe and the rest of the world are discovering discounters. In all developed markets, there is consumer pressure for more variety, quality, service, and value. These pressures will spread into less developed countries.

With retail formats so easily replicated, entrepreneurs in other countries will import the discount store concept. Adapting customer service, merchandise layout, and display for local tastes is less critical because the basic premise is simply price.[21]

In developing countries, there is a real need for the basic necessities. Because of regulatory constraints, the scarcity of land, and the lack of mobility of the population, discount stores will be smaller in size, offering limited lines of merchandise. Product categories are likely to include health and beauty aids, housewares, home appliances, bedding and bath products, and "basic" or "commodity" clothing.

Category Dominant Stores

Category dominant retailers like IKEA, Foot Locker, Toys 'R' Us, BabySuperstores, and Home Depot will march around the globe. Consumers are attracted by the depth and breadth of their merchandise selection and "value" pricing. Because retailing is so competitive, probably only a handful of stores in each merchandise category will survive in each market. See Box 16.6.

High-End Luxury Retailers

High-end retailers such as Tiffany, Cartier, Gucci, Chanel Hermes, and Burberry were among the first to begin implementing a global strategy.[22] This will remain a viable retail format.

As developing nations mature and trade barriers fall, these retailers will be able to open stores in new markets and increase their presence in existing ones. Reaching their target customers will be made easier by the fact that in most areas the highest income consumers tend to be clustered in easily identifiable locales, and they travel extensively.

Also, retailers of luxury goods can build on the global recognition of store name, brands, and products. They will not have to contend with the same margin pressures that affect other full-price retailers.

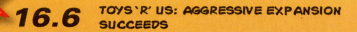

BOX

16.6 TOYS 'R' US: AGGRESSIVE EXPANSION SUCCEEDS

Toys 'R' Us is expanding aggressively into markets, becoming the dominant global toy retailer. By the early 1990s, the company had more than 700 stores located in the United States, Canada, the United Kingdom, and other countries, including Japan, Hong Kong, Malaysia, Singapore, and Taiwan. Sales were over $7 billion. By the end of the 1990s approximately 20 percent of its sales will come from international operations.

Toys 'R' Us achieves a high level of standardization in operations; at the same time it has local partners to help develop its own support structure in each different market.

The company takes advantage of its global buying power while also seeking out local vendors to create multinational products that meet local customer needs and regulatory standards.

Toys 'R' Us has had to downsize its store layout from an average-sized operation in the United States of 40,000 square feet to 13,000 square feet in Europe and Japan. It has also adapted to labor and trading laws. For example, in some European countries stores are not allowed to open on Sundays and have to close early Saturday evening.

6543217

Specialty Niche Retailers

The Body Shop, Gap, Virgin, Disney Stores, and Benetton are prime examples of specialty niche retailers that are taking a global approach to building their businesses. Their concepts will succeed by targeting specific demographic groups. For example, consumers over the age of sixty-five will be vastly greater in number by the year 2010. Store opportunities will exist to cater to their specific needs. Consider a "Grandparents store" where items can be sent directly to grandchildren who live not just in a different state but in a different country.

Consumer segments sharing similar lifestyles create opportunities for specialty niche concepts such as health and fitness. This is where some of today's specialty catalogers may excel in creating their own stores for the hobbyist.

Manufacturer-Owned Stores

Manufacturers of American brands often have worldwide recognition. Mass communication vehicles such as MTV and CNN give manufacturer-owned stores an advantage. As we suggested in Chapter 6, manufacturers are opening their own stores to regain power lost to global retailing giants. An example is Nike, which is opening stores in selected urban areas. Manufacturers may also be designing and operating their own stores within larger department stores.

NEW CUSTOMIZED FORMATS

We have suggested some of the changes in retail formats that will likely occur as we move into the twenty-first century. The overriding change that will dominate new formats will be specialization and customization to meet special market needs. You know a lot about retailing now. Expand your thinking, and envision what new retail formats might look like.

Customized Stores

Stores will have products tailored to individual tastes and levels of buying power. There will be age-specific stores to meet consumer needs and those that reflect specific cultures and lifestyles.

Efforts will continue to bring products closer to the actual consumers, and retailers will seek formats that allow them to develop closer relationships with customers. Instead of traditional merchandise classification, the emphasis will be on products that appeal to the same target customer group. More "point of view" stores will emerge, targeting consumers who share an interest in specific social issues. Stores with ecological themes are just the beginning.

Portable Stores

Truck and van **portable stores** will increase to meet the needs of the growing number of home office workers, as well as elderly consumers with reduced mobility. And, of course, there will be stores based on specific themes that are made possible through the use of virtual reality technology.

Customer-Made Stores

Other new formats will include stores where the customer makes everything. There will be no actual products, just the necessary technology and components. How about the "Just Do It—Woodworking Store." Grandma and Grandpa go there to make the grandbaby's crib. The merchant has equipment, plans, and materials for whatever you want to build. If you don't know how, lessons are also available. Some companies will engage in on-site production for you. IBM planned to team up with Blockbuster Entertainment Corporation to develop a system that allows customers to choose music and make compact disks on the spot. The alliance failed, but the concept is still viable. In-store kiosks would enable customers to select specific music and have it manufactured on a compact disk while they wait.

Merchandise Depots

We mentioned earlier the probability of **merchandise depots** for database retailers and the virtual store. Customers will be able to pick up products purchased from home via computer, interactive TV, mail, or telephone. Instead of just ordering a compact disk from EntertainmentMCI via 1-800-MUSIC NOW, you would call and tell them the artists and songs you wanted so that they could produce a custom CD that would be available for pickup at a merchandise depot with drive-through facilities.

Interactive Kiosk "Shopping Arcades"

There may also be "shopping arcades" where the interactive kiosks discussed in Chapter 15 are lined up. Shoppers will be able to view products, receive information, and make purchases. Merchandise will be picked up at a special "loading dock" or delivered to the home.

The Retail Theater

Many new formats will provide integration of information, entertainment, and retailing. As shopping and entertainment merge, we have what is in essence a **retail theater.** See Figure 16.2.

Merchandise displays will become "retail attractions" using multimedia to create excitement. Actual entertainment experiences will be added to the shopping experience. It will go beyond the Disney store with costumed characters, movies, and video games, or the country store integrated into the Cracker Barrel restaurant. For example, food-oriented formats may combine food, cooking schools, and/or demonstration areas in person and via video, with some transmissions via satellite. Perhaps you can go to a fully stocked and equipped restaurant and do your own cooking and not have to do the dishes!

FIGURE 16.2

The transformation of the view of retailing and entertainment.[23]

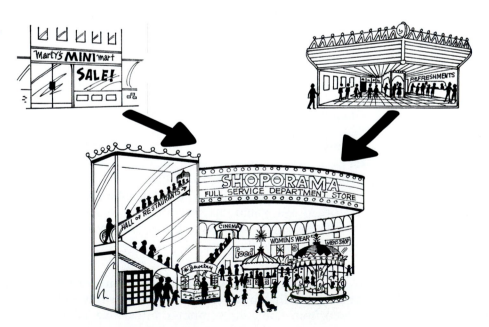

The concept of retailing as theater can be seen at The Forum Shops at Caesars in Las Vegas, which is an integral part of the bustling activity in the casinos. In one piazza, Bacchus, the Greek god of merriment and wine, hosts a party with Apollo, Pluto, and Venus, who join an astoundingly realistic, animated robotic feature that includes lasers, music, and sound effects. A great hall features an entertainment spectacular, "Atlantis."

Retailers who provide added entertainment value will attract more customers, increase customer loyalty, and probably achieve higher gross margins.

Service Malls

In Chapters 6 and 7 we discussed how malls are changing as customer demographics and store formats change. Many of the older malls may perhaps be converted to service malls. The service mall will have elements of an entertainment center as a department store is remodeled to become a basketball court and a community theater stage. Of course there will be the movie theaters and restaurants. Video arcades will be next to city and county government offices. At the service mall customers will visit the bank, renew their driver's license, have lunch, and see the dentist or doctor. There will still be merchandise retailers in the service mall, but many of them will be more convenience-oriented, focusing on the individuals who come to the mall for services rather than being merchandise shopping destinations.

Database Retailers and the Virtual Store

In Chapter 15 we covered the virtual store and database retailing. There are numerous issues concerning the future of database retailers and electronic in-home shopping formats. For example: How will these formats be paid for? Who will pay for the services? Which products and which traditional formats are most affected? In fact, the major question may be, What role will traditional retailers play? Only one thing is certain. In the next twenty years, especially in developed nations, database and electronic formats will account for a significant share of retail store sales.

H&M—REVISITED: GLOBAL STANDARDIZATION AND ADAPTATION

H&M has pursued an organic strategy for international expansion, financing its growth with self-generated funds. Company top management cautions that the cost of entering a new country and establishing an organization there is always much higher than anticipated. Therefore, achieving profitability also takes longer than expected. H&M emphasizes that for these reasons, it is critical that the balance sheet at home be strong and able to carry the weight of struggling new entities for several years.

Even with its fashion emphasis, the company nevertheless achieves economies in marketing, buying, and store design by not tailoring its merchandise offerings or store formats for different countries. H&M starts up cross-border businesses with key people from the home country and then hires local nationals. A Swede is always appointed in foreign countries to maintain and monitor performance at the local level through the financial control function.

The company is also able to achieve economies of distribution, marketing, and management when entering a new country by clustering new stores in one city before moving on to the next. H&M has no financial involvement in manufacturing, which is done primarily in Italy, Turkey, Portugal, England, and the Far East.[24]

The company has learned from its success in international expansion to centralize the "economy of scale" functions such as buying, marketing, and systems. However, it operates in each country in a decentralized fashion so that local management feels a sense of ownership and of being part of a team. At H&M both formal and informal communication between the head office and stores in all countries occurs daily. Local management is also encouraged to express opinions and contribute ideas for streamlining operations.

The company believes in maintaining key characteristics of the business—value offering, service policy, marketing approach—from country to country but allowing flexibility on other issues so that the local staff does not feel it is working in a foreign company, but rather in one that is sensitive to the needs of the individual country's working people.

1. Do you agree that Hennes & Mauritz's strategy of standardization with some local adaptation is a viable approach for entering the marketplace of other countries?
2. Why has it worked for them?

Summary

One of the major reasons retailers are moving into international markets is the high saturation that exists in the United States and other countries where the markets are maturing. The greatest opportunities for growth are overseas, where competition is not quite as intense and the actual market is enlarging.

Retailers seeking to enter international markets must initially decide how to effectively gain an entry. A formula that is successful for one retailer may not be successful for another, or for that same retailer in a different market. Merchants have several choices: going it alone, acquisitions and mergers, joint ventures, franchising, or concession and licensing.

Changes in consumer needs and tastes will alter the face of retail formats in the future. While the traditional formats like department stores will continue, new dynamic ones will be created. In order to be truly successful in the global markets, retailers must build on their core competencies while making sure they stay flexible enough to adapt to shifts in consumer preferences, competition, and culture.

Chain Store Age Executive presented a structured process developed by Coopers & Lybrand Consultants to guide a company toward an international strategy. In brief the report suggests that to be a player in the global marketplace, management must be deeply committed to global strategic thinking. It must:

1. "Focus on how the firm creates value and how it fits the local conditions.

2. Understand how to adapt the company's internal capabilities to fit targeted foreign markets.

3. Develop high-level strategies for targeted countries.

4. Have a global vision statement and implementation priority.

5. Develop country-specific strategies and implementation plans."[25]

In the year 2010, consumers will have more choices of products and retail outlets than ever before. However, as competitive as the world playing field will become, there will continue to be retail success stories. Some of these will be the further evolution of existing businesses, while others will represent the development and growth of exciting new concepts and the successful exporting of truly global retailing formats around the world.

Key Terms and Concepts

Acquisitions, 616

Concessions, 617

Customer-made stores, 627

Economies of scale, 612

Franchising, 617

Internationalization, 613

Joint venture, 616

Kiosk "shopping arcades," 628

Licensing, 617

Merchandise depots, 627

Organic growth, 616

Portable stores, 627

Retail theater, 628

QUESTIONS

1. Why should a retailer consider foreign expansion?

2. What type of problems will a retailer face when expanding into a foreign market?

3. Explain what a manager needs to do before expanding overseas.

4. When should retailers use the same format in foreign operations as they do in their home country?

5. What are the potential risks of entering a foreign market with a wholly owned subsidiary as opposed to using a franchise agreement? What are the benefits?

6. Contrast the different entry modes with regard to the degree of risk and potential reward.

7. Do you think entry of foreign retailers into a market can affect the culture of the market?

8. Researchers argue that sometimes the highest risk country is the best to enter because of the high profit potential. What do you think? What are the pros and cons?

SITUATIONS

1. You are in charge of buying for a large domestic retailer. An overseas competitor has just announced that it will cut prices on its goods by 20 percent. The domestic vendor that you normally use has decided it can cut prices only 10 percent. The deal from the international vendor is the better of the two. However, you realize that there are some extra problems when buying internationally. Should you choose your normal vendor or the international vendor? What is the basis of your choice?

2. You are in charge of a small retail operation in a recently established Middle East country. There are twelve male employees and four females. When it comes time to hire an assistant store manager, you review all the personnel files and find that a particular female employee has been outstanding. After deciding to promote her, you make the announcement to the staff. Eleven of the male employees threaten to quit on the spot. What should you do?

CASES

CASE 16A
Sourcing Overseas

John Chowdhury is the American buyer for a large U.S. retailer. As with many companies, his company assigned him overseas (in India) to groom for a promotion. He had been having problems with delivery of merchandise to several stores. When he contacted the transportation company, he was told rather directly that several thousand rupees in cash would cure this problem. John immediately contacted another buyer from a European retailer that he knew. The European told him to pay the bribe like everyone else. As a matter of fact, the European told him that most countries in Europe allow bribes to be deducted from their taxes. After a short discussion with his boss, John was told that the Foreign Corrupt Practices Act in the United States had outlawed such bribes. However, his boss also indicated that this was India, not the United States, and that the final decision was his. The last comment the manager made was "I don't care how you do it. We *need* that merchandise on time!"

1. *What should John do?*

2. *What are the future repercussions of each choice John faces?*

CASE 16B
Kmart: Trouble in Canada

In 1994 Wal-Mart changed the competitive equation in Canada when the firm announced it would acquire 122 Woolco general merchandise discount department stores. In addition to U.S.-based Sears and Kmart, Canadian firms such as Zellers, The Bay, and Eaton's are major competitors. Zellers is an aggressive firm in the discount end of the department store market.

By the middle of 1995, Wal-Mart's entry was driving speculation that Kmart was trying to sell its Canadian operations. In 1994 Kmart Canadian stores experienced an increase in sales in lo-

cal currency despite increased competition and the lingering depressed economic environment. However, the continuing deterioration of the Canadian exchange rate caused a negative sales comparison when converted to U.S. dollars.[26]

In July 1995, the *Edmonton Journal*[27] reported on the speculation of Kmart closing its operations. A Kmart spokesperson stated, "There are no facts behind the speculation. The company's 128 stores are open for business as usual for now and the foreseeable future." The newspaper quoted University of Alberta marketing professor Adam Finn as saying that in the face of intense competition from Wal-Mart and Zellers, Kmart faces one of three alternatives: "It must inject either a lot of money in renovation, relocating and relaunching its stores, sell out its operations, or face continually declining profits. . . . A recent consumer survey by the University of Alberta showed that Kmart scored the poorest in service and quality of all department stores in the Edmonton market." Additionally, the survey showed that fewer than 50 percent of the people had shopped at a Kmart in the last twelve months, the smallest percentage of the major chains. Kmart customers spent an average of only $11 per visit compared to $18 for Wal-Mart and $44 for Sears.

1. *What would you recommend to Kmart to improve its chances for survival in Canada?*

CHAPTER 1

1. Adapted from "A Brief History of the Gap, Inc.," Public Relations Department, San Francisco, Calif.

2. From the company's *Annual Report,* January 1995.

3. Karen J. Sack, "Survival of the Fittest," *Standard and Poor's Industry Surveys,* vol. 2, October 1993, p. R78.

4. Vince H. Trimble, *Sam Walton: The Inside Story of America's Richest Man,* Dutton, New York, 1990, pp. 33–34.

5. Gordon W. Weil, *Sears, Roebuck, USA,* Stein and Day, New York, 1977, p. 25.

6. For a complete look at Deming's approach, see W. Edwards Deming, *Out of the Crisis,* Massachusetts Institute of Technology, Cambridge, Mass., 1986.

7. Katherine Snow, "Category Killers Stalk Hometown Stores," *The Business Journal Serving Charlotte and the Metropolitan Area,* Sept. 7, 1992, pp. 7–8.

8. Mike McDermott, "The Revenge of the Little Guy," *Adweek's Marketing Week,* Sept. 17, 1990, pp. 21–24.

9. Reprinted with permission from *Entrepreneur Magazine,* Andrew Caffey, "Quest for Knowledge," January 1993, pp. 77–81.

10. Gregory A. Patterson, "Alive and Kicking: Department Stores, Seemingly Outmoded, Are Perking Up Again; Leaner Now, They Benefit from Trends Like Aging of the Baby Boomers," *The Wall Street Journal,* Jan. 4, 1994, p. A1.

11. *Chain Store Guide,* Discount Retailers, Business Guides, Inc., Tampa, Fla., 1993, p. 1.

12. Ross Kerber, "Discount Chains in the Northeast Get Squeezed," *The Wall Street Journal,* Oct. 9, 1995, pp. 1, 4.

13. Alice Bredin, "The Fight Begins," *Stores,* September 1993, pp. 23–26.

14. "Warehouse Club Owners Hope to Sign Up Everybody Eventually," *Marketing News,* Sept. 13, 1993, p. 1.

15. "Woolworth's Plans to Close 970 Stores," *Chain Drug Review,* Oct. 25, 1993, pp. 2–3; June Carolyn Erlick, "More Woolworth Closings," *Home Furnishings Daily,* Oct. 25, 1993, p. 1; Holly Haber, "Woolworth Corp. Maps Its Plans," *Women's Wear Daily,* Nov. 3, 1993, p. 26.

16. "Variety Chain Retailers Redefine Store Image," *Discount Store News,* July 5, 1993, p. 86.

17. David P. Schulz, "Top 100 Specialty Stores," *Stores,* August 1993, p. 24.

18. "An Industry of Contradictions," *Standard and Poor's Industry Surveys (M–Z),* vol. 2, 1993, p. R83.

19. "Outlook Improving, Competition Sharpening," *Standard and Poor's Industry Surveys (M–Z),* 1993, pp. R89–R93.

20. "Progressive Grocer's Market Scope," *Progressive Grocer's Trade Dimensions,* Maclean Hunter Media, Inc., Stamford, Conn., p. 13.

21. David P. Schulz, "Top 100 Retailers," *Stores,* July 1993, p. 30.

22. "Directory of Supermarket, Grocery and Convenience Store Chains," *Chain Store Guide,* Business Guides, Inc., Tampa, Fla., I, 1993.

23. "Direct Marketing Statistics," Direct Marketing Market Place, National Register Publishing, New Providence, N.J., 1993, p. ix.

24. Betsy Spethman, "Toys: A Venerable Retail Technique Opens New Doors of Opportunity," *Brand Week,* Feb. 14, 1995, p. 38.

25. Adapted from *Gap Inc. 1993 Annual Report and Securities and Exchange Commission Form 10-K,* Mar. 28, 1994, San Francisco, Calif.

26. Stephanie Storm, "How Gap Inc. Spells Revenge," *The New York Times,* Apr. 24, 1994, p. 3-1.

27. Ibid.

28. Ibid

29. This story appeared in the August 26–September 1, 1994, issue of the *Dallas Business Journal*. It has been reprinted with permission of the *Dallas Business Journal*, and further reproduction by any other is strictly prohibited. Copyright 1994 by *Dallas Business Journal*.

CHAPTER 2

1. Adapted from the *Tiffany & Co. Annual Reports*.

2. David Jefferson, "Retailing: Rodeo Drive Mini-Mall Is Looking Smart," *The Wall Street Journal*, June 14, 1990, p. B1.

3. Adapted from a presentation by professor Douglas J. Tigert, Babson College School of Executive Education. Babson Park, Mass.

4. Walter K. Levy, "Beware, the Pricing Genie Is Out of the Bottle," *Arthur Andersen Retailing Issues Letter*, November 1994, p. 3.

5. Ibid.

6. Ibid.

7. Alex Witchel, "Minding the Store," *The New York Times*, June 4, 1995, p. 4E.

8. Harvey B. Braun, "Learning to Serve Your Customers Well," *Discount Store News*, Oct. 1, 1990, pp. 22–23.

8a. Thomas J. Peters and Robert H. Waterman, Jr., *In Search of Excellence*, Harper & Row, 1982.

8b. Thomas J. Peters, *Thriving in Chaos*, New York, Knopf, 1987.

9. Levy, p. 3.

10. From the *PetsMart Company Annual Report*.

11. The authors appreciate the contribution of Professor Bruce Woodworth, King Fahd University of Petroleum and Minerals.

12. W. Frank Dell, "Can TQM Save the Supermarket?" *Grocery Marketing*, May 24, 1992, pp. 14–16.

13. Sam Walton and John Huey, *Sam Walton: Made in America*, Doubleday, New York, p. 51.

13a. Stanley Marcus, *Minding the Store*, Boston, Little Brown, 1974, p. 1.

14. Professor Bruce Woodworth, King Fahd University of Petroleum and Minerals contributed to this section.

14a. Armand V. Feigenbaum, *Total Quality Control*, New York, McGraw-Hill, 1991; Richard A. Shores, *Survival of the Fittest: Total Quality Control & Management Evolution*, Milwaukee, ASQC Quality Press, 1988.

15. *Management Letters*, "Care and Compassion Must Be Delivered When and How It Suits the Customer," *TAI*, vol. 5, no. 1, p. 6.

16. Richard Halverson, "Target Empowers Employees to Be Fast, Fun, and Friendly," *Discount Store News*, May 3, 1993, pp. 65–66.

17. Jim Cory, "A Consensus on Quality," *Hardware Stores Management*, September 1993, pp. 81–83.

18. Oren Harari, "Ten Reasons Why TQM Doesn't Work," *Management Review*, January 1993, pp. 33–38.

19. Cyndee Miller, "TQM's Value Criticized in New Report," *Marketing News*, Nov. 9, 1992, pp. 1–2.

20. Teri Agins, "Marketing—On Fashion," *The Wall Street Journal*, Nov. 18, 1992, p. B1.

21. Gerald D. Sentell, Tennessee Associates International, Inc., 223 Associates Blvd., Alcoa, Tennessee.

22. W. Edwards Deming, *Out of the Crisis*, Massachusetts Institute of Technology, Cambridge, Mass., p. 141.

23. "Stores Share Secrets of Super Service and Satisfied Shoppers," *The Straits Times*, June 28, 1995, p. 22; "Shoppers Find Service as Good as in Stores Downtown," *The Straits Times*, July 3, 1995, p. 32; "Retailers in Tatters," *The Straits Times*, July 4, 1995, p. 22. This case was prepared by Charlotte Allen.

CHAPTER 3

1. Michael Garry, "The Lion Talks," *Progressive Grocer,* June 1993, p. 19.

2. Stephen Bennett, "Ready to Rumble," *Progressive Grocer,* February 1993, pp. 53–58.

3. "Executive Briefing," *HRMagazine,* September 1993, pp. 9–10.

3a. Milton Friedman, *Capitalism and Freedom,* Chicago, University of Chicago Press, 1962, p. 193.

4. David A. Aaker and George S. Day, "Introduction: A Guide to Consumerism," in *Consumerism,* David A. Aaker and George S. Day (Eds.), Free Press, New York, 1974, p. xvii.

5. Richard S. Buskirk and James T. Trothe, "Consumerism—An Interpretation," *Journal of Marketing,* October 1970, pp. 61–65.

6. Aaker and Day, pp. 8–15.

7. Ibid., pp. 361–371.

8. "When Money's Not Enough," *Dealerscope Merchandising,* vol. 35, no. 12, December 1993, p. 34.

9. Jack Epstein, "Child Labor Flourishing in Brazil Shoe Industry," *Dallas Morning News,* Oct. 21, 1995.

9a. *Bloomsbury Thematic Dictionary of Quotations,* London, Bloomsbury Publishing, 1990.

9b. John Bartlett, *Familiar Quotations,* Emily Monison (Ed.), Boston, Little Brown, 1980, p. 698.

10. "When Money's Not Enough," p. 32.

11. Norma Rusbar, "Rethinking the Obvious in Retail," *National Real Estate Investor,* October 1993, pp. SS8–SS10.

12. Mary Ann Linsen, "Safety First," *Progressive Grocer,* December 1993, pp. 83–91.

13. Quoted from the company's *Annual Report,* January 1995.

14. "Food Lion Inc. Is Sued in Class-Action Filing Alleging Racial Bias," *The Wall Street Journal,* May 20, 1994, p. A5.

15. Tony Cantu, "Group Targets Outdated Items at Food Lion," *Denton Record-Chronicle,* Aug. 23, 1995, p. A11.

16. Yumiko Ono, "Shopping Lessons: As Discounting Rises in Japan, People Learn to Hunt for Bargains, Giant Department Stores, Little Shops Are Hurt, but U.S. Firms Benefit Middlemen Are under Fire," *The Wall Street Journal,* Dec. 31, 1993, p. 1; Jim Landers, "Japan's Economy Stuck in Doldrums," *Dallas Morning News,* July 30, 1995, pp. 1H, 6H. Case written by Charlotte Allen.

CHAPTER 4

1. Joan Delaney, "Frozen Yogurt: The Latest Scoop," *Management Review,* August 1990, pp. 58–60.

2. Carol Caspar, "Market Segment Report: Ice Cream & Yogurt," *Restaurant Business,* May 1, 1992, pp. 209–230.

3. Kathleen Deveny, "Marketscan: Candy-Crammed or Free of Fat, Frozen Yogurt Is Selling like Hot Cakes," *The Wall Street Journal,* June 2, 1994, p. B1.

4. John A. Goodman and Dianne S. Ward, "The Importance of Customer Satisfaction," *Direct Marketing,* December 1993, pp. 23–26.

5. "Catalogs Cut Shipping, Handling Fees to Inspire Early Christmas Shopping," *The Wall Street Journal,* Oct. 24, 1995, pp. B1, 15.

6. Abraham H. Maslow, *Motivation and Personality,* Harper & Row, New York, 1954.

7. Melvin S. Hattwick, *The New Psychology of Selling,* McGraw-Hill, New York, 1960.

8. Martha Farnsworth Riche, "Psychographics for the 1990's," *American Demographics,* July 1989, pp. 25–26, 30–32.

9. Alison Fahey and Laurie Freeman, "Retailers Adding Touches of Green," *Advertising Age,* Dec. 10, 1990, p. 58.

10. *Marketing News,* Sept. 13, 1993, p. 42.

11. Ronald W. Hasty, Joseph Bellizzi, and Fernando R. Diaz, "A Cross-Cultural Study of Ethical Perceptions of Whites and Hispanics toward Question-

able Retail Practices," abstracted in *Enhancing Knowledge Development in Marketing,* pp. 400–401, Ravi Achrol and Andrew Mitchell (Eds.), proceedings of the 1994 AMA Educators' Conference.

12. "Retail Trends," *American Demographics,* October 1993, p. 18.

13. Alexa Bell, "Searching for Generation X," *Restaurant Business,* Oct. 10, 1993, pp. 50–54.

14. "Boomers Flex Muscles at Retail," *Discount Stores News,* Apr. 3, 1995, p. 27.

15. Jeffery Green, "Changing Consumer Demographics," *Discount Merchandiser,* January 1993, pp. 68–70.

16. Jennifer Pellet, "Bringing Up Baby Sales," *Discount Merchandiser,* September 1990, pp. 46–50.

17. Richard S. Teilbaum, "Children a Mixed Blessing? Not to These Stocks," *Fortune,* Nov. 29, 1993, pp. 27–28.

18. Alfred L. Kroeber and Talcott Parsons, "The Concept of Culture and of Social Systems," *American Sociological Review,* October 1958, p. 583 (italics added).

19. See, for example, John A. Howard and Jagdish N. Sheth, *The Theory of Buyer Behavior,* Wiley, New York; James F. Engel, David T. Kollat, and Roger D. Blackwell, *Customer Behavior,* 3rd ed., Holt, Rinehart and Winston, New York, 1978; and David L. Loudon and Albert J. DellaBitta, *Consumer Behavior,* 4th ed., McGraw-Hill, New York, 1993.

20. Deveny, p. B1.

21. "TCBY's Yogurt in the Middle East," *The Wall Street Journal,* Mar. 19, 1994, p. B2.

22. Jerry A. Tannenbaum, "NAFTA to Boost Mexican Business," *The Wall Street Journal,* Nov. 17, 1993, p. B2.

23. Case prepared by Phil Wilson.

24. Adapted from Anne L. Balazs, "Positioning the Retail Shopping Center for Aging Customers," *Stores,* April 1995, pp. RR10–RR11. Case written by Charlotte Allen.

CHAPTER 5

1. Donald Lander et al., "The Body Shop Goes beyond Profits," *Business Quarterly,* Winter 1993, pp. 10–14.

2. Adapted from *The Body Shop Company Annual Reports.*

2a. "Shopping Should Be Fun, for All Generations," *Discount Store News,* July 3, 1995, p. 11.

3. Robert O. Metzer and Sukhen Dey, "Affluent Customers: What Do They Really Value?" *Journal of Retail Banking,* Fall 1986, pp. 25–35.

4. David Luck, Hugh Wales, and Donald Taylor, *Marketing Research,* Prentice-Hall, Englewood Cliffs, N.J., p. 75.

5. Mark Hinricks, "Marketing to Minorities," *U.S. Government Small Business Reports,* no. 17, pp. 47–55.

6. Richard L. Lysaker, "Data Collection Methods in the U.S.," *Journal of the Market Research Society,* October 1989, pp. 477–488.

7. Rust Langbourne, "Observations: How to Reach Children in Stores: Marketing Tactics Grounded in Observational Research—Part 2," *Journal of Advertising Research,* November–December 1993, p. 68. Copyright © 1993 by the Advertising Research Foundation.

8. Ibid., p. 69.

9. Jean Simmons, "Tales, Luxury Scent Big Cedar Lodge," *Dallas Morning News,* July 30, 1995, pp. G1, G6; Jean Simmons, "Lose Yourself Indoors at Outdoor World," *Dallas Morning News,* July 30, 1995, pp. G1, G3. Case written by Charlotte Allen.

10. Adapted from Susan Reda, "Motor Oil: Hands-On Approach," *Stores,* May 1995, pp. 48–49. Case written by Charlotte Allen.

Chapter 6

1. Compiled from *1994 Wal-Mart Stores Inc. Annual Report to Shareholders;* John L. Gann, Jr., "Manager's Journal: Main Street vs. Wal-Mart," *The Wall Street Journal,* Aug. 30, 1993, p. A8; and Bob Ortega, "Wal-Mart Looks beyond North America, Plans to Expand in Argentina, Brazil," *The Wall Street Journal,* June 6, 1994, p. A3.

2. Robert Kahn, "Good-Bye to the Myth That Wal-Mart Stores Are Only in Small Towns," *Retailing Today,* September 1995, p. 2.

3. Richard Gibson, "Location, Luck, Service Can Make a Store Top Star," *The Wall Street Journal,* Feb. 1, 1993, p. B1.

4. Gary Davies, "Bringing Stores to Shoppers—Not Shoppers to Stores," *International Journal of Retail and Distribution Management,* January 1995, pp. 18–23.

5. John R. Beaumont, "Retail Location Analysis: Some Management Perspectives," *International Journal of Retailing,* vol. 2, 1987, pp. 22–35.

6. "Consulting Firms Examine Global Markets," *Discount Store News,* Feb. 7, 1994, p. 37.

7. "Information: Key Ingredient to Connect Supply with Demand," *Automatic I.D. News,* July 1995, pp. 34–35.

8. Rebecca Piirto, "VALS the Second Time," *American Demographics,* July 1991, p. 6.

9. Joseph Kahn, "Japan's Yaohen Opens Supermarket That Sells Chinese Food in Shanghai," *The Wall Street Journal,* May 31, 1994, p. B1.

10. James Mammarella, "Baby Stores Duel It Out in Texas," *Discount Store News,* Sept. 4, 1995, p. 1.

11. Craig R. Smith, "Rising Rents Turn Hong Kong Retailers into Workaholics; Shopkeepers Put In Long Days Struggling to Keep Pricey Roofs over Their Heads," *The Wall Street Journal,* Apr. 18, 1994, p. B1.

12. Gregory A. Patterson, "Retailing: All Decked Out, Stores Head Downtown," *The Wall Street Journal,* Feb. 15, 1994, p. B1.

13. David Huff, *Determination of Intra-urban Retail Trade Areas,* Real Estate Research Program, 1962, University of California, Los Angeles.

14. Lisa O'Malley, Maurice Patterson, and Martin Evans, "Retailing Applications of Geodemographics: A Preliminary Investigation," *Marketing Intelligence & Planning,* February 1995, pp. 29–35.

15. Terance Moloney, "Retailers Large and Small Jump on the GIS Bandwagon," *Computing Canada,* Jan. 6, 1992, p. 26.

16. Ian Clarke and Jennifer Rowley, "A Case for Spatial Decision-Support Systems in Retail Location Planning," *International Journal of Retail Distribution Management,* March 1995, p. 4.

17. *1992 Census of Retail Trade,* Missouri and Louisiana volumes, SIC 5713, 4, 9.

18. Sylvia Lewis, "When Wal-Mart Says 'Uncle,'" *Planning,* August 1994, pp. 14–19.

19. David J. Burns, "Image Transference and Retail Site Selection," *International Journal of Retail and Distribution Management,* September–October 1992, pp. 38–43.

20. Laura Richardson, "Consumers in the 1990s; No Time or Money to Burn," *Chain Store Age Executive,* August 1993, pp. 15A–17A.

21. Kenton L. Ownbey et al., "Ingredients of a Successful Shopping Center," *Commercial Investment Journal,* Fall 1994, pp. 22–24.

22. Alan Giltman, "Redefining the Regional Mall," *Chain Store Age,* August 1992, p. 96.

23. Suzanne Sutro Rhees, "Mall Wonder," *Planning,* October 1993, pp. 18–23.

24. Gay Nagle Myers, "After One Year, Mall of America Emerges as Major Attraction," *Travel Weekly,* Oct. 14, 1993, p. G14.

25. Bryon Paege, "A Darker Shade of Mall," *Alberta Business,* December 1992, pp. 15–17.

26. "Factory Outlet Centers Keep Their Distance: Manufacturers Prefer to Avoid Competition with Regional Malls," *Chain Store Age Executive,* April 1990, pp. 39–42.

27. F. Wayne Boling, "Pursuing the Factory Outlet Development," *Economic Development Review,* Spring 1995, pp. 89–90.

28. Wendy Hower, "Black Businesses Flee Inner City for Suburbs," *Boston Business Journal,* Aug. 5, 1991, p. 1.

29. See, for example, "Return from the Crypt," *Financial World,* Mar. 2, 1993, pp. 52–53.

30. Gregory Patterson, p. B1.

31. Richard J. Bertman and Dan Pinck, "Street-Front Shops in Taller Office Buildings," *Real Estate Finance,* Summer 1992, pp. 76–78.

32. "Industry Performance," *Retail Tenant Directory,* Maclean Hunter Media, Inc., Stamford, Conn., 1993.

33. "Retailer Outlook," *Retail Tenant Directory,* Maclean Hunter Media, Inc., Stamford, Conn., 1993.

34. Kevin Farrell, "Sites and Saturation: Risky Business," *Restaurant Business,* July 1, 1993, pp. 72–75.

35. Alex Finklestein, "Walgreen Shops Free-Standing Sites," *Orlando Business Journal,* Oct. 9, 1992, p. 4.

36. Kathleen Deveny, "Movable Feasts: More People Dine and Drive," *The Wall Street Journal,* Jan. 4, 1994, p. B1.

37. Terry Meyer, "Site Selection vs. Site Evaluation: Techniques for Locating Retail Outlets," *Real Estate Issues,* Spring–Summer 1988, pp. 25–28.

38. "Computer Imaging as a Design Tool," *Chain Store Age Executive,* May 1995, p. 146.

39. "Retailer Outlook."

40. Nora Aufreiter, Nancy Karch, and Christiana Smith Shi, "The Engine of Success in Retailing," *McKinsey Quarterly,* vol. 3, 1993, pp. 101–116.

CHAPTER 7

1. Compiled from *Kmart 1995 Annual Report to the Stockholders;* Laura Zinn, "Attention, Shoppers: Kmart Is Fighting Back," *Business Week,* Oct. 7, 1991, pp. 118, 120; and Christina Duff, "Retailing: Adding Groceries, Super Kmarts Try to Be More Things to More People," *The Wall Street Journal,* June 7, 1993, p. B1.

2. Jay L. Johnson, "Kmart Unveils Its Prototype Store for 1993," *Discount Merchandiser,* January 1993, pp. 48–53.

3. Mary Ellen Kelly, "Kmart Seeks Higher Yield with New Top Secret Test," *Discount Store News,* February 1994, p. 1.

4. Cyndee Miller, "Glitzy Interiors Transform Stores into 'Destinations,' Boost Sales," *Marketing News,* Aug. 30, 1993, p. 1.

5. Pete Hisey, "IMRA: 'Be Distinctive' in Store Design," *Discount Store News,* Dec. 17, 1990, pp. 7–8.

6. See, for example, "The Impact of ADA: Accessibility Is Key," *Chain Store Age Executive,* December 1991, p. 12B.

7. Quoted and adapted from Walter F. Loeb, "Innovative Retailing: An Urgent Need for the Nineties," *Arthur Andersen Retailing Issues Letter,* March 1994, p. 1.

8. David Dillon, "All the Store's a Stage," *Dallas Morning News,* May 31, 1995, p. C1.

9. Ibid.

10. Gary Robins, "CADvantages: Computer Aided Design Boosts Productivity at Dillard's, Mervyn's," *Stores,* December 1991, pp. 25–31.

11. Dianne M. Pagoda, "At Macy's: Turning Windows into Worlds," *Women's Wear Daily,* Nov. 30, 1992, p. 12.

12. "Hermes Beach Party," *Women's Wear Daily,* July 20, 1990, p. 9.

13. David Moin, "At Bloomingdale's: Fashion First; Whimsy Second," *Women's Wear Daily,* Nov. 30, 1992, p. 14.

14. Michael Garry, "Space Shots: Are You Allocating Too Much or Too Little Shelf Space to Your Categories?" *Progressive Grocer,* December 1992, p. M42.

15. "Window Fashion Merchandising Reaches New Tier at Mass Retail," *Discount Store News,* May 4, 1992, p. S14.

16. Arthur Markowitz, "Tracking Shopper Traffic May Improve Service," *Discount Store News,* Mar. 16, 1992, p. 10.

17. Robert E. O'Neill, "Customer Behavior: Seeing Is Believing," *Progressive Grocer,* January 1993, p. 57.

18. Brookman, p. 54.

19. Joseph Bellizzi, Ayn Crowley, and Ronald W. Hasty, "The Effects of Color on Store Design," *Journal of Retailing,* September 1983, p. 43.

20. "Lighting and Retailing," *Chain Store Age Executive,* December 1991, p. 4A.

21. "Introduction—Lighting Management," *Chain Store Age Executive with Shopping Center Age,* December 1992, p. 13.

22. "Stemp's Markets' Retrofit; Energy-Efficient Program Has Quick Payback," *Chain Store Age Executive with Shopping Center Age,* July 1993, pp. 66–67.

23. "Design Options," *Chain Store Age Executive with Shopping Center Age,* December 1992, p. 86.

24. "Space Management in the 90s: The Window to Market Dominance," *Drug Store News,* Sept. 24, 1990, p. S1.

25. Renee Rouland, "Space Management for Category Management," *Discount Merchandiser,* January 1992, pp. 56–58.

26. "Sears 'MAPS' Customized Assortments: Space Management Software Draws Up Planograms, Product Lists," *Chain Store Age Executive,* October 1991, pp. 62–63.

27. Elliot Zwiebach, "Tesco Produces 2 Million Store Planograms a Year," *Supermarket News,* Aug. 31, 1992, p. 14.

28. "Choosing the Right Signage; Focus on What's Important to Your Customers," *Chain Store Age Executive,* July 1991, p. 81.

29. Laura Liebeck, "Kmart to Unveil New Super K Prototype in '96," *Discount Store News,* June 1995, p. 3.

30. Leah Rickard, "Kmart Searches for Agency to Ignite Change," *Advertising Age,* Jan. 16, 1995, p. 36.

31. This case was written by Phil Wilson.

CHAPTER 8

1. Adapted from the *1995 Woolworth Corporation Annual Report to the Stockholders,* cited references, and Woolworth Corporation News Releases provided by Frances E. Trachter.

2. Penny Gill, "American Spirit Award," *Stores,* June 1993, p. 59.

3. Marianne Wilson, "Legislation Could Cost Millions: The Americans with Disabilities Act Mandates Revamped Stores," *Chain Store Age Executive,* July 1990, pp. 29–31.

4. "Breast Cancer Awareness Saves Lives and Money," *Business and Health,* 1993, pp. 20–25.

5. "Can You Qualify as a Supervisor?" *Goodall News,* June–July 1969, pp. 1, 2.

6. Adapted from Rich's, Atlanta, Georgia, *Head of Sales Manual.*

7. Adapted from Terri Kabachnick, *Arthur Andersen Retailing Issues Letter,* September 1995, p. 3.

8. *The Home Depot—1993 Annual Report,* p. 13.

9. *Wal-Mart Annual Report 1994,* p. 3.

10. John Naisbitt and Patricia Aburdene, *Megatrends 2000: Ten New Directions for the 1990s,* William Morrow and Company, Inc., New York, 1990.

11. *Kmart Corporation Corporate Profile,* Kmart Corporation, Troy, Mich., 1994, p. 8.

12. Elaine Fearnely, "Scheduling Smarter Improves the Checkout Line and the Bottom Line," *Chain Store Age Executive,* September 1993, p. 72.

13. Mark S. Ain, "A Solution in Comprehensive Labor Management," *Discount Merchandiser,* October 1993, pp. RT4–RT5.

14. "Incentive Pay Plan Replaces Wage Hikes," *Chain Store Executive,* February 1989, pp. 78–79.

15. "Company Settles Lawsuit over Back Pay for Sales Reps," *Marketing News,* Feb. 15, 1993, p. 12.

16. Paul M. Mauzer, *Principles of Organization Applied to Modern Retailing,* Harper & Brothers, New York, 1927.

17. Nancy Brumbak, "Silo's Chicago Beached at Marshall Field's," *Home Furnishings Daily,* Sept. 20, 1993, pp. 112–113.

18. Michael Garry, "Fast Friends," *Progressive Grocer,* March 1993, p. 10.

19. Sharon Nelton, "Winning with Diversity," *Nation's Business,* September 1992, pp. 18–24.

20. Don McNerney, "The Bottom-Line Value of Diversity," *HR Focus,* May 1994, pp. 22–23.

21. Faye Rice, "How to Make Diversity Pay," *Fortune,* Aug. 8, 1994, pp. 78–86.

22. Dean Elmuti, "Managing Diversity in the Workplace: An Immense Challenge for Both Managers and Workers," *Industrial Management,* July–August 1993, pp. 19–22.

23. John Martin, "Unleashing the Power in Your People," *Arthur Andersen Retailing Issues Letter,* September 1994, p. 4.

24. Joseph Pereira, "In Reebok-Nike War, Big Woolworth Chain Is a Major Battlefield," *The Wall Street Journal,* Sept. 22, 1995, p. A1.

25. This case was prepared by Charlotte Allen.

CHAPTER 9

1. Adapted from *Dillard's Annual Report 1993,* pp. 1–13.

2. Laura Bird, "Macy's Lead by Altar and Big Alterations: Plans Include Reducing Costs While Streamlining Key Operation," *The Wall Street Journal,* Nov. 18, 1994, p. B4.

3. Adapted from *Dillard's Annual Report 1993,* pp. 14–27.

CHAPTER 10

1. Susan Caminite, "The New Champs of Retailing," *Fortune,* September 1990, pp. 85–100.

2. Gretchen Morgenson, "Here Come the Cross-Shoppers," *Forbes,* Dec. 7, 1992, p. 90.

3. Ibid., pp. 90–101.

4. Ibid.

5. Norta Aufreiter, Nancy Karch, and Christiana Smith Shi, "The Engine of Success in Retailing," *McKinsey Quarterly,* vol. 3, 1993, pp.101–116.

6. Mort Haaz, "Make Buying Your Bottom Line: An Open-to-Buy Plan Takes the Guesswork out of Purchasing," *Playthings,* October 1993, p. 35.

7. Robert S. Reichard, "Garbage In, Garbage Out," *Purchasing,* Feb. 20, 1992, p. 36.

8. Duane Shader, "Projecting Sales by Seasonal Trends," *Boating Industry,* March 1989, pp. 66–67.

9. Alan Miller, "To Detect Long-Term Trends, 5-Year Figures Vital," *Drug Store News,* June 26, 1989, p. 20.

10. "Thrift Measures True Dollar/Unit Loss from Theft," *Drug Store News,* Aug. 5, 1991, p. 32.

11. "Loss Prevention Trends in Retail: An Executive Overview," *Chain Store Age Executive,* January 1992, pp. S6–S7.

12. Quoted from the *1994 Annual Report to the Stockholders.*

13. Laura Bird, "Some Counsel Modest Approach to Victoria's Secret Parent IPO," *The Wall Street Journal,* Oct. 23, 1995, p. C1.

CHAPTER 11

1. Contributed by Mr. Steve Speck, vice president of sales, Russell-Newman, Inc., Denton, Texas.

2. Zachary Schiller and Wendy Zellner, "Clout! More and More Retail Giants Rule the Market Place," *Business Week,* Dec. 21, 1992, pp. 66–73.

3. Terri Agins, "Industry Focus: Apparel Makers Are Refashioning Their Operations: Manufacturers Scramble to Adjust," *The Wall Street Journal,* Jan. 13, 1994, p. B4.

4. Ibid.

5. Karyn Monget, "Sleepwear Firms Target Discounters," *Women's Wear Daily,* Aug. 29, 1994, p. 6.

6. Adapted from Kevin Heliker, "Final Final Sale! Stores Unload Buyers' Efforts," *The Wall Street Journal,* Nov. 4, 1994, p. B1. Used with permission.

6a. Adapted from Jeremy Main, "The Winning Organization," *Fortune,* Sept. 26, 1988, p. 56.

7. James Mammarella, "Retailing Goes Global—With Glitches," *Discount Store News,* January 1995, pp. 1, 70.

8. Bob Ortega, "Broken Rules: Conduct Codes Garner Goodwill for Retailers, but Violations Go On: Factories in Latin America Still Hire Minors Illegally and Unionists Get Killed, Drastic Solution at Wal-Mart," *The Wall Street Journal,* July 3, 1995, p. A1.

9. "Who's Minding the Gun Counter?" *Business Week,* Oct. 25, 1993, p. 120.

10. Elena Hart, "Russell-Newman Adds Men's Robes," *Daily News Record,* Jan. 14, 1994, p. 6.

11. Richard Alm, "Trade Group Names JEFA International Exporter of the Year," *Dallas Morning News,* May 26, 1994, p. 11D.

12. Mark Hendricks, "The Bloom's Still on the Yellow Rose; Improved Marketing, Free Trade and Better Technology Could Put Texas at the Center of a Pan-American Boom; Clothing Industry," *Apparel Industry Magazine,* August 1993, p. 20.

13. Elena Hart, "Tommy Hilfiger Licenses Name for Men's Robes; Cypress Apparel Group," *Daily News Record,* Sept. 26, 1994, p. 24.

CHAPTER 12

1. Rahul Jacob, "Beyond Quality and Value," *Fortune,* Autumn–Winter 1993, pp. 8–11.

2. Jay Palmer, "Toys 'R' Nest," *Barron's,* Sept. 27, 1993, p. 12.

3. Stephen H. Epstein, "Understanding the Consumer in the 90's," *Discount Merchandiser,* December 1992, pp. 44–45.

4. Karen J. Sack, "Survival of the Fittest," *Standard and Poor's Industry Surveys* (M–Z), May 13, 1993, p. R76.

5. "On the Bargain Counter," *Barron's,* Mar. 29, 1993, pp. 8–9.

6. "Marketing & Media: Kmart, in a Departure, Plans Manhattan Site for a Discount Store," *The Wall Street Journal,* Dec. 8, 1995, p. B4.

7. Allison G. Burgess, "Technology Update," *Law Practice Management,* March 1993, pp. 10–14.

8. Walter K. Levy, "Beware, the Pricing Genie Is Out of the Bottle," *Arthur Andersen Retailing Issues Letter,* November 1994, p. 3.

9. Julie Liesse, "Price War Bites at Pet Food Ad $," *Advertising Age,* Apr. 5, 1993, p. 12.

10. See, for example, "One-Price Selling Improves Profits and Perceptions," *Boating Industry,* May 1993, pp. 44–45; Danna M. Jones, "Dealers, Manufacturers Turn to One-Price Policies for Cars," *The Business Journal,* Sept. 20, 1993, p. 7; Brad Smith, "One-Price Car Buying?" *Colorado Business Magazine,* October 1993, pp. 52–55.

11. Steve Weinstein, "Is High-Low More Profitable?" *Progressive Grocer,* June 1993, p. 11.

12. Susan Reda, "Active Outerwear," *Stores,* April 1992, pp. 44–45.

13. "Who Wins with Price-Matching Plan?" *The Wall Street Journal,* Mar. 16, 1994, p. B8.

14. Adaptation of *Bullock's Markdown Reminder Card* from *198 Ways of Controlling Markdowns,* National Retail Federation, New York, pp. 57–59.

15. Frank P. Spinella, "Business Electronics and the Coerced Supplier," *Commercial Law Journal,* Summer 1990, pp. 230–246.

16. Alan L. Gilman, "Innocents Abroad—Prepare for Globalization," *Chain Store Age Executive,* September 1993, p. 98.

CHAPTER 13

1. "Sears: In with New . . . ," *Fortune,* Oct. 16, 1995, p. 96.

2. Gregory A. Patterson, "Marketing and Media—Advertising: Sears Will Show Its 'Softer Side' in Blitz Pushing Women's Wear," *The Wall Street Journal,* Aug. 24, 1993, p. B5.

3. Kevin Goldman, "Advertising: Research in Advertising," *The Wall Street Journal,* April 13, 1994, p. B8.

4. Patterson, p. B5.

5. Ann Cooper, "For Big or Small, Image Is Everything," *ADWEEK Eastern Edition,* Mar. 8, 1993, p. 28.

6. Nancy Zimmerman, "Today's Retailer: The New Power in Promotion," *Incentive,* October 1990, p. 42.

7. "Methodology for LNA," *Advertising Age,* September 1994, p. 72.

8. Pat Sloan, "Avon Looks beyond Direct Sales," *Advertising Age,* Feb. 22, 1993, p. 32.

9. Betsy Spethmann et al., "Nine Trends That Will Drive Business in 1994," *Brandweek,* Jan. 3, 1994, pp. 18–23.

10. Christy Fisher, "Retailers Target Ethnic Consumers," *Advertising Age,* Sept. 30, 1991, p. 50.

11. Arthur Buckler, "Wal-Mart Told to Tone Down Its Claims," *The Wall Street Journal,* May 26, 1994, p. B9.

12. Charles L. Whitter, *Creative Advertising,* Holt, Rinehart and Winston, New York, 1955, pp. 56–60.

13. Ibid., p. 62.

14. Michael Ducey, "Balancing the 'Threats' to Paper," *Graphic Arts Monthly,* March 1992, p. 102.

15. *Advertise . . . to Promote Your Business, to Sell Your Goods,* The National Cash Register Company, Dayton, Ohio, 1960.

16. George Garneau, "The Retail Ad Revolution and Newspapers," *Editor & Publisher,* Nov. 7, 1992, pp. 24–25.

17. Laurie A. Shuster, "Retail Advertising: What Works, What Doesn't," *Hardware Age,* September 1991, p. 71.

18. Peter Viles, "The Storm Passes: Radio Posts Healthy Gains," *Broadcasting and Cable,* Sept. 6, 1993, p. 38.

19. Debra Aho, "What Cart? Turn On the TV to Buy Food," *Advertising Age,* Jan. 10, 1994, pp. 1, 39.

20. Kevin Goldman, "Advertising: Spending on Billboards Is Rising; Vital Tool Makes Buying Easier," *The Wall Street Journal,* June 27, 1994, p. B8.

21. Hugh M. Cannon and Edward A. Riordan, "Effective Reach and Frequency: Does It Really Make Sense?" *Journal of Advertising Research,* March–April 1994, pp. 19–28.

22. Robert D. Wilcox, "Co-Op Advertising: Getting Your Money's Worth," *Sales & Marketing Management,* May 1991, pp. 64–68.

23. Jennifer Pellet, "The High Cost of False Price Claims," *Discount Merchandiser,* July 1990, pp. 79–80.

24. Peter F. Drucker, "The Retail Revolution," *The Wall Street Journal,* July 15, 1993, p. A12.

25. Gilbert A. Churchill, Jr., and J. Paul Peter, *Marketing,* Richard D. Irwin Co., Homewood, Ill., 1995, p. 103.

26. Sudhir H. Hale, "Cultural Specific Marketing Communications: An Analytical Approach," *International Marketing Review,* no. 2, 1992, p. 18.

27. Phillip Cateora, *International Marketing,* Richard D. Irwin Co., Homewood, Ill., 1993, p. 499.

28. Ibid., p. 501.

29. "Legislation Passed by the European Community Which Directly Affects Advertising," *International Journal of Advertising,* vol. 10, no 1, pp. 79–81.

30. Syed H. Akhter, *Global Marketing,* South-Western College Publishing, Cincinnati, Ohio, 1994, p. 119.

31. Gregory Patterson, "Advertising: Sears Raises Its Marketing Budget amid a Shift into New Projects," *The Wall Street Journal,* Feb. 16, 1994, p. B3.

32. Kevin Goldman, "Advertising: Sears, Seeking to Change Image, Plans to Sponsor Phil Collins Tour," *The Wall Street Journal,* Jan. 4, 1994, p. B2.

33. Kate Fitzgerald, "Sears, King World Link for Infomercials," *Advertising Age,* Nov. 8, 1993, p. 8.

CHAPTER 14

1. Adapted from D. Lakner, *Nordstrom, Inc.—Company Report,* Oppenheimer and Co., Inc., Copyright 1994, Thompson Financial Networks Inc.; and the *Nordstrom Annual Report 1995.*

2. Cyndee Miller, "Nordstrom Is Tops in Survey," *Marketing News,* vol. 27, no. 4, 1993, pp. 12–13.

3. Ted Gladson, "How to Incorporate the Art of Personal Selling," *Drug Topics,* Sept. 6, 1993, p. 6.

4. Kerry J. Smith, "Still Climbing," *Promo,* July 1993, p. 7.

5. Ibid., p. 81.

6. Ibid., p. 81.

7. Ibid., p. 81.

8. Ibid., p. 18.

9. Rhoda M. Gilinsky, "Corporate Sponsorship Has Been Provided By . . . ," *Corporate Meetings and Incentives,* June 1993, p. 19.

10. "Window Fashion Merchandising Reaches New Tier at Mass Retail," *Discount Store News,* vol. 31, May 4, 1995, p. S14.

11. "P-O-P Industry Rallies, Despite Slow Start," *Promo,* July 1993, p. 81.

12. "Company Settles Lawsuit over Back Pay for Sales Reps," *Marketing News,* February 1993, p. 12.

13. Jean Bozman, "Retailer Has Client/Server Make-Over," *Computerworld,* Feb. 22, 1993, p. 47.

14. Carlene Thissen, "Frequent Shopper Update," *Discount Merchandiser,* October 1992, p. 50.

15. Kevin T. Higgins, "Mr. Plastic Joins the Marketing Team," *Credit Card Management,* June 1993, pp. 26–27.

CHAPTER 15

1. Hershell Gordon Lewis, "How Powerful and How Sincere Is Your Guarantee," *Catalog Age,* November 1993, p. 153.

2. Lynn Hayes, "1992 American Catalog Award—Sporting Goods: Still the Mail Order Giant: L. L. Bean," *Catalog Age,* September 1992, p. 97.

3. Dawn Anfuso, "At L. L. Bean, Quality Starts with People," *Personnel Journal,* January 1994, p. 60.

4. Dawn Anfuso, "L. L. Bean's TQM Efforts Put People before Processes," *Personnel Journal,* July 1994, p. 72.

5. Anonymous, "Hello, Caller. You're on the Screen," *Catalog Age,* April 1993, p. 22.

6. James Rosenfield, "L. L. Bean," *Direct Marketing,* February 1992, p. 17.

7. John Lang, "Joshua and the Box," presented by Stephen Boxustow Productions, Los Angeles, California, 1970.

8. Adapted from Richard Cross and Janet Smith, "Retailers Move toward Customer Relations," *Direct Marketing,* December 1994, pp. 20–21.

9. International Mass Retail Association with Coopers & Lybrand, *Navigating through Changing Channels,* International Mass Retail Association, Washington, D.C., 1993, p. 3.

10. "Gates Shares His Vision of the Info Superhighway," *Discount Store News,* July 17, 1995, p. 3.

11. Ibid., p. 4.

12. Ibid., p. 5.

13. Ibid., p. 251.

14. William Gates, *The Road Ahead,* Viking, Penguin Books, New York, 1995, pp. 94–96.

15. Joan E. Rigdon, "Blame Retailers for Web's Slow Start as a Mall," *The Wall Street Journal,* Aug. 16, 1995, p. B1.

16. Joan E. Rigdon, "Coming Soon to the Internet: Tools to Add Glitz to the Web's Offering," *The Wall Street Journal,* Aug. 16, 1995, p. B1.

17. "Wal-Mart, Microsoft Align" *Marketing News,* March 11, 1996, p. 1.

18. Suzanne Oliver, "Virtual Retailer," *Forbes,* Apr. 24, 1995, pp. 126–127.

19. "Reinventing the Store," *Business Week,* Nov. 27, 1995, pp. 84–96.

20. Robert Maynard, "The Truth about Internet Commerce," *Special Advertising Section, Texas Business,* November 1995, p. 2.

21. Cyndee Miller, "Marketers Demand Real Research Results from Cyber Efforts," *Marketing News,* Aug. 28, 1995, pp. 1, 12.

22. "Learn How to Do Business on the Internet," *Dallas Morning News,* Oct. 15, 1995, p. 11Q.

23. Laura Castaneda, "New Medium, Old Message," *Dallas Morning News,* Jan. 7, 1996, pp. H1, H2.

24. Joe Abernathy, "Untangling the Web," *Texas Business,* November 1995, p. 63.

25. Maria Halkias, p. H1.

26. Laura Zinn, "Retailing Will Never Be the Same," *Business Week,* July 26, 1993, p. 54.

27. Sari Bonnon and Julie L. Belcove, "Shopping without Shoving: Pushing Crowds Can't Impede Those at Home, Phoning Orders for What They See on TV," *Home Furnishings Daily,* June 21, 1993, p. 10.

28. Gregory Patterson, "Marketing & Media: Spiegel and Time Warner to Scale Back Cable Shopping Venture, Use Internet," *The Wall Street Journal,* Jan. 30, 1995, p. B6.

29. Patrick M. Reilly, "Entertainment + Technology (Special Report)," *The Wall Street Journal,* Mar. 21, 1994, p. R11.

30. Lewis Rose, "What the Government Looks For When It Watches DRTV," *Response TV,* March 1993, pp. 41–42.

31. Jennifer Rowley, "Multimedia Kiosks in Retailing," *International Journal of Retail & Distribution Management,* May 1995, p. 32.

32. "Windows-Based Kiosks Steal the Show at Best Buy's Concept III Stores," *Chain Store Age Executive,* January 1995, pp. 14C–15C.

33. Jennifer Rowley, pp. 32–40.

34. "Kiosks: Creative Ideas Abound, Return on Investment Unproven," *Chain Store Age Executive,* November 1994, pp. 35–42.

35. Elaine Underwood, "Lee Gets In Touch with Retail Kiosk," *Brandweek,* June 12, 1995, p. 42.

36. Virginia Matthews, "Screening Their Customers," *Marketing Week,* Mar. 17, 1995, p. 23.

37. "Electrolux Brings Virtual Reality to Kitchen Stores," *Marketing Week,* May 12, 1995, p. 9.

38. Richard Cross and Janet Smith, "Retailers Move toward New Customer Relations," *Direct Marketing,* December 1994, pp. 20–22.

39. "Spiegel Keeps In Touch," *Stores,* October 1993, p. 75.

40. "The Success of Service Merchandise," *Direct Marketing,* August 1992, p. 44.

41. Greg Gadus, "Kiosks Build Mall Loyalty and Database," *Direct Marketing,* October 1994, pp. 26–27.

42. Kelly Shermach, "Electronic Coupon Program Offers Data-Base Potential," *Marketing News,* Sept. 25, 1995, p. 6.

43. Hallie Mummert, "Tapping Hispanic America," *Zip/Target Marketing,* June 1994, p. 32.

44. Ibid., p. 37.

45. "The Marriage of Catalogs and Retail Stores," *Catalog Age,* June 1987, pp. 111–117.

46. Harlan S. Byme, "Shopping Made Easy," *Barrons,* July 25, 1994, p. 20.

47. Len Egol, "Photo CD Could Jazz Up Catalog Offers," *Catalog Age,* January 1993, p. 36.

48. Mollie Neal, "Dell Takes a Megabyte of the PC Market," *Direct Marketing,* May 1993, pp. 28–30.

49. Ko de Ruyter and Jean Gnap, "Customer Service Call Centers for Retailers," *Retail Control,* June–July 1992, pp. 17–21.

50. "How J. C. Penney Streamlined Telemarketing," *Communications News,* February 1995, p. 34.

51. Robert Ingenito, "It's Your Call: 900 Numbers," *Direct Marketing,* September 1990, pp. 49–52, 83.

52. Paul Miller, "Maintenance Warehouse," *Catalog Age,* November 1994, p. 65.

53. Eric Sandelands, "Penetrating the Japanese Market," *International Journal of Physical Distribution & Logistics Management,* March 1994, pp. 19–20.

54. "Micro-Marketing Pricing: Evidence of Grocery Store Payoffs," *Stores,* August 1994, p. RR4.

55. Renee Covino Rouland, "Mico-Marketing and Best Wishes," *Discount Merchandiser,* July 1992, pp. 64–65.

56. Murry Raphel, "The Return of Max Grassfield," *Direct Marketing,* April 1995, pp. 30–31.

57. Ibid., pp. B1–B4.

58. Laura Bird, "Department Stores Target Top Customers," *The Wall Street Journal,* Mar. 8, 1995, pp. B1–B4.

59. Ibid.

60. Kelly Shermach, "Shopping Malls Becoming 'Pretty Sophisticated,'" *Marketing News,* Sept. 25, 1995, p. 6.

61. Phyllis Berman, "Trouble in Bean Land," *Forbes,* July 6, 1992, p. 42.

62. Gregory Patterson, "U.S. Catalogers Test International Waters," *The Wall Street Journal,* Apr. 19, 1994, p. B1.

63. Justin Doebele, "Manager's Journal: Way to Japanese Heart Is through the Mail," *The Wall Street Journal,* Dec. 6, 1993, p. A14.

64. Len Egol, p. 36.

65. "Technology: America Online Plans to Acquire Redgate for about $35 Million," *The Wall Street Journal,* May 12, 1994, p. C21.

66. Bruce Caldwell, "GE's New Marketing Touch," *Information Week,* May 8, 1995, p. 78; Eric Cabrow, "Multimedia Is the Message," *Information Week,* Jan. 2, 1995, pp. 36–37; John W. DeWitt, "Kiosk Data Supports Manufacturing Flexibility," *Apparel Industry Magazine,* May 1995, pp. 42–46; Elaine Underwood, "Lee Gets In Touch with Retail Kiosk," *Brandweek,* June 12, 1995, p. 9. This case was prepared by Charlotte Allen.

CHAPTER 16

1. Seth Chandler, "Swedish Marketers Going Global," *Advertising Age,* April 1990, p. 38.

2. Carolina Johanson, "Sweden: Clothes Stores Have the Look of Success," *International Management,* May 1994, p. 6.

3. Mary Krienke, "Hennes & Mauritz," *Stores,* February 1993, p. 36.

4. Carla Rapoper, "Retailers Go Global," *Fortune,* February 1995, pp. 64–68.

5. Loretta Roach, "A Global View: 32 Million Retail Outlets in 1995," *Discount Merchandiser,* May 1995.

6. Jay L. Johnson, "Why American Retailers Are Going Global," *Discount Merchandiser,* September 1995, p. 35.

7. Michael Reid, "All the World's a Shop," *Economist,* Mar. 4, 1995, p. 334.

8. Arthur H. Good and Stephen Granovsky, "Retail Goes Global," *The Canadian Business Review,* Summer 1995, p. 31.

9. Jay L. Johnson, "The Globetrotters: Retail's Multinationals," *Discount Merchandiser,* September 1995, pp. 40–42.

10. David Begg, "What Does It Take to Be a Global Retailer?" *Discount Merchandiser,* Sept. 1995, p. 52.

11. Larry Katzen, "Retailing—The Global Mandate," *Arthur Andersen Retailing Issues Letter,* September 1993, pp. 1, 2.

12. David Swindley, "UK Retailers and Global Responsibility," *The Services Industry Journal,* July 1990, pp. 589–598.

13. "American Retailers in Europe Treble in Only Three Years," *International Journal of Retail & Distribution Management,* March 1995, p. 3.

14. Strephen Lewis, "Germany," *European Retail,* Aug. 30, 1994, p. 2.

15. Bob Davis, Peter Grenbal, and David Hampton, "To All U.S. Managers Upset by Regulation, Try Germany or Japan," *The Wall Street Journal,* Dec. 14, 1995, pp. A1–A5.

16. Ibid., p. A5.

17. Michael Reid, p. SS16.

18. Quoted in part and adapted from Neil Herndon, "Wal-Mart Goes to Hong Kong, Looks at China," *Marketing News,* Nov. 21, 1994, p. 2.

19. Alexa C. Lam, "Tapping the Retail Market in China," *China Business Review,* September–October 1995, p. 23.

20. O. P. Malik, "The Great Indian Bazaar," *Brandweek,* June 5, 1995, pp. 31–32.

21. "The Most and Least Suitable Retail Formats," *Discount Merchandiser,* September 1995, p. 49.

22. Ibid.

23. Based on *Retail . . . Vision of the Future,* AT&T Global Solutions, A presentation by Tom Doddridge, formerly area vice president.

24. Mary Krienke, p. 37.

25. Michael Bier and David Mish, "Best Practices in Retailing: Going Global: Best Practice and Strategy and Brand Development," *Chain Store Age,* November 1995, pp. 76–84.

26. *Kmart Annual Report,* January 1995.

27. Jac MacDonald, "Canadian Kmarts Still Strong Despite Sale Rumors, Official Says," *The Edmonton Journal,* July 21, 1995, p. 4.

PHOTO CREDITS

GLOSSARY

Above the market pricing: Prices are above those typically found for comparable merchandise with the expectation that customers will pay for exclusivity, quality, convenience, or service.

Accordion theory: It suggests that stores evolve in a general-specific-general pattern resembling the bellows of an accordion.

Acquisition: The purchase of other retailers to obtain access to market knowledge, buying expertise, new sources of supply, or desirable retail sites.

Additional markup: A price increase made in addition to the original markup.

Advanced dating: Vendors offer retailers more time in which to pay their bill in order to entice them to purchase their goods.

Advertising: A paid presentation of a message on behalf of a product, service or idea by an identified sponsor to a mass audience.

Advertising specialties: Items, often imprinted with the store name, offered to consumers free of charge in an attempt to build name awareness.

Affinity list: A list of names collected from non-competitors of consumers whose purchase behavior is similar to that of the store's current customers.

Age Discrimination in Employment Act of 1967: An act which makes it illegal for an employer to refuse to hire or discharge a person on the basis of age.

AIDA: A formula approach to a selling or advertising message which uses the form of attention, interest, desire, action.

Americans with Disabilities Act (ADA) of 1992: A federal law which requires employers to make reasonable accommodations to hire all persons regardless of mental or physical ability.

Anticipation discount: Discounts given by some vendors as an incentive for early payment in the form of a percentage rate per year.

Applied research: The application of basic principles and existing knowledge to the solution of a problem.

Asia-Pacific Economic Cooperation (APEC): Seventeen Pacific Rim countries whose primary focus is business development among the members.

Assets: Everything that a business owns.

Assorting: The evaluation of all of the different products that are available and offering to consumers an optimum array of products from which to choose.

Assortment: This refers to the depth of a product line, or how many different styles and brands a retailer carries in each product line.

Assortment plan: A bottom-up approach to merchandise planning. The designation of the specific items to be purchased and the dollars to be spent.

At the market pricing: Merchandise prices are comparable to those of most competitors. Customers neither look for the lowest prices nor are willing to pay higher prices. They shop for a combination of products and services.

Attitude (opinions): A predisposition or tendency of an individual to act in a particular way. An opinion is the verbalization of an attitude.

Auxiliary services: Services which are usually promotional in nature and are auxiliary to the operation of the store, such as gift-wrapping and fashion consulting.

Average inventory: Calculated by adding the inventory at the beginning of the period and the inventory at the end of the period and dividing by two.

Bait and switch: Products are advertised at an unusually attractive price, but the retailer has no intention of selling the low priced merchandise.

Balance sheet: An accounting statement of the value of all assets, debts, and net worth of the business at a particular moment in time.

Basic consumer rights: The right to safety, the right to be informed, the right to choose and the right to be heard.

Basic stock: Planned average stock for the season less planned average monthly sales for the season.

Basic stock list: An approach to assortment planning for staple merchandise for which there is a fairly constant demand and where fashion plays a relatively unimportant role. It is a precise statement of the items to be carried in stock.

Basic stock method: Requires buying adequate goods to begin the month so there is inventory that exceeds the planned monthly sales by a basic stock amount.

Book method: A perpetual method for valuing inventory. Values of inventory are entered at either cost or retail prices. The store's sales records show how much was sold. The ending inventory position can be obtained without taking a physical count.

Boutique: A limited-line store which is smaller and appeals to a more limited target market than a specialty store.

Boutique pattern of customer traffic flow: A natural extension of the free-flow pattern to create departments that sell related merchandise.

Breach of warranty: The retailer is subject to liability if there is proof that the product was defective and the proximate cause of injury.

Broker list: A list of potential customers compiled by and purchased from a broker.

Bulk breaking: The process of taking bulk shipments and breaking them into smaller sizes for consumers.

Buying plan: A plan which tells the buyer what kind of merchandise to purchase in what quantities as well as the dollars to be spent.

Buying power index (BPI): A single measure based on the relative purchasing power of consumers. The BPI combines effective buying income (weighted 50%), retail sales (weighted 30%), and population (weighted 20%).

C.I.F. (Cost, insurance and freight): The seller quotes the price including all transportation, insurance, and miscellaneous expenses.

C.O.D. (Cash on delivery): The seller requires that the buyer pay for goods at time of delivery.

Calendar date: The date for the beginning of a new selling season.

Carriage trade: A consumer segment of very financially well-to-do consumers.

Cash budget: Estimates of cash inflows and outflows during a planning period.

Cash discount: Deduction in price given by suppliers for prompt payment of invoice.

Category dominant limited-line stores (category killers): A limited-line discount retailer specializing in one or a few product lines with an extensive assortment and variety.

Caveat emptor: Let the buyer beware.

Census: The collection of data from the entire population of the universe included in a research study.

Central buying office: A buying office which works for a group of noncompeting stores.

Central business district (CBD): A shopping area located in the central downtown area or another area in the city with a concentration of businesses.

Chain: Multiple retail units under common ownership and management.

Civil Rights Act of 1964: A federal law which declares it to be illegal for an employer to discriminate in matters of employment or compensation against any person otherwise qualified because of race, creed, color, national origin or ancestry.

Clayton Act (1914): An amendment to the Sherman Antitrust Act which made illegal practices that might substantially lessen competition or tend to create a monopoly.

Clip strips: Attachments to the retail shelf on which small items can be clipped for display.

Cognitive dissonance: The tension that results from holding two conflicting ideas or beliefs at the same time, particularly the negative feelings that can occur after a commitment to a purchase has been made.

Collateral materials: Printed matter distributed to customers from either a point of purchase display or a sales associate.

Commission buying office: A buying office which receives income from commissions paid to them by manufacturers rather than fees from retailers.

Communication channel: The element of the promotion mix that carries a message to the receiver, such as a sales associate or newspaper.

Community shopping center: A general merchandise and convenience center of 100,000–350,000 square feet with two or more anchors, such as a discount store and a supermarket.

Competitive advantage: The development of a strategy which defines for the store its business relative to its competitors.

Computer aided design (CAD): Computer hardware and software which allows for planning store interior and exterior layout and design as well as fixtures, design, and location.

Concentric zones: Using maps to construct concentric zones based upon determining how far customers will travel to shop.

Concept-grounded merchandising: The concept of the store that determines the character of merchandise offered to targeted shoppers.

Concessions: A low-cost and low-risk form of entry into a new country that usually involves leasing a space within a store.

Consumer decision processes: The process by which customers engage in decision-making activities prior to purchase. The degree of involvement can range from routine involvement response or more limited-problem solving. Consumers engage in extensive-problem solving when they are considering new or infrequently purchased products.

Consequential ethic: See others ethic.

Consumer cooperatives: Retail operations owned and managed by consumers.

Consumer price index (CPI): The measure of the cost of living based upon the amount of price increase or decrease over time for a group of retail goods.

Consumer Products Safety Act: Sets specific responsibility of the retailer to monitor the safety of the products that they sell.

Consumerism: A term encompassing the activities of government, business, independent organizations, and concerned shoppers designed to protect the rights of consumers.

Consumers: Individuals who buy for personal, family or household use.

Continuity promotion: A program designed to encourage customers to engage in multiple purchases over a period of time.

Continuous quality improvement: A philosophy and program focusing on quality in everything the people and the store accomplish.

Controllable expenses (direct expenses): Expenses that can be controlled by a store manager, a department manager, or a buyer, such as payroll or advertising.

Convenience goods: Goods that consumers put a minimum amount of thought into purchasing.

Convenience stores: These stores carry a small, but balanced inventory of convenience items.

Cooperative advertising: Process whereby manufacturers or distributors share the cost of local ads with retailers.

Cooperative chain: A voluntary association of retailers who typically own a wholesaling organization.

Cooperatively owned buying office: A buying office that is controlled by member retailers.

Core competency: A concept that says a company should focus on what it does best and where its real competitive advantage lies.

Corrective advertisement: A remedy used by the FTC designed to overcome the effects that misleading advertising may have had on the consumer.

Cost method: A method of inventory valuation where all goods are recorded at cost and ending inventory values are determined by actually counting the goods in stock and recording values at the cost prices.

Cost of goods sold: The difference between the cost of total merchandise handled during a period (beginning inventory plus purchases) and the cost of ending inventory.

Cost-plus approach: Pricing based upon the cost of the product and a standard markup percentage.

Coupon: A certificate redeemable when offered as partial payment for goods or services.

Cross-border retailers: Retailers who venture only into markets adjacent to their home country.

Cross-seas retailers: Retailers who expand beyond adjoining countries, where language and culture may be significantly different.

Cross-shopping: The tendency of consumers to be drawn to an area where stores have similar retailing strategies based on merchandise quality, price lines, and service.

Cues: A prompt in the environment and/or individual which triggers a need recognition.

Culture: The complex of values, ideas, attitudes, and other meaningful symbols created by man, and the artifacts of that behavior as they are transmitted from one generation to the next.

Cumulative markup: The difference between total merchandise handled at cost and total merchandise handled at retail.

Cumulative quantity discount: The values of all orders in a period are added together for the calculation of quantity discounts.

Current ratio: Current assets divided by current liabilities, which indicates the ability of the business to pay its current liabilities with its current assets.

Customer focus: The orientation of a business toward satisfying customer needs rather than just making a profit.

Customer-made stores: A store which provides the technology and components for the customer to make the product.

Customer satisfaction: Correctly matching the needs of customers with the information, goods, and services offered by the store.

Customized stores: Stores which have products tailored to the individual customer at the point of sale.

Cyberspace retailing: Advertising and selling in the world of computer electronics where we cannot see what is taking place, but we know that somewhere somehow we are linked together and can communicate.

Database retailing: This is a computerized system whereby an electronic database of consumer information is used for both store-based and nonstore merchandising.

Deceptive advertising: The advertising message contains an intentionally false or a misleading claim, even though it may be true in a literal sense.

Decoding the advertising message: The receiver's interpretation of an idea from the signs and symbols into which it was encoded.

Delivery or lead time: The stock needed to cover the normal time between executing an order and receipt of the merchandise.

Demand: The amount of goods that people are willing to buy at various prices.

Demand communication: The communication of consumer demand information among all players in the supply chain including manufacturer, distributor, logistic provider, and retailer.

Demographic variables: Population characteristics that are used to describe consumers, such as age, income, and occupation.

Department stores: Stores which are departmentalized for the purposes of buying and selling, accounting, and general management.

Dialectic process: A theory which seeks to explain changes in retail structure by suggesting that change occurs through thesis, antithesis, and synthesis. For example, a concept such as a full service store (thesis) and a discount store (antithesis) combine (synthesis) to form a new concept such as a limited service everyday-low-price store.

Differential advantage: The sustainable competitive advantage which separates a store from its competitors.

Direct response television: A system which allows a customer to respond to a message on television by making a direct purchase.

Direct mail: Advertising that uses the mail to deliver the message.

Discount stores: A store with limited customer service and low markup which typically carries a diversified product line.

Discretionary income: Disposable income available after spending for basic household operations and fixed commitments.

Disposable income: Personal income after taxes.

Division of labor: Job specialization designed to allow tasks to be performed more efficiently as tasks become more and more complex.

Dollar control: The merchandise budget is a master control plan based on a top-down approach that specifies the dollars that can be spent on merchandise inventory in a given period.

Dollar margin concept: Pricing based on demand, appeal, and competition to achieve a profit, not on each item, but on the mix of products.

Drawing power: The natural ability of a store to pull customers to it based upon its own desirability and not location.

Drive-in locations: A special case of freestanding sites that are selected for the purpose of satisfying the needs of customers to shop in their car.

Economic Union (EU): A free trade area and agreement among twelve European countries.

Economic utilitarianism: The business influence on management decision-making processes.

Economies of scale: Efficiencies created by the increase in size of manufacturing, logistics, or sale of goods.

Effective buying income (EBI): The amount of personal income available in an area after such things as income, property, and social security taxes are subtracted. It is divided by the EBI of the United States to obtain a percentage.

Effective reach: The number of target market members who have received enough exposure for advertising to have the desired effect.

Elastic demand curve: When a small percentage change in price brings about a relatively large percentage change in sales.

Electronic data interchange (EDI): A system whereby retailers and their vendors are linked together by computers to improve the ordering process.

Employee discounts: Discounts given to employees to purchase that store's merchandise.

Empowerment: The concept of allowing subordinates to have decision-making power that usually is only in the hands of managers.

Encoding of the advertising message: The process of translating an idea into signs and symbols that have meaning for the receiver.

End caps: Stacks of merchandise or displays constructed at the ends of aisles.

E.O.M. (End of month): Under E.O.M. dating, the ordinary period does not begin until the end of the month of the date shown on the invoice.

Equal Employment Opportunity Act: A federal law which allows the EEOC to bring legal action against any employer who does not comply with the provisions of civil rights legislation.

Equal Employment Opportunity Commission (EEOC): The federal agency responsible for enforcing the Equal Employment Opportunity Act.

Equal Pay Act of 1963: A federal law which prohibits gender discrimination in salaries and fringe benefits.

Exclusive dealing: An agreement with a supplier whereby a retailer does not sell competitive products.

Exclusive territories: A supplier grants a retailer an exclusive right to sell the supplier's products within a specified geographic area.

Expense budget: Estimates of expenses during a planning period.

Express warranty: A statement of fact or promise about a product made by retailers to buyers.

Extra dating: One type of advanced dating which lengthens the time that retailers have to take advantage of cash discounts.

F.A.S. (Free alongside ship): At a named port the seller quotes a price for the goods including charges for delivery and loading alongside a vessel.

F.O.B. (Free on board): Merchandise is placed on board a truck, railroad car or airplane with title to goods passing from seller to buyer at the F.O.B. point.

Factory outlet center: Manufacturers outlet stores occupying 50,000–400,000 square feet.

Factory outlet stores: A limited-line store owned and managed by the manufacturer, often offering production overruns, seconds, and returned merchandise.

Fair Labor Standards Act of 1938: A federal law which deals with minimum wages, equal pay, maximum hours, overtime pay, and child labor.

Family life cycle: The identifiable stages through which a family passes based upon the age of the family members.

Family Maternity Leave Act (1993): A federal law requiring employers to allow eligible workers unpaid leave of up to twelve weeks for serious illness, birth or adoption of a child, or caring for a seriously ill parent, spouse, or child.

Fashion/specialty center: A shopping center of 80,000–250,000 square feet with higher-end fashion-oriented tenants.

Federal Trade Commission (FTC): The agency that enforces most sections of the Clayton Act and its amendments.

Feedback: The reverse flow of information from the receiver back to the sender from which the success of the communication can be judged.

Financial leverage ratio: A business's total assets divided by its net worth. It indicates the extent to which the retailer's assets are funded by debt.

Flow-through replenishment: This concept is based on having information on consumer demand that allows the flow of goods to be regulated by the actual needs in the retail stores.

Foreign exchange risk: Operating in an international environment subjects the retailer to foreign exchange risk. The transaction risk relates to the fact that foreign exchange rates may change between the time that a transaction is booked and the time it is settled. Economic risk can affect the competitive relationship between two companies that are sourcing and/or selling in different countries and different currencies.

Foreign trade zone: A trade zone which enables retailers and manufacturers to delay paying duties on imports, avoid duties on exports, and reduce duties paid on goods processed from imported goods.

Formal balance, displays: The arrangement of products in a symmetrical manner with similar items placed equal distance from the center.

Formal organization: The planned structure created by management to establish relationships among people, material, and other resources.

Format, retail store: The total mix of merchandise, services, advertising, and promotion, pricing policies and practices, location, store design, layout and visual merchandising used to implement a sustainable competitive advantage.

Formula approach to selling: A standardized sales presentation containing statements that lead the customer through stages to a purchase.

Forward buying: Buying ahead of needs to ensure inventory will be in stock when desired by customers.

Franchising: An association of independent retailers created by a contractual agreement. A franchise system may be sponsored by manufacturers, distributors or service firms.

Free flow pattern of customer traffic flow: The use of a minimum of structural features within the store, with counters arranged for maximum visual interest and positioned so their angles will capture customers in the department.

Freestanding location: A retail store that stands alone, physically separated from other retail stores.

Frequency: The average number of times that a customer sees an advertisement.

Frequent purchase programs: A program that awards customers with prizes or discounts for purchasing at a store often.

Gap analysis: The identification of a gap between customer desires and other retailer's offerings which may identify an opportunity.

General agreement on tariffs and trade (GATT): An agreement among countries that has been instrumental in creating free trade by lowering tariffs and quotas.

General-line retailing: This refers to operations carrying a wide variety of product lines with at least some depth of assortment in each line.

Geodemographics: The combining of demographics of the population with the geographical dimensions of populations for use in location analysis.

Geographical information systems (GIS): A computerized system that utilizes information databases to construct digital maps of specified geographic locations.

Globalization: The movement of retailers beyond their national boundaries in the search for greater market potential.

Grid pattern of customer traffic flow: A layout pattern to control traffic flow in the store using main, secondary, and tertiary aisles.

Gross domestic product (GDP): A measure of the health of the overall economy expressed as the sum of the individual growth rate of four components: the labor force, employment rate, work week, and labor productivity.

Gross leasable area (GLA): The amount of space in a shopping center or store which can be leased.

Gross margin: Net sales minus cost of goods sold.

Gross margin position: The overall amount of gross margin achieved by the retail store.

Gross margin return on investment (GMROI): Gross margin dollars divided by average inventory at cost is a measure of how many gross margin dollars are returned for each dollar invested in inventory.

Gross margin return on labor (GMROL): Gross margin dollars divided by employee payroll dollars is a measure of the productivity of labor which can assist management in allocating payroll dollars.

Gross margin return on space (GMROS): Gross margin dollars divided by selling space is a measure of the productivity of space.

Hedging: When a firm sends funds to a foreign subsidiary it simultaneously purchases the needed currency in the financial market. This protects it against currency rate swings in the financial market.

Hedonism: The idea that the only justification for an action is the amount of pleasure derived for the decision maker.

Holistic approach, store design: The concept that a store's design should match the store's character to create an image that the merchant hopes to project.

Horizontal cooperative advertising: When advertising support dollars for one retailer flow from another retailer.

Horizontal price fixing: When competing retailers agree to set a common price. It is always illegal.

Huff's model: A gravitational model which helps estimate the trade area. It considers the size of the shopping center, how long it would take to travel to each center, and the type of product the consumer is looking for.

Hypermarche: Similar to a superstore combining general merchandise and food products, but on a much larger scale.

Hypertext links (http): "Http" stands for hypertext transport protocol, the computer code that enables users to instantly skip from information place to information place and search on the Internet's World Wide Web.

Image transference: The concept that the image of a retail business is positively or negatively influenced by the types of businesses that surround it.

Impulse goods: Goods which customers buy as unplanned purchases.

Independent buying office: A buying office from which a group of noncompeting client stores purchase professional services.

Index of retail saturation (IRS): A measure of the competitive structure of the market. The total market potential in the market for the SIC code is divided by total square feet of stores selling merchandise in that SIC code.

Industrial buyers: Individuals who purchase goods and services on behalf of manufacturing firms.

Inelastic demand curve: When a large percentage change in price brings about a relatively small percentage change in sales.

Infomercial: A longer version of a conventional commercial that uses product demonstration and information in an attempt to persuade potential customers to make a direct response purchase.

Informal balance, displays: Products arranged in a symmetrical manner with different sized goods and objects placed away from the center based on their relative size.

Informal organization: A structure which arises naturally out of the activities and interactions of personnel which establishes a natural flow of authority and communication.

Information superhighway: A name for a high-speed digital communication system which can handle computer data as well as television and telephone signals.

Information flow: The movement of information among customers, retailers, manufacturers, and logistics suppliers.

Informing: The function that a retailer provides consumers by supplying information which facilitates the completion of a transaction.

Infrastructure: The basic framework that allows business to operate including the network of highways, water and railways, the legal infrastructure, and technical infrastructure, such as computerization and communication.

Initial markup percentage (original markup) (cumulative markon percentage): It is calculated as gross margin dollars plus retail reduction dollars divided by planned sales dollars plus retail reduction dollars. This markup figure provides the basis for buying and pricing merchandise.

Inspection system: An informal method of making periodic merchandise counts by visual inspection.

Interactive television: A system which allows selecting on demand the program or product to be viewed as well as controlling and participating in product demonstrations.

Intermediary buyers: Wholesalers and retailers who buy merchandise for resale.

Internationalization: The expansion of retailers into countries beyond their home base.

Internet: A global computer network.

Invoice: A bill sent by suppliers calling for payment.

J-hooks: Attachments to the retail shelf on which small items can be hung for display.

Job analysis: An identification of needs in terms of what tasks people will perform in the firm.

Job description: A written record of duties, responsibilities, and requirements of a particular position.

Job evaluation: Determines the value of a job in relation to other jobs. It establishes the minimum and maximum salaries for the job.

Job enlargement: A concept which seeks to motivate employees by increasing the number of tasks an employee performs.

Job enrichment: Building into people's jobs possibilities for greater advancement and growth through more challenging and responsible work.

Joint venture: Expansion into a new country through partnership with a local operator.

Just-in-time delivery: The concept that merchandise arrives from the manufacturer or distribution center just as it is needed to replenish stock on the selling floor.

Just-in-time manufacturing: The concept that materials and components are delivered to the manufacturer just as they are needed for the manufacturing process.

Kiosk, electronic: A freestanding unit with an interactive computer system from which consumers can learn about product features and prices and make purchases without the help of salespeople.

Labor-Management Relations Act (Taft-Hartley Act) of 1947: A federal law which strengthened and clarified the National Labor Relations Act regarding employees rights to organize and bargain collectively.

Labor-Management Reporting Disclosure Act (1959): Clarifies certain areas of the National Labor Relations Act regarding employees right to organize and bargain collectively.

Laissez-faire: A doctrine opposing governmental interference in business affairs and advocating little interference in individual freedom of choice and action beyond the minimum necessary to maintain peace and property rights.

Learning: A term which refers to changes in behavior that result from experience.

Leased department: Leased space within a store or a specialized department operated by someone other than the management of the store itself.

Legalistic ethics: The use of law, or absence thereof, as justification for individual or business actions.

Liabilities: Everything that a business owes.

Licensing: An agreement with another company to use store name, products, or operating methods in return for royalty payments.

Lifestyle: An individual's manner of living.

Lifetime value (LTV): The dollar value of all of the sales that a store will receive over the lifetime of a customer.

Limited-line retailing: This refers to operations that carry a considerable assortment of goods within only one or a few related product lines.

Liquid crystal display (LCD) shelf tags: A shelf tag which uses a LCD display that can be changed electronically.

Liquidity: A measure of the firm's ability to meet its cash obligations as they become due.

Location analysis: The use of demographic, economic, cultural, demand, competition, and infrastructure to determine the area where a store will be placed.

Logistics: The physical movement of goods from vendor to retailers including transportation, warehousing, materials handling, order processing, and inventory management.

Loss leaders: Setting the price at a level which does not cover full cost of the item.

Machiavellianism: A term applied when a decision is made on the basis that the ends justifies the means.

Magnuson-Moss Warranty Act (1975): An act designed to ensure that consumers have accurate, understandable, and readily available information about product warranties.

Maintained markup: The markup percentage achieved from selling the goods. The gross margin is the maintained markup decreased by the amount of alterations and increased by the amount of cash discounts.

Malls: A shopping center configuration which is an enclosed, climate controlled facility with walkways between facing rows of stores.

Managing diversity: The concept of fostering an environment where workers of all kinds can flourish and reach their full potential and contribute at their highest level.

Margin sharing: A process whereby the manufacturer agrees to share losses of the planned gross margin incurred by the retailer.

Markdown: A reduction in the original retail price of an article.

Markdown cancellation: A price increase in any markdown already taken. Net markdown is the difference between markdowns and markdown cancellations.

Market: A retail market is any group of individuals who possess the ability, desire, and willingness to buy retail goods and services.

Market potential: The total dollar sales that can be obtained by all stores selling a particular product, product line, or group of services in a retail trade area.

Market segment: A group of customers who have some common characteristic(s).

Market segmentation: The identification of a homogeneous group of customers that a store can profitably serve.

Marketing: The process of planning and executing the conception, pricing, promotion, and distribution of ideas, goods, and services to create exchanges that satisfy individual and corporate objectives.

Marketing mix: The elements of product, price, promotion, and place (distribution and location) which comprise the product and/or service offering to customers.

Markup: The difference between the selling price of an item and its cost. It is frequently called original markup or initial markup.

Markup cancellation: A price reduction in any additional markup already taken. Net additional markup is additional markup minus markup cancellations.

Maslow's hierarchy of needs: Abraham Maslow's postulation that at any given time a person may be faced with a number of needs, but probably cannot act on all of them at the same time. Maslow's hierarchy included physiological, safety, emotional, self-esteem, and self-actualization needs.

Maximum operating stock: The amount of stock represented by the basic low stock plus safety stock plus stock needed to cover the reorder interval and the delivery time.

Measured media: National advertising expenditures in media with measured circulation.

Media: The means for transmitting advertising messages to the market, including printed, broadcast, traffic, and computer media.

Membership warehouse stores (wholesale clubs): Stores which require membership by business and/or consumers which succeed by volume selling at about half the expense rate of competitors.

Merchandise budget: The amount of purchases (in dollars) that will be made for an upcoming selling season.

Merchandise date: The date for the end of the old selling season.

Merchandise depots: A place where customers can pick up products purchased via computer, interactive television or telephone.

Merchandise flow: The movement of merchandise from manufacturer through logistics suppliers to retailers and their customers.

Merging: The adding of a new prospect or customer to an existing database.

Micromarketing: The identification of the needs and wants of the local marketplace and customizing marketing efforts at the store and individual level allowing the retailer to capitalize on differences in consumers and competition.

Mission statement: A general statement that answers basic questions about the store's business: In what business are we? What is the scope of the business? What is our vision? What is our growth direction?

Model stock plan: A breakdown of the seasonal or fashion goods that a store plans to stock. Merchandise is expressed in terms of the important features such as price lines, size, color, and style.

Minimum selection stock: The quantity of a given item below which inventory should not be permitted to drop.

Multiattribute weighted checklist: A checklist of site evaluation criteria which can be weighted to reflect the importance of each attribute to the particular retailer.

Multiple-unit pricing: Also called bundling. The practice of combining two units of a product and selling them together at one price.

National Labor Relations Act (Wagner Act): A federal law which gives employees the right to organize and bargain collectively. Also, employers cannot interfere with the efforts of employees to form, join, or assist labor organizations.

Natural selection theory: A theory which suggests that change in retail store structure is a natural reaction to retailers adapting to changes in the environment.

Needs: The basic underlying motivations that move people to action.

Negligence: The lack of reasonable care exercised in the manufacture or sale of products or failure to issue warnings about them.

Neighborhood shopping center: A convenience oriented center of 30,000–150,000 square feet typically anchored by a supermarket.

Net worth (owner's equity): Assets minus liabilities.

Net worth position: Total debt divided by net worth which reflects the relationship between creditors and owners and the ability of a firm to finance its operations.

Net working capital: Current assets minus current liabilities is a ratio that reflects the capital structure of the business.

Noise in communication: Any interference that arises during the communication process.

Nonstore retailer: The selling of goods and services direct to consumers through channels other than traditional stores.

North American Free Trade Agreement (NAFTA): An agreement among the United States, Canada, and Mexico designed to create greater trade opportunities through the lowering of trade barriers.

Objective and task method of setting advertising budgets: Advertising dollars budgeted to accomplish specific goals.

Observational studies: The collecting of information regarding the behavior of individuals by observation.

Occupational Safety and Health Act (OSHA): A federal law which provides employees with protection in their working environment.

Odd-number pricing: The practice of ending a price in an odd number.

Oddball pricing: The practice of selling an assortment of related merchandise at the same price. The price bears no direct relationship to cost or desired markup at any given time.

Off-price center: A shopping center that consists of a large variety of value-oriented retailers such as factory outlet stores and close-out outlets.

One-price selling: Practice of selling to all customers at the same price as opposed to variable pricing and negotiation.

Open-to-buy (OTB): The dollars available to the buyer for the purchase of merchandise. It equals planned purchases less merchandise on order for the period minus merchandise received during the period.

Organic growth: The company introduces its current format into new markets.

Organizational buyers: Individuals whose purchase behavior is guided by the need to sell a product effectively, efficiently, and at a profit.

Others ethic: An ethic which considers the effect a decision will have on others as well as self and society as a whole.

Out-of-the-box: A term used to describe retailing outside of the store.

Outshopping: Individuals within a retail trade area who go outside of that trade area to shop for similar goods and services.

Patronage motives: The underlying forces a store can use to influence consumer store choice.

Pattern advertising: A global strategy with a standardized basic message that also allows some degree of adaptation to local situations.

Penetration pricing: A policy of pricing the product as low as possible in order to attract many initial customers.

Percentage of sales budgeting for advertising: Setting an advertising budget based on a percentage of anticipated sales. The percentage may come from historical usage or industry averages.

Perception: An element of the complex process by which we sense, select, organize, and interpret sensory stimulation so that we receive a meaningful picture of the world.

Periodic inventory control system: A basic system of inventory control used for staple merchandise accomplished by monthly, weekly or daily inventory counts.

Perpetual control system: A system of inventory control which involves keeping track of inventory changes continuously through accurate computer or manual records.

Personal gross income: Income before taxes have been deducted.

Personal selling: Individual, face-to-face communication between a sales associate and a customer.

Personalized shopper database: An electronic database developed by capturing as much information as possible about individual customers.

Planned markup: See initial markup.

Planned purchases: The total amount of inventory at retail that needs to be purchased. It equals total merchandise needed minus expected beginning inventory.

Planogram: A graphical representation that visually shows the space to be allocated by describing where every stockkeeping unit (SKU) within a space is physically located.

Point-of-sale (POS) system: Electronic register and scanners which are linked to computers to complete a transaction and capture consumer data.

Portable stores: Stores in trucks or vans that can be moved to the home or office where consumers are located.

Power centers: This center has three or more category dominant anchors with a few small tenants in 250,000–600,000 square feet.

Predatory pricing: Pricing at a very low level with the intent to harm competition.

Preferred customer programs: Similar to a frequent purchase program in that customers are rewarded with prizes or discounts for amount and/or frequency of purchases.

Premiums: A complementary product offered as an inducement to the consumer to purchase a particular item.

Price: Value assigned to something bought, sold or offered for sale expressed in terms of monetary units.

Price-driven company: A company that consistently has a lower price than competitors.

Price lines: Establishment of a limited number of prices and placing all merchandise at one of the price levels.

Primary data: Data gathered through survey/interviews and/or observation to solve a particular problem.

Primary research: That which involves collecting original data to answer a specific problem.

Private label: A merchandise label owned by the retailer as opposed to the manufacturer or wholesaler.

Problem-solving need-satisfaction approach to selling: An approach focused on being genuinely concerned about individual customer needs based on asking questions and listening to the customer and then translating product features into benefits.

Pro forma balance sheet: Estimates of assets, liabilities, and owner's equity at the end of the planning period.

Pro forma income statement: Estimates of revenues, expenses, taxes, and profits for the planning period.

Product liability: The legal burden on both manufacturers and retailers concerning the safety of products and the dangers involved in using them.

Profit and loss (P&L) statement (income statement): An accounting statement which provides a picture of how successful the store has been in buying and selling goods and in controlling operating expenses.

Projective techniques: Indirect questioning where the purpose of asking the questions is disguised.

Promotion mix: The set of controllable elements that a retailer can use to communicate ideas including advertising, sales promotion, personal selling, public relations, and packaging.

Psychic income: Personal satisfaction that a person receives from work rather than monetary income.

Publicity: Any news-related event that broadcast or print media run on behalf of the store which is not paid for by the store.

Puffery: An exaggeration of the benefits of a product.

Purging: The process of deleting names from a database.

Push-money (spiff): A cash bonus received by a salesperson for selling particular items.

Quality: The features and characteristics of the store, product, service and people that combine to contribute to satisfy customer needs and wants.

Quantity discounts: A discount from the invoice offered to retailers who purchase a specified quantity.

Quick response (QR) inventory systems: An inventory management system whereby the inventory is scheduled to arrive from vendors or a distribution center only as it is needed on the selling floor.

R.O.G. (Receipt of goods): Under ROG dating, the terms of the discount do not begin until the date that goods are received in the store.

Reach: The number of people who would see a promotion or an advertisement at least once.

Real income: Purchasing power of today's income relative to the previous period.

Recency, frequency, and monetary value (RFM): A system which lets the retailer know when a customer's last order was placed, how frequently the customer orders, and what the monetary value is of the average sale to that customer.

Receiver: In retail communications, the individual towards whom an idea is being communicated.

Reductions: Consists of markdowns, shrinkages, and employee discounts.

Reference group: People with whom a person identifies.

Refusal to deal: The right of a supplier and a retailer to deal only with those they choose.

Regional shopping center: A general merchandise and fashion center typically in an enclosed mall from 400,000–800,000 square feet anchored by two or more department stores.

Rehabilitation Act Amendments of 1974: A federal law which provides that no qualified disabled person be subject to discrimination in employment.

Reilly's law: A gravitational model which states the distance a customer will travel to shop based on population of the shopping area and the distance between areas.

Reinforcement: Purchase behavior which is strengthened when a response to the need and cues produces satisfaction.

Reorder interval: The elapsed time between two consecutive reviews of an item (or the stock needed to cover this period of time).

Research design: The overall plan that determines information needed and how the investigation to obtain it will be conducted.

Research process: Steps involved in gathering and analyzing data to solve a problem.

Response: The behavior which is a result of a need or want following stimulation by a cue.

Retail method: A method of valuing inventory which provides information on both inventory investment and gross margin which does not require a physical count.

Retail profit margin accelerators (RPMA): A concept which forces merchants to make their analyses and decisions with regard to their potential impact on profitability.

Retail theater: A format which integrates information, entertainment, and merchandise retailing.

Retailing: Activities involved in the sale of goods and services to consumers for their personal, family or household use.

Return on net worth (RONW): Net profit divided by net worth which allows a comparison with alternative investments.

Rightsizing: A term used to explain the practice of finding the right number of employees to effectively and efficiently run an organization.

Robinson-Patman Act (1936): An ammendment to Section 2 of the Clayton Act which expanded the concept that it is unlawful to discriminate in price among different purchasers when the effect might be to substantially lessen competition or tend to create a monopoly.

Safety or reserve stock: Protection stock as a hedge against an unanticipated surge in demand.

Salary plus quota bonus: Salespeople are paid a fixed amount and a bonus based on the amount by which sales exceed a quota.

Sales forecast: The specific estimate of sales volume that a retailer expects to achieve within a retail trade area.

Sales per cubic foot: A relevant measure of space productivity where depth is important, such as in freezer and refrigerated cases.

Sales per linear foot: Common measure of productivity of shelf space for items like groceries and health and beauty aids.

Sales per square foot: The typical measure for the productivity of a store, department or freestanding display.

Sales per square foot of exposure space: The concept that space has height value as well as linear value. It is calculated as a length times height measure of vertical space.

Sales plan: A detailed estimate of the sales anticipated for a time period, typically six months.

Sales potential: The total dollar volume that a retailer might expect to obtain within a retail trade area if everything was maximized.

Sales promotion: A broad set of activities designed to induce an immediate response or provide a novel way to transmit a message.

Sales taxes: A state or local tax applied only to retail sales, typically a percentage of the selling price.

Sampling: The process of selecting a limited group to represent a larger group.

Scrambled merchandising: The combining of unrelated merchandise across categories.

Seasonal discounts: A discount retailers earn by ordering or taking delivery of merchandise before the normal selling period is done.

Secondary data: Information collected for some purpose other than solving a current problem.

Secondary motives: Needs and wants which are learned or socially acquired.

Secondary research: Use of data and information that are collected for a purpose other than solving the particular problem at hand.

Selective attention: The unconscious control of the reception of information by either paying attention or ignoring the information.

Self ethic: The basing of decisions on the welfare of the individual decision maker.

Self-liquidating premium: A premium offered as an inducement to purchase a particular item but which requires the payment of additional money.

Self-service scanning checkout: A device where customers can scan the bar codes on the products they wish to purchase. It calculates the amount owed and can accept credit or debit cards.

Service retailer: A retailer who sells services which may include pure services without merchandise or services with merchandise including rental-goods services and owned-goods services.

Services that facilitate sales: Services used by some shoppers that are tied directly to the kind and amount of merchandise purchased, such as credit and installation.

Services that provide convenience: Basic services which make shopping convenient and are used by most shoppers, such as adequate parking.

Shelf extender: Wire baskets or lips that attach to the stationary shelf to support impulse items.

Shelf talker: Printed matter attached to a display shelf for the purpose of attracting attention.

Sherman Antitrust Act (1890): Legislation designed to combat monopolies by making every contract combination, conspiracy in restraint of trade, or attempts to monopolize illegal.

Shop concept: See Boutique pattern.

Shopping goods: Goods for which customers are willing to search and compare for price, service or brand.

Shrinkage: The difference between the amount of merchandise listed on the books and what is on the shelves.

Single-event promotion: It is designed to encourage the retail customer to engage in a single purchase or trial of goods and services with the hope that future purchases will follow.

Site: The specific location selected for a retail store.

Situation ethic: The idea that a decision or act itself is not deemed right or wrong unless the situation in which the act takes place is specified.

Skimming: A pricing policy designed to "skim the cream off of the top" of the demand curve by selling at a high price before lowering the price to appeal to more price-sensitive customers.

Smart cards: A credit card sized device containing a micro-computer processor which can store large amounts of information.

Social class: The stratification of people into a group based upon a social variable such as occupation or education.

Social Security Act of 1935: A federal law which requires employers to make contributions for employees' retirement, disability, and unemployment insurance.

Societal ethic: The idea that what is considered right is what the majority considers to be right in a given time or place.

Source: In retail communications, the originator or processor of an idea who desires to communicate that idea to a receiver.

Span of control: A concept which refers to the number of employees a supervisor can manage effectively.

Specialty goods: Those goods for which customers have a preconceived need and for which they will make a specific effort to come to the store to purchase.

Specialty stores: A limited-line store which carries a few lines of merchandise within a broader category competing on uniqueness of offering rather than price.

Sponsorship system: An experienced employee is given the responsibility for mentoring a new employee.

Stimulus-response approach to selling: The basic premise is that for a given stimulus there is a particular response. The sales associate tries to find a stimulus that will result in a sale.

Stock turnover rate: Stock turnover is calculated in three ways. They are (1) Net yearly sales in retail dollars divided by average inventory in retail dollars, (2) Cost of goods sold during the year divided by average inventory on hand at cost, (3) Number of units sold during the year divided by average inventory on hand in units. It is a measure of whether there is too little or too much invested in inventory based on the number of times that stock turns over in a given period.

Stock-to-sales ratio: There are two ways to calculate the stock-to-sales ratio. (1) Twelve divided by planned turnover and (2) Beginning of the month stock divided by sales for the month. The stock-to-sales ratio helps retailers to determine how much stock needs to be on hand in order to generate a specific amount of sales.

Store as a brand: A means of competitive differentiation based upon merchandise which has the same brand as the name of the store. The store typically uses its powerful assortments rather than a price appeal to attract customers.

Store design: The architectural character or decorative style of a store that conveys to a customer "what the store is all about."

Store list: A database of the store's customers.

Storing: The function that a retailer performs when they acquire and keep safe an inventory of products so that they will be available when customers need them.

Straight commission: A method where salespeople are paid on the basis of total sales multiplied by a commission rate.

Straight salary: Employees are paid a specified amount for each pay period.

Strategic partnerships: The coordination between retailers and vendors to get the right products to the retailer at the right time to reduce costs and improve service.

Strategic profit model (SPM): A model which lets the retailer calculate the return on net worth and evaluate the main areas of financial management.

Strip shopping center: An attached row of stores or service outlets managed as a coherent retail entity.

Subculture: A segment within the dominant culture which has its own religion, language, or family structure.

Substitute selling: The salesperson suggests another brand or an alternative product when the exact product is not carried or does not best satisfy customer needs.

Suggestion selling: Salesperson suggests complementary products that tie in with a purchased product.

Supermarket: A complete, full-line, self-service, departmentalized food store.

Superregional center: A general merchandise and fashion center with more than 800,000 square feet and three or more full-line department store anchors.

Superstore: A store combining general merchandise and food products in a low-cost, high-volume, limited-service operation.

Supply: The amount of goods offered for sale at various prices.

Supply chain management: The optimization of inventory levels, customer service and logistics activities.

Survey: The questioning of respondents about past, current or intended behavior and attitudes including respondent characteristics. The survey may be administered by mail, telephone or personal interviews.

SWOT analysis: The assessment of the strengths, weaknesses, opportunities and threats of a retailer to correct weaknesses and identify opportunities.

Target market: The customer profile of a segment of the people within a geographic area that the store decides to serve.

Team construct: The concept that organizational structures are looser and more networked. Multifunctional teams set plans, make decisions, and monitor performance.

Telemarketing: Telephone solicitation of consumers from a database in an attempt to sell a product or service.

Terms of payment: Conditions under which retailers must make payment to vendors.

Terms of sale: Conditions under which merchandise is sold to the retailer.

Test stock: Purchases made for the purpose of gauging customer reaction to merchandise before large orders are purchased.

Theme/festival center: A leisure, service and tourist oriented center with numerous restaurant and entertainment formats occupying 80,000–250,000 square feet.

Total quality management (TQM): A participative management style that focuses on satisfying customer expectations by continually improving the way business is conducted.

Trade area: The retail trade area is the geographic area within which the retail customers for a particular kind of store live or work.

Trade discount: A price reduction granted to retailers or wholesalers for performing services.

Tying contracts: An illegal arrangement whereby the supplier allows the retailer to purchase the product only on the condition that the retailer buy certain specific items from the suppliers.

Unaffiliated independents: Establishments owned and operated as single owner operations.

Uncontrollable expenses (indirect expenses): Expenses that continue for a time even if the store is closed or the department eliminated.

Under the market pricing: Merchandise is priced under what most competitors are charging in an attempt to appeal to the bargain-conscious consumer who is willing to give up some services and convenience in return for the lower price.

Uniform Commercial Code: Federal legislation which defines the retailers' rights and responsibilities with respect to product warranties and establishes other aspects of the legal environment of vendor/retailer conduct.

Unit control: A system of recording units of stock on hand, on order, and sold in a given period.

Unity of command: The concept that employees should only have one supervisor.

Unmeasured media: Media whose circulation is not normally measured, including couponing, direct mail, etc.

Utility: A concept which refers to the ability to satisfy needs. Form utility is created by manufacturing and other means of production. Time utility is created when the retailer stores goods and makes them available when the customer wants to purchase. Place utility is created by the transfer of goods from the place of production to the place that they can be accessed by consumers. Possession utility occurs when the retailer assists the consumer in acquiring the good or service.

VALS™2: A copyrighted framework designed by SRI International to segment consumers into one of eight basic classifications.

Value-added tax (VAT): A tax levied at every transaction.

Variety: This refers to the number of different types or classes of products that a retailer carries.

Variety stores: A form of general-line retailing. Stores have a wide collection of merchandise in low price ranges.

Vendors: Manufacturers, wholesalers or importers who supply goods to retailers.

Vertical cooperative advertising: When advertising support dollars for a retailer flow from either the manufacturer or the wholesaler.

Vertical price fixing: When vendors set minimum prices for the sale of their products by retailers. It is illegal.

Virtual reality marketing research: A system using computer simulation to test store promotions, layouts, and product positioning as well as new products.

Virtual reality simulations and showrooms: A system whereby a shopper can sit at a computer screen and interact with images of genuine three-dimensional products.

Virtual store: Any communications and selling retail format that relies on electronic technology to interact with a potential customer.

Voluntary chain: An association of independent retailers sponsored by a wholesaler rather than by retailers themselves.

Want slips: A form for employees to use in recording merchandise requested by consumers which is not currently in stock.

Wants: The specific ways that people choose to satisfy their needs.

Warranty: Obligation of the seller with respect to a product that has been sold.

Warranty of fitness for a particular purpose: See Warranty of merchantability.

Warranty of merchantability: Goods must be adequate for the ordinary purposes for which they are used.

Warranty of title: The expectation by buyers that retailers have the right to sell the goods and can convey a legal title to them.

Week's supply method: This method is used to plan beginning inventory where it is desirable to cover sales planned on the basis of a number of weeks instead of monthly basis.

Wheel of retailing: A theory which seeks to explain the changes in the structure of retailing. An innovative retailer enters the market based on low price and limited service. In a trading-up phase they add services to reach additional markets. In a maturity phase prices are higher with additional service, selection, and better facilities. The retail concept is then venerable to another innovative retailer.

Wheeler-Lea Act (1938): This act makes unfair methods of competition and unfair deceptive acts or practices including false or deceptive advertising unlawful.

Wireless POS systems: A portable point-of-sale data capture device which does not require a wired hookup with the computer.

NAME INDEX

SUBJECT INDEX